NAVAL OPERATIONS

The Lords Commissioners of the Admiralty have given the Author access to official documents in the preparation of this work, but they are in no way responsible for his reading or presentation of the facts as stated.

NAVAL OPERATIONS

History of the Great War
Based on Official Documents

VOL. I

by

SIR JULIAN S. CORBETT

The Naval & Military Press Ltd

in association with

The Imperial War Museum
Department of Printed Books

Published jointly by
The Naval & Military Press Ltd
Unit 10 Ridgewood Industrial Park,
Uckfield, East Sussex,
TN22 5QE England
Tel: +44 (0) 1825 749494
Fax: +44 (0) 1825 765701

and

The Imperial War Museum, London
Department of Printed Books

Printed and bound by Antony Rowe Ltd, Eastbourne

PREFACE TO REVISED EDITION

THE first edition of this volume was published eighteen years ago. As it was also the first instalment of Official History to be issued by any of the belligerent States, the author, the late Sir Julian Corbett, had of necessity to base his narrative almost solely upon our own records, and laboured under the disadvantage of having only incomplete information as to the activities of our opponents.

A far more comprehensive study is now possible, for a mass of material has become available, notably in the issue of the German Official History, *Der Krieg zur See*, 1914-1918, the following six volumes of which have been consulted :—
Der Krieg in der Nordsee, Volumes I and II ; *Der Kreuzerkrieg*, Volumes I, II and III ; *Die Mittelmeer-Division.*

Many points that remained in doubt have thus been settled, details hitherto unknown added, the uncompleted accounts of incidents and operations elaborated, and the maps amended accordingly. The Chapter (VII) on the action in the Heligoland Bight on August 28, 1914, was invested with the greatest difficulties, for the author had to produce his narrative from unreliable and conflicting reports of the enemy's movements, and in many instances the names of the ships engaged were misstated. Much information has been derived from the series of monographs issued by the Naval Staff of the Admiralty, especially in connection with the cruise of the German raider *Berlin*. The original account of this vessel's movements came admittedly from a source not entirely trustworthy. It was based upon a report by one of her own crew interned at Trondhjem, and it has since been ascertained beyond doubt that her cruise began on October 16, 1914, and not on the 14th as stated. This difference of two days, affecting as it does the positions of the Grand Fleet Squadrons during the *Berlin's* activities, has necessitated the substitution of an entirely new narrative.

In the preparation of this revised edition I am greatly

indebted to Mr. C. V. Owen of the Historical Section, whose collaboration is acknowledged with gratitude. I have also to thank Captain A. C. Dewar, R.N., (Head of the Historical Section, Training and Staff Duties Division, Admiralty), for assistance given on many points of detail.

E. Y. DANIEL,

Lieut.-Colonel, R.M.

Secretary, Historical Section,

Committee of Imperial Defence.

August, 1938.

PREFACE

On June 28, 1916, the Prime Minister (Mr. Asquith) announced in Parliament that " In view of the demand which is likely to arise and the desirability of providing the public with an authentic account, it has been decided to prepare for publication, as soon as possible after the close of the war, an Official History dealing with its various aspects." The present volume is the first instalment of the promised work. Although full use has been made of enemy and Allied sources of information so far as they were accessible, the work is based throughout on our own official documents, not only naval, but also military and political. In this sense, but in this sense only, the work is to be regarded as official; for the form and character of the narrative as well as for opinions expressed the author is alone responsible.

The period dealt with in the volume includes the preparations for war during the years immediately preceding the outbreak of hostilities and the progress of the naval operations down to the time when the Battle of the Falklands gave us a working command of the ocean trade routes.

The aim has been to give in narrative form and free from technicalities an intelligible view not only of the operations themselves but of their mutual connection and meaning, the policy which dictated them, their relation to military and diplomatic action, and the difficulties and cross-currents which in some cases delayed their success and robbed them of the expected results. Endeavour has thus been made to present the various naval movements, actions and individual exploits in their just relations to the course of the war as a whole.

Owing to the complexity of the operations and vast arena they filled in the earlier stages of the war, the period covered by the volume is comparatively short. After the first year, however, this difficulty tends to diminish as the arena became more restricted and the leading lines less complicated. It is hoped, therefore, that the whole work may be completed in four or possibly five volumes.

It should be understood that the work is one of collaboration with the Staff of the Historical Section, without whose assistance it would have been impossible to extract a connected narrative from the mass of material that has been continually accumulating.

Even so, it has been found necessary to confine the narrative to the actual operations and relegate the important subject of their effect on sea-borne trade to a separate section of the work, which is being prepared by Mr. C. Ernest Fayle.

Similarly, in order to deal with the work of the Mercantile Marine more fully and more intimately than is possible in the general account of the operations, a third section of the work, " The Merchant Navy," has been entrusted to Mr. Archibald Hurd.

In the preparation of the maps and charts to illustrate the operations special provision was made by the Hydrographer of the Navy for giving the indispensable co-operation of his Department. Courses and bearings mentioned in the text are true unless otherwise stated.

Authorities.—The material on which the narrative is based is mainly :—

1. Reports, papers and records of the Committee of Imperial Defence.
2. The " In " and " Out " series of Admiralty telegrams.
3. Letters of Proceedings, Reports and Despatches of Admirals and Senior Naval Officers. These have been carefully checked, especially for actions, by Deck Logs, Signal and Wireless Logs and Engine-Room Registers, and wherever possible by reference to the officers concerned.
4. Admiralty correspondence with other Departments of State, especially the Foreign Office, War Office, Colonial Office and India Office.
5. Depositions of prisoners, captured documents and other intelligence reports.
6. War Office records of analogous nature so far as they relate to combined operations or affect the distribution and action of the Fleet.

As the official naval documents are not at present accessible to students, no particular references to them are given in the foot-notes. All, however, that are of historical interest are being collected and arranged by the Historical Section for future reference in a special series of volumes covering the whole period of the war. Where, on the other hand, unofficial sources have been used, references will be found. These consist mainly of published accounts of British, Allied and enemy origin, dealing with particular episodes.

J. S. C.

CONTENTS

CONTENTS

CONTENTS

MAPS, PLANS AND DIAGRAMS
IN VOLUME

MAPS AND CHARTS IN SEPARATE CASE

INTRODUCTION

In the long series of wars during which the British naval tradition had grown up, there was none that presented the same problems as those with which we were confronted in July 1914. Quite apart from changes in material—changes which in certain vital elements were still in a state of restless development—the fundamental factor was one of which there had been little or no experience. The bulk of our knowledge had been gained against enemies that lay to the southward. Never since the Dutch wars of the seventeenth century had we had to deal with a first class naval power which was based to the northward of the Dover defile, and it was on the inviolability of that defile and its long, difficult, and well-flanked approach from the south and west that the traditional distribution of our main fleet rested.

Now all that was gone. For the easily defended English Channel, in which the old enemy had no naval base of any importance, there was the expanse of the North Sea, with its broad and stormy outlet between Scotland and Norway, and the new enemy was so placed as to have entries to it at two widely separate points, which are linked together by a perfectly protected inland waterway. Finally, instead of our southern seaboard, rich in well-disposed naval ports, we had, facing the enemy, a long stretch of coast dotted with vulnerable commercial ports but without a single Fleet base of the first order, except Chatham, which, owing to navigational difficulties, was incapable of being adapted to modern war conditions.

To the right solution of this problem naval attention had long been devoted, but there were other problems which also differed from the old ones, and some of them—particularly those which arose out of the military developments of the war—were not foreseen with any clearness. It was known that the Navy might be called upon in the early days to transport our Expeditionary Force to the Continent; but how great that force was to grow and what a burden would be the work of its nourishment was beyond any man's ken. Again, assistance from the Dominions oversea was to be expected, but the outburst of imperial spirit that astonished the world was far from being fully gauged. Still less was it foreseen that India would take her place in the main theatre in line with the rest. In no one's mind was there a picture of convoy after convoy pressing to Europe at the very outset from all the ends of the earth, and in their eagerness to swell the efforts of the homeland cutting through our hard-strained system of commerce protection beyond all anticipation.

In the appreciations which preceded the war all this was dark, but the fundamental new problem had been fully realised and provided for by unceasing study. Still the solution was only beginning to take shape when war suddenly came upon us, and there are few achievements in our history finer than the way in which all departments made shift with the unfinished work, and in the stress of the struggle brought it quickly to completion.

The dominant problem had been to fix the disposition of the main fleet. The reversal of the old geographical conditions, which was the outstanding difficulty of a war with Germany, overrode all the considerations which had determined the key position of the fleet in former wars, and a new one had to be found from which it could best discharge its primary functions. What those functions had always been must be clearly apprehended, for of recent years, by a strange misreading of history, an idea had grown up that its primary function is to seek out and destroy the enemy's main fleet. This view, being literary rather than historical, was nowhere adopted with more unction than in Germany, where there was no naval tradition to test its accuracy. So securely was it held by our enemy that it seems to have coloured their naval policy with a sanguine expectation that we should at once seek out their fleet where it most wished to be found; and when they saw their hope unrealised they consoled themselves—probably quite sincerely—with taunts that the British Navy had lost its old spirit, and was no longer to be feared.

How the false conception which the Germans adopted arose is difficult to explain, unless it be that so often the most attractive personalities amongst our admirals had performed their most brilliant exploits when in command of secondary fleets, and that these exploits form the most stirring pages in the story. But the truth is that with rare and special exceptions, as when the enemy's chief naval force was not based in the Home Area, our main or Grand Fleet always operated from its Home Station. Its paramount duty was to secure the command of Home Waters for the safety of our coasts and trade. There was no question of seeking out the enemy, for normally his fleet lay behind his base defences where it was inaccessible. All our own fleet could do was to take the most suitable position for confining him to port or bringing him to action if he put to sea. There was always the hope that the pressure so exercised would sooner or later force him to offer battle. But until an opportunity for decisive action arose, it was by patient and alert vigil it sought to attain its ultimate object—that is, primarily to cover the squadrons and flotillas which formed our floating defence against invasion, and secondarily to cover those which operated in the home terminals of our trade routes for the protection of our own commerce and the disturbance of that of the enemy, so far as geographical conditions permitted of both duties being performed simultaneously. For defence against invasion the system was obviously the only one possible; for control of trade it had been found efficacious, and never more so than proved to be the case in the war of 1914. For since all the new enemy's home terminals lay within our own home waters, we could close them by the same disposition with which we ensured free access to our own. The result was an immediate paralysis of German oceanic trade, and it was due not to the operations of our distant cruisers but to the fact that access to the German home ports was barred by the Grand Fleet and the Home cruisers that it protected.

With these considerations in mind the right position for the Grand Fleet was not far to seek. It was found in Scottish waters, where it could control the approach to the North Sea just as the old Western Squadron controlled the Channel and its approaches. But the fact had to be faced that the new position was weak in the special elements in which the old one was so strong. In Portsmouth, Plymouth and Falmouth the old Western Squadron had excellent bases, both primary and subsidiary, but for the new position everything had to be created afresh, and here it was that, in spite of all the thought that had been given to the subject, so much remained to do.

It was not for want of study or foresight that we were found unprepared. It was due mainly to the never ceasing change in the power, range and character of naval material which left no stable factors on which a solid scheme could be built up. So rapid were the developments that, as experience had shown but too often, extensive naval works tended to be out of date before they could be completed. Nothing but the most careful consideration was likely to save the country from costly disappointment, and for this purpose committee after committee had been sitting up to the eve of the war.

After considerable hesitation it had been decided in 1903 to establish a first class base at Rosyth, but this was not expected to be completed at the earliest till the end of 1915. Of second class bases, like Pembroke and Queenstown, there were none in the North Sea, though so far as docking and repairs were concerned the Tyne gave similar facilities. In the third category classed as " war anchorages," such as Berehaven, Portland and Dover, there was only one on the East Coast. This was Harwich. There were, however, several defended commercial ports such as the Humber, the Tees, Hartlepool, the Tyne, the Tay and Aberdeen, which would serve the same purpose, but all of them were cramped river ports, which had nothing like the ample space of those of the south-western area, nor, owing to tidal conditions, had they the same freedom of access at all times; and finally, over and above these drawbacks, no one of them was far enough north to satisfy the fundamental strategical need. Furthermore, the use which had been made of the Elliot Islands and other similar localities in the Russo-Japanese War had impressed naval opinion with the great advantages of unfrequented natural harbours, not only as " war anchorages " but as " advanced bases of a temporary and auxiliary character." There were two ideal spots, the one Cromarty Firth, the other Scapa Flow in the Orkneys, and the need of such places was emphasised by an enforced recognition of the inadequacy of the designed base at Rosyth. In 1908 it became apparent that, owing to the increasing power of torpedoes, its outer anchorage was exposed to destroyer attack, and its defences had to be reconsidered. Even so it would not serve, for it was soon realised that the determined rivalry of Germany was swelling fleets to a size that could not have been contemplated when the new base was first designed, and it could no longer contain a fleet such as we needed. By 1910, therefore, Cromarty began to be regarded as indispensable for an advanced temporary fleet base, and Scapa Flow as one for minor forces.

At first it had been contemplated that both places should be treated in the Japanese manner, which was for the Fleet to establish them when they were required. But by 1912, when the new Board of Admiralty came into office, naval developments had reached a pitch that gave both Cromarty and Scapa Flow so much importance that both were seen to require fixed defences.

With this began a new series of difficulties due to other developments in naval material. Our system of defending ports was that the Army was responsible for creating and garrisoning the land defences on the basis of " a scale of attack " which was fixed by the Navy—that is, the Navy laid down for the guidance of the Army in organising the defence the nature and power of the attack which the importance of the particular port was likely to attract. But here, owing to the rapid progress of naval construction and armaments, and changes in the ports themselves, was a shifting foundation on which it was almost impossible to build. For instance in the Humber, which offered the best-placed and most convenient war anchorage between Rosyth and Harwich, large oil fuel stores and new docks in the lower reaches at Killingholm and Immingham had been established since the defences were erected, and they were now of little use. They had to be re-designed on the usual basis for defended ports— a combined attack by armoured cruisers and a small landing force. But by the time the War Office had worked out a new scheme and prepared the estimates they were no longer adequate. Dreadnoughts had rendered the older battleships unfit for the line of battle, and the enemy might well elect to risk these obsolescent units in coastal attack. Thus the scale of attack had to be revised and the work of designing the defences begun all over again on a new and higher scale.

These considerations applied to all defended ports and anchorages; but the continual sapping of the foundations did not end here. Apart from ships of force becoming available for coastal attack and the ever-increasing range and power of torpedoes, submarines began to obtrude themselves. This fresh menace specially concerned the new temporary war anchorages. When their defence had first been proposed the Admiralty had regarded them as beyond submarine range, but by the end of 1913 the sea-going power of submarines had so greatly increased that they could no longer be eliminated. Though Cromarty could easily be made impregnable to the new form of attack the estimates for doing as much for Scapa, owing to its numerous entrances, were found to be so great as to raise a doubt whether the work was worth the cost.

These were only some of the thorns that beset the question. There were others—and particularly those which grew from the inevitable differences between the Naval and the Military views of what was adequate defence—such, for instance, as radical divergencies as to the danger of military attack. This, however, was overcome in the case of Cromarty by handing it over entirely to the Navy. From the first this had been desired by the Admiralty, since one of the advantages of the advanced naval base was the elasticity with which it could be adjusted to the immediate needs of the naval situation—an elasticity which must necessarily be reduced unless the Admiralty had a perfectly free hand. The result was that by the end of July 1914 the whole of the fixed defences were complete and armed. In the Humber, on the other hand, the new heavy armament had not been begun, and the status of Scapa was still undecided. The last proposal of the Admiralty was that if its complete protection was found too costly it should be constituted an oil fuel base, and be given light defences sufficient to repel such a scale of attack as it was likely to induce. But this had not been settled, and when war broke out Scapa, except for the local territorial artillery, was without defence of any kind.

Still, by this time, although Rosyth was specified as the principal base and headquarters for the Grand Fleet, Scapa had come to be regarded as the best initial station. In one respect the position was very inferior to the old one. In another respect it was more favourable. For although in the old French wars, so far as the Atlantic was concerned, the Grand Fleet operating from the Channel could watch and blockade the main naval port of the chief enemy and control the rest of his western ports by detached squadrons in the Bay of Biscay, he had another seaboard in the Mediterranean, and this entailed a secondary fleet of considerable force operating within the Straits of Gibraltar or at its entrance. The case of a war with Germany presented no such complication. Seeing that her whole Battle Fleet was concentrated in the North Sea, the conditions permitted us a complete counter concentration in the new position, except for such force as was needed to secure the Straits of Dover, and this was mainly a question of torpedo craft and their supporting cruisers and minor battleships.

But it was not a war merely between ourselves and Germany that had to be considered. The premonitory symptoms indicated that when the war came we should find ourselves in line with France and Russia against Germany and Austria and possibly Italy. Here, then, was a condition which brought the Mediterranean into play as of old, and at the same time it placed upon our Home Fleets responsibilities which were entirely without precedent, and emphasised with added stress the need of concentration in the newly selected position.

The reason for this lay in the uncertainty which surrounded

the probable attitude of Italy. Though it was almost impossible to conceive a situation in which she would be found fighting Great Britain by the side of her natural enemy Austria, the French had no such comfort. They at least had to face the prospect of having to deal with the combined Austrian and Italian Fleets, and the result was a growing desire to concentrate their whole battle fleet in the Mediterranean, and to trust to the British Fleet for protection against the German Fleet in the Atlantic. So vital for the French was the command of the Mediterranean that any reasonable risk, it was felt, must be taken to secure it. Not only was it needed for the sake of the North African Colonies, which Germany was so obviously coveting, but it was of the essence of the French war plan that the Algerian Army Corps should be transported to France in the first days of the war. Nor did the risk seem great. Theoretically the French Atlantic coasts would lie open to invasion, but the advocates of the proposed combination held that if by its adoption the British Fleet was freed from all preoccupation with the Mediterranean, it would be able to concentrate in the North Sea and Channel such a force as would paralyse the German High Seas Fleet altogether. The doctrine of the École Supérieure de la Marine was that with an Anglo-French flotilla barring the way to the Channel and the British Fleet barring the north-about Passage, the Germans would be caught in a mouse-trap and there would be no fighting in the Atlantic.[1]

Though the British Admiralty took a less confident view, the French idea fell in with their own tendency towards extreme concentration, and they were inclined to adopt it even to its logical conclusion, which would divide the command of European waters between the two Navies, leaving the Mediterranean entirely to the French and the Atlantic entirely to the British. But in both countries the proposal met with marked disfavour mainly on moral and sentimental grounds. In France they spoke of " those waters laden with memories where lay the wrecks of Tourville's and Duquesne's ships and the bones of the *Vengeur's* crew," and deplored that the tombs of the dead who fought at sea and bred the race of French seamen were to be defended by British guns. In Great Britain the instinct that our position in the world was in some way bound up with the strength we could display in the Mediterranean was even stronger. It had become a canon of British policy—consecrated by repeated experience—that our Mediterranean Fleet was the measure of our influence in continental affairs, and the feeling had only increased since

[1] Lanessan : *Notre Défense Maritime,* 1914, p. 210.

the road to India lay that way, and Egypt and Cyprus had become limbs of the Empire.

The result was characteristic of both countries. In France the logical view prevailed over the sentimental. In the autumn of 1912—that is, on the eve of the first Balkan War—it was announced that their 3rd Battle Squadron, which was still based at Brest, was to join the 1st and 2nd which were already in the Mediterranean, and by the spring of 1913, in order to provide the concentrated Fleet with officers, the whole of their Atlantic defence flotillas were demobilised and the defence of the ports handed over to the Army. All that remained at the northern bases was their 2nd Cruiser Squadron, composed of six " Gloires," an old type of armoured cruiser, and the flotillas which were to co operate with the British in the combined defence of the Channel.[1]

On our side, on the contrary, it was the naval tradition that prevailed, and a Mediterranean Squadron was formed as powerful as was consistent with the minimum required for the northern concentration. It consisted of four battle cruisers, four of our best heavy cruisers and four light cruisers, but even this force was regarded only as provisional till the development of our building programme permitted more to be done. As it stood it had certain technical advantages in that the battle cruisers furnished an element in which the French Fleet was wanting. But as the Fleets of the Triple Alliance Powers increased it would not suffice, and the intention was by the end of 1915 to replace the battle cruisers by a full battle squadron.[2] In this way the extreme French views were met by a compromise. While they were left free to make a complete concentration of their battle fleet within the Straits, we did not commit the Mediterranean to their sole charge. Further than this, there was an informal understanding, without which the French might well have hesitated still longer in taking the final step. Although in accordance with our time-honoured policy we studiously refrained from developing the Entente into an Alliance, though we refused to bind ourselves to declare war with Germany if she attacked France, yet the Staffs of the two countries were permitted to discuss conditionally plans of joint action, and on November 22, 1912, Sir Edward Grey defined our mutual obligations at sea in a letter to the French Ambassador. The letter recorded an agreement that while the new distribution of the French and British Fleets respectively was not based on an engagement to co-operate in war, yet " if either Government had grave

[1] René La Bruyère : *Deux Années de Guerre Navale*, p. 21. Paris, 1916.
[2] First Lord's speech. *Navy Estimates*, March 17, 1913.

reason to expect an unprovoked attack or something that threatened the general peace, it should immediately discuss with the other whether both Governments should act together, and if so what measures they would be prepared to take in common." [1]

Guarded as was the formula agreed on, yet, taking note as it did of the distribution of the two Fleets, it did imply a definite sphere of naval action for each Power for the common purpose should the specified condition arise. Thus it was our Home Fleets, over and above their normal duties, became charged with others which were without precedent, and in these added duties the tendency to extreme concentration found its final justification. There were critics to whom it appeared excessive and a departure from British practice, but seen as a measure complementary to the French concentration in the Mediterranean designed to develop the utmost naval energy of the Entente, it was for the responsible authorities essential to our war plan.

With Russia no arrangement had been made, and indeed none at the time was possible, for the reconstruction of her Fleet, which had been taken in hand after the war with Japan, had not yet proceeded far enough to make it an effective factor in the situation. Her Black Sea Fleet for the purpose was off the board, and in the Baltic she had only four battleships in commission, two approximately of " Lord Nelson " type and two older.[2] She had also there four of her new fleet of eight " Dreadnoughts " which had been launched in 1911, but only two of them were approaching completion. Besides these she had the *Ryurik*, in which the Commander-in-Chief, Admiral von Essen, flew his flag, and four cruisers.[3] In spite of the reputation this brilliant officer had won in the Japanese War for bold and enterprising leadership, a force relatively so weak could only be regarded by the Military Authority, under whose supreme direction it was, as part of the defence of the capital. Their policy was one of concentration in the Gulf of Finland. Libau, a practically ice-free port, which in 1893 had been commenced as the chief naval station, had been abandoned as being too near the German frontier and its defences dismantled. The only naval ports that remained were Helsingfors and Revel inside the Gulf. Except, therefore, for such influence as the Russian Fleet could exert by

[1] Sir Edward Grey's speech in the House of Commons, August 3, 1914.
[2] *Imperator Pavel I* and *Andrei Pervozvanni* (four 12", fourteen 8"), *Tzesarevich* and *Slava* (four 12", twelve 6").
[3] *Ryurik* (four 10", eight 8", twenty 4·7"), *Gromoboi* (four 8", twenty-two 6"), *Bayan, Pallada* and *Admiral Makarov* (two 8", eight 6").

forcing the Germans to watch it with a superior force, it could have no effect upon our own disposition.

The arrangement with the French, on the contrary, necessarily affected the limits within which our distribution could be made. However advisable the division of labour, it was undeniable that it presented drawbacks, and in certain important aspects the drawbacks were more obvious than the merits. Chief among them was that the system entailed the practical abandonment of the Atlantic trade routes, and the disappearance of our cruisers from the localities where they had been accustomed to show the flag in time of peace. The inevitable consequence would be that on a sudden outbreak of war the great trade routes would be very slenderly protected, and this was the more serious since Germany not only had cruisers abroad but was credited with an intention to arm a large number of fast and powerful liners as commerce destroyers wherever they might happen to be at the outbreak of war.

The reason for this weakness was that, for our system to work, the main concentration must not only be overwhelming but instantaneous. The Grand Fleet which was to take the northern position must always be in instant readiness for war. The advantage of time and place demanded no less, and in this case the demand was specially urgent on account of precisely those defects in the intended position of the Grand Fleet which were still unremedied. The northern islands still lay dangerously open to attack by the enemy. By a blow before declaration the Germans might establish themselves there, and our whole system would then be in danger of collapsing. It was essential, therefore, that the Grand Fleet must be ready at the first tremor of strained relations to get into position and prevent any such attempt except at the cost of a fleet action, which of all things was what we most ardently desired.

But if we were to make sure of the key position it was impossible to keep cruisers in full commission all over the world except by greatly increased estimates which the country was in no mood to sanction. Active service officers and ratings were insufficient, and the choice consequently lay between risking the main position and risking some initial loss on the trade routes in the first weeks of the war. Given the conditions, the choice could not be in doubt for a moment, and just as the French had to demobilise their west coast defence flotillas to provide for the Mediterranean Fleet, so had we to demobilise our commerce protection cruisers to provide for the instant readiness of the Grand Fleet. In one particular, however, a modification of the policy had been found necessary. Owing to the disturbed state of Mexico and other circumstances, there had been a call for the restoration of the West Atlantic Station, that is, the area of the old West Indies and North American Squadrons, and to satisfy the demand one of the First Fleet Cruiser Squadrons had been detached there permanently.

To meet the needs of the situation the organisation in Home Waters was based on three fleets, in progressive states of readiness for war. In the First were a fleet flagship and four battle squadrons, the 1st, 2nd and 4th consisting of " Dreadnoughts," and the 3rd of eight " King Edwards," the last development of the " Majestic " type. In July 1914 the " Dreadnought " battleships in commission numbered twenty against the German thirteen, and ship for ship the German, though better protected, were inferior in gun power to our own, while against the *Agamemnon* and the eight " King Edwards " they had five " Deutschlands " and five " Braunschweigs " of inferior armament.[1] The First Fleet had also a squadron of four battle cruisers, all except

[1] DREADNOUGHTS

British

2 Iron Dukes .	.	.	10 13·5″	12 6″	
4 King George V ⎱	.	.	10 13·5″	16 4″	
4 Orions ⎰					
2 Colossus ⎱	.	.	10 12″	16 4″	
1 Neptune ⎰					
3 St. Vincents	.	.	10 12″	18 4″	
3 Bellerophons	.	.	10 12″	16 4″	
1 Dreadnought	.	.	10 12″	24 12 pdrs.	

German

5 Kaisers	.	.	10 12″	14 5·9″	
4 Ostfrieslands	.	.	12 12″	14 5·9″	
4 Nassaus	.	.	12 11″	12 5·9″	

PRE-DREADNOUGHTS

British

Agamemnon .	.	.	4 12″	10 9·2″	
8 King Edwards	.	.	4 12″	4 9·2″	10 6″

German

5 Deutschlands ⎱	.	.	4 11″	14 6·7″
5 Braunschweigs ⎰				

The *Agamemnon* was attached temporarily to the 4th Battle Squadron.

In addition to the above we had approaching completion two more " Iron Dukes " and two of the new " Queen Elizabeth " class, with eight 15″, and the Germans had three large " Dreadnoughts " of improved type, of which the *König*, the nameship of the class, was more advanced than our own.

one being of the latest type, with eight 13·5″ guns, against which the Germans could show on the North Sea three of an earlier type armed with 11″ guns. In cruisers our First Fleet entirely overweighted the High Seas Fleet.[1] Besides the cruisers attached to the battle squadrons, it had four squadrons, the 2nd, 3rd, and 4th (of which, however, the 4th was actually in the West Indies), and a light cruiser squadron. It had also attached to it the first four flotillas of destroyers, each comprising a cruiser leader and twenty units.[2] This was in effect the " Grand Fleet," which was intended to be in position to occupy the North Sea at the outbreak of war, and it was always kept in full commission ready for immediate action.

The Second Fleet consisted of the *Lord Nelson* (four 12″, ten 9·2″) as Fleet flagship with the 5th and 6th Battle Squadrons, that is, five " Duncans," eight " Formidables," and the *Vengeance*, each armed with four 12″ and twelve 6″, to which the Germans could oppose only five " Wittelsbachs " and five " Kaiser Friedrichs," armed with four 9·4″ and fourteen to eighteen 5·9″. These obsolescent German ships also formed a second fleet, designed, with the older armoured and protected cruisers, to operate in the Baltic and keep the Russian Fleet in check. Assigned to our own Second Fleet were two cruiser squadrons, the 5th and 6th, but this was for administrative purposes only. They formed no part of its war organisation, but, as will appear directly, were allotted other duties of immediate importance. In the same way there was nominally attached to it the bulk of the Home Defence Patrol Flotillas. They comprised seven flotilla cruisers, four patrol flotillas and seven flotillas of submarines. Except for the submarines this fleet was not on a war footing, but was manned by what were called " Active Service Crews," consisting of all the specialist officers and about three-fifths of the full complement of men. They could, however, be ready in a few hours, for " Balance Crews," consisting mainly of men going through courses of training, were kept together in various naval barracks ready to embark at the shortest notice. As the main function of the battle squadrons was to form the Channel Fleet in immediate proximity to its home ports, no higher degree of readiness was necessary.

[1] For details and organisation of the High Seas Fleet see Appendix A.
[2] The actual number of the Grand Fleet destroyers was 76, of which 33 had a speed of no more than 27 knots. Against these Germany had in Home Waters 96 of 30 knots or over and 48 others of from 30 to 26 knots fit for coastal work.

The remainder of the battleships and cruisers still on the active list formed the Third Fleet, which was in effect a " Reserve." It comprised the 7th and 8th Battle Squadrons —that is, five " Canopus " and nine " Majestics," with five squadrons of cruisers.[1] They were not in commission, but were distributed in groups in various home ports, and were manned by no more than " care and maintenance " parties. For full crews they had to rely on the various Reserves, and therefore could only be brought forward for service some time after mobilisation. The battleships were all on the brink of obsolescence, and as none of them had any definite place as active ships in the initial distribution, the system served well enough. They were regarded as available for subsidiary services, and shortly before the war four of the " Majestics " had been allotted as guardships for the Humber till its new defences could be completed.

With the cruisers, however, the case was different. Besides securing the position in Home Waters, the Home Fleets were responsible for commerce protection over all the trade routes in the Atlantic, and it was from the Third Fleet cruisers that the system had to be completed. During peace we had nothing in the Atlantic except one ship on the South American station, and the 4th Cruiser Squadron which, as we have seen, was engaged at the moment entirely in the West Indian area for the protection of British interests in Mexico. By the organisation, it will be remembered, it belonged to the First Fleet, and though the intention was that from time to time it should join the Commander-in-Chief's flag for manœuvres, it was in practice permanently detached in the West Atlantic. The next squadrons to be ready would be the two attached to the Second Fleet. Of these the 6th, which consisted of four " Drakes," though intended to support the flotillas in the south part of the North Sea, had to be diverted to take the place of the 4th Squadron in the Grand Fleet. The 5th, which on the eve of the war consisted of the *Carnarvon* and three " Monmouths," was assigned to the most important and exposed area in the Atlantic trade routes—that is, to the Mid-Atlantic area between the West Coast of Africa and Brazil, in which lay the converging points of the great southern trade.

All the nearer stations had to be filled from the Third Fleet Squadrons, some of which were actually required to complete the disposition in Home Waters. The 10th, for instance, was to act in close connection with the Grand Fleet and to

---

[1] Against these still efficient battleships with four 12″ guns and twelve 6″, the Germans could only show two " Brandenburgs " with six 11″ and eight " Hagens " with three 9·4″.

form what was known as the Northern Patrol—that is, the Patrol specially charged with exercising control of the trade route to Germany north-about. The 11th Squadron was to operate to the West of Ireland to cover the home terminals of the great Western trade routes, and the 12th to combine with the French cruisers in the approaches to the Channel, in accordance with the provisional arrangement which had been settled between the two Admiralty Staffs in October 1913. The 7th Squadron also acted in Home Waters, the greater part of it being employed in place of the " Drakes " with the flotillas which guarded the southern part of the North Sea. The remaining squadron—that is, the 9th (for the 8th had no ships assigned to it)—was to complete the protection of the great Southern and Mediterranean routes, its station being off the mouth of the Straits and covering the area Cape Finisterre–Azores–Madeira immediately north of the 5th Squadron in the Mid-Atlantic area. The general idea was to push out these ships as fast as they were mobilised, but as they were on the Third Fleet basis some delay was inevitable. So far as possible it was minimised by the fact that the nearest stations were assigned to them. Still the risk remained, and had to be accepted as the price paid for the immediate readiness of the First and Second Fleets.

Beyond the Mediterranean and Red Sea, for which, as we have seen, a special fleet was provided, our interests were guarded by four squadrons. The most important of them was that on the China station, with one battleship, two cruisers, two light cruisers, eight destroyers, four torpedo boats, three submarines and a flotilla of sixteen sloops and gunboats, ten of which were river gunboats. Next came the squadron provided by the Australian Commonwealth, with one battle cruiser, four light cruisers, three destroyers and two submarines. Associated with it was the New Zealand station with three old " P " class light cruisers and a sloop. Finally, there was the East Indies Squadron, with one battleship, two light cruisers and four sloops. Each squadron was an independent command, but an organisation had been worked out under which they could be formed into one force, known as the Eastern Fleet, under the command of the Commander-in-Chief of the China station. When so formed it would consist of two battleships, one battle cruiser, two cruisers, eleven light cruisers, eleven sea-going sloops and gunboats, eleven destroyers and five submarines. More loosely connected with this Fleet was the Cape station, which, with only three light cruisers, occupied South African waters between the Mid-Atlantic station and the East Indies station. The only other foreign stations were the West Coast of Africa with a single gunboat, the South-east Coast of America with one light cruiser, and the West Coast of North America with two sloops, both of which were on the west coast of Mexico watching British interests, like the 4th Cruiser Squadron on the Atlantic side.

In this way the vast extent of the Seven Seas was occupied in the traditional manner, not by patrolling the trade routes, but by guarding in such force as our resources permitted the main focal areas where they converged, and where the enemy's commerce destroyers were most likely to be attracted and had the only chance of making a serious impression upon the huge volume of our trade. At some of these points, and particularly those which had recently attained importance, such as the Fernando Noronha or Pernambuco area off the north-east shoulder of Brazil, our hold, as will appear later, was weak. To some extent, also, the system was distorted by the desire to watch ports which were frequented by enemy's ships capable of being converted into commerce raiders. In other words, the principle of watching focal points was at times crossed and confused by the principle of watching bases. But on the whole the system worked well, and when we consider the prodigious nature of the task, the unprecedented volume of trade, the tangled web which its crossing routes wove round the earth, and then how slender was our cruiser force beside the immensity of the oceans, and how in every corner of them the enemy was lurking, all defects are lost in the brilliance and magnitude of the success. We have now, after our manner, ceased to wonder at it, but the fact remains that, for all we may point to occasions and places where more might have been done, the success of the defence over the attack went beyond everything the most sanguine and foresighted among us had dared to hope, and beyond anything we had achieved before.

Nor did the task of the Navy end here. Over and above the burden that lay on our sea-going ships there remained the task of protecting our own shores from attack by lightly escorted raiding forces. To this function were assigned all the destroyer flotillas except the first four which were attached to the Grand Fleet, and the 5th which was in the Mediterranean. They were organised in " Patrol " and " Local Defence " Flotillas. The Patrol Flotillas, which were the 6th, 7th, 8th and 9th, with their attached light cruisers, were under a special officer designated " Admiral of Patrols " (a post then held by Rear-Admiral G. A. Ballard). The Local Defence Flotillas, which consisted of the older destroyers and

torpedo boats, were attached to the naval ports which their
function was to protect. Since in Naval opinion no raid
was likely to be attempted except across the North Sea, the
Patrol Flotillas were distributed along the East Coast. To
the 6th Flotilla, known as the Dover Patrol, was assigned
the defence of the Straits : the 7th was based on the Humber,
the 8th on the Tyne and the 9th on the Forth.[1] Beyond the
Forth Area the Scottish Coast was sufficiently safeguarded
by the Grand Fleet bases at Cromarty and at Scapa, to which
a special Defence Flotilla of two destroyer divisions was
assigned. The East Anglian Coast between the Dover and
Humber Patrols was equally well provided for by the active
force based at Harwich. Here was Commodore Tyrwhitt
(Commodore T) with the 1st and 3rd Destroyer Flotillas and
their attached light cruisers, and here, too, was the 8th or
"Oversea" Flotilla of submarines ("D" and "E" class) under
Commodore Keyes (Commodore S).[2] In view of the possibility of the enemy making an attack before declaration of
war, the first function of this force was to provide during the
period of strained relations a Destroyer Patrol for the defence
of the Thames Estuary, but as soon as the Nore Defence
Flotilla was ready to take over this duty the Harwich
Flotillas would assume their real place in the war plan, which
was to act offensively against the enemy's destroyers and
minelayers operating in the southern part of the North Sea.
Here, therefore, a Patrol Flotilla was unnecessary.

Under Commodore Keyes were also the five older flotillas
of submarines ("B" and "C" class), which were distributed
amongst the Patrol Flotillas and formed part of the patrol
organisation under Admiral Ballard. The oldest boats of
all (three flotillas, mainly "A" class) were attached to the
Local Defence Flotillas.[3]

Such in broad outline was the force and organisation on
which we had to rely to solve the problems which confronted
us when the storm broke. But it takes no count of the vast
auxiliary fleet that rapidly came into existence during the war
to second the efforts and fill the interstices of the established

	Light Cruisers.	Destroyers.	Torpedo Boats.
[1] Dover Patrol	2	22	—
Humber	1	22	12
Tyne	1	8	12
Forth	1	18	—

[2] The post of "Commodore S" was originally instituted as an administrative appointment at the Admiralty, but under Commodore Keyes it
tended to become an active command.

[3] The total number of submarines completed was 74, which, excluding
3 in China, 3 at Malta and 3 at Gibraltar, left 65 in the nine Home Flotillas.

Navy. To a small extent assistance from the Mercantile Marine had been counted on, but it proved to be no more than a germ of the vast organisation which was quickly developed. A few liners had been retained as auxiliary cruisers, and in 1911 a commencement had been made in organising an auxiliary minesweeping service of hired trawlers to be manned by a special section of the Royal Naval Reserve. It was recruited from the ordinary fishing crews, and placed under an officer designated Captain-in-Charge of Mine-sweepers. The organisation was on a basis of seven areas with nine " Trawler Stations " under the Admiral of Patrols.[1] Such good progress was made that during the crisis of 1913, Captain Bonham, who was then Captain-in-Charge, was able to report that in the event of war eighty-two trawlers would be immediately available. In the year before the war steps were also being taken to form a Motor-boat Reserve, but all these things were only a beginning. After the outbreak of war the system developed so rapidly that soon the auxiliary vessels far outnumbered those on the Navy List. The armed merchant cruisers rapidly multiplied; trawlers, drifters and yachts were taken up in scores for minesweeping and anti-submarine patrols, and steam-craft of all kinds for the Examination Service which controlled the flow of trade in our Home Waters. There had been nothing like it since the distant days when the Mercantile Marine was counted as part of the Navy of England— nothing to equal it even in the heyday of privateering or in the days of our floating defence against Napoleon's Invasion Flotilla. Faced with a struggle, the gravity of which was quickly recognised, the country not only fell back to the mediæval spirit in which its sea power had been born, but infused into it a new and wholly modern energy and method. The whole seafaring population, in so far as it was not needed for other work vital to the national life, gathered to the struggle before it was six months old. As on the Continent it was seen to be a contest not of armies but of armed nations, so by the end of 1914, and without any previous preparation, our nation was in arms upon the sea. Such a reawakening of the old maritime spirit which had lain dormant for so many ages must always remain as one of the most absorbing features of the war, and the strangeness of the revival is the more impressive when we remember that it was mainly the mine and the submarine, the very last words of the Naval art, that threw us back to the methods of the Middle Ages.

[1] Cromarty, the Forth, the Humber, Harwich, the Nore, Dover, Portsmouth, Portland and Devonport.

CHAPTER I

PREPARATION FOR WAR AND THE PERIOD OF STRAINED RELATIONS [1]

AMONGST the many false impressions that prevailed, when after the lapse of a century we found ourselves involved in a great war, not the least erroneous is the belief that we were not prepared for it. Whether the scale on which we prepared was as large as the signs of the times called for, whether we did right to cling to our long-tried system of a small Army and a large Navy, are questions that will long be debated; but, given the scale which we deliberately chose to adopt, there is no doubt that the machinery for setting our forces in action had reached an ordered completeness in detail that has no parallel in our history.

It must be said, however—and nothing is more eloquent of the widespread belief that the world had grown too wise for Napoleonic convulsions ever to recur—that the work was not completed till the eleventh hour. Much had been done by various Departments—particularly since the South African War and the rapid expansion of the German Navy. For some years past the Admiralty had been keeping a " War List," in which was laid down in detail the action which was to be taken by the Navy and the Admiralty Departments during what was known as the Precautionary Period and on Declaration of War, and to secure co-ordination with the other Departments immediately concerned. They were regularly informed of all intended action which would affect them. Still the arrangements were to a large extent independent, and it was not till the end of 1910 that an effort was made to reach a complete co-ordination. Mr. Haldane was then completing his reorganisation of the Army for the work it was likely to have to perform in a great European war, and at his instigation Mr. Asquith, in January 1911, set up at the Committee of Imperial Defence a strong standing Sub-Committee for "the co-ordination of Departmental Action on the outbreak of war." It was composed of highly-placed representatives from the nine Departments concerned: two from the Admiralty, three from the War

[1] See Map 1 in case.

Office, and one each from the Foreign Office, Home Office, Colonial Office, India Office, Board of Trade, Board of Customs and Excise, and Post Office, with Sir Arthur Nicolson, Permanent Under-Secretary for Foreign Affairs, as Chairman, and Rear-Admiral Sir Charles Ottley, Secretary to the Committee of Imperial Defence, as Secretary.[1]

Its labours resulted in the production of a " War Book," in which was tabulated what every department had to do, and how and when it was to do it. Each Department had its own chapter, arranged on an identical plan in sections, each of which dealt with a successive phase of the preparation. First came departmental arrangements in peace time to secure instantaneous and accurate working of the machinery. Then followed the Precautionary Stage which was initiated by the Foreign Office informing the Cabinet that relations with a certain Power or Powers were strained. To save time, however, as soon as the Foreign Office had decided to take this step they were privately to communicate the decision to the Admiralty, War Office, and Post Office. The next step was the issue of a " Warning Telegram," which formally set on foot the period of " Strained Relations." From being a vague historical expression it had been given a technical, administrative, political and strategical meaning which connoted certain definite defensive actions being taken, such as Mobilisation of Naval Centres and Signal Stations, Protection of Vulnerable Points, Harbour Traffic, certain preliminary stages of Navy and Army Mobilisation, Censorship, Control of Aliens, Treatment of Enemy Merchantmen in Port, Trading with the Enemy, and many other similar measures down to such internal arrangements as the suspension of certain Acts, if found necessary. The four Sections that followed dealt with the Mobilisation of the Navy and Army, Intelligence, Control of Wireless and Cable Censorship, all of which steps could be taken separately or together as required. Finally came the decision to declare war, and the steps that automatically followed.[2]

[1] The Admiralty members were the Director of Naval Intelligence and the Secretary, those of the War Office the Directors of Operations and of Military Training and the Assistant Secretary. Most of the other Departments were represented by their permanent heads. On Admiral Ottley's retirement in 1912, his successor, Captain M. P. A. Hankey, R.M.A., became Secretary. The Clerk to the Privy Council and a representative from the Treasury were afterwards added, and when the Naval War Staff was set up its Chief also became a member.

[2] Major A. Grant Duff, Assistant Secretary, was mainly responsible for the design of the " War Book," and later the work was carried on by Major J. A. Longridge, Indian Army, both afterwards killed in action.

Each departmental chapter was arranged so as to show at a glance not only what the particular Department had to do at each stage, but also the correlative or consequential action of the other Departments, and the precise method by which every message or letter required for operating the system was to be transmitted. In order to secure the utmost degree of decentralisation and provide for executive action being taken automatically on receipt of the " Warning " and " War " Telegrams, these general instructions were worked out in supplementary War Books kept by each Department to meet its own needs and organisation. During the three and a half years the Sub-Committee was at work these details, by constant revision, and particularly by the experience gained during the Agadir crisis at the end of 1911, were carried to a high degree of precision. Special arrangements were made so that in every office responsible officials should be ready at all hours to take immediate action. The requisite telegrams—amounting to thousands— were carefully arranged in order of priority for dispatch in order to prevent congestion on the day of action; every possible letter and document was kept ready in an addressed envelope; special envelopes were designed so that they could be at once recognised as taking priority of everything. All necessary papers, orders in council and proclamations were printed or set up in type, and so far was the system carried that the King never moved without having with him those which required his immediate signature.

The fundamental lines of the system were not settled without doubt and difficulty, for the whole structure had to rest on that unstable ground where the opposing tendencies of the diplomatic and the fighting services never reach equilibrium. The period of " Strained Relations " is the " No Man's Land," where political action and war overlap. The tendency of all Foreign Offices is inevitably to postpone till the last moment a declaration that they cannot guarantee the attainment of their object by political means; the desire of the fighting services is to set their machinery in motion at the earliest possible moment. A compromise is inevitable. Even in Germany, where the military side was all powerful, it had to submit at the last moment to political exigencies. The lines within which the compromise is determined are fixed by the period of Strained Relations, the time at which it is declared, and the action that is permissible when it is instituted. Any sign that the machinery is in motion tends to prejudice a political solution at its acutest and most delicate stage. No less hazardous for a solution by arms may be even a few hours' delay in starting the machinery. To minimise the difficulty, the possibility of establishing a precautionary period was considered, during which measures not likely to disturb public opinion might be permitted, but it was found that nothing of value could be done secretly enough not to arouse excitement—except in the Navy. Owing to the stealth of naval movements and the fact that the principal part of the Fleet was always on a war footing, certain preliminary steps could be taken without danger. It was understood, therefore, that the Admiralty would be free to take such precautionary steps as long tradition had sanctioned, and on this basis the Admiralty War Book was framed.

For the " Warning Telegram " which set up the Precautionary Period there were two alternative code words. The first put in action defensive measures of a purely naval character, such as guarding against surprise torpedo attacks before declaration. It authorised the mobilisation of flotillas, mine-sweepers, cable guard gunboats, examination service at naval ports, and the like. It also set on foot preparations to mobilise, while a separate word called out the " Immediate Reserves," a step which could be taken without touching civil life. The second word authorised all preparatory measures down to the retention of time-expired men, but not putting in force the Mobilisation Instructions or calling up the Civil Naval Reserves—that is, Royal Naval Reserves and Royal Naval Volunteer Reserves, Trawler Reserves and Pensioners. Finally, there was a word, for use in extreme emergency, which covered everything, including not only full mobilisation but all action indicated by the " War Telegram." The Navy was thus ready at any moment to adapt its action to all conditions, from a comparatively extended Precautionary Period to a " Bolt from the Blue."

The whole system was complete and brought up to date by June 1914, with the exception of the work of certain subordinate Committees which had been appointed to work out special war arrangements that crossed the normal flow of civil activity. The chief of these were four in number : one charged with providing for the Control of Railways, which eventually took the form of a Communications Board, consisting of representatives of the Admiralty, War Office, Home Office, Board of Trade and the Executive Committee of Railway Managers. Another was dealing with the Control of the Press. The two others were specially concerned with the sea. One was the Diversion of Shipping Committee, whose function was to provide against the possible inaccessibility of our North Sea ports by arranging to handle the trade elsewhere. The other was the Maintenance of Trade Committee, which was working out a system of State Insurance against war risks at sea. It had long been recognised that a serious obstacle to maintaining our seaborne trade in war-time would arise from the dislocation of the Marine Insurance market, and in order to find a remedy a thorough investigation of the whole question had been going on for some time. Three months before the outbreak of war the Committee had produced a complete scheme, but the expediency of its adoption was considered too controversial for immediate action, and it was held up for further consideration. The work of the other Committees was also well advanced, but none of them had actually reported.

So far as the Navy was concerned, everything was in order. The Home Fleets were even in a state of readiness beyond what the War Book provided. In March 1914 it had been announced in Parliament that instead of the usual summer manœuvres a test mobilisation would be held. It was to begin about the middle of July, and after carrying out exercises at sea the various fleets and flotillas would disperse on the 23rd. It was in no sense a surprise test, nor was it a real war mobilisation, for the Reserves were invited to attend—not called out—and officers were appointed as convenient, and not to their true war stations. The composition of the cruiser squadrons also differed in some cases from that of the War Organisation.

Operation orders were issued on July 10 for the ships to assemble at Portland under the command of Admiral Sir George A. Callaghan, who was completing his third year as Commander-in-Chief of the Home Fleets. All told, counting fleet auxiliaries, not less than 460 pennants were in orders for his flag. They included the whole of the Home Fleets, except the 4th Destroyer Flotilla, which, owing to the unhappy state of affairs in Ulster, was tied to police duty in the Irish Sea. The response of the Reserves proved all that could be desired, and by July 16 the whole of the vast Fleet was assembled in a state of mobilisation.

Outwardly the European situation seemed calmer than it had been for two years past. The murder of the Archduke Ferdinand and his wife at Serajevo at the end of June had produced no ostensible complications : the German Emperor was in Norwegian waters, where the High Seas Fleet was carrying out summer manœuvres, for which it had sailed on July 15, and on the 13th the French President had started for the Baltic to visit the Tsar with the *France* and *Jean Bart.*

Accordingly, at the conclusion of the exercises on the 23rd, Admiral Callaghan informed the Admiralty that he was beginning to disperse the Fleet, and was himself returning to Portland for a Conference of Flag Officers which was to mark the conclusion of the mobilisation.   Then in a flash everything was changed.

Whether by coincidence or design it was on this memorable day—July 23rd—that Austria presented her harsh and peremptory ultimatum to Serbia, and the long-dreaded hour seemed at hand.   Early on the 24th its text was communicated to our Foreign Office.   It was found to contain a time-limit of forty-eight hours, and to be so provocative in its terms that the Admiralty immediately countermanded the Flag Officers' Conference.   Still no steps were taken to stop the dispersal and demobilisation of the Fleet, and, in acknowledging the order, Admiral Callaghan reminded the Board that if nothing was done the dispersal would be complete by Monday the 27th.   By that day, since the First Fleet would be entirely broken up, he himself would be at Berehaven with the 2nd Battle Squadron, the 3rd would be at Lamlash, and all the rest at their home or other ports giving manœuvre leave, while the Second and Third Fleets would have returned to a peace footing.

Still the Government felt bound to avoid the semblance of menacing action.   The forty-eight hours were being employed by the Entente Powers in a strenuous effort to persuade Austria to extend the time, and then to induce her to accept as a basis of negotiation the almost abject reply which, on Russia's advice, Serbia had returned to the ultimatum.   All was useless against Germany's sinister influence. On the 25th, when the forty-eight hours expired, the Austrian Minister left Belgrade, and the advantage we had gained by the test mobilisation was fast slipping away.   But the diplomatic situation was more delicate than ever.   Though neither Russia nor Austria appeared to be irreconcilable, popular feeling in both countries ran so high as to be almost uncontrollable.   Austria could not give way, and Russia had to intimate that she could not stand by and see Serbia attacked.   The only chance our Foreign Office could see of avoiding a general conflagration was to bring together the two Powers immediately interested, and meanwhile to keep everything as quiet as possible.   The Admiralty, therefore, had to rest content with filling up the war flag appointments, and nothing further was done.

Next day, however (the 26th), the outlook was much more menacing.   It was now known for certain that the

Serbian reply had been rejected. At Vienna war was regarded as imminent, the Emperor William was suddenly returning to Berlin, in Germany the measures for the Precautionary Period were being put in force, and news was received that the previous day the High Seas Fleet had had orders to concentrate on the Norwegian coast. Inaction was no longer possible, and at 4.0 in the afternoon a telegram went out to the Commander-in-Chief that no ships of the First Fleet, or any of its attached flotilla, were to leave Portland till further orders, and that the ships of the Second Fleet were to remain at their home ports in proximity to their balance crews. For Admiral Callaghan the order came at the eleventh hour. The battle squadrons were to disperse the following morning, many minor units had already left, the *Bellerophon*, of the 4th Battle Squadron, was on her way to Gibraltar to refit, and six of his cruisers, most of the destroyers and all his minesweepers were at the home ports, with half their crews away on leave. Still, he was able to stop the dispersal before it had gone too far, and on the 27th steps were taken to restore the condition of the Fleet, so far as the now highly-critical state of Europe warranted. The negotiations for a settlement had been broken off abruptly by Austria's withdrawing her Minister from Belgrade. An effort to induce Germany to intervene had failed, but there were fresh indications that direct negotiations between Russia and Austria were not impossible. At Petrograd it was thought that the chief hindrance was an impression which prevailed in Berlin and Vienna that in no circumstances would Great Britain intervene. Sir Edward Grey was able to reply that this impression ought to be removed by the orders given to the First Fleet not to disperse for manœuvre leave.[1] At home all necessary steps were being taken to make the measure a reality. Men on leave were not recalled, but the balance crews were to remain in the ships they had joined for the test mobilisation, the training schools were not to reopen, and no leave was to be given to the second detachments. Subject to this, and so far as resources allowed, the Second Fleet, thirty-six coastal destroyers and some others were ordered to complete to full crews, and all officers temporarily appointed for the test mobilisation were to rejoin the ships in which they had been serving. Both the Second and Third Fleets were to complete with coal, stores and ammunition, but all was to be done as quietly as possible. Quietly, too, the Admiralty proceeded to take other precautionary actions which had

[1] To Sir George Buchanan, Petrograd, July 27.

been left open to it. To provide for the safety of the Humber, four "Majesties," *Mars, Hannibal, Magnificent, Victorious,* which were not in the Fleet organisation, were directed to proceed there as soon as they could complete to active crews, the intention then being to form them into a separate squadron under the Admiral of Patrols. This officer was to be responsible for the Scottish coasts, including the Forth and Shetlands, but not Cromarty and the Orkneys. The *Forward,* which was on police duty in the Irish Sea, was ordered to proceed to Lerwick to take charge of the four destroyers, which were to form the Shetland Patrol. The eight destroyers of the special patrol for the northern anchorages were also to get into position, but they were not able to leave the Nore till the 31st. In the course of the day, moreover, a telegram went out to all Foreign Stations warning them that the European political situation rendered war not impossible, and that they were to be ready, as unobtrusively as possible, to shadow ships of the Central Powers, but that they were not to regard this message as the " Warning Telegram." For the Commander-in-Chief in the Mediterranean was added an order to concentrate his fleet at once at Malta.

Next day, July 28, a further degradation of situation took place. Though conversations between Russia and Austria had begun, and France and Italy had accepted the British proposal for a Conference of Ambassadors in London to discuss its settlement, Germany had refused. It is true she at the same time expressed a desire to co-operate in preventing war, but the insincerity of her attitude was reflected by a telegram from our Ambassador in Vienna, saying that the Foreign Minister had categorically refused to delay operations against Serbia, or to negotiate at all on the basis of the Serbian reply to the Austrian ultimatum. The news was followed quickly by a telegram from Belgrade to say that Austria had declared war.

The gravity of the situation could no longer be disguised. Still, hope of a peaceful solution was not yet entirely lost, and the Foreign Office did not give the word for inaugurating the Precautionary Period. The War Office, however, proceeded rapidly to complete its preparations, and the Admiralty took yet more drastic steps. The flotilla precautions against surprise were further developed, and all the patrol and local defence flotillas first for service were ordered to complete to full crews, so far as might be without recalling men from leave or disturbing the general mobilisation arrangements. Finally, at 5.0 in the evening, when the worst was known,

4

an order went out for the First Fleet to proceed next morning to its preliminary war station at Scapa. Under the war plan it was to proceed west-about, except in case of a sudden crisis. In that event it might expect an order to face the risk of going east-about up the North Sea, particularly if the conditions promised a chance of bringing on a fleet action. Seeing that our last news of the High Seas Fleet was that it was concentrated off the coast of Norway, that chance was clearly in view, and the order was for the east route. To minimise the risk of torpedo attack the fleet was to steer out into mid-channel, and then carry on eastwards so as to pass the Dover Strait by night without lights. Seeing what our engagements were to France, no less could be done. At the same time Vice-Admiral Sir Cecil Burney, who had taken to the Nore the ships belonging to that port for manœuvre leave, was ordered to assemble the 5th and 7th Battle Squadrons and the 5th Cruiser Squadron at Portland.

At 7.0 a.m. on the 29th the First Fleet put to sea. It was high time, for during the day things took a still uglier turn. The Austrians began to bombard Belgrade, Russia was mobilising her southern forces, and Germany was threatening complete mobilisation unless all preparations for war were discontinued in Russia. As it was a demand that could not be complied with, nothing but a miracle could now avert war, and this was the moment when the machinery of the War Book was definitely set in motion. It was not done by the issue of the prescribed intimation from the Foreign Office. Although the idea of mediation by the four Powers had practically been negatived by Germany, a more conciliatory attitude at Vienna gave some hope that a European conflict might yet be avoided by direct conversations between Russia and Austria. But to the Admiralty that hope appeared too slight to justify further inaction. Accordingly, when the Cabinet met that morning the First Lord pressed strongly for the initiation of the Precautionary Period. His view was accepted, and during the afternoon the " Warning Telegram " went out both from the War Office and the Admiralty. The form used by the Admiralty was the second, which authorised everything short of full mobilisation. Certain steps, however, which could not be kept secret were negatived. The Examination Service was to be prepared but not put in force, and the diversion of steamship sailings was not to take place. But by the evening the war cloud was so dark that the Admiralty ordered all officers and men on leave to be recalled by telegraph.

Concealment of our precautionary measures was no longer

possible, even had the Government desired it. But, in fact, that afternoon Sir E. Grey had definitely warned the German Ambassador that he must not be misled into thinking we should necessarily stand aside if France became involved. This frank hint, backed as it was by our naval preparations, had a startling result, for it was a few hours later that the German Chancellor made his notorious proposal to our Ambassador for inducing us to leave France to the mercy of her old enemy. What it meant, as Sir Edward Grey instructed our Ambassador, was that on condition that no soil of France were annexed we were to stand by while her colonies were torn from her and she was crushed down to the status of a helpless satellite of Germany. To preserve our neutrality by such a bargain would be a disgrace from which the good name of the country would never recover. So the reply went forward next day. Still all hope was not lost. Negotiations between Russia and Austria were on foot; they were not without promise and were progressing in a reasonable spirit when, on July 31, Germany suddenly broke everything down with an ultimatum to Petrograd demanding demobilisation in twelve hours.

War was now very near, but we were ready. The machinery of the War Book was working smoothly, and everything was slipping into its place without further orders. During the two days of suspense all units of the First and Second Fleets had reached, or were on their way to, their war stations. Admiral Callaghan, when the First Fleet was ordered north, had been summoned to the Admiralty for a final conference on war plans, and the fleet proceeded under Vice-Admiral Sir George Warrender. While steaming up Channel he had exchanged salutes with the *Jean Bart* and *France* returning from the Baltic, and after passing the Straits of Dover the course was set up the middle of the North Sea, direct for the Skagerrak, till shortly before noon they were abreast of Terschelling. Here a German cruiser was sighted hull down. She probably was able to report the movement, but perhaps wrongly, for when they dropped her the course was altered direct for Scapa, the *Iron Duke* parting company to pick up the Commander-in-Chief in the Forth. Nothing else was seen of the enemy. The High Seas Fleet was, in fact, all in port. On July 26 it had been hurriedly recalled. The North Sea ships were back at Wilhelmshaven by the evening of the 28th, those from the Baltic were early next day at Kiel, and the last destroyers from Norway were coming into Wilhelmshaven as our Fleet passed wide of it.

On July 31 Admiral Callaghan rejoined the *Iron Duke* at

Queensferry, and proceeded to Scapa. To strengthen the staff of the Fleet, Vice-Admiral Sir John R. Jellicoe had been appointed Second in Command. For Chief of the Staff he was given Rear-Admiral Charles E. Madden, who had been commanding the 2nd Cruiser Squadron and was now succeeded by Rear-Admiral The Hon. S. A. Gough-Calthorpe, while Admiral Jellicoe's place as Second Sea Lord was filled by Vice-Admiral Sir Frederick T. Hamilton.

It says much for the skill and completeness with which our preparation for war had been elaborated during the past ten years that the general situation was so far secured without any recourse to a complete mobilisation by the time the critical day arrived. By August 1 the tension had so much increased for the worse that it was scarcely possible we could avoid being involved in the coming struggle. During the previous day Sir Edward Goschen had seen the German Chancellor, and communicated to him Sir Edward Grey's stern reply to his attempt to purchase our betrayal of France. The Chancellor could scarcely listen. They had just heard, he said, that the whole Russian Army was being mobilised. They must therefore at once declare " Kriegsgefahr," which corresponded to our " Warning Telegram," and mobilisation would follow almost immediately. Upon this news it was found necessary the same evening to ask from both France and Germany an assurance that in the event of war Belgian neutrality would be respected. As the telegrams were going out (7.0 p.m.) Sir Francis Bertie at Paris heard from the Foreign Minister that Germany had presented her ultimatum at Petrograd demanding the arrest of mobilisation within twelve hours, and that in default of submission a complete mobilisation of the German Army would take place, on both the Russian and the French frontiers. The replies about Belgium did not come to hand till the early hours of August 1. From France came a full and frank assurance; from Germany practically a refusal to reply. Thereupon the German Ambassador in London was given formal notice that if Belgian territory was violated, we might be forced to take action. As the day advanced things grew rapidly worse. Early in the afternoon the Admiralty received news direct from our Ambassador in Berlin that British ships were being detained in Germany, and that they were forbidden to leave Hamburg on account of " important naval manœuvres " which were to take place the following day.[1]

Within half an hour of the receipt of this news the Admiralty had decided to proceed with mobilisation, and at

[1] Sir Edward Goschen to Admiralty, August 1, received 1.45 p.m.

2.15 p.m. the word went out to act on the Mobilisation Instructions, followed by the word for taking up supply and hospital ships, colliers, and oilers. All the recently appointed Third Fleet flag officers were ordered to join and hoist their flags at once, and Port Admirals were directed to report if the Third Fleet ships were ready to receive their crews. This was followed by the word for controlling wireless in merchant ships, and it only remained to take the final step of calling out the Reserves. Before this was done, however, the Admiralty felt an even more warlike precaution must be taken. The dominating apprehension was that the Germans meant to deliver a blow at sea before declaration—as the Japanese were assumed to have done at Port Arthur—and it was highly probable that it would take the form of offensive mining. The Chief of the Staff, therefore, submitted that the time had come for our patrol and local defence flotillas to be but at night, and this step was at once approved. Orders went out accordingly, but with the proviso that the submarine flotillas were not to be employed in patrol duty during the precautionary period. It was not till some hours after these movements were sanctioned that the Admiralty set on foot the last stage of mobilisation which would render the Third Fleet active. Late that night news came in that Germany had declared war on Russia, and as soon as it was known at the Admiralty, it was felt that the final step could no longer be delayed. At 1.25 a.m., therefore (August 2), without further consultation they gave the word to mobilise the Naval Reserves, and their action was formally sanctioned by the Cabinet later in the day.

Thus it will be seen that, contrary to an impression that became current owing to a misapprehension on the part of a Foreign Representative, there was no prolongation of the test mobilisation.[1] Not only had it lapsed, but manœuvre leave had been given in the Second Fleet and in part of the First. The actual mobilisation was an independent act ordered by the Admiralty after a definite war movement had been ordered. It was not completed till 4 a.m. on August 3, and was not even ordered till the First and Second Fleets were so far assembled at their war stations as to render a serious surprise impossible. Admiral Burney was at Portland, Vice-Admiral The Hon. Sir A. E. Bethell had hoisted his flag in command of the Third Fleet battleships, and all the remaining flag officers appointed on July 25 had taken up their commands. It was also decided, in order to complete our cruiser system, to take up nine liners as armed

[1] *French Yellow Book*, No. 66, August 27.

merchant cruisers.[1]   We were thus prepared for any eventuality, and it was none too soon.

For France the situation was critical.   At any moment a German force might appear on her western coasts, and the desperate resolve was taken to order Admiral Rouyer, who was in command of the 2nd Cruiser Squadron, " to proceed forthwith to the Straits of Dover and dispute the passage of the enemy." [2]   All he could hope to do was, with the help of the French Channel destroyers and submarines, to inflict severe loss on the Germans before his own squadron was destroyed.   But the anxiety did not last long.   Clearly the conditions had now arisen under which, by the terms of the understanding of 1912, mutual discussions between France and England were called for.   The French Ambassador had been instructed to move accordingly, and on approaching Sir Edward Grey he was assured during the afternoon of August 2 that the British Fleet was mobilised, and that the Cabinet next morning would be asked to agree to certain measures for preventing an attack on France by sea.   About the same time it was known that the German mobilisation by sea and land, which had been in secret progress for nearly a week, was in full swing.   Before the Cabinet met they knew that German troops had seized the railways in Luxemburg, and Sir E. Grey was authorised to give the following undertaking to the Ambassador : " If the German Fleet comes into the Channel or through the North Sea to undertake hostile operations against French coasts or shipping, the British Fleet will give all the protection in its power."   The Ambassador, however, was made clearly to understand that the assurance was given in order to enable France to settle the disposition of her Mediterranean Fleet, and that it did not bind us to go to war unless the German Fleet took the action indicated.   It was further explained that in view of our enormous responsibilities all over the world and the primary exigencies of Home Defence, there could be no question at present of a promise to send our Expeditionary Force, or any part of it, to France.[3]

[1] *Aquitania, Caronia, Macedonia, Marmora,* and *Armadale Castle,* all in port ; *Oceanic, Lusitania,* and *Mauretania* due at Liverpool August 7th, 10th, and 17th respectively, and *Osiris* in the Mediterranean.   *Lusitania* and *Mauretania* eventually were released, the cost of fuelling being judged out of proportion to their usefulness.   *Aquitania* had a collision early in August and was returned to her owners, but on August 6 eight more were listed for service : *Carmania, Kinfauns Castle, Alsatian, Otranto, Mantua, Victorian,* and two ships of the Indian Marine, *Dufferin* and *Hardinge.*

[2] La Bruyère : *Deux Années de Guerre Navale,* p. 21.

[3] Sir Edward Grey to Sir F. Bertie (Paris) August 2.   Dispatched 4.50 p.m. M. Paul Cambon to M. Viviani, August 1, and same to same, August 2.   Orders accordingly were sent to the Fleet the same evening.

The only step taken in regard to the land forces was an order issued this day (August 2) for mobilising half the Territorial Garrison Artillery for the protection of the Orkney Islands, where Admiral Callaghan was already extemporising batteries for the defence of Scapa Flow. This measure became urgent, owing to a report that three transports had passed the Great Belt on August 1. The Shetlands had nothing but the *Forward* and the four destroyers of the 8th Flotilla, which formed its special patrol. They were now at their base in Dales Voe, but a prompt reinforcement was necessary. The Commander-in-Chief, therefore, dispatched Rear-Admiral Pakenham with five cruisers, *Antrim*, *Argyll*, *Devonshire*, *Cochrane*, and *Achilles*, at full speed, and ordered his battle cruisers, under Vice-Admiral Beatty, to Fair Island in support. These ships were in position on August 3, and on the same afternoon Admiral Rouyer, with the French 2nd Cruiser Squadron, took up his position to guard the Straits of Dover. To the Admiralty it now seemed imperative to set up without further delay the dispositions which had been provisionally arranged in October, 1913, for the combined defence of the Channel. At 5 p.m. an urgent request was sent to the Prime Minister and Sir E. Grey, pressing for authority to do so, with an intimation that unless forbidden they would act at once. Approval came promptly and orders immediately went out for the Dover Patrol and the Cross Channel Patrol, which was to act with the French, to take up their war stations next morning, but neither was to attack unless attacked. Admiral Wemyss's Squadron, with which, according to the plan of operations, Admiral Rouyer's was to combine, was not yet ready for sea.[1] The *Challenger*, however, was in the Bristol Channel to guard against minelayers, and Commodore Tyrwhitt was standing by to carry out an extensive destroyer sweep which he had already designed with the same object in the Southern Area of the North Sea, so as to intercept anything that tried to operate in it from the Heligoland Bight, and Admiral Campbell was under orders to support it with part of his squadron of cruisers.[2]

So far, then, as naval readiness could secure the country against invasion, there was now no reason why part at least of the Expeditionary Force should not leave. The Germans seemed to be more concerned with meeting a descent than with making one. Our intelligence was that their destroyers

[1] Twelfth Cruiser Squadron, known as Cruiser Force G., *Charybdis* (flag), *Eclipse, Diana, Talbot.*

[2] *Bacchante, Aboukir, Euryalus,* of the 7th Cruiser Squadron (Cruiser Force C).

and submarines were spread fifty miles north and south of the Elbe, and that the shores of Borkum and the approaches to their North Sea ports had been mined and the light-ships removed, while the High Seas Fleet had not stirred. That night, however, there was a report, now known to have been unfounded, that the Germans meant to get a number of commerce destroyers to sea before the outbreak of war, and at 4.0 in the morning of August 4 the Grand Fleet received orders to carry out a movement in force to intercept them.

But it was not made under Admiral Callaghan. His term of command had already been extended a year, and in spite of the fine work he had done in bringing the Fleet to the high state of efficiency it was showing—work which the Admiralty recognised in a special letter of acknowledgment—it was thought better to commit the arduous work ahead to a younger officer. Accordingly he was ordered to strike his flag, and Sir John Jellicoe succeeded him, with the acting rank of Admiral. He took with him to the *Iron Duke* Admiral Madden as Chief of the Staff, and at his special request the continuity of the old regime was maintained by his being permitted to keep Commodore Everett as Captain of the Fleet. If it was not Admiral Callaghan's fortune to wield the weapon he had brought to so fine an edge, he could at least lay it down knowing it was ready and in place to meet with a heavy reckoning anything the enemy could attempt.

At 6 a.m., some two hours before the Grand Fleet could execute the order to put to sea, news came in that the Germans intended to cross the Belgian frontier at 4.0 that afternoon. At 9.30 the Foreign Office sent off an emphatic protest requesting an immediate reply. Meanwhile, in accordance with the concerted procedure, contained in the War Book, to meet this contingency, steps had been taken by the Board of Customs and Excise and the Admiralty to detain German ships in our ports in retaliation for what they had already done at Hamburg, and in particular two mail boats which had just put into Falmouth, one with a very large amount of gold for the Bank of England. At noon came the German reply. It merely gave an assurance that no part of Belgian territory would be annexed, but that they could not leave the Belgian line of attack open to the French. That was the end. Two hours later the Fleet was informed that an ultimatum had been sent to Berlin which would expire at midnight, and that at that hour the " War Telegram " would go out.[1]

[1] The telegram said midnight, G.M.T., but what was intended was midnight, Central European Time, that is, 11 p.m. G.M.T., at which time the " War Telegram " was actually sent out from the Admiralty.

When the ultimatum was sent Admiral Jellicoe was already at sea commencing the precautionary movement which he had been directed to make. The general idea which had been laid down by the Admiralty was that he should take his four battle squadrons, with their attached cruisers and the 4th Destroyer Flotilla, to within 100 miles of the Norwegian coast, leaving the battle cruisers and Admiral Pakenham's squadron to watch the Shetlands. The 2nd Cruiser Squadron and six other ships of different squadrons, which with the 2nd Destroyer Flotilla, were at Rosyth, were to meet him at a mid-sea rendezvous, and then make a sweep south and west, and at 8.30 a.m. on August 4 he had sailed to carry out the movement.

In the Mediterranean the Precautionary Period found us less well placed. There, indeed, the moment Germany had chosen to precipitate hostilities was peculiarly favourable to the enemy—that is, assuming the enemy would be the Triple Alliance, and all Admiralty appreciations had to take into account the possibility of Italy being drawn into the struggle against France. In the Adriatic Austria had six battleships, two light cruisers and about twelve torpedo craft, which were based on Pola. In the Adriatic, too, was the German battle cruiser *Goeben*, which during the recent Balkan troubles had been dominating Turkish sentiment at Constantinople, and had just completed a thorough dockyard refit at Pola. Italy, besides more or less obsolescent types, had in commission three Dreadnoughts at Taranto, and four other good battle-ships at Gaeta, near Naples.

Against this force France, in spite of her policy of con-centration, could only show one Dreadnought, six " Dantons " —good ships, approximately of the " Lord Nelson " type— and five others. Of her other three Dreadnoughts, two had been away in the Baltic with the President, and one was just being completed at Brest.

As for our own Fleet, which was under the command of Admiral Sir Berkeley Milne, only three ships of the 2nd Battle Cruiser Squadron were on the station; the 1st Cruiser Squadron under Rear-Admiral Troubridge was complete, and so was the Light Cruiser Squadron, but the ships were much scattered.[1] The flagship *Inflexible*, with the *Indefatigable, Warrior, Black Prince*, the four light cruisers and fourteen destroyers, were at Alexandria, about to proceed to Malta. The *Indomitable* and *Duke of Edinburgh* were at Malta for their annual refit; while Admiral Troubridge in the *Defence*, with the destroyer *Grampus*, was in the Adriatic

[1] See Appendix C.

off Durazzo, in company with the French cruiser *Edgar Quinet* and the German light cruiser *Breslau*, taking part in an international demonstration in support of the Conference which was sitting at Scutari for the settlement of Albania.

When on July 27 the preliminary warning went out to all stations, a special clause was added for the Mediterranean directing Admiral Milne to return to Malta as arranged, and to remain there with his ships filled up with coal and stores. He was also to warn Admiral Troubridge to be ready to join him at any moment. He left accordingly next morning, and was well on his way to Malta when, in the evening of the 29th, he received the " Warning Telegram." Next day he was informed of the general situation and what he was to do in the case of war. Italy would probably be neutral, but he was not to get seriously engaged with the Austrian Fleet till her attitude was declared. His first task, he was told, should be to assist the French in transporting their African Army, and this he could do by taking up a covering position and endeavouring to bring to action any fast German ship, particularly the *Goeben*, which might try to interfere with the operation. He was further told not to be brought to action in this stage against superior forces unless it was in a general engagement in which the French were taking part. In thus assuming the duty of assisting the French to protect their transports we went beyond our undertaking; yet, seeing how weak our Ally was at the moment in the Mediterranean, and how anxious we were to do all in our power for her at sea, the order was natural enough, but, as will be seen later, it had very regrettable consequences.

In order to carry out his instructions, Admiral Milne had reached Malta in the forenoon of July 30. On the previous day, when the " Warning Telegram " was issued, the Admiralty, with the concurrence of the Foreign Office, had recalled Admiral Troubridge from Durazzo. Admiral Milne thus had his fleet well concentrated, and decided to keep it so till he had leave to consult the French Admiral. Considering it unsafe to spread his cruisers for the protection of the trade routes, he contented himself with detaching a single light cruiser, the *Chatham* (Captain Drury-Lowe), to watch the south entrance of the Strait of Messina. Of this he informed the Admiralty next day (July 31). With this exception, by the following afternoon the whole Fleet was concentrated at Malta, filling up with coal and stores. The same morning Rear-Admiral Souchon, commanding the German Mediterranean Division, put into Brindisi with the *Goeben* and *Breslau*, and then proceeded to Messina. After some trouble with the Italian Government, both vessels filled with coal on August 2 and sailed during the night.

By the time Admiral Milne had concentrated his fleet he received an order to detach one ship of the 1st Cruiser Squadron to Marseilles to embark Lord Kitchener, the Sirdar, and some other officers, who were hurrying back to Egypt. Accordingly, the *Black Prince* left on August 1, but was recalled next day by wireless when it had been decided that Lord Kitchener should join the Cabinet as Secretary for War. The Admiral was also charged with the withdrawal of the British troops which had been guarding the Conference at Scutari, and for this purpose he chartered the P. & O. mail steamer, *Osiris*. Then in the afternoon came further orders which overrode the disposition he had decided on. Informing him that Italy would probably remain neutral, the new instructions directed that he was to remain at Malta himself, but to detach two battle cruisers to shadow the *Goeben*, and he was also to watch the approaches to the Adriatic with his cruisers and destroyers. The whereabouts of the *Goeben* and *Breslau* was uncertain. They were reported to be at Taranto or Messina, but the last trustworthy intelligence was of their being off Brindisi. Admiral Troubridge was therefore ordered to the southern approaches of the Adriatic with his own squadron (*Defence, Warrior, Duke of Edinburgh*), reinforced by the *Indomitable* and *Indefatigable*, and accompanied by the *Gloucester* and eight destroyers, the *Chatham* being directed to join him after searching the Strait of Messina and the south coast of Italy.

This was the position when, on August 2, our undertaking in regard to the Channel and North Sea was given, and authority was sent him to get into communication with the French Admiral. Admiral Milne, unable to get any response to his wireless calls all next day, sent away the *Dublin* in the evening with a letter to Bizerta in quest of his colleague. The fact was there had been a delay in getting the fleet to sea. By the time-table of the war plan it should have been covering the Algerian coasts by August 1, but so anxious, it is said, were the French to avoid every chance of precipitating a conflict, that sailing orders were delayed till the last possible moment. Ashore, for the same reason, they had suffered no movement of troops within a certain distance from the German frontier.[1] Whatever the real cause, it was not till daybreak on August 3 that Admiral de Lapeyrère put to sea with orders " to watch the German cruiser *Goeben* and protect the transport of the French African

[1] La Bruyère : *Deux Années de Guerre Navale*, p. 32.

troops." [1] Thus both Admirals had the same principal object, but no co-ordination of their efforts had yet been possible, nor could anything further be arranged when, in the evening of the 4th, Admiral Milne received word through Malta that the British Government had presented an ultimatum to Germany which would expire at midnight.

In Berlin it had been decided at once to send no reply, and Sir Edward Goschen was taking his leave of the Chancellor. From Dr. von Bethmann Hollweg's agitation and voluble reproaches it was apparent enough how great was the shock of the German miscalculation. Face to face with the intangible, the almost mysterious power of the sea (for at that time it was not our army that counted), his fears found expression in inconsequent recrimination. In spite of the three clear warnings which he had ignored, he denounced our loyalty to the Belgian treaties as "unthinkable." For him it was a stab in the back upon a kindred nation—and all for a word "neutrality"—all for "a scrap of paper." Brought up in the narrow school of German history, he knew not that that scrap of paper was the last consecration of a political tradition, centuries old, under which the sea power that he now saw cutting across the laborious German plans had gained the subtle influence he feared. It was always here in the Netherlands—the borderland between Teutons and Latins—that we had sought to use that influence so that neither race should dominate the other. To this cardinal fact in British history German eyes had been closed by the self-centred teaching of recent years, and the shock of the awakening was in proportion to the depth of the self-deception. That our honour in observing a solemn international compact was as deeply engaged as our national instinct was nothing : "At what price," he cried, "will that compact be kept? Has the British Government thought of that?" We had paid the price many times before and knew it well, as he should have been aware. In the Chancellor's strange appeal we can hear other words that more truly expressed his thought. "What will our blind miscalculation cost Germany? How can we measure the power we have raised up against us?" The power of armies they could calculate to a nicety—of the power of the sea they had no experience. All that was plain was that Great Britain was as ready as ever to play the old game, and had set the board with all the old skill.

[1] Sir F. Bertie to Foreign Office, Paris, August 3, 6.50 p.m.

CHAPTER II

OPENING MOVEMENTS—HOME WATERS AND
TRADE ROUTES

WHEN Admiral Jellicoe took over the command of the Grand Fleet it consisted of twenty Dreadnoughts, eight " King Edwards," four battle cruisers, two squadrons of cruisers and one of light cruisers, though a few units had not yet joined.[1] Like his colleague in the Mediterranean, he received notice of the ultimatum at sea. The signal was taken in about 5 p.m. on August 4, and having been informed that the movements laid down for covering the passage of the Expeditionary Force would not be required for the present, he carried on with his sweep in the North Sea. It was at once suspected the Germans were already trying to locate him, for a trawler was encountered with carrier pigeons. She was detained, and all other trawlers met with were searched. Several more were found next day, also with carrier pigeons. Some, after the removal of their crews, were sunk, and some sent in to Scapa or Cromarty. No commerce destroyers were seen, but, as afterwards appeared, one escaped him, and by hugging the coast of Norway got clear away into the Atlantic round the north of Iceland. She was the *Kaiser Wilhelm der Grosse* of the Norddeutscher Lloyd Company.

Her escape was due to the northern area being still short of its proper complement of cruisers, and particularly to the absence of the Northern Patrol. The 10th Cruiser Squadron which was to form it, being on a Third Fleet basis, had not been able to move till the mobilisation of the reserves was complete, and was only just leaving the Channel; while the 6th Cruiser Squadron,[2] which was intended to fill the place of the 4th Squadron as an integral part of the Grand Fleet cruiser force, had had to be diverted, as will appear directly, to other duties. The battleship force, however, was being reinforced. It had long been the intention, under certain conditions, that the " Duncans " of the 6th Battle Squadron should form part

---

[1] For organisation and details see Appendix B.
[2] *Drake, King Alfred, Good Hope, Leviathan.*

of the Grand Fleet.   When the war telegram was sent out
Admiral Jellicoe was asked if he wished to have them, and
on his replying in the affirmative the *Russell*, *Albemarle* and
Exmouth, which were all that were ready, were ordered to
join him at once west-about.

By noon on August 5 he reported his sweep complete,
and he was then directed to keep his fleet to the northward
so as to hold the entrance to the North Sea, unless there were
tactical reasons against his doing so.   Accordingly, as there
were reports of a German submarine base being established
in the Norwegian Fjords, and also of a number of merchant
ships arming at the Lofoten Islands, he directed the 2nd and
Light Cruiser Squadrons to make a sweep up the Norwegian
coast, and continued his battle squadron at sea in support.

In the lower part of the North Sea a complementary sweep
had been carried out by what was soon to be known as the
Southern Force.   At present it was organically part of the
Grand Fleet, and was nominally under Admiral Jellicoe's orders.
Based at Harwich, it consisted of the 1st and 3rd Destroyer
Flotillas under Commodore Tyrwhitt and the "oversea"
submarines under Commodore Keyes, and they had for their
support some of the 7th Cruiser Squadron—old armoured ships
of the "Bacchante" type—under Rear-Admiral Campbell.
The sweep on this occasion had been planned by Commodore
Tyrwhitt, and, as he expected, it led quickly to an encounter.
Leaving Harwich at dawn on August 5, with the *Bacchante*,
Aboukir and *Euryalus* in support, he himself in the *Amethyst*,
with two submarines, proceeded to look into Heligoland Bight,
which he found protected by a cordon of trawlers fitted with
wireless.   While the 1st Destroyer Flotilla swept up the
Dutch coast, Captain C. H. Fox in the *Amphion* followed with
the 3rd Flotilla.   He had not gone far before he encountered
the first sign of the ruthlessness with which Germany was to
conduct the war.   A stray trawler informed him there was a
suspicious vessel in the vicinity " throwing things overboard
twenty miles north-east of the Outer Gabbard."   While the
flotilla spread in search, two destroyers, *Lance* and *Landrail*,
were sent ahead to investigate the spot.   About 11 a.m. they
sighted the minelayer *Königin Luise*, which had left Borkum
the previous night.[1]   A hot chase ensued in which the
Amphion joined; by noon they had sunk her by gun-fire, and
so we drew first blood.

The crew of the sunken ship were taken on board the
Amphion and the sweep was continued without further

---

[1] The movements of the *Königin Luise* are detailed in a letter of one of
her crew found in a bottle on the scene of action.

incident, till the return.   Then there was another tale to tell.
In the early hours of the morning the *Amphion* had changed
her course so as to avoid the minefield the enemy had been
laying.   But at 6.30 a.m. (August 6), just when she believed
she was clear, a violent explosion shattered her.   " Abandon
ship " was promptly ordered, but almost immediately she
struck another mine and went down so quickly that it was
impossible to save all the crew.   One officer and 150 men
perished, as well as many prisoners from the *Königin Luise*.

Such was the immediate success of the policy of mining
in international waters which Germany had chosen to adopt.
The indications were that the minefield had been laid between
3° E. long. and the Suffolk coast—that is, in the open—
regardless of neutrals and of all the time-honoured customs
of the sea.   It was the first opening of our eyes to the kind
of warfare we had to deal with, and four days later the
Admiralty declared themselves forced to take similar measures
in self-defence ; but it is now known that the *Königin Luise*
had orders to lay her mines as near as possible to the coast.
The flotillas were promptly ordered back to Harwich, and the
cruisers to the Downs, while immediate steps were taken to
clear the suspected area.   The Admiralty also thought it
expedient to order the Admiral of Patrols to patrol the coast
day and night to prevent further minelaying operations.   They
thus began under pressure of the enemy's insidious form of
attack to break into the sound system of coast defence which
the War Plans had provided.   That system was based on concentration of flotillas at well chosen points, a system which
could not be adhered to if continuous coastwise patrols were
to be maintained.

The incident, moreover, could only add to the Commander-
in-Chief's anxiety for his base, especially as by the second day
of the war it was fairly clear the enemy had located him.
Not only had more trawlers with pigeons been overhauled,
but several ships were reporting periscopes, and though no
attack was made there was good reason to believe the fleet
was being shadowed by the enemy's submarines.   Actually,
on August 9 ten enemy submarines reached Fair Island
Channel, where U 13 and U 15 were sunk.

Since the order to hold the north-about route had compelled him to recall the battle cruisers and the 3rd Cruiser
Squadron to his flag, the Orkneys and Shetlands had been
left uncovered, and he pressed the Admiralty to send him
the 6th Cruiser Squadron and the *Invincible*, which he had
been led to expect.   But the exigencies of commerce protection stood in the way.   A dominating factor in pre-war

studies had always been the fear of a food panic in the first weeks, and in many parts of the country it was showing signs of development. At almost any cost, therefore, it was essential—if only for the moral effects—to prevent captures on the food routes, and so serious was the tension that rumours of enemy ships being upon them were perhaps too easily credited. The result was that the 6th Squadron was scattered in all directions. The *Drake* had gone out to meet the *Carmania* from New York and bring her in. The *Leviathan*, which had been ordered to take station 500 miles west of the Fastnet, was suddenly ordered to the Azores on rumours of enemy cruisers and colliers being there. The *Good Hope*, on the point of sailing for Scapa, was hurried away to the south of Newfoundland on a liner's report that German merchant cruisers were working on the trade route there. The *King Alfred* was not ready for sea, and as for the *Invincible* she was to go to Queenstown to stand by for chasing any of the enemy's battle cruisers that might break out into the Atlantic. In the end the *Drake* was the only ship that could be sent, and she went up as soon as she returned. Meanwhile, however, on August 6 Admiral de Chair, Commanding the 10th Cruiser Squadron, appeared with his six " Edgars," and after sweeping round the Orkneys proceeded to establish the Northern Patrol in the latitude of the Shetlands. Admiral Jellicoe thus had the rest of his cruisers free; and for the protection of his undefended anchorage, as the eight destroyers he had were insufficient for the duties of harbour defence and sweeping the approaches, four more were sent him from the Tyne Patrol Flotilla. This, then, was his position when, early on August 7, he put into Scapa to coal, and his first movement, the precursor of so many that were to prove equally disappointing, came to an end.

So far, except for the loss of the *Amphion*, all had gone well. No attack upon our commerce had taken place, and not a single loss had been reported on any of the routes, and the prearranged system for their protection was fast taking shape. During the afternoon of August 4 Admiral Wemyss had got his squadron to sea from Plymouth, and in the following forenoon Admiral Rouyer, who had been recalled from the Straits of Dover, joined him, and so completed the combined Western Patrol.[1] In the mid-Atlantic areas, through which passed the great routes from the Mediterranean, the Cape and South America, the dispositions were not made

---

[1] Admiral Rouyer had with him *Marseillaise* (flag), *Gloire* (flag of Rear-Admiral Le Cannellier), *Admiral Aube, Jeanne d'Arc, Dupetit Thouars, Gueydon, Desaix, Kléber* (all armoured cruisers), and the light cruiser *Lavoisier*.

without difficulty and much anxiety.   To the southern or Cape Verde–Canaries station was assigned the 5th Cruiser Squadron under Rear-Admiral Stoddart; while the northern or Finisterre station was to be occupied by Rear-Admiral de Robeck with the 9th Cruiser Squadron.[1]   But as this squadron was on a " Third Fleet " basis it was necessary for Admiral Stoddart to occupy both areas till it could be mobilised.   He also had instructions to detach one of his fastest cruisers to join the *Glasgow* on the South American station, since she was the only ship we had on that part of the route.   His general instructions, in order to expedite the occupation of his station, were that he should consider the protection of our own trade as taking precedence of attacking that of the enemy, and he was therefore to regard " interference with unarmed merchant ships not carrying contraband as of minor importance."   If any such vessels were seized he was to send them in with a prize crew, or " in extreme cases " they might be sunk.

It was on July 31, two days after the " Warning Telegram," when it was known that Germany had refused to give an undertaking to respect Belgian neutrality, that he got away alone in the *Carnarvon*.   He was to go to Gibraltar and await orders, but now that war seemed inevitable his instructions were changed.   The German light cruiser *Strassburg* was known to be in his area, and had last been reported in the Azores.   He was therefore directed to proceed along the trade route towards Madeira to get into communication with four important ships which were on their way home from the Cape and South America.   Going down Channel, however, he met the *Strassburg* hurrying home in response to the general recall which the Germans had issued a few days before.   The two ships passed each other without saluting and carried on.

During the next two days the *Cumberland* and *Cornwall* followed him down, and by August 3 he had communicated with the vessels he had been sent to warn.   Orders then reached him to carry on down the trade route, as two German cruisers had been reported at Las Palmas in the Canaries. The report was but one of the rumours which some of our own and our Allies' consuls kept sending in with too little verification, and which did much to hamper our commerce protection arrangements in the early days of the war.   The wonder is they did not cause more mischief than they did. In this case a serious deflection resulted.   The report made the French keenly anxious for the safety of their transport

[1] Fifth Cruiser Squadron : *Carnarvon* (flag), *Cornwall, Cumberland, Monmouth.*   Ninth Cruiser Squadron : *Europa* (flag), *Amphitrite, Argonaut, Vindictive, Highflyer, Challenger.*   See Map 2 in case.

line from Casablanca, where they were about to move some of their Morocco troops to France, and they begged our assistance in protecting it.   The area should have been guarded by their Mediterranean Fleet, but these ships were fully occupied with covering the main line of passage from Algeria, and since we regarded it as a paramount obligation of our Navy to safeguard the French military concentration, the *Cornwall*, instead of joining Admiral Stoddart, had to be detached for the duty.

The call was a severe one.   The *Monmouth* was still in dockyard hands, and none of Admiral de Robeck's ships had yet reached their station.   The Spanish and Portuguese ports were full of German ships—some sixty of them—all using their wireless actively, and any of them, as we believed, might be arming as commerce destroyers.   In particular, there were two Norddeutscher Lloyd steamers, the *Prinz Heinrich* at Lisbon and the *Goeben* at Vigo, both apparently on the point of coming out to operate, and Admiral de Robeck's squadron could not be in place for some days.

He himself in the *Vindictive* had left Plymouth on August 4, with the *Highflyer*, but on his way down he had stopped the *Tubantia*, an afterwards famous Dutch liner, with German gold and reservists on board, and the *Highflyer* had to be sent back with her.   Thus, owing to our devotion to French interests, which were paramount at the time, we had at the critical moment not a single ship on the Peninsula coasts. But, so far from Germany using the opportunity as she might have done, Admiral de Robeck was doing all the attacking. A hundred and twenty miles north of Cape Ortegal he captured the Norddeutscher Lloyd *Schlesien* and sent her in to Plymouth with a prize crew.   On August 7 he was off Vigo, where he induced the port authorities to remove the wireless installation from the S.S. *Goeben* and the German cable ship *Stephan*, which was suspected of being after our cables.   The *Highflyer*, when she rejoined, was sent to Lisbon, and on August 9 she was able to report that the *Prinz Heinrich* would not be allowed to leave if she had arms on board, and that the Portuguese authorities had dismantled the wireless of twenty-six other German vessels that were in the inner harbour.

The inactivity of the Germans while their chance lasted is only to be explained by their definite policy to avoid any measure unfriendly to us so long as our decision was delayed. Their failure to take action immediately war was declared may have been partly due to the promptitude with which we had dealt with their cables.   It was a subject to which special atten-

tion had been given in preparing the War Book. The lines
of the most immediate importance were the five German
cables which from Emden passed through the Channel to
Vigo, Tenerife and the Azores, and as early as the summer
of 1912 arrangements had been made for their being cut by
the Post Office, with Naval assistance, as soon as the Admiralty
gave the word. When the Warning Telegram went out the
Admiralty settled with the War Office what enemy cables
should be cut, and the issue of the request to the Post Office
on a Priority Form was one of the steps which followed
automatically upon the " War Telegram."   At Dover everything stood ready to act; the order came down from the
Admiralty in due course, and on August 5, when the Germans
could think of nothing more effective than their mining
venture with the *Königin Luise*, all five cables were cut.

The difficulties in the way of the enemy organising an
attack on our commerce where it was most vulnerable were
thus very great, and by the end of the first week of the
war their opportunity in this area had passed away. Two
more ships, the *Argonaut* and *Sutlej*, had joined Admiral de
Robeck; by August 13 he had a firm grip on his station from
Finisterre to Gibraltar, and French and British trade, which
hitherto had been held up in Spanish and Portuguese ports,
began to move again in freedom and security. Even across
the Bay, where there was a gap between his squadron and
that of Admiral Wemyss at the mouth of the Channel, there
was little or no danger, for one of Admiral de Robeck's ships
was almost continually upon the route on her way to or from
his main coaling base at Plymouth.

Only the southern section about Madeira was beyond his
reach as yet, and this had to be left to Admiral Stoddart.
But for this he could now spare the *Cornwall*, for on August 7
he was informed that the French were sending three cruisers,
Bruix, *Latouche-Tréville* and *Amiral Charner*, to guard the
Casablanca transport line, and two light cruisers, *Cosmao*
and *Cassard*, as a permanent patrol for the Morocco coast
under the orders of the British Admiral. On August 8 he
himself, with the *Carnarvon* and *Cumberland*, had reached
Las Palmas, having found, after searching the Salvage and
Canary islands, that all the wild reports of German cruisers
and German bases were false. Not a single British ship
had been molested, while German trade was at an absolute
standstill. By August 13 the *Monmouth* had arrived, and
he was able to dispatch her, as being the fastest ship of his
squadron, to the vital Pernambuco area, while he himself
completed the occupation of his station by carrying on down

to Cape Verde. For it was here at St. Vincent Island that, according to his instructions, his "principal position" was to be, with Sierra Leone for his coaling base.

On the other side of the Atlantic the difficulties of the opening were no less great but the results less fortunate. Though by organisation it was one station known as the "West Atlantic," strategically it comprised two areas, the West Indies and North America, and while all the cruisers that we or the enemy had were in the southern section, the gravest anxieties of the Government lay in the northern one. As we have seen, we had in the West Indies, under Rear-Admiral Sir Christopher Cradock, the 4th Cruiser Squadron, consisting of four 23-knot "county" cruisers and one 25-knot light cruiser.[1] The French maintained there one old light cruiser, *Descartes*, but in view of the Mexican troubles they had recently sent a larger and more modern ship, the *Condé*.[2] Germany, as it happened, also had two. Her interests on the Mexican coast were being watched by the *Dresden*. She was under the orders of Rear-Admiral Paul von Hintze, the German Envoy to Mexico, with whom Admiral Cradock had been acting in cordial co-operation. When, indeed, on July 17 it was decided that the *Dresden* should remove the family of the ex-President to Jamaica, he offered to place his cruisers at Admiral von Hintze's disposal for the protection of German interests, and for "the marked generosity which dictated this noble act," he received a glowing letter of thanks from the German Admiral emphasising the excellent relations and good comradeship which happily existed between the two navies. In his letter Admiral von Hintze spoke of the *Dresden's* temporary absence on a special mission, but in fact she was on the point of being relieved by the *Karlsruhe*.[3] The two ships were to meet at Kingston, Jamaica, to exchange captains, but as there were reports of trouble at Haiti the *Karlsruhe* was ordered to Port-au-Prince. On the way she passed the *Berwick* coming back from there, and the two captains exchanged friendly compliments. The *Dresden*, after dropping the family of the Mexican ex-President at Kingston, went on to Port-au-Prince

---

[1] Fourth Cruiser Squadron: *Suffolk* (flag), *Lancaster*, *Essex*, *Berwick*, all of 9,800 tons with fourteen 6" guns, and *Bristol* of 4,800 tons, with two 6" and ten 4" guns.

	Tons	Trial Speed.	Guns.
[2] *Condé* (1904) . .	10,233	21·3	2 7·6"; 8 6·5"; 6 3·9".
Descartes (1896) .	3,970	19·6	4 6·5"; 10 3·9".

	Tons.	Designed Speed.	Guns.
[3] *Dresden* (1908) . .	3,592	24	10 4·1"
Karlsruhe (1914) . .	4,820	27¼	12 4·1"

and there on July 25 Captain Köhler of the *Dresden* took over the *Karlsruhe*. Next day he sailed for Havana, while two days later the *Dresden* proceeded to St. Thomas to coal. This Danish island was practically the German base on the station, and since it was the West Indian headquarters of the Hamburg-Amerika Line, it was well adapted for the purpose. It is further to be noted that the island is a focal point for the trade from South-east America to New York and the American cotton ports. It had, therefore, a special importance in the eyes of our Admiral on the station.

But it was for the northern section of the station that the Admiralty was most gravely concerned; for although there were no enemy cruisers there, the United States ports, and especially New York, were full of great liners capable of being converted into the most formidable commerce destroyers, and the route they frequented was our all-important line of food supply from Canada and North America. This, moreover, was the route which lay most exposed to hostile cruisers breaking out of the North Sea, and consequently in pre-war studies it had received special attention. For its protection, as we have seen, the Admiralty had drawn on the 6th Cruiser Squadron, which was one of those belonging to the Grand Fleet. But this was only a temporary measure till Admiral Cradock's squadron could be permanently increased. Meanwhile he had to do the best he could with the slender force at his disposal.

When, on July 27, the preliminary warning reached him at Vera Cruz, neither of the German cruisers was on the coast. His intelligence was that the *Dresden* had arrived at Port-au-Prince in Haiti on the 25th, and that the *Karlsruhe* had left that port next day for an unknown destination. He therefore ordered the *Berwick* (Captain Clinton Baker) to proceed to Jamaica as a good central position for shadowing her. The *Essex* was sent to join the *Lancaster*, which was docking at Bermuda, and together they were to look after the North American routes. He himself in the *Suffolk* remained at Vera Cruz, with the *Bristol*, to wait for the " Warning Telegram," when he intended to proceed to Haiti in order to shadow the *Dresden*, and to send the *Bristol* down to Pernambuco to work with the *Glasgow*. However, as Admiral Stoddart was sending a cruiser there, he was relieved of this part of his duty, and on the 30th was told he might keep all his force for the rest of his station. The two French cruisers were not available. Together with the *Friant* at St. John's, they had been called home, and he himself had passed them the order.

On the 29th it was known that the *Karlsruhe* had put into Havana, and thither the *Berwick* hurried at full speed, but only to find her gone again, no one knew where.[1] She had, in fact, arrived on the 28th, intending to coal and carry on to Mexico; but hearing that Austria had declared war on Serbia, Captain Köhler decided to wait a day. Next day news came in that relations were seriously strained between the Central and Entente Powers. As he believed the French and British ships to be concentrated at Vera Cruz, he thought it best to give up the idea of going there, and to await events in the vicinity of Havana. In the morning of the 30th he put to sea, and being in wireless touch with the shore station, he next morning received his Warning Telegram. He knew the *Bristol* had been detached, and now fully expected the *Berwick* would also be on his track. So when on August 1 he heard she was at Havana, and at the same time got the order to mobilise, he had no doubt of what was coming.

Meanwhile the *Berwick*, finding him gone, had coaled and made off to the Florida Channel as the most likely place to fall in with him. Though the *Karlsruhe* remained somewhere out of sight near Havana, Captain Clinton Baker's move was well judged. By August 3 Captain Köhler knew that war had broken out with Russia and France. He was then near the spot where, in 1870, the comic opera duel between the *Meteor* and *Bouvet* had come to an ignominious end by both ships drifting helpless into territorial waters and being towed into Havana; but in the lapse of years the incident had been nurtured into a legend of victory in the German Navy, and the coincidence was taken as a happy omen. Being convinced that war with Britain would follow in a few hours, he decided to move nearer the great American trade route, where he intended to strike his first blows. Accordingly, after steaming a false course to the westward, he doubled back east for Plana Cays, near Crooked Island in the Bahamas, in order to lie concealed there away from all steamer tracks and await developments.[2]

As for the *Dresden*, all that was known was that she had left Port-au-Prince on the 28th, and in the next few days, as war became more and more inevitable, anxiety for the North Atlantic trade rapidly increased. Out of the large number of German liners in New York and the adjacent ports, no

---

[1] See Map, p. 50.

[2] The main authorities for the *Karlsruhe's* movements are (1) Aust.: *Die Kriegsfahrten S.M.S. Karlsruhe*, and (2) *S.M.S. Karlsruhe*, by her First Officer (Studt.). While hiding at Plana Cays the *Karlsruhe* received the Wireless Press telegram twice a day from Sayville (New York), and also the War Telegram from the Admiralstab at Berlin.

less than fourteen were on our list as being fitted for conversion into commerce destroyers, and furthermore, our
wireless station in Newfoundland and other centres reported
both the *Dresden* and *Karlsruhe* in those waters.   The *Essex*
had been able to leave Bermuda for the north at midnight
on August. 2–3, but the *Lancaster* was still there in dockyard
hands, and Admiral Cradock, who had reached Jamaica, was
directed by the Admiralty to send up another cruiser for
Newfoundland waters.   The *Bristol* had joined him, and as
she was no longer required for the Pernambuco area, he
ordered her northward.   All this time the *Berwick*, working
up the Florida Channel, was getting indications that the
Karlsruhe was near her.   She herself kept quiet till, in the
early hours of August 4, she was directed to jam the *Karlsruhe's* signals.   This she did, and, on information received
from one of the United Fruit Company's steamers, began to
search the anchorages near the Great Isaac Light; that is, at
the point where the N.W. Providence Channel enters the
Florida Strait.   During the afternoon the Admiral received
from the Admiralty an appreciation that the danger point
of his station appeared to be in the vicinity of New York, and
that our trade had been advised not to sail till some of his
cruisers arrived.   As the *Essex* was the only ship near the
spot, he himself at once left Jamaica in the *Suffolk* for the
north.

This, then, was the position when, at 7.30 p.m. (local time)
on August 4, he received the war telegram.   The German
Government may have sent out theirs some hours earlier,
for the *Karlsruhe* got it in the afternoon, and was able to
open her sealed orders.   She was still lying concealed at
Plana Cays, some 400 miles south-east of where the *Berwick*
was looking for her, and at once left her hiding place on a
northerly course.   About the same time Admiral Cradock
heard definitely from the Admiralty that the *Dresden* was
off New York, though, in fact, she was off the Amazon, running away south to join Admiral von Spee in the Pacific.
More trustworthy news he got from the *Berwick*, who on the
evening of the 5th, having passed through the Providence
Channel to search Cat Island, could hear the *Karlsruhe* calling
up a ship which she took to be the *Friedrich der Grosse*, one
of the German liners in New York; but in fact she was the
Kronprinz Wilhelm, with whom Captain Köhler was arranging
a rendezvous in order to arm her as a consort.   Feeling he
could now leave the *Karlsruhe* to the *Berwick*, the Admiral
held on to the northward for Bermuda.   Next morning, the
6th, he was abreast of Watling Island and in wireless touch

with the *Bristol*, which was nearly 400 miles ahead of him, making for Newfoundland. The *Karlsruhe* could still be heard. The rendezvous she had fixed for the *Kronprinz Wilhelm* was, in fact, right on the track the Admiral was following, and at 11 a.m., 120 miles north-east of Watling Island, he saw her, apparently coaling, not from the *Friedrich der Grosse* but from the *Kronprinz Wilhelm*, the last German liner to get away from New York before war was declared.

The process of arming her with two 3·4″ guns was just finished, and although she had only had time to take in one-third of her ammunition, the two ships separated, the *Kronprinz* going off north-north-eastwards and the *Karlsruhe* north. To her the Admiral gave chase, calling to the *Bristol* to intercept her, and also giving the news to the *Berwick*. That ship, however, was then searching the vicinity of Windward Passage on her way back to Jamaica to coal, but the *Bristol* at once turned south at full speed and continued to steer for the *Karlsruhe* as the Admiral indicated her position. For him it was soon apparent the chase must be a long one. The *Karlsruhe* had a knot or so the advantage of the *Suffolk*, but the Admiral could still hope he might get his chance when the *Bristol* headed her off, and to improve the position he signalled the *Berwick* to proceed to a rendezvous sixty miles north-east of Mariguana Island in case the chase should double back and try to get away by the Caicos Passage.

By nightfall, though there was plenty of moonlight, the *Karlsruhe* had gained so much as to get out of sight, but it was only to fall foul of the *Bristol*. At 8.15 p.m. Captain Fanshawe, as he ran south, could make out the German cruiser right under the moon three and a half points on his port bow. She was steering north, only six miles away, but being as yet unable to see the *Bristol* she held on. Hopes naturally beat high—for Captain Fanshawe it was a splendid position, and to make the best of it he turned seven points to port so as to bring his starboard battery to bear and to cut across the enemy's course.

The range was falling rapidly, and when it was down to 7,000 yards the *Bristol* opened fire. The *Karlsruhe* then woke up, immediately replied and turned sharply to the eastward, bringing the *Bristol* abaft her beam. For a time they held on thus on parallel courses in the moonlight. As the superior speed of the *Karlsruhe* began to tell, the range was opening out again till she had gained enough and could turn to port to cross the *Bristol's* bows. To counter the manœuvre the *Bristol* had to alter to north-east by east, and in a few minutes more the *Karlsruhe* seized her chance to turn away to south-east and made off, hidden in her cloud of smoke.   Thus, as with the *Suffolk*, she was able to set the *Bristol* a stern chase. Had the British ship been able to develop her proper speed it would have been by no means hopeless.   Nominally the *Karlsruhe* had less than a knot's advantage, but in spite of all she could do the *Bristol's* speed kept falling.   It was down at last to eighteen knots instead of twenty-four, and by 10.30 p.m the *Karlsruhe* had run out of sight—but not out of danger.

When three hours earlier Admiral Cradock lost sight of her he had turned to the eastward to cut her off if the *Bristol* drove her south, and he was now only about twenty miles to the westward of the chase.   Hearing from the *Bristol* what the enemy's course was, he turned to about S.S.E., while the *Karlsruhe*, finding she had too little coal left to reach St. Thomas—only, indeed, just enough to take her direct to Puerto Rico at economical speed—dropped to twelve knots and made for that port as being the nearest one at which she could safely re-fuel.   The course of the two ships diverged slightly at first, but shortly after 3.0 a.m. Admiral Cradock inclined to the south-eastward, and at daylight altered to the eastward straight across the course the *Karlsruhe* was taking. At this time Captain Köhler could hear the wireless of the British cruisers obviously converging upon him, but his lack of coal allowed of no divergence of his course, and those on board fully expected the end would come with full daylight. In fact, when Admiral Cradock turned to cross her course he was only twenty miles to the westward, with the chase on his port bow.   Shortly after 8.0 a.m. he must have passed astern of her, only just out of sight.   With the luck a few minutes more on his side he must have caught her, and she had no longer coal enough to run away from him.   The judgment he showed surely deserved better fortune, but as it was he missed her by a bare sea chance.

Even so she was not yet clear of the trap he had set.   After her narrow escapes from the *Suffolk* and the *Bristol*, she continued her course direct for Puerto Rico at economic speed, but her relief at finding no ship in sight as the sun rose was short-lived.   As she proceeded she began to hear the *Berwick*. This ship, it will be recalled, after her search of the Bahamas had been making for Jamaica to coal, when she was ordered by Admiral Cradock to try to intercept the chase, and she at once made north-eastward from the Windward Passage. Though the indications of her presence came closer and closer, the *Karlsruhe* dared not venture either to increase speed or take a circuitous course; but when escape seemed impossible, the calls began to grow weaker, for the *Berwick*, after running out nearly across her course, turned back to the westward for a further examination of the southern Bahamas. So the *Karlsruhe* got through, and by daybreak on August 9 put into Puerto Rico with only twelve tons in her bunkers.

The affair added one more to the long list of proofs that for commerce protection armament without speed is of little avail. Without the speed a decision cannot be counted on— the enemy may be disturbed and forced to seek other hunting ground, but that is all, and in this case so much was gained. The intention obviously was for the *Karlsruhe* to make a dash at the main Atlantic routes, and this Admiral Cradock was able to prevent.[1]

Captain Köhler's intention was now to raid some of the British and French West Indian Ports, but at Puerto Rico he could not obtain coal enough for the venture. On August 4 three, if not four, colliers had sailed from Newport News and St. Thomas to find him, but he had been driven away from the rendezvous. His only course was to seek fuel else- where. To St. Thomas he dared not go, as it was too notorious a coaling place. The only other possibility was the distant Dutch island of Curaçao. By taking in all the coal he could lay hands on, he found he had just enough to bring him there, and at night he stole out again, and picking his way through the difficult Virgin Passage, as Drake had done before him, he reached the Dutch port without further adventure at dawn on August 12.

Meanwhile, in the absence of definite intelligence, Admiral Cràdock could not regard the North Atlantic trade routes as safe. He had therefore hurried on to Bermuda, cap- turing on his way the German oil-tanker *Leda*. At Ber- muda he found the two French cruisers, and learned that the day after we had declared war the French Govern- ment had cancelled their recall and placed them under his orders. This relieved his anxiety for the southern area, for he was able to send the *Condé* to watch the entrance of the Gulf of Mexico, with Jamaica for her base, and the *Descartes* to patrol the Caribbean Sea from St. Lucia. He also heard that two German liners, the *Vaterland* and *Barbarossa*, were ready to sail from New York, and as he could not yet be sure the *Karlsruhe* had not doubled back to the northward, he hurried on to take the *Bristol's* place off Sandy Hook. His presence in the north was the more necessary as Canadian rumours placed a hostile cruiser in the Cabot Strait, where the *Lancaster* had been watching till she was obliged to leave in

[1] Aust.: *Die Kriegsfahrten S.M.S. Karlsruhe*, p. 10.

THE ESCAPE OF
S. M. SS. KARLSRUHE AND DRESDEN
July and August 1914.

SRUHE at Port au Prince 25th to 29th July 4 p.m. at Havana.
        28th to 30th July 10 a.m. at San Juan. 9th Aug. 5 a.m. to 7 p.m.
SDEN Left Port au Prince 28th July coaled at St. Thomas 31st July.
FOLK Left Vera Cruz 30th July 8.12 a.m. arrived Jamaica 2nd Aug. 2 11 p.m.
        Left Jamaica 4th Aug 5 p.m.
TOL at Jamaica 2nd Aug 11 p.m. to 3rd Aug 6 10 p.m.
WICK Left Vera Cruz 29th July 9.25 a.m. at Havana 31st July 12.30 p.m.
        to 2nd Aug 11.30 p.m.

Longitude 75° Weenwich.

Ordnance Survey, 1919.

Prepared in the Historical Section, Committee of Imperial Defence
1540/88.

order to coal.   The Ottawa Navy Department also believed
the Germans were bent on establishing a base at Miquelon
and St. Pierre Islands, and all local shipping had been held up.
By the 13th, however, the situation was cleared by definite
intelligence that both the *Dresden* and *Karlsruhe* were to the
southward.   On the 12th the S.S. *Drumcliffe* reported she
had been stopped by the *Dresden* off the Amazon on August 5,
and on the 13th the *Karlsruhe* was located at Curaçao.

Admiral Cradock being thus assured that the northern
route was safe for the time, went on to Halifax to coal.
Here he met the *Good Hope*, which had been sent out during
the first period of anxiety as a temporary reinforcement for
the trade route; she was being followed by the battleship
Glory, and also by the armed merchant-cruiser *Carmania*,
which was to be a permanent addition to the station.

At Halifax the Admiral received an enthusiastic welcome, which was given practical demonstration by the
citizens assisting to coal his flagship.   There was, in fact, an
intense relief throughout the area.   Not a single German liner
had ventured to put to sea since the *Kronprinz Wilhelm* left
just before the declaration of war, and the Admiralty's attention was now shifted to the southern area.   The Admiral was
asked if he could not reinforce that section of his command,
and his reply was that he could if he might keep the *Good
Hope*.   A ship of her speed was essential for dealing with the
two German cruisers, and although she had only just been
commissioned and was still quite a raw ship, he proposed to
shift his flag to her and go down himself.   This the Admiralty
approved, and he accordingly sailed, leaving Captain Yelverton of the *Suffolk* in command of the northern area, where
he would have under his command the *Essex, Lancaster* and
Carmania, with the *Glory* as supporting ship.

So by August 14, less than ten days after the declaration of
war, the northern trade routes were completely secured, and
on that day, in response to an inquiry from Paris, the
Admiralty could report, " The passage across the Atlantic is
safe.   British trade is running as usual."

This, contrary to universal expectation, was true of all
routes, and it was due not only to the skill and rapidity with
which the Admiralty had handled their not too adequate force
of cruisers, but also to the courage of the merchants and
owners.   To them a large share of the credit is due.   There had
long been a doubt whether, when war should come, they would
face the risks of the early days.   If they did the Admiralty had
no fear but what they could reduce the losses to an insignificant percentage.   If they would not, nothing the Navy could

do would prevent a serious shortage of supplies. The position had been placed frankly before the Chambers of Commerce during peace, and now in the partnership between navy and merchant shipping the owners played their hands with a boldness of which any nation might be proud. Except in areas where the Admiralty issued a special and temporary warning, there was practically no holding up of sailings, and the result was that the incipient food panic which threatened in the first days of the war died down before it had well shown its head.

This happy result was in a large measure due to the rapid completion and adoption of the reports of the two committees which had been appointed to supplement the preparatory work of the Co-ordination Sub-committee. It will be remembered that the Report of the Maintenance of Trade Committee recommending State Insurance had been reserved for further consideration, and no action was taken. But as soon as relations grew strained it became every day more obvious that, in the absence of some such expedient, British shipping would be brought to a standstill for a period, the duration of which could not be foreseen. Three days before war broke out action became imperative, and amongst other drastic and unprecedented measures which the Cabinet had the courage to take at this time was the adoption of the scheme in its entirety. The effect was immediate, and from the complications which would necessarily hamper our sea-borne trade the factor of an unsteady Insurance Market was practically eliminated.

It was a stroke of policy that required some boldness, but whatever its drawbacks it proved to have other advantages. By the power the Government retained of refusing re-insurance for routes that were dangerous or otherwise undesirable, it acquired a valuable control over the movement of shipping, which proved very effective in maintaining our own supplies and restricting those of the enemy.

The Diversion of Shipping Committee had also just completed the investigation of another difficulty—that is, how to cope with the probable congestion of our western and southern ports owing to ships avoiding ports in the North Sea, and to get over it they had ready a detailed scheme for ascertaining the daily position as regards accommodation and for notifying ship-owners and merchants accordingly. This committee sat at the Admiralty under the chairmanship of Vice-Admiral Sir E. J. W. Slade, so that there was immediately available machinery for giving effect to the measures recommended, and the functions of the committee for assisting the flow and safety of trade could be enlarged as experience was gained. Closely affiliated to the Trade Division of the War Staff, they carried out the work with conspicuous smoothness and efficiency. But for the thoroughness with which these two precautions had been thought out and the prompt decision with which the Government enforced them it is probable that the movement of our trade would have been seriously disturbed and the food panic difficult to allay, no matter how prompt and well-directed our cruiser operations.

CHAPTER III

In the area of the Eastern Fleet the opening had been even more successful than in Home Waters and the Atlantic, but the operations in this theatre were so much entangled with combined expeditions that they can best be made clear at a later stage. It was only in the Mediterranean, where Admiral Souchon was in command of the *Goeben* and *Breslau*, that we had met with failure, and even there so little was its gravity recognised that generally it was regarded almost as a success. It will be recalled that the day after Admiral Milne had concentrated his force at Malta he had been ordered to detach Admiral Troubridge's squadron, with the *Indefatigable, Indomitable, Gloucester* and eight destroyers, to shadow the *Goeben* and watch the entrance to the Adriatic. The *Chatham* was to look into the Strait of Messina, and the *Dublin* had gone to Bizerta to get into touch with the French Admiral. About 1 a.m. on August 3, to give further precision to their orders, the Admiralty directed that the watch on the mouth of the Adriatic was to be maintained, but that the *Goeben* was the main objective, and she was to be shadowed wherever she went. Taking this as a repetition of the previous order which instructed him to remain near Malta himself, Admiral Milne stayed where he was and left the shadowing to Admiral Troubridge.

The whereabouts of the enemy was still uncertain. Circumstantial rumours told of their having arrived at Messina to coal, but by 8 a.m. the *Chatham* had run through the Strait and signalled they were not there. A report had also been received that there was a German collier at Majorca. Concluding, therefore, they must have gone west, and mindful that his primary object was to protect the French transport line, he ordered Admiral Troubridge to detach the *Gloucester* and his eight destroyers to watch the Adriatic, and with the rest of his force to proceed to the westward along the south coast of Sicily. In this way the Admiral did his best to reconcile his instructions to watch the Adriatic, to shadow the enemy's cruisers, not to be brought to action by superior force and to cover the French transports.

An idea now arose at the Admiralty, owing perhaps to the unprotected state of our trade routes, that the *Goeben* and *Breslau* were making for the Atlantic. Early in the afternoon a patrol was ordered to be set up at Gibraltar, and Admiral Milne decided to take up a station in the Malta Channel. Accordingly he gave orders for Admiral Troubridge to turn back for the entrance of the Adriatic with his own squadron, and for the two battle cruisers to carry on to a rendezvous twenty miles north-east of Valetta, where he would meet them. But at the Admiralty anxiety for the Atlantic trade routes had grown more insistent, and at 8.30 p.m. came an order for the two detached battle cruisers to proceed to the Strait of Gibraltar at high speed to prevent the *Goeben* leaving the Mediterranean. The Toulon Fleet had sailed at 4.0 that morning, and for over sixteen hours it had been making its way at twelve knots towards the Algerian coast, where it would bar any such attempt on the part of the Germans.[1] But we had not then sent our ultimatum, and organised connection between the British and French Admiralties had not yet been established. Consequently, the departure of the Toulon Fleet for the Algerian coast was not known to Admiral Milne till about noon on August 4, after the *Dublin* had reached Bizerta. Our Admiralty were informed sooner, but not till late on the night of the 3rd, through the Foreign Office. Nor was it till next evening that it was known from Paris that the transportation of the troops was not to begin at once, owing to the presence of the German ships. Consequently, they had to play up to the French hand as best they could, and Admiral Milne gave orders accordingly. Recalling the *Chatham*, who had reported nothing on the north coast of Sicily, he himself remained during the 3rd in the Malta Channel with the *Weymouth, Hussar* and three destroyers, while the two battle cruisers hurried off to the westward under Captain Kennedy of the *Indomitable*.

Though Admiral Souchon had gone west—having left the Straits ahead of the *Chatham*—it was not for Gibraltar he made. He was, in fact, making a dash at Bona and Philippeville to hamper the transport of the Eastern Division of the Nineteenth Army Corps.[2] Of what his ultimate destination was to be he as yet knew nothing; the probability was either Gibraltar or the Adriatic. Orders were hourly

---

[1] Commandant Vedel: *Nos Marins à la Guerre*, p. 34–5. La Bruyère: *Deux Années de Guerre Navale*, p. 24.

[2] *Der Krieg zur See : Die Mittelmeer Division*, p. 7.

expected. About 6.0 p.m. he heard that war had been declared, and three hours later off the south coast of Sardinia the two ships separated, the *Goeben* making for Philippeville and the *Breslau* for Bona. At 2.35 a.m. on August 4 his orders reached him. He was told that an alliance had been concluded with Turkey and that the two ships were to proceed to Constantinople.

During the 3rd it would seem some kind of an arrangement had been made at Berlin on which it was assumed that he would be permitted to enter the Dardanelles. Long afterwards it became known that on the following day the Kaiser informed the Greek Minister that an alliance had been concluded between Germany and Turkey, and that the German warships in the Mediterranean were to join the Turkish Fleet and act in concert. This statement would appear to have been at least premature. Whatever may have been arranged with the Young Turk leaders, events went to show the Turkish Government was no party to it.

Though the new orders to Admiral Souchon were marked " of extreme urgency," he did not take them to cancel the enterprise in hand, and he carried on. At daybreak (August 4) both ports were subjected to a short bombardment. Some damage was done to the railway stations, and at Philippeville a magazine was blown up, but that was all. Nowhere were the troops embarking as had been intended. By the French Staff plan they should have been on their way in transports, sailing singly and unescorted under cover of the whole fleet operating to the eastward, but when on August 2 the *Goeben* was reported near Bizerta, Admiral de Lapeyrère stopped the movement and informed the Minister he must now proceed to form convoys. After firing fifteen rounds Admiral Souchon left to rejoin the *Breslau*. His idea was first to proceed westward to give the impression that he intended to quit the Mediterranean. The two ships were then to meet at a rendezvous to the northward, and thence run back to the eastward.

Admiral Souchon of course desired to obtain as long a start as possible towards the Dardanelles before England's entry into the war, which was expected every moment, but, owing to the boiler defects of his flagship which greatly reduced her radius of action, the voyage to the Dardanelles (about 1,150 miles) could not be made at normal cruising speed without coaling again. Therefore he chose the fifty miles longer detour through the Straits of Messina because the chance of being able to fill up with coal there seemed better than elsewhere. The result of his choice of route was that he ran straight into the two British battle cruisers as

they were hurrying westward. It was just after 10.30 a.m.,
some fifty miles westward of Galita Island, when the
Indomitable sighted the two German cruisers coming eastward. The *Goeben* was seen at once to alter course to port,
and Captain Kennedy altered to starboard in order to close,
but the *Goeben* promptly turned away, and in a few minutes
the two ships were passing each other on opposite courses
at 8,000 yards. Guns were kept trained fore and aft, but
neither side saluted, and after passing, Captain Kennedy led
round in a wide circle and proceeded to shadow the *Goeben*,
with his two ships on either quarter. The *Breslau* made off
to the northward and disappeared, and early in the afternoon
could be heard calling up the Cagliari wireless station.

By the time the Admiralty heard the *Goeben* had been
found the decision was being taken to send an ultimatum
to Germany. Two hours before it went out they begged
authority to order the battle cruisers to engage the *Goeben*
if she attacked the French transports. That Bona had
been bombarded was already known, and the authority was
granted, subject to fair warning being given, but the message
did not reach Admiral Milne till 5 p.m. At 2.5 p.m. word
was sent him that the ultimatum had gone out, to expire
at midnight, and he was told that this telegram cancelled
the permission to attack the *Goeben*. This had not yet
reached him, and it did not affect the situation.

Indeed, even before the permission came to hand, it
was clear the *Goeben*, though, according to the German official
history, finding the greatest difficulty in maintaining a speed
of 22 knots, was getting away from our comparatively slow
ships. In her efforts to escape it was said she did two knots
over her official speed, while the *Indomitable* could not reach
her best. Captain Kennedy then ordered the *Indefatigable*
and the *Dublin*, which had joined the chase from Bizerta,
to carry on. Still the *Goeben* gained, and as the hours of
our ultimatum were expiring only the *Dublin* had her in
sight. Then she, too, lost the enemy, but found her again
about 5 p.m., with the *Breslau* in company. She asked if
she might engage the light cruiser, but the answer was " No ! "
and an order to continue shadowing.

Exasperating as it was to miss so good a chance just as
the sands were running out, our ships were well disposed for
trapping the enemy at Messina. It was Captain Kennedy's
intention to hold off for the night so as not to give away
his position to observers on the Sicilian coast. During the
dark hours he meant to form a patrol in case the enemy
should break back, and then close in so that at 4 a.m. he
would be off Messina. But this he was not permitted to

6

do, for at the moment a political difficulty arose which could
not be ignored and materially altered the strategical outlook.
At 6 p.m. when Captain Kennedy was disposing his ships
for closing the northern exit from the Straits, Admiral
Milne received a message from the Admiralty to say that
Italy had declared neutrality, and that in accordance with
the terms of the declaration no ship was to go within six miles
of her coast. The declaration, therefore, seemed to bar
Messina to both belligerents, and implicitly forbade any of
his ships entering the Straits. It at least confirmed the
impression that Admiral Souchon would go west, and on this
supposition Admiral Milne made his dispositions for the
night. The two detached battle cruisers, instead of carrying
on to Messina, were to steer west at slow speed to intercept
the German ships which, it was thought, might make for
Majorca to coal. The *Dublin* was to keep in touch, but she
soon lost the chase, and about 10.0, being then off Cape San
Vito, she turned to the westward and received an order to
rejoin the *Indomitable* in the morning. The Admiral took
station off Valetta, with the *Chatham* and *Weymouth* watching
on either side of Pantellaria. Admiral Troubridge was
patrolling between Cephalonia and Cape Colonne in the heel
of Italy, but with his cruiser squadron and the *Gloucester*
only, for about midday, when Admiral Milne knew that war
was imminent, he had ordered him to send the flotilla to
Malta to coal.

Though the news of the ultimatum was sent off at 2 p.m.,
it did not reach Admiral Milne till 7.0. An hour and a half
later he issued a new general order which was dominated by
his original charge to cover the French transport line. The
destroyers were turned back to the Greek coast and coal
was to be sent to meet them, but there was considerable
delay in getting the colliers away. Admiral Troubridge was
to detach the *Gloucester* to watch the southern entrance of
the Strait of Messina, and with his squadron to stand fast
where he was, taking care not to get seriously engaged with a
superior force. Then at 12.8 a.m. (5th) the flagship proceeded
to the westward to join the other two battle cruisers and pick up
the *Chatham* and *Weymouth* on the way. " My first consideration," the Admiral explained in his report, " was the protection of the French transports from the German ships. I
knew they had at least three knots greater speed than our
battle cruisers, and a position had to be taken up from
which the *Goeben* could be cut off if she came westward."
Nevertheless, he had left the line of attack from Messina open,
but, apart from this serious defect in his dispositions, they

were in accordance with his original instructions. The order that the French transports were to be his first care had not been cancelled, though, in fact, there was now no need for him to concern himself with their safety.

It was at 4 a.m. on August 3, a few hours after it was known that the *Goeben* had put into Messina, that Admiral de Lapeyrère put to sea with orders to seek out the enemy with his whole fleet and cover the transit of the troops in accordance with the Staff plan. To him, however, the situation had seemed too uncertain to adhere to it. Germany had not yet declared war, the attitude of Italy remained doubtful, and it was quite unknown whether Great Britain would come into the war or not. It was in these circumstances he had decided to abandon the Staff plan and to form convoys, and to this end he organised the fleet into three groups. In the first group, under Vice-Admiral Chocheprat, were the six " Lord Nelson " type battleships of the 1st Battle Squadron, *Diderot* (flag), *Danton*, *Vergniaud*, *Voltaire*, *Mirabeau*, and *Condorcet*, the 1st Division of the Armoured Cruiser Squadron, *Jules Michelet* (flag of Rear-Admiral de Sugny), *Ernest Renan* and *Edgar Quinet*, and a flotilla of twelve destroyers. This group was to proceed to Philippeville. In the second group were the Dreadnought *Courbet*, carrying the Commander-in-Chief's flag, with the 2nd Battle Squadron *Patrie* (flag of Vice-Admiral Le Bris), *République*, *Démocratie*, *Justice* and *Vérité*, the 2nd Division of the Armoured Cruiser Squadron (*Léon Gambetta*, flag of Rear-Admiral Senès, *Victor Hugo*, *Jules Ferry*) and twelve more destroyers. This group was destined for Algiers. In the third group were the older ships of the Reserve Squadron, *Suffren*, *Gaulois*, *Bouvet*, and *Jauréguiberry*, under Rear-Admiral Guépratte, who was to go to Oran. The idea appears to have been that on reaching the latitude of the Balearic Islands the three groups would separate and each proceed to its assigned port.[1]

This point was reached in the morning of August 4, when the Fleet was about twenty-four hours out, and the news of the attack on Bona and Philippeville reached the Admiral and forced him to reconsider the plan. The situation was so far cleared that he knew Italy had declared her neutrality the previous evening, and so far as she was concerned it was possible for him to seek out the German cruisers and destroy them. But, on the other hand, the co-operation of the British Fleet was still uncertain, and an attempt to get contact with the enemy might leave the transports exposed

[1] Vedel: *Nos Marins à la Guerre*, pp. 34–7, and Chart, p. 28.

to attack. There was the further possibility, emphasised by the reported presence of a German collier in the Balearic Islands, that Admiral Souchon would seek to leave the Mediterranean and attack Algiers on his way to Gibraltar. Instead, therefore, of sending his first group to Philippeville, he ordered it to proceed with the second group at high speed to Cape Matifou, just to the eastward of Algiers, and there to take station on guard from 3 p.m. on the 4th till next day.

There was thus no occasion for Admiral Milne to trouble about the Western Mediterranean or the French transports, but he had received no word of Admiral de Lapeyrère's movements. Consequently, when at 1.15 a.m. on August 5 the order to commence hostilities against Germany reached him, and no modification of his general instructions accompanied it, he held to his disposition. After effecting his concentration to the west of Sicily he detached the *Indomitable* to Bizerta to coal and the *Dublin* to Malta, and with the *Inflexible, Indefatigable, Weymouth, Chatham,* and one division of destroyers proceeded to patrol between Sardinia and the African coast on the meridian 10° E., that is, to the northward of Bizerta.

At this time Sir Rennell Rodd, our Ambassador at Rome, was trying to get a telegram through to say the enemy were in Messina, but, owing probably to the pressure on the wires, the message did not get to London till 6 p.m. Though the Germans were using Italian wireless freely, nothing came through from our Consul at Messina to the *Gloucester,* which was now watching the southern entrance of the Strait. At 3.35 p.m., however, Captain Howard Kelly telegraphed that the strength of wireless signals he was taking in indicated that the *Goeben* must be at Messina. She was, in fact, there coaling from a large East African liner, *General,* and several colliers and lighters. Admiral Milne, however, made no change in his dispositions; the last he had from the Admiralty was that, although Austria was not at war with France or England, he was to continue watching the Adriatic for the double purpose of preventing the Austrians emerging unobserved and preventing the Germans entering.

Admiral Troubridge was then cruising between Cape Colonne and Cephalonia with this object. He regarded the *Goeben,* owing to her speed and the range of her guns,[1] as in daylight a superior force to his own, with which his instructions were not to engage, but his intention was to neutralise the German advantage by engaging at night. Accordingly

---

[1] *Goeben* (1912) Trial speed 27·2. Guns 10-11''; 12-5·9''.

in the afternoon of the 5th he steamed across towards Cape Colonne, but about 10 p.m., as Admiral Souchon had not come out, and as he knew there were Italian torpedo craft about, he turned back for his daylight position off Cephalonia. This he did with less hesitation, since, believing the French were guarding the approaches to the Western Mediterranean, he fully expected his two battle cruisers would now be returned to him. Indeed his impression was that when they were first attached to his flag it was a preliminary step to the whole command devolving on him. For in the provisional conversations with France it was understood that the British squadron at the outbreak of war would come automatically under the French Commander-in-Chief—an arrangement which necessarily involved the withdrawal of an officer of Admiral Milne's seniority. Admiral Milne, however, took an entirely different view, and feeling still bound by his " primary object," began at 7.30 a.m. on August 6 to sweep to the eastward, intending to be in the longitude of Cape San Vito, the north-west point of Sicily, by 6 p.m., " at which hour," so he afterwards explained, " the *Goeben* could have been sighted if she had left Messina," where he considered she was probably coaling.

The *Indomitable* at Bizerta was greatly delayed in coaling, so that it was not till 7 p.m. she was ready to sail, and then she received her orders—but they were not that she should reinforce Admiral Troubridge.[1] At 11 a.m., in response to an inquiry from the Commander-in-Chief, she had reported that the French transports had begun to move, and that Admiral de Lapeyrère, who had been last heard of at Algiers, was devoting his battle fleet—not on the British plan to cover the line of passage—but entirely to escort duty, and that it would not be free till the 10th. The French Admiral was, in fact, no longer at Algiers. For on the 5th, finding the Germans did not appear, he had broken up the Cape Matifou guard and proceeded himself, with the flagship and two ships of the 2nd Battle Squadron, to search the Balearic Islands, leaving the rest of the squadron to carry on with the escort programme,[2] and apparently detaching a squadron of four armoured and three or four light cruisers to Philippeville. For, with the other information, Admiral Milne heard

[1] The cause of the delay was that Captain Kennedy, finding the briquettes which were ready for him were no good, wished to coal from a British collier he found there with a suspiciously large cargo—over 5,000 tons—consigned on German account to Jiddah and Basra, and he required the Commander-in-Chief's authority to requisition it, though he began helping himself before the authority came.

[2] Vedel : *Nos Marins à la Guerre*, p. 37.

from the *Indomitable* at Bizerta that this squadron had left Philippeville that morning at 8.0 for Ajaccio in Corsica. The messages, however, were not very clear and seem to have left Admiral Milne unchanged in his conviction that his duty was to close the northern exit of the Straits of Messina. The *Indomitable* was therefore ordered to join him thirty-five miles west of Milazzo, so that with his full force he could proceed to bar the Germans' escape for the night. If they eluded him, he intended to chase to the northward for the Strait of Bonifacio, or Cape Corso in the north of Corsica.

The reason for these dispositions was clearly a belief that the Germans might still have an intention to attack the French convoys, and so long as this was a practical possibility the Admiral could scarcely disregard his strict injunctions to protect them. We know now that Admiral Souchon had no such reckless intention. From all accounts he believed himself caught. At Messina he had hoped to coal, but facilities of wharfage were denied him, and he had to do what he could from German colliers he found there. His belief was that the French cruisers were watching to the northward, and that the main part of the British Fleet was about the Strait of Otranto, with its scouts off the Strait of Messina. The urgent order from Berlin that he was to endeavour to make the Dardanelles had not been cancelled, and the danger of the situation was apparent to all, but did not shake their calm sense of duty. So desperate indeed was the chance that in spite of the ominous outlook in the Near East it was the only one which had not entered into our calculations. Our relations with Turkey were severely strained, owing to our having, the day before war was declared, requisitioned the two Dreadnoughts which were just being completed for her in British yards. We knew she was mobilising and that the German Military Mission was taking charge of her army, but we also believed the Dardanelles was being mined. Nothing of all this vital information was communicated to Admiral Milne, except advice as to the mine-laying, and if this detail had any effect upon his judgment it would tend to show that Constantinople was barred to all belligerents alike. That Germany, with the load she already had upon her, intended to attempt the absorption of Turkey was then beyond belief.

All this was in the dark when Admiral Milne, feeling bound by his instructions that " the *Goeben* was his objective," made his last dispositions to prevent her escape to the northward. But scarcely had he issued his instructions when Captain Kelly in the *Gloucester*, being then off Taormina, signalled the enemy coming south. Admiral Souchon's intention, as his one chance of escape, was to steer a false course till nightfall, towards the Adriatic, and as his reserve ammunition had been sent to Pola, this was probably the original plan before the intervention of Great Britain rendered that sea nothing but a trap. The orders he issued were that the *Goeben* would leave at 5 p.m. at seventeen knots ; the *Breslau* would follow five miles astern, closing up at dark ; the *General* and three colliers were to meet him at convenient points on his route. The two cruisers, after steering their false course till dark, would make for Cape Matapan. Half an hour after issuing these orders Admiral Souchon received a telegram from the Admiralty Staff : " Arrival Constantinople not possible at present for political reasons." He, however, decided to make no alteration, for he knew Turkey well, and judged the outlook favourable for drawing her into the war on the German side. In accordance with this plan, Admiral Souchon, the moment he sighted the *Gloucester*, altered course to port so as to keep a'ong the coast of Calabria outside the six-mile limit.

When at 6.10 p.m. Admiral Milne got the news he was thirty-five miles north of Marittimo, proceeding eastward to his new rendezvous north of Sicily, but as the passage of the Strait was denied him he at once turned back. His idea was that Admiral Troubridge, with his squadron and his eight destroyers, besides two more which were being hurried off to him from Malta in charge of the *Dublin*, was strong enough to bar the Adriatic, and that there was still a possibility of the Germans making back to the westward along the south of Sicily. The Admiralty, however, an hour and a half later sent him an order to chase through the Strait if the enemy went south. Unfortunately, it did not come to hand till midnight, too late for the Admiral to modify the movement to which he was committed.

All this time Captain Kelly was clinging to the two German ships and reporting their course. It was not done without difficulty. At 7.30, being on their seaward beam, he began to lose sight of them against the land in the gathering darkness, and he saw his only chance was to get the inshore position and have the moon right when it rose. But to effect his purpose he must steer straight for the *Goeben*, well knowing if she opened fire he would be blown out of the water. Yet he did not hesitate, and by his daring move succeeded in gaining the desired position well upon the enemy's port quarter. This position he held till the *Breslau* altered towards the land and forced him, after a struggle, to fall astern for lack of sea room. Then she turned to cross his bows, as though she meant fighting. Captain Kelly altered to meet her and they passed starboard to starboard at about 4,000 yards. Still feeling it his duty to follow the *Goeben*, he did not open fire, and the *Breslau* disappeared east-south-eastwards, presumably to ascertain if the main British force was in that direction. So the shadowing went on till about 10.45, south of Cape Rizzuto, the *Goeben* suddenly turned to about S. 60° E., and began trying to jam the *Gloucester's* signals.[1]

By this time the *Breslau* had probably reported all clear in that direction. Admiral Troubridge was, in fact, off the Greek coast. When the *Goeben* came out of the Strait he was patrolling with his four cruisers[2] off Cephalonia on the look out for a German collier. His destroyers, with scarcely any coal in their bunkers, were all either at Santa Maura or patrolling outside.[3] His intention, as we have seen, had been to seek an engagement only at dusk, but Admiral Milne had ordered him to leave a night action to his destroyers. On hearing the enemy were out, he at once steamed north-north-east towards Santa Maura, thinking they might be making for his base behind the island, and, with the same idea, he ordered his eight destroyers to be under way and hidden in Vasilico Bay by midnight. As soon, however, as he knew the *Goeben* was heading for the Adriatic, he held on for the position he originally intended to take at Fano Island, just north of Corfu, where he hoped the confined and shoal waters would enable him to force an action at his own range. Even when Captain Kelly reported the *Goeben's* change of course he believed it was only a device to throw him off, and it was not till midnight, when the *Gloucester*, in spite of the *Goeben's* efforts to jam, reported her still going south-east, that he was convinced her original course was the false one and that she was making for the Eastern Mediterranean, either to operate against our trade or to repeat at Port Said and Alexandria what she had done at the Algerian ports. He then turned to the south to intercept her, called out his destroyers, and signalled to Captain John Kelly, who in the *Dublin* was bringing up the two destroyers from Malta, to head off the chase. The *Dublin* had already received orders to the same effect from Admiral Milne, who, as soon as it became clear that

---

[1] According to the German Official History the *Breslau* was to the northward of the *Gloucester* and *Goeben*, from 11 p.m. (6th) to mid-day (7th), but the account does not describe the movements in sufficient detail to make a close comparison and a definite conclusion practicable.

[2] *Defence* (flag), *Warrior, Duke of Edinburgh, Black Prince.*

[3] Their collier had been ordered to Port Vathi in Ithaca, but the Greek skipper had gone to another port of the same name.

the enemy was making to the eastward, ran for Malta to coal so as to be able to keep to the chase.

Guided by his brother's signals, Captain John Kelly and his two destroyers made for the zone in which it seemed the two German ships were intending to get together again, and about 1 a.m. he saw smoke. It was now brilliant moonlight, so that the work in hand was extremely hazardous. Still, as soon as he had gained a good position for delivering an attack he carried on to close the chase, till in a few minutes he became aware from the *Gloucester's* signals that the ship he was after must be not the *Goeben* but the *Breslau*, and that the *Goeben* must be between him and his brother. He therefore turned to meet her, and after getting across her course so as to have the moon right, he ran up to attack from ahead. It was a most promising situation. But he was doomed to disappointment. The *Goeben* was nowhere to be seen. Possibly warned by her consort, she had altered course to avoid the torpedo menace, but the failure may have been due to some confusion between local and Greenwich time in taking in the *Gloucester's* signals. Whatever the cause, she had given the *Dublin* the slip, and there was nothing to do but to carry on to the Fano rendezvous according to previous instructions.

At the same time (3.50 a.m.) Admiral Troubridge, being then abreast of Zante, and judging it to be inexpedient to quit his position in the absence of specific instructions, also gave up the chase. His intention had been to engage the *Goeben* if he could get contact before 6 a.m., since only darkness or half light offered a chance of his being able to engage her successfully outside territorial waters, and when he found it impossible he thought it his duty not to risk his squadron against an enemy who, by his superiority in speed and gunpower, could choose his distance and out-range him. Still, he only slowed down, and held on as he was, in expectation that his two battle cruisers would now be sent back to him, with instructions for concerting action. But they did not come, and about 10 a.m. on August 7, by which time the *Goeben* had passed ahead of him, he went into Zante preparatory to resuming his watch in the Adriatic.

When Admiral Troubridge made the port, the Commander-in-Chief steaming at moderate speed was nearing Malta. During the night he had received from the French Admiral an offer of a squadron which he had requested should patrol between Marsala and Cape Bon to watch the passage between Sicily and Africa.[1] Being thus relieved of anxiety in that

[1] The ships were the armoured cruisers *Bruix, Latouche-Tréville, Amiral Charner* and the cruiser *Jurien de la Gravière.*

direction he had moved away to the eastward at fifteen knots.
The *Indomitable* was coming up astern at twenty-one knots,
and when she reached Malta he did not send her on,
but kept her there till his other two ships had coaled.
Thus Captain Kelly in the *Gloucester* was left to carry
on the chase alone. So perilous was his position that,
about 5.30 a.m., Admiral Milne had signalled to him to drop
astern so as to avoid capture; but he chose to take the
signal as permissive only, and held on as doggedly as ever
in spite of every effort of the Germans to shake him off. By
10.30 a.m. the *Breslau* had rejoined, and, after taking station
astern of the flagship, kept crossing the *Gloucester's* course
as though to drop mines. But Captain Kelly did not flinch.
He steamed on undisturbed and with so much persistence
that off the Gulf of Kalamata the *Breslau* began to try to
ride him off by dropping astern. By 1 p.m. it became clear
that something must be done if he was to keep the *Goeben* in
sight. By engaging the *Breslau* he would be able either to
force her to close the flagship or bring the flagship back to
protect her. At 1.35, therefore, he opened fire with his
forward six-inch gun at 11,500 yards. The *Breslau*, who
was two points on his port bow and had her starboard guns
bearing, returned the fire smartly and accurately. Captain
Kelly then increased to full speed, ran up to 10,000, and,
turning 10 points to port, brought the enemy on his starboard
quarter. As soon as the two ships were engaged broadside
to broadside, the *Goeben*, as Captain Kelly expected, turned
16 points to come back, and, though far out of range,
she opened fire. Having thus gained his object, Captain
Kelly at 1.50 ceased fire and, with admirable judgment, broke
off the action, considering it his duty to preserve his ship
intact for fulfilling his main duty of keeping hold of the *Goeben*,
and as soon as she turned again to resume her eastward
course he informed the Commander-in-Chief and continued
to shadow. Admiral Milne, who was coaling, had not yet
felt able to leave Malta, and was getting very anxious for
the *Gloucester*. Knowing she must be short of coal, he
sent her orders not to chase further than Cape Matapan, and
then to rejoin Admiral Troubridge, but no other cruiser was
sent to take her place. By 4.40 p.m. the *Gloucester* had
reached the specified point, the *Goeben* and *Breslau* could be
seen holding eastwards through the Cervi Channel, and with
this last report of their movements Captain Kelly turned
back.

For his conduct throughout the affair he was highly
commended by the Admiralty. " The *Goeben*," so ran the

minute on his report, " could have caught and sunk the
Gloucester at any time . . . she was apparently deterred by
the latter's boldness, which gave the impression of support
close at hand. The combination of audacity with restraint,
unswerving attention to the principal military object, viz.
holding on to the *Goeben* and strict conformity to orders,
constitute a naval episode which may justly be regarded as
a model." In endorsement of this judgment Captain Kelly
received the honour of Companionship of the Bath.

His conduct was the one bright spot in the unfortunate
episode. The outcome of a situation which had been so
promising, and which might well have resulted in a success,
priceless at the opening of the war, was a severe disappointment. But on his return home the Commander-in-Chief was
able to give explanations of his difficulties which satisfied
the Board and he was exonerated from blame. In view of
the instructions which the Admiralty had given him in their
anxiety to protect the French transport line and to respect
the neutrality of Italy, it is clear that what blame there was
could not rest solely on the shoulders of the Admiral. His
failure was due at least in part to the fact that owing to
the rapid changes in the situation, it was practically impossible for the Admiralty to keep him adequately informed.
The sudden pressure on an embryonic staff organisation was
more than it could bear, but the fact remains that intelligence
essential for forming a correct appreciation of the shifting
situation either did not reach him, or reached him too late,
and, what was more embarrassing, his original instructions
as to his " primary object " were not cancelled when they
were rendered obsolete by the action of the Toulon Fleet.

After due consideration it was felt that the failure of
Admiral Troubridge to bring the *Goeben* to action required
investigation. A month later, therefore, he was recalled to
justify himself before a Court of Inquiry. On its report, a
Court Martial was ordered, before which he was charged under
the Third Section of the Naval Discipline Act, that "from negli-
gence or default he did on August 7 forbear to pursue the chase
of H.I.G.M.'s ship *Goeben*, being an enemy then flying." But
before a full Court of his brother officers Admiral Troubridge
had no difficulty in proving his case. The Court found that
he had acted in accordance with his instructions, that he
was justified in regarding the enemy's force as superior to
his own in daylight, and that, although if he had carried on
the chase he might have brought the *Goeben* to action in the
Cervi Channel, he would not have been justified in quitting
the station assigned to him without further orders. Con-

sequently they declared the charge not proved, and the Admiral was " fully and honourably " acquitted. There the matter ended.

Much as there was in these crowded opening days to excuse the failure, it must always tell as a shadow in our naval history. But it is only right to recall that the circumstances of the case are closely analogous to those in which Nelson in 1805, preoccupied primarily with the security of Sicily and the Eastern Mediterranean, allowed Villeneuve to escape to the west, as Admiral Souchon had been permitted to escape to the east. Nor is this the only precedent; for it was in these same hide-and-seek waters that Nelson's great successor Collingwood had missed Ganteaume and Allemande in 1809. Tried beside the failure of the two great masters in whom all our old naval lore culminated, it will perhaps be judged most leniently by those whose wisdom and knowledge are the ripest.

What makes the whole episode more unfortunate is that, had we been able to know it in time to take action, there was still a possibility of making good the failure of the first blow. Whatever may have been the truth about the alleged alliance between Germany and Turkey, it was clearly not working. For scarcely had Admiral Souchon shaken off the *Gloucester* and entered the Ægean Sea when a message reached him that he must not proceed at once to the Dardanelles, as the Turks were making difficulties about allowing him to enter. He was still, therefore, in a highly precarious position, and immediately took steps to get contact with the *Loreley*, the German guardship at Constantinople. To this end, at the risk of revealing his position, he signalled to the *General* to make forthwith for Smyrna instead of Santorini in order to act as wireless link. He also ordered up the first of his three colliers and, having found a convenient bay to hide her, proceeded to cruise slowly eastward amongst the islands. During the 8th, while thus engaged, he fell in with two French passenger ships with a large number of reservists from the Bosporus, but as they kept within Greek waters he had to leave them alone. In the afternoon he sent away the *Breslau* to fetch the collier and bring her into Denusa, a small and sparsely inhabited island east of Naxos, where he anchored at 5.32 a.m. on the 9th, and completed coaling at 5.0 a.m. on the 10th.

Meanwhile Admiral Milne had taken up the chase again, but it was not till midnight (the 7th–8th) that he left Malta, and as in default of intelligence he steamed very slowly, at 2.30 p.m. on the 8th he was no more than half

way to **Matapan**.   Then fortune played another trick, for
here he received from the Admiralty a warning, which had
been sent out by mistake, that hostilities had commenced
against Austria.   He could not yet tell whether the *Goeben's*
objective might not be Alexandria and our Levant and
Eastern trade, but since his last news of the French Fleet
was that it would not be free to co-operate with him
before the 10th, his only course seemed to be to turn back
and re-concentrate his fleet.   He therefore proceeded to a
position 100 miles south-westward of Cephalonia so as to
prevent the Austrians cutting him off from his base, and
ordered Admiral Troubridge to join him.   The *Gloucester*
and the destroyers were to do the same, while the *Dublin*
and *Weymouth* were left to watch the Adriatic.   Later on
in the day (August 8) he was informed that the alarm was
false, but as, at the same time, he was instructed that relations
with Austria were critical, he continued his movement for
concentration till noon on the 9th.   Then came a telegram
from the Admiralty to say definitely we were not at war with
Austria and that he was to resume the chase.   Accordingly,
leaving Admiral Troubridge to watch the Adriatic, he proceeded south-eastwards with the three battle cruisers and the
Weymouth, calling the *Dublin* and *Chatham* to follow.   The
movement involved some risk, since, for the time, it left
Admiral Troubridge in the air, but as the Admiralty were
inviting the French to use Malta as their base it could not
be long before they would arrive to join him.

Since Admiral Milne came down the Greek coast at only
ten knots, presumably to allow his light cruisers to come up,
it was not till 3 a.m. on August 10 that he entered the Ægean,
some sixty hours after the *Goeben* had passed the Cervi
Channel, and he was still entirely without information as to
her whereabouts or object.   Admiral Souchon was actually
still at Denusa, waiting to hear that permission to enter the
Dardanelles had been negotiated.   But not a word could the
General pass him of any alteration in the situation, although
she had succeeded in establishing communication with Constantinople.   The previous day (9th) had passed in increasing
anxiety, till about 9 p.m. he had begun to hear the wireless
of the British.   As it came nearer and nearer his position
became too dangerous to hold, and although he was still
without a word from Constantinople, he received an order
through the *General* presumably from Berlin, at 1.0 a.m. on
the 10th, directing him to enter the Straits.   He put to sea
at 5.45 a.m. and at 12.10 p.m. received a message direct
from the German Admiralty : " It is of great importance that
Goeben enters Dardanelles as soon as possible."

At this time Admiral Milne having rounded Cape Malea, was heading about north-east on a course that was rapidly converging with that of Admiral Souchon. He was well in sight of Belo Pulo Light, and little more than 100 miles to the westward of the German cruisers. But close as he now was upon their track it was too late. Even had he known what their destination was he could scarcely have been up in time to prevent them being piloted safely through the Dardanelles minefields. Nor had he any good reason for making the effort. So far as he was informed of the state of affairs, the immediate danger was for the safety of Alexandria and the Suez Canal. Apart from this there was still a widespread opinion that Admiral Souchon's intention was to rejoin the Austrians. He had had plenty of time to coal amongst the islands; indeed, there was a report that he had gone to Syra for that purpose. Admiral Milne's main preoccupation, therefore, was to make sure the enemy did not break back to the southward, and with this object in view he spread his force so as to bar the passages through the islands between the mainland and the Cyclades, while the *Weymouth* was detached to look into Milo and Syra. Soon, however, German signals were heard near by, and a sweep was made to the southward. Then the German colliers were heard calling distinctly to the northward, and so the sweep turned in that direction to occupy the passage between Nikaria and Mykoni, while the *Weymouth* scouted as high as Smyrna, and *Chatham*, who after searching round Naxos had just joined, was sent to the eastward to examine the vicinity of Kos. But all doubt was soon to be at an end. Shortly before noon on the 11th, before the sweep was complete, the Admiral heard from Malta that the *Goeben* and *Breslau* had entered the Dardanelles at 8.30 the previous night. They had, in fact, arrived off Cape Helles about 5.0 that evening, still not knowing whether they would be received. But on calling for a pilot, a Turkish torpedo-boat came out and signalled them to follow. They anchored off Chanak at 7.35 p.m. As soon as the news reached Admiral Milne he hurried off after them, and in the course of the afternoon received an order to blockade the exit.

So the unhappy affair ended in something like a burst of public derision that the Germans should so soon have been chased out of the Mediterranean to suffer an ignominious internment. How false was that consolation none but the best informed could then even dream. It was many months before it was possible to appreciate fully the combined effrontery, promptitude and sagacity of the move. When we consider that the Dardanelles was mined, that no permission to enter it had been ratified, and that everything depended on the German powers of cajolery at Constantinople, when we also recall the world-wide results that ensued, it is not too much to say that few naval decisions more bold and well-judged were ever taken. So completely, indeed, did the risky venture turn a desperate situation into one of high moral and material advantage, that for the credit of German statesmanship it goes far to balance the cardinal blunder of attacking France through Belgium.[1]

[1] It would appear that the final decision was taken by Admiral Souchon himself. According to Admiral von Tirpitz, when on August 3 news was received of the alleged alliance with Turkey, orders were sent to Admiral Souchon to attempt to break through to the Dardanelles. On August 5 the German Embassy at Constantinople reported that in view of the situation there it was undesirable for the ships to arrive for the present. Thereupon the orders for the Dardanelles were cancelled, and Admiral Souchon, who was then coaling at Messina, was directed to proceed to Pola or else break out into the Atlantic. Later in the day, however, Austria, in spite of the pressure that was being put upon her from Berlin to declare war, protested she was not yet in a position to help with her fleet. In these circumstances it was thought best to give Admiral Souchon liberty to decide for himself which line of escape to attempt, and he then chose the line of his first instructions. (Von Tirpitz, *My Memories*, pp. 349-350. Eng. ed.)

CHAPTER IV

PASSAGE OF THE EXPEDITIONARY FORCE

JUST as the transport of the Algerian Army was completed, that of our own Expeditionary Force was beginning. On August 6 the immediate dispatch to France of four of its six Infantry Divisions and one Cavalry Division was sanctioned, and before the Navy had had even time to get out its commerce protection cruisers, it found itself saddled with a task which in difficulty and magnitude was quite beyond its experience. The question whether such an operation was a legitimate risk of war before a decided command of home waters had been established had long been in debate. Still, the risk had been measured, and so vital did our own and the French General Staff consider it to get our Army upon the left of the French line at the earliest possible moment, that the risk, with all its hazards, had been accepted by the Admiralty. During the past three years every detail had been worked out between the two Services for landing the Force in the north-west of France, and a plan of operation settled which promised to reduce the risk to a minimum. For a landing in Belgium, which would involve a much higher sea risk, there was no plan at all.

The general idea involved the use of several ports of departure and two of arrival. The lines of passage consequently varied, but all were within waters that lay well for cover by the Fleet. The main port of embarkation for troops in England, as well as for horses and hospital ships, was Southampton, and thence the bulk of the transports were to make for Havre, the main port of arrival, though some proceeded up to Rouen and a few went to Boulogne. Certain units stationed in Scotland were to embark at Glasgow, while the Vth and VIth Divisions,[1] which were stationed in Ireland, were to start from Dublin, Queenstown and Belfast. For stores Newhaven was the principal port, but the heavier kinds, and the mechanical transport, were shipped at Avonmouth

---

[1] To avoid confusion with Naval units, Military divisions are specified throughout by Roman numerals.

and Liverpool.   At the last moment, however, the scheme was modified.   The original idea had been to send five divisions, and transport to that amount had actually been taken up, but finally it was decided to be unsafe at the outset to leave the country with less than two regular divisions.   The VIth Division, therefore, instead of going direct to France from Ireland, was ordered to come to England first and concentrate to the north of London about Cambridge.

A special feature of the plan, in order to minimise the risk, was that there were to be no convoys.   Transports were to sail singly or in pairs as they filled up and to proceed independently to their destination.   The system of protection, in fact, was the reverse of that which the French had been employing in the Mediterranean.   There was to be no escort : everything depended on the Covering Squadrons.   The plan was new.   To a certain extent it had been used, somewhat precariously and not without loss, by the Japanese ten years before, but our more favourable geographical position enabled us to carry the principle to its logical conclusion.

The system of cover was based on closing both ends of the Channel against raids, while the Grand Fleet took up a position from which it could strike the High Seas Fleet if the Germans should choose to risk it in an effort to prevent our Army joining hands with that of France.

It was on August 5 that the decision was taken by the War Council.   The day mentioned for the movement to begin was August 7, and the Admiralty had intimated that transports would all be ready by that time, and that from then onwards they could guarantee safe passage to the French ports designated.   The Army Council, however, had to notify them that the troops could not reach their ports of departure so soon.   The difficulty was that large numbers of Territorials who had just gone into training camps had had to be recalled for embodiment, and the railway time-table could not work until the labour of transporting them had been completed.   The whole operation, therefore, had to be postponed till the 9th.

The utmost secrecy was observed, and it was not till the morning of the 7th that the Admiralty had the word to put their operation orders in action.   At the same time the Channel Fleet was given a new organisation adapted to the special work in hand.   As we have seen, the " Duncans " of the 6th Battle Squadron had been ordered to join the Grand Fleet, and the three units which were ready for sea had already sailed for Scapa.   This squadron, which had been Admiral Burney's own, was now suppressed, and of the remaining ships the *Lord Nelson* and *Agamemnon* were to join the 5th

Squadron and the *Vengeance* the 8th under Admiral Tottenham. These two squadrons with the 7th under Admiral Bethell were now to form the Channel Fleet, with the *Lord Nelson*, as Fleet flagship, flying Admiral Burney's flag. The remaining battleships on the active list—that is, the seven " Majestics "—never actually formed part of it, being withdrawn for special service. The four that were stationed in the Humber were intended to form the 9th Battle Squadron —*Hannibal* (flag), Captain J. F. Grant-Dalton; *Victorious*, Captain R. Nugent; *Mars*, Captain R. M. Harboard; *Magnificent*, Captain F. A. Whitehead; but when Admiral Jellicoe decided to make Scapa his main base he had asked for a senior officer to take charge of it and for some better defence. Accordingly Rear-Admiral F. S. Miller was appointed to the post and on August 7 was ordered to hoist his flag in the *Hannibal* and proceed to Scapa with that ship and the *Magnificent*. The *Majestic* and *Jupiter* were in dockyard hands, and the intention was to pay off the *Illustrious* in order to provide a crew for the *Erin*, the completed Turkish Dreadnought which had just been requisitioned.

On August 7, therefore, the Channel Fleet was constituted as follows :—

Fleet Flagship: *Lord Nelson.*
Vice-Admiral Sir Cecil Burney, K.C.B., K.C.M.G.
Captain J. W. L. McClintock.
Attached light cruiser, *Diamond*, Commander L. L. Dundas.

FIFTH BATTLE SQUADRON

Rear-Admiral Bernard Currey.
Rear-Admiral C. F. Thursby, C.M.G.

Prince of Wales (flag)	Captain R. N. Bax.
Queen (2nd flag).	Captain H. A. Adam.
Venerable	Captain V. H. G. Bernard.
Irresistible	Captain The Hon. Stanhope Hawke.
Bulwark	Captain G. L. Sclater.
Formidable	Captain D. St. A. Wake.
Implacable	Captain H. C. Lockyer.
London	Captain J. G. Armstrong.

Topaze, Commander W. J. B. Law

SEVENTH BATTLE SQUADRON

Vice-Admiral The Hon. Sir A. E. Bethell, K.C.B., K.C.M.G.
(Commanding 3rd Fleet)

Prince George (flag)	Captain A. V. Campbell.
Cæsar	Captain E. W. E. Wemyss.
Jupiter [1]	Captain C. E. Le Mesurier.
Majestic [1]	Captain H. F. G. Talbot.

Sapphire, Captain H. G. C. Somerville.

---

[1] In dockyard hands.

EIGHTH BATTLE SQUADRON

Rear-Admiral H. L. Tottenham, C.B.
(2nd in Command 3rd Fleet)

Albion (flag)	.	.	.	.	Captain A. W. Heneage.
Goliath	.	.	.	.	Captain T. L. Shelford.
Canopus	.	.	.	.	Captain Heathcoat Grant.
Glory	.	.	.	.	Captain C. F. Corbett.
Ocean	.	.	.	.	Captain A. Hayes-Sadler.
Vengeance	.	.	.	.	Captain Bertram H. Smith.

Proserpine,[1] Commander G. C. Hardy.

The squadrons proceeded immediately to assemble at Portland, and so well had the whole scheme for the Expeditionary Force been worked out, that by the time specified for its passage Southampton and Newhaven were closed to commerce and all squadrons were in position. Admiral Burney himself with the 5th Squadron was cruising between the longitudes of Dungeness and the Owers (off Selsea Bill).   He was given a free hand in case the enemy tried to break through the Strait of Dover, the Admiralty merely suggesting a certain position as the most favourable for meeting such an attempt with advantage.   To provide him with a cruiser force the southern area of the North Sea was drawn upon.   Admiral Campbell, after the loss of the *Amphion*, had been ordered, as we have seen, into the Downs with the *Bacchante, Euryalus* and *Aboukir*.   There the *Cressy* had joined him, and at noon on the 8th all four were directed to pass the Strait before dark and join Admiral Burney's flag at Portland.   The Strait itself was held by the French destroyers and submarines of the Boulogne Flotilla in combination with our own Dover Patrol —that is, the 6th Flotilla—which since it had taken up its war station on August 3 had been examining all vessels that passed, directing all traffic through the Downs, and dealing with British ships under order for Baltic and North Sea destinations which their owners desired to have diverted to Home ports.   Immediately in advance of this patrol was another line held by Commodore Keyes with the *Firedrake* and twelve submarines, and this ran from the North Goodwins through the Sandettie light-vessel to Ruytingen.   Still further to the northward, as a special precaution for the detection of hostile submarines, a seaplane and airship patrol was established between the North Foreland and Ostend, and beyond this, again, were the 1st and 3rd Destroyer Flotillas at Harwich, ready to form an advance patrol in the waters off the Dutch

---

[1] In dockyard hands.

coast, known as the Broad Fourteens, and elsewhere as might be directed.

The western entrance of the Channel was similarly guarded by the Anglo-French cruiser squadron, which was dealing with traffic in the same way as the Dover Patrol. Under Rear-Admiral Wemyss were the light cruisers *Charybdis*, *Diana*, *Eclipse* and *Talbot*, and the French had five armoured cruisers, subsequently reinforced by two light cruisers. They were now under Rear-Admiral Le Cannellier, Admiral Rouyer himself having returned to Cherbourg with the other three armoured cruisers of his squadron. The special instructions of this force were to prevent disguised ships laying mines on the Army's lines of passage, and all doubtful ships that could not be searched at sea were to be passed into Falmouth. In support of this cruiser patrol was Admiral Bethell with the 7th and 8th Battle Squadrons, but at first his station was somewhat removed from the cruisers. His assigned functions in the plan were to support the transports on the western side of the main line of passage in order to give confidence to the troops and to assist the transports with his boats in case of need. But when after the first night he found the presence of battleships along the line of passage was a source of danger rather than security, and when also a Life Saving Patrol organised by The Hon. Sir Hedworth Meux at Portsmouth appeared on the route, he was directed at his own suggestion to take station further west, and he then proceeded to patrol the line between St. Alban's Head and Cherbourg—that is, just to the eastward of the line between Portland and Cap de la Hague, which was being held by the Cherbourg submarines. From this port, also, Admiral Rouyer, with the remainder of his squadron, operated in concert with Admiral Bethell. Thus there was nothing actually on the main line passage except the Life Saving Patrol, and this was in no sense an escort. It was composed of any small craft that could be pressed into the service, and they sailed unarmed under the blue ensign with the Red Cross at the main.

So far, then, as protection against cruiser or flotilla raids was concerned, the system was very complete and strong, but with the arrangements for dealing with the High Seas Fleet, should it come out, things proved more difficult. As Admiral Jellicoe, on the morning of August 8, was proceeding to take up the position he had selected, three ships, which had been detached for firing practice, reported submarines in the vicinity of Fair Island; one of the three was actually attacked unsuccessfully. They were at once recalled, but the Admiral, taking all precautions, held away for his chosen area,

which he believed to be free both of mines and submarines.
As he approached it, however, its supposed security became
more and more doubtful.   In the evening a periscope was
seen by the flagship, but still he carried on, with constant
alterations of course, for a rendezvous where the 2nd Cruiser
Squadron and the light cruisers were to meet him.   He
reached it at 4 a.m. on the 9th, just as the advance parties
of the Expeditionary Force were embarking, and here the
Birmingham reported that a short time previously she had
rammed and sunk the German submarine *U 15*.[1]

It was the first achievement of the kind, and so far as it
went gave a certain confidence that the new weapon, if boldly
met, was not so formidable as it was generally supposed to
be.   Still, it was obvious that the area was not free from
danger, especially as there was a strong suspicion that the
enemy were using, or intended to use, the northern islands as
bases for their submarines.   In reporting the occurrence to
the Admiralty, Admiral Jellicoe proposed taking his battle
fleet west of the Orkneys as soon as the troops were across.
Till then he was ready to accept the risk and held his ground
all day in case the High Seas Fleet should move.   Of this
there was still no indication, and in the evening came an
order from the Admiralty directing him to take the whole of
his heavy ships north-west of the Orkneys at once well out
of the infected area.   This he did, proceeding to Scapa himself
to organise a scheme for clearing the waters he had left with
his lighter vessels.

One of the chief anxieties was a continuance of the reports
that the Germans were endeavouring to establish submarine
bases in the vicinity of the anchorage.   They were said to
have ships at the Faeroes and Lofotens.   To the Faeroes were
sent two ships of the Northern Patrol under Rear-Admiral
Grant, who had just joined, in the *Drake*.   Circumstantial
intelligence also came in that they were using the Stavanger
Fjord, and the Light and 3rd Cruiser Squadrons, which were
sweeping in that direction from Kinnaird Head, were ordered
to pick up the 4th Flotilla and examine the place, but
with strict orders not to violate Norwegian neutrality unless
the Germans were actually operating in territorial waters.
Nothing was found, except that Norwegian officers were
keeping a strict watch, and nothing came of it except that,
unfortunately, a ship was searched within the three-mile limit,
and for this a full apology was promptly sent to Christiania.
At the Faeroes no suspicious signs were discovered, and the
search of the Lofotens was countermanded.

[1] See *ante*, p. 39.

In view of how Germany had behaved to another weak neutral, these precautions against the Norwegian Fjords and islands being used by our enemy could not be regarded as other than moderate. Seeing how exposed was the Grand Fleet's position, without so much as a defended anchorage, even more might have been excused. The temporary defences which Admiral Jellicoe had been able to devise were wholly inadequate as a protection against submarines. It was owing to this precarious state of things that he had asked for two old battleships as guardships, with a flag officer to take charge of the anchorage, and that Admiral Miller was ordered up with the *Hannibal* and *Magnificent*, from the Humber, leaving the defence of that harbour to the *Mars* and *Victorious*. But even this was not enough. The worst feature of the case was that Admiral Jellicoe could no longer shut his eyes to the fact that the Germans, as was only to be expected, had already located his anchorage. He therefore further submitted to the Admiralty that it was essential for the Fleet's security to provide another as an alternative. This also was at once sanctioned, and steps were immediately taken to establish a second war-anchorage on the north-west coast of Scotland at Loch Ewe. Having arranged these matters, the Admiral rejoined the Battle Fleet. In advance of it his cruiser squadrons were working from Cromarty, and in this way the Grand Fleet, according to instructions, kept at sea while the Expeditionary Force was passing.

So far the operation had worked without hitch and according to programme—indeed, the only variations appear to have been due to transports being ahead of time. During the first three days the work was mainly concerned with advance parties of various kinds, and it was not till August 12 that the bulk of the force began to cross. On the 13th the Vth Division was to begin moving from the Irish ports to Havre, and special measures had to be taken for its protection. For this purpose the 11th Cruiser Squadron, whose station was off the west of Ireland, had to be called away from its commerce protection duties. While one ship watched the North Channel, the other three, with the armed merchant cruiser *Caronia*, which had recently been added to it, patrolled between Queenstown and Scilly to guard against mine-laying and to hand on the transports to the Western Patrol.

Of hostile movements there had been no sign. By some the enemy's mysterious inaction was explained—in view of his obvious nervousness about a British descent in some unexpected quarter—by a conjecture that in his eyes the Expeditionary Force was less to be feared, or at least less disturbing, in France than anywhere else. But of course it was not then known how the German Staff counted on annihilating it at the first blow, and the ominous stillness seemed rather to portend a sudden counterstroke, either to prevent its transport being completed or to terrorise the country after it had gone.[1] While, therefore, the precautions in the Channel were relaxed by resting half the submarines and withdrawing Admiral Bethell's squadron to a watching position at Portland, new orders were sent to the Grand Fleet. On August 12 the Admiralty informed Admiral Jellicoe that in view of the possibility of an attempt at invasion he ought to be nearer the decisive area than had hitherto been contemplated. They proposed, therefore, that he should bring the fleet back east of the Orkneys. If any attempt of the kind was in contemplation it would prove most telling after August 15, by which time the bulk of the Expeditionary Force would have left the country. It was to meet this situation that the VIth Division was to come over from Ireland and concentrate at Cambridge, and in response to the Admiralty's suggestion Admiral Jellicoe made arrangements for a full occupation of the North Sea during the critical period. The Grand Fleet was to move to a mid-sea position about the latitude of Aberdeen in full force— even Admiral de Chair, with four of his cruisers, was called from the Northern Patrol to take a part. From that position the cruisers would sweep down to the Horn Reefs, and to complete the disposition he proposed a northward sweep of the 1st and 3rd Destroyer Flotillas from Harwich, with the 7th Squadron cruisers in support.

These ships were no longer under his immediate command. As early as August 8, finding communication with the southern area very difficult, he had requested the Admiralty to take over its direction, and this had been done by their issuing orders direct to Rear-Admiral Campbell and Commodores Keyes and Tyrwhitt. The system was now regularised by constituting the flotillas and the supporting cruiser squadron an independent command under Rear-Admiral Christian. Admiral Campbell's squadron comprised the *Bacchante* (flag), *Hogue*, *Aboukir* and *Cressy*, the *Euryalus* being taken for the new Admiral's flag. The whole became known as the " Southern Force," and its functions were to protect the Belgian coast, to prevent the Schelde being blocked, and to give notice of any attempt to interrupt our communications with France in the Channel. In carrying out this general idea the Admiral was given a free hand in arranging patrols, subject only

[1] See *Military Operations (France and Belgium)*, Vol. I, p. 10, note 3.

to orders from the Admiralty when special operations were required.

The first of these special orders was for the movement which was to combine with that of the Grand Fleet. During August 15th, 16th and 17th the operation was carried out so that on the 16th—the day on which the largest amount of transport was passing—the Heligoland Bight was completely blockaded. To the north was disposed the Grand Fleet in full force, with Admiral de Chair and his four cruisers watching between it and the Skagerrak, while its extreme right was connected up with Terschelling by the Southern Force, consisting of the four " Bacchantes," three light cruisers and thirty-six destroyers, with four submarines in pairs, watching the mouths of the Jade and Ems. During these three days the transports made 137 passages—the tonnage passing being well over half a million—but still there was not a sign of the enemy moving, and on August 17 both forces returned to their normal stations, Loch Ewe being used by the Dreadnought squadrons for the first time.

No sooner, however, was our Fleet well out of the way than the Germans took heart. August 18 was the last heavy day for the transport work, the number being thirty-four vessels, totalling 130,000 tons, or only just under the average of the past three days. Admiral Bethell's squadron had since the 14th been entirely withdrawn, his attached cruiser, the *Sapphire*, being added to the Southern Force, but Admiral Rouyer had spread his Cherbourg cruisers further north to take his place. To the northward of the Strait of Dover, after the big movement was over, the normal Watching Patrol of the Broad Fourteens was resumed by the 1st Destroyer Flotilla under Captain William F. Blunt in the light cruiser *Fearless*. Proceeding to their station, they at 5.40 a.m. were nearing Brown Ridge, when they sighted the large German cruiser *Stralsund*. She at once gave chase, and the patrol ran off to the westward, calling up Admiral Christian at the Nore and Admiral Campbell, who two or three hours earlier had anchored in the Downs. Commodore Tyrwhitt also got the alarm at Harwich, and by 7.20 was away at full speed with the *Amethyst* and the 3rd Flotilla. Half an hour later Admiral Campbell also got his squadron away. Meanwhile the *Fearless* had become engaged with the *Stralsund*, supposed at the time to be the 3rd-class cruiser *Rostock*. At 7.0 she gave up the chase, and as soon as Captain Blunt had collected his flotilla he proceeded to chase in turn, while Commodore Tyrwhitt headed to cut the enemy off from the Bight. The search was kept up all day and through the night, but nothing more was seen of her.

The *Stralsund* and *Strassburg* with the submarines *U 19* and *U 24* had arrived in the area at 7.0 p.m. on the 17th and, having sighted nothing, started home at 4.0 a.m. next morning.   At 5.39 a.m. the *Stralsund*, then unsupported, sighted and opened fire on the *Fearless*.   When the latter was joined by a second cruiser, however, the German commander, realizing that no support could reach him in time, broke off the action.

As the transportation of the first part of the Expeditionary Force was now practically complete, and there was no prospect of the High Seas Fleet being tempted out by any smaller attraction, further sweeps southward by the Grand Fleet had been forbidden.   The idea was to shift our destroyer patrol further south, where it could keep in touch with its supporting cruisers, and at the same time to provide a second force so placed as to be able to cut off the enemy's retreat if they attempted anything to southward.   For this force the Humber was the base chosen, and as it was evident that faster and more powerful ships were required, two battle cruisers were ordered there, under Rear-Admiral Sir Archibald Moore, whose flag was in the *Invincible*.   The lack of enterprise which the Germans were showing rendered her detention at Queenstown unnecessary.   She was therefore available, and though she had been promised to Admiral Jellicoe she had to be diverted.   With her was detached the *New Zealand*, and three of the " Arethusas," the new light cruisers which were nearly ready for sea, were to follow.   The places of the two battle cruisers in the Grand Fleet were to be filled from the Mediterranean.   On the day the Broad Fourteens Patrol was chased off, the *Inflexible*, as will appear later, had left Malta for home, and next day—August 19—the *Indomitable* was ordered to leave the Dardanelles for Gibraltar and there await orders.

The urgent need for strengthening our hold on the lower part of the North Sea was that the work of transporting the Expeditionary Force had received a sudden extension.   By the programme the first movement was to be complete on August 20, but owing to the success of the Germans in forcing the Belgian frontier, the situation had to be reconsidered.   The Belgian Government and Field Army had retired to Antwerp, the enemy were in Brussels, and so precarious was the position of the British Army owing to the breakdown of the French opening, that it was decided to send over another division.   The one selected was the IVth, which was then distributed along the East Anglian coast as a defence force, and on the 20th all the covering squadrons and flotillas

were ordered to stand fast for another five days. So smartly,
however, was the work done, and so urgent the call for
reinforcing Sir John French, that by the 23rd the bulk of
the troops were across. In the afternoon Admiral Burney
received permission to leave the position he had been holding
between Beachy Head and Boulogne and to return to Portsmouth to overhaul his ships. At the same time, also, the Life
Saving Patrol was withdrawn. There remained, of course,
the permanent task of protecting the lines of supply, and for
this purpose Admiral Burney was to hold half his fleet in
readiness for prompt action, while Admiral Bethell was to
stand by to join him at short notice with what was left of his
command.

By this time it had been greatly reduced. The first draft
upon him had been for the four "Majestics" which were now
guarding the Humber and Scapa. In consequence of this
reduction the 6th Battle Squadron had been amalgamated
with the 5th, and the 7th and 8th had been merged into one,
denominated the 7th. By the time the first four divisions
of the Expeditionary Force were across, a further call had
been made upon him. An idea was growing that the in-
explicable inactivity of the High Seas Fleet possibly por-
tended that the enemy was contemplating an organised
attack with his heavy cruisers on our weak commerce
protection squadrons that were scattered on the great trade
routes. For the Grand Fleet to guarantee that battle
cruisers could not break out was impossible, and as in the old
days it was the practice to strengthen such squadrons with a
lesser ship of the line, so now it was thought well to detach
some of the oldest battleships to furnish them with a rallying-
point. The *Glory* had already gone to the Halifax area, and
now three more of the "Canopus" class were taken from
the 7th Battle Squadron—the *Canopus* herself for Admiral
Stoddart on the Cape Verde station, the *Albion*, with Rear-
Admiral Tottenham's flag still flying, for Gibraltar to support
Admiral de Robeck on the Cape St. Vincent–Finisterre station,
and the *Ocean* to Queenstown. For the defence of the new
Grand Fleet anchorage at Loch Ewe another "Majestic"—the
Illustrious—was taken, so that Admiral Bethell had now
nothing left but the *Vengeance*, to which he had shifted his
flag, *Prince George*, *Cæsar* and *Goliath*, with the *Proserpine* as
attached cruiser. The rest of the arrangements for securing
the lines of supply stood as they were, but on the day it was
all settled, as will be seen later, the system received a rude
shock which for a time threatened to upset it altogether.

CHAPTER V

FOR the Mediterranean Fleet, seeing how the position in those waters was developing, the call on its battle cruisers was a severe one. True, it was less than our original war plan contemplated, but things had taken an ugly and unexpected turn. On August 6 a naval convention had been concluded with France by which the command of the Mediterranean was to be left entirely in her hands. As soon as the *Goeben* and *Breslau* were disposed of, all our armoured ships, except Admiral Troubridge's flagship the *Defence*, were to be withdrawn, and the rest of the fleet was to come under the orders of the French Commander-in-Chief, Admiral Boué de Lapeyrère, who would be responsible for the Austrian Fleet and the protection of British trade. In all other parts of the world the British Admiralty were to have the general direction of naval operations, the French ships in those seas were to be under the flag of the British officer commanding the station, and we have seen how in the West Indies the *Condé* and *Descartes* had been promptly placed at Admiral Cradock's disposal.

It was also in accordance with this convention that the French had been invited to use Malta as their advanced base. This was essential; for seeing that Italy's neutrality was now assured and the Germans had been driven out of the sea, the Austrian Fleet was the only source of danger. Still, owing to the diplomatic situation, it was some time before any combined plans could be settled. As yet, though Austria was at war with Russia, she had made no overt movement against France, and was giving plausible assurances to Paris. Though transparently insincere, they were accepted by the French Government at their face value, as a means of postponing the inevitable declaration of war till their fleet was free to take up the Malta position. For us the situation was an uneasy one; for Russia it was a source of grave anxiety. The need to get our armoured ships away did not arise solely from the situation in home waters; another urgent call had arisen. Owing to the critical state of the military situation in France it was necessary to get the Egyptian and Mediterranean garrisons home as soon as possible, and in order to replace them two divisions were under orders to sail from India on August 24. The *Königsberg*, and possibly another German cruiser, were operating on their route,[1] and on August 10, before the French had made any move for Malta, it had been found necessary to order Admiral Troubridge to detach two of the 1st Cruiser Squadron, *Black Prince* and *Duke of Edinburgh*, to the Red Sea. For Russia the apprehension was that Austria, before declaration, intended to dispatch her fleet to join the Germans in the Dardanelles, in order to overawe the Turks, penetrate to the Black Sea and force Bulgaria into the arms of the Central Powers. To our Admiralty this danger was not very real. Italy had not only refused to join the Central Powers, but was mobilising her fleet, and the prospect of Austria abandoning the Adriatic seemed too remote for serious consideration. Still, on general strategical grounds we were no less anxious than Russia to see the uncertain situation brought to a head. At Paris, therefore, we supported the urgent Russian request to have the position secured by a prompt declaration of war, and the final step was taken. On the 11th the French Ambassador left Vienna, and Admiral de Lapeyrère, who had just completed the transportation of the Algerian Army Corps, was ordered to concentrate his fleet at Malta. Next day Admiral Milne was informed of the convention, and that he, as being senior to the French Admiral, would have to come home, leaving under the orders of the French Commander-in-Chief Admiral Troubridge and Admiral Carden, who was commanding at Malta.

At midnight these instructions were followed by news that we, too, had declared war on Austria, and that he was to sail for Malta at once in order to hand over the command to Admiral Carden, and to leave two battle cruisers and one light cruiser to watch the Dardanelles under the senior captain. Of the other two light cruisers that were there he was to take one to Malta, and to send the other to Port Said, where she was required to assist in protecting the Indian Transport route. Reaching Malta on August 14, he found that the French Fleet had concentrated there two days earlier, and that Admiral de Lapeyrère, with his 1st Battle Squadron and

---

[1] See *post*, p. 152.

a division of cruisers, had sailed to join Admiral Troubridge at the entrance of the Adriatic.[1]

Next morning the rest of the ships and nearly all the destroyers followed, and on August 15 the junction took place in a dense fog that did nothing to damp the scene of high enthusiasm that marked the event. But no time was lost beyond what was needed for a conference of flag officers, at which the French Admiral explained the immediate action he meant to take. His intention was to break up the Austrian blockade of Montenegro next morning. His plan was with his own battle squadrons and destroyers to steal up the Italian coast, without lights, as high as the latitude of Cattaro. Thence in the early morning he would strike across till he made the Montenegrin coast, while Admiral Troubridge and the French light cruiser squadrons would sweep from Fano island up the Albanian coast to drive the enemy into his arms. The movement was carried out with precision, but nothing was found but a small cruiser, the *Zenta*, and one or two torpedo craft. The latter escaped inshore, but the *Zenta* was caught, and though she was brought to a standstill by

---

[1] The French main fleet was now composed as under :—

DREADNOUGHT DIVISION

Courbet (Admiral de Lapeyrère).
Jean Bart.
(Attached cruiser) *Jurien de la Gravière.*

FIRST BATTLE SQUADRON

Diderot (Vice-Admiral Chocheprat).
Danton.
Vergniaud.
Voltaire (Rear-Admiral Lacaze).
Condorcet.

SECOND BATTLE SQUADRON

Vérité (Vice-Admiral Le Bris).
République.
Patrie.
Démocratie.
Justice (Rear-Admiral Tracou).

FIRST CRUISER SQUADRON

Jules Michelet (Rear-Admiral Ramey de Sugny).
Ernest Renan.
Edgar Quinet.
Léon Gambetta (Rear-Admiral Senès).
Victor Hugo.
Jules Ferry.

FLOTILLA

Forty Destroyers.
Six submarines.

the first salvos of the *Courbet*, she gallantly refused to sur-render. In ten minutes she was a mass of flames and blew up, but her devoted crew, who had abandoned the ship in time, managed to reach the shore. Still, the blockade had been raised, and Admiral de Lapeyrère retired for the night to the southward to get his fleet out of torpedo danger, and prepare for further action.

His plan of campaign was by no means completed; indeed, the operation which had just been carried out was but the first step to something much more ambitious. The first obstacle to establishing a permanent blockade of the Adriatic was the advanced Austrian base at Cattaro, the southernmost of her ports, of which Montenegro formed the hinterland. Its capture would require more force than was at present avail-able, but an idea prevailed at the time that Italy was about to join the Entente Powers. Her co-operation would make an attack in force possible, and the recent operation had been designed not only to break up the blockade of Montenegro, but as a means of getting into communication with the king and arranging with him for the investment of the Cattaro forts on the land side. Seeing how the war was likely to develop—and as in fact it did—the success of the contem-plated operation would have been inestimable. But the hour for Italy's intervention was not yet ripe; nor was this all. The opening operation was destined to be the last piece of combined work which the French and British Fleets were to carry out in those waters for many a long day. At mid-night, as the Allied Fleet swept southward, Admiral Troubridge received an order from the Admiralty that he was to proceed at once to the Dardanelles in the *Defence*, taking with him all his destroyers and their parent ship *Blenheim*, and leaving the *Warrior* and the two remaining light cruisers, *Weymouth* and *Dublin*, with the French Admiral for the present.

Already the true significance of the escape of the *Goeben* and *Breslau* was declaring itself. Even before their arrival in the Bosporus the feeling at the Porte had become so much embittered over our detention of their two dreadnoughts that, as early as August 9, our Chargé d'Affaires—for the Ambassador, Sir Louis Mallet, was unfortunately away on leave—had to enter a formal protest against German vessels being allowed to arm in Turkish ports. Next day, when the *Goeben* and *Breslau* entered the Dardanelles, another protest was delivered against their being permitted to pass the Strait, and Sir Edward Grey—for whom the news left no illusions—telegraphed an immediate warning to Cairo. " If con-firmed," he said, " this means that Turkey has joined Germany and may attack Egypt." The effrontery with which our demand was met only deepened the sinister impression. To our protest the Porte replied that they had bought the two German ships, and that they were to be handed over to Admiral Limpus, the head of the British Naval Mission. Admiral Limpus himself was asking to be recalled to active service; but the Grand Vizier, who throughout was honestly opposed to a breach with us, protested he only required them as a means of bargaining with the Greeks for the return of the islands they had occupied during the Balkan War and not in any way for designs against Russia, and he begged that the Mission might be allowed to remain; to recall it was to leave the field to the Germans. It was, therefore, thought well to accept the Grand Vizier's assurance for the time, and Admiral Limpus, in spite of his urgent request, was ordered to remain. He did not leave till September 16.

But acquiescence did not mean inaction. Already, as soon as Sir Edward Grey's warning was sounded, orders had gone to India for all possible efforts to be made to advance the arrival of the first echelon of troops in Egypt by four or five days, and we have seen how the *Black Prince, Duke of Edinburgh* and *Chatham* had been detached to the Red Sea to clear their line of passage. Finally, when a warning came from our Embassy at Constantinople of persistent rumours that two Austrian cruisers were going to try, with the connivance of the Porte, to join the *Goeben* in the Dardanelles, it was decided to strengthen the blockade. It was then, in the afternoon of August 15, that Admiral Troubridge was ordered to take command of the blockading squadron.[1]

Owing to his being engaged in Admiral de Lapeyrère's movement, it was over thirty hours before the order came to his hands, and in that time the cloud over the Bosporus had ominously darkened. Instead of the German ships being handed over to our Mission, Admiral Limpus and his officers had been suddenly superseded by Turkish officers, and Admiral Souchon was appointed Commander-in-Chief of the Turkish Forces Afloat. He asked for a considerable number of German officers and men to help to train the Turkish Navy, and these arrived on August 29. The hand of the Germans overmastering our friends in the Ministry was plainly visible, and in Egypt it was no less strongly felt. There, too, intrigues, like that which was entangling Turkey, were stirring on all hands, and with so much craft and activity

[1] By an order of August 18 Admiral Carden was to be Senior Naval Officer, Malta; Admiral Troubridge to be in command of ships at sea, both officers being under the French Commander-in-Chief.

that it was to be feared if war broke out with the Suzerain Power, the internal situation of the country might be critical. We knew already that at Constantinople the mischievous Minister of War, Enver Pasha, was a German puppet, and that his dream was to use the European War to recover Egypt by force of arms. The Turkish Army was being mobilised; troops were reported in Syria moving towards the Egyptian frontier, and in the Red Sea ports transports were embarking troops for passage through the Canal. Not only was there nothing to prevent their landing on its banks, but the gravity of the situation was increased by the knowledge that the numerous German ships detained at Suez and Port Said were full of reservists. Immediate precautions were necessary, and on August 16 the *Black Prince*, which had been ordered to Aden, was directed by an order from Malta to remain at Suez, where a Turkish gunboat was in continual communication with Constantinople.

The *Black Prince* had started down the Red Sea two days before, but a happy chance had just brought her back. On the previous afternoon, shortly after leaving the Gulf of Suez, she met and captured two Hamburg-Amerika ships, the *Istria* of 4,200 tons and the *Sudmark* of 5,100. With her two prizes she turned back to Suez, passing the *Duke of Edinburgh*, who had just started for Aden, and she in her turn captured the Argo Company's *Altair* of 3,200 tons and took her into Port Sudan. Late on the 16th the *Black Prince* reached Suez, but only to find that her previous orders had been superseded by one from the Admiralty. The protection of the Indian convoy was too pressing a need for her to be spared from Aden. Accordingly she was to carry on there. To take her place for the defence of Egypt the *Warrior* had to be withdrawn from the Adriatic, her instructions being to call at Port Said in order to take on the *Black Prince's* prizes to Alexandria, where she was to remain. The *Chatham*, which was then at that port with an Austrian prize she had captured off Crete, was to move at once to Suez.[1] Thus the last of our armoured ships was removed from the French Admiral's flag, and only the two light cruisers *Weymouth* and *Dublin* were left at his disposal at Malta.

Here, then, were the first effects of the unhappy escape of the *Goeben*. The prospect of joint operations with the French in the Adriatic were at an end, and two of our best cruising ships were condemned to the duties of guardships,

[1] This was the *Marienbad*, but she was released shortly afterwards under Art. III of the Sixth Hague Convention (" Days of Grace "), to which Austria, but not Germany, had subscribed.

and this at a moment that was peculiarly inopportune. For this was the time, as we have seen, that Admiral Bethell's squadron in the Channel was being broken up to provide battleship support in the Commerce Defence areas, and that the order went to Admiral Troubridge to send one of his battle cruisers to Gibraltar to await orders.

On August 20 the *Indomitable* parted company, leaving Admiral Troubridge to carry on the Dardanelles blockade with only two ships of force, the *Indefatigable*, which now carried his flag, and the *Defence*. Still Sir Louis Mallet, who had hurried back to his post, was reporting an improvement in the situation. The forces in favour of neutrality, headed by the Grand Vizier, were gaining ground; the Minister of Marine had even promised to admit our ships if the German officers and crews did not leave Constantinople. Nevertheless, the Ambassador foresaw the possibility of a *coup d'état* by Enver Pasha, with the assistance of the *Goeben* and the German Military Mission, who now had complete control of the Army. The only counter weight was the British squadron. But quite apart from political considerations, it could not follow the German ships in, for Enver, as Minister of War, had control of the defences. All it could do was to remain where it was as a moral support to the Grand Vizier and his party. This the Ambassador advised it should do, and at the same time he suggested the propriety of considering " how far the forcing of the Dardanelles by the British Fleet would be an effective and necessary measure in influencing the general outcome of the war should the situation develop suddenly into a military dictatorship."

In Egypt, on the other hand, there was no improvement, and the anxiety for the Canal increased. Now that the troops were moving from India, and the East Lancashire Territorial Division—one of the two originally intended for Ireland—was on the point of starting from home to replace them, it was more than ever imperative to prevent it from being blocked. At the urgent request of our Agent-General, therefore, the Admiralty ordered the *Warrior* to return to Port Said, and a division of destroyers from Malta to be detached as a patrol for the Canal.[1] The same considerations seemed also to demand special protection for the route between Port Said and Malta, and for this purpose the French Admiral placed at Admiral Carden's disposal the *Weymouth* and *Dublin*, the last of the ships which had formed the combined fleet. Almost immediately, however, he had

---

[1] *Foxhound, Mosquito, Racoon, Basilisk.* They arrived at Port Said on August 21.

to ask for one of them to proceed to Jaffa on the Syrian coast, where Russian subjects were crying out for protection.   The Admiralty, who never shared the anxiety for the Malta–Port Said line while both the Adriatic and the Dardanelles were blockaded, at once ordered the *Dublin* on the required service.   In their view the two cruisers were much more urgently required for hunting down the *Königsberg*, and they wished both of them to proceed in chase of her without delay, but in deference, apparently, to French opinion neither of them went.   The *Dublin*, after doing what was needful at Jaffa, joined Admiral Troubridge, and the *Weymouth* remained at Port Said.

This was the more hazardous, for as the month wore away things grew worse at Constantinople.   The diplomatic struggle centred on the release of some British ships which had been detained in the Dardanelles on the plea that the exit was mined, and the pro-German faction was obviously getting the upper hand, for a direct order of the Grand Vizier for their release was disobeyed.   Moreover, so far from the crews of the *Goeben* and *Breslau* leaving the city, numbers of German officers, seamen and marines, were known to be passing through Bulgaria for the Bosporus.   Two Turkish gunboats in the Red Sea were getting active, and the southward movement of troops in Syria continued.   So critical was the situation that Sir Louis Mallet, though still regarding it as not quite hopeless, warned the Government to be prepared to deliver a rapid blow if hostilities broke out.   Russia was particularly anxious about the command of the Black Sea if, in combination with the *Goeben*, the Turkish Fleet, reorganised, officered and largely manned by Germans, chose to dispute it.   In these circumstances, though it was assumed that the mine-fields had been extended under German direction, he again on August 27 recurred to the possibility of forcing the Strait.   This time his despatch was accompanied by an appreciation from our Military Attaché, who reported the operation as possibly feasible, but at the same time he pointed out that, even if the mine-fields could be passed, little good could be done without a considerable military force.   This view the Ambassador endorsed in his dispatch, and it concluded with a warning that " failure, or even partial success would have an effect that would be disastrous."

On this appreciation, as there was no prospect of our having troops available to act with the fleet, there was nothing to do but to avoid precipitating hostilities, and no orders could be given to Admiral Troubridge except to attack the

Goeben and *Breslau* if they came out. The moment was, indeed, peculiarly unfavourable for extending our military engagements, for in the main theatre events were occurring which threatened to bar indefinitely all prospect of combined operations in the Mediterranean. The darkest days of the war were upon us, and we were face to face with the possibility already alluded to, that owing to the alarming military situation our whole distribution in home waters might break down before the week was out.

CHAPTER VI

ALTHOUGH on August 20 it had been decided to send the
IVth Division of the Expeditionary Force to Flanders at once,
the naval arrangements were to remain as they had been
settled for the permanent defence of the Army's lines of supply.
Admiral Jellicoe was ordered not to repeat his sweep down
the North Sea, but to rest his fleet, and use the opportunity
for tactical exercises. Instead of attempting to hold the
North Sea with the whole Grand Fleet, the Admiralty, as we
have seen, had strengthened the Southern Force by detaching
two battle cruisers to the Humber. In view of the military
situation it was the southern area which at the moment
was vital.

Sir John French had practically completed the concentration of his force on the 21st and had moved forward to
positions which he considered most favourable to assist in
the operations planned by General Joffre, on the line Binche-
Mons-Condé, so as to prolong the French left, which was
about Charleroi. On the military side there was thus no
immediate anxiety. From the naval point of view, however,
the situation was unsatisfactory in one special point. On the
21st it was known that the Belgian troops had evacuated
Ostend in order to join the concentration at Antwerp, and
Ostend, if it fell into Germans hands, must prove a disturbance to the arrangements for covering the Army's lines of
supply. In the evening the menace became more serious on
intelligence that a force of German cavalry was expected to
appear before the town next day, and as a precaution Admiral
Christian was ordered to make a demonstration off the port
with a light cruiser and two divisions of destroyers; two
" Bacchantes " were also to be in support outside the shoals.
He was specially enjoined not to fire on the town, but to
confine his attentions to any bodies of the enemy that gave a
target outside.

On August 22 the operation was carried out, but Admiral

[1] See Map p. 126, and Map, 1 in case.

Christian, on landing, was informed by the Burgomaster that it had been decided not to defend the place. The Civil Guard had been disarmed and their arms sent to Antwerp. No enemy troops had been seen, but eighty German motor-cars had entered Ghent and gone forward on the Courtrai road. In the decision that had been taken the Admiral concurred, mainly because he found the sand dunes along the coast masked the roads from the north, and those from the south and south-east could only be held by a military force at a point three miles from the town where the roads crossed the Bruges Canal. It was obvious that under these conditions no adequate support could be given from the sea with the force under his command. He therefore withdrew the flotilla to the outer roadstead, and, returning to his flagship, asked for further instructions. The reply was an order to withdraw the whole force.

Next day (August 23) our Army was violently attacked at Mons, and although in face of greatly superior force they brilliantly held their position all day, by nightfall it became evident a retirement was inevitable. With equal violence the French had been attacked at Charleroi; as a result they were retreating to their own frontier, and in sympathy our force had to fall back with its right on the fortress of Maubeuge. So difficult was the operation that no one could tell how or where it would end, and our anxiety for Ostend spread to Boulogne and even to Havre.

So imminent was the danger to both those ports that the Admiralty began to make arrangements for withdrawing from them all stores not immediately required by the Army. The intention was to transfer them to Cherbourg, and before noon on the 24th word went out that no transport was to sail for Boulogne or Havre till further orders. Cherbourg was the new base favoured by the War Office in view of the ease with which the Cotentin Peninsula could be made an impregnable place of arms so long as we had command of the Channel. But for a really effective command of the Channel it was highly important that the Flemish ports should not pass into the hands of the enemy. The Admiralty, therefore, while pushing on all preparations for the transference of the base, were in no mind to abandon the more easterly Channel harbours without an effort to save them. Whether the Army required them or not, their naval value was permanent and indisputable.

Representations were therefore made to the French Admiralty as to the importance which, for naval reasons, we attached to defending Dunkirk, Calais and Boulogne as long as possible. For this object our Admiralty expressed their willingness to release Admiral Rouyer's squadron from the Western Patrol and to support him with a battle squadron. Dover was also offered as a base for the Calais and Boulogne flotillas, and transport was ready to bring their stores across. They further joined with the War Office in asking for particulars of the land defences at Dunkirk, Calais, Boulogne and Havre, and also as to the permanent defence of the neck of the Cotentin Peninsula. At the same time Admiral Jellicoe was informed of the serious consequences which seemed to be developing out of the battle of Mons, and warned to consider the possibility of having to fix a new position for the Grand Fleet should the Germans get control of Calais and the adjacent French coast—that is, in fact, if they succeeded in breaking into the Dover defile. Here, then, as the direct result of a military reverse, we were faced with a by no means remote prospect of the fundamental distribution of our Fleet no longer sufficing for the exigencies of the war.

At first the French Admiralty took a less grave view of the danger and its consequences. In their opinion no readjustment of the allied naval force was called for, but in the evening (24th) they adopted the British view and ordered Admiral Rouyer to leave his light cruisers with Admiral Wemyss, and bring his armoured ships to Cherbourg, where he was to hold himself in readiness to co-operate in defence of the threatened ports. Sir John French, in his telegram explaining the necessity of his retiring on Maubeuge, had particularly desired that immediate attention should be given to the defence of Havre, and as there seemed no need for the moment for a radical shift of base, the stores from Boulogne were transferred to that port, and Cherbourg was left for further consideration.

This same evening, however (the 24th), the security of Ostend came again into the field of our naval operations. Detachments of German cavalry had been scouring the country round, and the authorities though unwilling to make a hopeless resistance to a serious attack, were fully prepared to stand on their defence against marauders. Accordingly at 7 p.m. the Belgian Minister in London received from the Burgomaster an intimation that the immediate dispatch of British ships and a landing force was desirable. Preoccupied as the Admiralty were with keeping out of German hands any port which could serve as a submarine base for operations in the Channel, they did not hesitate to take action. The first idea, it would seem, was merely to land a few hundred men from the ships, sufficient in co-operation with the local gendarmerie to drive off the enemy's cavalry patrols. But so important was the place, and so great the need to do anything that was possible to relieve the ever-increasing pressure on our Army, that the scale of the project rapidly developed. On the 25th it became known that the Maubeuge line had proved untenable, and that the Army was falling back still further on Le Cateau, under conditions which made its extrication a matter of the gravest doubt.

On the other hand, the rush of the Germans in pursuit was exposing their communications in a most tempting manner to a blow from the sea. Could it be delivered—could it even be threatened—there was at least a chance of relieving the strain on our hard-pressed Army. In such circumstances it was impossible for the Navy to sit by and not try to hold out a hand to the sister service. No matter the risk, no matter how small the chance of success, the instinct to act even desperately was bred in the bone of the Navy. If troops were available so much the better, if not, then the Admiralty must make shift with their own resources. For just such a venture the Royal Naval Division was being raised, but it was still in embryo and quite unfit for service. There was nothing approaching readiness except the Marine battalions at Devonport, Portsmouth and Chatham, some 3,000 men, but even these were mainly composed of as yet unseasoned reservists and recruits. Still, with the *pied-à-terre* established, better troops might follow. Our VIth Division had not yet sailed for Havre, and as the Belgian Army was contemplating offensive operations from Antwerp, a comparatively small force acting in combination with it would have a fair prospect of bringing about an effective check to the enemy's advance.

So in the evening of the 25th the order went out for the four battalions (one R.M.A. and three R.M.L.I.) to proceed to Ostend under Brigadier-General Sir George Aston. He was to create a diversion on the western flank of the German advance and to sustain the Belgian forward movement. The Chatham Battalion was to be carried in the cruisers of the Southern Force, and the others in Channel Fleet battleships. For this purpose Admiral Burney was to detail the *Prince of Wales, Venerable, Formidable* and *Irresistible* under Rear-Admiral Currey, who would take on the Portsmouth battalions, while Admiral Bethell, who was at Portland, would fetch the Plymouth Battalion in what was left of his squadron (*Vengeance, Goliath, Prince George* and *Cæsar*). These four ships, with the light cruiser *Proserpine* and six destroyers, were also to support the operation, but in this duty they were to be assisted by a recent addition to the Fleet.

Three monitors, just completed at Barrow for the Brazilian Government, had been purchased in the first days of the war. It was a type essential for coastal operations, especially in shallow seas, but in spite of former experience of their utility and the value the Japanese had obtained from such craft, the type was absent from our Navy. The " blue water " trend of modern naval opinion inclined to treat all such craft as heretical, in that they were unfit to take part in a fleet action, and they had been pilloried with the designation of " Coast Defence Vessels." This unfortunate misnomer had served to throw into oblivion their function of " coast attack," and the type had died like a dog with a bad name. The first breath of war, however, had blown away the misconception, and these three vessels, each armed with two 6" guns and two 4·7" howitzers, had been added to the Fleet as the *Severn, Humber* and *Mersey*.

With this powerful support the co-operation of Admiral Rouyer was no longer necessary, especially as the French had been able to give full assurances as to the land defences of Calais and Dunkirk. His orders, therefore, were to continue his co-operation with Admiral Wemyss on the Western Patrol. A strong hold on the mouth of the Channel was in any case desirable, for the severe losses the Army had suffered in the retreat had to be made good; Southampton was closed again to civil traffic, and for some days troops would be once more pouring across to Havre.

A striking feature of the enterprise was the movement that served for covering it. While Admiral Bethell's battleships remained to support the occupation of Ostend, the whole of the Southern Force, including the Humber battle cruisers, was to carry out an offensive demonstration up to the Heligoland Bight. As the sweep to the Bight would absorb all the Harwich destroyers as well as Admiral Campbell's cruisers, the flotilla for Ostend was provided from the Dover Patrol, and, at the request of the Admiralty, Admiral Rouyer sent destroyers from Cherbourg to replace it, and with his three armoured cruisers, which were not required in the Western Patrol, moved from Brest to Cherbourg in readiness to weigh at four hours' notice in case the landing at Ostend should tempt the German Fleet to make a sortie. It will thus be seen that the dual object which had always been a feature of these enterprises recurred. Though as a diversion the landing might fail, there was always a hope that it might bring on an action at sea, and this hope, in the eyes of such masters as Lord Anson, was the real justification for the much-derided pinpricks of his time.

In this case the enterprise was certainly of a sufficiently hazardous nature to provoke the enemy to attack; for owing to the difficulty of combining the three contingents of the landing force for the immediate action that was required, the ships had to be exposed for many hours in thick and heavy weather. The idea was for the Chatham and Portsmouth contingents to rendezvous off the Goodwins on the 26th and proceed in company. But when in the morning it was found that Admiral Currey could not arrive before night, Admiral Christian was ordered to go at once to Ostend to make a demonstration. It was now known that the Belgian gendarmerie had been in conflict with Uhlans three miles from Ostend, and as it was possible by this time that the town itself might be in the hands of the enemy, a careful reconnaissance was necessary before any action could be taken. He was off the port by 6 p.m. with General Aston and the Chatham Battalion, but before he could ascertain that the place was still free of the enemy, the weather had grown too bad for the Marines to land. Not till 3 a.m. on the 27th did it improve enough for the disembarkation to begin, and as soon as the ships were cleared Admiral Christian sent away Admiral Campbell's cruisers to the rendezvous for the Heligoland demonstration, and remained himself to see the landing completed.

Owing to the weather, Admiral Currey had had to anchor for the night, in spite of the position being exposed to torpedo attack; but weighing at 3.30 a.m., without lights, he was off Ostend by 6.30. Still, he could not begin landing, as the tugs which should have been there had not arrived. By 8.0, however, the Belgian authorities sent out the mail boat *Princesse Clémentine*, which had just finished landing the first contingent. At 4 p.m. Admiral Bethell arrived, but owing to the congested state of the quays the Marines had to be kept afloat till next morning. Admiral Bethell, however, was able to take over the command according to instructions, and, while Admiral Currey left to rejoin Admiral Burney's flag in the Channel, Admiral Christian got away to conduct the covering operation of the Southern Force. Early in the morning of the 28th the tugs arrived, and the Plymouth Battalion was soon ashore with the other three.

As we have seen, the original conception of the force which was now in occupation of Ostend was that of an advance guard to seize a *pied-à-terre* for the inlet of further forces. It was recognised as being incapable either by training or equipment for field operations, and General Aston's instructions were that he was to keep his force in close proximity to the coast. In pursuance of these orders he was entrenching on the perimeter of the town, with small bicycle patrols thrown out, when word came from the French that they were ready to embark 4,000 Belgians at Havre and 12,000 more on the 30th and 31st if we could guarantee their safe landing at Ostend or Zeebrugge. These were the troops that had retreated from Namur into France,[1] and for a time there was hope that the Ostend enterprise would develop into something effective. As things were, the position there was anything but satisfactory. The monitors, having only just reached Dover from the westward, had not yet appeared. All, therefore, depended on Admiral Bethell's squadron. This meant not only that it must remain dangerously exposed with insufficient flotilla protection, but as Admiral Christian had already reported, that should the inadequate garrison be attacked, the height of the sand dunes rendered effective support by ship fire impossible. Still, the prospect of affording some real help to the Army was now too promising for the project to be abandoned, and the Admiralty decided to hold on, and inform the French that they could guarantee the safe transport of the Belgian troops. There was, in fact, no longer any risk about it, for away to the northward events were happening which promised to keep the Germans quiet at sea for some time, and served to throw an enheartening ray of light over the unrelieved gloom which seemed to the Government and public at home to have settled over the fortunes of the Allies in France.

[1] Namur, with its circle of nine forts, succumbed to the German heavy howitzers after an intense bombardment which commenced on August 21. Two days later five of the forts were in ruins, and at midnight the Belgian IVth Division and the 8th Brigade (which had fallen back upon Namur from Huy on the 19th) withdrew southwards, and finally, after sustaining a loss of 5,500 men, made good their escape into France, whence they ultimately rejoined the main Belgian Army at Antwerp.

CHAPTER VII

THE ACTION OFF HELIGOLAND, AUGUST 28 [1]

THE operations in question took place off Heligoland.
That they also served to cover the Ostend diversion was in
some measure an afterthought. In their first conception
they were dictated by a desire to assert our command of the
North Sea right up to the enemy's gates. The plan was based
on a proposal made by Commodore Keyes on August 23.
Since the first days of the war the submarines of the 8th, or
" Oversea " Flotilla, had been keeping a constant watch off
the ports in the Bight. It was a risky and exciting service in
which there were continual encounters with the vigilant and
well-handled destroyers of the enemy and several hairbreadth
escapes. Still, with such boldness and persistence was the
reconnaissance maintained that the German patrol ships
were in continual danger, and on August 21 a large cruiser
of the " Roon " type was missed by sheer fatality in circumstances that made her escape miraculous. By extraordinary
bad luck not a ship was touched ; but, on the other hand,
very full information had been obtained as to the routine
of the German guard.

It was evident that their practice was for light cruisers
to lead out a number of destroyers every evening to certain
points where the destroyers fanned out to seaward. On their
return at daylight they were usually met towards 8.0 a.m. by
the light cruisers about twenty miles north-west of Heligoland. It had further been ascertained that enemy patrols
also put to sea before dark and came back at dawn. This
valuable information, which had only been obtained at great
risk and by noteworthy skill and daring on the part of the
submarine officers, the Commodore was anxious to turn to
account. Little could be done in the daytime, for continuous
guard was kept up both north and south of Heligoland by a
large number of destroyers steaming at high speed on some
regular system which was evidently designed to prevent mine-
laying and to foil submarine attacks. But the Commodore
was of opinion that a well-organised drive, commencing

inshore before dawn, should inflict considerable loss on the returning night patrols.

At the time the proposal was made no special activity was contemplated. Indeed, a design which the Commander-in-Chief had just submitted for a sweep to the Heligoland Bight, in co-operation with the Southern Force, had been postponed by the Admiralty on the ground that as another division of the Expeditionary Force would be crossing it was necessary to maintain the Broad Fourteens patrol in place ; and when on August 23 it was no longer needed it was withdrawn, and its supporting cruisers directed to go to target practice.[1]

Commodore Keyes's scheme was then considered as a separate undertaking, and after consultation with Commodore Tyrwhitt its general lines were modified to this extent : instead of the destroyer sweep commencing from inshore before dawn so as to inflict loss on the returning night patrols, the actual drive was not to commence until 8.0, when the night patrols would have been safely in port. The expectation was that our flotillas would thus intercept the enemy destroyer day patrols, who were to be lured out to sea by an outer line of submarines. Otherwise the scheme was on the general lines suggested by Commodore Keyes. An inner line of three submarines (*E 4*, *E 5*, *E 9*) was to be first formed north and south of Heligoland, and till a certain moment they were to remain concealed so as to be in a position to attack any cruisers that might come out to drive off our destroyers, and also any they might catch of those returning. An outer line of three others (*E 6*, *E 7*, *E 8*) would be placed some forty miles out, and their function would be to show themselves and try to draw the enemy's destroyers to sea. Two others (*D 2*, *D 8*) were to take station off the Ems to deal with anything that might come out or try to get in. The attacking force was to be the 3rd and 1st Flotillas and their leaders, *Arethusa* and *Fearless*. The *Invincible* and *New Zealand*, which had just taken up their station in the Humber, were to act as supports, while Admiral Christian with Admiral Campbell's squadron was to be in reserve off Terschelling. The plan of operations was that while the submarines were getting into position, the battle cruisers and destroyer flotillas would get into touch to the south-east of the Dogger Bank, and during the night proceed to the north-eastward so that at 4.0 next morning

---

[1] The Southern Force supporting cruisers were now *Euryalus* (flag of Rear-Admiral Christian), with *Amethyst* as attached light cruiser, and Rear-Admiral Campbell's Cruiser Force C ; that is, *Bacchante* (flag), *Cressy*, *Hogue* and *Aboukir*.

the destroyers would be twenty-five miles south-west of the Horn Reef light-vessel, and the battle cruisers further to the westward. The destroyers were then to commence the actual raid by running down to the southward with the battle cruisers on their starboard-quarter till they had reached a point twelve miles to the westward of Heligoland at 8.0 a.m., when they would begin the drive to the westward.

Such was the plan as originally sanctioned, but it soon expanded into something more considerable. On August 25, when the diversion to Ostend was approved, it was decided to carry out the scheme at once by way of a covering attack for the expedition. The Commander-in-Chief was informed of what was intended and warned that the Ostend expedition might lead to a movement of the High Seas Fleet. Assuming from this that his co-operation was required, he proposed moving down the Grand Fleet cruisers and destroyers to a supporting position with the Battle Fleet near. In reply he was told the Battle Fleet would not be wanted, but that his battle cruisers might support if convenient. Early on the 27th he informed them he was sending Admiral Beatty, with his three remaining battle cruisers, *Lion*, *Queen Mary*, *Princess Royal*, and Commodore Goodenough's six light cruisers to meet the Humber battle cruisers next morning at their rendezvous. He also asked that directions should be sent to Admiral Beatty as to what the light cruisers should do, and the answer was that they should make for the destroyer rendezvous and follow their sweep in support. Shortly after noon a message went out from the Admiralty explaining all this to Admiral Christian and the two flotilla Commodores. The message was duly received in the *Euryalus*, but by some mischance it never reached either Commodore, and they began the elaborate movement with no knowledge that the Grand Fleet cruisers were taking part in it. Consequently when, at 3.30 a.m., the light cruisers were sighted by the flotillas they narrowly escaped being attacked. Their identity, however, was quickly discovered, the junction was effected as arranged, and punctually to time Commodore Tyrwhitt began his run to the southward according to programme with the light cruisers following in support and the five battle cruisers some thirty miles distant on his starboard-quarter.

The defences of the Bight consisted of two lines of patrolling vessels : an outer line, 25 miles west of Heligoland, of nine new destroyers (the 1st Flotilla), and an inner line of nine older vessels (the 3rd Minesweeping Division), 12 miles from the

outer line. Four light cruisers and the 5th Destroyer
Flotilla were also stationed near the island, but on August
28 only three of the light cruisers were on duty.

When, at 5.26 a.m. on the 28th, the outpost destroyers
reported a submarine, the 5th Flotilla and an airship were at
once ordered out to investigate. At 7.6 two of the patrolling
destroyers sighted British ships, but owing to the jamming
of their signals, their reports were not received in the *Köln*[1]
until about half an hour later. This was the first time that
British surface warships had been sighted in the Heligoland
patrol area, but they were not unexpected. Pre-arranged
counter measures were immediately put into force, and two
of the light cruisers patrolling off the island, the *Frauenlob*
and *Stettin*, were despatched to support the destroyers.
The third light cruiser, the *Hela*, was too weak in armament
for any serious engagement, and after 10 a.m. she remained
in her position behind the destroyer patrol line. Six other
light cruisers (*Strassburg, Köln, Ariadne, Stralsund, Danzig*
and *Kolberg*), though not so quickly available, left harbour
independently between 9.30 and noon. The battle cruisers
and heavier ships were unable to cross the bar of the Jade
before 1.0 p.m. owing to the state of the tide. The *Moltke*
and the *Von der Tann* left at 2.0 p.m., and the *Seydlitz*
(Admiral Hipper's flagship) later. [2]

What had happened on our side was that Commodore
Tyrwhitt was leading down for the 8 o'clock rendezvous
west of Heligoland in the *Arethusa*—the nameship of a new
class of armoured light cruiser to which he had transferred
his broad pendant the day before the operation began.
The 3rd Flotilla was with him in cruising order—that is, in
divisions line ahead, disposed abeam to port, the columns
being five cables apart. Two miles astern was Captain
Blunt in the *Fearless*, leading the 1st Flotilla similarly disposed.
Following them at an interval of eight miles was Commodore
Goodenough, in the *Southampton*, with his six light cruisers
in three divisions two miles apart. [3]

In this order they had proceeded for nearly three hours
when, shortly before 7.0, one of the German patrol destroyers
was sighted to the south-eastward—that is, on the port bow
—about three and a half miles away. Without altering

---

[1] Flagship of Admiral Maass, the Senior Officer of Destroyer Flotillas.
Admiral Hipper, as Senior Officer of Scouting forces, was in command of the
defence of the German Bight.

[2] See *post*, p. 119.   [3] See opposite page.

course himself, Commodore Tyrwhitt detached his 4th Division in chase—that being the division nearest to the enemy. The enemy's destroyer at once made off south-eastwards into the Bight, and our chasing division soon made out a number of other German destroyers, which it continued to chase and engage, but at so great a range that the firing was ineffective on both sides. In half an hour's time they had got so far away from the Commodore that he could not see what was happening. Though it was a perfectly fine morning with a smooth sea and clear to seaward, as the land was approached the visibility was greatly reduced, and as the firing increased, the Commodore, although he had just sighted other destroyers to the south-south-west, decided he must go to the support of his detached division. He there-fore signalled for four points to port, leaders together, and increased speed. In a few more minutes he was able to make out ten German destroyers with which his own were engaged. At 7.40, therefore, he altered another two points to port, and forming line abreast settled down to a full speed chase with the *Fearless* and her flotilla following. With the mist thickening towards the shore the range was too great for effective firing, nor could his utmost speed reduce it. The enemy's destroyers could be seen on both bows, and first one and then another group was chased, but still without gaining on them. Yet for nearly half an hour the action was kept up, heading at full speed into the Bight. A few minutes before 8.0, however, a light cruiser of the " Stettin" class was

THIRD FLOTILLA

Arethusa, 3,500 tons, 28·5 knots (designed), 2 6″, 6 4″ guns.

Division 4.	Division 3.	Division 2.	Division 1.
Laurel	*Laforey*	*Lark*	*Lookout*
Liberty	*Lawford*	*Lance*	*Leonidas*
Lysander	*Louis*	*Linnet*	*Legion*
Laertes	*Lydiard*	*Landrail*	*Lennox*

FIRST FLOTILLA

Fearless, 3,440 tons, 25·4 knots, 10 4″ guns.

Division 5.	Division 3.	Division 2.	Division 1.
Goshawk	*Ferret*	*Ariel*	*Acheron*
Lizard	*Forester*	*Lucifer*	*Attack*
Lapwing	*Druid*	*Llewellyn*	*Hind*
Phœnix	*Defender*	——	*Archer*

The 4th Division of the 1st Flotilla (*Badger, Beaver, Jackal, Sandfly*) had been detached to accompany the Humber battle cruisers. Destroyers attached to the submarines were *Lurcher* (Commodore Keyes) and *Firedrake*

LIGHT CRUISER SQUADRON

Division 2.	Division 1.	Division 3.
Nottingham	*Southampton*	*Falmouth*
Lowestoft	*Birmingham*	*Liverpool*

seen coming up from the north of Heligoland.[1] From the peculiar arrangement of her three funnels it was believed that she was the *Stettin* herself, and Commodore Tyrwhitt altered four points to the eastward to engage her while the flotilla closed in. As he did so another cruiser, with two funnels, was seen coming up on the port quarter of the first, and proved to be the *Frauenlob*. She at once turned about sixteen points inwards, and Commodore Tyrwhitt altered to the south-eastward on a parallel course. The *Stettin* held on upon the opposite course, and for a time he engaged her apparently without result. By 8.5 the *Stettin* had come in sight of the *Fearless*, who, with her flotilla was some four miles away. Altering course to the eastward, the *Fearless* opened fire, but the *Stettin* turned sixteen points to starboard and retired in a south-easterly direction. Firing continued at approximately 8,000 yards till about 8.12 when, owing to the range, the *Fearless* turned back to the westward. The *Arethusa* was thus left alone with the smaller of her two antagonists.

At 8.10 the *Frauenlob* turned to the southward, down the west side of Heligoland, and Commodore Tyrwhitt altered to a slightly converging course. A running fight ensued with the range continually diminishing, till when it was below 4,000 yards the Commodore fired two torpedoes. Neither, he thought, took effect, and as the *Arethusa's* guns were being put out of action one after the other her position began to be serious. Some of his destroyers were attending to a Norwegian steamer on her way to Bremen which they mistook (as had the *Stettin* half-an-hour before) for a minelayer. Others were heavily engaged with a German minesweeper, which ran in from the westward, and though they thought they sank her she was eventually taken in in a pitiable state, lashed between two destroyers. Thus not only was his force somewhat scattered, but he was getting dangerously close to the forts of Heligoland, and sure enough the island suddenly loomed up to port. Promptly the Commodore made the signal " W. ¼ S." (mag.)—that is, for the drive to the westward to begin. The *Fearless* and her destroyers were already on that course, having left the *Stettin* to disappear in the mist. The Commodore, however, still held on and continued the action with the *Frauenlob*, till by 8.25 the only gun he had in action was one 6″, but as it happened it was enough. For at this moment it got home apparently under the enemy's fore bridge, and she sheered off and made for the protection

[1] See Plan. Phase 8.0 to 8.25.

of the Heligoland batteries. So badly, indeed, was she hurt that it seemed doubtful whether she would survive, but she did get in to Wilhelmshaven at 10.30, having received ten hits with the loss of nine killed and twenty-eight wounded, and a report that she had totally disabled the *Arethusa*. But this was far from the case, for as soon as she turned away Commodore Tyrwhitt signalled again to start the drive westward.

So the first phase of the operations ended, but it was scarcely over before the second phase developed.[1] The *Fearless*, who with the 1st Flotilla had begun the outward sweep a quarter of an hour earlier, had almost immediately caught a stray destroyer in her net. At 8.15, three minutes after she got Commodore Tyrwhitt's signal to turn to the westward, *V 187* was sighted ahead. She was the flotilla leader's boat, which had been scouting beyond visual distance, but on getting a wireless signal from another destroyer that she was being chased, *V 187* was steaming about east-south-east to her assistance. After making the challenge Captain Blunt opened fire and ordered the 5th Division to chase, but just then he took in a signal from Commodore Keyes, who in the *Lurcher* had been searching for enemy submarines, according to plan, on the line of the battle cruisers' advance. He seemed to be coming in from seaward, and Captain Blunt, fearing it might be the *Lurcher* he was attacking, ceased fire and cancelled the signal to chase. He then lost sight of *V 187*, who appears to have turned away. At 8.25, however, the 5th Division sighted her going south-south-west only 6,000 yards away, and gave chase. At first she went off to the westward, but soon turned to southward. On this course *V 187* tried to get away with shells falling thick about her, when she was suddenly aware of two of our " Town " class cruisers which could only have been the *Nottingham* and *Lowestoft*, Commodore Goodenough's port division which, as will be seen directly, he had detached to support the flotilla. They opened fire on her, and she at once turned to try to break through our destroyers to the northward. She passed the 3rd Division with little damage, but four more destroyers—the 1st Division—appeared on her port bow. The 3rd Division had also turned and re-opened fire, so that the *V 187* was now in a trap, fired upon from the north-west and the south-east. Before she could win through she was circling helplessly, and in another minute she had almost stopped and nothing could be seen of her but a cloud of black

[1] See Plan. Sinking of *V 187*.

smoke. It was now 8.50, and seeing the enemy helpless, Captain Blunt left her to the 3rd and 5th Divisions, and with the other two went off to the southward to rejoin the Commodore. At nine they were together again, and reforming cruising order Commodore Tyrwhitt held on to the westward according to plan.

Up till this time they had seen nothing of either the battle cruisers or the light cruisers. Admiral Beatty had already reached his supporting position, fifty miles about west-north-west from Heligoland, and there, awaiting a call, he was marking time with successive eight point turns at good speed, so as to avoid submarine attack. At 8.30 Commodore Goodenough had also reached his allotted position west-south-west of Heligoland. His ships were not all in company, for at 8.5, having received a delayed signal from Commodore Tyrwhitt that he was engaged, he had detached the *Nottingham* and *Lowestoft* to assist him. They were soon chasing a destroyer to the eastward, which they quickly lost in the mist, but as they ran down abreast of Heligoland other boats appear to have been chased in various directions, and at 8.50, when they had passed the island, they saw more destroyers to the south-west and gave chase in that direction. These must also have been German; for when, twenty minutes later (9.10), having apparently lost them, the two cruisers turned north-west, they almost immediately saw and passed the reunited British flotillas steering to the westward.

Elsewhere the situation was in considerable confusion. When the action began Commander Keyes, in the *Lurcher*, was still unaware that Admiral Beatty's force was present, and having searched for submarines in the water over which the *Invincible* and *New Zealand* were to pass, according to the original plan of operations, he was making to the eastwards towards the sound of the guns. In doing so he was aware of two four-funnelled cruisers looming out of the mist. They were difficult to make out, and in all probability were the western division of the Light Cruiser Squadron. At all events they were steering the same course, but Commodore Keyes, having no reason to suppose any British cruisers of the class were in the vicinity, signalled to the *Invincible* that he was in touch with two of the enemy and proceeded to shadow them.

At 8.15—that is, shortly after the *Nottingham* and *Lowestoft* had been detached—Commodore Goodenough took in the signal, and decided to go to the *Lurcher's* assistance. He

was just approaching the final position from which he was
to sweep seawards in conformity with the general movement.
At 8.30 he turned to the westward, but not finding her,
at 8.53 he altered to the northward.   The movement quickly
brought him in sight of the *Lurcher*, but the result was only
to increase the confusion.   For Commodore Keyes now
thought he was in the presence of four enemy cruisers instead
of two, and he held away about north by west towards the
position where the battle cruisers were marking time.   Our
own ships followed, and he signalled to the *Invincible* that he
was being chased by four cruisers and was trying to lead them
on to her.

It was not, however, for long that Commodore Goodenough
followed the false lead.   Something was evidently wrong, and
at 9.5 he turned to the westerly course laid down by the programme which he now knew the flotillas were taking.   Unfortunately this led to further confusion, for it soon brought
him upon the outer line of our submarines, of whose position
he was still unaware.   A little before 9.30 he came upon *E 6*
(Lieutenant-Commander C. P. Talbot) and made a prompt
attempt to ram her.   So close and quick was he that the
submarine only escaped by diving under the flagship, but,
thanks to Lieutenant-Commander Talbot's skilful handling,
no harm was done, nor did he, being uncertain of his assailant's
nationality, make any attempt to attack.   Commodore
Goodenough now continued his westerly course, while the
Nottingham and *Lowestoft*, having quite lost touch, carried on
about north-westward towards where the battle cruisers
were marking time.   But, in fact, Admiral Beatty was
just moving from his first position, for having ascertained
that the seaward drive had begun, he, too, held away W. ¼ S.
(mag.) and signalled his intention to the three Commodores,
but as the *Nottingham* and *Lowestoft* did not get the signal
they held on as they were and were thrown out for the rest
of the day.

To complete the confusion, at about a quarter to ten the
other submarine leader, *Firedrake*, passed to the *Arethusa* the
Lurcher's signal that she was being chased.   Commodore
Tyrwhitt immediately stopped his westerly course and turned
back eastward with his destroyers to go to her assistance.
Almost at once they had sight of a three-funnelled enemy
cruiser, which was probably the *Stettin* again.   She was
chased, but quickly disappeared in the mist.   Then about
10.0 appeared the 3rd and 5th Divisions of the *Fearless's*

flotilla coming back from finishing *V 187*. The Commodore now broke off the chase, and fearing he was getting too close to Heligoland, turned back 16 points to the westward. No enemy was in sight, and it seemed a good chance of doing some repairs to the *Arethusa*, whose speed had been dropping more and more owing to the injuries she had received from the *Frauenlob*. Accordingly at 10.20, leaving his own flotilla to carry on to the westward, under Commander Dutton of the *Lookout*, at 10 knots, he closed the *Fearless* and signalled to her and the 1st Flotilla to stop engines.

He was now able to get the story of the last hours of the German flotilla leader. They had been unexpectedly full of incident, and had afforded the first evidence of a spirit in our enemy for which we were little prepared. As we have seen, it was at 8.50 that the *Fearless* had left her two divisions to finish with the helpless destroyer, and after they had passed, firing into her at 600 yards, with every shot telling, she was seen to be badly down by the bows and apparently sinking. Our destroyers then stopped and sent away boats to rescue her crew. No flag of truce was flown, though the colours were still flying, and the enemy's idea seems to have been that our object was to board and capture. The Germans had no intention that their gallant defence should have so tame an end, and an officer was seen to train and fire the after gun at the *Goshawk*, the leader of the 5th Division, which was only 200 yards away. The shot hit her in the ward-room, and it was clearly necessary to destroy the gun before the work of rescue could proceed. Fire was reopened and with such effect that at 9.10 *V 187* went down. The boats then closed to pick up survivors, but almost at once a cruiser appeared out of the mist and began a heavy fire. She was the *Stettin*, who, after the *Fearless* had left chasing her, returned to assist the 1st Torpedo Boat Flotilla.[1] With the best will in the world it was impossible to continue the work of mercy. Yet all that was possible was done.

[1] The *Stettin's* wireless was damaged by gunfire from our destroyers, and after firing four salvos she turned away. She remained near Heligoland giving orders to the submarines—for she had the Chief of the 2nd U-boat Flotilla on board—until about 11 a.m. when, having repaired her wireless, she again turned westward. At 12.40 she sighted the *Ariadne*, and five minutes later, hearing heavy firing, she turned sixteen points to starboard towards the direction from which it came and very soon recognised the *Lion*, which, she states, opened fire on her at 1.5 p.m. She then turned away, and at 1.20 sighted the *Danzig* to the southward and also saw the *Ariadne* in flames. Realising that the British cruisers were not pursuing and that the *Danzig* had gone to the assistance of the *Ariadne*, the *Stettin* returned to Heligoland to regain touch with her flotilla.

With our men there was nothing but admiration for the gallant fight the enemy had made. The *Stettin* claims that she arrived eight minutes after the *V 187* went down, and therefore did not realize that our destroyers' boats were engaged on the work of rescue. Our two divisions recovered their boats' crews and proceeded at full speed to the north-west, taking as prisoners two officers, including the Commodore and twenty-six men. In one case only had it been found impossible to pick up our own men. The *Defender*, rear boat of the 3rd Division, had drifted away from her two boats and was under such heavy fire that her commanding officer thought it his duty to save his ship and leave his boats to shift for themselves.

To all appearance they were irretrievably lost, and but for one man's gallantry and resource they would have been. Lieutenant-Commander Leir of the submarine *E 4* had been watching the whole affair through his periscope. Having seen the cruiser coming up he had made a bold attempt to torpedo her, but she apparently detected the rush of air, and by a sudden change of course straight for the submarine she just avoided the torpedo. *E 4* then dived to avoid being rammed, and about 9.30, when all seemed quiet, came to the surface again. The cruiser was nowhere to be seen, but the boats were still there and she closed them. They were full of badly-wounded Germans, and our men had done their best to tend them by stripping to their trousers and tearing up the rest of their clothes for bandages. There were also two officers and eight men unwounded. To leave men who had fought so well to their fate was impossible, even in face of what the cruiser had done. So what Lieutenant-Commander Leir decided to do, besides taking on board the *Defender's* men, whom he had so miraculously rescued, was to take one officer, and two men prisoners, " as a sample," so he said, and leave the rest to look after the wounded. Then, having seen they had water and biscuits enough and a compass, and given them the course for Heligoland, at 10.10 he made off for the sound of guns in the south-west.

It was just at this time, as we have seen, that the re-concentration of the flotillas was completed by the 3rd and 5th Divisions of the 1st Flotilla rejoining the *Fearless*. By this time also the mystery of the *Lurcher* and her phantom chasing ships had been cleared up. About 10.0, as the general movement seaward had brought the Light Cruiser Squadron into a clearer atmosphere, she had so much doubt as to whether she was really in the presence of enemy ships that she ventured to make the challenge. It was answered, and the mistake was soon explained. The explanations, however, could only increase the anxiety of both Commodores, for though Commodore Keyes now knew that the Light Cruiser Squadron was taking part, his submarines did not know. They would now be moving westwards; it was impossible to warn them of the misunderstanding, and Commodore Goodenough signalled to the Admiral that he considered it best to withdraw from the danger area. So the westerly movement continued, with the battle cruisers conforming to the northward. At 9.30 Admiral Beatty had proceeded W. ¼ S. at 20 knots till about 10, when he again began to mark time. Meanwhile Commodore Goodenough signalled to his two stray ships, the *Nottingham* and *Lowestoft*, to join the battle cruisers.

The second phase of the operations was now at an end, and, indeed, it might have seemed that the whole affair was over with disappointing results. But, in fact, it was only a pause before the last and most productive phase began.

When Admiral Beatty received Commodore Goodenough's signal explaining the situation and suggesting a retirement to get clear of our submarines, he replied by directing him not to get too far south, but to keep well to the northward of the flotillas. At 10.30, therefore, the light cruisers, which, having carried on with the westward sweep were now some thirty miles to the westward of the *Arethusa*, turned north. About the same time the *Arethusa* had managed to get all her guns, except two 4″, into working order again, and was once more ready for action. But as Commodore Tyrwhitt feared that if he searched in the direction from which he had come, he would be getting too near Heligoland, he signalled (10.37) for a westerly course (N. 75° W. mag.), hoping it would bring him into touch with the light cruisers. Meanwhile, as his ship could only maintain 10 knots with difficulty, he directed the *Fearless* to keep him in sight. The wisdom of the precaution was quickly apparent. They had been little more than ten minutes on the westerly course when (10.55) a large four-funnelled cruiser of the " Breslau " class was seen to the south-east coming up on a northerly course. This ship was the *Strassburg*. She at once opened an accurate fire on the Commodore, and in view of the crippled condition of the *Arethusa*, his position was obviously critical. He therefore ordered the *Fearless* and the 1st Flotilla to attack with torpedoes. The whole flotilla turned upon the enemy as she held to the northward, and in face of the overwhelming force she quickly sheered off.

The Commodore did not follow. Scenting a snare to entice his ships towards Heligoland, at 11 a.m. he negatived the chase, and being anxious for the retirement to continue without further interruption, particularly as the *Goshawk*, leader of the 5th Division, had been somewhat badly hit in the action with *V 187*, he signalled to carry on to the westward. Meanwhile the 3rd Flotilla, under Commander Dutton in the *Lookout*, had also been retiring westward, but at the first sound of the guns they turned 16 points towards the fight. In a few minutes, however, the 1st Flotilla were seen to the eastward, and Commander Dutton returned again to his westerly course. At the same time the *Fearless*, in response to the Commodore's signal, was just turning to rejoin him when at 11.5 another cruiser appeared to the eastward. It was the *Köln*, and she began to engage at once, but rapidly disappeared. The *Arethusa* and *Fearless* again turned to the westward, when at 11.16 the *Strassburg* reappeared to the northward. Another sharp action began. At 11.23 Commander Dutton once more turned his flotilla back east-south-east where the *Arethusa* and *Fearless* could still be heard in hot action. Five minutes later the *Acheron*, who was ahead with the 1st Division, having just taken in a signal from the *Fearless* to attack with torpedo, turned to the south-eastward and made for the position where she had last seen the *Arethusa* and *Fearless*.

Almost at the same time the rest of the 1st Flotilla sighted another enemy cruiser to the westward on their line of retirement. The new-comer was undoubtedly the *Mainz*. At 10 a.m. she had been seen by our submarine, *D 2*, which was stationed off the Western Ems, coming out of the estuary and then making at high speed to the eastward. According to prisoners she had been lying at Borkum when the action began. She then put to sea and was hastening towards Heligoland when, on receipt of an order to go to the assistance of the *Strassburg*, she turned north-eastward, and thus ran up to our destroyers as they were retiring westward. When the 1st Flotilla sighted her at 11.30 she was to the west-south-west on their port bow and heading northerly across their course.[1] The *Ariel*, who was leading the 2nd Division, at once swung round

---

[1] See Plan. Phase 11·30 to noon.

to the northward to get into position for attacking her ; the
3rd and 5th Divisions followed in line-ahead, and all three
divisions continued their action to the northward with the
Mainz at long range till in about twenty minutes they were
surprised to see her suddenly turn back 16 points.   The fact
was, as they quickly perceived, she had been headed off by
Commodore Goodenough, who at that moment appeared from
the northward with the four light cruisers that he had kept
with him in line-abreast and had opened fire on her.   The
5th Division at once turned back on a parallel course to the
enemy, while the other two divisions made to cross her wake
towards our own cruisers.

The explanation of Commodore Goodenough's opportune
appearance was this.   All the time the 1st Flotilla had been
engaged with the *Mainz*, Commodore Tyrwhitt, after driving
off the *Köln*, had been in hot action with the *Strassburg*.
At 11.16 she had reappeared from the northward, and so
severe and well-directed was her fire that, although the
Arethusa was not hit, her position was again so critical that he
ordered his destroyers to attack with torpedoes, and sent an
urgent signal to Admiral Beatty asking for assistance.   Till
10.45 the Admiral had been marking time, some forty miles
away to the west-north-westward, but then having sighted
the light cruisers coming north he had begun to move to the
eastward to close them.   Almost immediately, however, (11.0)
his movement was checked by an alarm of a submarine.   It
was a false alarm, but the consequent alteration of course
caused a short delay.   At 11.20, before he got the *Arethusa's*
call for help, he had ordered Commodore Goodenough to
detach two light cruisers to Commodore Tyrwhitt's assistance,
and they went off east by south making for the sound of the
guns.   Five minutes later the whole of the 1st Light Cruiser
Squadron was ordered away to support Commodore Tyrwhitt.

What was Admiral Beatty to do ?   He was now leading
the battle cruisers on a course about S. 30° W., and all he knew
went to show that the situation of the flotillas was extremely
critical.   Commodore Tyrwhitt's message spoke of a large
cruiser, for in the bad light the four-funnelled *Strassburg*
had been taken for something much more formidable than she
was.   The Admiral, moreover, had to consider that fighting
had been going on for nearly four hours, and that since 8.0
a.m., when the westward sweep was to begin, it seemed only
to have advanced about ten miles.   The flotillas were consequently dangerously near two of the enemy bases—the

Jade in their rear, and the Ems on their port bow. He calculated, therefore, that the Germans would have had time enough to be getting a powerful force to sea in order to deal a retaliatory blow, and the Commodore's signal that he was engaged with a large cruiser looked as if they were actually doing so. In these circumstances there was obvious danger of the light cruisers being outmatched unless support reached them in time. But to be effective the support must be overwhelming and brought to bear with the utmost speed. The battle cruisers alone could give what was wanted, but, on the other hand, the risk of taking them in would be great. Not only did he believe enemy submarines were in action, but our own were also operating in the area, nor could the contingency of his meeting a battle squadron be ignored. Seeing how the mist was thickening to the eastward the risks were certainly great. With due deliberation they were calculated, but all together they were not found to outweigh the duty of rescuing the flotillas. The still air, which caused the mist to hang, gave also so glassy a sea that submarines could easily be seen in time for his high speed to enable him to avoid them, nor was it very likely that a more powerful force could be on the spot in time if he made his swoop immediately and at his utmost speed. So, at 11.30, as the third call from the *Arethusa* came in, the Admiral's mind was made up. Commodore Goodenough was already away with all he had, and the Admiral himself led away eastward at full speed to cover the forty odd miles which lay between him and the position Commodore Tyrwhitt had given (54° N, 7° E.).

The bold and well-judged decision was taken at the last possible moment. The 3rd Flotilla which had been ordered to close the Commodore at 11.20, after the *Köln* had been driven off, was just re-forming cruising order on the *Arethusa* when salvos began to fall amongst the destroyers from an unseen ship to the northward, which in a few minutes, as we have seen, proved to be the *Strassburg*. The *Arethusa* and *Fearless* opened a hot fire, and at the same time the *Acheron's* division, which was coming down south-east in response to the *Fearless's* signal to attack the *Köln* with torpedo, sighted the *Strassburg* and attacked her. To avoid her the *Strassburg* turned to north-westward. This was the moment when the Commodore, feeling himself outmatched by the heavier enemy, had ordered his destroyers to attack with torpedoes. All four divisions sped off to obey, and the two leading divisions, going away to the north-westward, soon found the enemy and engaged her. Several torpedoes were fired, none of which hit, but they had the effect of forcing the cruiser to turn away and disappear. Meanwhile, the 3rd and 4th Divisions, being to the southward of the Commodore, could not see the cruiser, and after an attempt to locate her, which brought them in touch with the *Acheron's* division, they rejoined the *Arethusa* and *Fearless*. The other two divisions also came back, and all were resuming the westward course in cruising order, when suddenly, shortly after noon, a three-funnelled cruiser loomed up ahead.[1]

It was the *Mainz*, still running to the southward from the fire of our light cruisers. They were coming down on her starboard quarter at full speed, continually reducing the range, and she had no choice but to run on to the southward to cross Commodore Tyrwhitt's bows. The *Fearless*, which was to the north of the *Arethusa*, turned promptly on the opposite course to the enemy and engaged her. She also fired a torpedo, but it ran in a circle and she had to manœuvre to avoid it. She then turned back to assist the *Arethusa*, who had altered a little to starboard to bring her guns to bear. Commodore Tyrwhitt was again in hot action at 5,000 yards, and not knowing that our light cruisers were close on the *Mainz's* heels, had signalled the five divisions of destroyers that were in company to attack her. The 1st Division of the 1st Flotilla and the 1st and 2nd of the 3rd Flotilla, which were to the northward of the *Arethusa*, formed line-ahead and swung to starboard on the opposite course of the *Mainz*, the other two being to the southward held on to the westward, and upon the 4th Division, which was outermost, the *Mainz* turned all her energy as she came down. Her fire was extraordinarily well-aimed and calibrated, and just after the *Laurel* had fired her two torpedoes and was turning away the fourth salvo hit her badly. Besides other damage, the lyddite in the after ready racks detonated, put the after gun and its crew out of action, and so damaged the after funnel that she was lost to view in a smother of smoke. She was thus able to limp away as fast as her crippled engines and boilers would allow. To some extent the smoke also hid her next astern—the *Liberty*—but she, too, as she turned away was hit forward. Her mast was brought down, and her captain, Lieutenant-Commander Nigel Barttelot, killed. Still, she carried on under Lieutenant Horan, and continued to fire till the *Mainz* was lost in the mist. The *Lysander*

[1] See Plan. Phase 12.5 to 12.30.

(Commander H. F. H. Wakefield), which came next, had better luck, for the salvo aimed at her as she turned missed, and she proceeded to attack another cruiser which had just come in sight to the northward, which seems to have been the *Köln*. Last came the *Laertes*, and she received her salvo with such precision that every shell hit her, and though her casualties were only two killed and six wounded, she was brought to a standstill with no water in her boilers.

So the *Mainz* brilliantly repulsed the torpedo attack, but by this time, under the cross fire of the light cruisers and the flotilla and its leaders, she herself had suffered severely. She was on fire fore and aft, but was still gamely in action. For Commodore Tyrwhitt the situation seemed still critical, for he assumed that a concentration of German cruisers was taking place to north of him. The *Strassburg* had returned to the attack, for the *Arethusa* had caught a glimpse of her through a break in the mist, and given her a salvo. The *Fearless*, as she ran down across the *Arethusa's* wake to assist the shattered 4th Division, had become engaged with the two cruisers, the *Strassburg* and the *Köln*, and coming up astern of them was a third cruiser, the *Ariadne*. But the anxiety was soon at an end. As the *Fearless* ran on she was again able to engage the *Mainz* and draw her fire, so that when the destroyers of the 3rd Division delivered their attack not a shot seems to have been fired on them. When the 4th Division attacked her rudder had jammed and she was circling to starboard. This change, of course, prevented all the boats of the 3rd Division attacking with torpedo, but the *Lydiard* was credited with one fairly home. Possibly a second reached her as well, but in any case her hour had struck. Her sudden turn brought her within decisive range of the light cruisers, and by the time the torpedo attack was over she had stopped and was practically silenced.

Still, where she lay at her last gasp, after the unequal action which she had maintained with so much skill and spirit, there still was apprehension that the tables might be turned by her consorts to the northward, who as yet, had given her no effective support. Just as she was stopping, indeed, it looked as if this was to be the end. Four cruisers appeared out of the mist, coming down from the northward in line-abreast at high speed. There was a moment of acute suspense, and then it was clear they were not her friends. It was Commodore Goodenough with his four cruisers coming down in accordance with Admiral Beatty's decision.

As soon as Commodore Tyrwhitt recognised them he signalled " cease fire," and calling his destroyers to re-form cruising order, he left the *Mainz* to Commodore Goodenough and resumed the retirement westward. But the danger was not yet over. As in obedience to the *Arethusa's* signal the uninjured divisions were closing her to re-form, salvos began to fall near them from the northward. In that direction they could now make out dimly two enemy cruisers—one was the *Köln*, flying the flag of the German Flotilla Admiral, and the other, some way astern of her, was the *Strassburg*. It was obviously within their power to turn the fortunes of the day, and the situation was extremely critical, when another surprise broke into it. Suddenly, out of the haze to the westward, the shadowy form of a very large cruiser loomed up coming on at high speed. There was another moment of breathless anxiety, and then she was seen to be the *Lion*. Nor was she alone. Astern of her appeared one by one the other four battle cruisers with the 2nd and 3rd Divisions of the 1st Flotilla, who, after their attack on the *Mainz*, had met and joined the *Arethusa*.[1]

So Admiral Beatty reaped the fruit of his difficult decision. Having taken it he had held on after the light cruisers, until, just when they turned to close the beaten *Mainz* and finish her, there was a burst of firing away to the eastward, and he promptly steered for it. What he heard was the *Köln* and *Strassburg* firing on the *Fearless* and the destroyers she had collected (*Lysander* and 5th Division of the 1st Flotilla). Having passed astern of the *Arethusa* to the rescue of the shattered division of the 3rd Flotilla, she was away to the eastward when the *Köln* and *Strassburg* appeared. She was still engaging them with her utmost energy to draw the fire from the *Arethusa* and the destroyers she was trying to rescue. Bold as was her action she was too much overmatched for the furious struggle to last long. But in a few minutes the tables were turned. Suddenly she saw her leading antagonist turn back sharply to the eastward and make off. In another minute she had sight of the *Lion* and knew that it was Admiral Beatty rushing in from the westward who had headed off the enemy. The *Strassburg* probably also got the alarm and broke back, for she, too, disappeared, and the *Fearless*, seeing how completely the Admiral had the situation in hand, could turn away and resume her work of rescue.

Prompt as had been the action of the German Admiral,

[1] See Plan. Phase 12.30 to 1.40.

it was too late. Admiral Beatty had the speed of him and was in position to cut him off from Heligoland. As he overhauled the doomed ship he altered a little to port to reduce the range and in two or three minutes, under the storm of fire, the German flagship was a blazing cripple, limping off to the north-eastward in an effort to open out the range. She did, in fact, get a respite. For at this supreme moment (12.56) another cruiser took shape in the mist steering eastward directly ahead of the *Lion*. From the *Arethusa* Admiral Beatty had learned there was a second enemy near ; she could not be allowed to get away, nor was it possible to detach ships in chase. Seeing how close they were to the enemy's bases and that a battle fleet might be met with at any moment, it was necessary to keep the squadron together. All five battle cruisers, therefore, held on to the eastward. But the ship ahead of them was not, in fact, the *Strassburg*. That ship was out of sight somewhere to the northward and eastward and so got clear away. The new arrival was the little *Ariadne*, and for her, as for the *Köln*, there was no possibility of escape.[1] Though she was running at high speed across the bows of the *Lion*, and thus continually altering the range, the shooting was too good for her. In ten minutes she was a mass of flames, with a heavy list, and was obviously sinking. So Admiral Beatty left her, for the destroyers had reported floating mines to the eastward, and the work for which he had risked his ships was done. At 1.10, therefore, half an hour after his first shot was fired, he made the general signal " Retire."

Before, however, he himself led the battle cruisers back to the westward he circled to port to get back to the spot where he had been obliged to leave the crippled *Köln*. About 1.25 the mist suddenly cleared and he had her in sight again crawling away to south-eastwards with her colours still flying. There was nothing, therefore, to do but finish the work, and the *Lion* leading round to port across her wake opened fire. The second salvo got home and only one more was needed. At 1.35 she suddenly sank. Every effort was made to rescue the survivors of her gallant fight. Admiral Beatty immediately ordered his four attached destroyers to the spot. But all was in vain ; the only trace of her they

[1] The *Ariadne* had apparently come out of the Bight, for at 12.10 p.m. she was seen by our Submarine *E4* steaming to the westward. Shortly before 1.0 this submarine saw her again proceeding eastward, so that she must have turned back, probably on learning from the *Köln* of the approach of our battle cruisers.

could find was a single stoker. The Flotilla Admiral and his whole complement of 380 had perished.

Even with the *Mainz* the work of rescue was difficult and hazardous. In a few minutes, after the light cruisers opened fire on her, she was reduced to a shapeless wreck, and at 12.50[1] she was observed to strike. There was nothing but admiration for the splendid fight she had made, and Commodore Keyes, who had just come up, closed in with the *Lurcher* and *Firedrake* to rescue the men that were jumping overboard. Commodore Goodenough, though he made off at once in the direction where the other enemy cruisers could be heard firing on our retiring flotillas, left the *Liverpool* behind to stand by, and she lowered three boats. Numbers of men were then picked up, but as Commodore Keyes's two destroyers came near, it could be seen that the burning decks were crowded with wounded. At great risk, therefore, he ordered the *Lurcher* to be laid alongside, and by the devoted exertions of his company had managed to remove all the survivors except two officers who refused to leave their ship, when at 1.8 the *Mainz* turned on her beam ends and went down so suddenly that the *Lurcher* narrowly escaped being smashed by her propellers. The two officers who had remained on board were subsequently picked up by the *Liverpool*, and in all, 348 officers and men out of a complement of 380 were rescued. Amongst them were 60 wounded, many seriously, and of these several died of their wounds before they could be landed. At the same time, away in the mist to the eastward, the *Ariadne*, whom Admiral Beatty had left in flames, was also going with nothing near to help. With her were lost her captain, two other officers and sixty-one men killed, and sixty wounded. Later on the few survivors of her crew were picked up by the *Von der Tann*, which, with the other battle cruisers, *Moltke*, and, later, the

[1] At this time the *Stralsund* arrived in the area. Leaving Wilhelmshaven lock at about 10.0 a.m., she received a signal on passing the *Seydlitz* to go at once to the assistance of the *Köln*. Half-an-hour later the *Köln* reported, erroneously, that mines had been laid in certain areas, and in avoiding these the *Stralsund* was prevented from joining her. At 11.20 she passed the outer Jade and steered for the *Strassburg* of whose engagement (with the *Arethusa*) she had heard at 10.27, and on the way she was fired at by one of our submarines. Several signals to the *Köln* brought no reply, and the *Stralsund*, proceeding to the westward, arrived in the area of operations at 12.50. At 1.6 she sighted our light cruisers and opened fire on the *Southampton*. The fire was returned and the *Stralsund* was hit, and, though not seriously damaged, she was forced to turn away. Continuing on a north-easterly course she proceeded to the assistance of the sinking *Ariadne*, and at 3.35 joined up with her battle cruisers three-and-a-half miles from the spot where the *Ariadne* had gone down.

Seydlitz, had come out by order of Admiral Hipper, but too late to save the situation.

At 8.20 a.m. the German Commander-in-Chief had ordered two battle cruisers, the *Moltke* and *Von der Tann*, then lying in Wilhelmshaven Roads, to be in readiness to support the light cruisers. By 11 a.m. they were prepared, and at 12.7 received their orders to proceed, but owing to the state of the tide they could not pass the Outer Jade until 2 p.m. They reached the *Ariadne*, then abandoned, by 2.25 and saw her sink an hour later. At 3.0 p.m. they were ordered not to go beyond 54° 9′ N., 7° 15′ E., but to wait there for the *Seydlitz*, Read-Admiral Hipper's flagship, which had been delayed by condenser trouble. She joined them at 3.10, but at 2.41 the Commander-in-Chief had already signalled to them not to become engaged with our armoured cruiser squadron. They, therefore, with three light cruisers (*Kolberg*, *Stralsund* and *Strassburg*) and the 8th Torpedo Boat Flotilla, carried out only a short reconnaissance movement to the north-north-west, which was chiefly a search for the missing *Köln* and *Mainz*. At 4.0 p.m. the *Blucher* (delayed by being in dock) joined the battle cruisers ; dispositions for the night patrol were made, and by 8.23 p.m. the *Seydlitz* and her squadron were once more at anchor. By that time aircraft had established that none of our forces was within a hundred miles of Heligoland.

Our own losses were exceptionally light. The *Arethusa* alone had suffered at all severely and was eventually towed in by the *Hogue*. Her losses were Lieutenant Westmacott and ten men killed, and one officer and sixteen men wounded. That they were comparatively so light after the punishment she had received was recognised as being due to her armour, and the first trial of the new type in action was held fully to justify its design. In the destroyers the losses were almost negligible, except for what the 4th Division of the 3rd Flotilla had suffered, and the total casualties for all ships engaged did not exceed thirty-five killed and about forty wounded. Moreover, every destroyer came in, two only being at all badly damaged. The enemy, on the other hand, had lost three light cruisers, *Köln*, *Mainz* and *Ariadne*, and one destroyer, and in killed, wounded and prisoners their total losses in all ranks were 1,242, including the Flotilla Admiral and Destroyer Commodore.[1] In the end, of course, thanks to Admiral Beatty's movement, we had been in overwhelming

---

[1] *Frauenlob*, 37 ; *V 187*, 71 ; *Mainz*, 437 ; *Köln*, 506 ; *Ariadne*, 129. Total, 1,180, besides losses in other cruisers and torpedo craft.

force, but it was not so in the earlier stages of the affair. Till our light cruisers came up the Germans had a decisive superiority in that type of ship, but it was neutralised, apparently, by the loose and ill-concerted manner in which they were handled. As it was, however, the *Arethusa* was twice engaged with superior forces, and was only saved by the power of her 6″ guns, the timely support of the *Fearless*, and the devoted covering attacks of the destroyers. Seeing, then, how our plan was confused by the unlucky wireless message, that did not get through, and how the intended surprise was disconcerted by counter action on the part of the enemy, the day undoubtedly reflects high credit on all concerned. It should live as a fine example of making good a tangled situation, which but for the decision and resourcefulness displayed on the spur of the moment might well have been very far from the enheartening success which the moment so sorely needed.

The moral effect upon the enemy can be measured with less certainty, but in the opinion of the most competent judges at the time it was at least as important as the material loss they suffered. It cannot be doubted that at a time when the Germans were methodically fostering the spirit of their untried Navy by ridiculing the inactivity of the Grand Fleet and nursing a belief that it dared not operate in the North Sea, the sudden appearance of part of it off the Bight was very disconcerting. In gauging the extent of the success, therefore, its deterrent effect must not be forgotten, and to its credit, at least in part, must be placed the continued disinclination the enemy displayed to venture his ships beyond his own coastal defences.

In their official history the Germans admit that their defensive system, in spite of the triple line of vessels, had failed entirely to fulfil its main purpose, and a fundamental change had, therefore, to be made. Admiral Hipper recommended that minefields should take the place of the advance patrol lines; the Fleet Command adopted the suggestion and in September minefields were laid off Heligoland and the Bight was closed.

CHAPTER VIII

THE EVACUATION OF OSTEND AND CHANGE OF THE ARMY BASE TO ST. NAZAIRE [1]

THE immediate result of the Heligoland action was that Ostend was rendered safe for the landing of the Belgian troops that were to come from Havre, and Admiral Bethell could maintain his supporting position with less fear of torpedo attack. Nevertheless, as we have seen, the situation at Ostend was for technical reasons very unfavourable. It was not only that the height of the sand dunes obscured the field of fire inland, but should an attack render a sudden evacuation necessary, the large civil population would seriously restrict operations for covering the withdrawal of the landing force. These objections to Ostend as a *pied-à-terre* led to a proposal for using Zeebrugge instead. Its superior advantages were concurred in by the French as well as by both Admiral Bethell and General Aston. The civil population was small, the quay accommodation better, and the difficulty of ship co-operation could be got over by the monitors entering the Bruges Canal.

The adoption of Zeebrugge, however, had not been decided when, in the forenoon of August 30, the first echelon of 4,000 Belgians began to arrive. By 2.30 p.m. they had all been landed and were at once railed up country as pre-arranged, while our Marines continued to do their best to hold the 5½-mile perimeter of Ostend. Meanwhile, another suggestion had come from the French, which was that Dunkirk should be used, as being much the best port of the three. Not only were its harbour facilities excellent, but with its well-designed land defences, its schemes for a protective inundation and its garrison of 20,000 men, it was practically secure against any force the enemy was likely to have available for its reduction. The only objection was that its greater distance from Antwerp made co-operation with the Belgian Field Army less easy. Still, the alternative might have been adopted, but that the developments in the main theatre brought the whole conception of a thrust from the sea to an

[1] See Map p. 126, and Map 8 in case.

121

9

end. The work it had been designed to do had been effected by General Sordet and a French cavalry corps operating on the British left towards Cambrai. The effect had been to reduce the strain on our over-burdened Expeditionary Force; at Le Cateau on August 26, in a hard-fought action, General Smith-Dorrien had been able to check the German rush, and in the next two days had outstripped the pursuit. By the 29th the whole of Sir John French's army had gained a position behind the Oise and was able to complete the re-organisation which had been already in progress during its march. On either flank its new line was prolonged by fresh French troops from the South, but the position was still not what was required, and after a visit by General Joffre to the British Headquarters it was decided, for strategical reasons, to fall back to the Marne.

It was a movement in which the French staked their own subtle strategical conceptions against the enveloping rush that characterised those of the enemy. They were untried, to some extent hazardous, and might well fail. Failure would mean to Sir John French the loss of his main supply line from Havre; and in any case it was endangered, for he had been drawn away from Amiens and the Germans had appeared there. The line was thus already menaced, and the question of a shift of base further to the westward, which had been raised as early as August 24, became insistent. On that day, pending a decision, all movements of stores and troops to Boulogne and Havre had been stopped, and our Government were discussing with the French the propriety of a shift to Cherbourg and Caen. The situation was still too obscure for a definite decision to be arrived at, and, though the War Office asked for six transports to be kept at Havre in readiness to evacuate it, stores and reinforcements continued to be directed there; but so uncertain was the outlook that the stores were not allowed to be disembarked. Boulogne, however, was definitely ordered to be cleared and closed down. For two or three days longer the uncertainty continued, with increasing strain on the Admiralty as transports were held up at Havre and the port became more and more congested. But the situation ashore was deteriorating too rapidly for the matter to remain open for long, and by August 29 it was clear that if the Expeditionary Force continued to rely on its original base it would have to face the possibility of a great disaster. To shift a main line of supply, even for a victorious army, is always a serious step. It is doubly serious on the top of an exhausting retreat, with heavy losses to replace, and above all when the army is based upon the sea,

and the change means shifting the base from narrow to open
waters. Yet this is what a change entailed.   In the Channel
there was no port now, not even Cherbourg, which would give
a new line that was reasonably secure, and nothing would
serve but a port on the west coast. Great as were the
difficulties, by August 29 it was clear they must be faced.
On that day Sir John French had decided that an immediate
shift had become imperative, and that a new base must be
established at St. Nazaire at the mouth of the Loire.

The Admiralty thus found themselves suddenly confronted
with a new and difficult task, which involved a wide change in
their dispositions for protecting the Army's communications.
Had it been merely a question of safeguarding the line of
supply the necessary redistribution would have been complicated enough, but it was more. The transportation of the
Expeditionary Force was not yet complete; this very week
the VIth Division was due to sail for France, and it was to
St. Nazaire it had to go. The factors of the problem differed
widely from those which they had hitherto successfully dealt
with. It was no longer the comparatively simple task of
protecting short routes within the Channel; the main sea-
lines would now run outside and round Ushant into the
Bay of Biscay. The patrol of this route, for reasons which
will appear directly, was difficult, and for a force to cover it
there was nothing to draw upon except the Channel Fleet.
Obviously, therefore, its strength could not be spent on such
a subsidiary object as the occupation of Ostend, which, however desirable, had now lost its primary importance.

Of this there could be no doubt, for it had been found that
the 10,000 Belgians, on whom the possibility of effective
operations from that point depended, were in such a state of
exhaustion after the terrible experiences they had gone
through, that they could not be fit for active service without
a long rest. Accordingly, at midnight on August 30–31
Admiral Bethell received a sudden order to re-embark the
whole Marine Brigade at once. To enable him to carry out
the order he asked that three Bacchantes might be sent him,
and after some delay Admiral Campbell, who since the
Heligoland action had been holding the Broad Fourteens
with his squadron and a division of destroyers, was directed
to come down with his cruisers to assist in the operation.
At 4 a.m. on the 31st General Aston got the order and
the work began at once. The force of well over 3,000
men was distributed over an arc now extending to seven
miles, with heavy weights of ammunition, tools and provisions, and some 200 tons of stores and equipment. There

was only one approach to the quay, and only one crane available. Yet, in spite of all difficulties, everything was on board Admiral Bethell's ships by 5 p.m., before he knew that Admiral Campbell was coming. Nor were the difficulties confined to the land; during the morning, in the height of the work, call signs were intercepted which indicated that the two German battleships, *Pommern* and *Braunschweig*, were out, and it was for this reason that Admiral Bethell decided not to wait for his colleague, who might well be otherwise engaged. Nothing, however, came of the alarm, and by 8.30 p.m. the squadron was able to weigh and proceed, in detachments, to land the Marines at their respective home ports.

Little as the Ostend enterprise had to show in material effect upon the campaign, its conduct was such as to give confidence for what the new force might achieve under more favourable conditions. In approving General Aston's management of the affair, the Admiralty wrote : " The whole operation has been carried out in such a way as to be a credit to the Marine Corps. Considering the suddenness with which the Expedition was dispatched, and the impossibility of previous arrangements for Staff, etc., the promptitude with which the Brigade was embarked, landed, and re-embarked was highly creditable." What effects had been produced were entirely moral. It is probable the Germans had no intention to enter Ostend, but the population could not know this. The Expedition found them depressed and even inclined to panic, and it left them in good heart, amidst enthusiastic farewells for men who seemed to have saved them from the fate of Louvain and Malines. It was at least some evidence that Britain did not mean to leave Belgium to her fate if by any possibility she could help it, and at this stage of the war, seeing what Belgium was suffering, this counted for not a little.

The moment the evacuation was complete the work of shifting the base began. It was no light task. At Havre and Rouen, besides the various disembarkation staffs, there were, with reinforcements held up there, 15,000 officers and men and 1,500 horses, and amongst the vast quantities of stores that had accumulated in the two places there were no less than 60,000 tons of oil, about which the French Government, who on September 2 withdrew from Paris to Bordeaux, were specially anxious. For the bulk of this our Admiralty had to provide tankers as well as transport for the troops and our own stores, and this was by no means the end of what they had to do for our Ally, besides the transfer of our own Army's base. The retirement towards the Marne had left isolated

the French troops at Dunkirk and in the northern departments. With the Germans at Amiens, their withdrawal
by land was too hazardous a risk, and it had to be done by
sea. Of the troops at Dunkirk, so many as were not required
for a garrison, the French were able to embark in their own
transports, and to transfer them to Honfleur; but for the
rest that lay out in the departments to the number of 25,000,
mainly Territorials, the assistance of the Admiralty had to
be sought. It was readily granted, and in due course all
were embarked in British ships and landed at La Rochelle.
Besides these, 2,000 Belgians at Havre, who had been found
fit for service, were also carried with 2,000 horses to Ostend,
and 10,000 French from Calais to Cherbourg; yet our
Transport Department, as usual, was equal to the task. In
about a fortnight after the word was given, Rouen and
Havre, as well as Boulogne, were clear, and by September 16
the last store-ships had reached La Rochelle and Bordeaux.
In the final six days of the evacuation there had left Havre
20,000 officers and men, 4,000 horses, and 60,000 tons of stores.
Seeing how heavily the Admiralty was burdened in every
other direction, it is a feat to be remembered.

It was in this way—rather than by the landing at Ostend
—that the British Navy was able to take a direct hand in
that famous retreat that was destined to defeat the enemy's
long-prepared purpose. It was but a subsidiary service;
but, met as the sudden call was with a scarcely credible
promptitude and sufficiency, it affords one more example
of the freedom of manœuvre which a fleet may give to a
Continental army by a firm hold on the coastwise lines of
supply and passage. There had been nothing comparable
to it since 1818 when Wellington, as suddenly and with as
little notice, called on the Navy to shift his base from Lisbon
to the difficult ports in the inmost recesses of the Bay of
Biscay—it was a *tour de force* carried out by the Admiralty
and Lord Keith as promptly and smoothly as was the shift
from Havre to St. Nazaire, and though almost forgotten in
the glory of the Vittoria campaign to which it contributed
so much, it was essential for that crowning victory, and
deserves to be enshrined in national memory no less proudly
than the similar feat of our own time.

The service which, at Sir John French's call, the fleet
rendered to the common cause at the critical juncture is
the more striking since it was done at the peril of the naval
position. The denuding of the northern coast of France
immediately raised again the old anxiety for the safety of
the ports on which our hold on the Channel so much depended.

Once more the Admiralty applied to Paris for a detailed account of the defences of Calais and Dunkirk. " Those places," they said, " being of very great importance to our naval arrangements, we are anxious to form an exact impression of their military strength." They were soon reassured. About Calais and Dunkirk the French had no anxiety, but Boulogne, being indefensible from the land side, was abandoned as a military port, and all preparations were made for blocking it any moment when it might be threatened by the enemy.

The anxiety of the Admiralty as to the inherent strength of the ports in the Dover Strait was natural, since the change in the line of supply for our army involved a gravitation of the Channel Fleet to the westward. The main protection of the new route, along which the VIth Division was about to pass, must lie with the Western Patrol, but in order to provide it with cover and support, Admiral Burney, having been rejoined by Admiral Bethell's squadron, moved his whole fleet to Portland on September 3. The Western Patrol, which it will be recalled was an Allied Squadron, was now under the command of Admiral Wemyss—this arrangement having been made when on August 25 Admiral Rouyer, at the request of the Admiralty, had withdrawn his armoured cruisers so as to have them in readiness to support the Ostend diversion. The squadron that remained under the British Admiral was still a strong one for its purpose. Besides his own four light cruisers, *Charybdis, Diana, Eclipse, Talbot,* he had a French contingent of four armoured cruisers and three armed merchant cruisers, and with these he was carrying on the routine of the Patrol. But when the shift of base saddled him with the protection of the new route, it was clear he could not cover the whole ground. It was exposed not only to the unlocated German cruisers in the Atlantic, but also to the ships which had taken refuge in Spanish and Portuguese ports. As some of them were suspected of being armed, Admiral de Robeck had been doing his best to watch them, but his squadron was too much overweighted with commerce protection and convoy work to do it effectively. By the original plan his function had been to guard the waters between Ushant and Finisterre. But later on his principal position had been shifted to the southward—" on the trade route off the coast of Portugal." Moreover, as must now be told, events were occurring which fully occupied his attention still further to the southward, and neither he nor Admiral Stoddart, to the south of him, could spare a ship. To add to the difficulty, within a week or so Admiral Wemyss would

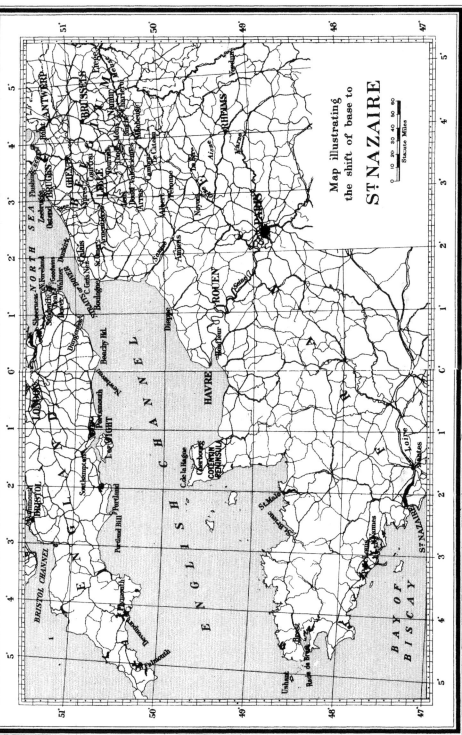

Map illustrating
the shift of base to
ST. NAZAIRE

0 10 20 30 40 50 60
Statute Miles

Prepared in the Historical Section of the Committee of Imperial Defence.
1540/38.

Ordnance Survey 1919.

have to take his cruisers to the St. Lawrence to bring home the Canadian convoy, and about the same time the East Lancashire Territorial Division would be sailing for Alexandria.

But for the French Atlantic Squadron the problem would have been very difficult to solve; it was they who came to the rescue. On August 31, the day the decision to change the base was announced, Admiral Rouyer was requested to take charge of the Ushant–Finisterre route with his second division, and to keep the first at Cherbourg in readiness to move east or west as might be required.

CHAPTER IX

THE causes which held the attention of Admiral de Robeck and Admiral Stoddart to the southward were due to influences which were beginning to make themselves felt all over the world. We have seen that by the middle of August both their squadrons had established a good grip on the stations assigned to them, so far at least as the coast of the Peninsula and the west coast of Africa were concerned. But no sooner was this accomplished than their commerce protection functions were disturbed from two sources. The first was the beginning of the Imperial Concentration—that is, the bringing home of the Imperial troops from abroad, which, unfortunately, the opening of the Continental campaign had rendered pressing and imperative; the second was the commencement of our offensive operations against German oversea possessions. At first sight it would appear that with so much on our hands in Europe, operations in the latter category were premature and unwise, as tending to dissipate our military force. But the question had been thoroughly gone into in all its aspects, and decisions taken on well-considered strategical grounds.

For the study of what operations might be undertaken a special body called the Offensive Sub-Committee of the Committee of Imperial Defence was appointed on August 5 to deal with oversea attack. It was composed of representatives of the Admiralty, and the War, Foreign, Colonial and India Offices. In practice, however, the naval element was predominant, its President being Admiral Sir Henry Jackson, who had just vacated the office of Chief of the War Staff and had been nominated for the Mediterranean command as successor to Admiral Milne. The Sub-Committee was closely associated with the War Staff, and its instructions were to submit to the Cabinet proposals for combined expeditions which would produce a definite effect on the course of the war.

[1] See Map 2 in case.

At the outset of its deliberations the Committee recognised the principle that no force must be dissipated on enterprises which would prejudice the Imperial concentration in the main theatre and the safety of the great trade routes, and further that all expeditions for the conquest of distant territory were faulty in conception unless and until we had established a working command of the sea in all quarters. This being so, no objective would be legitimate which could not be dealt with by local forces, and no such objective could have a definite effect on the course of the war unless it tended to confirm our hold upon sea communications.   As long as the enterprises were kept within these lines, so far from dissipating force, they would tend to assist and strengthen the main concentration of effort by keeping open the flow of trade and the Imperial lines of passage and communication.   Unless this was done effectively a free concentration of effort in the main theatre was impossible.

The objectives within these limitations were not far to seek. They must all be naval, and of these the most important were the enemy's foreign bases and centres of intelligence. Long experience had shown that until such positions were in our hands the task of clearing the seas of hostile commerce destroyers must be precarious and indefinitely prolonged. The governing principle, therefore, on which the Committee set out, was that all operations were to be regarded primarily as designed for the defence of our maritime communications and not for territorial conquest.   The single object was to deprive the enemy of his distant coaling and telegraphic stations.

Of these Tsingtau was the most important, but its reduction was too formidable an undertaking for the forces then available. Among other tempting objectives were Luderitz Bay in German South-West Africa, with the adjacent high power wireless station at Windhuk, and on the east coast Dar-es-Salaam.   But Luderitz Bay had to be ruled out as requiring too large a military force, while an attack on Dar-es-Salaam must depend on the local naval situation, and upon what troops India could spare over and above those she was sending to replace the Mediterranean Garrisons.

Besides these three points, there were others less difficult to deal with which fell well within the limitations laid down by the Committee.   All were mainly important as centres of communication.   The key of the whole German system of telegraphic communication for the Atlantic was in Togoland in the Gulf of Guinea, adjoining our Gold Coast colony.   Here the high-power station at Kamina made direct connection

with Nauen near Berlin and linked up the capital with the
German West African possessions, and thence with South
America by the three German cables from Monrovia in
Liberia to Pernambuco. Since these cables, though German
owned, had both terminals in neutral countries, it had been
decided not to interfere with them. All that was required
would be gained without friction by destroying their feeding
station at Kamina. It was therefore a point to strike at
once, and, moreover, was within the power of the local
forces. It happened that General Dobell, the Inspector-
General of the West African Frontier Force, was at home,
and in conference with him a scheme was soon worked out
for doing the work with troops from the Gold Coast and
Sierra Leone. The capture of the adjacent German Cameroons was also taken in hand as an object of special and
immediate importance. For in its excellent harbour at
Duala several ships of the Woermann Line had taken refuge,
and possibly the intention was to equip them as raiders.
The operation was to be undertaken by the garrison of
Nigeria if the force could be brought up to sufficient strength
from elsewhere. In the Pacific similar points were arranged
for with the help of the Australian and New Zealand forces.
The principal centres were in German New Guinea, which
included the Bismarck Archipelago; [1] the island of Yap in
the Western Carolines; Nauru south of the Marshall Islands;
and Apia in the Samoa Group. Omitting for the present any
attempt to occupy German New Guinea as being scarcely
within the limitations laid down, it was decided, as a beginning, that its principal port, Rabaul, should be seized by
the Australian forces as a base of operations against the
cable and wireless stations at Yap, Nauru, and Angaur in
the Pelew Group. To complete the scheme, New Zealand
was invited to take similar action against Samoa.

Besides being charged with these world-wide operations,
Admiral Jackson was also entrusted with the management
of the Imperial Concentration. The dual function, if not
quite logical, was eminently practical. For the pressing work
of transporting to Europe the Colonial Garrisons and the
various Dominion and Indian Contingents necessarily con-
flicted with the development of the oversea attacks which
were the primary function of the Committee. For successful
achievement there was need of the nicest adjustment of
force and plans, and particularly an adjustment of naval

---

[1] The two main islands were Neu Pommern and Neu Mecklenburg,
which, until the allocation of spheres of interest in 1885–6, had been New
Britain and New Ireland.

force between the calls for escort and the exigencies of commerce defence.   Although the fundamental idea was that all
the oversea attacks were to be regarded as subservient to
commerce defence, yet as the calls of the main European
theatre became ever more insistent they tended to override
the exigencies of trade protection, and the oversea attacks
assumed more frankly the object of securing territory to
balance the enemy's acquisitions in Europe.   Such a development was probably inevitable, and was at any rate a recurrence
of what always took place in former wars when the line
between operations for the capture of distant bases and the
conquest of colonial territory as " compensations " never
preserved a clear definition.   In the present case the old
tendency was emphasised by the moral importance of
responding frankly to the outburst of Imperial enthusiasm
in the self-governing Dominions, particularly as this was a
factor which the enemy had omitted from his calculations,
and which came upon him as a complete and disturbing
surprise.   Not only was it necessary to listen to the keen
desire of the daughter states to get their troops as quickly
as possible in line with those of the homeland, but our desire
was also to give all possible rein and assistance to the aspira-
tions of each of them to remove the enemy permanently
from its own doors.   The problem, therefore, was of a complexity and delicacy beyond anything with which our enemies
or our Allies had to deal, and a typical instance of the kind
of complication it raised was the difficulty already alluded to
of modifying our naval distribution to meet the call of the
new line of supply to St. Nazaire.

On August 14, when Admiral Stoddart had got his squadron
complete and well disposed upon the Cape Verde–Canary
station, Admiral Jackson's Committee had just recommended
that not only should Kamina in Togoland be at once dealt
with, but also the German wireless station at Duala in the
Cameroons.   Thanks to the promptitude of Mr. Robertson,
the Acting-Governor of the Gold Coast, and the ready co-
operation of the Governor-General of French West Africa and
the Lieutenant-Governor of Dahomey, the operations against
Kamina were already well advanced.   On the first day of
the war a force consisting of the Gold Coast regiment and
other local details was mobilised under Captain (temporary
Lieutenant-Colonel) Bryant, and an officer was sent to Lome,
the chief German port, to summon the colony to surrender.
The Germans had proposed its neutrality.   This we bluntly
refused, and on August 7 the Acting-Governor abandoned
Lome and agreed to surrender it, with a large part of the

hinterland. It was immediately decided to occupy the place as a base for further operations against Kamina, while other Allied columns from Northern Dahomey, Nigeria and the Gold Coast threatened the northern hinterland. So promptly did Colonel Bryant act that by August 12 he had landed his whole force at Lome, and there he rapidly organised his column for an advance on Kamina.

It was no easy task. The wireless station lay 100 miles inland on the hills near Atakpame. The only approach to it was by the railway and road, which formed practically two continuous defiles through almost impassable jungle, and though several locomotives and much rolling stock had been captured at Lome, the Germans were destroying the bridges as they retired. Skill and rapidity, however, overcame every difficulty. Nothing but rear-guard opposition was met with till at Agbelufoe station the advanced guard was hotly attacked. It succeeded in defending itself till the main body approached, and then the enemy fled, leaving thirty more miles of the railway in our hands intact. After a three days' halt to get up supplies the advance was resumed, with the force increased by a company of Senegalese Tirailleurs, and on August 21 the enemy were found strongly entrenched on the Chra river, twenty-five miles short of Kamina. A sharp action ensued on the 22nd, but by dark Colonel Bryant had so far succeeded that during the night they fled. With that all resistance ceased. A French column under Major Lacroix was closing on Kamina from Dahomey and one of ours from the Upper Gold Coast, and during the night of August 24–25, when Colonel Bryant was ready to resume his advance, the wireless station was blown up, and next day the whole colony was surrendered unconditionally. It was all as smart a piece of work as could be wished,[1] and withal so valuable to the Navy that the Admiralty sent a letter to the Colonial Office expressing their high appreciation of Colonel Bryant's conduct.

Duala in the Cameroons was to prove a much more serious matter. For this operation the Nigerian troops were to be mainly employed, and the French had promised to assist with a force from Senegal. It was not till August 15, at a conference with French Staff Officers held at the Admiralty, that the general plan of operations was settled. A cruiser was to proceed at once to Fernando Po to blockade the Cameroons, and, as this step would give an alarm, the troops were to be pushed up as rapidly as possible. In three weeks'

[1] See *Official History of the War : Military Operations, Togoland and the Cameroons*, 1914-1916.

time the French would have ready 2000 men at Dakar, with six guns; Sierra Leone would send 600 and Nigeria 1700, with ten guns. The base would be Fernando Po, Calabar River or Lagos, and all troops would be conveyed in British transports.

In accordance with this arrangement, Admiral Stoddart was ordered to send the *Cumberland* to Fernando Po at once, and on her way she was to cover the passage of the Sierra Leone Contingent to Togoland, since it had nothing but the gunboat *Dwarf* as escort. This he did, and from this time the *Cumberland*, one of his most powerful units, was practically removed from his squadron.

Scarcely had the Admiralty given the order when the danger to our commerce defence system which Admiral Jackson had foreseen declared itself. In a few hours it was known that a German merchant cruiser had broken into the station and was playing havoc with the trade. This ship was the *Kaiser Wilhelm der Grosse*, which in the early days of the war, before the Northern Patrol could be established, had broken out, as we have seen, into the Atlantic. Leaving Bremen on August 4 for a rendezvous off Heligoland, she had stolen up the Scandinavian coast and so out into the North Sea, making for the north-east of Iceland, where she lay a day in the ice. In this vicinity she captured and sank the trawler *Tubal Cain*, and then, keeping wide out in the Atlantic, made for the focal point which Admiral Stoddart had to guard. Here during August 15 and 16, to the south-westward of the Canaries, she captured four British ships : the *Galician* from South Africa, the New Zealand Shipping Company's *Kaipara* from Montevideo to Bristol with frozen meat, the R.M.S.P. Company's *Arlanza* from Buenos Aires, and the Elder Dempster liner *Nyanga*, with a cargo originally consigned to Hamburg. The enemy's treatment of these ships was very good. The *Galician* and *Arlanza*, having passengers, were allowed to proceed after their wireless was removed; the other two were sunk and their crews taken on board the cruiser.

Owing to the disturbance of the station by the Togoland and Cameroons expeditions the *Cornwall* was the only ship in the vicinity, and she did not get the news till the 17th, when she spoke the *Arlanza* coming out of Las Palmas. It was not the *Arlanza's* fault the alarm was not spread sooner. Having a spare set of wireless she had rigged it as soon as the German cruiser was out of sight, but atmospherics had prevented her getting any message through. The Admiralty, however, had already received the news from Las Palmas, and immediately took measures to reinforce the area. As a first step Admiral de Robeck was ordered to send the *Highflyer* down to assist his colleague, while he himself was to have the *Challenger* from the Bristol Channel and *Minerva* from the Irish station, and for Admiral Stoddart the merchant cruiser *Macedonia* was coming down. Three other ships of the same class were also passing through the area, *Armadale Castle* and *Kinfauns Castle* for the Cape, and *Otranto* for South America, and the search was soon hot.

Its first result was that on August 22 the *Kinfauns Castle* captured the German barque *Werner Vinnen*, with 4000 tons of coal, and sent her into Sierra Leone. Next day Admiral Stoddart himself, while on his way to the same port to coal, captured the steamship *Professor Woermann*, which, as her log showed, had been hanging about Brava Island, Cape Verde, for some days as though expecting a friendly cruiser. Still the *Kaiser Wilhelm* was unlocated, but on August 24 our Consul at Las Palmas reported that on August 17—the day after her last captures—she had put into Rio de Oro, a desolate Spanish anchorage on the Sahara Coast some 300 miles south of the Grand Canary. In company she had the steamship *Duala*, which had recently been in Las Palmas, and after staying forty-eight hours, in spite of the Spanish Authorities, had cleared on the 22nd, ostensibly for New York.

Captain Buller in the *Highflyer* was promptly informed, and getting away at once found the chase in the afternoon of the 26th coaling between two ships off the Rio de Oro. A third collier was standing off stopped—showing what lavish arrangements the Germans had made in this area for keeping their commerce destroyers supplied. Captain Buller being in much superior force, summoned the enemy to surrender.[1] The prompt answer was, " German warships do not surrender. I request you to observe Spanish neutrality." The obvious retort was that she was violating it herself. This Captain Buller signalled, adding that he would sink her if she did not surrender, and warning her tenders to cast off. There was a second refusal, and after giving her an hour and a half to strike or put to sea, during which the tenders made off and the *Highflyer* manœuvred to get a range clear of the land, Captain Buller at 3.10 p.m. fired a challenging shot. The German at once opened fire, the *Highflyer* replied, and the unequal action began. For an hour and a half it

---

[1] *Highflyer*, 5,600 tons, 20·1 knots, eleven 6″ and eight 12 pdrs. *Kaiser Wilhelm* had six 10·5 cm. (about 4″) guns firing 38-lb. shells.— (Diary of J. Peters, her assistant engineer).

lasted briskly, but at 4.25 the *Kaiser Wilhelm* ceased fire and boats were seen to be leaving her. To save further bloodshed, Captain Buller signalled her to haul down her flag and sent off boats under the Red Cross with medical assistance. But before they could reach the battered ship she went down in shallow water. As the crew ashore had taken up a menacing position behind the sand-hills, Captain Buller recalled the boats and left the Germans to their fate.[1]

So it was that the only commerce destroyer that had started from Germany ended her career ten days after she reached her cruising ground. What her losses were is unknown. Those of the *Highflyer* were one man killed and five slightly wounded, while the material damage was so small that she held her ground in spite of the Admiralty authorising her to return to Gibraltar to refit. The British prisoners from the *Galician, Kaipara, Nyanga,* and *Tubal Cain* suffered not at all : for the German captain, with the humanity that had distinguished him throughout, sent them on board one of his colliers before the action began, and she on August 28 set them free at Las Palmas. The capture of this ship was specially happy, for it seems to have gone some way to break up one of the only combinations which the Germans appear to have arranged against our trade. From a captured diary it is known she was under orders to proceed at once to South America, where, as will be related in its place, she would have met a consort in a weakly-protected area. As it was, so far as she was concerned, the scheme was nipped in the bud.

Naturally, the Spanish Government complained of our violation of neutral waters; but on our being able to show that the *Kaiser Wilhelm* had used the lonely harbour as a base for nine days and had there been met by no less than four colliers and supply ships, they admitted both sides were to blame and presented a friendly but energetic protest to each Power. After careful inquiry our own Admiralty decided that Captain Buller had been fully justified in what he did. It was clear that for over a week the Spanish Government had been unable to enforce its neutrality against the enemy. To have left the offending ship untouched would have been to invite hostile commerce destroyers to seek sanctuary in similar unfrequented anchorages all over the world. A letter of apology in this sense was sent, the apology was accepted, and, in spite of a vigorous German Press campaign in Spain, no more was heard of the affair.

In face of this outburst of German activity it was obviously impossible for Admiral de Robeck to attend

[1] See note, p. 186.

to anything north of Finisterre. As soon as the depredations of the *Kaiser Wilhelm* were heard of he had been ordered to send down his armed merchant cruiser *Marmora* to join the *Highflyer*, and when they were fully known and before her destruction was reported, he left his usual station off Lisbon to the *Sutlej* and hurried off in his flagship to Madeira. While there he heard from the Admiralty that there were indications that the Azores required attention. The *Vindictive* was ordered there, and on September 8 she captured a German collier with 5000 tons of Welsh coal—a capture which made a prolongation of her cruise clearly imperative. About coaling in the Portuguese Colonial ports there was no difficulty. The attitude of that Government was that though they were neutrals in the war they were also allied to Great Britain, and therefore intended to afford every help to British ships.

Besides these preoccupations, both of the Mid-Atlantic Squadrons had now to be concerned with guarding the safe passage of the oversea garrisons which were beginning to move homewards, and the outgoing of the Territorial troops that in certain cases were to replace them. But these movements did not develop till September, and by the time they were under way the Admiralty, as we have seen, had taken steps to strengthen the areas concerned with some of the older battleships.

NOTE.—Four hundred and fifty of the *Kaiser Wilhelm der Grosse's* crew were transferred to her tender, the *Bethania*, which, with her own crew of fifty, immediately set out with the intention of reaching Charleston, U.S.A. The feeding of so large a number on board a vessel usually carrying not more than forty was a considerable problem, the supply of fresh water presenting the greatest difficulty. It was hoped, however, that the provisions could be made to last out for the thirteen days in which she had set herself to reach Charleston, but her anxieties, in this direction at least, were ended on September 7 when she was captured by the *Essex*, taken to Kingston, Jamaica, and there interned.

CHAPTER X

THE EASTERN FLEET—FROM THE OPENING OF THE WAR TO THE INTERVENTION OF JAPAN [1]

In the Pacific during the period in which the *Kaiser Wilhelm der Grosse* inaugurated the German attack on our commerce, the plans of the Oversea Attack Committee had been maturing—but not without difficulty, owing to the strength of the German squadron in those seas, and the intrusion of the Imperial Concentration which quickly absorbed the attention of the Cape and East Indian Stations.

When on July 28 the preliminary warning reached Admiral Jerram he was at Wei-hai-wei, where he had just returned from a cruise with the *Minotaur* (flag), *Hampshire, Yarmouth,* the gunboat *Thistle* and five destroyers (*Welland, Ribble, Usk, Colne* and *Kennet*). His second light cruiser *Newcastle* was at Nagasaki fuelling. Three other gunboats were at Shanghai and six in the Yang-tse-kiang, while at Hongkong was the battleship *Triumph,* demobilised and in dock, and the sloop *Clio* refitting. At Hongkong, also, was the rest of his squadron: three more destroyers (*Jed, Chelmer* and *Fame*), four torpedo boats and three "C" class submarines, with their parent ship *Rosario,* as well as four other gunboats.

He was still at Wei-hai-wei when on July 30 the Warning Telegram reached him, and he forthwith proceeded to act on his War Orders, the principal step being to direct the *Triumph* to be mobilised at once and to lay up the four gunboats on the Lower Yang-tse-kiang to provide her with a crew. He then put to sea to take up a position in view of war breaking out as seemed best to meet the situation as he knew it. According to his latest intelligence there was nothing at Tsingtau except the German cruiser *Emden,* four German gunboats (*Iltis, Tiger, Luchs* and *Cormoran*) and one old Austrian cruiser (*Kaiserin Elizabeth*). The gunboat *Jaguar* was at Shanghai. Neither of the two powerful units of the enemy's squadron was located; the *Scharnhorst* (flag) was believed to be out in

[1] See Maps 7 and 14 in case.

the Pacific somewhere near Yap, and the *Gneisenau* was reported to have just left Singapore, but the intelligence was discredited, and was, in fact, an error; the ship in question was really the gunboat *Geier*, and the *Gneisenau's* whereabouts was quite unknown. The other two light cruisers belonging to the German Pacific Squadron, *Nürnberg* and *Leipzig*, were believed to be upon the west coast of North America.[1] In these circumstances the Admiral intended, pending instructions from home, to place his squadron between the ships in Tsingtau and those at sea. Just as he was starting, however, he received an order to concentrate at Hongkong, where the *Triumph* was now mobilising, and where three Canadian Pacific liners and one P. & O. which had been taken up locally to reinforce his squadron were to receive their armament. They were the *Empress of Asia*, *Empress of Japan* and *Himalaya*, to be complete by August 13, and *Empress of Russia* by August 21.

In view of the prevailing naval opinion that the great difficulty in commerce protection would be dealing with enemy auxiliary cruisers of this class, these ships had a special importance. We have already seen how deeply their menace affected our cruiser dispositions in the Atlantic; in the area of the Eastern Fleet the preoccupation was no less insistent. Of the possible raiders in East Indian waters three remained, *Tabora, Zieten* and *Kleist;* the *Derfflinger* on reaching Port Said had been detained, and the *Sudmark* had been captured by the *Black Prince* when that ship was detached into the Red Sea with the *Duke of Edinburgh*. At

---

[1] The force of the two squadrons was as under :—

GERMAN

	Completed.	Tons.	Trial speed.	Guns.			
Scharnhorst. . . .	1907	11,420	23·2	8	8·2″	6	5·9″
Gneisenau	1908	11,420	23·5	8	8·2″	6	5·9″
Emden	1909	3,592	24·1	10	4·1″		
Nürnberg	1908	3,400	23·5*	10	4·1″		
Leipzig	1906	3,200	22·4	10	4·1″		

BRITISH

Captains.	Completed.	Tons.	Trial speed.	Guns.			
Minotaur (E. B. Kiddle)	1908	14,600	23·1	4	9·2″	10	7·5″
Triumph (M. S. Fitzmaurice)	1904	11,985	20·1	4	10″	14	7·5″
Hampshire (H. W. Grant)	1905	10,850	23·5	4	7·5″	6	6″
Yarmouth (H. L. Cochrane)	1912	5,250	25·8	8	6″		
Newcastle (F. A. Powlett)	1910	4,800	26·1	2	6″	10	4″

* Designed speed.

Tsingtau were the *Yorck* and *Prinz Eitel Friedrich*. In the Philippines was the *Princess Alice ;* at Shanghai two Austrians, *China* and *Silesia*, and in Australian waters the *Seydlitz*. All together they formed a serious menace, which for a long time complicated the problem for all the Admirals of the Eastern Fleet and added materially to the difficulty of seeking out the enemy's main squadron.

Seeing how uncertain was intelligence about the *Scharnhorst* and *Gneisenau*, Admiral Patey on the Australian Station was no less concerned with them than Admiral Jerram. His last information was that the *Gneisenau* had left Nagasaki on June 23, probably with the *Scharnhorst* in company. If, then, they were not at Tsingtau he inclined to the view that the German Admiral was probably concentrating in the vicinity of New Guinea, where there were two comparatively important ports at his disposal, the one Friedrich Wilhelm Harbour in German New Guinea and the other Simpson Harbour in the adjacent island of Neu Pommern, where stood Rabaul and the capital Herbertshöhe. But, in fact, Admiral von Spee was nearly 1000 miles away at Ponape in the Caroline Islands. About the end of June he had left Tsingtau for a cruise to Samoa with the *Scharnhorst* and *Gneisenau* and a tender, the *Titania*, and, having reached Ponape on July 17, he called the *Nürnberg* from San Francisco to join him. She left that port on July 21 and Honolulu on July 27. It was not till August 6 that his preparations were complete. On that day the *Nürnberg* joined him, and without any delay he put to sea.[1] Beyond a vague report of a German cruiser moving westward from Honolulu nothing of this was known to Admiral Patey. He could only act on the appreciation he had formed, and his idea was to concentrate his squadron south of British New Guinea, where he had Port Moresby available, and endeavour to get contact with the enemy.

On July 30, when the Warning Telegram arrived, Australia took steps to place her squadron at the disposal of the Admiralty. New Zealand had already attached her battle

---

[1] The main German authority for Admiral von Spee's movements is *Das Kreuzergeschwader, sein Werden, Sieg und Untergang*, by Admiral C. Dick (Berlin, 1917), but on points of detail it has been found to differ from diaries kept by German officers at the time. In the *Kieler Neueste Nachrichten*, January 10, 1915, the *Titania* is described as an auxiliary cruiser, but the identity of the ship is uncertain. She does not appear under this name in *Lloyd's List*, but elsewhere is described as a cargo vessel of about 2500 tons displacement and 1300 I.H.P., used as a storeship for Tsingtau. She was presumably armed, as on November 2 she captured the Norwegian sailing vessel *Helicon* and took her into Mas a Fuera, where she (*Titania*) was eventually scuttled by the *Prinz Eitel Friedrich*.

cruiser *New Zealand* to the Grand Fleet, and three light
cruisers on the station now became available for general
service.[1] Besides these ships there was also somewhere in
the Pacific a French Squadron consisting of two armoured
cruisers and two gun-vessels, under Rear-Admiral A. L. M.
Huguet, with his flag in the *Montcalm*. She was known to
be approaching Admiral Patey's station, and at the moment
was making for Tahiti *en route* for the French port of Noumea
in New Caledonia, where the gun-vessel *Kersaint* was awaiting her. At Tahiti was another gun-vessel, the *Zélée ;* the
other cruiser, *Dupleix*, was in Chinese waters. All these ships
the French at once placed at the Admiralty's disposal, but
owing to Admiral Huguet being unlocated the order was a
long time reaching him.[2]

Admiral Patey's first step was to assemble at Sydney all
his ships except the *Sydney* and the three destroyers, which
were sent northward to Moreton Bay near Brisbane. The
Melbourne was to go to her war station at Fremantle in the
south-west and the rest to the rendezvous south of Port
Moresby. He would thus have the bulk of his fleet concentrated, so far as local considerations permitted, in the waters
where he expected to find the enemy, and if no news was to
be had of them his intention was to proceed to Simpson
Harbour in Neu Pommern and destroy whatever he found

[1] Australian Fleet

		Captains.	Tons.	Trial speed.	Guns.	
Australia	(battle cruiser)	S. H. Radcliffe	18,800	25·8	8	12″
Sydney	(light cruiser)	J. C. T. Glossop	5,400	25·7	8	6″
Melbourne	(light cruiser)	M. L. E. Silver	5,400	25·7	8	6″
Encounter	(light cruiser)	C. La P. Lewin	5,880	20·8	11	6″
Pioneer	(light cruiser)	T. W. Biddlecombe	2,200	19·7	8	4″
Yarra						
Parramatta	(destroyers)			26·0*	1	4″
Warrego						

Submarines *A.E. 1* and *A.E. 2*. Parent ship, *Protector*.

New Zealand Squadron. Captain Marshall, S.N.O.

	Completed.	Captains.	Tons.	Trial speed.	Guns.
Psyche	1899	H. J. T. Marshall	2,135	20·5	8 4″
Philomel	1891	P. H. H. Thompson	2,575	19·0*	8 4·7″
Pyramus	1899	Viscount Kelburn	2,135	20·7	8 4″

[2] French Squadron

	Completed.	Tons.	Trial speed.	Guns.	
Montcalm	1902	9,177	21·1	2 7·6″	8 6·4″
Dupleix	1903	7,432	20·9	8 6·4″	
Kersaint	1897	1,276	16·1*	1 5·5″	5 3·9″
Zélée	1899	637	13·3	2 3·9″	

* Designed speed.

there, including the wireless station, which was reported to be at Rabaul opposite Herbertshöhe.

In view of the strength of the German Pacific Squadron and of the fact that it was unlocated, the detaching of so useful a unit as the *Melbourne* was obviously unsatisfactory, but this was quickly remedied. On August 6, the day Admiral von Spee left Ponape, Admiral Patey as he was proceeding northward received from the Australian Naval Board a report that the German cruisers had been heard near Malaita to the east of the Solomon Islands, and that they seemed to be steaming south-east. This could only confirm the impression that Admiral von Spee intended to concentrate in the vicinity of Australia, and the menace to the detached cruisers could not be ignored. Admiral Patey therefore took immediate steps for a counter concentration by arranging for the *Pioneer* to take over the *Melbourne's* duty at Fremantle and for the *Melbourne* to join him in St. George's Channel, which leads up to Simpson Harbour through the Bismarck Archipelago. Admiral von Spee, however, was actually proceeding north-westward to Pagan Island in the Ladrones to complete his mobilisation in the seclusion of that remote spot. At Tsingtau his supply ships were being loaded in feverish haste, but in face of the possibility of an Allied concentration he had no intention of returning there. They were to come out to him at his island base disguised as British East Asiatic ships, and there, too, he summoned the *Emden*. This afterwards notorious cruiser had put to sea from Tsingtau on the last day of July on a cruise to the entrance of the Japan Sea. War with France and Russia had not then been declared, but she had received the "War Imminent" signal, and her object possibly was to catch the Russian cruiser *Askold*. In this she failed, but in the Strait of Korea she did capture the *Ryasan*, a ship of the Russian Volunteer Fleet, and took her back to Tsingtau on August 6.

The only indication of Admiral von Spee's movement was that in Australia the *Scharnhorst's* signals were found to be growing weaker; but Admiral Patey, so far from changing his plan, was trying to call up Admiral Jerram and suggest his combining in the sweep he was bent on making in New Guinea waters. There was no reply. Admiral Jerram by this time was making a movement of his own which required complete wireless silence. By the time war was declared he had completed his concentration at Hongkong. Of the two French cruisers *Montcalm* and *Dupleix* which had been placed at his disposal, the *Dupleix* had joined him, but the flagship was still out of touch and much anxiety was felt for her safety.

He, too, had received the vague reports about the *Scharnhorst* and *Gneisenau* and also one, more precise, that the *Emden*, with four colliers, had left Tsingtau on August 3 as soon as his back was turned, though in fact she did not sail till three days later. He had also heard that the *Leipzig* had left Mazatlan in Mexico, and that the Norddeutscher Lloyd liner *Yorck*, which was fitted for conversion as a cruiser, had left Yokohama on the 4th full of coal and provisions. His appreciation on these data differed from that of the Australian authorities, and was less wide of the mark. It was that Admiral von Spee would concentrate somewhere in the South Sea, and then either attack our trade in the South American area, or seek out the *Montcalm*, or return to Tsingtau. On the last hypothesis it was obviously his primary duty to bar the enemy access to their base. Still, it seemed extremely probable that both the *Emden* and *Yorck* would make for Yap, the German telegraph centre in the Pelew Group, and it was just within his power to provide for this eventuality as well as for barring the Admiral's return to Tsingtau.

By dint of great exertions the *Triumph* was ready for sea. Her manning had been a difficult question. As the crews of the demobilised gunboats were insufficient to complete her, it had been intended to fill up with native seamen. None, however, were found willing to serve in a ship of war, but the difficulty was quickly solved by an appeal to the sister service. By permission of General F. H. Kelly, commanding the troops in South China, the Admiral called for volunteers from the garrison; almost the whole of it wished to come forward, and eventually two officers, 100 men and six signallers were selected from the 2nd Battalion of the Duke of Cornwall's Light Infantry. By this display of the old spirit the *Triumph* was completed and Admiral Jerram was able to do what he wanted. Whether or not the *Emden* was making for Yap, the island was of the greatest importance as an intelligence centre, for not only did it possess a high-power wireless station, but it was in cable communication with Shanghai and so with Tsingtau, as well as directly with the Dutch islands and Rabaul in the Bismarck Archipelago. If, then, its wireless station could be destroyed at once the German operations must be seriously hampered. By steaming fifteen knots he calculated he could reach it before the *Emden* if she had colliers with her. It meant a big detour on the way to Tsingtau, and only the *Minotaur, Hampshire* and *Newcastle* had sufficient coal endurance to do it. But now that the battleship was ready for sea he could safely make his sweep with those three ships, while the *Triumph, Yarmouth* and *Dupleix* with five destroyers went directly up the trade route under Captain Fitzmaurice of the *Triumph* to establish a watch on Tsingtau and prevent colliers and merchant-cruisers getting out. For such a movement to succeed secrecy was essential, and for this reason on August 6, the day he started, he forbade the use of wireless. Consequently, although on August 9 he heard the *Australia* calling, he made no reply.

On August 11 as he approached his objective he was rewarded by capturing the German S.S. *Elsbeth* with 1800 tons of Government coal from Tsingtau to Yap. As a prize crew could not be spared and the weather was too bad to coal from her, she was sunk by gunfire. The capture, however, was in a measure disappointing. She was not one of the colliers which the *Emden* was believed to be escorting, and this and other indications left little doubt that both the *Emden* and the *Yorck* had gone to some other theatre. Still, he decided to carry on, being unable to divine that Admiral von Spee was, in fact, still waiting at Pagan for the *Emden* to join him.

By this time the *Hampshire* was so short of coal that the Admiral ordered her back to Hongkong with the *Elsbeth's* crew, and at 8 a.m. next morning (the 12th) he appeared before the Yap wireless station. A small party had just arrived there from Rabaul in the surveying vessel *Planet* to garrison the place. They were busy entrenching the landing place when Admiral Jerram appeared but were not seen by him. No landing was attempted, but after giving due warning for the operator to clear, he opened fire at 9.30. His 7·5 with lyddite at 4500 yards made short work. The second shot set fire to the buildings, and in a quarter of an hour the 200 feet steel trellis mast was down and the oil stores and whole station irretrievably burning. Although the *Emden* had eluded him, Admiral Jerram could be content with a piece of work valuable both to himself and Admiral Patey, and by 10 a.m. he was away again to rejoin Captain Fitz-maurice and the rest of his squadron.

The rendezvous was at the Saddle Islands off the mouth of the Yangtse, and in order to lose no chance of intercepting any commerce destroyers that might have come out of Tsingtau, his two ships proceeded by different routes. The *Emden*, in fact, though she did get away, had between the Admiral and Captain Fitzmaurice a fairly narrow escape. When on August 6, the day she returned from her cruise to the Korean Strait, she had left again in response to Admiral von Spee's call, she had with her a large tender, the *Marko-mannia*. The *Prinz Eitel Friedrich*, which had been manned as an armed merchant cruiser, left the same day with a convoy of supply ships. It was also on the 6th that Captain Fitzmaurice began to sweep northwards. On the 8th he reached the Saddle Islands, and as he started to coal there with all speed the *Emden*, about 100 miles away, was passing southwards between him and Quelpart. Her whereabouts was not unknown to him. Through the French wireless station at Shanghai he had word that at 10 a.m. on the 7th she had been sighted 120 miles south-east of Tsingtau. During the 8th he took in signals which seemed to place her sixty to eighty miles away, and next morning as soon as he could he made a sweep to the north-east. There was keen expectation. He actually crossed her track, but it was forty-eight hours after she had passed Quelpart, and nothing was seen of her or the *Prinz Eitel Friedrich* and her convoy. Still, he had now made good the ground as high as Shanghai and could advise all shipping to continue trading. This he did on the 9th, and next day as he turned back to his rendezvous at the Saddle Islands another vessel came out from Tsingtau. This was the Russian volunteer ship *Ryasan*, the *Emden's* prize, now converted as a merchant cruiser and renamed *Cormoran*. Two raiders had thus been fitted out in Far Eastern waters, but it does not seem that Germany had made special provision for arming such ships. In most cases, at least, they could only be armed at the expense of regular ships of war. In this case the *Prinz Eitel Friedrich* drew her armament and crew from the gunboats *Luchs* and *Tiger* and the *Ryasan* from the old *Cormoran*.

Though all the German squadron was thus at sea and unlocated, Admiral Jerram was now in a much stronger position. Besides watching Tsingtau, he was able on his return from Yap to establish patrols from Shanghai to Fuchau and Japan, and also by means of his armed merchant cruisers another from Hongkong to Singapore. He had thus less to fear from the enemy's auxiliary cruisers, and on August 10 his squadron was further increased by the two Russian cruisers *Askold* and *Zhemchug* being placed under his command. But what was of far more importance was that as he was leaving Yap he heard from the Admiralty that Japan intended to declare war that day upon Germany, and that as soon as she did so he was to open communications with the Japanese Commander-in-Chief. He was further told that he could now leave the protection of the trade north of Hong-kong to Japan, and concentrate his attention on co-operating with the Australian Admiral in trying to destroy Admiral von Spee's squadron. He therefore altered course for Hongkong in the *Minotaur*, but for the *Newcastle* there were other orders.

So strong was the position now in Chinese waters that it was felt that something could be done for the other side of the Pacific, where the situation was causing no little anxiety. On the west coast of America we had nothing but two sloops, *Shearwater* and *Algerine*. The naval base at Esquimalt had been taken over by the Canadian Government, and they maintained there the old light cruiser *Rainbow*. When war became imminent both sloops were on the Mexican coast, together with the Japanese cruiser *Idzumo*, the German light cruiser *Leipzig* and an American squadron under Admiral Howard.[1]

Owing to the disturbed state of the country there was some difficulty in getting the Warning Telegram through to our ships, but thanks to Admiral Howard the difficulty was surmounted, and on August 3 both sloops made away secretly for Esquimalt. Though they thus got clear of the dangerous Mexican waters they were far from safe, for there was still the *Nürnberg* unaccounted for. As we have seen, this ship— a sister of the *Leipzig*—had left San Francisco on July 21 for Honolulu. She arrived on the 27th, and sailed again the same day for an unknown destination. She had, in fact, been ordered to join Admiral von Spee. This, of course, was unknown to the Admiralty, and the prevailing impression was that both the *Leipzig* and *Nürnberg* would operate along the trade routes on the west coast of North America.[2]

Meanwhile, the two little sloops were toiling northwards against head seas which sometimes reduced the *Shearwater's* speed to a single knot, and nothing could be heard of them. Anxiety for their safety grew, and not only for theirs but also for that of Esquimalt. True, it had been strengthened by two submarines recently completed at Seattle for Chile, and these the Canadian Government had just purchased and placed at the disposal of the Admiralty, but till crews could be provided they were of no use. The *Rainbow*, however,

		Completed.	Tons.	Trial speed.	Guns.			
[1] *Rainbow*	(light cruiser)	1893	3,600	20·2	2	6″	6	4·7′
Idzumo	(armoured cruiser)	1900	9,750	22·0	4	8″	14	6″
Leipzig	(light cruiser)	1906	3,200	22·4	10	4·1″		

[2] According to Admiral Dick (p. 98) it was the intention that *Leipzig* should do this, her special objective being the Canadian Pacific " Empress " liners. She expected to arrange for a continuous supply of coal from San Francisco, but as she failed to do so, the plan of operations broke down.

was ready, and having also been placed at the Admiralty's disposal, she was ordered south to try to get touch with the *Leipzig* and protect the trade routes from Vancouver southward to the Equator. Though she was able to get to sea on August 3, the day the sloops left the Mexican coast, day after day went by and nothing more was heard of them. It was feared both were lost, and something had to be done for the station. For this reason the Admiralty on August 11 directed Admiral Jerram to send one of his light cruisers there by way of Yokohama, and he detached the *Newcastle*. So serious, however, did the situation appear, as nothing further was heard of either of the sloops or of the *Nürnberg*, that the following day he was directed to detach the *Hampshire* as well, as soon as ever Japan declared war.

For another reason the increase of the Allied force on the China Station by the intervention of Japan was specially opportune. From now onward Admiral Patey had his hands more than full with the Australian and New Zealand Expeditions which were being organised against the German possessions in the Bismarck Archipelago and Samoa, and Admiral Jerram had received orders to cover the passage of the troops. While the operation at Yap was proceeding, Admiral Patey was engaged in his raid on Simpson Harbour and Rabaul. On August 9, when Admiral Jerram first heard him calling, his ships were assembled at his first rendezvous south of Port Moresby, and there he explained to his captains the plan of operations. His intention was for the *Sydney* to go forward with the destroyers, and at dark to make a torpedo attack on anything that was found at Simpson Harbour. What he expected to find was the *Scharnhorst*, *Gneisenau* and *Nürnberg*, with possibly two armed surveying vessels, *Komet* and *Planet*. If nothing was there they would try the adjacent Matupi Harbour. If both places were empty they would land parties to destroy the wireless station which was supposed to be at Rabaul. The whole plan had been worked out locally without reference to the Admiralty, but no sooner were Admiral Patey's arrangements complete than there came to his hand a message from Whitehall to impress on him the importance of doing immediately just what he was engaged in doing. The telegram, no doubt, was sent to ensure that his attention should not be diverted to other calls. These the Admiralty knew to be imminent, though in fact nothing had yet reached him. He therefore could have no doubt how to proceed, and the programme was duly carried out.

But not a ship of any kind was found, nor, though parties were landed, could any trace of the wireless station be dis-

covered either at Rabaul or Herbertshöhe. He had therefore
to be content with destroying the Post Office and all telegraph
and telephonic communications. He did, however, capture a
vessel from Nauru, which was bringing gear and an engineer
to complete the wireless station. By this means he learnt
it was hidden far in the bush, and not in good working order.
Nothing more could be done without a landing force, and as
the ships required coaling he proceeded to return to his
rendezvous, searching the coasts on the way, and leaving the
Sydney to make a fresh attempt to find the wireless station.

It was not till he had completed his work that the call
reached him which the Admiralty had feared might distract
him from the paramount duty of seeking out the enemy's
ships and dealing with their centres of intelligence. That
night (August 12–13) he received from the Governor of New
Zealand a telegram to say that a force for the occupation of
Samoa was ready to start, and asking if the route was safe.
It was the first word he had heard of the expedition. The
Australian Naval Board, indeed, was expecting that his next
objective would be Nauru. Having found no colliers in the
neighbourhood of Herbertshöhe, Admiral Patey inclined to
believe that the pressure was growing too great for the Germans
and that they were moving away to Nauru, possibly by way
of Samoa, and that their destination was South America.
Here, again, he was on the right track. On August 12 the
Emden, with *Prinz Eitel Friedrich* and *Markomannia* joined
Admiral von Spee at Pagan Island. This same day, it
will be recalled, was the date on which it was first believed
Japan would commence hostilities, and up to this time it
would look as though the *Emden* was intended to form part
of the main squadron. But on the day the *Emden* joined,
Admiral von Spee heard of the coming Japanese ultimatum,
and whether or not she brought him fresh orders from home,
he detached her and her tender on a special mission to the
southward.[1] He then decided that it was too dangerous for
his force to remain at Pagan, and that he would proceed
towards the west coast of America where he would find coal
and supply facilities. His idea was to disappear for a time
in order to escape destruction from a superior force, cause
anxiety to the enemy, and reappear elsewhere when opportunity occurred to do good service. The enemy, he thought,
would be expecting him to return to Tsingtau, and out in the
Pacific it would be hard to find him. Once on the American

[1] According to Lieutenant von Mücke of the *Emden*, a not very trustworthy authority, she was detached at the suggestion of her commander
Captain von Müller.

coast he would have only inferior force to meet him : in Asiatic waters, on the other hand, the enemy would be in superior force. The *Australia* was his special apprehension. She alone, he considered, was superior to his whole squadron, and it was his plain duty to give her a wide berth.¹ On August 13 he could hear British wireless, as it seemed, not far off, and came to the conclusion that the German wireless station at Yap had been put out of action. That evening he sailed to the eastward for his next coaling place at Enivetok or Brown Atoll in the western extremity of the Marshall Group. Admiral Patey's appreciation was thus very near the truth, and believing what he did he could only reply to the New Zealand Government that an escort much stronger than the old " P " class cruisers of their squadron could supply was essential. But as he thoroughly approved of the project, he at once made arrangements for meeting the Expedition with the *Australia* and *Melbourne* 400 miles south of Suva in Fiji, and proceeded to Port Moresby to coal. His other two cruisers and the destroyers were to be left to co-operate with Admiral Jerram in case the Germans should by chance come to the westward by way of Batavia.

On August 16, however, before he could reach Port Moresby, he heard that the New Zealand expedition had already started. To the Admiralty it appeared that the route, at least as far as Suva, was sufficiently covered by the China and Australian Squadrons, and that the Expedition might safely proceed so far under escort of Captain Marshall's three light cruisers *Psyche*, *Philomel* and *Pyramus*, especially as the *Montcalm* had now been located at Suva and was under orders to take part in the operation instead of joining Admiral Jerram. As for Admiral Patey's squadron, the Admiralty plan was that the *Australia* should meet the Expedition at Suva, while the *Melbourne*, *Sydney* and *Encounter* looked after the Australian expedition for German New Guinea, which Admiral Patey now learnt was about to leave for Port Moresby. This, however, was a plan which, in view of his failure to locate the German Squadron, the Admiral could not endorse. He wished to take to Samoa the *Melbourne* and *Sydney* as well as his flagship. In Australia, however, so keen was the desire to strike the blow that had been prepared that a postponement of the attack on Rabaul was very unpalatable. Eventually, however, it was arranged by the Admiralty that Admiral Patey, with the *Australia* and *Melbourne* and also the *Montcalm*, should meet the New Zealand Expedition at Noumea while the *Sydney*

¹ Letter to his wife, August 18, 1914.

and *Encounter* escorted the Australian transports to Port Moresby in readiness to act at the earliest possible moment.

On August 22 the whole New Zealand expedition was assembled at Noumea; three days later it reached Suva, its last halting place, and by that time the whole situation in the Pacific had changed. We have seen that on the 12th when the two British Admirals appeared at Yap and Simpson Harbour they had been informed that Japan was coming into the war that day, and Admiral Jerram had redistributed his squadron accordingly. The event, however, was not so sudden. It was not till August 15 that Japan presented an ultimatum to Germany demanding the unconditional surrender of Kiao-chau, and it was not to expire for a week. The delay was unexpected and especially unwelcome as war had now begun with Austria, and two more possible commerce destroyers were added to the list, the *China* and *Silesia*, which were both at Shanghai. However, during the period of strained relations Japan undertook to place cruisers on the trade routes to protect British ships as well as their own. Still, it was a period of some difficulty for Captain Fitzmaurice, on whom lay the duty of watching Tsingtau. In order to communicate the vital intelligence to his Admiral he had had to throw out the *Dupleix* and *Yarmouth* to form a wireless chain, and though his squadron had been reinforced by the *Empress of Asia*, it was not till August 20, after the two detached cruisers had rejoined, that he was able to establish anything like a close watch on the German base.[1] He then at once captured four German steamships coming out of the port, in two of which were 8000 tons of coal, 100 head of cattle and sixteen German officers. He learnt that their destination was the Dutch East Indies, and on August 22, when it was certain that Germany would reject the Japanese demands, he moved away to leave a clear field for the Fleet of our new Ally. The last act of the British blockade was a bold effort of the destroyer *Kennet* to cut off a German destroyer that was making for the port at sunset on the 23rd. But she was out-paced, and not only did the enemy get away, but punished the *Kennet* so severely that she had a gun put out of action and lost three men killed and six wounded, two of whom subsequently died.

In the coming operations for the reduction of Tsingtau, it

---

[1] Considerable difficulty was found in manning the *Empress of Asia* and the other three merchant cruisers, *Empress of Russia*, *Empress of Japan* and *Himalaya*, but it was overcome again by General Kelly's help and that of the French. The crews, which were mainly R.N.R. men, were finally completed from the French Yangtse gunboats, R.G.A. and Pathan Sepoys.

had been agreed that British troops from Tientsin were to take part, together with the *Triumph* and a destroyer. The *Triumph*, therefore, proceeded to Wei-hai-wei, where she had to disembark her volunteers, as the regiment was under orders to proceed to India. The parting was with much regret, for the revival of the old practice had proved a success. The soldiers had put their hearts into their new duties and had rapidly become efficient members of the crew. In return for our assistance the Japanese placed at Admiral Jerram's disposal their fine armoured cruiser *Ibuki*, a more powerful ship than the *Triumph*, as well as the light cruiser *Chikuma*.[1] They also signified their intention of keeping the *Idzumo* on the North American coast, which enabled Admiral Jerram to cancel the *Hampshire*'s orders and recall her to his flag. By this time both the sloops had arrived safely at Esquimalt, where they were paid off, their crews proceeding to Halifax to man the Canadian cruiser *Niobe*. As for the *Newcastle*, she arrived the day the Japanese ultimatum expired, and her commander, Captain Powlett, took over the station as senior officer.

The news of the Japanese intervention reached Admiral Patey at Suva. As the north-western Pacific would now be closed to the Germans, his inference was that they would be forced either eastward to America or south-eastward towards his own convoy, his actual information being that they were probably either in the Mariana or the Marshall Islands, the nearest of which was little more than 1500 miles to the north-westward of Samoa. If, therefore, the expedition against that place was to continue, no risks could be taken, and he decided to carry on with his whole force. His conjecture, as was afterwards known, was very accurate. From August 19 to 22 Admiral von Spee was actually in the Marshall Islands at Brown Atoll. The day before he reached it he had heard from Nauru that the *Australia* and two cruisers had been sighted off Rabaul steering south. After coaling he moved to Majuro at the other end of the group. He was there on the 26th, having heard the previous day that Japan had declared war. At this anchorage he was joined by the *Cormoran* from Tsingtau with two more store ships. On his way to it he had detached the *Nürnberg* to Honolulu for further supplies, and to take letters and telegrams for transmission to the German Naval Staff and auxiliary supply bases. Early

	Completed.	Tons.	Trial speed.	Guns.		
[1] *Ibuki*	1910	14,600	20·8	4 12″	8 8″	14 4·7″
Chikuma	1912	4,950	26·8	8 6″		

on the 30th the German squadron sailed. But Admiral
von Spee did not intend to leave the Pacific untroubled.
With this object, and also in the hope of giving a false impression of his movements, he left behind him at Brown Atoll
the *Prinz Eitel Friedrich* and *Cormoran,* with orders to
operate against trade in Australian waters, while he himself
proceeded again eastward towards Christmas Island, just
south of Fanning Island. But Admiral Patey was at work
before him. On the morning of the 30th (Eastern time) the
New Zealand Expedition was before Apia, the capital of
Samoa. There was no resistance. At the Admiral's summons the place surrendered, and during the afternoon the
British flag was hoisted and the New Zealand troops landed.
Next day, having seen the new garrison installed, he left
with the *Australia, Melbourne* and *Montcalm* to pick up the
Australian Expedition, directing the two empty transports
and Captain Marshall's cruisers to go back to New Zealand,
where the contingent that was to proceed to Europe was
eagerly awaiting their arrival.

The first work which now lay before Admiral Patey with
the Australian Expedition was the seizure of Rabaul and
Herbertshöhe. Then, in accordance with the original plan,
a base was to be established there, and three expeditions
sent out to occupy Nauru, Yap and the adjacent island
of Angaur. So he informed Admiral Jerram on August 31
before leaving Samoa. Admiral Jerram being anxious, as
all naval opinion was, to seek out the enemy before any
further occupation of territory was attempted and before
the troops began to move to Europe, still wished to have the
Mariana and Marshall Islands searched, and being unable to
do it himself, he had asked his colleague if he would undertake
it. But this was out of Admiral Patey's power, for not only
had he the Herbertshöhe Expedition on hand, but he had
also been warned that before long his ships would be required
to escort homewards the large Australian contingent which
was rapidly being enrolled for Europe.

The inability of Admiral Jerram to make a sweep out
into the Pacific was due to his feeling compelled to concentrate his fighting force in the south-western part of his station,
and this necessity arose out of the situation that had developed
in the neighbouring East India waters. The station was very
inadequately furnished. Admiral Peirse, who commanded it,
had nothing but the battleship *Swiftsure,* two light cruisers,
Dartmouth and *Fox,* and three sloops, *Alert, Odin* and *Espiègle,*
one of which was required in the Persian Gulf, and one was
under orders to stand by to complete the crew of the *Triumph,*

The intention had been to reinforce him with two new ships, *Falmouth* and *Nottingham*, but the demand for light cruisers in home waters was so great that they could not be spared. Based at Dar-es-Salaam was the fast German cruiser *Königsberg*. Though actually within the Cape station, she was an immediate menace to his own, nor was the Cape Commander-in-Chief, Rear-Admiral King-Hall, in a position to deal with her effectively.

His force consisted of three comparatively old and slow light cruisers, *Hyacinth* (flag), *Astræa* and *Pegasus*.[1] When the preliminary warning went out he was on a cruise to Mauritius. He at once concentrated his squadron at Diego Suarez, and as there was no other enemy ship on his station except the gunboat *Eber*, which had got away from Cape Town on July 30, he proceeded north for Zanzibar to look after the *Königsberg*. But seeing how Admiral King-Hall was situated when the period of strained relations began, Admiral Peirse considered it necessary to take steps for shadowing the *Königsberg* himself, and to this end he ordered the *Dartmouth* to get away out of the station to Zanzibar as soon as she was out of dockyard hands. There was a standing order that station limits were not to fetter urgent movements of this nature, and in fact he was only anticipating an order from the Admiralty which reached him a little later.

The necessity for his action was quickly apparent. On July 31, as Admiral King-Hall was coming north, the *Pegasus*, which had been sent ahead, sighted the *Königsberg* steaming out of Dar-es-Salaam, but the German cruiser quickly showed her a clean pair of heels and disappeared. Two hours later the *Hyacinth* came across her in the dark and was equally unable to keep touch for lack of speed. As it was impossible to tell where she would go, Admiral King-Hall decided he could not leave his cardinal focal area unprotected. He therefore decided to return to the Cape and leave the *Astræa* and *Pegasus* to carry on for Zanzibar.

Here, then, was another case of getting touch with an enemy cruiser just before war was declared and losing her from not having sufficient speed. In this instance it was peculiarly unfortunate, since there was no ship really capable of dealing with the *Königsberg* immediately available. The orders for the *Dartmouth* stood, but she was still in dock at

	Completed.	Tons.	Trial speed.	Guns.	
[1] *Hyacinth*	1900	5,600	19·2	11 6″	
Astræa	1894	4,360	19·7	2 6″	8 4·7″
Pegasus	1898	2,135	21·2	8 4″	
Königsberg	1907	3,350	24·0	10 4·1″	

Bombay and not expected to be ready for sea till August 8. It was further known that four large German liners, believed to be armed as commerce destroyers, were moving within the station, and Admiral Peirse had nothing left to deal with them except two of the Indian Marine ships, *Hardinge* and *Dufferin*, which by a long-standing arrangement incorporated in the War Book were transferred to the Royal Navy on the issue of the War Telegram.

In these circumstances it was not easy for him to decide how best to dispose his force. The three principal focal points in his area were Aden, where the Mediterranean station joined his own, Singapore, where almost the whole of the Far Eastern trade and much of the Australian streamed through the Strait of Malacca and, thirdly, the waters south of Colombo, where most of the trade routes converged. Between the two latter it was particularly difficult for the Admiral to choose his position. On the one hand, the Colombo area was most exposed to the *Königsberg*, and on the other Singapore was menaced by Admiral von Spee's squadron. He knew, when in the first days of the war this squadron was believed to be concentrating in the vicinity of New Guinea, that his colleague on the China Station had been directed to concentrate at Hongkong and would have his attention fixed primarily on Tsingtau. There was nothing, therefore, to prevent Admiral von Spee breaking into the Indian area through the Strait of Malacca or by the south of Sumatra, and it was in the Singapore area that Admiral Peirse saw his best position. Accordingly, in response to an inquiry from the Admiralty, he informed them on the first day of the war that he was proceeding to Singapore in the *Swiftsure*, and leaving the *Espiègle* to do her best with the Colombo area. The Admiralty, however, knowing that Admiral Patey was concentrating the Australian squadron to deal with the New Guinea area, informed him that the *Swiftsure* would not be required at Singapore. Admiral Peirse, therefore, took up the Colombo position and proceeded on August 6 to patrol the route to Aden in his flagship, leaving the *Espiègle* to watch the focal point, and here, three days later, she was joined by the *Fox*. By August 7 the Bombay dockyard had succeeded in completing the *Dartmouth*—that is, a day ahead of time—but the Cape Squadron ships were now in the north of the station and there was no chance of finding the *Königsberg* near Dar-es-Salaam. She was therefore ordered next day (August 8) to proceed to Aden and patrol the Aden–Colombo route in concert with the flagship.

That same morning the general situation was improved by a smart piece of work done by the *Astræa*. We have seen how, when Admiral King-Hall on receipt of the Warning Telegram had turned back for the Cape, he had directed the *Astræa* and *Pegasus* to watch Dar-es-Salaam. This was specially important since, although the *Königsberg* had got away, the *Tabora*, a liner of 8000 tons, had been located there. She was one of the four possible commerce destroyers which were supposed to be somewhere on the Colombo-Suez line and which were a source of considerable anxiety to Admiral Peirse. On July 30 she had put into Zanzibar, where it was found that she had on board an aeroplane and its pilot, and from there she had gone into Dar-es-Salaam. Captain Sykes of the *Astræa* was in charge of the detachment, and as soon as war was declared he was ordered, in conformity with the line we were taking everywhere, to close the port and to destroy its wireless station by gun fire. This was done early on August 8, and as the Germans themselves sank their floating dock to bar the entrance of the harbour, the *Tabora* was shut in and the place rendered useless as a base for the *Königsberg* for some time at least.

One danger point had thus been rendered innocuous, and the arrangements of the East Indian station were considerably facilitated. But not for long, for the day after the work was done everything was upset by the need to provide escort for troops. The critical diplomatic situation at Constantinople rendered imperative immediate steps for the protection of the Suez Canal, and a division of the Indian Army was to proceed to Egypt at the earliest possible moment. Moreover, the operation which the Oversea Attack Committee had projected for the reduction of German East Africa was also to be taken in hand, and would require further escort and support. The force for Egypt was expected to be ready to leave on August 15, and on the 9th Admiral Peirse was told that the *Swiftsure* and *Dartmouth* were to return with all speed to Bombay and that all the Indian Marine ships were to assemble there. Of these there were now five, for besides the *Dufferin* and *Hardinge*, three others, *Northbrook*, *Minto* and *Dalhousie*, were being armed for his command and were to be ready by the 15th. It was the same call which had compelled the Admiralty to detach the *Black Prince* and *Duke of Edinburgh* from the Mediterranean to Aden in order to take over the Egyptian convoy from Admiral Peirse. For trade protection he therefore had nothing left but the *Fox* and *Espiègle* in the Colombo area, while that of Singapore had to be left to the old French torpedo gun-vessel *D'Iberville* and three French destroyers, which were then searching for the *Geier* in the vicinity of the Malacca Strait.[1]

Thus, although the main Indian convoy from various causes was unready to sail till August 28—nearly a fortnight later than the Home Authorities hoped—from the 10th onwards Admiral Peirse had to devote all his attention to the Bombay-Aden route, and the Colombo and Singapore areas were at the mercy of the *Königsberg*. Hence, also, Admiral Jerram's anxiety to move to the Malay end of his station when Admiral Patey, having ascertained that the German Pacific Squadron was not concentrating at New Guinea, moved away for Samoa. Admiral King-Hall was equally unable to give help, for he soon had to call the *Astræa* to the Cape to assist him in escorting homewards the Cape Garrison, for whose speedy return to England the military situation in France was urgently crying.   On all sides, in fact, the paramount military necessity for completing the Imperial Concentration in the European theatre was overriding naval needs, cutting into the Admiralty system of commerce protection and forcing them to submit to the subversion of their most cherished strategical traditions.   From Wei-hai-wei to Quebec it v is everywhere the same, and the strain continued to grow more tense. The primary need of restoring the situation in France could not be denied, and the navy loyally submitted, with now and then a protesting growl as some new and unexpected call for convoy strained the tension almost beyond their power to endure.

Such demands were frequent, for besides getting home the Imperial Garrisons their places had to be filled from elsewhere.   Thus, when on the Indian station the Admiralty were groaning over the fortnight's inactivity that had been forced on them by the premature call for convoy at Bombay, there came without warning a demand for escort to take an Indian Battalion to Singapore and another to Mauritius. Every draft was met, but not without paying the penalty. The risk that was being run was emphasised when on August 21 it became known that on the 6th the Hall liner *City of Winchester* had been captured in the Gulf of Aden by the *Königsberg*, and a week later had been sunk in Khorya Morya Bay on the south Arabian coast. The German cruiser must have had a narrow escape from the *Dartmouth*, who went on to Aden after her recall before returning to Bombay, but by the time the loss was known there was nothing available to search for the intruder and she got clear away.

	Completed.	Tons.	Trial speed.	Guns.	
[1] *D'Iberville*	1893	952	21·5	1 4″	3 9-pdrs.

Whether by luck or good arrangement the *Königsberg* must have received a certain amount of intelligence. The German S.S. *Zieten*, which left Colombo on July 29, met her on August 7 at Makalla on the Arabian coast, where she first conducted her prize, and there took away part of the captured crew to Mozambique. The same day the *Ostmark* also met her there and went on to Massawa. The *Sudmark* communicated with her in the Gulf of Aden, and at Khorya Morya the *Goldenfels* was with her and took away the rest of the *City of Winchester's* crew to Sabang. All these ships got clear away before we were able to occupy the Aden area, but the *Zieten* had her wireless removed and her crew disarmed by the Portuguese authorities at Mozambique, and another ship, the *Essen*, was served the same way at Lourenço Marques.

It was just after the loss of the *City of Winchester* became known that the Japanese ultimatum to Germany expired and Admiral Jerram was able to move down to the Singapore end of his station, where he would be in the best position to support his colleague should the German Pacific Squadron break into the Indian Ocean. He had indeed some reason to believe that Admiral von Spee was coming to the back of Sumatra with the intention of using the Dutch islands as a base of operations against our trade. In this he was not altogether wrong. For this was precisely the special mission on which the *Emden* and *Markomannia* had been detached at Pagan Island. On August 23, the day the Japanese commenced hostilities, the *Emden* had just passed through the Molucca Passage, and by the end of the month was steaming westward along the south coast of Java preparatory to making her famous raid into the Indian Ocean. The only error in Admiral Jerram's appreciation was that he expected his opponent to carry out the operation with his whole force. Accordingly, after having disposed his merchant cruisers and the Russian ships to maintain a patrol of the trade route, he concentrated the rest of the Allied Squadron at Singapore and sent a message to Admiral Patey suggesting that the Australian Squadron might search the Mariana and Marshall Islands in case the enemy was not coming west. But that was out of the question. Admiral Patey, as we shall see, had barely time to carry out the occupation of Herbertshöhe before he, too, was entangled in the military concentration and powerless for any other duty.

CHAPTER XI

WE have now traced what may be regarded as the deployment of the fleet all over the world so far as it could be carried with the material available. All stations were short of fast light cruisers owing to what was regarded as the prior claim of the Grand Fleet on the new ones as soon as they left dockyard hands, but most stations had received their battleship supports as well as their armed merchant cruisers, of which there were now seventeen in commission. Thus by the beginning of September the general deployment was practically complete, and the war at sea began to take on the dead and uneventful character with which our ancestors were so familiar and which public opinion at first found hard to reconcile with its expectations.

Scarcely anywhere, indeed, had the expected happened. The great opportunity for an organised attack on our trade by means of armed merchant cruisers had passed by unused; and in home waters there had been no attempt to stop the passage of the Expeditionary Force to France either by direct attack during its transit or indirectly by a raid on our shores. It was this inertness of the High Seas Fleet that was the greatest surprise to naval officers. Knowing how German doctrine was saturated with the spirit of offence, and knowing well what they themselves would have done in like circumstances, they found the enemy's inaction difficult to explain. Yet it was but a repetition of what occurred in the old French wars when France had the inferior fleet. By massing an overwhelming concentration at the vital point the Admiralty had made sure of the command of the Narrow Seas upon which their whole system was built up. They had also made sure of a crushing decision on " the day," but incidentally they had made it inevitable that " the day " would be indefinitely postponed. All experience shows that in conditions such as our home concentration had set up an enemy will never risk a battle except for some vital end

[1] See Map 1 in case.

157

which cannot be obtained in any other way.   For the Germans
the stoppage of the transit of our Expeditionary Force did
not fulfil that condition.   Believing, as their High Command
certainly did, that they could make an end of our few divisions
in their first rush, it was obviously better for them that our
Army should expose itself to that rush on a naked flank
than that it should be held in reserve at home where it could
strike at any time and never be struck.   In any case it was
far easier for them to deal with our Expeditionary Force on
land than upon the sea, and the interruption of its passage
was certainly not an object for which Germany could wisely
risk any substantial part of her fleet.   Nor must it be forgotten that since the German High Command certainly
believed the war would be a short one—too short for our
blockade to make itself felt—and that they then also regarded Russia as their most formidable enemy, they were
more immediately concerned with the command of the
Baltic than with that of the North Sea.

During the last half of August its importance had declared
itself in a startling manner.   Beyond all expectation Russia
had found herself able to invade East Prussia in a devoted
attempt to relieve the alarming pressure upon France.   The
operation was undertaken by two armies under Generals
Rennenkampf and Samsonov, the first moving from the
Niemen and the other through the Masurian Lake district
from the Narev.   The opening was a complete success.
Between the 16th and 20th the weak German forces were
defeated at Gumbinnen on the Berlin–Petrograd railway and
at Frankenau, south-east of Königsberg.   The result was
that the German armies were split in two, part retiring
in haste westward and part to the sea at Königsberg.   The
Russians quickly pushed as far as Allenstein in the western
part of the Masurian marshes, and by the 25th General
Samsonov's cavalry patrols had reached the Vistula.   Here
the tide suddenly turned.   The Holy Land of the Prussian
aristocracy had been profaned, a flood of panic-stricken
fugitives was carrying the alarm into the heart of the kingdom,
and, by exertions no less remarkable than those of the Russians,
the Germans quickly had an army together under General
von Hindenburg to purge the sacrilege.   By August 26, near
the classic battle-ground of Eylau, he had contact with General
Samsonov at Tannenburg between Allenstein and Soldau,
and by a flank movement to his left he succeeded during the
next two days in involving the Russians hopelessly in the
marshes.   By August 31 they were completely cut in two,
and though one half succeeded in escaping the net, the other

was annihilated, leaving, it is said, some 90,000 prisoners in German hands. Having thus dealt with Samsonov, Hindenburg turned on Rennenkampf, but here he failed of complete success. Rennenkampf succeeded in getting his army away, but not without a loss of perhaps 30,000 prisoners and a large part of his artillery. Thus for the time the danger was met, but in view of the shock which the sudden activity of the Russians had given to the confidence of the Germans and the evidence that their offensive power had been underestimated, the Baltic, with its all-important ports of Dantzig and Königsberg, asserted itself in all its old historic force as a vital element in the position.

There can be little doubt, then, that the policy they adopted in their Home Waters was the most correct for them and the most annoying for ourselves. It was a policy, so far as their fleet's activities indicated its nature, akin to that by which the French had so often and skilfully wearied our superior strength. The High Seas Fleet was simply kept in being while our fleets were harassed and our command disputed by every form of minor attack which modern development in material had placed within the Germans' reach. In the old French wars such minor attacks had been confined to privateering, with an occasional raid by a flying squadron, but that system could never be of any avail except against our trade : it tended in no way to break down our fighting superiority. But now all this was changed. By the enormously increased power of minor attack Germany could at least hope to reduce our margin of superiority so low as eventually to warrant her taking the offensive. Her policy had, therefore, even greater justification and greater promise than that which the French had been wont to adopt in analogous circumstances. Where France for redressing the balance of force could only look to the weather and the wear and tear of our long blockades, Germany had the minelayer and the submarine. It is with a legitimate pride that we look back upon the silent endurance with which the seamen of the old era clung on to their thankless task year after year through storm and sickness, but no one can feel aright the part our modern Navy has played unless he remembers how they, too, had to cling on in face of dangers beyond anything that Hawke or Cornwallis or Nelson had to face. It was the humour of the German Press to picture our Grand Fleet lying always securely in some inaccessible harbour. How far was it from the truth !

By the end of August, on the eve of the Heligoland action, the Admiralty became aware of how the enemy were anticipating our minor offensive by a form of attack which, at the Hague Conference of 1907, they had solemnly deprecated in the name of German humanity. The minefields which were then discovered off the Tyne and the Humber were at first believed by the Admiralty to have been laid surreptitiously by trawlers under neutral colours, and this belief, though responsible naval officers doubted the capacity of small craft for the work, was confirmed by reports from neutral sources. The Germans lost no time in publicly declaring that the mines were laid by ships of the Imperial Navy, and there is now no doubt that it was so. Illegitimate as was their action, judged by the hitherto sacred traditions of naval warfare, it is clear they were embarking on a considered minor offensive with the probable object of forcing the Grand Fleet into some such hazardous enterprise as they wished to see it attempt.

A raid on the fishing fleet off the Dogger Bank was actually carried out on August 21-22 by three light cruisers, the *Strassburg, Rostock* and *Hamburg*, with the 6th Destroyer Flotilla and three submarines. A fourth light cruiser, the *Mainz*, was in support 90 miles west of Heligoland, and three battle cruisers had steam up in the Schillig Roads. An unsuccessful attack was made on the *Rostock* by one submarine *D 5*; but eight British trawlers were sunk and their crews, 90 men, were taken as prisoners to Wilhelmshaven. On the 24th, encouraged by impunity, a similar force started again, in two groups, one for the Humber (*Mainz, Nautilus,* 3rd Destroyer Half Flotilla), the other for the Tyne (*Stuttgart, Albatross,* 11th Half Flotilla). In making for Flamborough Head which was again their landfall, the Tyne group encountered another fleet of fishing craft about 70 miles east of the Humber. Ten of them were sunk by the destroyers, while the cruisers carried on to the westward. Later in the day the Humber group sank six more trawlers. Thirty miles off the Humber, where it will be remembered the *Invincible* and *New Zealand* had just arrived, the *Mainz* laid a minefield, while the *Stuttgart* and *Albatross* laid another the same distance off the Tyne. The whole force then retired without having been seen by our Coast Patrols.

The work appears to have been done in the early hours of August 26. The first victim was a Danish fishing vessel which was blown up that evening in the Tyne minefield. On the same day also the Humber field was located by the *City of Bristol* trawler, which exploded a mine in her nets. Thus the discovery was made in time to prevent a disaster to the two battle cruisers who were under orders for the

Heligoland raid, and who now proceeded to their assigned rendezvous round the south of the dangerous area. Sweeping operations were quickly set on foot, but till the extent of the minefields could be definitely ascertained both the Tyne and the Humber were unsafe as bases, and for this reason after the Heligoland action the two battle cruisers were ordered to the Forth. So much the Germans gained in military advantage and so far their unprecedented action was justified by what they called military necessity. In a short time a number of merchant and fishing vessels, the gunboat *Speedy* and two minesweeping drifters had been sunk. Meanwhile a minesweeping patrol of thirty-two trawlers, based on the Humber, had been formed, but after these losses the Admiralty directed that the minefields were to be left alone and sweeping operations confined to clearing a swept channel along the coast.

The minefields, indeed, were soon recognised as a blessing in disguise. The main reason why the Germans had not been detected was that by the War Orders the local Patrol Flotillas were to be kept concentrated and ready to deal with attempts to raid our coast. As the Germans themselves had barred to so great an extent the approaches to the Tyne and Humber districts, it was now possible to use these flotillas to extend the system of continuous coastwise patrol which had been organised for the East Anglian zone after the affair of the *Königin Luise*, and eventually the German minefields were not only left untouched but were actually reinforced by our own minelayers.

Had this form of minor offensive stood alone it would have been comparatively easy to contend with, but it was supplemented by an ever-increasing activity on the part of the enemy's submarines. Both methods of attack were forms of hostility of which we had no experience, and with which the fleet itself could not deal; they could only be met by small craft specially equipped for the work. Already by September 1, besides the regular flotillas and minesweepers, there were in commission some 250 trawlers, drifters and similar craft, besides seaplanes, entirely devoted to meeting the submarine and mine attack. Even so they were proving all too few and were being rapidly increased in number, but as yet they had been given little organisation, and for a long time to come they would be unequal to the work they had to do. The duties of the several classes of these craft were to sweep for mines, to guard the swept channels, to patrol for submarines and examine vessels to see that they were not being employed as submarine tenders or as mine-layers.

But swarming as the North Sea was with neutral traffic of all kinds, they were too few to examine more than a tithe even of the ships they sighted, and for all that could be done submarines were continually being reported in all directions.

At Scapa the Grand Fleet was given no rest. In the old days when gales drove our fleet from its station it had at least a secure port in which it could enjoy complete relaxation, but Admiral Jellicoe had none. Except for such makeshifts as the fleet itself could provide, Scapa was still an undefended anchorage; by three or four channels it was possible for submarines to enter, nor could the fleet even go in or out until the waters it had to pass had been elaborately swept. On August 24 the Committee specially appointed to consider the defence of the anchorage had recommended, with certain modifications, a scheme drawn up the year before. It provided for increasing the armament and for closing some of the entrances with blockships and others with mines. But in the fleet it was considered that the tidal streams were so strong that the danger of mines getting adrift forbade their use, and that blockships must be used everywhere.

A typical incident which occurred on September 1 will give the best idea of what the strain of this insecurity meant. The three Dreadnought squadrons with the light cruisers and a few other ships were at anchor in the Flow at three hours' notice preparing for a new movement. It was a typical Scapa day; the desolate anchorage was shrouded in a driving wet mist, and all conditions were favourable for a surprise attack. About 6 p.m., when dusk was beginning to add to the gloom and the strain of the look-out was more than usually exacting, the *Falmouth*, near the north-eastern entrance, was suddenly seen to be firing. Shortly afterwards she ceased, and reported that she had seen a periscope inside the anchorage and believed she had sunk a submarine. The report was not entirely credible, but in any case the risk was too great to run, and the Commander-in-Chief resolved to get to sea. While steam was being raised the *Drake*, to the westward, also reported a submarine, one or two other ships fired, and the destroyers were hunting feverishly all over the Flow. In the last of the twilight the whole fleet went out and returned again at sunrise. Subsequent investigations made it fairly certain that it had been a false alarm. On several occasions ships had fired on seals, which while swimming in a bad light were easily mistaken for periscopes, and later information proved that no submarine had entered the harbour.

Still, true or false it made little difference. For so

stealthy was the form of attack which the Germans were
pursuing, that false alarms and unfounded reports were
inevitable and must be taken seriously till they were proved
to be untrue.   The strain was therefore none the less continuous, nor was any relaxation to be expected till Scapa was
adequately protected and the new-born system of floating
defence perfected.   Till that time came Admiral Jellicoe
looked for security in almost continuous activity at sea.   The
movement for which he was preparing when the alarm of
September 1 took place was a full strength sweep of the
North Sea in combination with the Southern Force in hopes
of catching the enemy's submarines and mine-layers as they
made their way home.   The Admiralty, however, who had
other operations in view, requested him to defer the movement, and as he had been warned by them that they had
information of a cruiser and submarine raid which was about
to be made from the Baltic on his base, he substituted a
sweep to the Skagerrak to endeavour to intercept the threatened expedition.   The sweep was carried out as planned by
the cruisers and destroyers with the battle fleet in support,
but nothing was found, and on September 5 he took the
battle fleet into his alternative base at Loch Ewe to coal.

This same day we suffered our first naval loss from
submarine attack.   The victim was the flotilla leader
Pathfinder (Captain Martin Leake, commanding the Forth
Destroyer Patrol), lost with nearly all hands off St. Abb's
Head.   She went down in four minutes, and at first it was
reported to be a mine.   But Captain Leake, who though
wounded was saved, made it clear that it must have been a
torpedo from a submarine which probably exploded the
magazine.[1]   The means already adopted for dealing with the
trouble were clearly insufficient.   In seas so thick with traffic
the enemy by using false colours could sow mines as they
pleased almost with impunity, and to those who believed
that this was the method employed there seemed no adequate
remedy short of closing the whole of the East Coast ports
to traffic and also forbidding fishing in the same area; but this
remedy was regarded as worse than the disease, and it was
decided to rely on the existing system in increased force
and with better organisation.   So much at any rate was
rendered necessary by the skill and boldness with which the
enemy's submarines were being handled, particularly in and
about the Forth, where Admiral Lowry reported that his
existing force was being worn out by almost incessant patrolling.   During September, though the patrol boats had been

---

[1] Subsequently it was ascertained that the attack was made by *U 21.*

attacked nine or ten times, one submarine was all they could claim. Stalking by submarines had proved ineffective, and it was clear that surface vessels, more numerous, faster and better armed, were the only radical cure.

It was as the unwelcome news of the *Pathfinder's* loss reached him that Admiral Jellicoe received instructions from the Admiralty for the movement they wished him to make. They had by no means despaired of forcing the High Seas Fleet to action, and their hope had been increased by learning from prisoners taken in the recent Heligoland action that the Germans had then intended to use their battle cruisers, though they had not been able to get out in time. It was possible, therefore, that a repetition of the movement supported by the whole Grand Fleet might lead to a decision.

The great retreat on land had just terminated beyond the Marne, the Germans had been drawn by General Joffre into just the position he required for an offensive return, and the moment had come for throwing every available man into the conflict if the failure of the German opening was to be turned against them. The transports conveying the British VIth Division to the new base at St. Nazaire were to begin moving on September 8, and at dawn on the 7th the battle fleet left Loch Ewe, but there was no connection between the two operations, and there is no trace of the Commander-in-Chief having received any information about the sailing of the division. The transport line was patrolled by the French cruisers, and the Channel Fleet was thus left free to take part in the main combination by moving up in support of the Southern Force. In the morning of the 10th all units were in position, and the Harwich flotillas carried out the raid into the Bight. The conditions were ideal for the Germans to accept action close to their base and with full advantage of their torpedo craft. It was a hot, still day with a haze and glare that brought visibility very low and the Commander-in-Chief considered it inadvisable to attempt a closer approach to the enemy's base. If ever the Germans had a chance—and a fairly safe chance—of dealing the kind of blow they wanted it was then. Yet not a ship stirred—not even a destroyer came out, and nothing was seen except a cordon of apparently neutral vessels 150 miles from Heligoland that were believed, erroneously, to have warned the Germans of the presence of the battle fleet. Accordingly, after coming down within 100 miles of Heligoland Admiral Jellicoe broke up the combination and led the Grand Fleet north again. It was thought that the Germans had submarines on his line of retreat, and the *Zeelandia* claimed to have sunk one, but this was not substantiated.   Owing to the bad visibility and the shortage of aircraft the enemy did not even know that the Grand Fleet was at sea.   Meanwhile the VIth Division had been moving without interruption, and by the 11th was safely landed at St. Nazaire.

If the German war direction found no energy to spare for taking action with the fleet it is no matter for wonder. While Admiral Jellicoe was carrying out his provocative sweep they were reeling amazed under the blows which brought their whole war plan to the ground.   On September 3 the Russians entered Lemberg.   Shortly afterwards the Germans on the Marne suddenly discovered a new French army on their right beyond the British Force ; on the 9th as the Grand Fleet swept down the North Sea to take up its position for supporting the raid into the Bight and the Channel Fleet moved up to meet it, General Joffre was brilliantly breaking through the German centre on the Marne, and next afternoon as Admiral Jellicoe turned north again the shattered German line was in full retreat on th Aisne.

Though the covering movement of the Grand Fleet had failed to bring about an action and the prospect of getting a decision against the High Seas Fleet seemed more remote than ever, our minor offensive, which we were incessantly carrying on by means of submarines, was more successful. At midnight on September 12, as Admiral Jellicoe returned to his base, *E 9* (Lieutenant-Commander Max Horton) was lying on the bottom at 120 feet 6 miles south-south-west of Heligoland.   At daybreak she rose and at once sighted a light cruiser less than two miles away.   The weather, which had been thick, was clearing, and she immediately attacked.   Two torpedoes were fired at a range of about 600 yards, and as *E 9* dived one explosion was heard.   Rising again, she could see the cruiser had stopped, with a heavy list to starboard, but shots from an unseen vessel splashed round the submarine, and Lieutenant-Commander Horton dived once more.   When, an hour later, he came up to see the result there was nothing but four or five trawlers where the cruiser had been.   The lost ship proved to be the *Hela*, whose fate was afterwards officially admitted by the German Admiralty.[1]   All the rest of the day *E 9* was kept down by destroyers, but was able to charge her batteries during the night.   Next day when she rose to reconnoitre nothing but trawlers were to be seen, and after suffering from heavy seas which made it impossible either to proceed on the surface or

[1] *Hela*, 1896; 2004 tons; 19·5 knots (designed); 2 15-pdrs. 4 4-pdrs.

rest on the bottom, Lieutenant-Commander Horton brought his boat safely back to Harwich, having fully retaliated for the *Pathfinder's* loss.

The military reverses of the Germans produced the inevitable reactions at sea. Their attention became fixed on the Baltic. Here they had recently had warning that they could not yet regard it as a German lake. In the last week of August one of their best light cruisers, the *Magdeburg*, a sister of the *Breslau*, while operating with destroyers at the entrance of the Gulf of Finland, took the ground on the Island of Odensholm and was there caught by the *Pallada* and *Bogatuir* and destroyed. The importance of the Baltic as a military highway for Germany was now so great that the recurrence of such incidents could not be risked, and it was soon known that the High Seas Fleet, or a considerable part of it, was occupied in covering the coastwise transport of troops and supplies to East Prussia. The moment was, therefore, favourable for resting the Grand Fleet and making good the minor defects which had developed by its almost continual cruising. Instructions to this effect were issued, and the occasion was also seized by the First Lord to hold a conference with the War Staff and the chief officers of the fleet to consider future plans. It was fixed to take place at Loch Ewe on September 17, and till then all but the routine cruiser patrols were suspended. Amongst other questions discussed was the possibility of assisting the Russians to dispute the command of the Baltic by sending them some of our submarines, and so obviously desirable was this for the common cause that measures were set on foot for ascertaining how far it was feasible. There was also the question of meeting the German method of warfare by similar stealthy means. The Commander-in-Chief, finding the device of stopping trade and fishing on our eastern coast was impracticable, had proposed an extensive system of offensive mining in the open sea. But with so much detestation was this practice regarded by the Admiralty that they still held back from adopting it. Moreover, they still clung to their old creed of free manœuvre in the open sea, and any measure that tended to curtail that freedom was too much against the old tradition to be adopted till all other means had failed.

So in spite of all the insidious dangers that surrounded it, the Grand Fleet had to settle down patiently to its hold on the north-about Passage. The actual work of intercepting ships was mainly done by Admiral de Chair with the 10th Cruiser Squadron which formed the Northern Patrol between the Shetlands and the coast of Norway. The Grand Fleet cruiser squadrons which worked from Cromarty and Rosyth formed a cordon more to the south, thus screening the Battle Fleet and constituting a second blockade line. In this duty, the older battleships, especially those of the "Duncan" class, also assisted from time to time. So heavy and complex was the administrative work of this quasi-blockade that it had been found to be beyond the power of the Base Admiral to deal with it. The bulk of it still fell upon the Commander-in-Chief, and to relieve him, in the first week in September the post of Admiral of the Orkneys and Shetlands was created. Under the Commander-in-Chief he was to be responsible in the islands for naval defence, naval establishments, and naval shore duties. The Base Admiral would be under his command, and the Admiral of the Coast of Scotland became henceforth a separate and co-ordinate authority, with no responsibility for the islands. Vice-Admiral The Hon. Sir Stanley C. J. Colville was appointed to the new command, and took it over directly after the Staff Conference at Loch Ewe. The need of such an appointment was the more pressing since the tendency was, under the exigencies of war, for Scapa Flow to pass from the status of a mere war-anchorage to that of a flying base, and to increase its powers of dealing with repairs it had already been decided to send up the old "Fisgards" which had been fitted as workshops for training boy artificers at Portsmouth. After careful inspection and special preparation they had been pronounced fit to make the voyage, and on September 16 they started in tow of two tugs. They were to proceed west-about, but next day they encountered a gale which forced them to seek refuge. *Fisgard I* managed to get into Plymouth later on, but the *Fisgard II* was not so fortunate. She made for Portland, but was taking in water through her hawse-pipes very badly. As there was no way for it to escape she was soon in serious distress, and before she could reach the shelter of the Bill she foundered, with the loss of twenty-three out of the sixty-four naval and dockyard ratings by whom she was manned. Thus the full equipment of the Flow to meet the needs of the Grand Fleet was still further postponed. A further loss which it suffered at this time was the fine armed merchant cruiser *Oceanic* of the Northern Patrol, which on September 8 ran aground in the Shetlands and became a total wreck.

CHAPTER XII

By the middle of September it seemed that the part of the
Navy in the war, so far as the European theatre was concerned, was to be confined to the weary and precarious watch
to which it had settled down, and that its activities were to
have little direct connection with the main operations on the
Continent. The centre of military energy had drifted far
away from the sea, and never, perhaps, since Blenheim had
our army in a great war seemed so entirely divorced from
the fleet. Yet so abiding are the advantages of the connection that the divorce was scarcely complete when the army
began to look to the distant fleet and call for assistance.

The situation which had arisen and was to develop rapidly
out of the battle of the Marne was one of the most revolutionary as well as the most permanently dominating of the
many unexpected features which the war was destined to
assume. The pursuit of the Germans from the Marne had
been checked at the River Aisne sufficiently to allow them to
dig themselves in on the heights north of the river, and by
September 16 General Joffre had recognised that the enemy's
new front could not be forced with the resources he had at
his disposal. On that day, therefore, he decided to change
his plans and endeavour to turn their western flank, which
was then about Noyon, with General Maunoury's army—
the same that had turned the flank on the Marne. It is
possible that he foresaw that with the inferior force he had
the movement was not likely to be a complete success. The
Germans would probably reply, as they had done on the
Marne, with a counter-turning movement, which would have
to be met by a further prolongation of the Allied Line to the
northward. The process would then be repeated, and in all
probability would continue till both the opposed lines reached
the sea. The best that could happen for the Allies was that
they would be able to join hands with the Belgian Army that
was now concentrated about Antwerp. This would keep the
enemy away from the sea altogether, and at the same time

[1] See Map p. 126 and Map 1 in case.

preserve the rich industrial and mineral districts of Flanders. Of this, however, there was little hope. New German forces had already appeared at Valenciennes and Cambrai; they had already compelled the Belgian Army to withdraw within the fortifications of Antwerp, and it seemed rather that we were threatened with the worst that could happen. The worst was that the enemy would reach the sea somewhere to the south of Boulogne, and, by gaining possession of the Flemish and Northern French ports, be in a position to dispute our hold on the Channel and upset our whole disposition in the Narrow Seas. At almost any cost this had to be prevented, and the Allied army must at least make an effort to reach the sea at some point midway between the two extremes, say about Ostend. In any case it would be a neck-and-neck race if General Joffre's turning movement failed, and it must have been obvious that the main chance of success lay in the prospect of the British being able to stretch out a hand from the sea to meet the northward movement.

Whether or not this was the precise process of reasoning on the part of the French Higher Command, it is certain that the day after General Joffre decided to change his plan of attack he sent through our Embassy a request which was destined to bring forward the British hold on the sea as a possible solution of the military problem. In the long roll of our wars similar attempts to relieve a Continental situation had been frequent, and, as was only natural, the suggestion had originally come from London. A week earlier—on September 11—only ten days after the Marines had been withdrawn from Ostend, a scheme of operations on the old lines had been put forward. By that time it was clear that the German war plan had broken down : the rush on Paris had just been stopped by the battle of the Marne. For the Allies it was no longer a question of securing a retreat or even of defensive operations. The way was opening for an offensive return, and the only doubt was whether the Entente forces were in sufficient strength to make it a success. So equally balanced did the opposing armies appear to be that very little might serve to turn the scale, and what our Government had in mind was that that little might possibly be found in a demonstration from the sea against the German communications. The idea was referred to General Joffre, but it was not till he found himself brought to a standstill before the enemy's new front that a reply was received.

He now intimated that " owing to the new German movements towards the north of France " (which obviously imperilled the success of his intended turning movement), he would like to see it put in execution. What he asked was that all available troops should be sent to Dunkirk and eventually to Calais " to act effectively and constantly against the enemy's communications, and thus hinder their operations in that region." In forwarding the request our Ambassador said the French Government desired to recommend it to the earnest consideration of His Majesty's Government, and Lord Kitchener at once marked the telegram " Very urgent." To the Admiralty the scheme seemed " Very important "; in any measure to secure the ports of the Strait of Dover they were directly concerned. The First Lord and the War Staff officers who had been at Loch Ewe had just returned, and without hesitation the Marine Brigade of the Royal Naval Division (about 2,600 strong) was offered as an advanced guard, if the War Office would provide the necessary mounted troops. They offered a Yeomanry Regiment (the Queen's Own Oxfordshire Hussars) and a party of Royal Engineers, and that night (September 18) the necessary orders were issued by the Admiralty and War Office. The Marine Brigade was to sail the following afternoon, and the Yeomanry in the evening. By September 20 the landing was to be complete at Dunkirk, where the force would be strengthened by the aeroplanes and armoured cars which had been left there under Commander Samson when the Marines were withdrawn from Ostend. More armed cars and motor transport were to follow.

General Aston was given the command of the whole. His instructions were that while he must regard his force as too weak for anything but demonstrations and minor enterprises to cut railway lines, he was to endeavour to give the impression that he was the advanced guard of a considerable British force destined to act against the enemy's communications. He was further reminded that the enemy could bring to bear upon him overwhelming forces whenever they chose, but if he forced them to concentrate for such an eccentric movement he would be achieving the object.

Seeing how fast the available British forces at home were ripening to efficiency, there was reason to believe the German Higher Command would not be able to ignore the threat. All past experience went to show that it was what lay behind such expeditions rather than their own strength that was the measure of their military value. And by this time we had troops that must be reckoned with. Part of the Mediterranean Garrisons were already at home : on the day the order was issued the Cape Garrison reached Southampton, and the famous VIIth Division, as well as the IIIrd Cavalry Division

of the old army, were being rapidly formed. Behind them,
moreover, the Territorial Troops were showing a surprising
capacity for fitting themselves for the field. It was therefore
quite possible that the little demonstration would develop
into something much more important, and it was a possibility
with which the Navy as well as the enemy must reckon.

For protecting the waters over which the new line of
communication would have to pass no special arrangements
were made. The Admiralty were relying on the Southern
Force, although it had recently been much reduced in
strength. Its main support had been the Second Battle
Cruiser Squadron, *Invincible* and *New Zealand*, which had been
stationed in the Humber for the purpose; but since their withdrawal to Rosyth after the discovery of the German minefields
they had been under Admiral Jellicoe's direct command. The
New Zealand, however, was now in the First Squadron, the
Inflexible, on her arrival from Malta, having joined her sister
ship in the Second. The Channel Fleet, from which support
could be looked for, had also been weakened owing to the
dominating call of the Imperial Concentration. By the end
of the month the Canadian Contingent was to be ready to
sail, and to provide it with escort Admiral Wemyss on
September 10—that is, as soon as the VIth Division had
been passed to St. Nazaire—had been ordered to leave the
Western Patrol and proceed with his four cruisers to the St.
Lawrence. Their place had to be taken by Admiral Bethell
with the 7th Battle Squadron, so that he was not available
as he had been during the Ostend landing.

The Southern Force, under Admiral Christian, at this
time consisted of his flagship *Euryalus* and his attached light
cruiser *Amethyst*, together with the 7th Cruiser Squadron
under Admiral Campbell (*Bacchante, Cressy, Aboukir, Hogue*),
and the Harwich Flotillas (1st and 3rd Destroyer and ten
submarines of the 8th or " Oversea " Flotilla), with their
attached light cruiser *Fearless*. The *Arethusa* had not yet
made good the damage she had suffered in the Heligoland
action, and Commodore Tyrwhitt was flying his broad pendant in the *Lowestoft*. Under the original War Orders of
July 28, 1914, the cruisers were based on the Nore " in
order to ensure the presence of armoured ships in the Southern
approaches to the North Sea and the Eastern entrance to the
Channel, and to support the 1st and 3rd Flotillas operating
in that area from Harwich." The object of these flotillas,
it was explained, was " to keep the area south of the 54th
parallel (which runs a little south of the Dogger Bank and
Heligoland) clear of enemy torpedo craft and minelayers."

Cruiser Force " C," it was added, " was to support them in the execution of these duties, and also, with the flotillas, to keep a close watch for enemy war vessels and transports in order that their movements may be reported at the earliest moment."

Subsequently two patrol areas had been established for the Harwich flotillas—one off the Dogger Bank and one in the Broad Fourteens. As a rule the bulk of the cruisers were to the northward supporting the Dogger patrol, but from time to time at critical junctures, such as the crossing of the Expeditionary Force and the shift of base to St. Nazaire, they had been concentrated in the Broad Fourteens. The normal disposition which it was sought to maintain was three cruisers for the Dogger area and one for the Broad Fourteens, but frequently, owing to coaling exigencies, only three of them were available. This was so on September 16, and Admiral Christian, who was then in the Dogger area with the *Euryalus, Bacchante* and *Cressy*, and had been ordered to re-establish both patrols, was given permission to keep only two cruisers to the northward and to send one to the Broad Fourteens. On this permission he did not act at once. His own view, as he explained to the Admiralty on the 19th, was that it was better to keep his available cruisers concentrated in a position south of the Dogger where he would be able to support either patrol as occasion required. At the moment, however, there was no question of support, for towards the evening of the 17th the weather turned so bad that both flotillas had to be ordered in to the base, and he reported that he was patrolling the Dogger area himself with three cruisers—that is, *Euryalus, Hogue* and *Aboukir*, the *Cressy* having gone in to coal and the *Bacchante* for docking and repairs.

Meanwhile, ever since the supporting battle cruisers had been withdrawn from the Humber, it had become obvious that the situation of the Southern Force area left much to be desired, and the day after the receipt of Admiral Christian's telegram stating that he was concentrated in the Dogger Bank area, the question of its reorganisation was put forward for consideration at the Admiralty. Experience was showing more clearly every day not only that more powerful and closer support was required by the strategical situation as it was developing, but also that the " Bacchantes " were tactically unfit for the work of close co-operation with the flotillas, work which in default of more suitable ships had to be assigned to them when the War Plan was settled. Now, however, that the eight light cruisers of the new

" Arethusa " class were coming forward, it would be possible to relieve the " Bacchantes " by those which were first ready for sea, and use them with advantage elsewhere for duties which they were well able to perform.[1]

All this time the weather continued to be so bad that neither flotilla patrol could be re-established, and Admiral Christian continued to watch to the northward with his three cruisers. On the 19th it was a little better, and the patrols made an attempt to take up their stations, but at 6 a.m. the Admiral had to order them all back to harbour, and in informing the Admiralty he expressed his intention of carrying on with the three cruisers in the Dogger area. By the afternoon, however, it had been decided to withdraw the Dogger Patrol altogether during the equinoctial weather and to maintain that of the Broad Fourteens only. An order accordingly went out calling him down from the position he was recommending as strategically the best. " The Dogger Bank Patrol," it ran, " need not be continued. Weather too bad for destroyers to go to sea. Arrange with cruisers to watch Broad Fourteens." The telegram went out at 4.40 before the Admiral's appreciation can have reached Whitehall. At the same time the transports carrying Marines to Dunkirk were just about to leave Dover, but the order appears to have had no connection with this movement, about which the Dover Patrol had received special instructions. It was supplemented by one to Commodore Tyrwhitt directing him to re-establish the Broad Fourteens flotilla patrol next morning, if possible, by which time the cruisers would have arrived to support it.

During the night both the Marines and the Yeomanry, under the protection of the Dover Patrol, reached Dunkirk unmolested. At 5 a.m., on the 20th, Admiral Christian was off the Maas Light Vessel with the *Hogue* and *Aboukir*, and there the *Cressy* joined him from the Nore. An hour later, since his flagship (*Euryalus*) was due for coaling and had had her wireless disabled, he parted company, leaving the squadron in command of Captain Drummond of the *Aboukir*. His intention had been to transfer his flag to her and remain out himself, but so high a sea was running that no boat could be lowered. For the same reason the *Fearless*, which was bringing out the destroyer patrol, was obliged to take them back to Harwich.

Thus all that day as well as the 21st the three cruisers were left to maintain the watch without a flotilla screen. The area they were to patrol was specially dangerous, since it lay

[1] See Appendix D1.

between the German minefield and the Dutch coast, and thus left little room for variations of course. But as the cruisers had recently been supporting the Dogger Bank Patrol, Admiral Christian considered that this area was the one in which the enemy were least likely to look for them, and before parting company he gave special directions as to how the patrol was to be conducted so as to minimise the risk. In particular he recommended alterations of course to guard against submarines till the destroyers could come out again. On this score there was no special reason for anxiety. It was a generally received view that the short steep seas which a gale sets up in the locality, and which even the best destroyers could not face, rendered successful submarine operations impossible. Moreover, the Admiralty had information that the enemy's attention was turned to the north. This same day they sent word to the Commander-in-Chief of a report that a mixed force of light cruisers, destroyers and submarines had been seen from Esbjerg, in the south of Denmark, going north, and Admiral Jellicoe at once organised and carried out a sweep with his full force as far as the line between Flamborough Head and Horn Reefs, but again without meeting anything.

Nor were the three isolated cruisers exposed for long, for during the night the weather began to abate, and Commodore Tyrwhitt started off himself for the Broad Fourteens with the *Lowestoft* and eight destroyers. He was well on his way when, early on the 22nd, the wireless room at the Admiralty began to make out the words, "*Aboukir, Hogue*, sinking," constantly repeated; and then the position "52.18 N. 3.41 E.," that is, about thirty miles west by south from Ymuiden. Eight more destroyers were immediately ordered to join the Commodore, and Admiral Christian made for the scene of danger with the *Amethyst* at full speed. But before any of them could arrive all was over, and one more tragedy was added to the tale of those useless sacrifices which never cease to darken naval memory.

It was part of the directions given to the captain of the *Aboukir* that he was to move to the south of his beat during the hours of darkness and patrol northward again at daylight. This precaution, which was enjoined by the original war orders of the squadron, was usual when the main danger to cruising ships was from destroyers, but it had no relation to the new conditions. To steam towards the enemy's base in daylight without flotilla protection was to increase the risk of submarine attack. Since the sea had gone down the better course, so the Admiralty held, would have been to keep to the southward till the destroyers returned. But for some reason which we do not know this was not done, and to make matters worse the squadron was proceeding abreast two miles apart without zigzagging and at barely ten knots. Still, a special look-out for submarines was being maintained, and at least one gun on each side was kept loaded and its crew closed up.

This, then, was the position when, just before 6.30 a.m., there was a violent explosion under the *Aboukir's* starboard side. No sign of a submarine was seen, and Captain Drummond, believing he had to do with a line of mines, signalled the other two ships to close, but to keep ahead of him. The wounded *Aboukir* quickly took a list of 20°, then steadied, and an effort was made to right her by flooding the opposite wing compartments. But suddenly the list began to increase again so rapidly that it was clear she was going. "Abandon ship" was sounded, but only a single cutter was available—the other had been broken up by the explosion, and there was no steam with which to hoist out the boom boats. Every one had to take to the water, and twenty-five minutes after the blow the *Aboukir* turned over and floated awhile bottom upwards.

By this time Captain Wilmot Nicholson in the *Hogue* was at hand. He had warned the *Cressy* to look out for submarines while he closed the *Aboukir*, and he was now a cable or two ahead of her stem on. One watch was at the guns and two were hoisting out boats and getting up mess-tables, stools and hammocks to throw overboard to their comrades in the water. His intention was, in spite of the danger, to steam through them to give what help he could, but for some minutes he could not move as the boats were in the way. As soon as they were clear and he had put the telegraph "Ahead," he was struck by two torpedoes, and immediately afterwards a submarine came up on his port quarter. The *Hogue* promptly opened a brisk fire, but although at first it was believed that the damage was not vital, in five minutes the quarter-deck was awash; still the men stood devotedly to their guns, nor did they cease fire till she was almost on her beam-ends, and the word was passed for every one to shift for himself.

Her boats were just beginning to return with the survivors of the *Aboukir*. The *Cressy's* boats were doing the same, and she was herself standing by and making the signal which gave the Admiralty the first word of the disaster. Ten minutes after the *Hogue* was struck she went down, and then at 7.17 the *Cressy* (Captain R. W. Johnson) began calling for help, still without moving. At this moment a periscope was seen on the starboard quarter two cables away, and then the track of a torpedo. " Full speed ahead, both," was the order, but before she could gather way she was hit abreast the after funnel, though a second torpedo passed just clear of her stern. Then another conning tower was reported on her port beam; the gunner opened fire and the men were cheering what seemed to be a hit, when a third torpedo hit her just before the after bridge. It seemed to come from yet another submarine masked by the *Hogue*, for it passed over the spot where she had just gone down. It was the *Cressy's coup de grâce*—she turned over on her beam ends and lay awash for a quarter of an hour, when she, too, disappeared. Her case was perhaps the worst of all. All her boats were away and filled with survivors from the other two ships, and nothing else was near but a couple of Dutch sailing trawlers, who hesitated to close for fear of mines; nor was it till an hour later that a Dutch steamship, the *Flora*, from Rotterdam to Leith, appeared on the scene and, regardless of all danger, came boldly up and began a strenuous work of rescue in a manner that excited general admiration. " I cannot," wrote Captain Nicholson, " speak too highly of the captain of the *Flora* in closing when he was unaware whether the ships had been struck by mines or torpedoes, and who thus incurred a great risk in the interests of humanity." As much might be said for the *Titan*, another steamer belonging to the same owners, which rescued 147 officers and men, as well as for the Lowestoft sailing trawlers *Coriander* and *J. G. C.* As for Commodore Tyrwhitt, for all his prompt departure he was still fifty miles away when he took in the call, and it was not till 10.45 a.m. that he was able to get up.

The loss of life was consequently very great. In all 60 officers and 777 men were saved, which meant that as many officers and nearly 1400 men were drowned. To give the last touch of bitterness, the old cruisers, being amongst the latest to mobilise, were manned mainly by Royal Naval Reserve ratings, most of whom were married men with families. Yet in spite of the rawness of the crews and the appalling nature of the disaster, by every testimony the discipline displayed was admirable and the conduct of the men beyond all praise both before and after the ships went down. As for the ships themselves, their loss was a small matter. They were already ripe for being sent to slumber out their obsolescence on the Mother Bank, and were but ill-adapted for naval warfare in its recent developments. But the crews, seeing how devotedly they had come forward from their civil occupations at the country's call, were a national loss to be lamented, the more since so much magnificent material perished helplessly by such insignificant means.

At first it was believed that at least five or six submarines had shared in the attack.   In the space of an hour six torpedoes had been fired, and when the Germans announced that only one boat had been engaged the claim was scarcely to be credited.   As soon as it was known that Commodore Tyrwhitt had reached the scene the 1st Destroyer Flotilla was ordered to Terschelling to cut off the enemy's retreat, but nothing was seen.   The whole work had been done by one comparatively old boat, *U 9* (Lieutenant-Commander Otto Weddigen), which had not been out before during the war. She had left Heligoland early on the morning of September 20 with orders to attack troop transports.   After considerable difficulty owing to weather conditions, Commander Weddigen found himself in a position to attack the three cruisers in succession.   He fired his six torpedoes and then returned to his base for more, safely arriving at Heligoland on the 23rd.

Nothing that had yet occurred had so emphatically proclaimed the change that had come over naval warfare, and never perhaps had so great a result been obtained by means relatively so small.   The result of the Inquiry that was held was that the disaster might have been avoided had the senior officer complied more closely with the general instructions which the Admiralty had issued to provide as far as possible for the safety of ships exposed to the new danger; but at the same time it was held that his error of judgment was amply atoned for by the exemplary conduct he displayed during the attack.

It remains only to note a question of international law to which the fine conduct of the captain of the *Flora* gave rise. He had taken on board no less than 28 officers and 258 men, and with these, seeing that submarines were still believed to be about, he hastened into Ymuiden.   The Foreign Office claimed their repatriation on the ground that Article XV of the Hague Naval Convention relating to internment only applied to belligerent persons landed by their captors.   This view the Netherlands Government adopted spontaneously, and on September 26 all the officers and men, after receiving the most generous hospitality, were repatriated.

CHAPTER XIII

Coming when it did, the effect of the loss of the three "Cressys" was deep and widespread, and to appreciate how the Navy rose superior to its moral oppression it is necessary to realise its full extent. The first result was a general order that henceforth it was to be recognised by all commanding officers that if one of several ships in company was torpedoed by a submarine, or struck a mine, she must be left to her fate and the rest clear out of the dangerous area, calling up minor vesssels to render assistance. "This," the order added, "is a further application of the rule of war to leave disabled ships in a fleet action to look after themselves." It was, in fact, a considerable stretch of the old rule. The original article of the first Fighting Instructions of the seventeenth century, as drawn up in 1653 by Blake, Deane, and Monk, was that if in action a ship was in danger of sinking and made signal to that effect, the nearest ships were strictly required to relieve her. It was only when not in danger of sinking or capture that she was to be left to herself. The rule was maintained, with only slight modifications, all through the eighteenth century. It appears in Howe's Instructions of 1799, and also in the last Instructions of the Great War period which were drawn up in 1816. In its final form it ran as follows : " If any ship should be disabled so as to be in great danger of being destroyed or taken . . . the ships nearest to her and which are least engaged with the enemy are strictly enjoined to give her immediately all possible aid and protection." No rule so stern as that of the new order had ever been formulated in our Service, and its appearance furnishes one of the many recent indications of how drastic and ruthless warfare had become for the seamen of to-day compared with anything their predecessors were called upon to face.

Another effect of the disaster was an order that for the future armoured ships, so far as possible, were not to board merchant vessels for examination. The process exposed

[1] See Maps 1 and 8 (inset) in case.

them too dangerously to submarine attack, and steps were taken for attaching to the various squadrons suitable armed vessels for doing the actual work of examination.

The dispositions of the Fleet also had to be modified. The War Plans provided for the Channel Fleet in cases of emergency being moved up into the North Sea, and the day before the three cruisers were lost it had been the intention to bring Admiral Burney and his 5th Battle Squadron to Sheerness, to be at hand should any serious attempt be made on the new line of passage, but as soon as the disaster was known the project was deferred. Again, since the mining and submarine activities of the enemy had so much increased, a new cruiser area had been established off the east coast of Scotland. It was frequently patrolled by the old battleships from the Humber, but now an order was issued that it was not to be patrolled by armoured ships at all.

To add to the difficulties, the suspicion that the enemy were using trawlers to lay mines in the open sea was increasing in strength. Though we now know the belief was erroneous, it was by this time so strongly held that the Admiralty came reluctantly to the conclusion that Admiral Jellicoe's suggestion for dealing with the trouble must be adopted, at least in part. Accordingly, they issued an order that from October 1 all the East Coast ports were to be closed to neutral fishing craft. Nor was this all. A certain war area was declared. North of the latitude of Whitby (54° 30′ N.), it extended to longitude 1° E., and south of Whitby to longitude 2° 30′ E., and all neutral fishing craft found within these limits were to be treated as under suspicion of mine-laying. Innocent vessels were to be warned off; those defying the prohibition were to be seized and treated as guilty of unneutral action. To such a high-handed recurrence to the practices of the old *Mare clausum* were we forced by Germany's flagrant contempt for the time-honoured customs of the sea. Distasteful as these measures were to our maritime conscience, it was now clear that the niceties of the old naval code must be abandoned. The insidious form of attack, which it had been expected Germany would adopt, was bidding fair to produce results as drastic as the firmest believers in the power of the new methods had expected. Never since the invention of the torpedo had it achieved so sweeping a success as on September 22; still less had the submarine anything like such an exploit to its credit, and it was useless to shut our eyes to the fact that the old methods would no longer serve. As

the Commander-in-Chief pointed out when asked for his
opinion how to deal with the problem, the policy Germany
was adopting was obviously the proper one for a belligerent
in her position, in order to weaken our battle line before the
main action was fought. Our policy, he submitted, should
consequently be to resist all temptation to activities which
entailed undue risk to our heavy ships, and meanwhile to
devote ourselves to strangling the enemy's trade and destroying his submarines by every possible device. If Germany
used fishing craft for warlike purposes, let us do the same.
" The method of destruction," he said, " should be to use
trawlers as freely as possible," and he proceeded to sketch
a system on which they might be employed.

   To realise a new danger meant for the Navy nothing
more than devising new means to deal with it. That had
always been the spirit; yet we need not be insensible to the
fortitude the attitude displayed. Nor without bearing in
mind the shock which the old tradition had received can we
realise how severe was the fresh call that had to be made
upon the Admiralty while the recent blow was still smarting.

   The new demand upon them arose from the military
situation in France. The race for the sea was nearing its
crisis. By reciprocal flanking movements the Allied and the
German lines had stretched northward as far as Arras and
Douai respectively, and between the Allied left and the sea
at Dunkirk was a gap of some fifty miles very weakly held.
At the suggestion of the French, the bulk of our Marine
Brigade had moved inland to Cassel, with one battalion
thrown forward as far as Lille; further to the eastward was
a French force at Tournai; but, as against the strength
which Germany was developing in the north, such forces
were negligible. Nor could the Belgian Army help. The
offensive movement which it had commenced from Antwerp
against the German communications had just been crushed
by the new forces that were pressing in from Germany; on
September 28 it had been forced to withdraw within the
line of the outer forts, into which the first German shells were
already beginning to fall.

   Simultaneously a profound modification of the situation
in the main theatre was taking place. This same day the
attempt of the Germans to break through the Allied Centre
about Rheims had finally failed. It was this characteristic
clinging of the Germans to their original plan which seems
to have been the main cause of their otherwise unaccountable
neglect to make more of their opportunity of reaching the
Channel Ports. They seemed now awake to their error,

their attention was evidently turning to the northward, and Sir John French saw the time had come for removing the whole of the British Expeditionary Force from where it was embedded in the French armies to its natural and original position on the sea flank. The proposal was at once accepted by General Joffre. The only hope of succeeding in his attempt to outflank the German right now depended on the possibility of a combined movement of French, British, and Belgian troops in Flanders. It was a moment, therefore, when the security of Antwerp and the field army it held was of special importance, for military reasons now as well as naval. It was, moreover, a typical situation which offered all possible advantages for a force to be dropped in from the sea at the decisive point. We had now the VIIth Division and the IIIrd Cavalry Division ready to take the field. Assuming the Navy was prepared to undertake the undoubtedly grave responsibility of transporting them, they could easily be thrown in from Dunkirk or Ostend, but without the co-operation of the Belgian Army they would be too weak to effect anything. There was, moreover, a further reason why direct action from the Flemish coast might be necessary in any case. Since the first week in September, when the fate of the frontier fortresses had revealed to the Belgian Government the impossibility of Antwerp resisting a formal attack, they had been asking the Allies to promise them 25,000 troops to secure the retreat of the Field Army by way of St. Nicolas, Ghent, Bruges and Ostend.

For the Admiralty such a development of the campaign meant a very heavy task. For with the whole British Army moving to the northward, St. Nazaire would no longer serve as a base. In addition to shifting it back to Havre, the Navy would have to protect the new lines of communication to Dunkirk and Ostend, and it was just at this moment that an incident occurred which redoubled the difficulties that had to be faced, and involved the previously simple plans in a tangle of complexities.

On September 27, the day the Belgian offensive was checked, the light cruiser *Attentive* (Captain Charles D. Johnson, commanding the 6th Flotilla, Dover Patrol) was attacked near the Strait by two submarines. Two torpedoes were fired, both were avoided, and the submarines dived and disappeared. Captain Johnson at once searched the area with his four divisions of destroyers. Commodore Tyrwhitt also sent a division to the North Hinder to cut off the enemy's retreat, but nothing more was seen of them, and the inference was that they had perhaps gone into the Channel. All sailings of transports were therefore stopped, except those from western ports to St. Nazaire or Nantes, and till further orders no vessels were permitted to move in daylight.

In view of the critical military situation the sudden insecurity of our cross-Channel lines of passage was intolerable. On September 29 fresh intelligence came in of reinforcements reaching the German right, and, if the situation was to be saved, something must be done to secure for the Army its indispensable communications. Something more effective than the existing system was required, and nothing seemed likely to meet the case but a policy of extensive mining. This idea now began to be pressed upon the Admiralty. They were as unwilling as ever to adopt the obnoxious expedient, and so restrict the freedom of the Grand Fleet, and before consenting they referred the question to Admiral Jellicoe. The military situation was laid before him, and he was asked whether on naval grounds, apart from all others, he objected to the proposed comprehensive scheme; and in particular as to whether he would apply it to the Heligoland Bight, or confine it to the narrow waters of the Southern Area. It will be recalled that about three weeks earlier he himself had made a similar proposal, and he had not changed his mind. The opinion, therefore, that he expressed was that, though generally opposed to any attempt to mine the Bight or the entrances of the German ports, since the risk would be great and the effect merely temporary, for minefields in those localities could not be watched, yet on naval grounds he regarded the mining of the Southern Area as desirable.

His answer came to hand early on October 2, and orders for the minefield to be laid were issued forthwith. At the same time, however, the example which the Germans had set of keeping such minefields secret was one we were not prepared to follow, great as were its advantages. Their action was a direct breach of Article 3 of the Hague Mine Convention, which provided that " When anchored automatic contact mines are employed every possible precaution must be taken for the security of peaceful navigation." The Germans had taken no such precaution. Our Admiralty at once decided to take the obvious one of announcing the existence of the minefield, and, accordingly, an official notification of the limits of the danger area was immediately issued and given the fullest possible publicity.

In accordance with Admiral Jellicoe's opinion the minefield was to be confined entirely to the narrow waters. The danger area was announced to be a parallelogram whose southern base was a line from the middle of the Goodwins to just north of Ostend. The northern limit was a line running eastwards from the Kentish Knock. Two minelayers, *Iphigenia* and *Andromache*, were told off for the work, but before they could begin it was clear they would have no easy task. During the morning (October 2) Submarine *B 3* of the Dover Patrol had been attacked unsuccessfully by a hostile submarine off the south end of the Goodwins. The work, therefore, could only be done at night and under destroyer protection.

The delay entailed was specially regrettable, for by this time the situation in Belgium had reached a crisis. On October 1, Forts Waelhem and Wavre St. Catherine in the south-east sector of the outer ring of the Antwerp defences had fallen and the Germans were pushing in through the gap. To the Belgian Government there seemed no hope of saving the city unless a diversion could be made against the left of the attacking army. To this end they appealed for help. The attacking force was believed to be no more than the equivalent of two army corps, while the German Governor of Brussels had at his disposal little more than one brigade of second line troops. The Belgians had in the fortress about 70,000 garrison troops besides their Field Army, numbering 80,000 men. Of the six divisions composing it, four were occupying the two southern sectors of the defences, one was at Termonde, and one in reserve with the cavalry on the flanks; but possibly two divisions, the cavalry in any case, could be spared to co-operate with an Allied force to make the required diversion. The French had promised a Territorial Division. We had already sent some heavy naval guns, and Rear-Admiral Oliver, the Director of Naval Intelligence, and two representatives of the War Office had gone over to report on the situation. Though our War Office was ready to respond with two divisions, provided the French could send regulars, they naturally hesitated, after recent experiences, to send them to undertake so hazardous and difficult an enterprise in concert with second line troops. The point was still under discussion between the two Governments when, late in the evening of October 2, came the startling information that the Belgian Government had suddenly decided to retire to Ostend and to withdraw the Field Army from Antwerp, leaving the fortress troops to hold it as long as they could.

It was a position that the British Government could not accept without an effort to prevent the breakdown of

our plans that it meant—particularly since the measure
seemed from our reports to have been dictated not so much
by immediate military necessity as by a sense of being abandoned by the Allies. The French, moreover, had now
promised two Territorial Divisions, with a full complement
of cavalry and artillery, and were pointing out that they
were no longer the raw troops which had so unhappily left
our Expeditionary Force in the air at the first shock. The
great difficulty was time. The diversion was decided on,
but for the moment it was impossible to say when the troops
would arrive. The main point was to enhearten the Belgians
to hold on for a few days, and for this some prompt and
practical evidence that they were not forgotten was necessary. It was decided, therefore, that the First Lord of the
Admiralty should proceed forthwith to Antwerp on behalf
of the Government and see what could be done. At the
same time, as an earnest of what was to come, the Royal
Marine Brigade was ordered to proceed at once to Antwerp to
assist in holding the place. General Paris, who had succeeded
to the command on General Aston being invalided, was then
at Dunkirk, and had withdrawn his advanced battalion
from Lille to Cassel as the French, under the increasing
menace of the German right, fell back from Tournai. He
was therefore able to start without delay.

The effect of these preliminary steps was immediate.
As soon as the Belgian Government were informed of them
they agreed to make no move until Mr. Churchill arrived.
Travelling through the night, he reached Antwerp on the
morning of October 3, and it was quickly apparent that
the Belgians were as ready as ever to play a bold game so
long as there was a shadow of hope. By the afternoon a
provisional agreement had been come to which promised
at least a substantial gain of time for General Joffre's plans
to develop without any undue risk to the Belgian Field
Army. The arrangement was that the Belgian Government
would at once make energetic preparations to resist for at
least ten days, and that within three days we would state definitely if and when we could launch a large operation for their
relief. If within three days we could not give a satisfactory
assurance of substantial assistance, they were to be free to
abandon the defence and withdraw the Field Army, and in
that case we were to cover its withdrawal by sending troops
to Ghent or elsewhere on the line of retreat. A further
condition was that, in the meantime, we were to assist the
local defence in all minor ways, such as with guns, marines,
and naval brigades.

The acceptance of this last condition was a desperate expedient to meet a desperate situation. The immediate importance, it will be seen, was to do something at once to gain time for the larger operations contemplated, and this was the only means available. Besides the Marine Brigade, which was already well on its way, we were organising two Naval Brigades so as to form a complete Naval Division, but as yet the force was wholly unfit for active service. It was still only in process of development from the original idea of a small flying force for the occupation of advanced naval bases. The minute which had inaugurated the expansion was dated August 17, 1914, and it was not till next day that even the Marine Brigade already formed had been ordered to train for field service. The idea was to raise two more brigades from superfluous men of the Fleet Reserve, the Royal Naval Reserve, and the Royal Naval Volunteers, with a few active ratings, and the War Office offered to lend officers to train them as infantry. Each brigade consisted of four battalions, which were named after famous admirals.[1]

It was not till the last days of August that the new formations were in camp at Walmer and at Betteshanger near Sandwich. They had thus had barely a month's training, and it had included practically no musketry. Arms for them had to be drawn from the Fleet, and it was the end of September before all received service rifles. Even so they were without proper equipment or entrenching tools, the majority of the officers and men were as yet quite raw, and a considerable proportion of the ranks were newly-raised recruits who had never served in the Reserves. Still, they were on the spot close to Dover, capable of being hastily embarked, and there was nothing else. It was, of course, little more than a forlorn hope, but they were only needed for garrison duty, and the troops they would have to meet were known to be of inferior quality. These considerations, coupled with the desperate condition of affairs at Antwerp at the crisis of the race for the sea seemed to justify the measure at least on moral and political grounds; and in telegraphing the heads of the agreement he had made, Mr. Churchill begged that, if they were approved, the Admiralty should be instructed to order the two Naval Brigades to embark at once for Dunkirk. The arrangement was approved, and orders were issued accordingly.

[1] The battalions of the First Brigade were: (1) Drake, (2) Benbow, (3) Hawke, and (4) Collingwood; those of the Second Brigade were: (5) Nelson, (6) Howe, (7) Hood, and (8) Anson. The Royal Marine Brigade also had four battalions, numbered 9 to 12, and named after the Royal Marine Divisions at the Naval ports.

Inferior as were these troops, it must be remembered that they were only intended to stiffen and enhearten the local defence for the vital three days. By that time, or possibly a day or so later, it was practically certain that a combined Franco-British force capable of co-operating with the Belgian Field Army against the besiegers' left would be concentrated at Ostend. For their second Territorial Division the French had substituted a complete Naval Brigade, which they regarded as a superior force. It consisted of two fine regiments of Fusiliers Marins, and one regiment of Zouaves, in all 8,000 men, with sixteen naval machine-guns. It was to go by rail from Paris, while from Havre would come by sea the LXXXVIIth Territorial Division, consisting of twelve battalions, two squadrons of reserve cavalry, and two brigades of 90-millimetre guns. As for our own contingent, the Admiralty had accepted the risk of its transport, and marching orders had also been given to the VIIth Division and the IIIrd Cavalry Division, which were to arrive during the 6th and 7th. All told, therefore, the combined force assembled at Ostend would number 42,000 men, 68 British guns, besides those of the French and besides the 8,000 men of General Paris's Naval Division and the heavy guns. Such a force suddenly dropped into the gap, and threatening the besiegers' left, could certainly not be despised, especially at the moment when General Joffre's and Sir John French's great effort to turn the right of the German main army was developing.

While waiting for the relieving movement to mature the Belgians were carrying out their part of the arrangement by establishing themselves on the line of the Great and the Little Nethe, the position to which they had fallen back when the outer ring of forts was forced. Here the Marines joined. Having reached Antwerp with the Royal Engineer detachment brigaded with them, they had been ordered early next morning to Lierre, which, standing as it does on an island site formed by the junction of the Great and Little Nethe, constituted the key and main bridgehead of the river position. Here three battalions occupied a section north of Lierre on the Little Nethe, with the fourth battalion in reserve and Belgian troops on either flank. All this section of the line, with the Belgian troops allotted to it, was placed under General Paris's command. It was already under heavy bombardment, and the field defences very imperfect, shallow, and without head cover. The engineers at once set to work to improve the trenches and clear the field of fire, and by the evening the lines were much strengthened.

All night, however, the bombardment continued with increasing violence, and the Belgians who had hitherto been holding the east bank of the Little Nethe were forced to retire behind the river. At the same time, some twenty-five miles away to the west-south-west, the enemy passed the Dendre, the river which flows northward into the Schelde at Termonde and so continues the main line of defence for Flanders towards the French frontier. They were thus able to begin an attempt to cross the Schelde itself at Schoonaerde and Termonde, a movement which seriously threatened the line of retreat from Antwerp. To make matters worse, by noon next day (the 5th) the German infantry succeeded in occupying Lierre, and, though they could not debouch from it, they effected a crossing of the Great Nethe below the town and drove back the Belgian regiment which was on the right of the Marines. A counter-attack by another Belgian regiment was quickly organised, and, assisted by bombs from our naval aircraft, it was successful. By 4.30 p.m. the original line was re-occupied by the Allies, but the enemy were able to retain their lodgment on the west bank of the river. To the southward, however, there was no improvement. There the weak Belgian division which was guarding the line of retreat on the Schelde was being so hardly pressed, especially at Schoonaerde, that the situation was reported as critical.

An urgent request was now sent to Bordeaux that the Fusilier Marin Brigade, instead of stopping at Ostend, should proceed direct to Antwerp, and, in spite of all discouragement, a Council held by the King that evening, at which the First Lord was present, decided to hold on and fight it out. Scarcely had the resolution been taken when word came in that the Germans had forced a passage of the Little Nethe just north of Lierre. Some desperate effort seemed now necessary unless the river line was to be wholly lost.

About 1.15 in the morning (the 6th) an order came from the Belgian Headquarters for a general attack to drive the enemy back over the river. The message had been greatly delayed in transit, and, as the attack was timed for 2.0 a.m., General Paris, who in any case doubted its wisdom, had to say he could not arrange it in the time. Two Belgian regiments, however, made the attack alone with great dash, drove the Germans back over the river, and by 4.30 had restored the position. Till the morning they held it, but at daylight on the 6th the Germans attacked again with fresh forces and succeeded in penetrating the right of the Belgian line south-west of Lierre at Boomlaer and Hulst. Another gallant effort was made to recover the lost trenches; it was materially assisted by the naval aeroplanes dropping bombs upon the Germans, but, although part of the lost ground was recovered, it was no longer possible to hold the ill-constructed trenches against the enemy's shell-fire, and by 11.0 a.m. General Paris found it necessary to order his Belgians to retire to a position a little further back, between the river and the inner forts. As this movement exposed the right of the Marine Brigade, and as they were already under heavy shell-fire, they were ordered to withdraw to Vremde, a village about two miles in advance of Fort No. 3 of the Inner Ring.

By this time the 1st and 2nd Brigades of the Royal Naval Division had arrived. After being delayed at Dover by the non-arrival of a transport, they had crossed to Dunkirk in the night of October 4–5, and had begun to reach Antwerp by rail at 2.30 a.m. on the 6th, by way of Ghent and St. Nicolas, across the head of the German advance at Termonde, and had then gone into billets round Wilryck near Fort No. 6 of the Inner Ring. The idea of the Belgian Headquarter Staff was that, as the line of the Nethe seemed no longer tenable, they should occupy a system of trenches extending across the Lierre–Antwerp road from the military depot on the Malines railway to Vremde. General Paris, however, wanted them to reinforce his right, where the Germans, having established themselves across the Nethe on the Malines road south-west of Lierre, were forcing the Belgians to retire. But so exhausted were our Allies by this night attack, that it was very doubtful whether they could be supported in time, and at 10.30 a.m. he ordered the two Naval Brigades to occupy the system of trenches that defended the intervals between the inner forts so as to cover a further retirement should it become necessary. By 11.30 they were busy trying to improve the trenches with such tools as they had been able to get hold of, but in about an hour's time it became evident that the Germans were not pressing their attack, and General Paris ordered the 1st Brigade to advance along the Lierre Road and to throw forward one battalion to support the Marines at Boschoek, and another to Château Weyninekx so as to prolong the Marines' line westward to the Malines railway.

The situation seemed now to be fairly hopeful, but on the Schelde things had been going hardly with the Belgian troops who were covering the line of retreat. Attempts by the enemy to force a passage of the river at Baesrode, Termonde and Schoonaerde had never ceased. All were repulsed, but so exhausting was the effort that another whole division had to be withdrawn from the front of attack and sent across the Schelde at Tamise to reinforce the threatened points. But this was not all. The right of the German main army, which had been defeated on the Marne, was reported to have reached the vicinity of Lille and to be sending a mixed force of 5,000 cavalry and infantry in motor-cars through Mouscron towards Ostend. There was therefore an obvious danger of the Belgian Army being cut off from those of the Allies. Its retreat, in fact, was being threatened from a new direction, and if the situation was to be saved it was necessary to reach out further up the Schelde and occupy Ghent at the great eastward bend of the river.

It had been hoped that the place would have been secured by the British VIIth Division. " Since the 4th," says a Belgian report, " the General Staff, convinced that Ghent must be occupied at all costs, and having no force available for the purpose, had urgently informed England, who was showing herself disposed to hold out a hand to prolong the defence of Antwerp, of the necessity of occupying Ghent. The intervention of the British VIIth Division, then disembarking on the coast, had been promised, and at the same time some French forces were to take part in the movement." [1] But of these succours there was still no sign at the crucial point. Neither the French Marine Brigade, nor the Territorials, nor our own VIIth and Cavalry Divisions had been heard of.

The fact was that considerable difficulty had been experienced in getting the British divisions into place. The orders directed that they were to leave Southampton during the night of Sunday the 4th, at the same time that the Naval Brigade left Dover. By that time the new protective mine-field would be completed, but, owing to the insecure condition of the Channel, further precautions had to be taken to safeguard their passage. The French were asked to provide all available torpedo boats to form an anti-submarine patrol from Selsea Bill to Dover. The Admiral of Patrols was to provide a special destroyer guard for the Strait, and Commodore Tyrwhitt was to use a sufficient number of the Harwich destroyers between the German and the British mine areas to prevent any enemy submarines getting through.

The French at once did what was required, and even went beyond what was required by the British plan. The Territorial Division which they were throwing into the gap was to come from Havre to Dunkirk by sea, and, according

[1] *L'Action de l'Armée Belge* (English translation), p. 60.

to their traditional views, the transports required cruiser escort. They were still unconvinced by the British system of cover and patrol, and accordingly they suddenly recalled for the duty their four armoured cruisers from Admiral Bethell's Western Squadron. He represented at once that the withdrawal of these ships rendered his squadron wholly inadequate to maintain an effective watch on the mouth of the Channel, and the Admiralty lost no time in begging the French to retain the ships in the covering position; but they still apparently preferred their own system—useless as such ships were against submarines. At the last moment, therefore, the western cover broke down.

Nor was this the end of the trouble. The orders for the VIIth Division and the Cavalry Division were to proceed to Dunkirk and Boulogne. But in the afternoon of the 4th, when it was known that the French Division was going to Dunkirk, the order was changed to Calais or Boulogne. Since the British reinforcements numbered 20,000 men, 68 guns, besides horses and vehicles, a clear port was evidently necessary for their reception. The Admiralty proceeded to give instructions accordingly, but the arrangements were barely complete when the War Office, owing apparently to the rapid development of the military situation in Flanders, suddenly asked that the troops should be taken on to Zeebrugge.

Nothing can speak more highly of the patient endurance of the Navy than that the demand was not at once and definitely refused. Sorely against their will, and solely to meet urgent military needs, they had consented at great risk to lay a minefield to protect the passage to Dunkirk, and now they were asked to take the transports through it. For the minefield blocked the approach to Zeebrugge, and a channel would have to be swept before the troops could pass. Still, having set their hand to the work of saving the military situation, they were not going to turn back. By midnight it was known that the Belgian troops had retired behind the Nethe, and the thing was settled. In the small hours of October 5 the orders began to go out for the transport staff from Nantes and Dunkirk to hasten to Zeebrugge, for the two southern groups of mine-sweepers which were then working between the Kentish Knock and the North Foreland to sweep the necessary channel, and for no ships of the convoy to proceed beyond Dover without orders. The weather was very bad for sweeping, but the attempt was made, and two of the vessels engaged were never heard of again.[1] Moreover, the submarines were still teasing.

[1] *Princess Beatrice* and *Drumoak*.

Early in the morning the *Coquette* of the Nore Defence Flotilla reported having chased one off the North Foreland and having lost her when she dived. It was necessary, therefore, to provide one, and, if possible, two destroyers to accompany each transport. It was also deemed essential to guard against a naval attack on Zeebrugge, which was likely enough to be attempted as soon as it was known we were using it. Consequently, the best of the Harwich submarines were told off to protect the new base, but the Ems patrol was maintained, and here on October 6 Lieut.-Commander Horton in *E 9* caught and sank the destroyer *S 116.*

Under this system of protection, in spite of the fact that the narrow course the transports had to take forbade all deviations, the passage proceeded without incident till the evening of the 6th. The ships were organised in batches, and those of each batch were proceeding singly at intervals of ten minutes. Submarines were certainly about. The *Mohawk*, one of the patrol destroyers, was actually attacked. No harm was done, but as seven transports passed over the spot within an hour and a half, it was clearly not for lack of danger that the whole of them escaped. It was nothing but the skill and vigilance displayed and the masterly versatility in conforming to the sudden changes of the military plans that saved them. So the work went on, and by the morning of October 7 the whole of the VIIth Division was safely across. The Cavalry convoy was a still more difficult matter, and the problem was complicated by the disovery that Zeebrugge was not fitted for a cavalry base and that they would have to use Ostend. To add to the trouble, the French were asking for special flotilla protection for their base at Dunkirk. Here, then, was another surprise to face. As things stood, it was impossible to provide destroyers enough for this duty as well as for escort, and the cavalry transports had to be ordered into the Downs till other arrangements could be made. Eventually, however, by calling down eight more destroyers from Harwich and giving the transports a new route through the Dunkirk defended area and then along the coast, the delicate and dangerous operation was carried through without accident.

Yet, the difficulties of getting the troops into position were by no means at an end. When Major-General Capper, commanding the VIIth Division, arrived he was pressed by the local military authorities at Ostend to entrain at once for Antwerp, but in view of reports of the attempts the enemy were making to pass the Schelde below Ghent he felt bound to decline. Having been specially cautioned by

Lord Kitchener and the Chief of Staff not to get shut up in
the fortress, he decided to billet his division about Bruges
till the situation became clearer.   Lieut.-General Sir Henry
Rawlinson, who had come up by car from the Aisne to command the whole force, endorsed his view and established
his headquarters at Bruges.

By this time, indeed, the idea of raising the siege by
operating as originally arranged had been practically
abandoned.   In view of the way the situation in Belgium
was developing, General Joffre and Sir John French had held
a conference, at which they agreed generally that the best
way now of relieving Antwerp was to carry out as rapidly
as possible the great operation for turning the German right
flank about Lille upon which they were then concentrating
their main effort.   In pursuance of this idea General Joffre
ordered the Fusilier Marin Brigade to conform to the movements of the Royal Naval Division, presumably with the
idea that Antwerp would then be able to hold out for the
required period, but the Territorial Division he diverted to
Poperinghe just west of Ypres, and at the same time ordered
a second Territorial Division from Paris to Cherbourg, there
to embark for Dunkirk.   Unfortunately, by some oversight
these orders were not communicated by the French Staff
to Sir John French or our War Office.   General Rawlinson
was thus left in ignorance that the combination on which
his operations depended had been cancelled, and he was
at a loss what to make of it.   All that was clear was that the
expedition could not now be carried out as designed.   He had
still nothing but the VIIth Division in sight—the cavalry
had not yet arrived, the Royal Naval Division appeared to
be already shut up in Antwerp, and of the French Marines
and Territorials there was still no news.   Moreover, while the
situation at Antwerp was still obscure, it was certain that
large bodies of hostile cavalry were concentrating about Lille as
though to turn the French left, and by the evening of the
6th it was known the communication between that town
and Dunkirk had been cut.

Meanwhile at Antwerp, owing to the loss of the line of
the Nethe and the continued pressure of the Germans on
the line of retreat, it had been decided that the time had
come for extricating the Field Army in order to ensure its
ability to co-operate with the expected relieving force.
General Rawlinson had gone on there to concert measures
with the Belgian General Staff, and in the afternoon of
October 6 a conference took place at which Mr. Churchill
was again present.   The outcome was that, in view of the

fact that from the lost ground the Germans could bombard the city and that the troops were becoming exhausted both physically and morally, a general retirement to the line of the inner forts must be carried out at once. General Paris, with the Naval Division and Belgian support, would hold the intervals to the utmost so long as the city endured the bombardment, and the rest of the Belgian Field Army was to be withdrawn immediately to an entrenched camp across the Schelde. From that position they would be best able to assist in any relieving movement from the westward which might still be possible, while General Rawlinson organised the relieving force at Ghent and Bruges. At the same time the Belgian Government decided to retire to Ostend.

The plan for withdrawing the Field Army was for three of the remaining four divisions to move across the river during the night while General Paris covered the retirement. He at once gave the word for the whole of his force to retire to the trenches in the intervals between the forts—the forts themselves being occupied by fortress troops. The 1st Naval Brigade, which led the retirement, took post on the left, Drake being between Forts Nos. 5 and 4, Collingwood between Nos. 4 and 3, Hawke on the extreme left between Nos. 3 and 2, and Benbow in reserve. The 2nd Brigade continued the line from No. 5 to 7, while one battalion of the Marine Brigade was between Nos. 7 and 8, with the rest in reserve at Waesdonck. Here the defences were also found to be very weak, and all that day and during the night strenuous efforts were made, with the assistance of the Royal Engineers and some Belgian troops, to improve them. So much progress was made that the 1st Brigade, at any rate, were fully prepared to hold on. While the work was proceeding during the 7th all was comparatively quiet, but during the night a heavy bombardment of the city took place. As, however, the Government had left for Ostend and the civil population had been streaming across the Schelde after the army, this caused no immediate anxiety. But in the morning of the 8th the Germans began to shell vigorously the trenches which the Royal Naval Division was holding, and at the same time to develop a strong attack on Forts 1 and 2. General Paris, who was already convinced that the ill-prepared position was untenable under shell fire, at least for the raw and exhausted troops at his disposal, had telephoned at 7.5 a.m. to General Rawlinson at Bruges that he could not hold out beyond the day, and that he would then retire to the westward. To add to his anxiety, he now saw that the attack on the forts was endangering his left flank, and gave warning to this effect. Still, it was many hours before any definite orders for the retirement reached the division. Everything had been too hurried for proper staff arrangements to be made, and communication was very difficult. At 2.30 p.m., though no fresh instructions had reached the 1st Brigade, it was found that the Belgians had evacuated Fort No. 4. The 1st Brigade then occupied it with a company from the reserve battalion, and by sending another company to Fort No. 3, induced the Belgian garrisons both there and at Fort No. 2 to hold on. They had still no thought of letting go, and shortly after 4.0 the Marine Brigade sent a whole battalion to reinforce them. They were not, however, to be permitted to retain their hold. Already early in the day, on a false report that the northern forts had fallen, a decision had been come to at Headquarters in Antwerp that the British Force and the remaining Belgian division should be withdrawn across the Schelde during the night to join the main Belgian Army. This decision was now confirmed. They were to retire through the city and cross the two bridges of boats which had been constructed at Burght and St. Anne, and thence march to St. Nicolas, where trains would be waiting to take them on.

This order was received about 6.0 p.m., and in an hour's time the 2nd and Marine Brigades were marching away through Antwerp to cross the river by the Burght bridge. The Drake Battalion, which was on the right of the 1st Brigade, followed them, but the order did not reach the rest of the Brigade. They therefore stood fast till nearly 7.0 p.m., when a staff officer arrived with orders that they were to retire outside the city to the Gare de Formation—a railway depot opposite Burght—and that the 2nd Brigade would cover and follow the retirement. The movement was to begin at 9.0 p.m. It was not till an hour or so later that they found that the rest of the division had already gone, and even so they could not get away at once. The Hawke Battalion, which was furthest north, found the village in their rear was being shelled, and they had to make a detour. Finally, it was fully 10.0 p.m. before they could move off, and then with nothing on their right it was unsafe to proceed by the Military Road as had been intended. They had to go by by-ways and through a wood in single file. Ably led as they were by three officers who had reconnoitred the route during the day, progress was very slow, many men fell out exhausted, and it was not till 1.30 a.m. that Brigade Headquarters reached the Gare de Formation and began to cross the river in a steamer to Burght.

By this time the general situation was extremely critical. When in the morning of October 8 General Rawlinson received General Paris's message that he would scarcely be able to hold out during the day and must retire in the night, he was back at Bruges. But there was no longer any thought of organising his force for the relief of Antwerp. He knew the Belgian Army was retreating westward from the entrenched camp, and he was in doubt whether he was even in a position to cover its retirement. There were indications of strong German forces moving northward, as though intending to drive the retreating army over the Dutch frontier, and it was essential to do something to save it as well as our own Naval Division. Ghent had been occupied by some 1,500 Belgians; he also knew that some at least of the French Fusiliers Marins had left Dunkirk to assist them, but of the lost Territorial Division he had still no news. The VIIth Division was concentrated and could reach Ghent next evening, and so could the Cavalry Division, which was then disembarking at Zeebrugge. He therefore announced his intention of making an effort, desperate as it seemed, to keep the road open unless he received definite orders not to attempt it.

At home there was grave doubt at the time whether it could be effected. In view of the increasing German concentration about Lille, something had to be done to protect Dunkirk, where the French Territorials were beginning to arrive. A detachment of 900 Royal Marine Artillery, with sixteen field guns, had just landed there with orders to proceed at once to Antwerp. They were now ordered to send on only half the number, the rest to stay with the guns, and the Oxfordshire Hussars were also told to stand fast and assist the defence of the place.[1]

Ostend was an equal source of anxiety. On receipt of General Paris's message from Antwerp, the Cavalry, as it landed at Zeebrugge, was ordered to march to that port and billet, and the heavy guns to remain there. To cover this movement General Rawlinson had ordered General Capper with the VIIth Division to take up a position on an arc four miles out of Ostend. For the moment, then, they could not move. Indeed, so menacing was the unexpected strength the enemy was developing that it was still uncertain whether the whole force would not have to be withdrawn, and at 10.45 a.m. on October 8 came a message that motor-transport

---

[1] This detachment of Royal Marine Artillery was organised under an Order of September 22, to consist of four batteries of 4 12-pdr. Q.F. guns and 331 men, to furnish field artillery for the Naval Division.

was not to be unloaded pending a Cabinet decision, and all
empty transports were to remain. At 2.30 p.m. Headquarters
moved into Ostend, and five minutes later the Cabinet
decision was made known. The disembarkation at Zeebrugge
was to continue, but the transports were to stand fast till
further orders. Similar orders were subsequently sent to
Ostend.

The Cabinet had decided that the force should remain,
at least to make an effort to cover the retirement from
Antwerp. It had already made fair progress. The previous
morning (the 7th) all the Belgian troops, except the rear
guard, were on the west bank of the Schelde, and although
the enemy succeeded in forcing a passage of the river at
Schoonaerde, and so were directly threatening the line of
retreat, they were held at Berlaere and could get no further
that day. German troops were also reported in the vicinity
of Ghent, but with the Belgian Brigade that had been detached there the place would be safe till the Allied troops
could reach it.

Definite orders to protect the retirement both of the
Belgian Army and the Naval Division reached the British
Headquarters at 5.45 p.m. on the 8th. By this time it was
known that the French Marine Brigade had been railed to
Ghent to join the Belgian Brigade that was holding the
place, and, in fact, the last battalion was just detraining.[1]
The General therefore decided to support them, and sent
off to Ghent two brigades of the VIIth Division with some
artillery to co-operate in the Belgian plan. The other
infantry brigade was to move back to Bruges as a reserve,
and one cavalry brigade to Ecloo, where the Belgian Headquarters was established on the 9th.

Owing to the inexperience of an improvised railway
staff, these dispositions took a long time to carry out, and
they were still in progress when at 9 a.m. on the 9th the
Naval Division was reported to have reached Selzaete, behind
the Terneuzen Canal, and to be " coming along all right."

So far all was well. The bulk of the Belgian Army was
getting into position behind the Terneuzen Canal from Selzaete on the Dutch frontier to Ghent, with one division in
reserve at Ostend. On this line it was hoped to make a
permanent stand against the German invasion, and to
connect up with the left of the Franco-British Army as it
extended northwards. Rear guards had been left at Loo-
christy, Lokeren, Wachtebeke and Moerbeke to cover the
retreat of the Naval Division and the Belgian Division. This

---

[1] Vedel : *Nos Marins à la Guerre*, p. 257.

rear guard the Germans were endeavouring to force by a strong attack upon Lokeren. The statement, however, that the Naval Division was " coming along all right " was not entirely true. The 2nd Brigade and the Marines, with the Drake Battalion, made their way in good order through the narrow streets of Antwerp to the south-west corner of the city. Here they had to pass out again to proceed along the river to the bridge at Burght. The whole route was flanked by the oil tanks which the Belgians had fired and which were sending up vast columns of smoke. The heat of the conflagration was almost unbearable, but the pall of smoke had prevented the Germans from destroying the bridge by shell fire, and the river was crossed in safety. From Burght the march continued to Beveren Waes on the railway that goes to Bruges by way of St. Nicolas and Lokeren. Here there was a hitch. A report had come in that the Germans had driven in the Belgian covering force at Lokeren and were advancing on St. Nicolas. It had accordingly been hastily decided that our men must proceed by the railway which ran near the Dutch frontier, and they had to strike off to their right front for St. Gilles-Waes, where they were informed trains would be found to take them direct to Ostend. On the new and devious route they struck the main line of retreat from the St. Anne Bridge, along which the Belgian Division was retiring. It was further choked with transport and throngs of refugees. There were no staff officers to control the traffic, and the brigades soon lost cohesion in the utter confusion that ensued. Still they toiled on, and eventually reached St. Gilles-Waes and were able to entrain for Ostend.

The attempt of the Germans to break through the covering force at Lokeren had, in fact, been checked. For a time it was certainly dangerous, and as soon as the British Cavalry Brigade reached Ecloo the Belgian Staff had asked for an offensive movement on that point to relieve the pressure. Preparations were at once made for an advance, but before they were complete the Belgian Headquarters announced that all anxiety was over in that direction, but that a more serious danger was threatening in the direction of Alost. The movement was therefore abandoned, and with serious results.

Meanwhile the rest of the 1st Brigade had reached Zwyndrecht on the main road west from Antwerp. Here they expected to find the Divisional Headquarters, or orders, but they found nothing but crowds of refugees, and it was not for some time that they heard the rest of the division had passed through Beveren and had gone on to St. Gilles-Waes. There was nothing for it but to press forward. The men, who had had no food since noon on the previous day, could do no more than put one foot before another. Still they struggled on, mixed with a helpless stream of fugitives, at a mile an hour, and eventually some 1,500 of them reached St. Gilles-Waes in the afternoon. There they found that the rest of the division had left some eight hours previously, and about 4.15 they were able to begin entraining. But long before the work could be completed news came in that the Germans had cut the line to the north of Lokeren beyond Moerbeke and were advancing upon St. Gilles-Waes. It would seem that about 4 p.m. a detachment which had been pushed out from Lokeren with artillery had attacked a train in which Colonel Luard was retiring with the 10th Battalion of Marines. The attack was met, but effective resistance soon proved impossible. All his efforts were frustrated by a throng of panic-stricken refugees who had boarded the train, and though he himself succeeded in extricating 150 men and reached Salzaete, the rest (five officers and 931 other ranks) were forced to surrender. A second train, seeing what was happening, went back to tell the tale. The last exit to the west seemed closed, the brigade was utterly exhausted by its march during the day and the previous night, it was without guns, ammunition, transport, food or water, and Commodore W. Henderson decided there was nothing to be done except to march north-east along the railway and try to cover the few miles between them and Dutch territory. This was done, and about 5 p.m. the frontier was reached. Here some thirty or forty men, with two officers, elected to try to escape along the border line, and they succeeded, but all the rest of the brigade and the engineer detachment, which had stood by them till the last, gave up their arms, and next day were removed by rail for internment.

With this exception, by the morning of October 10 the withdrawal from Antwerp was successfully accomplished, and, as was soon known, all might have escaped. The railway was still open. The Germans, after their coup at Moerbeke, appear to have retired hastily to Lokeren, possibly for fear of several thousand Belgian troops who, having chivalrously given up the trains to the British, were endeavouring to get away by road. The train the Germans had stopped was taken on later by a Belgian officer who could drive a locomotive. Another train with about 200 of our men passed later still, and other small parties got away on foot. Among them were the men who had been sent to re-occupy

Fort No. 4, under Lieutenant Grant, R.N.V.R. No order to retire reached him till midnight. When he reached the river he found the bridge blown up, but, crossing by a steamer, he caught up the battalion that was retiring over the Dutch frontier. As soon, however, as he knew what their intention was he broke away westward. Another officer who got away was Flight-Lieutenant Marix of the Royal Naval Air Service, who on the 8th had made a flight to Düsseldorf and had there destroyed a Zeppelin in its shed.

But though the threat to the line of retreat from Antwerp had not materialised, new grounds for anxiety quickly declared themselves. The French left was as far away as Arras, and the British Army from the Aisne, which was to fill the gap, had only just begun to detrain its leading units at Abbeville. Added to this, the effort of the Germans to interpose themselves between the Belgians and their Allies, which was developing about Ghent and Alost, was getting serious. In the course of the day Antwerp capitulated, so that in a few days the siege army would be free for the field; and the trouble culminated in the news that three, and possibly four, newly formed German Reserve Corps, whose existence had been unsuspected, were entering Belgium. In these circumstances it was obviously impossible to hold the line of the Terneuzen Canal, or even that of Schipdonck Canal which lay immediately to the westward. For the Belgians further retreat was imperative to some position which was not only capable of prolonging defence, but which would also ensure an effective junction with the Franco-British forces. Such a position was to be found no nearer than the Yser. To that line a retreat was therefore ordered under cover of the Allied Forces which were now gathering about Ghent.[1]

Such a movement entailed grave danger to our base ports at Zeebrugge and Ostend, and, indeed, their eventual abandonment. It was to Ostend the Naval Division had been ordered to retire. Having served its immediate purpose it had done all—and more than all—it was then fit for, and was now to be withdrawn to England. There was as yet plenty of time, but as a precaution, in case the Germans should succeed in breaking through in the vicinity of Ghent, the Admiralty ordered the three monitors to Ostend to cover the re-embarkation and the evacuation of the base so far as was immediately advisable. The work which these new dispositions unexpectedly threw upon the Transport Department and the Flotilla in the Strait was very

[1] *L'Action de l'Armée Belge* (English translation), p. 64.

heavy. The instructions were that the Naval Division, numbering now between 5,000 and 6,000 men, including the Marines, were to be embarked that night and sent into camp at Deal. Some 1,500 Belgian recruits and volunteers at Ostend were to be embarked for Cherbourg and 11,000 more Belgian recruits to be transported to the same place. Zeebrugge was also to be evacuated, and all transports there to leave at once. In addition to all this labour, the orders provided for dealing with the removal of Belgian stores and of from 8,000 to 10,000 wounded then at Ostend. But this work was to be subject to the need of our troops in case they required assistance, and there was a special instruction that enough transports to re-embark the VIIth Division and IIIrd Cavalry Division were to be kept in immediate readiness with steam up for the next forty-eight hours. Although it was unlikely they would have to be brought off, preparations for the emergency were to be made, and General Rawlinson was to telephone direct to the Admiralty the moment the situation rendered his re-embarkation likely. The three monitors were also held at his call, and all the naval armoured trains, armed motor-cars and aircraft (except those under Commander Samson at Dunkirk) were handed over to him.

The emergency never arose. General Rawlinson's Force, though too late and, owing to unforeseen developments, too weak to save Antwerp, was yet dropped in from the sea in time and strength enough to stop the enemy's efforts to cut off the Belgians altogether. It remained in Flanders, and from now onward, in co-operation with the French troops acting with it, became absorbed in the movements of the rest of the British Army which culminated in the first battle of Ypres. The battle had already begun with the cavalry in contact north of the Aire-Bethune Canal, and the race for the sea had reached the decisive phase, as the remains of the Naval Division re-embarked.

Though the combination which had been planned for the relief of Antwerp had never materialised, and the Naval Division had been left without support, it had something to show for the severe losses it had suffered (52 officers and 2,558 other ranks, of whom 37 officers and 1,442 other ranks were interned). In a general order some days after their return the Admiralty summed up the results. After complimenting all ranks on the way they had borne the ordeal, it was explained that they had been chosen for the work as the nearest available force and the most quickly embarked. "The Naval Division," it was further stated, "was sent to Antwerp not as an isolated incident but as part of a large operation for the relief of the city. Other and more powerful considerations prevented this from being carried through. The defence of the inner lines of Antwerp could have been maintained for some days; and the Naval Division only withdrew when ordered to do so in obedience to the general strategic situation, and not on account of any attack or pressure by the enemy. The prolongation of the defence, due to the arrival of the division, enabled the ships in the harbour to be rendered useless and many steps of importance to be taken. It is too early now to judge what effect the delaying even for four or five days of at least 60,000 Germans before Antwerp may have had upon the fortunes of the general battle to the southward. It was certainly powerful and helpful."

The claim that the work of the Naval Division had not been wholly barren is certainly justified. Whether by prolonging the defence of Antwerp it really did anything to save the Belgian Army for the brilliant part they were destined to play in the operations for the defence of the Channel coast is doubtful. The justification of the attempt is rather to be sought in the concluding words of the Admiralty's general order. At the crisis of the race for the sea the German army of the north had been held for several days before Antwerp. But for the promise of the Naval Division the evacuation of the city would have begun on October 3; as it was, the surrender did not take place till the 10th. This was just the critical week. Unless something had been done, the army besieging Antwerp would have been free by the middle of it to prolong the right of the main German line. As it was, before they could move, there had been time to throw our two divisions and the French Marine Division into the gap between Ypres and the sea. There had also been time for a French Territorial Division to reach Dunkirk, and, what was of the last importance, time for our Expeditionary Force to get well forward with its flank march and to obtain a hold on the new ground it was to occupy south of Ypres.

Nor in judging the whole episode must it be forgotten that Belgium in its extremity had appealed for assistance, and it was an appeal which in honour could scarcely be disregarded short of absolute inability. It was this aspect of the affair which, when all was over, seems at least to have remained uppermost in the mind of the Belgian Cabinet. " I am to inform your Excellency," wrote the Foreign Minister to Sir Edward Grey, " that if the British co-operation did not avail to save Antwerp, the King's Government is none the less grateful to Great Britain for having complied with its request."

14

CHAPTER XIV

SPREAD OF THE GERMAN SUBMARINE ATTACK AND THE
CANADIAN CONVOY [1]

NOTHING is more eloquent of the effective control which
the Navy was exercising over the North Sea, than that no
attempt was made by the German Fleet to interrupt the
operations for filling the Flanders gap. The startling success
which the enemy had just achieved against the cruisers of
the Southern Force seemed to have opened the way for a
telling blow at the new line of passage, and, as we have seen,
an attempt was expected and prepared against as far as was
possible at the moment. For this work the Southern Cruiser
Force was no longer available; it had ceased to exist. On
October 2 both Admiral Christian and Admiral Campbell
had been ordered to strike their flags, and their flagships,
Euryalus and *Bacchante*, were told off for other duties, to the
westward, where, as the Admiralty had indicated before the
late disaster, their most suitable field of action lay, and where
they were now urgently required.

The Wessex Territorial Division was about to sail for
India to replace the troops that were proceeding to Europe,
and the passage across the Bay was no longer guarded. The
Cruiser Patrol, which the French had been asked to establish
from Ushant to Finisterre, when the Army base was shifted
to the mouth of the Loire, had suddenly been withdrawn as
soon as it was known the base was to be shifted back to Havre.
The idea of the French in taking this step was to use the
cruisers to reinforce Admiral Bethell, whose force at the mouth
of the Channel had been so badly weakened by the withdrawal of the French armoured cruisers as escort for the
French Territorial Division from Havre to Dunkirk. Beyond
Finisterre, Admiral de Robeck's squadron was more than fully
occupied with the special duties of the station, and it had
become necessary to provide escort for the outgoing division
as far as Gibraltar. This much-frequented section of the
Mediterranean and Eastern transport route had always been
difficult to guard, and had been a serious disturbance to the

[1] See Maps 2 and 9 in case.

work of the squadron concerned. Its importance was growing, and likely to grow.   It was therefore decided to furnish it with a regular and permanent escort service, and for this purpose the *Euryalus* and *Bacchante* were now attached to the Western Squadron. At the same time, to provide for a continuous patrol of the Bay, the French were requested still to maintain three cruisers between Ushant and Finisterre.

For another reason—and again a military reason—the security of the western area was specially important at the moment.   A further development of the great Imperial Concentration was on foot, and this was the sailing of the first Canadian contingent.   We have seen how, as early as September 12, Admiral Wemyss had taken his four light cruisers from the Western Patrol to fetch it, and how Admiral Bethell had replaced him with his reduced battle squadron. The convoy was expected to sail on September 23, but from various causes it was delayed till October 3, and by that time the Canadian Government had become seriously apprehensive for its safe transit.   The convoy in the St. Lawrence consisted of thirty-one ships, and was to be joined off Cape Race by two more—one with the Newfoundland contingent and one with the 2nd Battalion of the Lincolns from Bermuda, where it was being replaced by the Royal Regiment of Canadian Infantry. For such a force, when it came to the point of sailing, the escort provided seemed to the Canadian authorities wholly inadequate, and on October 2 the Admiralty, in the height of their preoccupation with Antwerp and the Flanders gap, found themselves being urgently pressed to increase it.

The demand, it would seem, was made under a misapprehension as regards both the strength of the escort, which had been already arranged, and the principle of covering squadrons on which the Admiralty was mainly relying.   Of these covering squadrons there were two—the Grand Fleet that lay between the line of passage and the German Home ports, and the North-American Squadron (now under Admiral Hornby) which was watching the German liners in New York and the adjacent ports.   It was from one of these two points that attack was alone possible, except, perhaps, from the *Karlsruhe*, *Dresden* and *Kronprinz Wilhelm* which were known to be in the Atlantic. It was but natural that a Government unfamiliar with the methods of naval warfare should ignore these two important elements and fix its anxious attention on the comparatively slender escort in sight.   But this had, in fact, been materially increased.   At first, when it was understood that the convoy would consist of no more than fourteen ships, Admiral Wemyss's squadron was considered by the Admiralty as sufficient, but later, when owing to the splendid response which Canada made to the Imperial call, it was known that double the number of transports would not suffice, important additions to the escort had been made. From Admiral Hornby's squadron his battleship, the *Glory*, was taken, and the *Majestic* from Admiral Bethell's was ordered to meet the convoy at a certain rendezvous on the secret route which had been given far out of ken of the usual track. At the same rendezvous the convoy would also be met by one of the best battle cruisers of the Grand Fleet, and for this purpose Admiral Jellicoe had been ordered to detach the *Princess Royal*. All this had been explained to the Canadian Government as early as September 19—that is, all but the last item. Had this been known there would probably have been no complaint, but it could not be revealed. In view of what the functions of the Grand Fleet were, its battle cruisers were all important—so important, indeed, that the detaching of one of them was dictated not so much by military considerations as to afford testimony of how highly the Canadian effort was appreciated by the Mother Country. It was much to ask of Admiral Jellicoe, but it was in accordance with the old principle that such detachments from the Main Fleet were within its normal action and involved little risk if they could be kept secret from the enemy while they lasted. Secrecy, in fact, was the essence of the expedient, and the value of secrecy was as yet scarcely realised by the Canadian Press. Details of the convoy and the force it carried had been published in the papers and telegraphed home *en clair*. It was necessary, therefore, to keep the secret of the *Princess Royal* between the Admiralty and the Commander-in-Chief; even Admiral Wemyss was not informed. Naturally, the conduct of the Admiralty was misunderstood, but it was only one more of the many misunderstandings which they were content to suffer patiently, so long as additional safety was secured for all it was their hard duty to protect. They were content, in fact, to know that when, on October 3, Admiral Wemyss led the convoy out of the St. Lawrence its passage was as secure as skill and force could make it.

As a covering force for the New York Area were the *Suffolk*, the *Caronia* and the Canadian cruiser *Niobe*, but as the escort would be sufficient without her the *Niobe* did not sail. Admiral Hornby himself, in the *Lancaster*, accompanied the convoy as far as longitude 40° W. On October 5 they met the *Glory* and the Lincolns off Cape Race; the Newfoundland contingent also joined, and together they proceeded on their secret route. On the 8th Admiral Hornby turned back, and next day they were in touch with the *Princess Royal* and *Majestic*, which for over two days had been waiting for them at the mid-Atlantic rendezvous. So, with ample escort, they carried on for the defended area off the mouth of the Channel.

With the Grand Fleet Admiral Jellicoe had made a disposition which rendered it almost impossible for any force equal to the Canadian escort to reach the convoy route from German ports. On September 30 he had returned to Scapa after a three-days' sweep to the Skagerrak in support of a submarine reconnaissance that was being made inside the Skaw. He then issued his new scheme of operation, which was to begin on October 2 and last a week while the Canadian Convoy was passing. Its main feature was the occupation of the cruiser areas, which he had established between Peterhead and the Norwegian Coast, by the 2nd, 3rd and most of the 10th Cruiser Squadron, as well as the light cruisers with the four battle squadrons in support.[1] In addition, however, there was a second line so placed as to sight in the morning anything that passed the main line in the night. It was in three sections on the line of the islands. The Pentland Firth was declared closed to all ships of war passing from east to west, and the destroyer patrol had orders to fire on any attempting to do so. West of Fair Island, to watch the passage between the Orkneys and Shetlands, was the 1st Battle Cruiser Squadron, without, of course, the *Princess Royal*, who parted company for her escort duty the day the scheme started. North of the Shetlands and extended towards the Faeroes was the 2nd Battle Cruiser Squadron (*Invincible* and *Inflexible*), with the *Sappho* and the three minelayers. The cover was thus stronger than it had been at any time during the war, and it was maintained in full strength till October 10, the day on which the convoy continued its voyage with the *Princess Royal* and *Majestic* in company.

It had been Admiral Jellicoe's intention to coal at Loch Ewe after the operation, but on October 7 he had gone to Scapa with the *Iron Duke* to confer on certain matters with the Fourth Sea Lord. Amongst the subjects discussed was the organisation of a system of trawler patrol areas as a means of curbing the activity of enemy submarines in the vicinity of the Grand Fleet bases, and while it was being considered its urgency was emphasised by the unwelcome intelligence that one, or possibly two submarines had appeared inside Loch

[1] These cruiser areas were established by the Commander-in-Chief by Fleet Order 84, August 1, and were subsequently modified by orders of August 8 and September 14. (See Map No. 1 in case.)

Ewe. There seemed to be no doubt about it, for the repair ship *Assistance* came to report exactly what had happened. No torpedo had been fired—probably, so it was thought, because no ship of high military value was in the anchorage at the time.   Nevertheless it was considered no place to coal the fleet ; the *Assistance* remained at Scapa, and the Commander-in-Chief rejoined the fleet there. No submarine, however, had, in fact, visited Loch Ewe.

On rejoining he found further annoyance from submarines. Our Minister at Christiania reported one accompanied by four cruisers off Skudesnæs. These waters were being patrolled by Admiral Pakenham with the 3rd Cruiser Squadron (*Antrim, Argyll, Roxburgh, Devonshire*). They had seen nothing of the reported cruisers, but during the afternoon of October 9 the flagship *Antrim* was attacked by a submarine about twenty miles south-west of Skudesnæs. Two torpedoes were fired ; she eluded both and steamed full speed straight at her assailant, with what result was uncertain, but Admiral Pakenham was of opinion that the submarine escaped. No more was seen of her, but three miles away was a steamer like a large trawler, which was stopped and seemed to be attending her. In view of what had happened to the " Cressys " it was too great a risk to examine her, and, in accordance with the recent Admiralty order, she had to be left alone.

Here was a striking instance of the crying need for more boarding vessels to be attached to the cruiser squadrons. Till they were forthcoming the submarine trouble could never be dealt with adequately, and, indeed, this was one of the points which the Commander-in-Chief had just been settling with the Fourth Sea Lord at Scapa. The question was all the more urgent since our mining of the Southern Area must inevitably tend to increase the flow of traffic north-about. Cruisers were already reporting an abnormal volume of trade entering the Skagerrak ; much of it could not be examined at all, and with the approaching season of bad weather and short days the work would be more difficult than ever. The Commander-in-Chief reported that, in spite of all he could do, food and supplies were reaching the enemy in considerable quantities, and in his opinion the only cure was to require all neutral vessels to call at a British port for inspection. Those neglecting to do so should be sent in by the cruisers. After inspection innocent vessels would be allowed to proceed flying a private signal. His proposal was too great a stretch of belligerent rights to be adopted at once. As yet it was only at sea that it was fully realised how profoundly changed were the conditions of search and blockade by the advent of the submarine, but another striking illustration was soon to be provided.

When, on October 12, Admiral Jellicoe brought the Dreadnought Battle Squadrons into Scapa for a few days' rest and refit, the battle cruisers and light cruisers made a sweep down to the Dogger Bank, while the rest occupied the north-about passage.   The bulk of the 10th Cruiser Squadron (*Crescent, Edgar, Endymion, Theseus, Hawke* and *Grafton*) were still detached from their normal duty on the Northern Patrol, which was left to the "Duncans" and the rest of Admiral de Chair's command.   He himself, with the above six ships, was occupying the central station between Peterhead and the Naze. At the moment, however, he was not with them, having taken his flagship, the *Crescent*, into Cromarty to coal, but he had left definite instructions for the method of cruising so as to minimise the risk of submarine attack.   These instructions they were carrying out, with the *Edgar* as senior ship, when at 1.20 p.m., on October 15, the *Theseus* reported she had been attacked by submarines.   She was not hit, and the *Edgar* ordered all ships to steam north-west at full speed.   All replied except the *Hawke* (Captain Hugh P. E. T. Williams). The Commander-in-Chief, on hearing of the attack, ordered the squadron, as well as its neighbouring one, to clear away to the northward, and at the same time hurried off the *Swift*, a special type of flotilla leader of exceptional speed, to make search for the *Hawke*.   On nearing the position in which the missing cruiser had last been heard of the *Swift* reported having seen a submarine, but no sign of the missing cruiser.   After a two hours' search, however, a raft was picked up with one officer and twenty men of the *Hawke*, and her fate was known.   On the morning of October 15 the five cruisers that were in company were spread in line abreast at ten-mile intervals, with the *Endymion* to starboard and the *Hawke* next.   At 9.30 the *Endymion* was signalled to close to enable the *Hawke* to get mails from her.   Both ships stopped on closing, and the *Hawke* sent a boat for the bags.   The *Endymion* then passed under the *Hawke's* stern to close the other ships, and the *Hawke*, having hoisted in her boat, was proceeding at 12 or 13 knots to regain station when, about 10.30, there was an explosion abreast the foremost funnel.   The engines were stopped immediately and she started to list.   There was only time to lower the two sea boats; one of them drifted away with three officers and forty-six men and was subsequently picked up by a Norwegian steamer and brought in to Aberdeen.   What became

of the other is unknown. She was probably crushed by the
ship, which rapidly turned over, and then, after floating a
few minutes bottom upwards, went down bow foremost. It
seems to have been thought at first that the cause of the
disaster was a mine, but Captain Williams, while floating
in the water, told an officer who was rescued that he had
seen the track of a torpedo. Though the search was diligently
continued, not another survivor was found, so that nearly
five hundred lives were lost with the ship.

Captain Williams was right ; two submarines (*U 9* and
U 17) were in the area and it was the *U 9* that sank the
Hawke. Shortly after finding the raft the *Swift* was herself
attacked by the *U 17*. A few hours later another division of
destroyers, patrolling off the eastern entrance of the Flow,
were attacked by the *U 9*. All escaped, but only by the
skin of their teeth. The division at the time disposed in
line-abreast to starboard (*Lyra, Nymphe, Nemesis, Alarm*)
was steaming at 13 knots, and at 1.30 p.m. in Lat. 58°

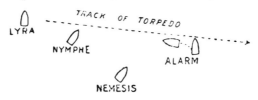

47′ N., Long. 2° 7′ W.,[1] was just altering course. The *Nymphe*
had increased to 15 knots to gain station, when she sighted
a periscope 3 points on the port bow, distant about 300 yards.
The order was immediately given " Hard-a-starboard," and
" Full speed both " to attempt to ram. " The submarine," so
Lieutenant-Commander R. M. King's report continues, " at the
same time fired a torpedo at us. . . . I was in the chart house
at the time and heard Lieutenant Creswell's order to the guns,
and rushed on to the bridge. I saw the submarine's periscope
disappearing, and her wake almost right ahead 200 yards off.
. . . The torpedo missed our stem by about two feet, and,
the ship being under full helm, the track of the torpedo
passed along the starboard side, about two feet off, abaft the
after funnel, when it went under the stern and crossed about
200 yards ahead of the *Nemesis* and 100 yards ahead of the
Alarm. . . . As soon as the torpedo had passed our stern I
put the helm hard-a-port and steered straight for the wake
of the submarine, which I went over. She was still close to

[1] So *Nymphe's* report. *Alarm* made the time 1.20, and the position
Lat. 58° 43′ N., Long. 2° 5′ W.

the surface, and the wash from her propellers could be plainly seen as our stern went over them.   I don't know if we touched, as we felt no shock. . . . I am certain if it had not been for the prompt action of Lieutenant Creswell the ship would have been torpedoed."

According to the *Alarm* her escape was much closer than it appeared to the *Nymphe*.   She saw the *Nymphe* hoist the submarine flag and fire, and then was aware of a torpedo coming straight at her.   Her Commander then says in his report : " I immediately rang down ' Hard-a-starboard ' and ' Full speed ahead both ' and just managed to avoid the torpedo, which passed down my starboard side not more than ten yards distant.   I had to go hard-a-port to prevent my stern swinging on to the torpedo."

Coming, as the *Hawke* disaster did, so soon after the loss of the three " Cressys," its impression was the more telling; nor was this the end of the Commander-in-Chief's trouble.   In the evening of October 16, as he lay at Scapa, having just heard the full extent of the *Hawke* disaster, the Switha Battery reported a submarine inside the anchorage.   Besides the *Iron Duke*, only three other capital ships were there, and as darkness fell all put to sea.   The rest were away at target practice or at their cruising stations and well out of harm's way, but the 3rd Battle Squadron (that is, the " King Edwards ") and the 1st Battle Cruiser Squadron were just leaving their stations to come in.   It was clear that the enemy was pushing vigorously his policy of minor attack, and his recent successes confirmed its correctness and its possibilities.   Indeed, the wonder is, in view of the results obtained, that a nation credited with so full a measure of the military spirit should so soon have turned its promising method of offence against a commercial objective instead of persevering against the naval one.   The Switha report, however, was another false alarm.

To the Commander-in-Chief it was at least clear that the German policy must be taken seriously, and to foil it he decided on a radical change in his whole dispositions.   In the first place he saw it was only playing into the enemy's hands to continue to use the anchorages they had discovered until they were adequately defended.   This was only a question of time.   At Cromarty a system of anti-submarine protection had been installed that gave every satisfaction.   He had already asked for a similar system for Scapa and Loch Ewe, and he had been informed that the necessary material would be put in hand with all speed.   How long it would take was uncertain, but until everything was ready he decided to seek other war anchorages.   It was one of the advantages of our geographical position that the west coast of Scotland provided such conveniences in abundance. The places he chose were two natural harbours well to the southward, in Skye and Mull, and as a third alternative Lough Swilly, a regular defended anchorage of old standing which was being used by the northern section of the Irish Cruiser Squadron.

In the second place he determined to shift his whole cruiser system further north. Instead of holding his advanced line between Peterhead and the Naze, he would draw it back to the islands—that is, to the position of his former second line, maintaining a new second line to the westward and southward. The new system would serve equally well for controlling the trade north-about. It, of course, left the North Sea itself more open, but this drawback was to be met by southern sweeps of the light cruisers at high speed. Finally, in communicating his intentions to the Admiralty, he begged for a dozen more armed merchant steamers to work with the cruisers as examination vessels. No time was lost in inaugurating the new system. On October 17 Admiral Colville reported another submarine inside Scapa; two destroyers had been attacked, again without result, and a vigorous hunt had produced no result. Accordingly, Admiral Jellicoe, next day, again urged the pressing need of the promised defences and began to move the fleet to its new positions.[1]

In the Channel Area the policy the Germans were pursuing required no less attention. Here there were unmistakable indications that they were trying to use their submarines against our communications with Flanders, and we have already seen the trouble they caused upon the new line of passage to Dunkirk; but the effect upon the Canadian Convoy was still greater. From the first the Admiralty felt the danger of bringing it up Channel, and the port they originally wished to use was Liverpool. Inquiry, however, showed that the dislocation of traffic in the Mersey would be too great, and Plymouth was substituted. Preparations to receive the convoy there were actually set on foot, but the War Office had objections. Southampton was the port for which all their arrangements had been made, and they pressed for its adoption. Again the Admiralty were at their wits' end how to meet the wishes of the General Staff. At the moment —it was the end of the first week in October—the Admiralty, at their request, were absorbed with arrangements for a sudden re-embarkation of the VIIth and IIIrd Cavalry Divisions, should the pressure on them in Flanders prove too great.

[1] Though the report was generally believed at the time, no German submarine ever penetrated the anchorage.

To protect the eastern half of the Channel was, therefore, a serious task, and, to add to the difficulty, St. Nazaire was just being closed and Havre substituted with Boulogne as a subsidiary base.   Nevertheless they once more gave way, and on October 10—the day the Canadian Convoy met the *Princess Royal* and *Majestic*—Southampton was settled as the port of disembarkation.   That the concession was not an easy one to make was proved next day by a French Patrol reporting a submarine off Cape Gris Nez, which was the actual landfall which the Flanders Transports had been ordered to make to avoid the new danger.   It all meant increased vigilance in the eastern part of the Channel, while what the War Office wanted called for equal vigilance in the western part.

Admiral Wemyss fully appreciated the difficulty of his task, and in order to minimise the danger he organised the convoy into three batches, and these, when it reached a certain point, were to come in separately, each with its own escort. The arrangement, however, could not be adhered to.   On October 13 call signs which appeared to come from German ships were taken in.   They were never accounted for, but Admiral Wemyss felt he must now keep the convoy and its escort concentrated till he reached Admiral Bethell's area, and the Admiralty approved the decision.   Even so, the position was not as satisfactory as could be wished, since the withdrawal of the French cruisers for escort work to Dunkirk had seriously reduced the efficiency of the Western Patrol; and as for Admiral Burney, seeing how heavy our responsibilities were in the Eastern Channel, he had to keep a central position at Portland.

As the convoy approached the difficulties only increased. Directly after Admiral Wemyss had adopted his altered scheme, the French reported that a submarine had been seen off Cherbourg that morning, and a few hours later our own torpedo boat No. *116*, of the Portsmouth Defence Flotilla, sighted one off Culver Cliff in the Isle of Wight.   She was only 1200 yards away, and the torpedo boat steamed for her at full speed, firing as the submarine dived, but she just missed ramming her by a few seconds.   This incident settled the question of what the convoy was to do.   Within an hour the Admiralty had decided their duty was to override all military exigencies—the safety of the convoy, for which they were responsible, was the paramount consideration.   It was clearly a case where the Navy must assert its time-honoured claim to the last word when troops were on the sea, and without more ado the convoy was ordered into Plymouth. Accordingly, as soon as Admiral Wemyss was inside Scilly he began to send forward the batches in succession. At 7 a.m. October 14 the first transports entered the Sound, and in due course all of them followed without further adventure. There was still a question whether the diversion to Plymouth was only temporary, but the Admiralty did not feel justified in taking any further risk. This same day they ordered the Admiral to proceed with the disembarkation of the troops at Devonport till the Channel was free from danger, and informed the War Office they had done so.

Nor was this the only dislocation of the War Office arrangements which the German effort entailed. Two other convoys of troops which were approaching had also to be diverted. The first was bringing home the remainder of the Egyptian Army of Occupation, and the second, four battalions and artillery from India. As Devonport was now full, both had to be directed to Liverpool, and there they arrived by the 22nd without incident.

So, in spite of the vigorous and well-designed offensive which the enemy was boldly pushing with his submarines all over the Narrow Seas, not a single transport or a single capital ship had yet been touched. They had gained nothing material beyond one flotilla leader, the *Pathfinder*, and four obsolescent cruisers, a loss which detracted little or nothing from our real power of command, and the Navy had demonstrated its ability to pass troops across the seas in all directions in spite of every attempt of the enemy to prevent them. Considering how new was the form of attack, how slender as yet the means of meeting it, and how wide and conflicting were the preoccupations of the moment, it was an achievement of which all concerned might well be proud. Our own submarines were no less insistent, though less fortunate. The diving patrol was maintained continuously in the Bight. In all weathers and in spite of the enemy's untiring efforts to keep them off with destroyers, submarines, mines and aircraft, they held their splendid grip on the outlets of the German ports; and of all they dared and suffered nothing was told, for no target came in their way. It was not from want of enterprise : every kind of risk was taken : yet only one boat was lost. This was *E 3*, who early in September had distinguished herself by rising as a German seaplane alighted on the water and capturing a flying officer and his mechanic. On October 18 while on the Western Ems patrol she was approached unobserved against the sun by the *U 27*, (Lt.-Commr. B. Wegener), which fired a torpedo at about 300 yards. *E 3* sank at once. Fearing another British submarine to be in the vicinity, *U 27* did not stop to rescue survivors.

CHAPTER XV

IF the Admiralty had been unable to meet the War Office in the matter of the Canadian Convoy, it was mainly because of a new call which the military situation was making upon them at the eastern end of the Channel. In Belgium, since the fall of Antwerp, the situation had developed in such a way as to afford another opening for interference from the sea, and this time it was a direct opening which the Navy could fill in a manner that was in shining contrast with what it had just attempted. It was no question of an immature landing force, but of clean coastal operations of a purely naval character.

Though, seen in the light of the vast forces which the war came afterwards to develop, the episode appears almost trivial, yet the special significance it had at the stage we have reached renders its progress of peculiar interest. Not only was the zone in question a vital point in the new plan of operations with which the Germans sought to restore the breakdown of their original plan on the Marne, but it was the first time that the power of ships was to be tested tactically in an effort to influence land operations under the revolutionary conditions which the struggle was so rapidly developing. The test was extremely severe, for the nature of the terrain rendered co-operation from the sea exceptionally difficult, and it is only by following the operations in some detail that it is possible to appreciate what was done.

With the decision of the Belgian Government to fall back to the Yser, the race for the sea may be said to have resulted in a draw. The Germans would reach the coast, but not at the point that was vital to their plans, and the question now was whether the line of the Yser could be held, or whether the Germans would be able to break through, and by turning the Anglo-French flank have Dunkirk and Calais at their mercy. It was a question, therefore, that concerned our naval position as nearly as it did the military; for with those two ports in the hands of the enemy, the protection of the lines of communication across the Channel might well prove an insoluble problem, and the whole situation in Home Waters would be undermined.

For the moment, at least, the worst had been warded off. There had been no need to re-embark the two British divisions. Whether it was due to the detention of the German forces before Antwerp, or to their heavy expenditure of ammunition, or other unknown causes, no adequate movement had been made in time or force enough to press our troops back to the sea. General Rawlinson, acting in conjunction with the French Marines at Ghent, had been able to cover the retirement of the Belgian army, and was now falling back through Bruges and Dixmude, with orders, in concert with the French troops with whom he was acting, to get touch with Sir John French's army and prolong its left north of Ypres. On his own left would be the Belgian army carrying the Allied front to the sea.

Ostend it would be impossible to save. It was to be abandoned, and the Belgian Government had decided to withdraw by sea to Havre. The Admiralty offered escort, and the ships selected for the purpose were the three river monitors, *Mersey*, *Severn* and *Humber*. They were now to see their first service and prove the wisdom of the purchase. For the special work, however, on which they were ordered they were too late. The sailing orders were issued on October 12, the day after the Naval Division re-embarked, and next day the evacuation of Ostend took place before they could arrive. The *Mersey*, however, was able to escort some transports that were leaving Dunkirk as far as Gris Nez. The other two went back to Dover, but not without incident, for half way across they were attacked at close range by the *U 8*. Neither was hit, nor was the attack repeated, and both reached Dover in safety and with increased confidence in the advantages of their shallow draft.

Zeebrugge was, of course, involved in the fall of Ostend, and from a naval point of view this was a more serious matter. The port had been found to be excellently adapted for a submarine base, and connected as it was by good waterways with Antwerp, it was likely, if left untouched, to prove a troublesome thorn in our side. The Admiralty had undertaken the work of evacuating the Belgian stores that had accumulated there, but in view of the naval possibilities of the port they also wished to complete their task by destroying its mole and harbour works. This unfortunately did not fit in with military views. The Higher Army Command was not yet prepared to accept the prospect of a deadlock. As yet the vast resources which Germany was capable of developing were underestimated, and there still existed a sanguine hope that when the British Army reached its new position it would be able, in concert with the Belgians, to carry out along the coast an offensive movement which would turn the German right and force it back from the sea. For such a movement to be carried through to its logical consequences Zeebrugge was essential as a port of re-entry, and the War Office pressed for its being left intact. The feasibility of the expected development was a purely military question which the Admiralty could not dispute. Deep, therefore, as was their sense of the risk that was being taken, they had reluctantly to acquiesce, and Zeebrugge was left intact, with what evil consequences time was to show.

At the moment, the prospect of Sir John French being able to accomplish his offensive return was certainly far from encouraging. On October 15 the withdrawal of the Belgian Army was complete, and it had taken up its new position. It extended from Boesinghe, four miles north of Ypres, along the Yser Canal to Dixmude, and thence north-westwards along the Yser itself to the sea at Nieuport. It meant a line of some thirty miles, and the Belgian Army that had to hold it was no more than six weak and exhausted divisions, without anything like its due complement of heavy artillery. No part of the Allied line gave so much cause for anxiety, though the situation of the British Army was bad enough. It was still in process of re-concentration. The First Corps had not yet come up from the Aisne, nor was it expected for five days. If, therefore, the Belgians were broken our left flank would be turned, and not only would all hope of an offensive along the coast be at an end, but Dunkirk and Calais would lie open to attack. Already, on October 15, the Germans had entered Ostend; their advance against the Belgian line could not be long delayed. Something had to be done to stiffen it, and that same evening the Navy received a call which was to inaugurate a long series of difficult and dangerous operations. It came from the Belgian Government. Their chief weakness was in the arm that was destined to dominate the whole war, and which was already asserting its control more clearly every day. Here, at least, the Navy could help, and the message that reached the Admiralty was that a British warship was anxiously desired to flank the Belgian line.

The Admiralty were ready for a prompt and full response. Seeing clearly what the fall of Antwerp and the continued vitality of Zeebrugge would mean to the Dover area, they had

lost no time in preparing for what was ahead. On October 12,
a new command was instituted out of that of the Admiral of
Patrols. The Straits were removed from his jurisdiction and
made a separate command under Rear-Admiral the Hon.
H. L. A. Hood, with the designation of " Rear-Admiral Commanding the Dover Patrol and Senior Naval Officer, Dover."
The force under his orders was to consist of the 6th or Dover
Destroyer Flotilla (twenty-four " Tribal " class), with its
attached light cruisers *Attentive* (Captain Charles D. Johnson
in command), *Adventure, Foresight* and *Sapphire ;* the 3rd and
4th Submarine Flotillas (13 " B " and " C " class), together
with the Downs Boarding Flotilla and all trawlers and
auxiliary patrol vessels within his area. At the same time,
the command of the Admiral of Patrols—who was left all
to the northward, and now shifted his headquarters to the
Humber—was re-organised in order to deal with its immense
extension which was on foot to cope with the submarine
attack. The submarine, indeed, was at the root of the
re-organisation. For the new Dover Patrol no coastal operations were in immediate anticipation, and of the few vessels
on the Navy List adapted for the purpose none had been
attached to Admiral Hood's Command, but the three monitors
were still at Dover, and within an hour of the Belgian
request coming to hand he asked for them.

They were given him immediately, but although this went
beyond what the Belgians had asked, the Admiralty did not
stop there. During the night news came in of vast bodies of
Germans swarming westward against the Belgian line, and
next day, October 16, a fuller request came from General
Joffre himself. Apparently he did not count on the Belgians
being able to stem the flood; for what he saw was operations extending to the North Sea between Ostend and the
outer defences of Dunkirk, and what he asked was that the
Allied fleets should take part in them by supporting the
extreme left and acting with long-range guns against the
German right if that flank was extended to the dunes;
and he expressed a wish that the navàl officer in command
would concert operations through Dunkirk with General
Foch, who was now in command of the extreme French
left. Within two hours Admiral Hood had his orders. The
three monitors, with a division of destroyers to protect them,
were to proceed at once to Dunkirk under Commander Eric
Fullerton of the *Severn.* The French also offered a division to
protect " the cruisers," but it had been explained that cruisers
were not to be risked on so hazardous a service. It was a
resolution the Admiralty soon saw cause to change. That

night the weather was so bad that the monitors could not put to sea. All that could be done for the moment was to direct them to sail as soon as ever the weather moderated, but this would not suffice. During the night the Germans made an attempt to surprise Dixmude, and about midday (October 17) came a message from Sir John French saying that 6000 of the enemy were advancing on Nieuport from Ostend, and anxiously inquiring when the monitors would come. A new apprehension was that the Germans were intending to move troops by sea to La Panne, the last town on the Belgian coast, a little east of Dunkirk. Everything for the moment seemed to hang on getting a naval force of some kind at the crucial point, and getting it there at once. To wait for the weather might mean to lose all; it was a question of hours, and the Admiralty without hesitation resolved to take the risk which, for naval reasons, they were most anxious to avoid. Cruisers must be used, and they gave the word for Admiral Hood's patrol scouts (an old type of light cruiser) and some of his destroyers to sail at once. In an hour one scout and eight destroyers were away; the monitors got off by 3.0 p.m., and Admiral Hood sailed a little later in the *Attentive*.

So the risk was taken, but it affected not only the ships themselves but also the main army communications; for with the bulk of the Dover Patrol occupied in coastal operations there was little or nothing left to guard the entrance to the Channel except the Harwich flotillas. To cover the intended operations they were maintaining a watch in the Broad Fourteens. Since the suppression of the Southern Cruiser force the cover was weak enough, but at this very time it was proving its efficiency in a way that cast a welcome ray of light across the prevailing gloom.

On October 16 the German 7th Half-flotilla was detailed to lay mines in the Downs. To meet such enterprises the Ameland-Terschelling patrol had lately been established. The *E 8* sighted the enemy but taking them for Dutch destroyers did not report them. Meanwhile the new light cruiser *Undaunted* (Captain Cecil Fox), which had just been commissioned and was attached as leader to the 3rd Destroyer Flotilla, sailed with the 1st Division (*Lance*, *Lennox*, *Legion* and *Loyal*) as routine patrol relief. By 2.0 p.m. on the 17th the *Undaunted* had reached her station east of Brown Ridge and was steaming east of north up the Dutch coast, when some fifty miles to the south-westward of Texel Island the smoke of four vessels was sighted about eight miles ahead. They were quickly made out to be German destroyers steaming in line abreast at about half a mile from one another on a course slightly more easterly than that of our flotilla. Very soon, however, they were seen to be spreading fan-wise, and the *Undaunted* signalled: "General Chase." The *Lennox* (Lieutenant-Commander C. R. Dane) and the *Lance* (Commander Egerton) then held away to head off the easternmost boats from the Bight, while the *Legion* (Lieutenant-Commander Allsup) and the *Loyal* (Lieutenant-Commander Burges Watson) made after the others. It was soon clear we had the speed of the enemy. The range fell fast, and as soon as it was down to 8000 yards the *Undaunted* opened fire with her 6″ bow gun. For a time, owing to the clever manœuvring of the Germans, the fire was ineffective, but as our ships continued to gain and the destroyers got into action the enemy began to suffer. By about 3.0 the *Lennox* and *Lance* had reduced the easternmost boat (*S 115*) to a sinking condition, and the *Legion* and *Loyal* had swept the westernmost clean of funnels, bridge and deck fittings and put her out of action. Seeing that escape by flight was impossible, the two centre boats, with a fine spirit, turned back to make a desperate attack on the *Undaunted* with torpedoes. The *Legion* and *Loyal* at once steered to head them off and received them with so hot a fire that they were compelled to turn away to the eastward without securing a hit on the *Undaunted*. Meanwhile the other two destroyers had joined in, and the result was a mêlée at close range, in which the doomed German boats were completely outmatched. In vain they fired their remaining torpedoes; they were avoided as easily as those they had expended earlier in the action, and by 4.30 the last German boat had gone down about west of the Texel. An effort was now made to pick up survivors, which resulted in saving the captain of one of the destroyers, who soon died of his wounds, one other officer and thirty-two men out of a total of 258. The German destroyers sunk proved to be *S 115, 117, 118* and *119*. Our own received very slight injuries, and the total British casualties were one officer and four men wounded.

It was a division of the Emden Patrol that had been destroyed. They were, however, so far beyond the usual limits of their area as to suggest that some plan was in the wind to disturb our operations on the Belgian coast. In any case this smart and successful affair was calculated to secure the Strait of Dover from attack for the moment, and Admiral Hood's personal supervision of the coastal operations was sanctioned. At the same time Commander Samson, who was in charge of our temporary air base at Dunkirk, was ordered to get in touch with him as soon as he arrived. There were eleven naval machines on the spot, but of these only five, so Commander Samson reported, were fit for war purposes. There were also ten belonging to the Military Wing, and two captive balloons were on their way out.

It was also known that the French had ordered the four destroyers they had offered to proceed at full speed to Dunkirk. It would seem that the French Military Authorities had also asked for two battleships of the "Formidable" class. The request was complied with, and at 2.30 p.m. Admiral Burney was informed that two of his ships were urgently required to support the eastern defences of Dunkirk. They were to arrive by daylight next morning, and he was to select ships with nets and good high-angle guns. At this time the affair with the Emden Patrol was not known. The news of it put an entirely new complexion on affairs. It was impossible to tell what further adventures it might not portend, and, when the news came in, orders were sent for the two battleships to proceed in the first instance not to Dunkirk but to Dover, and there await events.

The *Queen* and *Implacable* were selected for the service by Admiral Burney, and the same night they sailed from Portland. Though anxious to meet the views of the French Staff, it was obviously undesirable to use battleships, as they requested, unless they were indispensable. In forwarding to Bordeaux, therefore, information of the measures that were being taken, the Admiralty suggested that the French might help with their coast defence ships of the "Furieux" class. The French, who, almost as much as our own service, had lost sight of the true value of this type of ship, could only reply that none was available—all, except one which was at Bizerta, were out of commission, and some even without guns. As an alternative, they proposed sending the cruisers *Kléber* and *Desaix*, but this offer the Admiralty declined, explaining that the two ships would be better employed in their functions as cruisers. In the same spirit Admiral Hood, on the assumption that the monitors would be in position at daylight, was ordered to withdraw the Scouts during the night, leaving four to six destroyers to protect the monitors and co-operate with them.

About midnight on the 17th Admiral Hood reached Nieuport in the *Attentive* and established communication with the shore. On his way he had received from the Belgian Headquarters the latest information as to the actual military situation. The Belgian Army was in position along the left bank of the River Yser, from Nieuport to Dixmude, with advanced posts on the further bank. One was at Lombartzyde, about one mile north of Nieuport on the Ostend road and 2000 yards from low water mark; a second at Rattevalle, about two miles east of Lombartzyde; a third at a crossing of the Plasschendaele or Bruges Canal, and a fourth at Mannekensvere, a mile east of the point where the Yser Canal turns southward. The King was at La Panne. What was required of the ships was, firstly, to prevent any landing of German troops between Nieuport and La Panne; and, secondly, to check with their fire the forces of the enemy which were advancing on Nieuport.

By 3.0 a.m. on the 18th Admiral Hood was able to announce that the monitors would be in position at daylight, and that he would send back the *Foresight* and one division of destroyers, but was remaining himself in the *Attentive*. At an early hour the German attack on the Belgian advanced post began. In the Nieuport sector it was directed against Lombartzyde and Mannekensvere. The first information was that German infantry were advancing on Westende village, and that they had a battery in action at Westende Bains, and he ordered the flotilla to move past Westende and Middelkerke to draw the fire and endeavour to silence the guns. In the first object he was successful, and was soon in a shower of shrapnel.

At 10.0 a.m. his attention, by request of the Belgian Headquarters, was diverted to Lovie, a village in front of the Belgian advanced post at Rattevalle on the Bruges Canal, and to Blokhuis Farm, about half a mile to the north of it, both points being about 1500 yards inland from Westende Bains. The *Attentive*, as well as the monitors and the *Foresight* with her destroyers, took part and were hotly engaged all day. The casualties were very slight, but, on the other hand, owing to the height of the sand hills, the effect of the ship-fire was difficult to ascertain, and as yet the fire control from the shore was not well developed. Still, while the Germans succeeded in establishing themselves in part of the village of Mannekensvere and both Schoore and Keyem were lost, the attack on Lombartzyde entirely failed, thanks, so the Belgian Official Report records, " to the support of the British flotilla, which was soon completed by some French units. These ships of war bombarded the German troops all along the coast as far as Middelkerke, and they furnished throughout the battle an effective support to the defence." [1] In the afternoon the King of the Belgians sent the Admiral a special message of thanks for the services he had rendered.

[1] *L'Action de l'Armée Belge* (English translation), p. 75.

The first rush of the Germans had been held, and Admiral Hood, at the suggestion of the Admiralty, transferred his flag to the destroyer *Amazon* and sent the *Attentive* to Dover. The *Queen* and *Implacable* were also there standing by in accordance with their last orders. They had not long to wait. Further indications came to hand that the Germans meant to interrupt the coastal operations, on a formidable scale, with armoured and light cruisers. Commodore Tyrwhitt was therefore warned to be out and ready with his full force, and the *Queen* and *Implacable*, with the *Sapphire* as attached light cruiser, and four destroyers were ordered to proceed through the Downs to a supporting position, and Admiral Burney was called on for two more battleships for Admiral Hood.

The belief that the Germans intended counter operations seemed to have been confirmed. About midday on October 18 Commodore Tyrwhitt, having reached his assigned station, overhauled the German steamer *Ophelia*. She purported to be a hospital ship searching for survivors of the recent flotilla action, but was quite unsuited for such a purpose. Her movements which had been watched since dawn by our Terschelling submarine patrol, were so suspicious as to leave little doubt she was acting as a scout. Her wireless was therefore dismantled, and she was detained.[1] Next day, October 19, the precautionary movement with the battleships was carried out as directed by the Admiralty, but no enemy appeared. The Commodore thought it probable that if anything had actually been intended, the capture of the *Ophelia* had disconcerted the plan, and next day the normal patrol was re-established and the battleships withdrew to the Nore.

Under cover of the precautionary movement the monitors had been hard at work all day. Since dawn on the 19th their fire had continued almost without interruption. The sand dunes, of course, prevented all direct laying, but various targets were indicated from the shore. The bulk of the fire was given to a series of batteries extending from the Ostend road behind Westende Bains and Slype, some three miles inland. So hot was the fire that about 2.0 p.m. ammunition began to fail, and the Admiral sent an urgent message for more. The results of the bombardment could not be seen, but the Belgian Staff expressed themselves as highly pleased with the work, and begged for its resumption at dawn.

The military situation, indeed, called for all the support the squadron could give. The Belgian advanced post at Beerst had been lost, and the salient which the Yser forms between the Schoorbakke and Tervaete Bridges was exposed

---

[1] She was condemned by the Prize Court, May 21, 1915.

to enfilade fire. At all hazards the bombardment must be kept up. So urgent, indeed, was its continuance that, in view of the failing ammunition of the monitors, the Admiralty decided to send back the Scouts. They had orders to proceed the moment Admiral Hood called for them. But he had an alternative proposal. He found he could keep going for another day, and suggested the old torpedo gunboat *Hazard*, now a submarine depot ship mounting two 4·7″ guns, and another obsolete vessel, would serve better than the Scouts. The suggestion was immediately adopted, and so these discredited old craft came by their own, and under the realities of war were called from the neglect to which a long peace had condemned them. Besides the *Hazard* there was only one, the gunboat *Bustard*, immediately available, but anything that could serve as a gun vessel was called up—the obsolete cruisers *Sirius* and *Brilliant*, the sloops *Vestal*, *Rinaldo*, and *Wildfire*—while at Portsmouth the old gunboat *Excellent* was to be armed with a 9·2″ gun.

On October 20, then, Admiral Hood could carry on with less anxiety. The weight of the German attack this day fell on the village of Lombartzyde and Bamburg Farm, 1500 yards south-east of it, which formed the outposts of the Nieuport bridge-head, and the targets indicated were a number of heavy batteries in the area Westende–Middelkerke–Slype. His flag was still in the destroyer *Amazon*, and besides the monitors and five French destroyers he had six others of the 6th Flotilla, having lost only one, the *Viking*, disabled by the bursting of a 4″ gun. As the intensity of the German attack developed he was asked to concentrate on heavy batteries at Westende and Blokhuis Farm, and also upon a concentration of troops at Westende Bains. The monitors soon silenced Blokhuis; with Westende Bains he dealt himself. As the attack reached its crisis and the Westende battery was still firing, he rushed inshore at full speed with all the destroyers, firing rapidly in hope of creating a diversion. The effect was reported to be good, and he kept it up till at last the guns hidden amongst the Dunes got the range, and the *Amazon* was so badly holed that she was put out of action.

But the naval effort did not end here. So threatening was the German pressure on the Nieuport front that the Belgians had begged for a machine-gun detachment to work with them ashore. Twenty men from the monitors, under Lieutenant Wise, R.N., of the *Severn*, were therefore landed early in the morning. The Germans were attacking Lombartzyde from Westende, and were also working round it from

the direction of Slype down the Canal. To check this movement Lieutenant Wise was requested to occupy Bamburg
Farm, and with his detachment he proceeded straight across
the fields towards it. Before he could arrive the Germans
had forestalled him. In vain the troops in the neighbouring
trenches shouted a warning. It was not understood; the
detachment continued to advance in the open till it was fifty
yards from the Farm, when the Germans suddenly opened
fire. Lieutenant Wise was killed almost instantly, and in
a few minutes the detachment was destroyed.[1]

The loss of the Farm decided the fate of Lombartzyde.
From the new German position its streets could be enfiladed.
The Belgians who were holding it had to retire on the supports that were sent forward, and message after message
reached the squadron urging an increase of fire. The ships
closed in to half a mile and the shooting was reported good,
but by 5.0 p.m. all ammunition had been expended, and the
Belgians began an orderly retirement on Nieuport, which
the Germans did not venture to follow. Admiral Hood at
once reported that affairs had become critical, and urgently
repeated his request for gun vessels. He had just heard that
the Belgians were evacuating not only Lombartzyde but all
their positions to the east of the Ypres Canal, where up till
now they had appeared to be making good progress. He was
further informed that as soon as the movement was complete
he would be wanted to bombard the evacuated positions.
All he could do for the moment was to send his destroyers to
Dover for fresh ammunition and the monitors to Dunkirk to
await the arrival of theirs, while he himself remained on the
spot in the damaged *Amazon.*

By midnight the retirement of the Belgians had been
effected, and he received information that they were now
behind the river Yser, with a bridge-head position half a mile
north of Nieuport village, and that Lombartzyde should be
heavily bombarded at dawn. To-morrow, so the message
said, would be the critical day. Targets were reported at
Middelkerke, Slype and St. Pierre Cappelle, and this line, he
was told, could be enfiladed from the north without danger.

By this time the German concentration was complete;
they had seven full divisions before the Belgian front, and
as the crisis came the monitors were at Dunkirk awaiting
their ammunition, which, however, did not arrive from Dover
until 3.30 p.m. By daylight the *Foresight* had arrived with
the *Hazard* and four more destroyers (*Lizard, Lapwing,*

---

[1] *The Times* Correspondent, October 20. Five men were reported
wounded and six missing.

Crusader, Cossack). Shifting his flag to the *Foresight*, Admiral
Hood sent the *Amazon* home for repairs, and by 7.0 a.m. had
opened fire on Lombartzyde. The effect was again reported
good, and an hour later he was asked to extend his fire along
the German trenches as far as Groote Bamburg, where troops
and bridging material were being collected. Later came a
signal to turn attention to the area behind the enemy's line
in the vicinity of Schuddebeurze. At this point one of the
naval balloons had also located a heavy battery, although so
accurate was the German fire upon it at 4000 yards that it
had to descend in five minutes. Later it was sent up near
Coxyde Bains, at 9000 yards from the enemy, where it was
out of range, and from this point, which became the headquarters of the detachment, it was able to direct the ship-fire
on a battery at Roodepoort Farm, which was soon in flames
and the guns silenced. Whether or not owing to the ship-
fire, which prisoners afterwards reported as appalling, the
attack did not develop during the morning, but at 3·30 the
Admiral received a signal to say that the enemy was endeavouring to force the passage of the river, and that the hottest
possible fire was required on the targets already indicated.

It was a heavy day's work. In the evening the Admiral
reported that he had fired for eleven hours without stopping,
the *Foresight* alone expending 1100 shells, and he could see
no visible improvement in the situation. Still, the attack
was checked, and the enemy failed to force a passage of the
river at Groote Bamburg.

As yet there had been little interference from the enemy's
submarines. One of the monitors had been attacked on the
first day, but none had been seen since. Now, however,
there was a false report that Submarine *U 21* was at Ostend,
and the Admiral was warned to expect an attack that day.
Special arrangements were made for safeguarding the flow of
ammunition, while the Admiral, shifting his flag to the
destroyer *Crusader*, took charge of the protective patrol.
He also ordered the *Hazard* away, and directed the *Foresight*
to follow her as soon as the monitors reappeared.

No attack took place, and during the night the French laid
a protected minefield east of Ostend. Next day, the 22nd,
things were quieter on the sea flank. The ship-fire had apparently prevented the Germans from establishing themselves
in Lombartzyde; they were transferring their efforts further
inland, and during the day they succeeded in getting a firm
hold of the Tervaete salient. Desperate counter-attacks
failed to dislodge them, and they were able to dig themselves
in on the west bank of the Yser. But within reach of the

ships' guns the fortunes were reversed.   While the monitors and the *Bustard* kept up a curtain fire on the German rearward batteries, the Belgians were able to push a reconnaissance into Lombartzyde.   Prisoners taken next day reported that the ships caused great damage, and they certainly so far dominated the enemy's fire that the Belgians early in the afternoon were able to re-occupy Lombartzyde.

So ended what Admiral Hood regarded as the first stage of the operation.   The general result was that the German rush along the coast had been stopped, and for the time, at least, the situation was saved.   It is scarcely too much to say that the naval assistance for which all three of the Allied Armies had called had turned the scale.   It was not only the material support they had given to the exhausted Belgian Army.   The spirit of the weary Belgian troops had been ebbing away under the oppression of the enemy's heavy guns, to which they could make no adequate reply, and the moral effect of the British fire seems to have given just the heartening that was required.   " The intervention of the British Fleet," says a Belgian eye-witness, " during the height of the battle afforded the defence a most efficacious support." He thus vividly describes the impression it made as the sound of it rose above that of their own and the enemy's guns. " Suddenly," he writes, " as in the desert the roar of the lion drowns the voices of the lesser beasts, detonations distant but formidable began to overpower all this din.   Yonder off Nieuport on the tranquil sea the men-of-war had opened fire on the enemy's lines.   They were some three kilometres from us, and we but ten metres from our batteries, but their thunder was such that we heard nothing else.   For an hour we watched them shooting miles inland, taking the German trenches in reverse, destroying their batteries, making any advance on that side impossible.   And while at Dixmude the French Marines and Colonel Maiser's Belgians were only holding on by prodigies of heroism, Nieuport and its bridge-head remained unapproachable.   And he who holds Nieuport and its system of sluices can stop everything." [1]

[1] Emile Vandervelde : " La bataille de l'Yser: Impression d'un témoin."— *Nineteenth Century*, March 1916.

CHAPTER XVI

OPERATIONS ON THE BELGIAN COAST—SECOND PHASE: THE FIRST BATTLE OF YPRES [1]

So striking was the success on the sea flank that it led at once to a new development which seemed to give promise of breaking down the western deadlock before it could solidify, and securing something like a decisive result.

In the evening of October 22 Admiral Hood went to Dunkirk to meet our military liaison officer with the Belgians, and also Admiral Favereau, who had just been appointed to command the French forces in the Channel. He found that the French XLIInd Division had arrived on the scene. The Belgians, who had now lost the Schoorbakke bridge-head, as well as the Tervaete bridge, and were clinging precariously to the neck of the river salient, seemed to expect the reinforcement there. But General Joffre had a larger plan which he hoped to carry out with the help of Admiral Hood, and the new troops went into Nieuport instead. The British squadron was now considerably strengthened; the old cruisers and sloops were coming in, and after the conference he reported to the Admiralty that he had ships enough. Winter was approaching, and he had to point out that a sudden northerly gale would probably make an end of the monitors and the gunboats. This risk, however, he considered as less than that to which the ships must be exposed from submarines, and that, therefore, it should be taken if they were doing valuable work.

The plan now in hand certainly justified a high risk. The French division was intended, with the support of the squadron, to attempt a counter offensive up the coast in order, if possible, to recover Ostend and to deprive the Germans of the support of the sea on the right flank. The movement would be complementary to that of the main Allied Army. Since the 19th our First and Fourth Corps, in concert with the IIIrd Cavalry Division under General Byng, had been endeavouring to advance through Ypres and Thourout, with Bruges as their ultimate objective. Large German reinforcements checked the movement on the 21st,

[1] See Map 8 in case.

but as General Joffre expressed his intention of bringing up his Ninth Corps to Ypres, with further troops to follow, it was hoped that the offensive could be resumed.[1] His intention was, " in conjunction with the Belgian troops, to drive the Germans east," and the effort was to begin on the 24th.

To this movement the proposed Franco-Belgian advance was apparently preparatory. It was to be arranged in the greatest secrecy, and at 6.30 a.m. on the 23rd Admiral Hood was informed that the French would be moving out northeast from Nieuport till 9 a.m., and after that time he would be required to support them to the northward. Before anything could be done, however, the Germans anticipated the movement by renewing their offensive against Lombartzyde, and the squadron had to devote its attention to checking them. All reports showed the fire which was quickly developed against the enemy's batteries and troop concentrations was very effective. With this assistance not only was the attack stopped, but in the afternoon the French were able to advance through Lombartzyde towards Westende. For a time it looked as if the push along the coast might well succeed, but at this juncture the fire of the ships was required elsewhere. The weight of the German attack was now falling on the Belgian lines between St. Georges and the Tervaete salient, and in this section the trenches were being enfiladed by heavy batteries which at last had been accurately located about Roodepoort Farm and Blockhuis. Unless they could be silenced this part of the front would soon become untenable, and the ships had to come to the rescue. Still, for all they could do it was not enough. Before long the position grew so serious that the Belgians had to inform the French Staff that nothing but the largest possible reinforcement from the XLIInd Division could save it. So urgent was the call that the new plan had to be suspended. Till the centre was made secure an advance up the coast was obviously impossible, and though the French had pushed right up to the outskirts of Westende they had to stand fast, and during the night a whole brigade was detached to strengthen the neck of the Tervaete salient.

Yet the idea of the coastal push was not given up, in spite of the difficulties. Amongst them was a serious dilemma which once more brought naval and military exigencies into conflict. The advance admittedly depended upon how much the squadron could do to assist, and the squadron could never do its utmost if it was in ever-present danger of submarine attack. So long as Ostend was open as a submarine base it would not

[1] Sir John French's Despatch, November 20.

be safe for an hour. On the other hand, if the advance was to achieve its ultimate object, Ostend must be left intact as a port of re-entry. It was a dilemma extremely difficult to solve, and for several days opinion fluctuated. The Admiralty, of course, were for destroying the port; but it was not till noon on October 23, before the French advance had begun, that Admiral Hood received authority from the Belgian Headquarters to bombard it. It was clearly high time. Both the sloop *Wildfire* and the destroyer *Myrmidon* had just reported attacks by submarines. Both were false alarms, but the reports were enough, and without more ado Admiral Hood proceeded to bombard the harbour.

At home the anxiety for the squadron increased, and steps were being taken to mitigate, as far as possible, the risk it was running. The Admiral was ordered to send all ships not actually required into Dunkirk; three trawlers with anti-submarine sweeps were sent across; Commodore Tyrwhitt was ordered to lend a division of destroyers; the *Venerable* and *Irresistible*, which were now in Dover at Admiral Hood's disposal, prepared towing charges for them so that they could deal with submarines diving in shoal water; and barges with nets were equipped for the protection of the larger ships when in action. But all this would be of little avail so long as Ostend was open, and at midnight the Admiral received orders from home to destroy the basins and railway station, and, indeed, not to spare any part of the town where the enemy was located. Blockships for closing the port had also been prepared at Sheerness, and he was to report on the prospects of running them in under the fire of the squadron and sinking them in the entrance.

But by this time the French forward movement had reached Westende; the advance looked quite hopeful, and half an hour later the Admiral had orders to hold his hand till they could hear from Sir John French what the actual prospects were. Already, however, he had been informed from Dunkirk that the offensive was to be resumed in the morning, and that the French had begun a supplementary line of advance on the Plasschendaele Canal, with Bamburg Farm as its objective. During the morning of the 24th he devoted his attention to supporting the movement with the increased force at his command. He had lost the *Severn*—sent home to shift her 6″ guns—but besides the other two monitors, the *Excellent* and the *Bustard*, he now had the *Brilliant* and *Sirius*, the sloops *Vestal*, *Rinaldo* and *Wildfire*, besides eight British and five French destroyers. All the morning he was searching the targets indicated, and the work went on till about 3 p.m., when word came to cease fire as the French, having won Bamburg Farm, were about to push on into Westende.

Meanwhile, a further conference between the Naval and Military Authorities had decided, in view of the success of the advance, to wait a day or two before wrecking the quays and docks at Ostend. The Admiral, however, was directed to bombard the railway station and its approaches at once, and also to deal with any activity he might detect in the harbour. But by the time the order reached him the weather had turned so thick that nothing effective could be done, and as an air reconnaissance from Kingsnorth had reported all quiet in the harbour, he was told to take no action unless local circumstances required it, but to confine himself to supporting the Allied left.

Such support was again essential, for during the day the general situation changed for the worse. The Allied attempt to advance had been met with violent counter-attacks in ever-increasing force. Nowhere could any progress be made, and in the centre the situation had become desperate. The German attacks on the Tervaete salient increased in force and fury till the neck was won, and in spite of a brilliant counter-attack by the French Brigade, the Belgians had to fall back to the line of the Beverdyk. This movement reacted on the St. George's sector, and there, too, they had to retire over the Noord Vaart (Canal du Nord) and abandon the line of the canal. In these circumstances the Belgians found it necessary to insist once more on the need of reinforcing their centre, and the French Staff saw nothing for it but to give them nearly the whole of the XLIInd Division.[1] All present hope of the intended offensive had now to be given up, and while enough French troops were left to hold the posts they had occupied near Westende, the exhausted Belgians fell back to Nieuport.

On the 25th little could be done. The weather was still too thick for effective air reconnaissance; the heavy batteries that were annoying the new Belgian position were far inland, and the only one that could be located brought the French outposts at Westende and Bamburg Farm into the line of fire from the sea. Every effort the Admiral made to close in to a better position was met by guns newly posted amongst the Dunes, and finally he drew off. To make matters worse, it came on to blow so hard in the night that the monitors, which had gone to Dunkirk to replenish ammunition, had to stay there, and all small craft were forced to take shelter.

[1] *L'Action de l'Armée Belge* (English translation), p. 81.

Fortunately, it mattered less than was to be expected; for the Germans seemed too much exhausted to make a serious attack on the new Beverdyk position. On the coast all was quiet. The French, however, thought well to withdraw their advanced posts, and by the morning of the 26th the whole of the Allied troops in the coastal section were behind the Yser, except for the bridge-head a mile north of Nieuport, which was still held.

Of an offensive movement along the coast there was now less hope than ever. The inaction of the Germans meant only strenuous preparation. At an early hour they developed an attack so violent and in such force all along the line that by 10.0 the Belgian situation was pronounced to be critical. The Admiralty at once decided to take further risk, and ordered the *Venerable* to join Admiral Hood. Hour after hour, as in all haste she obeyed the order, the attack continued with undiminished energy, and it was only too plain that at any moment the defence might break. As for the squadron, it was now developing its utmost energy. By two o'clock all the ships were in hot action, and still the coast section held firm. But the enemy had not yet attained his maximum effort. Two hours later it became evident he was preparing a culminating blow from Lombartzyde, and an urgent signal came from Headquarters for the squadron to concentrate the heaviest possible fire on the village. It was done, and with the aid of the storm of heavy shell the stubborn defence of the sea flank was undefeated. But in the centre, where the Germans' main effort was made, their artillery fire could not be adequately checked, and, unable to endure more, the reduced Belgian ranks were forced to fall back to the embankment of the Nieuport-Dixmude Railway.

Here was the last possible stand, but if it could only be held long enough it would be made impregnable. It required but the stopping of the railway culverts to flood the whole country in its front and so develop the ancient Low Country defence which had so often baffled the invader. The work was already in hand, but it would require some time to complete; the water would take two days to rise, and it was more than doubtful whether it was physically possible for the exhausted Belgians to hold out long enough. Much would depend on what the squadron could do—so much, indeed, that it seemed only too likely it would be attacked in force. With the two battleships at Sheerness, and with Commodore Tyrwhitt's force, every preparation was made to meet the expected interruption, and Admiral Hood's Squadron held its ground. Early next morning (the 27th), with his flag in the *Venerable*, he had anchored in position, and on his asking for targets, all available units of the inshore flotilla were directed to engage Westende, Slype and Lombartzyde. But by this time the enemy had so many guns concealed amongst the dunes that the ships could not approach within 4000 yards of the shore, and their field of fire was greatly limited. Finally, indeed, in the afternoon the Germans got a heavy gun to bear, and they had to retire altogether.

The *Venerable*, of course, was unaffected by this fire, but she, too, had had to break off. From 7 a.m. till past 8, lying at anchor with the net barges round her, she was firing, and, as prisoners afterwards reported, with terrible effect. But at 8.15 a.m. one of her destroyer guard reported a submarine, and Admiral Hood decided to weigh and send the *Venerable* into Dunkirk. In doing so he reported he could do all that was wanted with his less valuable units. The German attack had, in fact, broken down; everywhere it was displaying less energy than on the previous days, and by noon the Admiral received a message from Headquarters to say that his fire had been splendid, and suggesting that he should economise ammunition.[1] So with a few parting shots at the more distant batteries, the *Venerable* went in to Dunkirk, and the Admiral informed the Admiralty he did not want her any longer. He felt that, given a steady flow of ammunition, he could go on doing what he had done indefinitely with the smaller ships, and as yet his casualties were no more than a score of wounded. But the *Venerable* was not recalled, and remained on the spot in case of need.

It was now clear that the military operations which Admiral Hood would have to support must continue to be of a purely defensive nature. It was no longer a question of recovering Ostend and pushing the enemy away from the sea. The incessant massing of German troops on the Yser front was evidence that it was no mere counter attack on which they were bent to stop the intended advance of the Allies. The growing concentration left no room to doubt that here they were developing their main offensive, and that what we had to face was a determined attempt to break through to Calais. From the sea to the French frontier the first battle of Ypres was raging; the Allies were definitely on the defensive, and the maintenance of the left flank was the vital concern of the fleet.

The main anxiety was the shortness of ammunition. Already the miscalculation common to all the belligerents,

---

[1] A letter from a German N.C.O. prisoner to his wife at this time stated that German troops had been obliged "to lead the life of cave-dwellers owing to the terrible artillery fire from the fleet." Their losses were very heavy.

which was destined to prove the dominant note of the first part of the war in all theatres, was making itself felt. In the evening of October 27 Admiral Hood was urged from home to husband his supply and confine himself to deliberate fire. But with this suggestion he felt unable to comply. During the day the work of closing the railway culverts had been completed, and at flood tide the Nieuport sluices had been opened. But till the water rose to its full height the situation would still be critical. It was a matter of holding on for the next forty-eight hours, and he pointed out that if he was kept to deliberate fire he could not give the indispensable assistance that the Belgians required. The answer was convincing, and he was promptly given full discretion " to obtain the best results." So by the time the German attack began on the 28th he had moved out of Dunkirk, and, with the *Venerable*, the three monitors and the *Bustard*, was in action again— not only against the old targets between Westende and Lombartzyde, but presently as far inland as St. Pierre Chapelle, where the morning air reconnaissance had located a heavy battery and a group of four artillery positions.

So effective had been the support all through that the Germans now seemed to regard the squadron as the determining factor in this part of the great battle. From now onward it became the chief target of their heavy batteries, and it began to suffer more than it had done since the beginning of the operations.

The most serious injury was to the *Falcon*. With another destroyer, the *Syren*, she was engaged on the patrol line in the N.E. Channel off Westende on the look out for submarines, when about 12.30 p.m. she came under a heavy and well-directed fire from the shore. She at once increased speed and opened fire with lyddite. For an hour and a half she gallantly held her position, till at 2 p.m. a shell hit her on the muzzle of the port foremost 6-pdr. and burst. The gun's crew was closed up at the time, and extra hands were assisting with the ammunition. The result was that her Commander, Lieutenant H. O. Wauton, was instantly killed, together with seven men, and the gunner and fifteen men were wounded, ten of them seriously. She was completely out of action and in a very dangerous position, but Acting Sub-Lieutenant C. J. H. du Boulay succeeded in bringing her into Dunkirk, a service for which he, together with Mr. Ernest Smith, the gunner, was highly commended.

With the slower ships of the main body of the squadron, serious injury was only avoided by continual alterations of course; but, as it was, the *Brilliant* had one man killed and several wounded, the *Rinaldo* had eight wounded, and the *Wildfire* was so badly hit on the water line that she had to be sent home for repairs.

Under these conditions of enforced movement and constant turns, indirect fire was extremely difficult. During the afternoon the work was again interrupted by the reported appearance of a submarine. All destroyers were sent in chase, and the *Venerable* took the ground on an ill-charted sandbank. Fortunately she was out of range, and as the tide rose she was got off with the assistance of the *Brilliant* without injury. Still, the enemy could make no progress ashore, and the Belgian bulletin for the day announced that the German fire had slackened, being subdued by the fleet guns. The truth was that it was to the subduing of the enemy's fire upon the Belgian position that Admiral Hood had been devoting nearly all his attention, with little regard to defending his squadron. The battle of Ypres was still undecided; the Germans were persisting with the utmost determination in their attempt to win through to Calais, and the Admiral's one idea was to do all in his power to prevent them, and to maintain the volume of fire inland which the Belgian Headquarters asked for. All this he explained to the Admiralty, and for reward he had authority " to go ahead " and an assurance that he had shown the enemy there was one flank they could not turn.

Events went to prove that this was probably a not too sanguine estimate of the effect that had been produced. Although the squadron remained on the coast for some time longer there was no serious call upon it. The spread of the inundations quickly rendered the Belgian position secure upon the coast, and the German effort on the Belgian front was mainly directed against Ramscappelle, the key of the railway position. Here, by means of a violent bomb attack, they succeeded in making a lodgment on the embankment, whence they began to push forward to the village. But at this point the ships could give some assistance by firing on the enemy's batteries on the line St. Georges–Schoorbakke, and on October 30 a brilliant Franco-Belgian counter-attack drove the enemy back from the railway and re-established the position.[1] Besides this long-range work, the usual bombardment of Westende Bains was kept up, and here, about 11 a.m., the *Vestal* was hit by the same battery that had disabled the *Falcon*, although the spot had been three times thoroughly shelled. The flotilla's casualties were twelve killed and forty-nine wounded. On this day Admiral Hood, in honour of the late addition to his command, flew his flag in

[1] *L'Action de l'Armée Belge* (English translation), p. 84.

16

the French destroyer *Intrépide*, but it was not for long. In the early afternoon it was known that the German attack had failed, and as all signs of activity died away the ships were rested.

During this period the position of the squadron had been getting every day more precarious, particularly from submarines, while, owing to the guns the Germans had now placed all along the coast, it was increasingly difficult for the vessels to get any result from their fire. Only by constantly keeping on the move at high speed could heavy casualties be avoided. Incessant vigilance had hitherto availed to foil the enemy's submarine attacks. As we have seen, on the 29th one had been reported off La Panne, where the *Venerable* was anchored ; this was a false alarm, but similar reports continued, and on the last day of the month some anxiety was felt for the seaplane-carrier *Hermes*, which, in the evening of October 30, had arrived at Dunkirk from Portsmouth with seaplanes. Early next morning she sailed for Dover, and at 9.30 was ordered to turn back, but ten minutes later the destroyer *Liberty* reported she had been torpedoed and sunk eight miles from Calais. She was destroyed by the *U 27*. Nearly all her crew were saved, but the incident raised the question whether the risk the ships were running was worth any further good they could do. The German batteries were now so well concealed that it was difficult to obtain any result from ship fire. The *Venerable* was therefore ordered to return, and the *Revenge*, an old battleship on the Sale List, which had been hastily prepared at Portsmouth for the service, was told to stand fast.

With this order the operations practically came to an end. For the next two days the struggle for Ramscappelle continued, but the railway embankment was firmly held, and on November 2 the Germans, as the water increased upon them, abandoned the left bank of the Yser, and as they fell back, leaving behind them guns, ammunition and wounded, the Allies began to advance on the roads through the flooded district. With this forward movement all pressure by the enemy on the sea flank ceased, and as it was not likely to recur for the present, Admiral Hood was directed to rest his force, still keeping touch with the military headquarters and ready to act at the shortest notice. But for him the rest was very short. Next day (November 3) came news that a serious attempt seemed intended by the enemy in the direction of the Straits, and leaving his gun-vessels under the *Vestal*, he hastened across with all his destroyers to resume his functions as Admiral of the Dover Patrol.

CHAPTER XVII

SINCE October 17 when the *Undaunted* and her consorts
had wiped out the four German destroyers there had been no
attempt in force to interrupt the operations on the Belgian
coast. The omission is the more remarkable, since the Grand
Fleet for the time was not in a position to deal promptly with
a sortie of the High Seas Fleet to the southward. During the
whole continuance of the operations Admiral Jellicoe had his
battle fleet upon the west coast of Scotland, with one or two
squadrons supporting his new cruiser lines, while the others
rested. The German submarines were still active. On
October 18 two of them were reported in the Minch, and were
said to have fuelled from a tanker at Stornoway. An active
destroyer search was instituted but no trace of them was
found for the very good reason that there was none there.
Still, as there were signs that information was leaking out,
further steps were deemed necessary to ensure secrecy, and
the Admiralty now took over the censorship of all the north
and west coast of Scotland and the north coast of Ireland.
To make it effective they even proposed to declare the whole
of Scotland north of the Caledonian Canal, including Inverness
and the Islands, a prohibited area, but this extreme measure
was as yet deemed unnecessary, and it was not adopted till
much later in the war. As an alternative the Commander-
in-Chief proposed a maritime prohibited area to extend from
Buchan Ness in Aberdeenshire, round the Shetlands and
Hebrides to Islay. This, he pointed out, would close the
Minch, the Pentland Firth and Fair Island Passage, and
greatly assist the operations not only against submarine
tenders but also against contraband trade. At the same
time the proposals he had made for establishing trawler
patrols at various focal points on the north coasts were
sanctioned, and the new patrol areas were filled up as fast
as the vessels came forward.

But this system would not entirely cover the ground.
The most northerly routes would still be open, and our
Minister at Copenhagen was reporting that a good deal of
contraband was reaching Scandinavia for Germany round
the north of the Faeroes, and then down Norwegian waters.
It was to stop this route that Admiral de Chair's Northern

Patrol had been established, but it had continually to be drawn upon for other work owing to Admiral Jellicoe never having had the 6th Cruiser Squadron. Of this squadron he still had only the *Drake*, and she, with the merchant cruiser *Mantua*, was away on a special mission to Archangel. He therefore asked for more armed merchant cruisers, a type of ship whose coal endurance rendered them specially fit for the purpose. They were promised him, and till they could arrive a division of Admiral de Chair's 10th Squadron was sent up to fill the gap, south of the Faeroes, while the merchant cruiser *Alsatian* cruised to the north of them. They found, however, but little traffic. During the whole month of October the Northern Patrol in its various positions examined less than fifty ships, nearly all Scandinavian, and only two, both Norwegians, were detained. To the westward the most notable capture was the S.S. *Oscar II*, which was sent in by the battleship *Hibernia*. She proved to have on board the Austrian Ambassador to Japan and his Staff on their way to Rome from Tokio. He, of course, warmly protested against the detention, and the ship was speedily released.

For the battle cruisers there was little rest. On October 20 the Admiralty had information, believed to be trustworthy, that certain German cruisers, with destroyers and submarines, which had been at Danzig had left for the North Sea, and Admiral Beatty had to cut short his harbour time. With the 1st Battle Cruisers and 1st Light Cruisers he was sent away at high speed to make a sweep from Fair Island to the Skagerrak in concert with the 4th Destroyer Flotilla from Cromarty. It was, however, quite probable that the object of the enemy's movement did not lie in the North Sea at all. Amongst other matters discussed during the recent conference at Loch Ewe was the possibility of sending submarines into the Baltic to attack the High Seas Fleet. It was heard of constantly exercising between the island of Bornholm and the southern entrance of the Sound, and the opportunity was too tempting to be resisted. The Commander-in-Chief was specially anxious for the attempt to be made, and at his instigation inquiries were set on foot to ascertain whether the Sound was mined. The upshot of them was that it was probably free, and on October 11 Commodore Keyes received instructions to carry out the operation. Three units were to be sent, and those selected were *E 1* (Lieut.-Commander N. F. Laurence), *E 9* (Lieut.-Commander M. K. Horton), and *E 11* (Lieut.-Commander Martin E. Nasmith). Their instructions were to pass through the Sound at night so as to avoid the cruiser and flotilla patrol which the Germans were known to maintain between Rügen and the Swedish coast. They would

then endeavour to attack the High Seas Fleet, and when their
fuel was expended they were to go to Libau and worl. from
there till further orders.   That Libau had been dismantled
and abandoned as a naval port, and that it was blockaded by
a large German minefield, appears to have been unknown to
our Staff.

Submarine *E 1* passed in safely during the night of October
17, and next morning Lieut.-Commander Laurence found himself within 500 yards of one of the patrol cruisers, known later
to be the *Victoria Louise*.   Diving at once to attack, he fired
two torpedoes at an interval of a minute.   The first ran
astern of the ship, and the second just missed her ahead as
she put her helm hard over to avoid it.   After submerging
for an interval *E 1* sighted another of the patrolling cruisers,
which she unsuccessfully attacked for six hours.   Nothing
could be seen of the Fleet, and next day he went to lie in
wait off Bornholm.   Meanwhile Lieut.-Commander Horton
had also passed in, but arriving too late to get through
as *E 1* had done before daybreak, and knowing that he must
be observed by the stream of traffic that was passing in both
directions, he had lain on the bottom all the 18th.   At dark
he carried on, and after several close encounters with
destroyers got clear past the patrol line on the 20th.   Lieut.-
Commander Laurence was then making a cast into Danzig
Bay, where, having dived right up to the entrance of Neufahr-
wasser, he found three cruisers in the basin, and as it was
impossible to get at them he went on to Libau.   Outside he
was met by a Russian officer who piloted him in, and then
for the first time he learnt that the port and dockyard
had been destroyed, and that he had gone right through
the German minefield.   Next day (October 22) *E 9* also
arrived in equal ignorance of the risk she had run, but also
unscathed, and there they awaited their missing consort.
But *E 11* had been less fortunate.   Being delayed by defects,
it was not till the 18th she was able to attempt the passage
of the Sound, and quickly she found she was being followed.
As it was possible that attempts might be made to ram her in
the shoal water ahead she was forced to retire.   Outside
the Sound (19th) she sighted a submarine, which she took
to be *U 3*, and tried to torpedo it.   It eventually proved to
be a Danish boat.   As her shots missed no harm was done.
Some hours later *E 11* was herself unsuccessfully attacked,
and next afternoon (20th) she was located by a seaplane
as she was re-charging her batteries for another attempt
to pass, and was hunted all night by destroyers.   Next day
she tried again, but only with the same result, and on the

22nd she decided to return to her base and wait for the hue and cry to die down.

The same day the other two boats were advised by Admiral von Essen, the Russian Commander-in-Chief, to seek safety at Lapvik, an anchorage he was using near Hangö, just within the Gulf of Finland. Still, they decided to wait a little longer for their consort, till two days later an order came from our Ambassador for them to go north. Even so they were not content to proceed direct without another try in the Gulf of Danzig. Three days were spent there and nothing seen but a destroyer, at which *E 1* fired a torpedo at 500 yards and again missed. This was on the 28th, and being unable to stay out longer they next day moved north. As a last chance they went by the German cruiser track west of Gothland, but luck was still against them. Nothing was seen, and on the 30th they put into Lapvik, where they were definitely placed under Admiral von Essen's orders. As an assistance to the Russians in disputing the command of the Baltic, their presence was little more than a token of good-will. But it was a beginning which the enemy could not permit to develop, and it is quite possible, therefore, that the German movements which had been reported to Admiral Jellicoe were designed to close the Sound and were not intended for offensive action outside. In any case the sweep of the Grand Fleet cruisers drew blank, and by October 25 Admiral Beatty's battle cruisers were back at Cromarty and the light cruisers at Scapa, where some further anti-submarine defences had been improvised from local resources.

The 2nd Battle Cruiser Squadron had also been busy. An air raid on the Cuxhaven Zeppelin sheds was on foot under Commodore Tyrwhitt, and on October 18 the *Invincible* and *Inflexible*, with a division of destroyers, were ordered down to the Bight to support the operation. The attempt was made on the 25th, but the weather turned against it. A deluge of rain prevented the seaplanes rising from the water, and the enterprise had to be abandoned.

Meantime, the enemy's submarine activity seemed to have died away. Possibly it had been foiled by the restless work of our patrols, but in any case the submarines had disappeared, and, so far as was known, without having succeeded in locating any of the new anchorages or the new cruiser areas. So the Grand Fleet was left in peace. It was not till October 26 that its comparative quiet was disturbed, and then it was from another cause. On that day, it will be recalled, certain dispositions were made in the Southern Area to meet an attack which it was believed the Germans were intending to make on Admiral Hood in order to stop his galling interference on the Yser. But these dispositions were only part of the action taken.   During the afternoon news that the German fleet was at Brünsbuttel reached Admiral Jellicoe, who, with the bulk of the Grand Fleet, was resting in Lough Swilly, and he at once took steps to concentrate his Fleet in its previous position.   All the battle cruisers were to assemble at Cromarty, and the pre-Dreadnought battleships, which were engaged in supporting the cruisers, were to coal at Scapa.   The 2nd Battle Squadron had just put out from the Mull anchorage for firing practice and was making for a rendezvous about thirty miles north-by-west of Tory Island (Lat. 55° 45′ N., Long. 8° 30′ W.), where the *Liverpool* was to meet them with the targets.   Since this movement would not prejudice a rapid concentration should it be necessary, it was not cancelled.   But the practice was destined never to be carried out; for just when the Grand Fleet seemed most secure it suffered its first heavy loss.[1]

The time for reaching the rendezvous was 5 a.m. on the 27th.   Four hours later the squadron was about twenty miles N. ¼ E. from Tory Island, steaming in line ahead, when the *Audacious* (Captain Dampier), being third in the line and just turning, struck something as she swung, and a violent explosion under her port side aft brought her to a standstill. Whether it was a mine or a torpedo no one could tell.   A minefield in those waters was hardly to be expected.   True, it was on the track between the Clyde and the West, and also on that from Quebec to Liverpool, which the Canadian Convoy had been originally expected to take, but the convoy had arrived nearly a fortnight before.   Though there had been no recent reports of submarines in the vicinity, a submarine seemed the most likely conjecture, and in obedience to the recent general order the rest of the squadron cleared away and called up assistance for the damaged ship.

At first it was thought she was sinking and unable to steam. The *Liverpool*, therefore, stood by, moving round her at high speed, and the tugs that had brought the targets closed in. For a while there was great anxiety, for a fairly heavy sea was running, which added seriously to the danger as the ship began to settle by the stern.   But presently the settling ceased, and it was found she could proceed slowly under her own steam.   Meanwhile all the fleet destroyers and every other available vessel were hurrying out from Lough Swilly, but nothing could be done to help her till, some four hours after she had been struck, the White Star liner *Olympic* appeared in answer to the S.O.S. call and offered to take her in tow. It was dangerous work.   As no second attack had been made it seemed probable it was a case of a minefield, and this was now confirmed by a signal that the S.S. *Manchester Commerce*

[1] See Map 9/10 in case.

had been blown up by a mine in the same waters the previous afternoon.[1]   Still, the *Olympic* would not hold back, and to see her clear the *Liverpool* boldly steamed ahead of her as she closed the *Audacious*.   But by this time the stricken battleship was so badly down by the stern that in the sea that was running she was almost unmanageable.   Even when the tow-line was passed it parted.   Then the Fleet collier *Thornhill*, who had just come up, tried her hand, but only with the same result, and all further efforts were seen to be useless.   She was still making headway, and up till 4.0 p.m., seven hours after she was struck, there was so much hope of saving her that the Commander-in-Chief telegraphed to the Admiralty asking that an officer of the Construction Department might be sent in order to report on patching her up. At the same time he submitted that every effort should be made to prevent the incident being published.

Being now sure the damage was due to a mine, he also ordered the *Exmouth* to proceed to the struggling ship and make another attempt to take her in tow.   But by the time she arrived on the scene all hope was gone.   The stern of the *Audacious* was awash, and all her crew had been taken off to the *Olympic*.   By extraordinary exertions and a fine display of seamanship she had been brought through the heavy sea fifteen miles from where she was struck.   But there it ended.   At 9.0 p.m., half-way to safety and after a twelve hours struggle, she suddenly blew up with great violence and went down.

Thus Admiral Jellicoe, having preserved his capital ships intact for the three most critical months of the war, cruising boldly in the most dangerous waters, and in spite of every German attempt to cripple him, now lost one of his finest ships by a stroke of sheer ill luck.   Whatever the enemy's object in laying the minefield off Tory Island, it is scarcely credible that he could have had information of the presence of the Grand Fleet in those waters in time to do it; it is even less credible that, had he intended it for the Grand Fleet, he would have laid it to the westward of Lough Swilly.   The Germans deserved the success even less than Admiral Jellicoe the calamity, but calamity it was, and the question of suppressing it had to be faced.

In announcing the loss the Commander-in-Chief had again urged that its publication should be withheld.   Considering what the juncture was, the request was natural enough.   The

---

[1] The information came from the Buncrana Naval Centre in Lough Swilly. It originated from the coastguard station at Mulroy.   The explanation of the delay was that on mobilisation all coastguard stations in this vicinity had been closed except for one chief officer at Mulroy, who was not in telegraphic communication with Buncrana.

operations on the Belgian coast were at their crisis. It was on this day the Nieuport sluices were opened; the Germans' attempt to reach Calais was reaching its highest intensity; the next forty-eight hours would decide the issue, and now if ever was the time for the German Fleet to strike a blow at Admiral Hood. At the Admiralty it was recognised at once that, owing to the *Olympic* having been on the scene, the loss could not be concealed for more than a week or ten days, but that would overtide the crisis. For concealment there was the highly successful precedent of the *Yashima* in the Russo-Japanese War. Still, concealment of loss was so contrary to all British tradition and sentiment, that the Admiralty would not decide without reference to the Cabinet.

When, indeed, it came to the point of a Cabinet decision it was not only or even mainly a question of the naval considerations on which Admiral Jellicoe had based his request. The Foreign Office, at the moment, was faced with what was to prove, and was even then recognised to be, one of the momentous crises of the war, and the announcement of the startling German success against the British Fleet might well turn the swaying scales in their favour. At Constantinople the struggle between the representatives of the Allies and those of the Central Powers had reached its height. The Germans were clearly doing everything in their power to force Turkey into the war; the *Goeben* and their Military Mission were gradually dominating the situation, and our Ambassador was reporting that the Turks could not be got to believe in any successes except those of the Germans. The tension could not last much longer, and any additional weight might snap the slender hold which the Entente Powers still maintained. Sir Louis Mallet informed the Foreign Office a day or two later that it was events in the main theatre that would in all probability decide the Turks one way or the other. The situation, he said, was in the last degree critical, as German and Austrian influence was clearly at its maximum. In these circumstances there was obviously every reason to conceal the loss as long as possible, and on October 28 Admiral Jellicoe was informed that, in view of the military and Turkish situation, the loss of the *Audacious* was not to be made public for the present, and that he was to use every endeavour to keep it secret locally. The news was not received in Germany until November 19, over three weeks after the disaster. The loss was not admitted officially by the Admiralty until the conclusion of the war.

So the departure from the time-honoured British practice, which proved so distasteful to public opinion, was sanctioned for high reasons of State. That the Turkish crisis, at least, was sharp enough to justify exceptional measures was soon made only too clear; for two days later, although till the last moment the Grand Vizier, and, indeed, the majority of the Turkish Ministers, were determined to maintain neutrality, their hand was forced, as must be related in its place, by the old Prussian device of a false telegram.

As for the minefield that had done the damage, why, when, and how it had been laid remained a mystery for some time. It was not till early in the New Year that it was ascertained the mischief had been done by the *Berlin*, a large Norddeutscher liner of 17,000 tons, that had been armed as a cruiser and equipped with mine-laying gear during August. She had originally started on her mission from Wilhelmshaven at the end of September, but on nearing the Naze she encountered some British warships which were cruising there on the look-out for two of our submarines returning from a reconnaissance in the Skagerrak.[1] Not venturing to proceed, she ran back to port, and did not start again till October 16.

Her orders were to mine the approaches to Glasgow between Garroch Head and Fairland Head in the Firth of Clyde, or, if this were not possible, to lay her mines between Pladda and Turnberry Point, at the entrance to the Firth. The *Pactolus, Bonetta* and submarines *A 10, A 11* and *A 12* employed in the defence of the Clyde as laid down in the War Plan, had been reinforced by the destroyer *Maori* at this date. The information of the *Berlin's* commander, Captain Pfundheller, was to the effect that he must expect to have to pass a British blockade line between Peterhead and Lindesnaes, as well as a northern line between the Shetlands and the Norwegian coast, near the 61st parallel; for the Germans as yet knew nothing of the far-reaching effect of their latest submarine offensive against the Grand Fleet and the withdrawal of the patrolling cruisers to the northward. They were aware that the Atlantic trade routes were watched, and that units of the Grand Fleet made use of ports in the west as coaling and repair bases; but they expected the *Berlin* would find but few patrols in the Irish Sea, the narrow approaches to which she would be able to pass under cover of darkness.

The German Admiralty could not have chosen a more favourable moment for the attempt to send a minelayer through the blockade line. Had the *Berlin* started only twenty-four hours earlier she would have had to run the gauntlet of several patrolling squadrons, and it is scarcely to be believed that she would have escaped the net. The

---

[1] This reconnaissance was preliminary to passing our " E " boats into the Baltic. The *Drake, Nottingham* and *Falmouth* with two destroyers met *E 5* on the 27th. The *Nottingham* was ordered to escort her in while the other cruisers continued to look for *E 1*.

entire Grand Fleet had withdrawn from the North Sea, the cruiser areas were deserted, and the *Berlin*, steering a north-north-westerly course, crossed the Kinnaird Head-Stavanger line in 2° 30′ E., just after dark on October 17, and altered course to north (true) to pass between the Shetlands and the Norwegian coast. Again fortune favoured her, for the Grand Fleet Cruiser Squadrons were working to the north-westward of the Shetlands, and none sighted her. Keeping well to northward she passed between Iceland and the Faeroes on October 19. Here leakages in the blockade were reported and the necessity of a patrol in this area was recognised by Admiral Jellicoe, but he had insufficient ships at the time to watch the ground, and it was not until 24 hours later that the *Alsatian* was dispatched to the area. On arriving on the meridian of 20° W., at 3 p.m. on the 20th, the *Berlin* altered course to the southward, and twelve hours later turned due east to make the Irish Coast after nightfall.

As the minelayer neared the Irish Coast she intercepted wireless signals which indicated that strong British forces were close to her ; and she was enabled to fix two squadrons one north-westward of the Hebrides and one off the North Channel. The former, though she did not know it, consisted of the 2nd Cruiser Squadron on patrol west of the Flannan Islands, and the latter of the *Albemarle* and *Exmouth* patrolling off Stanton Banks. At 4 p.m. on the 22nd these two battleships reached the southern limit of their patrol in 56° N., 8° 8′ W., and turned 16 points to a north-easterly course. The *Berlin* having arrived in 56° 32′ N., 11° 55′ W., at 3 p.m., now turned south-east by east for Tory Island. To the southward of the *Berlin*, the *Isis*, of Cruiser Force E, was patrolling west of Tory Island, but the minelayer's course took her no nearer to the *Isis* than 30 miles. The patrol of the North Channel at this date was being carried out by the *Tara*, one of four small steamships taken up by the Admiralty on August 16 and commissioned as fleet messengers.

It was clear to Captain Pfundheller that, contrary to his intelligence, the entrance to the Irish Sea was strongly patrolled, and he was doubtful of being able to penetrate to the Firth of Clyde. But hesitation appeared worse than useless, and increasing to his full speed of 17 knots he held on. As soon as darkness fell he made ready his 200 mines and cleared his six 10·5 cm. (4·1 in.) guns for action. At 10 p.m. the soundings showed him to be close under the land, but the night was dark and the coast-line could not be discerned. Suddenly Aran Island light shone to starboard and the *Berlin* put her helm hard over and altered course four points to port.[1] At 11 p.m. Captain Pfundheller reckoned he was off Tory Island, but neither that light nor Fanad Head was burning.

In the absence of coast lights he concluded it was hopeless to attempt the passage of the North Channel. This was a fortunate decision for him, for the armed boarding steamer *Tara* was patrolling in the North Channel, between the Mull of Cantyre and Fair Head. Since he could not lay his mines in the Firth of Clyde, the best position for the minefield seemed to be to the northward of Tory Island, and at 11.35 p.m. on October 22 the *Berlin* began to lay her mines in this position. She was undisturbed, for although part of the Grand Fleet was lying at anchor in Lough Swilly, thirty miles away, the patrolling destroyers forming the anti-submarine protection worked inside the Lough only. By 12.10 a.m. on the 23rd the minelaying was completed, and the *Berlin* turned to a north-west by west course to escape into the open sea.

Her luck still held. The *Albemarle* and *Exmouth* had turned at 9 p.m. on the 22nd and were making a southerly stretch. At 1 a.m. on the 23rd the *Albemarle* was in 56° 5′ N., 8° 25′ W., with the *Exmouth* some ten miles to the north-westward of her. The *Berlin*, closing them at an angle of 90°, was fifteen miles to the southward; but at 1 a.m. the two battleships turned 16 points to commence a stretch to the northward, and they rapidly drew away from the minelayer. The morning broke with mist and rain squalls which shrouded the *Berlin*, her speed reduced to 13 knots by dirty fires. But there was no need now for haste, for she had a clear run before her. Keeping well out into the North Atlantic she passed between Greenland and Iceland on October 30, intercepting on the 27th a British wireless warning which showed her that the minefield had béen discovered. A few days later the British wireless signalling showed that something of importance had occurred in connection with the minefield, but the German Admiralty made no sign to her by wireless for guidance. All indications of her character as a minelayer were now removed as far as possible, and an attempt was made to repair the boiler defects which had developed under the strain of high speed steaming.

Captain Pfundheller's orders had instructed him, if he were not forced to escape into the Atlantic, that he was to raid the Iceland fishing fleets. But the weather was so bad that he realised the fishing vessels would have taken refuge in harbour, and he accordingly steered eastward towards the

---

[1] Captain Pfundheller was actually some twelve miles to the north of the position given in his report.

Russo-Norwegian coast to carry out his third duty, the raiding of merchant traffic on the England-Archangel route. The ordinary traffic had ceased at the end of October with the icing up of Archangel, but food ships were still running to England and colliers were taking to Russia much needed coal, whilst there were also reports of three Russian volunteer fleet ships taking reservists home from Genoa, and of war material being shipped from Havre *via* Liverpool to Archangel. The *Drake* and *Mantua* had already left Archangel and returned to Liverpool on October 28 and there was no warship to obstruct the *Berlin*.

The conditions were not favourable, however, for commerce raiding. The *Berlin's* speed was seriously reduced, and the long, bright, moonlight nights rendered it doubtful whether she could overhaul any enemy merchantman before the latter found refuge in one of the numerous fjords and hiding places on the coast. Moreover, the coast was well furnished with telegraph and telephone communication for fishing purposes, and the *Berlin* could not long expect to remain unreported when once she commenced active operations. On the night of November 7-8, however, as the moon was obscured by clouds, Captain Pfundheller determined to close the Murman Coast to see what he could find.

At 10 p.m. he sighted his first ship. Whilst manœuvring to get between her and the land a second vessel came in sight. From the position of her lights she appeared to be a warship and Captain Pfundheller took her for a British cruiser guarding the trade route, an impression which was heightened when she stopped and began exchanging signals with the first vessel. The *Berlin* had no night sights for her guns and no shells, and under the circumstances Captain Pfundheller decided it was useless to attempt to fight, and under cover of a sudden snowstorm he escaped.

His fears had been groundless, for the vessel sighted was not a British warship ; but in the conviction that his presence on the Murman Coast had been discovered, Captain Pfundheller decided to move further south and try his luck southward of the Lofotens. Heavy weather again came on, however, causing a high expenditure of coal and rendering impossible all question of lowering boats to examine merchant vessels. In these circumstances it was hopeless to attempt to prosecute operations against trade.

On November 11 the *Berlin* got into wireless communication with the German Admiralty, and learned that a considerable volume of valuable war material was passing from

America to Archangel.   Meanwhile British wireless signalling
had been heard, indicating that enemy warships were off the
Lofotens and on the Norwegian coast, and that the patrol
line between the Shetlands and Norway was occupied.   This
was not entirely correct, for though the 10th Cruiser Squadron
was working off the Shetlands and the armed merchant
cruisers between Iceland and the Faeroes, there were no
British ships as far north as the Lofotens.

The   weather continued bad, with heavy gales, and on
November 15 Captain Pfundheller decided to take advantage
of a clause in his orders which permitted him, if any other
course was impracticable, to intern himself in a neutral
port.   His boilers were defective, coal was running short,
and in the bright moonlight nights now ruling he seemed
to have only a slight chance of evading the British warships
reported to be off the Norwegian coast, and of reaching home.
On the morning of November 17, in a thick snowstorm,
he entered Trondhjem and anchored in the harbour at
9 a.m.; twenty-four hours later the ship was interned.

Intelligence of her arrival duly reached the Admiralty.
It was known that the *Berlin* was fitted as a minelayer, while
the emptiness of her bunkers indicated that she had recently
completed a lengthy cruise ; but no less than three weeks had
now elapsed between the discovery of the minefield off Tory
Island and the arrival of the *Berlin* at Trondhjem, and the
Admiralty did not with any degree of certainty connect the
two with one another.

Precautions were at once taken to warn merchant ships,
to ascertain the extent of the minefield and to sweep channels
through it.   No further loss occurred, nor did the Commander-in-Chief shift his ground.   He did not, however,
remain with the Fleet, for on October 30, as our ultimatum
to Turkey was being dispatched, he was invited to London
to confer with the Admiralty, and on the last day of October
he said good-bye to the Fleet for the first time since he had
hoisted his flag.   Vice-Admiral Sir George Warrender was
left in command, and as the Commander-in-Chief departed
the telegram for war with Turkey came in.

It was a new Board he met.   In view of the rising agitation in the Press against every one German or of German
descent, Prince Louis of Battenberg thought it right to offer
his resignation as First Sea Lord.   On October 29 he had
signalled his farewell to the Fleet, and Lord Fisher resumed
the office which he had vacated four years before.   The
immediate result was one of those drastic measures which

the country had come to connect with his personality. The loss of the *Audacious* in one of the great highways of the Atlantic trade naturally forced to the front the necessity of dealing firmly with the increasing disregard with which Germany was treating the accepted limitations of naval warfare. Regardless alike of civilian and neutral life, she was sowing mines broadcast and surreptitiously in the highways of the world—and sowing them, as was then believed, under neutral flags. Even without this last aggravation, so ruthless a stretch of legitimate belligerent action could not be met within the old canons of war; that was clear. Admiral Jellicoe, as we have seen, in his proposal for a prohibited area had already indicated the lines on which a new departure should proceed, and under the stress of the recent outrage the new Board received sanction for something even stronger than he had suggested. But the measure that was to be adopted was at least not carried out surreptitiously or without due notice. On November 2 the decision was announced to the world in the following declaration :—

" During the last week the Germans have scattered mines indiscriminately in the open sea on the main trade route from America to Liverpool via the north of Ireland. Peaceful merchant ships have already been blown up with loss of life by this agency. The White Star liner *Olympic* escaped disaster by pure good luck. But for the warnings given by British cruisers, other British and neutral merchant and passenger vessels would have been destroyed. These mines cannot have been laid by any German ship of war. They have been laid by some merchant vessel flying a neutral flag which has come along the trade route as if for the purpose of peaceful commerce and, while profiting to the full by the immunity enjoyed by neutral merchant ships, has wantonly and recklessly endangered the lives of all who travel on the sea, regardless of whether they are friend or foe, civilian or military in character.

" Minelaying under a neutral flag and reconnaissance conducted by trawlers, hospital ships and neutral vessels are the ordinary features of German naval warfare. In these circumstances, having regard to the great interests entrusted to the British Navy, to the safety of peaceful commerce on the high seas, and to the maintenance within the limits of International Law of trade between neutral countries, the Admiralty feel it necessary to adopt exceptional measures appropriate to the novel conditions under which this war is being waged.

"They therefore give notice that the whole of the North Sea must be considered a military area. Within this area merchant shipping of all kinds, traders of all countries, fishing craft, and all other vessels will be exposed to the gravest dangers from mines which it has been necessary to lay, and from warships searching vigilantly by night and day for suspicious craft. All merchant and fishing vessels of every description are hereby warned of the dangers they encounter by entering this area except in strict accordance with Admiralty directions. Every effort will be made to convey this warning to neutral countries and to vessels on the sea, but from November 5 onwards the Admiralty announce that all ships passing a line drawn from the northern point of the Hebrides through the Faeroe Islands to Iceland do so at their own peril.

"Ships of all countries wishing to trade to and from Norway, the Baltic, Denmark and Holland are advised to come, if inward bound, by the English Channel and the Strait of Dover. There they will be given sailing directions which will pass them safely, so far as Great Britain is concerned, up the east coast of England to Farn Island, whence a safe route will, if possible, be given to Lindesnaes Lighthouse. From this point they should turn north or south according to their destination, keeping as near the coast as possible. The converse applies to vessels outward bound. By strict adherence to these routes the commerce of all countries will be able to reach its destination in safety, so far as Great Britain is concerned, but any straying, even for a few miles from the course thus indicated, may be followed by fatal consequences."

This, then, was the answer to the German provocation; but no sooner was it given than the enemy took another step in his rake's progress. The theatre of his offence was this time in the Southern area. It was the news of it that had brought Admiral Hood so suddenly back to Dover, and as suddenly it caused Admiral Jellicoe to hasten back to the Fleet.

CHAPTER XVIII

THE reports that had been coming in that the enemy
seemed to be contemplating some activity in the North Sea
had not ceased. They were still quite vague, and the concentration of the Grand Fleet, for which the Commander-in-
Chief had been preparing when the *Audacious* was lost,
had gone no further. The probabilities pointed to action
in the Southern Area, and on November 2, while Admiral
Jellicoe was still absent from the Fleet, a new disposition was
made. About noon on that day the 3rd Battle Squadron (that
is, the " King Edwards " and the " Duncans ") were ordered
to come south and join Admiral Burney's flag at Portland.
The squadron, though originally intended—at least in part—
for the Channel, had been supplying the Grand Fleet's shortness in cruisers, and had usually been employed in acting
with them for exercising command of the North Sea approaches. They were being so employed at the moment and
were widely spread; but Admiral Bradford, who commanded
the squadron, proceeded to concentrate, and then steamed
south.

In the Southern Area Commodore Tyrwhitt sent the
Undaunted and *Aurora*, with the 3rd Destroyer Flotilla, in
search of submarines and mines, the former to patrol in the
Terschelling area, and the *Aurora* in the Broad Fourteens ; the
Fearless had come in to coal ; and he himself was standing
by at Harwich in the *Arethusa*. Towards evening he recalled
the *Aurora*.[1] In pursuance of the declaration for closing
the North Sea that was issued this day, it was intended to
strengthen the barrier minefield which closed the northern
approach to the Channel, and the *Aurora* was required, with
six destroyers, to protect the minelayers. As for the other

---

[1] The *Aurora* was a new light cruiser nominally belonging to the 4th
Flotilla, but had not yet joined it. She was commanded by Captain Hotham
in September, and having completed her trials was specially attached to
Commodore Tyrwhitt, whom she joined on October 20. Map No. 11 in case.

ships in the Southern Area, there were four battleships at the Nore, *Queen*, *Majestic*, *Jupiter* and the *Venerable*, which had just come in from Dunkirk; the *Queen* being on guard at two hours' notice. At Dover was the *Irresistible*, also at short notice. To the northward the battle and light cruisers were at Cromarty, where the Commander-in-Chief had ordered them to concentrate. This was the position when, shortly after 7 a.m. on November 3, Commodore Tyrwhitt was surprised by a wholly unexpected signal. It came from the *Halcyon* (Commander Ballard) a mine-sweeping gunboat stationed at Lowestoft, which was then working near Smith's Knoll, and it was to say she was engaged with a superior enemy. At the same time big shells began to fall close to the beach at Yarmouth. In the mists of the autumn dawn no ships could be clearly made out. According to the German official history, a squadron of four battle cruisers, *Seydlitz*, *Moltke*, *Von der Tann*, and *Blücher*, and four light cruisers, *Kolberg*, *Graudenz*, *Strassburg* and *Stralsund*, had left the Bight the previous evening with orders to make a demonstration against the English coast. Making the Cross Sands light-vessel about daybreak, they surprised the *Halcyon* some four miles south of it, steering north-easterly. Two miles south-west of her was the destroyer *Lively* (Lieutenant Baillie-Grohman), patrolling to the eastward, and astern, near the Scroby Buoy, was another destroyer, the *Leopard* (Lieutenant V. S. Butler). On seeing the leading ships of the enemy coming out of the morning mist the *Halcyon* turned towards them and made the challenge. It was greeted with salvoes of 11″ and other guns, and she at once turned away to the south-west. Seeing her acute danger, Lieutenant Baillie-Grohman, who also had altered course towards the enemy, dashed across her stern and boldly turned down on a parallel course with her and set up a smoke screen between her and the enemy. For about a quarter of an hour the two ships were under heavy fire, but thanks to continual changes of course and the smoke screen neither was seriously hit when, at about 7.40, the enemy, who had been steaming parallel to and about ten miles from the coast, firing heavily on Yarmouth without, however, actually hitting the town, ceased fire and made off to the eastward. The *Leopard*, who all through had been under heavy fire, now turned to search down the coast while the *Lively* held after the enemy till she lost them in the mist. The other destroyers of the Yarmouth Patrol, though they had put to sea the moment they heard the guns, were unable to arrive on the scene before the enemy had made off. Still, it was owing to the bold action of the patrol that the *Halcyon* was able to escape with only trifling damage, and no more than three men wounded.

At 7.45 she reported that the enemy, whose force was still undetermined, was making off to the south-eastward. Upon this Commodore Tyrwhitt, who on the first alarm had ordered the *Aurora* and *Undaunted* to make for Smith's Knoll with all dispatch, and was himself hastily preparing to get to sea, decided to hasten off to Terschelling with the *Arethusa* and another division of destroyers to try to cut off the enemy's retreat, and ordered the *Aurora* and the *Undaunted*, with her destroyers, to do the same.

By 8.30 the *Halcyon* reached Yarmouth and was able to present a fuller report. She made out the enemy to be four Dreadnought battleships and four four-funnelled cruisers, and had lost sight of them steaming east-south-east about twelve miles off Lowestoft (Lat. 52° 33½′ N., Long. 2° 04′ E.). Owing to the inevitable delay in transmission and decoding it was some time before the Admiralty had the information. An earlier message from Gorleston stated that the enemy's force consisted of at least one battle cruiser and three or four others and was steaming south. In this form the intelligence was sent at 9.0 a.m. to Admiral Hood at Dunkirk, and also to Admiral Beatty at Cromarty, and at the same time the nearest East Coast Defence Patrols were ordered to the spot; all available submarines at Harwich were sent out to attack, and those at Dover were to get to sea ready for action. Admiral Burney was also warned, and the *Queen* and *Irresistible* were directed to take up a position to support the Patrols. By noon Yarmouth reported for certain that two battle cruisers and four light cruisers had been sighted, and this information was sent to the Commodore with a warning to beware of being cut off.

So far all the information pointed to a raid to the southward, but to ensure against the enemy doubling back Admiral Beatty was given discretion to proceed with all dispatch to an intercepting position north of Heligoland, where the Scapa light cruisers were to join him. This was repeated to the Grand Fleet; and the 3rd Battle Squadron, which, on its way to the Channel, was then off the N.W. coast of Ireland, was ordered to turn back and join the Commander-in-Chief at Scapa. There the concentration which he had prepared was now taking place, since the most likely explanation of what then appeared to be an unintelligible attempt of the enemy to bombard an open coast town was that it might be a diversion to distract attention from something more serious in the north. The Grand Fleet battleships would in any case

be too late for action in the Channel, and there other precautions were taken. Admiral Burney was to move up to
Spithead; the *Venerable* and five of the Nore submarines
were to join the *Queen* and *Irresistible* at the Tongue, and
the *Majestic* and *Jupiter* were to get ready to do the same.
At Gorleston were three " Oversea " submarines, *E 10* under
orders for the Cattegat, and *D 3* and *D 5* for Terschelling.
At the first sound of the guns they put to sea, but unhappily
as they were hurrying to the scene of action *D 5* struck a
floating mine. In less than a minute she went down, and
though two fishing drifters, *Homeland* and *Faithful*, regardless
of the danger, rushed to the rescue, nearly all hands were lost.

Though coastal bombardment appeared at first to be the
object of the raid, mining was the main intention, but not
where *D 5* was lost. The *Stralsund* had laid a line of mines
at 5.30 a.m. on her way to Smith's Knoll Passage, and
dropped her last twenty-eight behind her squadron when they
began their retirement. This was known as early as 11.0 a.m.,
when a fisherman coming in reported having seen the Germans
laying mines as they retired. One fishing boat had been sunk
at 8.30 a.m. Before noon a general warning had gone out
from the Admiralty.

In the meantime the Commodore, having provided as he
thought for Terschelling, had decided to take the Smith's
Knoll position himself with the *Arethusa* and six destroyers,
sweeping along the Suffolk coast on his way. The *Aurora*,
however, not having received his last order, apparently had
held on for the same position, and was waiting there for
instructions. The *Undaunted*, with her destroyers, was thus
making for Terschelling alone, and when she had reached a
position near the mid-sea rendezvous in Latitude 53° she
sighted to the southward four cruisers " looking like two
' Roons,' and two others." They were the *Strassburg* and
Stralsund, whose course slightly converged with that of the
Undaunted. Actually they were on their way home and did
not attempt to follow the British light cruiser. Captain
St. John signalled to all ships (9.55 a.m.) that he had sighted
the enemy and later (10.40) that he had resumed his course.
He was ordered (10.55) to try to lead the enemy south, but
they had also turned slightly northward, and the *Undaunted*
lost sight of them altogether. Meanwhile the Commodore,
who at 11.30 had reached the Corton light-vessel off Lowestoft
on his way to Smith's Knoll, started off to her assistance.
By this time, however, the Admiralty, having ascertained
the overwhelming force of the enemy, had recommended
him to concentrate. The *Undaunted* was accordingly re-

called. By 3.0 p.m. the Commodore had his three light cruisers and thirteen destroyers assembled at the mid-sea rendezvous, and with this force he proceeded to sweep past Terschelling to the Bight. But of the enemy no more was seen, and Admiral Beatty and the Scapa light cruisers were recalled. Towards midnight Commodore Tyrwhitt swept back again, and by noon on the 4th was off the Maas light-vessel, with his whole force barring the way down the Broad Fourteens. Still, there was no further trace of the raiders ; and as it was now evident that the German movement was nothing but an attempt to disguise the real purpose of the expedition, the normal routine was resumed, and the 3rd Battle Squadron carried on to join the Channel Fleet at Portland.

Though only the laying of a minefield had been contemplated, the force employed was certainly large enough to justify all the precautions that were taken by the Admiralty. According to German reports all their ships got back safely, but they admitted that the morning after the raid (November 4) the armoured cruiser *Yorck* fouled the minefield which defended Jade Bay and was lost with half her crew. She was one of the light cruisers screening the battleships. Developing defects which necessitated her going into dock, she struck the minefield on her way in the darkness of a dense fog. She and the *Roon* formed a class by themselves, but neither was with the raiding force, though the *Strassburg* and *Stralsund* had been mistaken for them.

To us, in view of the excellent opportunity they had had of a really telling interference with our operations on the Belgian Coast, the whole affair seemed peculiarly inept. The actual result was to leave the position on the Yser in so favourable a condition that the Belgian Headquarters determined to attempt a forward movement to recover their original line. This was made known the same night (November 3–4), and Admiral Hood, hoisting his flag again in the *Crusader*, went over with three other destroyers to assist. The advance was so far successful that the line of the Yser was reached and Lombartzyde re-occupied. Admiral Hood's force was now strengthened by the *Excellent*, and the *Revenge* was ready for him at Dover; but before he could act a night counter-attack drove the Belgians out of Lombartzyde, and they fell back to the Nieuport bridge-head. There they were soon firmly established, and, content with what they had regained, they decided not to press their offensive further. On November 7, therefore, Admiral Hood was recalled to resume his normal duty at Dover, leaving the

Vestal as senior ship with the *Humber, Rinaldo, Bustard* and *Excellent* to carry on in accordance with military requirements. His last day's work was directed against concentrations of troops between Westende and Lombartzyde. It was reported to have been very effective, but next day (November 8), when the operation was repeated in his absence, the ships found themselves received with so heavy a fire that they were forced to withdraw out of range. Though under fire for twenty-five minutes, the *Excellent* alone was hit; fortunately the shell did not burst. There were also submarine alarms, but only the *U 12* was near, and owing to navigational difficulties she could make no attack. The operations now terminated. So secure was the sea flank that no immediate assistance from the fleet seemed necessary, and next day (November 9) the whole force was recalled to Sheerness to remain organised as a flotilla, full up with stores and ammunition, ready for further orders.

So ended the three.weeks' operations, with the main object which they were designed to further fully attained. For although all hope of quickly recovering the lost ground in Belgium was given up, it was certain the enemy would not be able to reach Calais through Nieuport and Dunkirk. The operations had been carried out under every kind of difficulty. The movements of the ships had been greatly hampered by the shoals and banks on the coast and by the constant menace of submarines. Dunes, rising in places to fifty feet high, obstructed the view, and "the only way to find the enemy," so Admiral Hood wrote, "was to locate a prominent high object such as a tower or tree in the neighbourhood of which we were informed the enemy's troops or guns were congregated, and then to search the area round that object by gun-fire." The difficulties were much increased by the weather, which for the most part was unfavourable for air reconnaissance and observing, and fire control was always difficult owing to the slowness of communication with the shore. Yet severe loss both in guns and men was undoubtedly caused to the enemy, while our own loss was insignificant. All told, the casualties were two officers and ten men killed, and three officers and forty-six men wounded, and two-fifths of these had been caused in the destroyer *Falcon* by a single shot. Apart from the incidental loss of the *Hermes* the ships suffered very little. Several had to be sent home to shift worn guns, and besides the injuries to the destroyer *Amazon*, already recorded, there was one other casualty, the gunboat *Niger* sunk, without loss of life, by the *U 12* in the Downs on November 11.

In contrast with the risks that had been run to achieve combination between the Navy and the Army, the conduct of the Germans is noteworthy. In spite of the importance and difficulty of the task which their army had been set, and in spite of the fact that its object was ultimately naval, the Navy had made no real effort to assist it. The movement of October 17 and the Gorleston Raid were both mine-laying operations and nothing else, and, except for weak submarine attacks, the German Navy sat idly by and left the Army to break itself to pieces without holding out a hand to ease its task. There was a lack of co-ordination among the staffs of the German fighting machine, and the Fleet Command were not even aware that any special help was required. Furthermore, units and even whole squadrons of the Grand Fleet had been reported as being in almost every harbour in the British Isles, and the Kaiser was unwilling to take any risk with surface ships, especially at a time when there was no sure information as to the disposal of our fleet.[1] Such activity as the German Navy displayed was spent on the Gorleston Raid, an operation of no military significance whatever.

[1] *Der Krieg zur See : Nordsee*, Vol. II, Chap. IV.

CHAPTER XIX

WITH the conclusion of the operations on the Belgian coast and the knowledge that the sea flank of the Allies was secure and Calais beyond the reach of the enemy, the interest of the Naval War shifts to the High Seas. There the Odyssey of Admiral von Spee had come more and more to dominate the situation. The existence of his squadron had set up conditions of which the Navy had no experience. Again and again in the old French Wars we had had to hunt down wandering squadrons in the Atlantic and the Indian Ocean, but never had we had to deal with one at large in the vast wastes of the Pacific, with all our most distant possessions in three continents and the furthest limits of our trade routes exposed to its ravages. It was impossible to tell within thousands of desolate miles where it would strike, and so powerful was it that at all the possible points it must be confronted with concentrations of force which would strain our resources to breaking point.

Never perhaps had the Admiralty had a more difficult problem to solve. Yet, thorny as it was, its solution would have been comparatively easy but for the unrelated complications which entangled it. The first of these was the incessant calls of the military for convoy all over the world, and the second a happy inspiration of the Germans. For instead of concentrating the whole of their outlying cruisers under Admiral von Spee's flag, they had left two or three to operate singly as long as they could against our trade. The cruising grounds assigned to them, moreover, were chosen so as to cause us the utmost embarrassment. The chief of the detached ships were the *Emden* and the *Karlsruhe*, and the fields of their activity were respectively the Indian Ocean and the north-east of Pernambuco. Not only did these waters constitute two of the richest and most important focal areas on the great trade routes, but in relation to the Pacific they were also the most distant in which it was

---

[1] See Maps 2 and 12 in case.

possible for an enemy's cruiser to operate without the likelihood of immediate capture. As a combination of the concentration and dispersal of cruising force, the disposition had much to commend it. Whether it was not rather accidental than deliberately thought out by the Germans is more than doubtful, but certain it is that no other device could have caused us greater annoyance. No use to which they put their scanty force of cruisers, with the exception of the even happier inspiration which sent the *Goeben* and *Breslau* to Constantinople, was better designed for our discomfort. Every fleet and squadron from the Grand Fleet downwards became affected by the disturbance with more or less severity, and in tracing its reactions it will be well to begin with the North American Station. For not only was it one of the most distant from the German Pacific base, but it was the officer in command of it—Admiral Cradock— who was so unhappily destined to be the central figure when the problem reached its culmination.

It will be recalled how on August 12 it became known to him that the *Dresden*, which at that time appeared to have the function of an isolated cruiser, had been molesting British merchant ships off the Amazon, and that the *Karlsruhe* had appeared at Curaçao. Admiral Cradock had then, at his own suggestion, been authorised to move down with his flag in the newly joined *Good Hope* and take personal charge of his Southern or West Indies area. The force he left in the north under the senior officer, Captain Yelverton, comprised the *Suffolk*, *Essex*, *Lancaster*, and *Carmania*, shortly to be reinforced with the Canadian cruiser *Niobe*. The great subsidised Cunard liner *Mauretania* was also in Halifax waiting for conversion, but on August 16 it was decided she was not to be used, owing to the cost of fuelling her, but next day, in pursuance of the policy of stiffening the cruiser squadrons with battleships, the *Glory* reached Halifax. In the West Indies Area were the *Berwick* and *Bristol* and the two French cruisers *Condé* and *Descartes*, all engaged in patrol or local convoy duty on their assigned stations. Their special preoccupation was with the *Dresden* and *Karlsruhe*, both of whom seemed to be still hovering on the most southerly verge of the station and might at any time break back. That they had some such intention was the more likely, since this part of the station had just acquired a new importance; for on August 16, the day Admiral Cradock started south, the long-anticipated change in the strategical aspects of the Atlantic was consummated by the formal opening of the Panama Canal.

There was no more news of the *Dresden* having molested ships, and the last word of the *Karlsruhe* was that on August 12 she had been at Curaçao where she took in 1,200 tons of coal.   Upon this information Admiral Cradock, on his way down, called the *Berwick* and *Bristol* to meet him at St. Lucia.   His intention was to seek the two German cruisers in the southern extremity of his station, and he asked for coal to be sent to Trinidad.   In the evening of August 20, however, the Admiralty received news which involved a radical change in the whole plan.   It came from our Minister at Rio, who reported that the crew of the Houston liner *Hyades*, from Rosario to Rotterdam, had been brought in by a German auxiliary, and that their ship had been sunk by the *Dresden* on the 15th about 180 miles east of Pernambuco. Of the *Karlsruhe* there was no further information, but it was clear that with the ruthless turn the German operations had suddenly taken the Pernambuco area must have instant attention.   It was actually in Admiral Stoddart's command —that is, the Canary and Cape Verde Station—but for all its importance he had not at first been able to deal with it.   The original intention in our commerce defence scheme was that it should be occupied from the North American and West Indies Station.   But the presence of so many large German ships in United States ports and the immediate need of safeguarding the North Atlantic routes had forced a change of plan, by which the area was committed to Admiral Stoddart.   Accordingly, he was given instructions to detach there as soon as possible his fastest cruiser, and we have seen how on August 13, when the *Monmouth* joined him at Las Palmas from home, he ordered her away.

Still, she could not be definitely assigned to the focal area, for she was to be under the orders of Captain Luce, who with the *Glasgow* had to watch the whole south-east coast of America single-handed, and his station stopped short of the area.   It is true that the Cruiser Squadron War Orders of July 1914 provided that no station limits were to be regarded as rigid and impassable, but these Captain Luce had not yet received.   His task was, of course, impossible to discharge adequately.   Much had to be left unwatched, and regarding the northern part of his station as the more important at the moment, especially as a number of large German ships had by orders from Berlin taken refuge in Brazilian ports, he had decided to leave the River Plate open, and was working from a secret coaling base at Abrolhos Rocks off the Brazilian coast, where the *Monmouth* joined him.   At the River Plate, therefore, German shipping was free to come and go, but off

the Brazilian ports his activity proved so strong a deterrent
that the only prize he had taken was the Hamburg-Sud-
Amerika liner *Santa Catharina,* which had left New York
before war broke out and had no wireless.

Clearly, then, something more must be done. To all
appearance the *Dresden* was operating in the Pernambuco
area from a secret base. The conclusion that she had orders
to do so was natural enough, but, in fact, her presence was
fortuitous and her orders quite different. It will be remembered that she had been actually under orders for home
when war broke out, having been relieved by the *Karlsruhe,*
and it would seem that one of the first effects of the closing
of the North Sea by the Home Fleets was an order that she
was to join Admiral von Spee in the Pacific. On German
authority we now know that as early as August 1 she was
told that war had broken out, and that she was to carry
on cruiser warfare, presumably against France and Russia.[1]
On these orders, apparently, she proceeded south and
hovered about the Pernambuco area for some time. On
the 9th and 10th she was coaling at Jericoacoara (Lat.
2° 50′ S., Long. 40° 35′ W.), an obscure inlet between
Para and Pernambuco. Thence she struck across the trade
route towards the island of Fernando Noronha, and then
doubled back to Rocas Reef, where she coaled again on
the 13th from the Hamburg-Amerika S.S. *Baden.* Here,
possibly, she received orders which led to her ruthless treatment of the *Hyades.*[2] It would also seem she was told to
carry on for the Pacific, avoiding normal trade routes, for
the *Hyades* was keeping off the usual track when she was
taken, and the *Dresden* with the *Baden* in company continued south. As no shipping was seen in the area it was
assumed that we were diverting our steamers to other routes.

All this, however, was not known till long afterwards,
and the Admiralty could only act on the belief that she was
definitely engaged in commerce destruction. On August 21
this appreciation was confirmed by intelligence from our
Vice-Consul at Pernambuco that she seemed to be using
Rocas Reef as a base, and next day the Admiralty ordered
Admiral Cradock to go down and search for her. Thus

---

[1] Admiral Dick : *Das Kreuzergeschwader.*

[2] This, however, is not certain. The first three ships she stopped (on
August 6) were released. This may have been because she had then no
tender to which she could transfer the crews. Admiral Dick's explanation
is : "Several vessels met *en route* to Rio and River Plate, but all ignorant
of war, except *Hyades,* which is sunk." This ground for release, however,
does not appear in the article of the German Prize Code relating to Vessels
Exempted from Capture (Part I. § 6).

early did war experience bring out the importance of the Pernambuco area and the inadequacy of the original defence system in the Atlantic. It was quickly seen that the shift would have to be permanent, and a fortnight later (September 4) Admiral Phipps Hornby, who had been commanding the 11th Squadron on the Irish Station, was ordered out to take over Admiral Cradock's original command. Both stations at the same time were reinforced with merchant cruisers. Admiral Hornby went out in the *Caronia*, and the *Macedonia* was sent to join Admiral Cradock, while a third, the *Otranto*, was well on her way to Captain Luce, who by this time also had the *Monmouth*, Captain Brandt.

It was on August 22, the day Admiral Cradock's new orders were issued, that she joined. Next day Captain Luce, who had asked whether he was to act against the *Dresden* to the northward of his station, was told that if he had certain news of her she was to be his objective, and that his station limits were only to be taken as a general guide. Accordingly, having heard of her sinking the *Hyades*, he at once went off to search the infested waters with the *Glasgow* and *Monmouth*. The news was a week old, but there was nothing to indicate what the real orders of the *Dresden* were. The effect of the movement was to leave her free to get well away on her southward course.

On August 19 the *Dresden*, in company with her tender, the *Baden*, made Trinidada, a lonely island lying out in the South Atlantic some 500 miles from the Brazilian coast. There she found the gunboat *Eber*, from German South-West Africa, waiting for the liner *Cap Trafalgar*, whom her captain was to arm and take over as an auxiliary. There, too, was a supply ship, the *Santa Isabel*, which had come to meet the *Dresden*.[1] Having filled his bunkers, Captain von Lüdecke sailed again on the 21st, intending, according to German accounts, to lie in wait off the River Plate for British steamers, whose arrival was known to be impending.[2] It was his intention to cruise in that area, and he laid a course direct for the Plate, but owing to the slow speed of

[1] The *Santa Isabel* came from Buenos Aires. On August 5 our Intelligence Officer there reported her to be taking in large quantities of coal, apparently for a German cruiser. She also took in coal-bags, shovels, oil and forty bullocks. On August 9 she sailed with a clearance for Togoland. Later it was ascertained that a German ship, the *Sevilla*, met her at sea about August 16 and transferred to her her wireless installation and an operator.
[2] Admiral Dick: *Das Kreuzergeschwader*. His account of the *Dresden's* movements does not always accord with her captured log. Here he says she sailed on the 24th, while the log gives the 21st. The German Official History (*Der Kreuzerkrieg*, Vol. I, p. 378) says she sailed on the 22nd.

the *Santa Isabel*, the *Dresden* and *Baden* turned on a rather more northerly course on August 25, and this alteration brought Captain von Lüdecke for the first time upon the regular trade route, and on August 26, when nearly abreast of Rio Grande, he captured the British S.S. *Holmwood*, outward bound for Bahia Blanca with coal, and shortly afterwards the *Katherine Park* from Buenos Aires to Rio and New York.   The *Holmwood* he sank, and as the other ship's cargo was American-owned, he let her go after transferring to her the crew of the *Holmwood*, a pretty sure indication that he did not intend to remain where he was.   He did, in fact, carry on down the coast, keeping well shorewards of the trade route till he reached Gill Bay, 500 miles short of Magellan Strait.[1]

All this time Captain Luce was searching for her as high as Cape San Roque.   On the 28th he tried the supposed German base at Rocas Reef.   Not even a collier was found, but there the *Otranto* joined and the three ships went off together to his secret coaling base at Abrolhos Rocks; he had little doubt what the *Dresden* was doing, and was bent on getting off the River Plate as soon as possible.

Complete as was the failure, the reasons that had dictated his movements were sound enough.   If he had missed the *Dresden*, he had come within an ace of getting the *Karlsruhe* ; for on September 1 this ship appeared there, and she it was and not the *Dresden* that had been told off to the Pernambuco focal area.

But meanwhile Admiral Cradock was at hand.   On August 27 he had begun a sweep along the north coast of Brazil, with the *Good Hope*, *Berwick* and *Bristol*, leaving the two French cruisers to take care of the West Indies in his absence.   He was thus engaged when on August 29 a report reached him that the *Cap Trafalgar* was making for St. Paul Rocks, which lie about midway between the African and Brazilian coasts.   This ship had come out of the River Plate on August 22 while Captain Luce was to the northward, and it was not till September 1 she received her armament.   On that day, somewhere off Bahia, she met the *Eber*, who had come on from Trinidada, and received from

---

[1] The *Dresden* attempted to coal from the *Santa Isabel*, but bad weather drove her into Cayetano Bay.   Here she coaled and left again on September 2. On the 8th she reached Orange Bay where the *Santa Isabel* arrived (12th) with news of British cruisers to the east of Magellan Strait.   Captain Lüdecke then decided to operate west of the strait and arrived at the western entrance on the night of the 17th/18th.

her her two guns, and apparently her officers and most of her crew. The *Cap Trafalgar* was thus well to the south-ward and had not actually started her career when Admiral Cradock heard of her. But the report he received pointed to the possibility of the *Dresden* being also at St. Paul Rocks, as she had not been heard of for ten days, and the Admiral, although it meant a run of 1500 miles, decided to proceed there in his flagship, leaving the *Bristol* and the *Berwick* to continue the search of the Brazilian coast.

The same report reached Admiral Stoddart at the Canaries, and as St. Paul Rocks were actually in his station he, too, decided to make a cast. Since the merchant cruisers which had been sent him after the *Kaiser Wilhelm's* raid had arrived, he felt he could do something for his south-western area, and on September 1 he ordered away the *Cornwall*, not knowing what his colleague was doing. Next day Admiral Cradock reached St. Paul Rocks. Nothing was there, and he at once made back for Fernando Noronha. Here, though it was Brazilian territory, there was a French Cable Company's station, connected with Brest and with Dakar in Senegal. Originally British, the station still had a British manager, who was ready to accept code messages. The Admiral thus got into communication with the Admiralty and the *Glasgow*, and being now made aware of the general situation was able to realise the extraordinary complication of the problem that the Germans had set.

From Captain Luce he heard that a number of German vessels seemed to be gathering in the Strait of Magellan, and that he was proposing to take his squadron there to investigate. On this the Admiral submitted to the Admiralty the possibility of a concentration there of all the German cruisers in the Pacific and Atlantic.

It would seem that he felt that in the circumstances he ought not to return to the West Indies. If so he only antici-pated the conclusion the Admiralty had come to. Their latest news from China and Australia raised a strong impression that Admiral von Spee was making for South American waters, and they had already sent him through Pernambuco an order that he was now to remain permanently in command of the South American Station, and, like the other stations, it was to have a battleship which he could use as a guardship for his secret base. For this purpose Admiral Stoddart was to send him the *Canopus*, which had been acting as guardship at St. Vincent, Cape Verde. The *Albion* was to replace her from Admiral de Robeck's squadron, and Admiral Tottenham, who was still in the *Albion*, was to strike his flag and take over the Irish Station in place of Admiral Phipps Hornby, who, as we have seen, was now appointed to Admiral Cradock's original command. At the same time, however, there was great anxiety about the West Indies. One at least of the enemy's Atlantic cruisers did not seem to be destined for the expected concentration, for it was now known that the crew of the *Bowes Castle*, a ship taking nitrates to the United States, had just been brought into Maranham, on the north coast of Brazil, with news of the *Karlsruhe*. What they had to report was that the German cruiser had sunk their ship on August 18 450 miles south-east of Barbados. At the same time our intelligence officers reported renewed German activity at the island of St. Thomas, where colliers and supply ships were being sent out apparently to the *Karlsruhe*, and possibly, also, to the *Dresden*. In the face of this information the West Indies could not be neglected. For their safety the Admiralty hastened to provide. A cruiser was to be called down from the North American area with special orders to look into St. Thomas, and the *Essex* (Captain Watson), being nearest, was selected. The *Berwick* (Captain Clinton Baker) was also to return there, and in her place Admiral Cradock was to keep the *Cornwall* (Captain Ellerton), who, as he was returning from his examination of St. Paul Rocks, had been ordered to turn back to Pernambuco.

The new instructions were entirely in accord with Admiral Cradock's own appreciation of what was likely to happen, and as it was now certain that the German vessels in the vicinity of Magellan Strait were colliers the probability of his having to deal with the Pacific Squadron was increased. As soon, therefore, as he received his new orders he proceeded to Pernambuco to reconcentrate his squadron. Here, as some compensation for his disappointment at St. Paul Rocks, he found ample evidence of the paralysis of the enemy's trade. In the harbour were not less than fifteen large German ships, belonging mainly to the Hamburg-Sud-Amerika and Norddeutscher Lloyd Companies. Many of them had taken refuge there on the general orders from home in the early days of the war, and none had ventured to stir. On the other hand, it was clear that the exploits of the *Dresden* had shaken the confidence of traders all down the coast, and our consuls were crying out for a stronger display of force. But this was already provided for, and it was Admiral Cradock who was to see to it, instead of returning to his old station. Before moving he asked for the latest information as to Admiral von Spee's movements. The reply was that there had been nothing certain for nearly a month, but it was quite probable the enemy might make for the vicinity of the Strait, or even the Falkland Islands. On this he determined to move down to the River Plate, where confidence had been most severely shaken and the call for protection was most insistent, and to distribute his squadron to examine all likely places on the way. At the same time he ordered Captain Luce to carry on with his division to the southward, searching all unfrequented anchorages south of the Plate as far as the Strait, and as the *Dresden* was now known by her last capture to be to the southward, he was to take up a position there so as to prevent her getting away into the Pacific. This plan the Admiral proceeded to carry out, till, in the middle of the month, it was overridden by new orders from the Admiralty, which once more changed his sphere of action.

The developments which had been drawing Admiral Cradock to the southward had also had their reaction upon his colleagues on the other side of the Atlantic, and here the problem was complicated in a high degree by military requirements. We have seen already how the first effect was that Admiral Stoddart was called on to reinforce Admiral Cradock with the *Canopus* and *Cornwall*. The loss of these ships came at an inopportune moment and heavily taxed his power of meeting the exigencies of the army. His squadron now consisted of the *Carnarvon* (flag), the *Albion* on her way down from Cape St. Vincent to replace the *Canopus*, the *Highflyer* refitting at Gibraltar after her action with the *Kaiser Wilhelm*, and three armed merchant cruisers, *Victorian*, *Empress of Britain*, and *Marmora*. The *Cumberland* was engaged in the operations against the Cameroons, and with her were the *Challenger* and the French cruiser *Bruix*, which was escorting the Senegalese contingent. His immediate concern was the transports bringing home the Cape garrison, which, in charge of the *Hyacinth* of the Cape Station and the *Leviathan*, specially detached from the 6th Cruiser Squadron, were just entering his area, and there was one enemy ship which might interfere with them. This was the *Kronprinz Wilhelm*, which had been in company with the *Karlsruhe* when, on August 6, Admiral Cradock lost her off the Bahamas. Since then she had disappeared, but it was now known that on August 27 she had boarded a Russian ship about 500 miles north-north-west of the Cape Verde Islands. Out of his diminished squadron Admiral Stoddart had now to take over the convoy from the *Hyacinth* with one of his own ships. In view of the proximity of the *Kronprinz Wilhelm* he had nothing to spare, but was fortunately able to use the *Europa*, which had brought out a transport with General Dobell and the Cameroons Staff, and the *Challenger* had taken it on. Thus all would have gone well, but on reaching the northern limit of his station the *Leviathan* broke down and he had to take the convoy on himself in his flagship. An order for Admiral de Robeck to relieve him came too late, and he had to carry on to Lisbon. Here he was authorised to leave the transports to the *Europa*, for the rest of the route was now patrolled by the French, and another large convoy, powerfully escorted, was coming down. This was the East Lancashire Territorial Division bound for Egypt, and ultimately India, together with two Territorial Battalions for Gibraltar and Malta, all in charge of the *Minerva* and the *Ocean* on her way to replace the *Albion* at Cape St. Vincent. But so much reduced was Admiral de Robeck's Squadron, owing to continual trouble with the old cruisers, that he had to leave the Cape St. Vincent focal area to the French Morocco Division and send away the *Ocean*, first to Madeira and then to the Azores.[1] But further military exigencies compelled the Admiralty to cancel this arrangement, and to send both *Ocean* and *Minerva* to the East Indies, where the menace of the German Pacific Squadron, as will be seen directly, was causing special anxiety for the safety of the all-important Indian convoys. Nor did this kind of interference with Admiral de Robeck's commerce protection duties cease till, after the loss of the three " Cressys," the remainder of the 7th Cruiser Squadron were told off as regular escort between home and Gibraltar.

Meanwhile, before Admiral de Robeck could act on the orders which deprived him of the *Ocean* and *Minerva*, Admiral Stoddart, having heard that the *Kronprinz Wilhelm* was in his station, had gone back to Madeira. She was said to be at Rio de Oro on the Morocco coast, where the *Kaiser Wilhelm* had been caught, and with the *Highflyer*, fresh from refitting, he made a sweep for her. Unfortunately, he started just soon enough to miss an urgent call from the French. Among all the fine things they did in the war, few surpass the way in which General Lyautey, the Governor of Morocco, clung to his still raw province without drawing on the resources of the Mother Country. His force was slender in the extreme, and German agents were diligently making trouble by their well-known methods. Amongst other devices, with their reckless or ignorant disregard of

---

[1] The French Morocco Division at this time comprised, besides the *Bruix* at Duala, the cruisers *Friant* and *Amiral Charner* and the light cruisers *Cassard* and *Cosmao*.

the consequences of deceiving Orientals, they had been spreading a report that Great Britain had declared war on France. The result was considerable unrest amongst the turbulent tribesmen, and, as a direct means of contradicting the German falsehood, the French Government asked for a British ship to make a joint demonstration with the *Cassard* along the disturbed coast. The sweep Admiral Stoddart was making may well have given colour to the German story, and it was nearly a week before the instructions reached him. He then immediately ordered away the *Victorian*. On September 26 she met the *Cassard* off Cape Juby, and together they moved up the coast as high as Agadir, bringing home the object lesson with occasional bombardments of the villages they passed. The effect seems to have been all that was desired, and the tribal unrest died down.

It may appear that it would have been a better reply to the French if we had sent a regular cruiser to join the *Cassard* instead of the *Victorian*, but what was done was in accordance with a new cruiser policy which the Admiralty had just enjoined. In spite of all its complexities, the problem of exercising a general command of the sea was growing clearer. It was now established that the danger from the enemy's armed merchant cruisers was going to be much less than had been anticipated, and it was to deal with this class of ship that our own merchant cruisers had been commissioned. The altered circumstances were pointed out by the Admiralty in a general order on September 13, and a new function assigned to the auxiliary units. Henceforth they were, as far as possible, to work in conjunction with a regular cruiser in order to assist her in getting hold of enemy cruisers, and never to engage a ship they met unless she was distinctly of inferior force. By this system of coupling, the reach of the regular cruisers would be considerably extended, and the work of dealing with the elusive tactics of the enemy simplified.

But for Admiral Stoddart the work was heavy enough. For, besides his trade defence duties, he had still the Cameroons Expedition to cover, and it had developed in such a way as to make it clear that the cruisers attached to it could not be released for some time to come.

CHAPTER XX

IT had, of course, been recognised from the first that the Cameroons would be a very different undertaking from Togoland. The colony, since its extension by the Franco-German agreement of 1912, had an area of nearly 300,000 square miles, and from the borders of Nigeria to those of the Gaboon, which was now included in the French Congo, its sea-front stretched for some 200 miles. The Germans had in the colony 230 white troops, and, including police, 3,200 natives. It was therefore a question of a considerable expedition which was to be organised from our West African Frontier Force under General Dobell, the Inspector-General. Whether the French would be able to assist directly was at first more than doubtful. Owing to the recent cession of territory which they had made to Germany, the position of their Congo Colony was very weak. Not only had the Germans obtained a perfect interior position, but their frontier had been brought up so close to the main French line of communication with the Lake Chad region as to menace it along its whole extent. The idea of the French, consequently, was to act purely on the defensive, and by seizing certain strategical points to pin the Germans down to areas where they could do least harm. Such operations would, of course, be valuable as a diversion, and the French were also ready to provide naval co-operation on the coast.

We, on our part, in accordance with the defence scheme drawn up some years before the war, had mobilised three columns from the Nigerian Force: one based on Maifoni on the Maidugari River near Lake Chad, another on Nafada to the westward, and a third, which was the strongest of them, at Yola, midway down the frontier. In the coastal area were two others, the Cross River or Ikom column, and the Calabar column. Though they were intended primarily as observation

---

[1] See Map, p. 276 and Map 16 in case. For a full account of the campaign see *Official History of the War, Military Operations, Togoland and the Cameroons* 1914-1916.

forces, their commandant was anxious to take the offensive. This was forbidden as premature, and they were to be confined to their assigned functions of reconnaissance, though the Yola or principal column was authorised, at the commanding officer's discretion, to seize Garua, the German station just across the frontier. Nothing, however, was intended at present beyond movements, analogous to those of the French, to draw the enemy from the coast and to prepare for combined action with the main expeditionary force later on.

On further consideration, however, the French were not content with naval co-operation in the main zone. At Dakar they had ready, with transports, a force of nearly 2000 Senegalese, with six guns. It was intended for Morocco, where General Lyautey urgently needed reinforcement, and it was only awaiting escort. This force they decided to use at Duala, and on August 15, at a joint conference held in the Admiralty, the plan of operation was settled. Nigeria could provide 1700 men and 10 guns, and Sierra Leone 600 men. A flotilla for inshore and river work was to be formed from the Nigerian Marine. Before, however, any move could be made, it was necessary to ascertain whether the reports of German cruisers being based at Duala and of a German occupation of the Spanish island of Fernando Po were true. Not an hour was lost, and on the same day these decisions were come to Admiral Stoddart got the order under which Captain Fuller was detached in the *Cumberland* to clear up the situation.

On the 23rd he left Sierra Leone with the gunboat *Dwarf* in tow, and a transport with reinforcements for Togoland. Lome was reached two days after the colony capitulated, and there he took possession of a Woermann liner, whose native crew had mutinied and forced their German officers to take the ship into a British port. Then, after looking in at Lagos to arrange for the organisation of the Nigerian flotilla, he went alone to examine Fernando Po. He was there on the last day of August. No trace of German occupation was found, and he immediately proceeded to Duala, where he found nothing but what appeared to be an armed ship patrolling the entrance. It was now necessary to report the condition of affairs to Nigeria, and as Duala was jamming his wireless he had to go back to Calabar before establishing a blockade. There, on September 1, he found that all outstanding questions had been settled. At first there had been some doubt as to how the command should be shared. The French proposal was that they should have command of the troops, and the British officers the command at sea, but on our urging the special qualifications and ripe local experience of General Dobell, they handsomely agreed that both commands should remain in British hands. At the same time, as their gun-vessel, the *Surprise*, had broken down and would require some time for repairs, they consented to let the armoured cruiser *Bruix* come on with the Dakar troops and co-operate with Captain Fuller.

The plan of operations had also been settled. The original idea was to establish a base in Ambas Bay some twenty-five miles to the westward of the Cameroon River. Here lay Victoria, a port connected by a light railway with Buea, the former capital, ten miles to the northward on the slopes of the Cameroon Mountain. The objectives of the first phase of the operations were laid down as Victoria, Buea, Duala, and particularly the wireless station. It had, however, just been reported that the route between Victoria and Duala was impassable during two months of the rainy season, which would soon be at its height. If this proved true Duala would have to be attacked directly, and a cruiser light enough to enter the river would have to be attached to the expedition. For this reason the *Challenger* (Captain Beaty-Pownall) was ordered to Sierra Leone, where the allied troops were to concentrate on September 10.[1] On September 3 Captain Fuller was back at Fernando Po with orders to gather intelligence and carry out a thorough reconnaissance in preparation for the expedition. He was still anxious that Victoria should be occupied as a first step, for whether or not it was suitable for an army base he regarded it, now that the tornado season was coming on, as essential for a base for the flotilla. Next day, therefore, when the *Dwarf* rejoined him he went there to make a close investigation. Intelligence that he was able to gather from friendly Kroomen quickly convinced him that it was useless as a military base, but, on the other hand, it was reported to contain a large store of provisions. As the colony was said to be short of them it was desirable to seize it, and he accordingly sent in a flag of truce expressing his intention to land, and threatening a bombardment if any opposition was offered. The demand was accepted, and as it was clear no troops were in the vicinity, a party of seamen and marines was landed to inspect the town. It was soon found that the bulk of the stores had been removed since Captain Fuller first appeared on the coast. A few stocks, however, were discovered, and a guard of marines was left on shore to prevent their removal in the night. Similar precautions were taken at Bóta, a little port in the

[1] *Challenger*, 5880 tons, 11 6"; 8 12-pdrs.

west of the bay, through which passed the light railway from
Victoria to Buea. Here a large store of supplies was discovered, and Captain Fuller decided to land a force and
remove them in the morning. But no sooner had the work
commenced than the bush was found to be full of troops, and
presently a flag of truce came in to demand instant evacuation. As nothing was to be gained by resistance, the landing
parties were promptly withdrawn, and, after warning the
inhabitants, the *Cumberland* destroyed the store by gunfire.

It was now clear that the only adequate base was Duala
itself. It was the actual seat of government, and not only
had it an excellent harbour with good quays and a floating
dock, but it was the starting point of the two main railways.
From the town ran the Midland Line, of which 100 miles
were completed to Edea on the Sanaga River and on to Eseka
on the Nyong. At Bonaberi, on the opposite or northern
bank of the Cameroon River, began the Northern Line,
destined ultimately to reach Lake Chad, of which the first
section of 100 miles was completed to the Manenguba
Mountains. To Duala Captain Fuller could now turn his
attention, for on September 5 he was joined by eight vessels
of the Niger Flotilla.[1] Before leaving Victoria, however, he
decided to try their mettle in seizing some lighters that were
moored off the pier. The work was done in brilliant style
by the *Vampire* and *Walrus*, and a cutting-out party from
the *Cumberland* and *Dwarf*. The lighters were all captured
intact, and with this very useful addition to the flotilla he
proceeded off the Cameroon River.

The first essential need on that surf-beaten coast was to
secure a safe anchorage at some convenient point for his
small craft. The only place was inside Cape Cameroon and
Suellaba Point, that is, the entrance to the lagoon-like estuary
by which the river reaches the sea, and before this could be
accomplished it was necessary, in view of the Kroomen's
reports of extensive mining, to sweep the estuary and
approaches thoroughly. But, in fact, Duala was so wholly
unprepared for defence, that the Germans had not a single

[1] *Ivy* . . . Nigerian Government yacht.
Moseley . . . Steam lifeboat.
Vigilant }
Vampire } . . Dispatch vessels.
Walrus }
Balbus } . . Tugs.
Alligator }
Crocodile } . . Motor launches.

They were mostly commanded by retired R.N.R. officers in the Nigerian service. Two more armed tugs, *Remus* and *Porpoise*, joined about ten days later.

mine and were only just beginning to extemporise substitutes. Nothing, therefore, was found, and so rapidly did the sweeping proceed that on September 9, after the two points had been searched by gunfire, the *Dwarf* was able to pass into the estuary.[1] It was known that a barrage of sunken vessels had been formed to block the river, and she at once discovered it at Rugged Point, some seven miles below the town. The patrol ship had fled at the first sight of her, but, seeing the Governor's yacht, *Herzogin Elisabeth*, coming out, the *Dwarf* promptly engaged her, and she quickly retired, apparently on fire, revealing as she re-passed the barrage that there was a practicable channel round the south end of it. Next day (the 10th) the *Cumberland* moved into the estuary and established a temporary base for the river craft inside Suellaba Point. The patrol ship was also seized. She proved to be the Hamburg-Amerika liner *Kamerun* (3660 tons), and was found beached and abandoned off Manoka Point.[2]

The laborious work of preparing for the troops began at once. This same day two of the *Cumberland's* steamboats penetrated the Lungasi River as high as Pitti, just below where the Midland Railway crosses it. On their way they chased and sank a large steam launch, and at Pitti they, in their turn, came under fire from entrenchments. Nevertheless, they landed, destroyed the telephone installation and made a valuable capture of papers which disclosed the enemy's scheme of defence for the Midland Railway. The sweeping, meanwhile, had been carried on up to and beyond the barrage. The *Dwarf* then passed it by the channel the Governor's yacht had shown her, and took up a position to prevent the obstruction being completed. Her boldness soon got her into trouble; for next day, as she was firing on a launch with a lighter in tow, she got caught by two field guns in a well-masked battery which had been established at Yoss Point to protect the barrage. She replied vigorously, but wisely retired at once, and though she had one bad hit on the bridge she succeeded in setting the battery on fire, and it never spoke again.

[1] *Dwarf* (Commander F. E. K. Strong), 710 tons, 2·4", 4 12-pdrs.

[2] She had been loading timber in the Gaboon on August 1 when, war being imminent, she was summoned to Duala. She was given a guard of native troops and stationed in the estuary to give wireless warning of an enemy's approach. Her orders were to sink herself in the fairway if a large cruiser appeared, but to try to ram a small one. At the first appearance of the *Dwarf*, however, on the 8th, she ran full speed up the Manoka Creek till she grounded, and her people made off in the boats to Edea.—(Diary of W. Schmacher, chief engineer.)

By this time it was known to Captain Fuller that he was to have the valuable addition to his force which it had been decided would be necessary if Duala had to be attacked from the sea. The *Challenger* was coming with the troops, and if a way could only be made for her through the barrage the fate of the town would quickly be settled. The work began at once, and while it proceeded the flotilla was assiduously nosing into every hole and corner of the multitudinous creeks that open out from the estuary along the coast on either hand. It was arduous and exciting work, for the creeks were tortuous and narrow, and at any moment the boats could be sniped out of the dense mangrove swamps that fringed them, and sometimes they were surprised by an armed vessel. Nevertheless, every inch was surveyed, with trifling casualties, and a number of launches were destroyed, while the *Ivy* and *Dwarf* took turns as guardship to cover the destruction of the barrage.

Needless to say, the Germans, in spite of their unpreparedness, exhausted all their ingenuity to stop the work. The *Dwarf* engaged their special attention. For her benefit they constructed a kind of infernal machine made of steel gas cylinders with percussion fuses and attached them under the bows of a launch. One of these engines was sent against her on the night of the 15th, when she was barrage guardship. The attack was duly made and a loud explosion heard. In Duala they counted it a sure success, but in the morning there was the *Dwarf* as usual. She had, in fact, detected the attempt in time, and under her fire the man in charge lost his head, lashed the helm wrongly before he leapt overboard, and the torpedo exploded against the bank. Next day she was sent to look after an armed vessel called the *Nachtigal*, after one of the founders of the colony. She had attacked two of our boats the previous day and had been chased by the *Ivy* into the Bimbia River, the western outlet of the maze of creeks. There while the *Dwarf* was anchored for the night she suddenly appeared, and in spite of the point-blank fire that greeted her she was able to ram. The blow went fairly home, and the Germans might well hope the *Dwarf* was done for, but it was the *Nachtigal* that perished. When the two vessels separated the *Dwarf* quickly had her enemy in flames, and though badly holed was able to get back to Suellaba, where she speedily repaired her damages and was ready for her turn of barrage guard again. On the night of the 19th a second attempt on her was made with another infernal machine. Again a loud explosion was heard. But the launch had been detected and sunk by a steam pinnace, and again the morning revealed the irrepressible little ship off the barrage quietly guarding the boats that were mining a way for the *Challenger*.

The work was carried out by the divers and torpedo staff of the *Cumberland* under the most dangerous and difficult conditions. The first attempt, indeed, failed, but by the 22nd part of the obstruction had been sufficiently demolished to allow of a ship of 19 feet draught to pass. But even so the way was not clear, for the Germans had just succeeded in laying a field of their extemporised mines a little above it, abreast of the Yoss battery.

Still, all the preparatory work that was needed had been done when next day (September 23) the *Challenger* appeared with six transports carrying General Dobell and his staff and the British contingent of the expeditionary force.[1] The *Bruix*, with the French contingent, was following, but had not yet appeared. Nor had the *Surprise*, but she was known to be well employed elsewhere. No sooner were her repairs completed than there was an urgent call for her from Libreville, the capital of the Gaboon. There in Corisco Bay, where the territory ceded to Germany in 1912 reached the sea between the Spanish enclave and the new Gaboon frontier, two armed ships had been giving trouble. The *Surprise* was quickly on the spot, and by September 24 had destroyed both vessels, and driven the Germans from their entrenched position on the Okoko beach, and so eliminated one possible raiding base.[2]

At Duala, as there was already force enough, Captain Fuller and General Dobell lost no time in settling a plan of attack. A possible landing place had been found near Mbenga on the Duala side of the Lungasi River, from which point it was hoped to seize the Midland Railway and cut off

[1] British contingent, under Colonel Gorges, was composed as under :—

Artillery :
> 4 guns, Sierra Leone Company, R.G.A.
> 1st battery, Nigeria Regiment (4 guns).
> Section Gold Coast Artillery (2 guns).

Infantry :
> 6 companies West African Regiment.
> 4 companies 1st Battalion Nigeria Regiment.
> 4 companies 2nd Battalion, Nigeria Regiment.
> 2 companies Sierra Leone Battalion, W.A.F.F.
> 2 companies Gold Coast Regiment, W.A.F.F.
> 1 Pioneer Company, Gold Coast Regiment, W.A.F.F.

Total with army troops (engineers, railway, telegraph, etc.), 154 British officers, 81 British N.C.O.s, 2460 native rank and file, 10 guns, and 3563 carriers.

[2] *Surprise*, 1895, 617 tons, 2 3·9″, 4 2·5″.

the escape of the garrison that way, while the *Challenger*, who meanwhile had been lightened to 19½ feet, was to endeavour to pass the barrage and with her fire prevent anything crossing to the Northern Railway. Early on the 25th, at slack tide, she was cleverly scraped through the gap that had been blown away, and though the *Bruix* and her transports were close at hand it was decided to lose no more time. Captain Fuller, with the General, therefore went on board the *Challenger* and sent in a summons to surrender. Nothing was received but prevaricating replies, and the negotiation was prolonged till it was too late to do anything that day. The *Challenger*, however, was ordered to bombard next morning, and the commanding officers returned to Suellaba to greet the French who had just anchored there.[1]

As it was too late for them to take part in the attack, the operations went forward as arranged. Early on the 26th part of the flotilla, with advanced companies of troops, went up the Lungasi to try the Mbenga landing, while two transports, with the main body, waited at the mouth of the river till they heard the result. Two companies were landed by 6.30 and sent forward to occupy Yansoki, a village opposite Pitti, while the two powerful armed tugs, *Remus* and *Porpoise*, which had recently joined the flotilla from Nigeria, went on with another company to deal with the enemy's entrenched position at Pitti, and, if possible, to push on to the Yapoma Bridge and cut the railway. They were received with a heavy fire which it took them the best part of an hour to silence, but it was done at last, and, landing a party, they again destroyed the telephone. Further progress, however, proved impossible. A little further on a boom of felled trees was discovered; all attempt to examine it was prevented by heavy maxim fire, and as nothing further could be done they retired. At Mbenga things had gone no better. The advance party had found the swamps too bad even to reach Mbenga Village, and the troops were withdrawn.

The first attempt, therefore, seemed to be a complete failure, but, in fact, it was not. The governor and commandant had already left the town, and the threat of the

---

[1] The French contingent, under Colonel Mayer, was :—

    1 six-gun battery.
    1 section engineers.
    1 company European Colonial Infantry.
    1st and 2nd Senegalese Battalions (4 companies each).

In all, with transport, etc., 54 European officers, 354 other Europeans 1859 native rank and file, 1000 carriers, and 200 animals—making the total force under General Dobell, 643 Europeans, 4319 natives, 4563 carriers and 16 guns, besides the naval field guns.

reconnaissance on the main line of retreat was too much for
the nerves of those who had been left in charge. Next
morning (the 27th), as the allied commanding officers were
reconnoitring Yoss Point with a view to forcing a landing
there, loud explosions were heard and the wireless mast
collapsed. Simultaneously a white flag was seen over
Government House. Troops were promptly ordered up, but
as they could not arrive for some time Captain Fuller offered
to land his marines, and before evening Duala, with Bonaberi
and the immediate environs, was surrendered unconditionally.

The capture had proved a much easier affair than had
been expected, and the booty was large. All the railway
rolling stock had been got away, but besides a whole company
of 100 Europeans taken prisoners, there were still in the
harbour all the Woermann and other ships that had been
called in when the warning telegram was issued, though, as
the captains explained, they might easily have got away to
Brazil. Of these there were eight of the Woermann line
and one Hamburg-Amerika ship, amounting in all to over
30,000 tons. Except for parts of their engines all were intact,
and most of them had valuable cargoes and plenty of coal.[1]
Two others were subsequently raised from the barrage, and
the floating dock and dredger, both of which had been
scuttled, were also salved, as well as a number of other
vessels and launches, including the governor's yacht and a
gunboat. Except, indeed, for the wireless installation and
the rolling stock, there fell into our hands almost everything
that was required to establish a base for further operations.

So far as the naval purpose of the expedition was concerned the object was already attained by the occupation of
the port and the destruction of the wireless station, and
immediately the Admiralty heard of it they inquired of
Captain Fuller how soon he could return to the trade routes.
He could only reply that the enemy was in force on all sides
of the surrendered territory, which extended only 3½ kilometres
on the Duala side of the river, and 1½ on the other, and that
he could therefore give no probable date when the *Cumberland* could safely be spared. There could certainly be no
question of her leaving for some time, for, as had happened
in all the other enterprises of the same nature elsewhere, the
naval object of destroying a hostile base and intelligence
centre had insensibly merged into one of territorial conquest,

---

[1] The reason why these ships remained at Duala appears to have been
that in Germany, during the period of strained relations, insurance against
war risks could not be effected except on condition that ships should make
for the nearest safe port when war broke out and remain there.

and on the following day it was decided to inform General Dobell that the ultimate end of the military operations was the complete reduction of the German colony. He was therefore to give his views and proposals, having regard to his own and the enemy's strength, of how the next phase of the operations could proceed.

Such an expression of views was certainly necessary. It was now obvious that the resistance of the enemy in the interior would be a very different thing from that they had set up on the coast. It would seem, in fact, that their policy was to abandon the coast, confident, as they were or had been till recently, that the war would be brought to a victorious conclusion long before we could operate successfully in the interior. In the Hinterland, where reconnaissances had been allowed to develop into operations against strategical points within the German frontier, two of our columns had met with reverses. The Yola Column had failed in its attempt to seize Garua and had been forced to retire right back with serious loss. The Cross River Column had succeeded in occupying Nssanakang near the head of the Northern Railway on August 25, but on September 6 it had been surprised by a superior force brought up from Duala and driven out with the loss of two guns, five machine-guns and a heavy list of killed, wounded and prisoners. So serious was the resulting position that, so far from further offence being possible, preparation had to be set on foot for meeting the possibility of an attack on Calabar. In the north the French main column operating from Fort Lamy had had no better success. It had failed to dislodge the Germans from Kusseri, and our own Northern Column, which had seized a post across the frontier in order to join hands with it, had to be withdrawn to reinforce the shattered Yola Column. It was clear, then, that a steady push inwards from the sea on the natural lines of communication would be our main chance, and there was little prospect—at least till the operations had passed beyond their coastal character—of the *Cumberland* being released. It seemed a waste of such a ship, but the old exigencies as usual were reasserting themselves. In combined operations of this nature ships of force had always been found necessary, not for their own intrinsic fighting power, but because the support of the officers, crews, guns, boats and stores was indispensable to give effective weight and movement to the land forces.

Such assistance in this case, where it was a question of organising a sea base, was specially necessary—no less than for the operations which General Dobell had immediately in

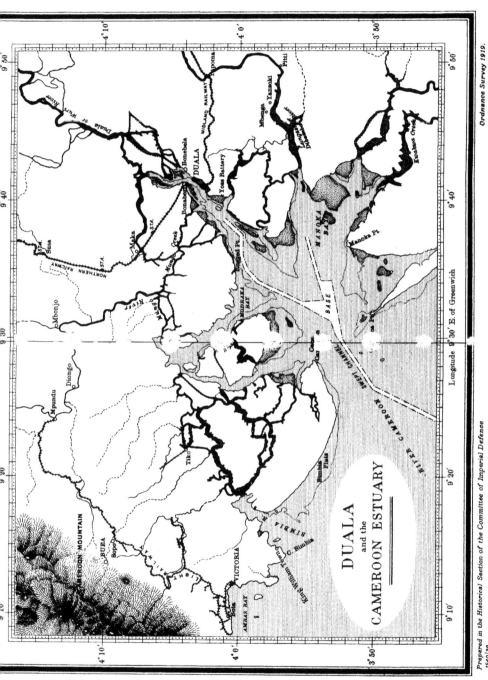

DUALA
and the
CAMEROON ESTUARY

Longitude 9° 30' E. of Greenwich

Prepared in the Historical Section of the Committee of Imperial Defence

1540/38.

Ordnance Survey 1919.

prospect. The Germans, reinforced by the crews of the captured ships, had retired on three lines, up the Northern Railway from Bonaberi, up the Duala or Wuri River to Ybassi, and on the Midland Line towards Edea. His intention was to press them without delay on all three lines, and the French were at once to drive the enemy beyond the Lungasi River and seize the Yapoma Bridge. In a couple of days they had forced the Germans to retire across the bridge, but they then found they could not get on without the field guns of the *Cumberland* and *Challenger* and the assistance of their marines and boats in the river. The assistance was promptly sent, and on October 6 the Senegalese were able in a brilliant rush to carry the bridge and establish themselves on the other bank. To the westward the flotilla had cleared the enemy out of Tiko and other posts to which they were still clinging on the routes to Victoria and Buea. The whole delta and estuary between the Bimbia and Lungasi Rivers was now in our hands, and the position at Duala sufficiently secure for further action. The same day that the Yapoma Bridge was taken, a reconnaissance in force, headed by the captured gunboat, re-named *Sokoto*, started up the river for Ybassi. There, however, so hot a reception was encountered that a retirement was necessary in order to reorganise. Meanwhile, the French ships and the *Ivy* had been detailed for patrolling the coast and dealing with the minor German ports. In these circumstances the *Cumberland* could not be returned to Admiral Stoddart, and Captain Fuller could only report that neither she nor the *Challenger* could be spared, at least until Edea had been taken, and that could not be expected before the end of the month.

For the present, then, there was no possibility of Admiral Stoddart providing for the distant section of his station off Pernambuco. For the African side he had enough—or rather would have had enough had it not been that he, too, came under the influence of the disturbance Admiral von Spee's movements were causing all over the world. As we have seen, on the other side of the Atlantic they had already drawn Admiral Cradock down to the southward, with the result that the Pernambuco area was again left without protection, and Admiral Stoddart, who had just heard the *Karlsruhe* had appeared there, had to recast the disposition of his reduced squadron in order to deal with her as best he could without the assistance of any of the British or French cruisers that were tied to the Cameroons.

CHAPTER XXI

WIDELY as the existence of the German Pacific Squadron affected the dispositions of our Atlantic squadrons, it was naturally those of the Eastern Fleet that were most seriously disturbed. The entrance of Japan into the war, of course, did much to simplify the general problem, but, nevertheless, the disturbing effect was destined to continue for some time. The reasons for this were not so much naval as military and political. Neither the Admiralty nor the Admirals on the spot had much doubt that, with the Fleet of Japan thrown into the scale, the main German Squadron must sooner or later be driven across the Pacific. Their concern was rather how to deal with the detached cruisers which were an abiding menace to trade and still more to the troop convoys. Of these cruisers there were two at large in the area, *Königsberg* and *Emden*, besides the *Prinz Eitel Friedrich* and the *Geier*. The *Nürnberg* was also a possible raider, and in the Dutch ports and the Philippines were a number of enemy steam vessels which might be converted into commerce destroyers or used as colliers and supply ships. The patrol of the trade routes had therefore to be maintained and supplemented by a strict watch on the ports where these ships lay. Still, if the Navy had only had a clean sheet to work on, the task would have been well within the capacity of the Eastern Fleet; but owing to the fact that the general military situation did not permit of the Imperial Concentration being postponed till there had been time to round up the enemy's prowling cruisers, the problem was difficult and complicated in the extreme. Indeed, it is not easy to see how the thing could have been done effectively but for the assistance which Japan so opportunely provided.

Her fleet, whose constitution differed considerably from our own, was admirably adapted for the work in hand. It was

---

[1] See Map p. 286 and Maps 7 and 14 in case.

the outcome, in fact, of rich and well-assimilated war experience only ten years old. Its backbone was a squadron of six modern battleships, two being Dreadnoughts, two similar to our "Lord Nelsons" and two of "King Edward VII" type. There were also five others dating from the late war, of which two were reconstructed Russian prizes; but it was its strength in cruisers that marked its special value to the common cause. Of these there were completed, or nearly ready, six battle cruisers, two being large ones of the British type and four smaller ones of a special Japanese design, and earlier in date than our "Invincibles," averaging about 14,000 tons and carrying four 12″ guns, besides a heavy secondary armament. Then came eleven armoured cruisers dating from before the Russian War, two of which were prizes, and then twelve good light cruisers, four of which had been added quite recently. Besides this sea-going fleet, Japan maintained, as the result of her recent experience, a large number of other vessels intended for coastal work and narrow seas. Most of them, but not all, consisted of obsolete types retained on the active list for this essential service. There were in all twenty-six of them (including three Russian prizes), classed as first and second class coast defence ships and first and second class gunboats; but if we may judge from the use to which they were put it was coastal attack rather than coastal defence for which they were intended.

The primary object of the Japanese Government was the reduction of Tsingtau. It was at once her own special interest in the war and the best service she could render to the Alliance. For this operation two fleets were constituted. The first fleet, or rather the main part of it, comprising three battleships (one "Dreadnought" and two "Lord Nelsons"), four light cruisers and a flotilla of destroyers with its leader, was told off primarily for escort duty, but, until the troops were ready to move, it took up a position in the south of the Yellow Sea to guard Japanese waters against offensive action by Admiral von Spee. It had also a division of battle cruisers, but these were used to form special squadrons for seeking out the enemy in the Pacific. The second fleet included three old battleships and two coast defence ships of the first class, all five of them being Russian prizes, three armoured cruisers and a destroyer flotilla with a light cruiser leader. This was the attacking fleet, and to it the *Triumph* and her destroyer, the *Usk*, were attached. Practically all the rest of the active cruiser force was devoted in co-operation with our Eastern Fleet to keeping control of the trade and transport routes, hunting down the enemy's scattered cruisers and depriving him of his minor bases. As a first step the second-class battle cruiser *Ibuki* was sent with the new light cruiser *Chikuma* to join Admiral Jerram's flag at Singapore. The Japanese also took over the guard of the Formosa Strait and its adjacent waters down to the approaches to Hongkong with a force designated " The Third Squadron," which consisted of the light cruiser *Tsushima*, two new first class gunboats and four of the second class. Admiral Jerram could thus devote his attention to the section of his station which extended from Hongkong to the Malacca Strait, and particularly to the Singapore area, to prevent Admiral von Spee from breaking into the Indian Ocean and attacking the Indian convoys.

The movement of these convoys constituted one of the most important factors in the situation. Their ports of departure were Karachi and Bombay, and the usual programme was that the convoys were composed of two groups of transports, one from each port, that from Karachi leaving the day after that from Bombay. They and their respective escorts then met at sea and made for a rendezvous at the British islands of Khorya Morya on the south Arabian coast. This formed the first stage of the voyage. The next was to Aden, and the third up the Red Sea to Suez. As the *Königsberg* was still unlocated, and believed to be cruising in or near the Indian Ocean, escort was a grave difficulty, since each group must be guarded by at least one ship capable of dealing with the German cruiser, and the Indian Marine ships did not come up to this standard. There was also the possibility that Admiral von Spee might appear on the scene. Not only, therefore, was the whole of Admiral Peirse's squadron absorbed in the work, but he had to be reinforced from the Mediterranean. It was for this reason that the light cruiser *Chatham* had been sent to him, as well as the *Duke of Edinburgh* and *Black Prince* from the 1st Cruiser Squadron, the two latter for the special purpose of dealing with the Red Sea. Moreover, in order to carry the rearrangement to its logical conclusion and bring the station limits into conformity with the strategical situation, the whole Red Sea, from Aden to Suez, was at Admiral Peirse's suggestion transferred to his command.

The first echelon of the main Indian Expeditionary Force consisted of the Lahore Division with part of the Secunderabad Cavalry Brigade. Being urgently needed for the security of Egypt, its first two groups were timed to sail on August 24 and 25, and the second two groups in the first days of September. The second echelon, consisting mainly of the

Meerut Division and the rest of the Secunderabad Cavalry, was to follow about the middle of the month.   There was also a single transport sailing for Mombasa with an Indian battalion, the advance guard of the reinforcements intended for British East Africa, and to her the *Fox* had to be devoted till she met the *Pegasus* of the Cape Squadron, a ship which, in spite of her inferiority in guns and speed, was held to be capable of giving a good account of the *Königsberg.*   Further, by the middle of September it was hoped to send an expedition against German East Africa and three more battalions to Mombasa for British East Africa. Even with the increased force at Admiral Peirse's disposal it was found impossible to keep strictly to the time-table. Still less was it possible for him, with so much convoy work on his hands, to deal adequately with the trade routes, or to attempt to form a covering force to the eastward against the German squadron.   Such cover, according to British ideas, was essential for regularising the position, and it was here the convention with the Japanese had an immediate effect.   For as soon as it was known that they had declared war, Admiral Jerram was able to supply the necessary covering force from his own squadron.   With this intention he had been concentrating his main strength at Singapore instead of making a sweep to the Mariana, Caroline and Marshall Islands, feeling sure that if the Germans were coaling there they would be gone before he could arrive.   He therefore contented himself with arranging for the *Askold*, when she joined, to search the Mariana group, and then, if possible, to destroy the German wireless station at Anguar in the Pelew group.

Such intelligence of the enemy as was reaching him indicated that if the Singapore position was to be made good there was no time to lose.   He had learnt that German auxiliaries were using the Dutch islands in the Java Sea, and there were other indications that pointed to at least a possibility that Admiral von Spee might be intending to concentrate to the southward of Sumatra for a raid into the Indian Ocean.   Seeing how entirely Admiral Patey was occupied with the Rabaul Expedition, such a plan was quite possible, and Admiral Jerram alone could fill the wide gap between him and Admiral Peirse.   He had decided, therefore, with the bulk of his squadron and the two Japanese cruisers, as soon as they arrived, to make a thorough search of the Dutch islands.   His auxiliary cruisers were to be employed on the trade routes between Hongkong and Singapore and in watching enemy ships in the Philippines.   The two sloops *Cadmus* and *Clio* with five destroyers were formed into a squadron corresponding to the Japanese 3rd Squadron at Formosa, and were based at Sandakan in British North Borneo to watch the channels south of the Philippines between the Celebes and South China seas. A similar squadron, composed of the French gun-vessel *D'Iberville* and three French destroyers, was based at Penang as a patrol for the western entrance to the Malacca Strait. This patrol the Admiral subsequently strengthened with the *Dupleix*, since her engines were so defective that she could not act with the main squadron, and her commander, Captain Daveluy, was placed in command of the whole patrol. As for the two Russian cruisers, the orders of the *Askold* had to be cancelled, for by the time she and the *Zhemchug* reached Hongkong both had to be diverted to escort duty in order to take charge of three transports which were to bring British regiments from Singapore, Hongkong and Tientsin to Calcutta, and amongst them was the company of the Duke of Cornwall's Light Infantry that had been doing so well in the *Triumph*. During the first fortnight of September, while group after group of the Indian Convoys were streaming away to Aden, the elaborately planned search of the Dutch islands was carried out by the *Minotaur, Yarmouth, Hampshire* and the two Japanese cruisers which joined on September 5. No hostile warships were seen or heard of, but no less than thirty-seven German steamships were found held up in the Dutch ports, besides twenty-two in the Philippines. Nearly every steamer met was British, trade was brisk, and there appeared to be no difficulty in getting cargoes. The safety of British trade seemed, indeed, as complete as in time of peace. Yet the truth was it was on the eve of receiving its first shock in Eastern waters, and the most interesting feature in Admiral Jerram's movement is how near it came to preventing that shock from ever being given.

On August 30 a rumour had come in that the *Königsberg* had appeared about Sabang at the north end of Sumatra. Since her capture of the *City of Winchester* in the Gulf of Aden on the second day of the war nothing had been heard of her, and as her base at Dar-es-Salaam had been destroyed by the *Astræa* it was quite possible she was seeking new ground. Admiral Jerram had therefore sent the *Hampshire* (Captain H. W. Grant) to Acheh Head at the extreme north-westerly end of Sumatra to clear up the situation. Between this point and the Nicobar Islands, about 100 miles north-west of it, all the trade of the Indian Ocean in and out of the Malacca Strait has to pass, and from now onward it became a regular patrol station. But for the moment it was unoccupied, for on

September 2, when the rumour of the *Königsberg* being in the vicinity proved to have no foundation, the Admiral ordered the *Hampshire*—in pursuance of his plan—to move down to search the west coast of Sumatra and the unfrequented chain of islands that lie along it. Nothing could have been better timed. For as the *Hampshire* started south to carry out her new instructions the *Emden* was coming up the same coast on the opposite course. . After being detached with her collier, the *Markomannia*, from Admiral von Spee's squadron in the Marshall Islands, she had coaled at the German station of Angaur in the Pelew group. Thence she had gone through the little used Molucca Pass, and so by the Flores Sea to the Bali Strait, where she passed out into the Indian Ocean. Keeping well out of sight to seaward, she then made her way along the south of Java and past the Sunda Strait till September 4, when, in order to coal again from her tender, she came into the Sumatra coast somewhere behind Simalur or Hog Island, the most northerly of the Sumatra chain. Here it was she had the first of her narrow escapes. For it so happened that the *Hampshire* had been searching this same island only the day before on a rumour that the *Königsberg* was there, but finding nothing she passed on down the islands, and so must have been within an ace of running into the *Emden* next day. As it was she missed her, and the *Emden* was left a free run into Indian waters, while on the opposite course the *Hampshire*, still searching the islands, carried on to Padang, and the Admiral was searching round Java.

In this operation of the China Squadron Admiral Patey could take no share. Admiral Jerram's suggestion that his colleague should supplement it by a search in the Marshall Islands was natural enough, for there Admiral von Spee was fairly certain to be if he was not coming to the Indian Ocean. He was, in fact, in the eastern part of the group when Admiral Jerram made the proposal. Thence it was that on August 29 he had detached the *Prinz Eitel Friedrich* and *Cormoran* with orders to carry on cruiser warfare in West Australian waters. They were given a collier, the S.S. *Mark*, with 3,400 tons of coal. After taking this precaution he himself put to sea and passed on eastwards into the solitudes of the Central Pacific. His movements and intentions were, of course, quite unknown, and in operating against Rabaul Admiral Patey had to use practically his whole force. The rendezvous which had been given for the concentration of the Australian squadron was Rossel Lagoon, in the islands off the eastern extremity of New Guinea, and here on September 9 Admiral Patey met the *Sydney* and *Encounter*, which

had brought from Port Moresby three destroyers, two submarines, five colliers and the Australian armed transport
Berrima with 1500 troops, under Colonel William Holmes,
partly Australian infantry and partly Naval Reserve.   The
Melbourne was to join later, but for the moment she was
detached on a special mission to destroy the German wireless
station at Nauru or Pleasant Island which lay 1000 miles
away in the direction of the Marshall Islands.   On September 10 the expedition proceeded for its objective, the
Sydney being sent ahead with the two destroyers to reconnoitre Simpson Harbour and the adjacent anchorages, primarily
to see if there was a defence patrol.   But there was also the
possibility that Admiral von Spee might be there.   By
3.0 a.m. on the 11th, however, the *Sydney* was able to report
all clear, and three hours later the Admiral arrived with the
Berrima, having captured a German collier as he came in.
The *Sydney* had on board two small landing parties of Naval
Reserve men, and these she was now ordered to disembark
at Herbertshöhe and Kabakaul.   The surprise was complete;
no resistance was made, and the two parties began to advance
inland to where the wireless station was now known to be.
The party from Herbertshöhe met with little opposition, but
had no luck.   They failed to reach the station and were
recalled in the evening.

With the Kabakaul party it was different.   The Germans
had fled inland, but natives were about who pointed out a
road leading to the wireless station.   It was a narrow trail
flanked by dense bush, and before the men had advanced up
it a mile they were fired on.   The Admiral at once ordered
the *Berrima* to the spot, and by 10 a.m. two more companies
of Naval Reserve and two machine-gun sections were ashore.
The advance was then resumed, but a force of about 150 black
police under German officers and non-commissioned officers
continued to resist.   The Australian troops, however, new as
they were, were equal to the occasion.   While Admiral Patey
was engaged in the Samoa Expedition they had had a long
wait at Palm Island in Halifax Bay, Queensland, and it had
been employed training them in landing and bush fighting.
They were therefore quite at home, and by fighting their way
through the bush, and avoiding the road which had been
mined and entrenched, they gradually pushed the enemy
back without much loss.   At noon four companies of infantry
were landed and moved up in support.   Still progress was
slow, and as there seemed no prospect of reaching the station
that day an order was given for the troops to retire to the
coast before dark.   But just then a formidable entrenchment

which defended the station surrendered, and by a smart piece
of work the whole wireless installation was seized.   As the
Germans had destroyed the tower before retiring it was useless for our people to hold it, and taking away all the gear
that the enemy had had no time to remove, the party returned
to the coast, with the loss of two officers and four men killed
and an officer and three men wounded.   For the Germans
further resistance was now hopeless, but the Governor, as
on Admiral Patey's previous visit, had retired to Toma, ten
miles inland, bent on making negotiations as dilatory as
possible.   This was the more annoying as the Admiral had
just heard that the *Australia* as well as the *Sydney* and
Melbourne would be required to escort the main Australian
convoy to Aden, and that it was to start on the 27th.   Early
on the 12th, therefore, a summons was sent up to Toma by
motor cycle, but by night there was no answer except that
one would be sent next day.   Meanwhile the *Melbourne*
had come in to report she had destroyed the wireless
station at Nauru, and the *Berrima* moved to Rabaul and
occupied it with four companies of infantry and one of
Naval Reserve.

Next morning there was a report that the missing *Geier*
was at Kawieng on the north coast of New Guinea with a
large merchant cruiser, and as the *Melbourne* was about to
start for Sydney she was ordered to examine the place with
the destroyer *Warrego*.   Nothing was found except the Government yacht *Nusa*, which was captured and sent back with
the *Warrego*.   From the Governor no answer came till 5.0 p.m.,
and it was then of so dilatory a nature that the Admiral and
Brigadier agreed that next morning an advance should be
made on Toma to arrest him.   Between Toma and Herbertshöhe was a ridge, and a plan had been captured showing
that it was fortified.   It was arranged, therefore, that the
Encounter should shell it next morning to clear the way for
the troops.   The plan was entirely successful, and when they
drew near the place in the afternoon they were met by a flag
of truce, saying that the Governor was ready to capitulate
and would come in next day.

So far all was well, but the success of the day was marred
by an unhappy accident.   The Admiral had sent out the
destroyer *Parramatta* and the submarine *AE 1* (Lieut.-Com-
mander T. F. Besant) to patrol east of Cape Gazelle.   In
the evening, according to orders, the *Parramatta* returned, but
she returned alone, and nothing more was ever heard of the
submarine.   A prolonged search failed to find any trace of her,
and so the first exploit of the Australian Navy was clouded

by the loss of their first submarine, with her commander, two lieutenants and thirty-two men.

For some time there was doubt about the Governor's good faith.   Information was obtained that there was a road which led from Toma westward to the coast at Pondo, and that he was probably intending to escape that way in the *Geier* or the *Komet*.   As a precaution the *Sydney* was sent round to clear the matter up.   The Governor, however, held to his word.   He kept his appointment on the 15th, and after four hours' discussion the preliminaries were agreed.   The capitulation covered not only Neu Pommern but the whole of German New Guinea—that is, all the German possessions in the Pacific which were administered from Rabaul, and these included all the Bismarck Archipelago, together with the populous island of Bougainville in the Solomons and Kaiser Wilhelm's Land in New Guinea, in all between 80,000 and 90,000 square miles.   Thus all the eastern half of New Guinea and all the Solomon group were now in British hands, and Neu Pommern and Neu Mecklenberg were once more New Britain and New Ireland.

A base for further operations could now be established at Simpson Harbour.   It will be recalled that under the original plan it was intended to use it for the occupation of certain German stations within reach—particularly Angaur and Nauru.   But, as the Admiral had already pointed out, there was a serious objection to this course.   The islands in question were not self-supporting, and to put a garrison in them would entail a regular system of supply ships.   As to Nauru, this was confirmed by the *Melbourne*, and it was decided to defer both enterprises.   The paramount call on Admiral Patey's squadron was for the escort of the Australian and New Zealand Expeditionary Forces for Europe, and their departure could no longer be delayed.   The plan had just been settled.   To avoid any possibility of an attack from Admiral von Spee the convoy was to proceed by the south of Australia, instead of by the usual route north-about through the Torres Strait.   Fremantle in Western Australia was to be its concentration point.   There it would be met by Admiral Patey in the *Australia*, and he would escort it across the Indian Ocean with the *Sydney* and *Melbourne*, as well as with the *Hampshire* from the China Squadron, which was to be detached for the purpose.   This Admiral Jerram could well afford to do.   He had returned (13th) to Singapore from his fortnight's search of the Dutch islands and had found nothing stirring in his waters.   He even suggested detaching three of his best ships, *Minotaur*, *Ibuki* and *Chikuma*, to

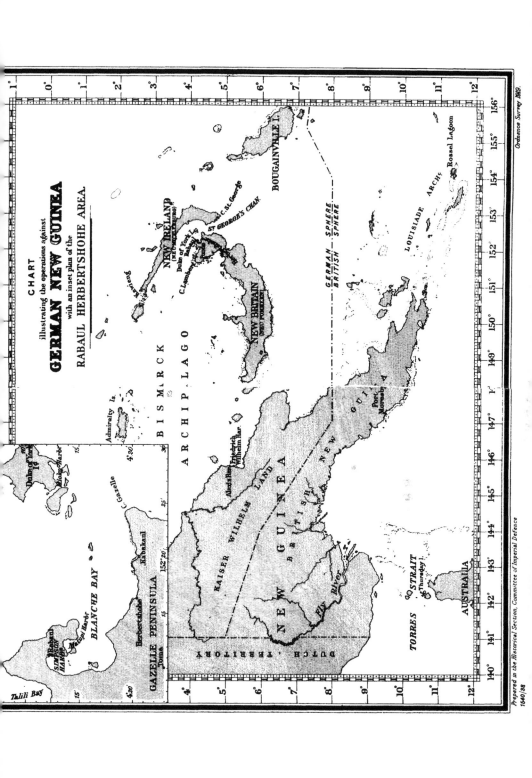

CHART

illustrating the operations against

GERMAN NEW GUINEA

with an inset plan of the

RABAUL HERBERTSHOHE AREA.

BISMARCK

ARCHIPELAGO

NEW IRELAND
(NEU MECKLENBURG)

BOUGAINVILLE I.

ST GEORGE'S CHAN.

C. St. George

Duke of York Is.

NEW BRITAIN
(NEU POMMERN)

GERMAN SPHERE
BRITISH SPHERE

LOUISIADE ARCHO

Rossel Lagoon

Admiralty Is.

KAISER WILHELM LAND

NEW GUINEA

BRITISH NEW GUINEA

Friedrich Wilhelm Har.

Aleris River

Port Moresby

DUTCH TERRITORY

FLY River

TORRES STRAIT

Thursday I.

AUSTRALIA

BLANCHE BAY

GAZELLE PENINSULA

Herbertshöhe

Kabakaul

C. Gazelle

Talili Bay

Ordnance Survey 1919.

Prepared in the Historical Section, Committee of Imperial Defence

1540/38

Simpson Harbour so as to cover the route of the Australasian convoy against a raid from Admiral von Spee.

It was to carry out this urgent escort duty that on September 15, as soon as the capitulation was signed, Admiral Patey sailed with the *Australia* and *Sydney*, leaving the guard of the new base to the *Montcalm*, which had just arrived from Noumea. He had not gone far, however, before he had cause to feel seriously anxious for the safety of what he was leaving behind him. In the evening of the day after he sailed he received from New Zealand news of the German squadron having appeared at Samoa,[1] and also heard from Admiral Jerram that the *Minotaur* and her Japanese consorts could not leave Singapore to take up their covering position till the 18th. It was not with any surprise, therefore, that in the night of the 17th he received from the Admiralty an order to return to Rabaul. Indeed, there was other news which had suddenly and profoundly disturbed the whole system in the East The convoy arrangements were thrown into confusion and a far-reaching redistribution of force became inevitable.

[1] See *post*, p. 291.

CHAPTER XXII

THE EASTERN FLEET—FIRST EXPLOITS OF THE *EMDEN* [1]

In the afternoon of September 14—that is, the day after the British flag was hoisted at Rabaul—a startling wireless message was received at Calcutta to say that a German cruiser was operating off the Hoogly. It came from the S.S. *City of Rangoon*, which had just left the river and was hurrying back. When only a few hours out she had met the Italian S.S. *Loredano*, which on the previous day had been stopped by the *Emden* about 300 miles down the trade route to Colombo, and the Italian captain had observed that the raider had four prizes in company.

The surprise was complete. Although the Japanese had ascertained that the *Emden* was not at Tsingtau, nothing had been heard of her since the war began, and it was taken as fairly certain she was with Admiral von Spee. That she should have slipped through the net which Admiral Jerram had spread and suddenly appeared far up in the Bay of Bengal was beyond all calculation. No part of the Eastern seas was regarded as more secure. Although, owing to preoccupation with the Indian convoys, we had not a single cruiser in the Bay, trade had quite recovered the shock of the outbreak of war, and so far as the shortage of shipping allowed was fast recovering its normal volume. So complete, indeed, was the sense of security expressed by the Indian Authorities that masters, in spite of Admiralty instructions, were in this section keeping to the usual track and steaming with undimmed lights. Had the most ordinary precautions been taken there must have been a much milder story to tell, but as it was the *Emden* had an easy task.

On September 5, when after so narrowly escaping the *Hampshire* she left her secret coaling place in Sumatra, in company with the *Markomannia* she had steamed straight for Ceylon, and on reaching a point about 200 miles from the coast she turned northward, striking the Colombo–Calcutta track about 150 miles south of the latitude of Madras. Here,

[1] See Maps 7, 13 and 14 in case.

early on September 10, she captured a Greek collier, the *Pontoporos*, with 6000 tons of Bengal coal, and kept her for her own use.   She then continued up the track, and about 250 miles south-east of Madras met the *Indus* of 3,413 tons, which was under charter as a transport for the next convoy from Bombay, and was on her way there empty from Calcutta. She was sunk by gun fire and her crew transferred to the *Markomannia*.   The following afternoon, about 150 miles further up the trade route and due east of Madras, she met another, the *Lovat*, of 6,102 tons, similarly employed, and her she dealt with in the same way.   Still proceeding up the track, she found nothing for some 250 miles, except about midnight on the 12th the *Kabinga*, a ship of 4,657 tons two days out from Calcutta to New York.   As her cargo was American owned, she was spared, but ordered to follow her captor.   Next morning, the 13th, the *Emden* had better luck, for on this day she made two good captures.   The first was the *Killin*, with 5000 tons of Bengal coal for Colombo. This ship, too, she sank by gun fire after transferring her crew to the *Kabinga*.   The same afternoon she stopped the *Diplomat*, with 7000 tons of general cargo for London, including 30,000 chests of tea.   None of these ships made any attempt to get away.   All were on the direct track and all steamed quietly to meet the *Emden*, assuming she was a British cruiser.   But now the luck turned.   The next ship she met was the Italian S.S. *Loredano*.   She, too, was stopped, and on her nationality being ascertained, she was asked to take over the prisoners.   This her master, Captain Giacopolo, refused to do on the ground that he had insufficient provisions, and on being dismissed he promptly made back for the Hoogly.   Thus it was he met and saved the *City of Rangoon*, a fine new ship with a cargo valued at well over half a million.   And not only her; for, being equipped with wireless, the *City of Rangoon* was able to spread the alarm instantly, and so all ships about to sail were held up, including three more chartered transports which might well have shared the fate of the other two.   She, too, returned to Calcutta, and it was not till she arrived that the details of the raid were ascertained.

But already the whole field was astir and the hunt was up.   Admiral Peirse, in the act of preparing to get the second echelon of the Indian troops away, could do little.   But Admiral Jerram on the 14th, when the first news came in, had just returned from his search round the Dutch islands, and had with his flag at Singapore the *Minotaur, Hampshire, Chikuma* and *Empress of Japan*.   The *Yarmouth* was also there in dock, the *Ibuki* was coming in from the Java Sea, and the *Dupleix* repairing at Penang. It was not till the night of September 15–16 that word of what had happened reached him. He at once ordered away the *Hampshire* and *Chikuma* in chase; the *Yarmouth* followed next day (the 17th). A few days later he took measures to watch the possible points in his own vicinity to which the *Emden* might return to coal. For this purpose the *Minotaur* and *Ibuki* were available for the moment. *Minotaur* was therefore sent to the west coast of Sumatra and *Ibuki* to the Cocos Islands, with orders to remain there until they were required for other duties which, as will be seen directly, the Admiralty had assigned to them.

The chasing ships were placed under Captain H. W. Grant of the *Hampshire*, and he was given a free hand. His plan was to make across to a point fifty miles east of Dondra Head in the south of Ceylon with the *Hampshire* and *Chikuma*, and then up the trade route to Madras and False Point; while the *Yarmouth* (Captain H. L. Cochrane) made for Rangoon, searching the Nicobar and Andaman Islands on the way; but as she developed machinery defects and had to put into Penang, he took her line himself and sent the *Chikuma* alone to Ceylon. The *Dupleix*, as soon as she was ready, was to take charge of the *D'Iberville* and the Malacca Strait patrol.

Such was the news that came hard on the heels of Admiral von Spee's appearance at Samoa. Up till this time his whereabouts had been quite uncertain. On September 7 the *Nürnberg*—last heard of at Honolulu—had appeared off the British cable station at Fanning Island in the Central Pacific, and after wrecking the apparatus and cutting the cable had disappeared again. Whether she was with the squadron or detached, as the *Emden* appeared to be, could not be known. The general belief was that Admiral von Spee was still lurking in the Caroline or Marshall Islands, and so strong was this impression that when it was found that neither Admiral Jerram nor Admiral Patey could get there, the Japanese had formed a special squadron to make the search themselves and incidentally to destroy the German base at Jaluit in the Marshall group. This force, which came to be known as the " First South Sea Squadron," was under Vice-Admiral Yamaya, and comprised two of the minor battle cruisers (*Kurama*, *Tsukuba*), one armoured cruiser (*Asama*), and a division of destroyers. It sailed from Yokosuka on September 14, the day the *Emden* was first heard of in the Bay of Bengal; but too late to have a chance of finding what it sought.

Admiral von Spee was far away in the Central Pacific. On September 7 he had anchored to coal at Christmas Island. On the previous day the *Nürnberg* had rejoined him, and next morning had been detached to Fanning Island. By this time he knew that Samoa was in British hands. He had heard it at sea as early as September 3, and had been able to detect the presence of the *Australia*, with three other British ships and one Japanese. To retake the island, he knew, was out of the question. He could not provide a strong enough landing party, nor did he wish to waste ammunition and destroy German property by a bombardment, but he thought there was a possibility of surprising the ships which would probably have been left there on guard. He now determined to make the attempt, and on the 8th, leaving the *Nürnberg* with his supply ships, he started south with the *Scharnhorst* and *Gneisenau*. On September 14 they approached Samoa from two directions to effect the surprise, unaware that the disposition which he was expecting to find had been deliberately avoided. It was just to frustrate such a venture that the defence of the place had been left entirely in the hands of the military. Not a ship of Admiral Patey's squadron was there, and without firing a shot the German cruisers disappeared to the north-westward.

With this episode the Admiralty had at last something on which it could take definite action, but the natural deductions were misleading. In the first place, since Admiral von Spee had come and gone without doing anything, it seemed fairly clear that, thanks to the rapid destruction of the German wireless stations, his information was defective, and that he had expected to find Samoa still a German possession. In the second place, his presence in the vicinity of Australasian waters tended to shake the conviction that the pressure of the Allied Fleets was forcing upon him a concentration in South American waters. The movement of the *Dresden* down the east coast and the disappearance of the *Leipzig* from Californian waters had tended to confirm the inference. Admiral Cradock, as we have seen, was moving down to the Magellan Strait in anticipation of Admiral von Spee's arrival, and on September 10 the *Defence* had been ordered out from the Dardanelles to enable him to deal with the on-coming enemy decisively. But the sudden discovery that the German Admiral was still in the Western Pacific, coupled with the appearance of the *Emden* in the Bay of Bengal, naturally modified the appreciation.

The *Defence*, which had reached Malta, had her orders cancelled; for now the immediate care was not South America, but the main Australian Convoy and the New Guinea Expedition, whose work was still unfinished, and on September 16 were issued the new instructions for the China and Australian Squadrons which had brought Admiral Patey back to Rabaul. The *Australia*, with the *Montcalm*, was now to cover the operation which the reserve of the Rabaul Expeditionary Force was about to carry out for the occupation of Friedrich-Wilhelm Harbour in German New Guinea, and when it was complete they were to go in search of Admiral von Spee's two cruisers. The instructions for the China Squadron were also reversed. To relieve the pressure on the Eastern Fleet the Japanese Government at this time had consented to place at Admiral Jerram's disposal another armoured cruiser, the *Nisshin*, one of the two they had purchased from the Argentine Government on the eve of the Russian War. With three Japanese cruisers now at their disposal, the idea of the Admiralty was that one of them with the *Minotaur* should take charge of the Australian Convoy in place of Admiral Patey, and, together with the *Sydney*, escort it from Fremantle to Aden. As there was still plenty of time, Admiral Jerram, as we have seen, detached the *Minotaur* and *Ibuki* to watch the west coast of Sumatra and the Cocos Islands on the look-out for the *Emden*. As for the chase itself, the Admiralty instructions were that it was to be carried on with the *Hampshire* and *Yarmouth*, while the *Melbourne* would remain at Admiral Patey's disposal. It was also hoped that the two remaining Japanese cruisers would be sent to Rabaul to assist him in bringing the *Gneisenau* and *Scharnhorst* to action. As the arrangement involved the China flagship leaving the station, Admiral Jerram was directed to shift the flag to the merchant cruiser *Empress of Japan*. But this seemed to him the waste of a good ship, and he had special use for her. On September 14 and 15 the Sandakan Patrol had captured two colliers, one the *Tannenfels*, a German ship from Batavia with 6000 tons of coal apparently intended for cruisers working in the Malay Archipelago, the other the *Rio Passig*, an American from Manila with 4000 tons, which had been to Yap, Angaur and Ceram in search of Admiral von Spee. It was a fine and timely haul by which the Sandakan Patrol well justified its existence, and Admiral Jerram was anxious to get the two prizes to Singapore. It was for this service he wanted the *Empress of Japan*, and in order to release her he received permission to fly his flag ashore.

So everything was satisfactorily arranged to meet the new situation as the Admiralty saw it. But now it was that the political deflections already referred to began to distort it. Under the existing arrangement the New Zealand Convoy, which had grown to ten ships and was assembling at Wellington, was to leave that port on September 25 to join the Australian Convoy at St. George's Sound, Albany, and was to be escorted there by the three " P " class cruisers of the local squadron. It meant a voyage of over 3000 miles, and, in view of the last news of German movements, the New Zealand Government began to feel uneasy for the safety of their troops. Though the " P " class cruisers were incapable of dealing with anything more formidable than armed merchant cruisers, this in the opinion of the Admiralty was all the protection that was required. An attack from Admiral von Spee seemed out of the question. So bad, apparently, was his information that he could not know of the New Zealand Convoy, and if he did it was inconceivable that he would venture to steam 2000 miles southward into waters where he could get no coal, and where, for all he could tell, he would meet the *Australia*. To increase the escort would mean that the further operations which lay before the New Guinea Expedition would have to be abandoned, and so successful had been the policy of destroying the German centres of intelligence that the Admiralty were very anxious to complete the work. This view the New Zealand Government accepted, though still with reluctance, and it was settled on September 21 that the convoy would sail on the 25th.

But in loyally deferring to the Admiralty view they had not reckoned with public opinion. It was, of course, impossible for the people generally to understand the situation. Even less familiar than the public at home with real naval history, they had no basis of appreciation, except a vague impression that the old naval wars were a succession of rapid and brilliant victories, which rendered a cowed and impotent enemy incapable of interfering with our control of the seas. The patient and arduous preparation which made these victories possible and the no less toilsome work of reaping their fruits were almost a sealed book. It was not to be expected that they could appreciate the prolonged and methodical operations by which the Admiralty were making the Pacific untenable to the Germans and by which alone it could be made untenable. All they could see were the failures— important cables cut, raiders breaking through our lines and the main force of the enemy moving apparently at its pleasure.

Nor was the feeling confined to New Zealand. It spread to Australia. At first the confidence had been complete— so much so indeed that, as in the case of Canada, the readiness of both Governments to send off their transports unescorted had had to be restrained by the Admiralty. The reaction was all the stronger. Open complaints were heard of the management of the Australian Fleet and regrets that the two Dominions had not kept the control in their own hands. Then, at least, they would have had their splendid contributions to the Navy—the *Australia* and *New Zealand*—to guard their own men.

Fresh news of the *Emden's* exploits added fuel to the fire. After dismissing the Italian ship on September 13 she had left the main trade route for False Bay to coal, in company with her tender and her two prizes, the Greek collier and the *Kabinga*. The move took her to the coastwise track, and in the evening of the 14th, about thirty miles south-east of False Point, she ran into the *Trabboch* from Negapatam to Calcutta. This ship Captain von Müller sank the same night, and then, as his wireless was telling him the *Loredano* had spread the alarm, he dismissed the *Kabinga* with his prisoners for Calcutta. He had first disabled her wireless, but he soon found it had been repaired and that she was talking to Calcutta.

Clearly he could not keep his cruising ground much longer, but his luck was not yet done. As he made for False Bay to coal, the *Clan Matheson* came up with her lights unobscured as usual, and she, too, was captured and sunk. But this was the end of it. All the 15th and 16th he cruised off the Sandheads, like Surcouf in the old days, but not a ship was seen. Wireless had closed the book on the game of the famous French privateers, and all sailings had been stopped. There was now no time to lose, and after coaling from the Greek collier off False Point he made across the Bay for Rangoon, in ignorance, of course, that that was the precise point for which Captain Grant was making in search of him.

In the evening of September 18, when the *Emden*, twenty-four miles south-east of the Rangoon River, was making over the crew of her last prize to the *Dovre*, a Norwegian ship with which she had fallen in, the *Hampshire* was coming north up the east side of the Nicobar Islands. Next day the *Dovre* put into Rangoon with her news, and about noon Captain Grant had it. He had unfortunately been compelled to proceed to Port Blair in the Andamans, for to his despair the Indian authorities kept sending him messages *en clair*, and he had to get to a cable in order to dispatch an urgent request that they should desist from thus revealing his presence. His chance of getting hold of the chase was already seriously compromised, but he held away again on a different course—keeping on to the northward instead of

going to Rangoon, in hopes of cutting the *Emden* off. At
the same time the *Chikuma* was passing westward across the
mouth of the Bay, and the *Yarmouth* was just completing
her repairs at Penang. Unfortunately, Captain von Müller
had taken in the unlucky signals, and they assured him that
several British cruisers were working to the south of him.
Knowing, therefore, that the mouth of the Bay was dangerous
ground, he coaled under way from the *Markomannia* in the
Gulf of Martaban, and then held away to the westward just
in time to cross ahead of the *Hampshire*, and thus he escaped
her for the second time. Meanwhile Captain Grant, not
finding the *Emden* where, with very accurate judgment, he
had expected to intercept her, had decided to make a sweep
round the head of the Bay to her previous cruising ground,
while the *Yarmouth*, which was able to sail on the 20th,
made a cast up to Rangoon inside the islands, and the
Chikuma held on for the Colombo focal point.

The depressing effect of the *Emden's* escape was all the
deeper since it did not come alone. Immediately on the
heels of the news there was something even worse. For
now the *Königsberg*, after her long disappearance, had come
to light again with a startling suddenness.[1] At Zanzibar was
lying the *Pegasus* (Commander Ingles). She had been
searching the coast about Dar-es-Salaam for intelligence of
the missing German cruiser, and in the course of her cruise
had developed defects which called for repairs. As Commander
Ingles's general orders were to protect Zanzibar, and the place
was inclined to panic whenever he left, he decided to do the
work there—especially as a supply vessel with stores and men
for his ship was due at the port. For some time there had been
no wireless signs to indicate that the *Königsberg* was in the
vicinity, but as a precaution the armed tug *Helmuth* was kept
out in the South Channel as guard. The men slept at the guns
during the night and steam was ordered at two hours' notice.
Still, the position was highly unsatisfactory. For so weak
and old a ship as the *Pegasus* to be left without support was
in any case full of danger, but the urgent call of the Indian
Convoy still stood in the way of a sounder disposition, and the
Königsberg cleverly seized her opportunity.

At 5.25 a.m. on September 20 the *Helmuth* observed a
vessel coming slowly up the South Channel. As this entrance
was forbidden to merchant vessels, the tug steamed out
to warn her off. The stranger at once broke the German
ensign, fired two rounds of blank and increased speed. She

[1] For the *Königsberg's* movements from August 6 to September 19 see
note, p. 302.

was clearly the *Königsberg*, but the *Helmuth* failed to get a warning to the *Pegasus*, which was lying off the town. At about 9000 yards the German opened fire, and before the *Pegasus* could reply she was straddled. In any case the British ship was outranged. She tried to return the fire, but all her shots fell short, and after about eight minutes, during which she fired some fifty rounds, all her engaged broadside guns were disabled. Notwithstanding her helpless condition, the *Königsberg*, after a pause of five minutes, continued firing on her, and then about half an hour after opening fire turned and steamed away without doing further damage.

The town was not touched. All the raider did ashore was to destroy a dummy wireless station. A large collier, the *Banffshire*, with several thousand tons of coal on board, was left alone, and with her boats did excellent rescue work; nor was the lighthouse or the cable interfered with. The *Pegasus* was still afloat, though she was badly holed on the water line and had lost twenty-four killed and fifty-five wounded, besides seven, including two officers, who died of their wounds. Her engines being found to be uninjured, an attempt was made to beach her, but it failed, and she turned over and sank. Hurried and nervous as had been the *Königsberg's* action, she had won a striking success. It is true such regrettable incidents were fully anticipated by the Admiralty when they found themselves involved in moving troops before they had had time to clear the seas. In this case the trouble was mainly due to the importunate demands of an outlying station for naval protection which there was no adequate means of providing. None the less, in public opinion a mistake had been made, and in Eastern waters the Navy had suffered an appreciable loss of prestige.

The best that can be said of the unfortunate incident is that it was not permitted to alter the policy on which we were launched. To the Indian Convoys the presence of the *Königsberg* was allowed to make no difference. The Bombay group of the second echelon had sailed that day, under escort of the *Swiftsure, Fox* and *Dufferin*, to the number of twenty-nine transports, including three with the balance of the force destined for Mombasa. The Karachi group of eleven sail started as usual next day (September 21) with the *Dartmouth* and *Hardinge*. Even the three Mombasa transports were not detained. In due course they parted company and proceeded independently with the *Dartmouth* and *Fox* for escort. Provision for hunting down the *Königsberg* was immediately made by ordering the *Chatham*, which had taken the last convoy up the Red Sea, to seek her out, and with her the *Dartmouth* was to work as soon as her convoy reached Mombasa. In addition, the *Weymouth* was ordered down from the Mediterranean for the same service, and thus to each of the German cruisers three of our own were devoted. It meant, of course, a further difficulty in providing for the Indian Convoys, but as the battleships *Ocean* and *Goliath* were already on their way to relieve the light cruisers of escort work, the difficulty would be overcome before the next big convoy was due to sail.

In face of the measures taken it was not likely that either the *Emden* or *Königsberg* could long keep going as they were, but this was a strictly naval view which could do little to quiet the prevailing uneasiness. All public opinion had to go upon was that, instead of the two raiding cruisers being brought to book, one of our own cruisers had been destroyed and half a dozen merchant ships sunk. To the Admiralty such events were but set-backs, incidental to their measured advance to a complete command of the sea, and inevitable if the lines of that advance were confused, as they necessarily were, by extraneous calls. But to the Australasian Governments, unversed in the inscrutable lore of the sea, they were only evidence that the Admiralty had failed; and with the *Scharnhorst* and *Gneisenau*, as it seemed, within striking distance of their convoys, they could no longer rest assured that the Navy knew its business. The prevailing anxiety was completed by a rumour that Admiral von Spee, after leaving Samoa, had gone to Fiji—that is, direct for the convoy route—and the result was that the New Zealand Government felt that it could not allow its troops to sail as arranged, and the concentration of the transports at Wellington stopped. Disconcerting as this resolution was to the nicely-adjusted plans of the Admiralty, it was immediately recognised that there was but one thing to do. The appreciation of the effort the Dominions were making for the Empire was so keen that, in spite of the dislocations that were involved, there could be no hesitation in meeting their views.

There was, furthermore, an additional reason for taking this attitude. The same evening that the New Zealand Government announced its decision, news spread that the *Emden* had struck another blow of even higher daring than before. Since she had been located off Rangoon all trace of her was lost. Indeed, so entirely did she seem to have disappeared that on September 22 the Colombo–Calcutta trade route was declared open again. Yet that same evening, about 9.30, she appeared off Madras and began bombarding the

Burmah Company's oil tanks which stood near the sea front. Two of them, containing nearly half a million gallons of kerosene, were set on fire and entirely consumed. A few shots also fell in the town, and some hit the British India S.S. *Chupra* which was lying there. In all five people were killed and a dozen or so wounded, but before more harm could be done the batteries opened fire and the *Emden* made off to the southward.

Once more her position was not a little precarious. Captain Grant, having searched False Bay that day, was coming down the coast; while the *Chikuma*, having coaled at Colombo on the 21st, was coming up the east side of Ceylon with two colliers for Madras in her charge. Thus when the *Emden* was off Madras the *Hampshire* was about 300 miles to the northward and the *Chikuma* little more to the southward, and she would have been much nearer but for the fact that by some misunderstanding she waited for instructions at Colombo after coaling instead of proceeding on her original orders to Madras. Nevertheless the *Emden* was still in danger. She spent several hours next morning (23rd) coaling from the *Markomannia*, and then shaped course for Pondicherry and Cuddalore, where she hoped to find British merchant ships, but was disappointed. At 2 p.m. she was reported from Pondicherry steaming away to the eastward. Her course was taken with a view to making for Simaloe Island (north-west of Sumatra) to coal, and to give further orders for colliers from the Batavia base, but Captain von Müller changed his plans and decided to turn back to the southward, intending to make a dash at the Colombo focal point. So for the third time the *Hampshire* missed him, and probably on this occasion, as the two ships had been steaming to meet one another, by not much more than three hours. Still the *Emden* was far from safe, for the *Hampshire* held on down the coast, and as she approached, the *Chikuma*, having reached the north of Ceylon, turned back by Captain Grant's orders, to protect Trincomalee, which might very well be the *Emden's* next objective.

Her attack on Madras had an injurious effect upon public opinion in India, for it had occurred only a few hours after the trade route to Calcutta had been declared " reasonably safe." The material loss she inflicted was not very great, for though she had taken seven ships, no less than sixteen got in or out of Calcutta unmolested, and twice she had been very near to being captured. Still, little as was the real impression she had made on the bulk of the trade, and nearly as our cruisers had come to success, the Madras episode was only another reason for deferring to New Zealand opinion. For again the trade routes concerned had to be closed, and once more the whole system of protecting the Australasian Convoys was thrown into the melting-pot. In order to meet the situation the Admiralty, while reiterating their conviction that the route from Wellington to Albany was safe, issued orders that the *Minotaur* and *Ibuki*, instead of acting as a covering squadron in New Guinea waters, were to proceed to Wellington to fetch the New Zealand Convoy, and then, after picking up the Australian transports at Fremantle, to escort the whole to Aden. Consequently the two cruisers had to be called away immediately from Sumatra and the Cocos Islands, where they were filling in time by watching for the *Emden*. By their original orders they were to pick up the convoy at Fremantle on October 4. Now they left their watching-stations in time to be there on September 29, and then carry on to New Zealand. Even so the sailing of the joint convoy would be delayed for at least three weeks, but there was no help for it, and the delay had to be faced.

As for the *Nisshin*, since she had no place in the plan, she was now at Admiral Jerram's disposal, and he ordered her away to reinforce the Sandakan Patrol, which seemed to be in danger. The *Geier*, *Prinz Eitel Friedrich*, and the *Cormoran* were still unlocated, and there were signs that the German colliers in the Philippines were getting suspiciously restless. One actually came out, but was at once headed back by the merchant cruiser *Himalaya*, and in these circumstances the possibility of a surprise attack on Sandakan could not be neglected.

Meanwhile the expedition to Friedrich-Wilhelm Harbour could proceed with the *Australia* and *Montcalm*. In pursuance of the previous arrangement Admiral Patey, just promoted Vice-Admiral, had returned to Rabaul with the *Sydney* in company on September 19, and on the 22nd, after detaching her to destroy the German wireless station at Angaur, started for his objective with the *Australia*, *Montcalm*, *Encounter* and the transport *Berrima*. On the 24th he was off Friedrich-Wilhelm Harbour. As the place had been included in the general capitulation signed by the Governor at Rabaul, he sent in a flag of truce to demand its surrender. No resistance was offered. In the afternoon troops and stores were landed, and after formally hoisting the British flag and proclaiming the occupation, the Admiral returned to Rabaul, leaving the troops in garrison.

The general situation in Far Eastern waters was now coming well in hand. The *Sydney* completed her work at

Angaur on the 26th.   Admiral Yamaya, moreover, was due
at Jaluit with the Japanese First South Sea Squadron on the
29th, and Tsingtau was invested both by land and sea.   So
by the end of the month the Western Pacific had been made
untenable for any serious hostile force, and there could be
little doubt—though, as we have seen, no undue risks were
taken—that Admiral von Spee would be forced away to
American waters.   If any doubt remained in the minds of
the naval authorities, it was now removed.   On the last day
of the month came news that on September 22—the day, as
it happened, that the New Zealand transports had been
stopped—the *Scharnhorst* and *Gneisenau* had bombarded the
French port of Papieté in Tahiti, the principal island of the
Society Group, and had sunk the gunboat *Zélée*.

On leaving Samoa Admiral von Spee had steamed for
Suvarov Island, a lonely British possession about 500 miles
on the way to the French group of the Marquesas, where the
Nürnberg was now bringing on the supply ships.   Two of them,
however, were to meet him at Suvarov.   As the swell proved
too great for coaling there, he took them on to Bora Bora,
in the Society Islands.   This group was also French, but
the native authorities, mistaking the German nationality,
allowed them to coal and buy provisions (September 21).
Thence on September 22 he went on to Papieté, the capital
of the group.   His intention, it is said, was merely to demand
supplies, but as the little batteries opened on him as soon
as he appeared, he replied, with the result that he quickly
sank the unarmed gunboat, whose guns were all ashore,
damaged a German ship in the port, and set the town on
fire.   In this he defeated his purpose; for the conflagration
spread so fast that he dared not enter the harbour, and so
had to sail away for the Marquesas without getting what he
came to seek.[1]

News of the incident could only confirm the view which
Admiral Patey had always held that the German squadron
would take the route by Samoa and Tahiti in moving away
to the American coast, and so sure now were the Admiralty
that this was the intention that they proposed that the New
Zealand transports should move off without further delay
and meet the *Minotaur* and *Ibuki* at sea.   Possibly the
proposal might have been accepted but for a new record of
failure that had to be scored to the Admiralty account; for
in the meanwhile the *Emden* had struck her blow at the
Colombo focal area.

Continuing on the southerly course which she had finally

[1] Admiral Dick : *Das Kreuzergeschwader*, p. 81.

adopted after leaving the Madras area, she ran down the coast of Ceylon, ahead of Captain Grant, and was not observed by the *Chikuma* at Trincomalee. The *Markomannia* was still with her, but the *Pontoporos* had been sent with a prize crew to a rendezvous on the west coast of Sumatra. It was not till they rounded the south of Ceylon that they found anything, but in the forenoon of September 25, some twenty-five miles south of Galle, they captured the *King Lud*. Being outward bound in ballast she was sunk at once by explosives, and in search of better luck Captain von Müller held boldly on for Colombo. Arriving off the port at nightfall, he saw a large ship coming out with all lights burning, dogged her till she was fifty miles out, and about midnight overhauled her. She was the *Tymeric*, with £60,000 worth of sugar on board. She was sunk, like the *King Lud*, and the *Emden* carried on for the south of Cape Comorin, where the tracks from Bombay and Aden to Colombo converge. Here, the following afternoon, she captured the *Gryfevale*, whose master was doing his best to keep off the converging tracks, and this ship Captain von Müller kept. With his prize and the *Markomannia* in company, he then made towards Minikoi, the island which is midway between the Laccadive and Maldive Groups, and on either side of which, through the Eight Degree and Nine Degree Channels, run the usual tracks from the Red Sea. Between that point and Cape Comorin he next day (September 27) captured three more ships, *Buresk*, *Ribera* and *Foyle*, all on or near the usual track. The last two, like the *King Lud*, were outward bound in ballast, and they were both sunk. But the *Buresk*, which was captured in the dead of night, was a real godsend. She was a ship of 4,300 tons, with a full cargo of Welsh coal for Hongkong on Admiralty charter, and yet she, too, gave herself away by steaming on the direct track with all lights brightly burning. She was naturally added to the little squadron, and by sheer neglect of ordinary precautions Captain von Müller's potentiality for prolonging his depredations was appreciably increased. After capturing the *Foyle* at 7 p.m. about 150 miles east of Minikoi, he did not tempt Providence further, but held away to the southward towards the Maldives to coal and clean his ship. The prisoners he dismissed in the *Gryfevale*, and it was early on the 29th when she put into Colombo that the whole story was known.

Regrettable as it was, the wonder is that the tale of loss was not much worse. In the three days the *Emden* was operating seven ships had been stopped by her, two into Colombo and five out, and in these usually thronged waters she had taken only half a dozen prizes, averaging less than 4000 tons, and half of them in ballast. Her cruise might well have been prolonged a day or two, for this time she was in little danger. The *Chikuma* reached Colombo to coal the same day as the *Gryfevale*, but Captain Grant, in the *Hampshire*, was half way across the Bay of Bengal steaming eastward. On the 26th, while the *Emden* was off Cape Comorin, he had put into Colombo to coal, and at 1.0 a.m. next morning, after calling the *Chikuma* from Trincomalee, he had left to proceed along the trade route to Singapore. The reason for this was that the *Dupleix*, which, it will be remembered, had been the supporting ship of the Penang Patrol, was coming westward with a vessel laden with French artillery, and the *Askold* and *Empress of Asia* were just starting with the three transports in which were our Far Eastern garrisons now all bound for Europe. It was to give further protection to this convoy that he was making eastward for Acheh Head when the news reached him at midnight of September 29–30. He immediately turned back, ordered the *Chikuma* to Minikoi and the *Yarmouth*, which was coaling at Penang, to Acheh Head. But all was too late. Even the *Chikuma* did not get away till 8 a.m. on the 30th, and by that time the *Emden* was lost in the trackless wastes in the middle of the Indian Ocean.[1]

Such, then, was the news which reached the New Zealand Government simultaneously with the Admiralty suggestion that their transports should not wait for the *Minotaur* and *Ibuki*. The exploits of the *Emden* had, of course, no real relation to the safety of the convoy, but the moral effect was none the less strong, and the result was a warm protest against any change in the arrangements. In the face of it the Admiralty at once acquiesced, and, as it was impossible to provide a separate escort for the Australian convoy, both of them had to be delayed the full three weeks.

NOTE.—The *Königsberg* spent the week following August 6 in attempts to coal among the Khorya-Morya Islands. On the 14th, realising that British cruisers were near, she left the area and made for Res Hafun, arriving there on the 19th. She left again four days later for Madagascar, hoping to attack French trade there, but, as she was reported at Majunga, all shipping took refuge in harbour. Her captain then decided to use his remaining coal to take him to German East Africa. His ship's engines were in urgent need of refit, and he made for the Rufiji delta—the only place where he could remain hidden. There the *Königsberg* arrived on September 3, and by the 19th was able to sail again and so sighted the *Pegasus* on the 20th.

[1] The *Emden* had arrived off Telidu Atoll in the Maldives on September 29. See *post*, p. 332.

CHAPTER XXIII

ADMIRAL VON SPEE CROSSES THE PACIFIC [1]

THE first week in October when the Australian Convoy should have sailed was marked with important developments in the general situation, both in the Atlantic and Pacific, where it still mainly turned on the movements of Admiral von Spee and the three detached cruisers, *Emden, Dresden* and *Karlsruhe.*

On the first of the month Admiral Patey, having secured our position in German New Guinea and the Bismarck Archipelago, had just put to sea with his squadron, *Australia, Montcalm, Encounter* and *Sydney,* with a view to intercepting Admiral von Spee if he should double back and try to enter the Indian Ocean. The two cruiser squadrons which the Japanese had formed for hunting down the enemy in the Pacific were now at sea, and the Admiral's idea was to cruise to the Carolines to try to get touch and concert operations with Admiral Yamaya, who, with the First South Sea Squadron, had left Yokosuka on September 14, the day Admiral von Spee was located off Samoa, and having occupied Jaluit on September 29, was now working in that area. In moving away from Rabaul Admiral Patey left behind him two German auxiliary cruisers, the *Prinz Eitel Friedrich* and her consort, the Russian Volunteer prize *Cormoran.* Intercepted calls had led him to suspect something was cruising north of New Guinea, and the *Sydney* had twice searched the suspicious area without success. The two German ships had, in fact, met at Angaur a week or so before the *Sydney* destroyed its wireless station. They had then separated in search of coal, and not knowing New Guinea was in our possession, had fixed their rendezvous at Alexis Bay, just north of Friedrich-Wilhelm Harbour. The *Cormoran* was actually hiding there when Admiral Patey was taking possession of the administrative capital, but was not discovered. When his back was turned both ships, finding Australasian waters too hot to hold them, had made off; *Prinz Eitel Friedrich* for the west coast of America, and *Cormoran* for the Western Carolines,

[1] See Maps 2 and 14 in case.

after narrowly escaping the *Satsuma* of the Second Japanese South Sea Squadron at Yap.

The *Geier* was also suspected of being somewhere about. She had not been heard of for over a month, but news of her had just come in. It was that on September 4 she had captured at Kusaie, in the Eastern Carolines, the British S.S. *Southport*, which was lying there ignorant that war had broken out. Having disabled her prize's engines so that she should not get away, the *Geier* left her in the harbour and went off on a fortnight's cruise. No sooner was she gone than the master of the *Southport*, Captain Clopet, made up his mind to escape. Desperate as was the chance and short the time, the crew agreed, and under the clever engineer, Mr. H. Cox, they set to work to repair the engines, in spite of the almost hopeless condition to which they had been reduced. The eccentric gear of the mean and high-pressure engines and the intermediate stop valve had been removed as well as a good many of the tools, but after eleven days' work, by fitting the astern eccentric of the low-pressure engine to the high-pressure cylinder, and cutting out the middle cylinder, they got a semblance of a compound engine. True, it would not go astern, and if it was stopped might get on a dead centre and refuse to start again. Nor was this the only trouble. They had over 2000 miles to go to reach a British port, and no provisions except what the island—which, like the rest, was not self-supporting—could provide. However, from the native king, whom the Germans had told to help him with food, Captain Clopet obtained 350 cocoanuts and 400 lb. of a root which the natives only eat in time of famine. With this equipment, after infinite difficulty in getting their unhandy craft to sea, they started on September 18 with only a day or so in hand. Still, they escaped, and on the 30th put into Brisbane with their news, and another brilliant page added to the record of resource and daring with which the mercantile marine was to glorify itself in the course of the war. The exploit was recognised by an Admiralty letter expressing high appreciation of the captain's and the engineer's seamanlike and skilful conduct, and to each of them the Board of Trade presented a piece of plate.

On the day of her arrival at Brisbane came the news that Admiral von Spee had bombarded Tahiti. It reached Admiral Patey on October 2, and as there was now no immediate prospect of danger to the Indian Ocean he turned back to Simpson Harbour to get into touch with the Admiralty. Though the general expectation was that the German Admiral was making for America, there was still a possibility that he might be intending to carry out similar attacks at Samoa, or even New Zealand, and the instructions Admiral Patey received were to proceed to Suva in Fiji and make that his base for operating in search of the elusive enemy.

This he could safely do, for on October 1 the Second Japanese South Sea Squadron left Sasebo for Rabaul, which was then intended to be their base for further operations. This squadron was under Rear-Admiral Tsuchiyama, and consisted of the *Satsuma*, a battleship with four 12″ and twelve 10″ guns, and two light cruisers, *Yahagi* and *Hirado*. But Admiral Jerram, whom the news from Tahiti convinced that Admiral von Spee was making for America, had a different arrangement to propose. His appreciation was that the Germans were bound for American waters to harass either the coast of British Columbia or our trade on the coasts off Chile and Peru, or possibly to pass into the Atlantic by the Panama Canal or the Strait of Magellan. With provision for the latter alternatives he had no concern, but for the first two he suggested that the First Japanese South Sea Squadron should move on from the Marshall Islands and cross the ocean as soon as it was certain the Germans had done so, and that Admiral Patey, with the *Australia* and *Montcalm*, should remain east of Australia. Meanwhile, during the absence of the *Minotaur* and *Ibuki* with the Australasian Convoy, he proposed that Admiral Tsuchiyama should co-operate with him west of longitude 140°, which passes approximately through Tokyo, Yap and the centre of New Guinea, and that the First Squadron should work with Admiral Patey to the eastward of that meridian. In both areas there would thus be a squadron capable of dealing with Admiral von Spee should he turn back, and at the same time the escape of colliers from the Philippines could be effectually prevented. But before any definite arrangement could be made the doubt as to the German intention was finally cleared up.

In the evening of October 4 (local time) the Suva wireless station intercepted a message from the *Scharnhorst* in the German secret mercantile code, a copy of which we had captured. It read : " *Scharnhorst* on the way between the Marquesas and Easter Island." As Easter Island lies half way between Tahiti and the American coast there was little doubt as to what was in the wind, especially as our station at Thursday Island, in the Torres Strait, had just taken in another warning. This message was *en clair*, and, translated, it ran : " Look out ! *Australia* and all the large English ships have left Rabaul going east. The Japanese squadron is all over the place. To-day the English established wireless communication with Rabaul. Look out ! "

If this intelligence was to be trusted—and, as will be seen directly, there was much on the American side to confirm it—the Eastern Seas were no longer threatened. The chief concern of the Admiralty was with the other side of the Pacific. Here, in North American waters, Captain Powlett was still operating with the *Newcastle*, *Rainbow* and *Idzumo*, trying to find the *Leipzig*, and protecting British and Japanese trade and the Canadian ports. But for this area there was little anxiety, for the Japanese had agreed to reinforce the squadron with the *Hizen* (formerly the Russian *Retvizan*), a small but fast battleship of 12,700 tons and 16,000 horse-power, built in America and captured at Port Arthur. Nothing had been seen of the *Leipzig*. Traces of her movements had been found by the *Newcastle*, but nothing definite was ascertained till early on October 1 a ship that had been attending her put into Callao with the crew of the British steamer *Bankfields*, which she had captured on August 25. On the same day there arrived at Guayaquil the master and part of the crew of the *Elsinore*, which she captured off Cape Corrientes in Columbia on September 11. They had to report that they had escaped from the Galapagos Islands, where they had been put ashore a week after being taken. These two pieces of intelligence could only raise a presumption that the *Leipzig* was operating to the southward, in expectation of Admiral von Spee's arrival.

All the probabilities, in fact, pointed to the waters in which Admiral Cradock was operating as the area most in danger, and his position was still far from secure. We have seen how, on taking over the South American station early in September, he had moved down to Montevideo with the intention of concentrating his squadron to the southward. His sweep down the coast—so far as the regular cruisers were concerned—was unproductive, but his armed merchant cruiser, the *Carmania* (Captain N. Grant), had met with better fortune. It fell to her duty in the southerly sweep to examine Trinidada Island, which was suspected to be a German coaling place, and where, in fact, the *Dresden* had coaled a month before on her way to the Pacific. Arriving there on September 14—the day the *Emden's* activities were first known—the *Carmania* found off the western end of the island a large liner coaling from two colliers. The liner was the *Cap Trafalgar*, a new ship of the Hamburg-Sud-Amerika Line, which on August 22, it will be remembered, when Captain Luce had moved north in search of the *Dresden*, had been able to escape from the River Plate. About a week later at a sea rendezvous she had met the gunboat *Eber* from South Africa, and had taken over her officers and her armament of two 4″ guns and six pom-poms. Since September 1 she had been cruising for our trade, disguised as a Castle liner, but as the air was full of British wireless signals her attention was more absorbed in keeping out of harm's way than in hunting prizes, and she had done nothing.[1]

It seems as if evasion was still her object, for before the *Carmania*, which was coming up at 16 knots from the north-east, had raised her hull she began making off to the south-ward, while her consorts dispersed. But very soon, as though she had ascertained the *Carmania's* class, she began to turn to the westward to close at 18 knots. By 12.10 the converging courses brought the range down to 8,500 yards, and the *Carmania* challenged the enemy with a shot across her bows and the German replied with her after gun. At 7,500 yards the *Carmania* began independent control fire from all her port guns, and the *Cap Trafalgar* answered with rapid fire. As the range continued to fall the action grew very hot. At 4,500 yards the *Carmania* changed to salvoes, the second and third of which were seen to hit all along the water line. Most of the enemy's shot went high, so that the *Carmania* only suffered in her masts, funnels and ventilators. But now, since the *Cap Trafalgar* continued to steer as though to cross the *Carmania's* bows, the range decreased so much that the German pom-poms began to tell. When, therefore, the range was down to 3,500 yards, Captain Grant began to turn away to starboard through about 16 points till his starboard guns bore. Till this time the *Cap Trafalgar* had kept her course, but she now began to sheer away to port, and Captain Grant, completing his circle, began chasing on her port quarter. It could be seen that her deck steam pipes had been cut : she was on fire forward and had a slight list to starboard. But the *Carmania* was also in trouble. A shell had passed through three thicknesses of plating without bursting, but had set fire to bedding under the fore bridge. As the fire main had been cut the flames could not be controlled, the fore bridge became untenable, and the fire dangerous. Still, as the wind was aft, the *Carmania*, by keeping

[1] Letter from her surgeon in *Weser Zeitung*, November 27, 1914. It is possible the intention was that she should cruise in South American waters in consort with the *Kronprinz Wilhelm* and *Kaiser Wilhelm der Grosse*, using Trinidada as a base. Three German colliers had been sent there, and the *Kronprinz Wilhelm* was in the vicinity when she sank the *Indian Prince*. If there was such a plan the fate of the *Cap Trafalgar* and the *Kaiser Wilhelm der Grosse* prevented it from maturing.

on the enemy's port quarter, was able to continue the action.

It had now resolved itself into a stern chase in which the *Cap Trafalgar* soon began to develop the better speed. So fast did she gain that by 1.30 she was out of range, and to all appearance she had escaped. But it soon became evident that her list was rapidly increasing, and that she was burning fore and aft. In this condition in a quarter of an hour she was suddenly seen, at 1.45, to turn 16 points to port, and then capsize and disappear bows foremost. The fact was that she was already doomed when the action ceased. She had four or five holes on the water line, the fire made her decks untenable, and her captain was killed. Orders were therefore given to abandon ship and sink her. She went down bows first with colours flying.[1]

So ended the first action that had been fought between two of the new class of armed merchant cruisers—the only one, in fact, in which one of ours had been able to perform the original service for which they were designed, that is, dealing with the enemy's armed merchantmen—and it so happened that the action was fought the very day after the new order came out which changed their function.[2] The first test of their powers had ended in a victory for the British ship, but the German had undoubtedly made a good fight of it. She had nothing but the *Eber's* armament, and that consisted of two 4·1″ and six machine-guns.[3] The *Carmania* had eight 4·7″ guns, and had suffered a good deal ; she had 304 holes from 79 projectiles, five on the water line, her fore bridge with all its steering, communication and fire-control gear and navigational instruments were destroyed, and she had lost nine men killed and twenty-six wounded. So precarious, indeed, was her condition at the end of the action that it was impossible to save the crew of the sunken enemy. The fire had still so strong a hold of her that Captain Grant had to keep on before the wind to subdue it. This course was the more necessary as smoke appeared on the horizon, and he believed it might well be coming from a German cruiser to which the *Cap Trafalgar* had been continually calling during the action. The *Eleonore Woermann*, one of the *Cap Trafalgar's* colliers, picked up the survivors a couple of hours later and took them to Buenos Aires, where they were interned. But of her the *Carmania* saw nothing. Captain Grant had enough to do to

---

[1] For the German account of this action see *Der Krieg zur See: Der Kreuzerkrieg*, Vol. III, pp. 26-38. Casualties in the *Cap Trafalgar* are given as six killed and fourteen wounded.

[2] See *ante*, p. 266.

[3] *Der Krieg zur See: Kreuzerkrieg*, Vol. I, p. 177.

save his ship, and as soon as the fire was got under he made for Abrolhos Rocks, calling for assistance. It was not till the next afternoon that the *Bristol* picked him up and stood by till the *Cornwall* appeared, by whom he was escorted to the coaling base.

These two cruisers were taking part in the general movement southward which Admiral Cradock had ordered in anticipation of its being Admiral von Spee's intention to come through the Magellan Strait and make an attack on our trade in that quarter. On the day the *Carmania* fought her action new instructions from the Admiralty confirmed his appreciation. He was informed that the *Canopus* was on her way to Abrolhos and that the *Defence* was coming from the Mediterranean to reinforce him, but until she arrived he was to keep at least the *Canopus* and one County class cruiser with his flagship. After leaving in the north sufficient force to deal with the *Dresden* and *Karlsruhe*, which were still unlocated, he was to concentrate to the southward a squadron strong enough to meet the *Scharnhorst* and *Gneisenau*, making the Falkland Islands his base. As soon as he had a force superior to the Germans he was to search the Magellan Strait, but was to be ready to break back and cover the River Plate if intelligence pointed that way.[1] The instructions reached him at Santa Catharina, some 250 miles south of Rio, where he had just found Captain Luce's detachment, *Glasgow*, *Monmouth* and *Otranto*. For on his

[1] The text of the telegram was as follows—

" From Admiralty to R.-A. *Good Hope*, via British Minister, Rio.—(Sent September 14, 1914, 5.50 p.m.)

" There is a strong probability of the *Scharnhorst* and *Gneisenau* arriving in the Magellan Straits or on the West Coast of South America.

" The Germans have begun to carry on trade on the West Coast of South America.

" Leave sufficient force to deal with *Dresden* and *Karlsruhe*. Concentrate a squadron strong enough to meet *Scharnhorst* and *Gneisenau*, making Falkland Islands your coaling base.

" *Canopus* is now *en route* to Abrolhos. *Defence* is joining you from Mediterranean. Until *Defence* joins, keep at least *Canopus* and one County class with your flagship.

" As soon as you have superior force, search the Magellan Straits with squadron, being ready to return and cover the River Plate, or, according to information, search north as far as Valparaiso, break up the German trade and destroy the German cruisers.

" Anchorage in the vicinity of Golfo Nuevo and Egg Harbour should be searched.

" Colliers are being ordered to the Falkland Islands. Consider whether colliers from Abrolhos should be ordered south."

The *Canopus* was officially credited with a sea-going full speed of seventeen knots ; that of the *Good Hope* and the " County " class was over twenty-two.

way down to the Magellan Strait, in accordance with his last orders to intercept the *Dresden*, Captain Luce had received a report that the *Dresden* had coaled near Santa Catharina. Being out of touch with the Admiral, he could only use his discretion, and he had turned back in search. The report was false. For the *Dresden*, after coaling at Gill Bay on August 31, had pushed on again, and without venturing to approach the Strait had run to the Horn. There, on September 5, she put into Orange Bay, a spacious natural harbour which lies hidden and completely land-locked amidst the snows and glaciers of Hoste Island.

This, of course, was quite unknown at the time, and the Admiral decided to go down to the Strait with the *Good Hope* and Captain Luce's detachment, leaving the *Bristol* to patrol between Santa Catharina and the Plate, and the *Cornwall* between Rio and Cape San Roque. The *Carmania* and *Macedonia* were to assist them, but as the *Carmania* was unfit for action and the *Macedonia* had to escort her to Gibraltar for a refit, the two cruisers had to watch the whole Atlantic coast between them as best they could. It was a vast field they had to cover, and the Pernambuco area was left with no protection except what the *Cornwall* could provide when she was in the region of Cape San Roque; nor although, on fresh news of Admiral von Spee's movements, the immediate anxiety for the Magellan Strait was removed and Admiral Cradock's instructions to concentrate there were promptly modified, was any change made in the dispositions to the northward. The reason his last orders had to be altered so soon was this : it was on the very day they were issued that Admiral von Spee had appeared at Samoa and gone off on a false course north-west. From this it was assumed he intended returning to his original station, and that there was no present fear for Admiral Cradock's Squadron. He was told therefore (September 16) there was now no need to concentrate, and was ordered at once to attack " German trade on the west coast of America and Magellan," for which two cruisers and an armed liner were suggested as sufficient force. The orders found him off the River Plate, where he intended to coal, but a succession of heavy gales so much delayed operations that it was September 22 before he could carry on to the southward. As he went down he obtained intelligence which emphasised the need of operating on the west coast, for it left no doubt the *Dresden* was there. It came from Captain Douglas Kinnier of the Pacific Steam Navigation liner *Ortega*, with which Admiral Cradock fell in on September 25. Captain Kinnier's report was that he had been fired upon by a three-funnelled cruiser on the other side of the Straits, and that the cruiser had a merchant vessel in company. It was clearly the *Dresden*, and her tender the *Baden*. Not only was this valuable piece of intelligence obtained, but Captain Kinnier had a story to tell which reflected the highest credit on his courage and resource.

He had sailed from Valparaiso with 300 French reservists on board, and had reached as far as Cambridge Island, about 100 miles short of the entrance of the Straits, when he was challenged by the cruiser. As he had only 14 knots and the German 21, escape seemed almost impossible. Still he resolved to try, and calling for volunteers for the stokehold he made away. The cruiser followed and opened fire. Such a chase could not last long, but behind Cambridge Islands opens the unsurveyed Nelson Strait, into which he knew the cruiser would not dare to follow him, and for this perilous passage he made at his utmost speed. " In order to realize the hardihood of this action," wrote our Consul at Rio in his official report, " it must be remembered that Nelson Strait is entirely uncharted, and that the narrow, tortuous passage constitutes a veritable nightmare for navigators, bristling as it does with reefs and pinnacle rocks, swept by fierce currents and tide rips, with the cliffs on either side sheer-to without any anchorage." Yet all these dangers he faced with his 8000 ton ship, and by heroic exertion in the engine-room was able to make the entrance of the Strait and drop his pursuer before he had been hit once. And not only this, but by feeling his way with his boats he brought his ship out into Smyth Channel without a dent in her plates. [1]

Upon this information it would seem that the Admiral decided to proceed with the squadron to the West Coast, and by this time the Admiralty had further information which made it fairly certain the *Dresden* was there. It was sent to him on September 26, the day after he met the *Ortega*, though it is uncertain when the telegram reached him. It was to the effect that on the previous day a three-funnelled cruiser, probably the *Dresden*, had passed Punta Galera near

[1] Admiralty Press *communiqué*, Nov. 20. An Admiralty letter was sent to the Company expressing " their Lordships' desire to place on record their appreciation of the courageous conduct of Captain Kinnier in throwing off his pursuer by successfully navigating the uncharted and dangerous passage of Nelson Strait." He was given a temporary lieutenant's commission in the R.N.R., and awarded a D.S.C. (January 1). The Chilean Government, who on hearing of the chase sent a destroyer to prevent a violation of neutral waters, found on her report that only blank was fired, and that the chase was abandoned when the *Ortega* entered Chilean waters. Captain Kinnier's report goes to confirm this. He says the *Dresden* fired twice at his ship, " both shots being ineffectual."

Valdivia some 800 miles up the Chilean coast, going north-wards. In corroboration of this report a private message stated that the *Seydlitz*, which for a month past had been lying at Valparaiso, was hurriedly coaling. Two days later the British ship *Galicia* reported having seen on the 26th a steamer without lights off Coronel exchanging signals with the German steamer *Santa Isabel*, which had reached the port on the previous day. All this indicated clearly that the enemy was becoming active on the west coast.

Whether or not Admiral Cradock knew all this, he now assembled his squadron off Cape Virgins and entered the Strait, intending to call for further intelligence at Punta Arenas. On the way there he was continually intercepting call-signs between German men-of-war and merchantmen. They could not be deciphered, but on arriving at Punta Arenas on September 28 he learnt from our Consul that the enemy were probably using Orange Bay as a base. It further appeared that one of the merchant ships in the harbour recently sailed with a large amount of live stock and fresh provisions, and had returned a few days later empty. There was every possibility, therefore, that at last he had run the chase to earth, and he immediately decided to attack. The movement was made in the utmost secrecy. Informing the Chilean Admiral who was there that he was bound for Valparaiso, he stole away without lights after midnight and made for the difficult Cockburn Channel. It was known at all times to be dangerous, and it had not been surveyed since 1820, but time was everything to the Admiral and he decided to take the risk. It was no light task. " The navigational abilities of Commander Scott," the Admiral wrote in his report, " in piloting the squadron in thick weather, with intermittent snow-storms, through this little charted channel, and again, to ensure arriving at daybreak off Orange Bay, round Cape Horn inside Barneveldt Rocks in snow storms and darkness, call for the most favourable comment."

Still the thing was done, and the Admiral had all fair to carry out the surprise he confidently expected. The idea was that possibly, besides the *Dresden*, the *Leipzig* and *Nürnberg* were also there with store ships and colliers. The bay had several good exits, and it was necessary so far as possible to dispose the force so as to guard them all. The ships were therefore made to close the place gradually from different directions, and then at the given signal each rushed in by a separate entrance. But not a thing was there. The bay was empty, nor could the picket boat that was sent ashore find a trace of the enemy having been there.

The disappointment was severe, but a new scent was quickly picked up. Wireless messages passing between the Peruvian and Chilean Authorities were intercepted, stating that two German cruisers had been off the south coast of Peru the previous day.

Before any action could be taken, however, it was necessary to go to the Falkland Islands to coal. It was not till October 3 that the *Glasgow* and *Monmouth* could start again to join the *Otranto*, which had been left in the Strait at Punta Arenas. Here she intercepted various messages which seemed to indicate that some enemy's ships were at Hermite Islands, just west of the Horn. The Admiral therefore proceeded there at once at high speed, and ordered the *Glasgow's* division to meet him at the island west-about. All ships had been much delayed by violent weather. It was now at its worst, and only by suffering all that the seas of that region can inflict could the movement be carried out. Again nothing was found, and the Admiral ordered Captain Luce to resume his sweep northward with his division as high as Valparaiso, and try to obtain stores and warm clothing. He himself, in the *Good Hope*, took another look into Orange Bay, but all he found was the *Dresden's* name written on a beacon, showing that the *Dresden* had been there on September 8, 9 and 10.

The situation, however, was now more clearly defined, for it was on the day before Admiral Cradock started to search Hermite Islands that the Fiji wireless station was intercepting the message from the *Scharnhorst*, which, as we have seen, left very little doubt that Admiral von Spee was making for Easter Island. At the same time New Zealand reported that he was calling up the *Dresden*. The Admiralty at once passed the information to Admiral Cradock, telling him to be prepared to have to meet the *Scharnhorst* and *Gneisenau*, and possibly a " Dresden " scouting for them, and that the *Canopus*, which had reached Abrolhos, was to " accompany *Glasgow*, *Monmouth* and *Otranto*, the ships to search and protect trade in combination." If, however, he meant to go himself in the *Good Hope*, the *Monmouth* was to remain on the east coast. This was important, for the east coast trade had now fully revived. It was of the utmost consequence to the vitality of the home country that it should not be again checked, and an Italian ship had recently reported having sighted the long-lost *Karlsruhe* in the Pernambuco area near St. Paul Rocks. The message which was sent off on October 5 missed him at the Falklands, nor did he receive it till the 7th, just as he was leaving Orange Bay to return for coal to his base.

21

It was only one of many such delays, and they must be appreciated if what followed is to be rightly judged. The fact was that communications with the south-eastern part of the Atlantic Ocean were specially slow and uncertain. We had a wireless station at Port Stanley in the Falkland Islands, to which the Uruguayan Government permitted the transmission of messages in cipher from their station at Cerrito near Montevideo, but from Punta Arenas the Chilean Government would only permit official messages *en clair*.[1] In addition to this difficulty the whole district is subject to frequent and continuous atmospherics, with the result that messages had generally to wait two or three days before they could be made, and in bad cases as much as a week would elapse. A previous warning of what was threatening had been sent by the Admiralty on September 30, but this never reached the Admiral at all. It was to inform him that the *Scharnhorst* and *Gneisenau* had bombarded Papieté and sunk the French ship *Zélée* on the 22nd, and had left steering north-east.

Admiral Cradock's own discovery that the *Dresden* had been in Orange Bay placed him in no little difficulty. On the information which the Admiralty had, their appreciation of what he had to deal with differed necessarily from his own, and he had no doubt they under-estimated Admiral von Spee's force. He therefore lost no time in telegraphing an account of his visit to Orange Bay and the deductions he made from it. Instead of only one light cruiser the Germans would almost certainly have three, *Dresden*, *Leipzig* and *Nürnberg*. Accordingly he informed them that he intended to concentrate at the Falklands to avoid a division of his force; also that he had ordered Captain Luce not to go beyond Valparaiso till the German cruisers were again located. At the same time, in view of his appreciation of the enemy's strength, he suggested that the *Essex* should be detached from the North American Squadron to relieve the *Cornwall* on the Rio–Cape San Roque patrol, so that the *Cornwall* could come south, and also asked whether the *Defence* was to join him.[2] She had, in fact, been stopped at Malta on September 16, two days after he was told to expect her, when the news was received that Admiral von Spee had appeared at Samoa. On the 18th she was ordered back to the Dardanelles, but no intimation to this effect had been sent him.

Still more disturbing was the strategical problem with which he was saddled. He could not see how it was to be solved with a single squadron acting on the west coast.

---

[1] British Consul (Punta Arenas) to Foreign Office, October 2.
[2] See Appendix D.

In a further telegram he submitted, therefore, that in the event of the enemy's heavy cruisers and others concentrating there it was necessary to have a British force on each coast strong enough to bring them to action. For if a single concentrated force were sent to the west the enemy might well evade it and destroy all our coaling bases on the Atlantic side, in which event the squadron would be unable to follow them, and they might possibly reach the West Indies.

Both messages he sent off on October 8, but for the best part of a week there was no answer. Persistent atmospherics baffled all the attempts of the Admiralty to get into communication with him. The second message was received on the 11th, the first not till the evening of the 12th. At Whitehall it was a moment of extreme pressure. The Naval Division was just completing its retreat from Antwerp, the question of evacuating Ostend, and possibly of having to re-embark the VIIth Division and IIIrd Cavalry Division was urgent, the new phase of the enemy's submarine activity was at its height, and the Canadian Convoy was on the point of making its perilous entry into the Channel. It is not surprising, therefore, that the Admiralty took a day or two to settle a plan for meeting the danger in the Pacific.

The menace to the West Indies and our South American trade was not the only one they had to face. Two other points had to be regarded as within Admiral von Spee's reach. The first was our expedition to the Cameroons. Here the base at Duala was still in process of organisation, and operations to drive the Germans from their points of retreat had commenced. They began on the river line at Ybassi with a combined naval and military column of some strength under Colonel Gorges. Besides six armed river craft, the flotilla had the *Mole*, a Nigerian dredger which had recently joined, and a lighter, each armed with a naval 6″ gun, and with them was a detachment of 100 bluejackets and a field gun, all under the command of Commander The Hon. Bertram Freeman Mitford of the *Challenger*. The military force, which was under Lieutenant-Colonel E. Vaughan of the West African Regiment, comprised eight companies of native infantry, half a company of pioneers and 600 carriers. Leaving Duala early on October 7, they easily overcame the opposition they encountered, and next morning the troops were disembarked three miles below the town for the attack. By 11.30 a.m. it was launched, but was suddenly met by so heavy a rifle and machine-gun fire from the dense bush that no progress could be made. Fortunately it was ill-directed, and eventually was silenced by the naval

6" guns.   A strenuous effort was then made to get a footing in the town.   But by this time the troops were too much exhausted by the heat for a final rush, and as they were fast losing cohesion Colonel Gorges decided to call them off for the night.   It was done without much loss, except that the *Balbus*, which was towing the armed lighter, took the ground so hard that she had to be abandoned.   On further consideration it seemed wiser to withdraw right back to Duala and reorganise the column in accordance with the knowledge they had obtained.   This was now being done, and at the same time reconnaissances of the Sanaga and Nyong Rivers were being carried out with a view to assisting the coming French advance against Edea.   The first reports were unfavourable, and with the failure of the first attempt on Ybassi it was clear that unless the base was made secure from an attack by sea there could be no prospect of reducing the colony within any calculable time.

Far more serious, however, was the case of German South-West Africa.   Here a considerable extension and modification of the original plan had been found necessary, and further naval responsibilities were entailed.   The idea of landing a column in the north at Walfisch Bay had been abandoned, owing to the difficulty of dealing with both that base and Luderitz Bay with the naval forces available.   After some delay incidental to getting home the Cape Garrison, the Luderitz Bay column was in place, and the last of the Cape Garrison had passed on homewards under convoy of the *Astræa;* but the column under Brigadier-General Lukin, which was based at Port Nolloth and was operating against the enemy's southern frontier, had received a check.   Whether, in face of the opposition he was encountering, he would be able to carry out the offensive operations which the plan assigned to him was now more than doubtful.   It was certainly highly inexpedient that he should try, for it was only too evident that the loyalty of the commandos on his right under Colonel Maritz was not to be trusted.   A new plan was therefore submitted by the Union Government on October 8.   It was based on concentrating practically the whole of their available striking force on a single effort from Luderitz Bay.   The troops already assigned to that line of operation were to be reinforced by fresh units from the Cape and by the bulk of the Port Nolloth force.   The plan further provided for forming as soon as possible a new column, which was to strike from Walfisch Bay along a railway which was to be built from the base to Swakopmund.   The escort work and base protection involved would absorb the whole capacity of the Cape Squadron, but the Admiralty cordially approved the plan and agreed to do what was wanted.

Here, then, was another point which might well be Admiral von Spee's objective. As things stood this was probable enough, but the danger was rapidly intensified. It was on October 10, two days before Admiral Cradock's anxious representation of the dilemma in which he found himself came to hand, that the new plan was approved, and next day the whole situation in South Africa was upset by news that Maritz had deserted to the enemy with his commando and was threatening to invade the Union territory with German help in order to raise a revolt. With the last of the regular garrison well on its way home, and with the Union forces already far involved in German territory, the situation was very serious, and the appearance of Admiral von Spee on the coast might well turn the scale. It was a possibility which could not be ignored, and it added the last complication to the problem which the Admiralty had to solve.

As a first step they sent the *Albion*, which was now with Admiral Stoddart, to Ascension, there to await orders from the Cape, and Admiral King Hall at once ordered her as guardship to Walfisch Bay to relieve the *Kinfauns Castle*. All further movement of troops was stopped, martial law was proclaimed, and the Union Government asked for the services of the *Hyacinth* and the two merchant cruisers *Kinfauns Castle* and *Armadale Castle*. In this request Admiral Jackson, who was still advising on the oversea operations, concurred, but at the same time he pointed out that special naval protection must be provided against the *Scharnhorst* and *Gneisenau*. It was of the first importance that they should not pass South America without being reported, and in his view the best initial disposition was a force strong enough to fight them concentrated at the Falklands, and numerically sufficient to watch for them at all salient points. To provide for this the old " County " class cruiser *Kent*, who had just completed her steam trials after commissioning for the North American Station, was already under orders to join Admiral Cradock instead by way of Cape Verde.

It was not entirely on the principle of a single concentration, nor on that suggested by Admiral Cradock for two adequate squadrons, that the Admiralty formed their plan. Something of a compromise between the two was adopted. When on October 12 the Admiral's messages of the 8th had come to hand, in which he pointed out the increasing difficulties of his position, and the doubt whether they could be met by a single concentration, the whole problem was again taken into consideration. One point at least was clear. All idea of cruising against the enemy's trade on the west coast must be postponed. For the moment Admiral von Spee's Squadron, and that alone, must be the objective, and, this being so, the cardinal need was to make such a disposition of the force available as to ensure as far as possible that the enemy should not get through into the Atlantic unfought.[1] As Admiral Cradock had himself submitted, there was an obvious danger of the Germans escaping in this way if the squadron went up the Chilian Coast, and of having our coaling stations and trade in the Atlantic at their mercy for an indefinite time. The outcome of the deliberations was that on October 14 a telegram went out to Admiral Cradock informing him that his plan of concentrating the *Good Hope, Canopus, Monmouth, Glasgow* and *Otranto* was approved " for combined operation." He was further told that a second squadron was to be formed for the River Plate Area, under Admiral Stoddart, who was to come down in the *Carnarvon* to Montevideo, where he was to have under his flag the *Cornwall* and *Bristol*, and the two merchant cruisers *Macedonia* and *Orama*, and where his squadron would be completed by the *Defence*, called once more from the Mediterranean, but the *Essex* was to remain in the West Indies.

Admiral Cradock's own proposal had been to concentrate at the Falklands, but as a new squadron was being formed for the east coast and combined operations were spoken of, he appears to have assumed that his original orders of October 5 stood, and that he was to concentrate all his squadron on the west coast "to search and protect trade" in co-operation with his colleague. For two reasons no concentration on either side could take place for some time. Captain Luce was already involved in the sweep up the Chilean coast which he had been previously ordered to carry out. After the barren search of Hermite Islands he had carried on northward, leaving the *Otranto* to guard a secret coaling base which he had established near the western end of the Straits, and in the evening of October 14 a message from him reached the Admiralty saying that the *Glasgow* was off Coronel with the *Monmouth*, and was going on to Valparaiso for supplies. Next day he was there, reporting the harbour full of German ships, some of which had been out supplying cruisers, but having ascertained the Government would not allow them to sail again, he went off, without disclosing his destination, to his secret coaling base, to await there the Admiral and the *Canopus*, according to his last instructions.

[1] See Appendix D.

The other difficulty was the *Canopus*. The Admiralty had calculated she would reach the Falklands on October 15, but, owing to bad weather, she did not appear till 10.15 p.m. on the 18th, and even then she required two or three days for an overhaul before she was fit for sea again. Her poor steaming powers were the Admiral's special anxiety, for it seemed to him to render it impossible to perform what he believed the Admiralty expected of him. As to the position he was to take up, it is clear he did not mistake the purport of the orders he received; for when the Admiralty knew that the *Glasgow* was at Valparaiso, they did not order Captain Luce to the Falklands, but merely repeated the order that he was not to go further north. Admiral Jackson's idea of a full concentration at the Falklands had, in fact, been dropped, and Admiral Cradock prepared to move to the west coast as soon as the *Canopus* should arrive, but not without misgiving. On October 18, when he knew how the old battleship had been delayed, he warned the Admiralty that so long as she was with him the strategical speed of his squadron could not exceed 12 knots, but he would trust that circumstances would enable him to force the enemy to action. These last words show that his order to " search and protect trade " led him to believe he was expected to seek out the enemy and bring them to action as best he could. Accordingly, on October 22, he sailed to join the rest of the squadron at the western coaling base. He could not wait for the *Canopus* to be overhauled. The time for Admiral von Spee's appearance was already past. He decided, therefore, to go round the Horn to see the enemy did not escape that way unobserved, and told the *Canopus* to meet him on the other side by way of the Straits. The *Canopus* sailed on the following day.

The calculation as to Admiral von Spee's movements was fairly accurate. He had reached Easter Island. There he was joined by the *Leipzig* and *Dresden*,[1] and after a stay of six days sailed again on the 18th, with his two heavy cruisers and three light cruisers, as Admiral Cradock was sending off his last message to the Admiralty. The destination of the German squadron was Mas-a-fuera, a lonely island some 500 miles west of Valparaiso, where they were to meet the colliers and supply ships that had been awaiting them in Chilean ports.

---

[1] He had with him also four auxiliary vessels : the *Baden, Göttingen, Yorck* and *Titania*. The *Leipzig* brought with her three more supply ships on the 14th.

CHAPTER XXIV

ON the day Admiral Cradock left the Falklands the situation was further complicated by the reappearance of the *Karlsruhe*, which up to this time he believed had joined Admiral von Spee in the Pacific. Since September 2, when news of the capture of the *Bowes Castle* off the Spanish Main had been received, nothing definite had been heard of her, but as several ships engaged in the South American trade were reported overdue, the Admiralty had left no stone unturned to locate her. Every rumour was carefully investigated by our Intelligence Officers, but in spite of all efforts she had hitherto succeeded in completely covering her tracks.

Now, however, it became known that before sinking the *Bowes Castle* on August 18 she fell in with the *Patagonia* of the Hamburg-Amerika Line—a collier that Captain Köhler had found at Puerto Rico and ordered to bring him coal to a rendezvous off Barbados from St. Thomas. He then proceeded along the Brazilian coast and coaled from her near the mouth of the Amazon. Thence the *Karlsruhe* carried on across the line to another rendezvous at São João Island, where a small collier she had found at Curaçao met her by appointment. This was the *Stadt Schleswig*, which was emptied and sent away to Maranham with the crew of the *Bowes Castle*.

Captain Köhler's intention now was to take up a cruising-ground north of Fernando Noronha, on the main trade route between Europe and the South American ports.[2] Having coaled again on August 30 at another secluded anchorage somewhere between Ceara and Cape San Roque, he made for his chosen station, and on the 31st got in touch with two Hamburg-Sud-Amerika liners, *Asuncion* and *Rio Negro* and the Norddeutscher Lloyd *Crefeld*, which had been dispatched from Brazilian ports to find him. All of them were ordered to a rendezvous off Rocas Reef, which he apparently intended to make his base, and to that point he proceeded himself, accompanied by his original tender the *Patagonia*.

---

[1] See Map 2 in case.   [2] See Map 12 in case.

Here he had one of his many narrow escapes; for on August 28, only two days before his arrival, Captain Luce, with the *Glasgow, Monmouth* and *Otranto*, had visited the place in search of the *Dresden* and her colliers. Nothing was then in the anchorage, and the swell was found to be so bad as to make it appear unlikely the Germans would be able to use the island as a base. Captain Luce therefore carried on with a sweep to the southward, and so missed the *Karlsruhe's* three tenders by about forty-eight hours.

Nor was this the end of Captain Köhler's good fortune; for as he approached the rendezvous he sighted and captured the British steamship *Strathroy* with over 5000 tons of Welsh coal for the Brazilian Government. It was a splendid windfall that was quite unexpected. She was, of course, taken on to Rocas, where, under the lee of the island, the three supply ships were found securely at anchor. But Captain Köhler, it would seem, found the place unsuitable for his purpose, as Captain Luce had expected, for on September 1 the prize was sent away, apparently to his last secret coaling place west of Cape San Roque, in charge of the *Patagonia*. This ship was then to proceed to Pernambuco with mails, and there is no record of her ever having rejoined. Captain Köhler, with the *Crefeld* in company to act as a scout, steamed northward to take up the station he had selected on the 2nd parallel, south latitude, about 100 miles north of Fernando Noronha, where the various tracks begin to converge closely and the trade normally assumes its highest density.

His chances of success were further increased by the fact that his original consort, the *Kronprinz Wilhelm*, was in the vicinity. Since Admiral Cradock, on August 6, had caught her with the *Karlsruhe* in the act of being armed, the two ships had been entirely separated, and the *Kronprinz Wilhelm* had been cruising independently. Near the Azores she coaled from the German supply ship *Walhalla*, and on the 27th boarded and released a Russian barque, the *Pittan*, about 1000 miles to the southward of the Azores on the direct line to Rocas Reef. It would look as though she may have heard where Captain Köhler was, for on September 3 she was with the *Asuncion*, which apparently had been left at a rendezvous near Rocas Reef with the *Strathroy's* crew on board. Next day she could be heard by Captain Köhler calling him, but he would make no reply for fear of attracting British cruisers, which his wireless room told him were not far away.

His precaution was natural. The area he had chosen for his cruising ground was precisely that which Admiral Stoddart would have been guarding had he had a cruiser available.

The area, however, was not altogether neglected. Apart from Captain Luce's recent visit, the *Macedonia* was passing through on her way to the South American station, and it was on September 1 that Admiral Stoddart had detached the *Cornwall* to search St. Paul Rocks. Admiral Cradock also, as we have seen, on his way down to South America was making an independent search of the same waters. Three days later Admiral Stoddart received orders that the *Cornwall* and *Canopus* were also to go to South America, and all these ships would pass through the area in which the *Karlsruhe* was operating.

In spite of the fact that the South American trade was just recovering from the first shock of the war, Captain Köhler had no great luck at first. But on September 3 he had another welcome windfall. This was the *Maple Branch*, a ship of 4,338 tons, with a general cargo for Chilian and Peruvian ports. It comprised everything he most wanted : live stock, tools and marine and other stores of all description. Full justice was done to her contents, and then she was sunk.

While this was going on the *Kronprinz Wilhelm* was equally fortunate. Getting no reply to her call she had gone off to the southward, and on September 4, some 200 miles to the eastward of Pernambuco and well off the track, she fell in with and captured the *Indian Prince* from Brazil to New York with a general cargo. This ship was treated like the *Maple Branch* and was sunk on the 9th. The *Kronprinz Wilhelm* then disappeared, and nothing more was heard of her for a long time. For the *Karlsruhe*, also, there now came a barren period. Owing to vessels observing the Admiralty instructions for diversion nothing more was seen for three days, and then the *Karlsruhe* had to move off for coal to the secret place where her prize the *Strathroy* was lying. So far, then, the *Karlsruhe's* cruise had been anything but as productive as she had expected. But, on the other hand, the good fortune that had saved her from the *Glasgow* had not deserted her. While she had been revelling in the good things the *Maple Branch* brought, Admiral Cradock in the *Good Hope* passed her about fifty miles to the eastward as he hurried back from St. Paul Rocks to join his new squadron at Pernambuco and to look into Fernando Noronha on his way. Nor did the German luck end here. For while the *Maple Branch* was being sunk the *Cornwall*, who after examining St. Paul Rocks had carried her search further on, reached a point not fifty miles to the eastward of where the *Karlsruhe* was cruising, but then by sheer perversity of fate she turned back according to her instructions in order to coal at Sierra Leone. Before she had gone far, however, she received her new orders to join the South American Squadron, and steamed away for Pernambuco, as the *Karlsruhe* was making for her secret base on the coast of Brazil. Having coaled there from the prize *Strathroy*, Captain Köhler was on the way back to resume his station, when he again narrowly escaped falling in with the *Carmania*, who at this time was coming down from Admiral Hornby to join the new squadron, and must have crossed his track very close. By September 10, however, he was back again un-observed on his old ground, and there he lay stopped with the *Crefeld* and *Rio Negro* thrown out on either hand as a screen against enemy cruisers, while at the same time they served as scouts to increase his range of vision. Yet for three days not a ship was seen. Everything kept out of their way, but at 6 a.m., September 14, they fell in with the *Highland Hope* —a frozen meat ship of 5000 tons from Liverpool to Buenos Aires in ballast. She was caught steaming without lights but close to the track, and here her captor was again in jeopardy. For now the *Canopus* was coming along straight down the trade route, and was very near. At the same time a Spanish passenger ship homeward bound saw the little throng of ships and inquired by wireless what they were. The *Karlsruhe* answered, "Convoy of British ships," and the *Canopus*, taking in the Spaniard's signal, asked for her position. The *Karlsruhe*, of course, heard the British message, and it was enough to warn her that her station was too dangerous to hold. Accordingly, without a moment's delay, she sank her prize and hurried off to the westward, and so left the *Canopus* to pass on without finding a trace of her.

Her intention now was to transfer her activities to the route between New York and South America which passes round the shoulder of Brazil, and here, some 300 miles from the scene of her last capture, she took a new position. At first this route seemed as deserted as the other, and she was just about to leave it in despair in order to coal when one of her scouts saw smoke about fifty miles to the eastward. It proved to come from the British steamer *Indrani*, which was carefully avoiding the usual track in accordance with Admiralty in-structions. She was chased and captured, and found to contain 7000 tons of coal from Virginia for Rio. Insured for £62,000 besides her cargo, she was one of the most valuable prizes yet taken, but the raiders' satisfaction was somewhat marred by a wireless message taken in a few days later from the German Consul at Pernambuco asking if they knew where she was, as he had bought the cargo. Presumably the purchase was made for the benefit of the German cruisers. The ship, at any rate, was exactly what Captain Köhler wanted. She was therefore retained, and while the *Karlsruhe* carried on with the *Asuncion* to the secret base, she was left in charge of the *Crefeld* and *Rio Negro*. Manned by a prize party and the Chinese part of her crew, she henceforth became part of the squadron, and under the name of *Hoffnung* continued to serve the German cruiser as a tender till the end came.

In spite of this fortunate capture, the *Karlsruhe's* career was still far from encouraging. Since her escape from Admiral Cradock on the second day of the war she had been cruising for four weeks and had only taken five ships, while she had been nearly caught four times. But now prizes came faster. On September 20, having picked up the *Crefeld* and *Rio Negro*, she was back on her old ground across the trade route north of Fernando Noronha. Here on the 21st and 22nd she took three more prizes of 8000 to 4000 tons: the *Maria*, a Dutch ship with wheat for Ireland, and the British outward bound ships *Cornish City* and *Rio Iguassu* with coal for Rio. As most of it was of inferior quality both these ships were sunk, and so was the *Maria*, notwithstanding that she was neutral and wheat had not been declared absolute contraband. On this day, also, the Italian ship *Ascaro*, homeward bound, was overhauled, but was allowed to proceed, and she it was who a week later, on her arrival at St. Vincent, gave the first news of where the *Karlsruhe* was working. A Swede was also stopped on her way to Buenos Aires, but she made no report of what she had seen.

At this time Admiral Cradock was making his sweep southward to deal with Admiral von Spee. The *Cornwall*, *Bristol* and *Macedonia* had been left to look after the Northern Area, but as the limit of their patrol area was Cape San Roque, the fertile zone which the *Karlsruhe* had chosen was left undisturbed. For the enemy it was a fine opportunity, but having as yet no knowledge of Admiral Cradock's movements, Captain Köhler made little use of it. The time, in fact, was chosen for overhauling his ship. For four days he was engaged on the work in the deserted waters to the westward of the route, and on September 28, when the work was completed, he had to make for his secret base again to coal. On the way, however, he met the *Asuncion*, which had cleared the last of the *Strathroy's* coal and then sunk her. He accordingly coaled from the *Asuncion* at sea, and after sending her away to get intelligence from the coast, made back to his original hunting-ground, labouring heavily with deckloads of coal that barely left the guns free to be worked, so that his ship was in no condition either to fight or run had an enemy cruiser appeared.

He arrived on October 1, and next day the *Asuncion* appeared with information that Admiral Cradock, with the *Good Hope*, *Monmouth* and *Glasgow*, had gone south, and the less welcome news that the *Cap Trafalgar* had been sunk by the *Carmania*. Feeling now fairly safe, he took a position off the east side of the track and about 100 miles from St. Paul Rocks. But although the Argentine maize was now beginning to move and the route was more crowded, two more barren days passed. As it became clear that the trade was not following the main track, the *Crefeld* was sent out forty miles to the eastward, where she would be on the Las Palmas–Pernambuco track, and there, on October 5, she sighted smoke. After a two hours' chase the ship was captured, and proved to be the *Farn* from Barry to Montevideo, which in avoiding her proper track had got upon the other. She had on board nearly 6000 tons of best Welsh coal. It was the last thing he wanted at the moment, for he could not take another ton, but he sent her away to a rendezvous to the westward where the *Asuncion* was waiting, intending to dispatch her to Admiral von Spee as soon as he knew his position.

The great gain from his last capture was that it seemed to indicate that he had found the line on which the trade was proceeding. But now he was once more disturbed. Again and again he had been forced to move by hearing British cruisers near him, and now another was calling. She seemed to be patrolling the route where he was working, and during the night her wireless grew so strong that to avoid her he moved his squadron right away to the eastward. The precaution was certainly a wise one. The three ships which Admiral Cradock had left behind in the northern section of his station had just begun a thorough search of the *Karlsruhe's* zone of operations. While the *Bristol* examined the north coast of Brazil where the German base lay, the *Cornwall* and *Macedonia* dealt with the focal area. On October 6 Rocas Reef was visited, and the *Cornwall*, after looking into Fernando Noronha, made up the trade route for St. Paul Rocks, so that during the morning of the 7th she actually passed over the spot where the *Farn* had been captured some thirty-six hours before.

The fact that she thus missed her prey was not the end of our ill luck; for the movement which drove Captain Köhler off the usual track, also pushed him upon that which a great part of the trade was actually taking, and so by pure accident he stumbled upon his richest spell of success. On each of the next four days a ship was captured—on October 6 and 7 two grain ships, *Niceto de Larrinaga* and *Lynrowan*, from Buenos Aires to London and Liverpool; on the 8th and 9th two, *Cervantes* and *Pruth*, with grain and nitrates from the west coast. All four of these ships, after useful stores had been removed, were sunk by explosives.

Captain Köhler had now to move to the westward to the rendezvous where his colliers, *Asuncion* and *Farn*, were waiting. The latter was the ship he intended to send to Admiral von Spee, but till he could arrange a rendezvous he meant to use her for a scout and decoy. As he approached the rendezvous three ships were seen upon it instead of two, and one of the three made off. The mystery was soon explained. The *Farn* by hoisting the red ensign had induced a British ship to approach, and the flying ship was the *Asuncion*, which had mistaken the *Karlsruhe* for an enemy.

The British ship which was by this ruse entrapped was the *Condor*, from New York to South American ports with a rich general cargo of provisions, dynamite and oil—everything, in fact, that the *Karlsruhe* wanted most, and it was only the purest bad luck that had sent her into the German hands, for she was keeping wide of the general track—so wide, indeed, that she had reached the unfrequented spot which Captain Köhler had chosen for his rendezvous. During the 12th and 13th, while our nearest cruiser, the *Macedonia*, was patrolling the trade route between Rocas Reef and St. Paul Rocks, and the *Edinburgh Castle*, on her way to join Admiral Stoddart, was coming down to the eastward of her, the prize was emptied amidst great rejoicing, and then sunk.

It was now high time for the *Karlsruhe* to be coaling again, but an important step had first to be taken which could no longer be delayed. Owing to so many captures—six in the last week—the number of prisoners was becoming a serious anxiety. There were now over 400 on board the *Crefeld*, of twenty different nationalities, and already, before the last batch of captures, there had been trouble with them owing to overcrowding and insufficient food. Not but what Captain Köhler did his best, and the stores of the last prizes had eased matters, but it was impossible to keep them much longer. Accordingly, he decided at the cost of revealing his whereabouts to send the *Crefeld* to a neutral port, and on October 13 she parted company.

Her destination was Tenerife, with orders that she was not to put in there till the 22nd. For another ten days, therefore,

Captain Köhler considered he could remain safely where he was. But, in fact, his sphere of operations was already known. A fortnight earlier, on September 28, the *Ascaro*, the Italian ship he had stopped and released, arrived at St. Vincent, Cape Verde, and though several other neutrals had been spoken, she was the first to report what she had seen to the north of Fernando Noronha. Beyond the fact that many ships on the route were overdue, the extent of the *Karlsruhe's* depredations was unknown, and though the area was in Admiral Stoddart's station, he still felt unable to spare a ship to occupy it. As we have seen, however, three of Admiral Cradock's cruisers were working it, but as soon as Admiral Stoddart knew that his colleague was moving into the Pacific to meet Admiral von Spee's squadron, he informed the Admiralty that he intended to search the area of St. Paul Rocks, Fernando Noronha and Rocas Reef with the *Carnarvon*, *Albion*, *Marmora* and *Empress of Britain*. Before he was ready to start, however, Admiral Cradock's suggestion for forming a second squadron for South America had been received and adopted by the Admiralty, and it was now, on October 14, that they had directed Admiral Stoddart to proceed with his flagship to Pernambuco and take up the new command, as "S.N.O. north of Montevideo." On arrival he was to proceed down the trade route to Montevideo and take under his orders the *Cornwall*, *Bristol*, *Macedonia* and *Orama*. He was also to have the *Defence*, which had been ordered out from the Mediterranean and was already on her way to join him, and his special instructions were "to keep sufficient force ready to concentrate in case the German squadron from the Pacific escapes past Admiral Cradock."

His immediate objective, however, was the *Karlsruhe* and her consorts. By October 18, after fuelling at sea, they were back across the trade route north of Fernando Noronha, and on that day they captured the *Glanton* with coal from Barry to Montevideo. As they were full up with fuel and could not spare another prize crew, she was sunk. For six days longer Captain Köhler maintained his position, so that had Admiral Stoddart been allowed to carry out his intended sweep down the route he could scarcely have failed to run into the *Karlsruhe* and her auxiliaries. As it was, he left St. Vincent on October 15, and on the 20th passed within ten miles of the spot where the *Glanton* had been captured on the 18th ; but although the German ships were still in the vicinity, he reached Pernambuco next day without having seen anything. The *Defence* followed him down at about a week's interval, but she had no better luck, for by that time Captain Köhler was gone.

By October 22 he knew that the *Crefeld's* arrival would give away his position, and he thought he might hear that British cruisers were about him. But, in fact, they were all as far away from him as they had ever been. The *Defence* had just left St. Vincent. Admiral Stoddart had just reached Pernambuco, where he heard a credible report that on the 20th the *Karlsruhe* had been taking in supplies a little east of Macau, about seventy miles west of Cape San Roque, and he at once ordered the *Bristol,* which was coaling at Abrolhos Rocks, to search the place, and the *Edinburgh Castle,* which having coaled there was on her way to Pernambuco, to assist her in the same region. The *Cornwall* was also at the base waiting for Admiral Stoddart, and acting as guardship there while the *Macedonia* was coaling and overhauling machinery. Captain Köhler could not, of course, know all this, but he had reason to anticipate a dangerous stir amongst the British cruisers in his vicinity, and to feel that the *Karlsruhe* would incur too great a risk of capture by remaining where she was. Moreover, for some time she had found little but neutrals on the trade routes, and it was clear that British ships were being diverted.[1] Captain Köhler therefore determined to change his plan of action entirely. His idea was now to leave the trade alone till it had had time to recover confidence and revert to his original scheme of raiding West Indian ports.

This operation appears to have held an important place in the original German war plans, for two rendezvous for colliers and storeships had been arranged in West Indian waters. One was close to the *Karlsruhe's* original hiding-place at Plana Cays in the Bahamas, and the other about 250 miles east of Trinidad. Both had been discovered by our West Indian cruisers, and on September 12 the *Berwick* had found at the latter the three vessels which had left port the day war was declared or shortly afterwards.[2] One, at least, had been originally to the northern rendezvous, but she had been called down about August 16, and ever since it would seem they had been waiting where they were found, a fact that would indicate that the arrangements of the German Admiralty for supplying their cruisers were not so complete as at one time they were popularly supposed to be. All three ships were captured and brought in by the *Berwick,* but

---

[1] It is said that the *Farn,* when she approached the *Condor* under British colours, got her to pass the Admiralty warning to take a course west of the usual track. Studt: *Der Karlsruhe.*

[2] See *ante,* p. 50.

whether the loss was known to the *Karlsruhe* does not appear.[1]

Important as was the new venture, Captain Köhler seemed loth to leave the waters where he had done so well. Till the last safe moment he clung to his cruising ground, and on October 23 was rewarded by capturing the *Hurstdale* of Liverpool with 4,600 tons of maize from Rosario to Bristol. She was sunk at once. The next day—the last one that was safe—brought nothing, and on the 25th, after detaching the *Rio Negro*, *Asuncion* and *Indrani* with instructions for the next few weeks, he held away with the *Farn* to carry out his raid on the West Indies.

Meanwhile, since Admiral Stoddart had left the Canary-Cape Verde station, there had been no little anxiety lest the *Karlsruhe* should appear there, and owing to the passing of transport convoys the moment was anything but opportune for Admiral Stoddart's departure. When on October 15 he started for Pernambuco, he left Captain Buller of the *Highflyer* in command of the station, but later in the day he received an order from the Admiralty that the *Highflyer* was to take over from the *Astræa* the transports that were coming up from the Cape, as that ship was urgently required in connection with the new plan of operations against German South-West Africa. This left nothing for patrol routine except three merchant cruisers, and at the same time intelligence came in that a German collier was at Las Palmas waiting to supply German cruisers. There was a strong probability that the expected cruiser was the *Karlsruhe*. The *Kent* was therefore ordered to join Captain Buller's command instead of going on to Admiral Cradock, and to her the *Astræa's* convoy was to be handed over. On reaching Admiral de Robeck's station she was, in her turn, to hand over to the *Vindictive* and return to search the Canaries, where there were fresh indications that the Germans were preparing a base.

No sooner had the *Kent* started than the rumour of the *Karlsruhe* being in the vicinity gathered strength. On October 21 the *Victorian*, which had been refitting at Gibraltar, reached Las Palmas to find the collier had gone to sea and that signal lights, believed to come from the *Karlsruhe*, had been seen off the south of the island. As the *Kent* and her convoy were passing she hurried off to warn her, and in

---

[1] The prizes were *Spreewald*, German merchant auxiliary from St. Thomas; *Lorenzo*, American, and *Thor*, Norwegian, chartered at Newport News ostensibly for the Hamburg-Amerika Co. *Lorenzo* and *Thor* had between them over 3000 tons of coal and nearly 200 tons of stores.

doing so passed another German ship in the dark without seeing her.   The collier, which was the *Walhalla*, got into Tenerife, and so did the other ship.

She proved to be the *Crefeld*, and to have startling news. For fourteen hours the Spanish Authorities kept it concealed, but then it became known that she had on board the crews of no less than thirteen vessels which the *Karlsruhe* had captured or destroyed between August 31 and October 11.

It was clear drastic measures must be taken promptly, but what they should be was not so evident.   The immediate effect of the news was to give increased colour to the rumour about the *Karlsruhe* being in the Canaries and Cape Verde Area, since she was not likely to remain on the scene of her recent exploits for fear of capture.   Indeed, Admiral Stoddart's first care on reaching his new station had been to order the *Bristol* and *Edinburgh Castle* to search the coast where the *Karlsruhe's* secret base was believed to be.   He also ordered the *Kent* to co-operate with them, not yet being aware that she had been held back on his old station.   To secure that station further it was necessary to call on the Coast of Spain station.

There, in spite of the difficulty of maintaining a watch on the Peninsular ports with his decadent squadron, Admiral de Robeck had managed to make a sweep to the Azores, where he captured a large Hamburg-Amerika liner, the *Grœcia*, which had been hovering there for a month calling up German warships.   His freedom of action had, indeed, been considerably enlarged by the recent detailing of the *Bacchante* and *Euryalus* as regular convoy ships between Home and Gibraltar.   But for this he could scarcely have left the convoy route.   Two groups of transports were moving in his station, besides the Cape Garrison.   One was homeward bound with the last of the old Mediterranean Garrisons, and the other, consisting of twelve ships, outward bound with the 1st Wessex Territorial Division for India.   As it was, he was able to make a thorough search round the Azores, and on completing it he went down himself to the Canaries in his flagship the *Amphitrite*.   And there he remained ; for he found the Spanish Authorities so lax in the matter of interning the German auxiliaries that were there that he decided not to leave till he had seen the situation regularised.   This he skilfully accomplished in a remarkably short time, considering how strong was German influence in the islands.

Nor was this the only point his vigilance was able to make. Here, as elsewhere, the successful protection of our trade rested in a great measure on our power of cutting off communication with the enemy's cruisers. This we had not been able to do entirely, for, as the Admiral found out, a private wireless installation was being constantly used by German and Austrian consular officers. No such privilege for consulates was generally recognised. Cipher wireless messages, indeed, could serve no special purpose except for communicating secret intelligence and orders to ships at sea. One intercepted by the *Victorian* on September 6 was actually sent to and acknowledged by Captain Köhler of the *Karlsruhe*. On these grounds, at the Admiral's instigation, our Foreign Office made representations to Madrid. The Spanish Government pointed out that the privilege was permitted to both sides. But, as the Admiral objected, the privilege was of no use to us, while it practically furnished the Germans with a means of communication which was otherwise out of their power. For this reason what was being permitted amounted to unneutral service. After some negotiations, thanks to Admiral de Robeck's persistence, cipher wireless messages were altogether forbidden. He also successfully demanded the internment of the German S.S. *Macedonia* at Palma Island on October 31, but the *Duala* and *Arucas*, though known to have coaled the *Kaiser Wilhelm der Grosse*, were kept in harbour at Las Palmas but not officially interned.

The Canary–Cape Verde area was thus well secured against any attack that was likely to be made upon it, but on the Cape station things had rapidly gone from bad to worse. The movement which Maritz had initiated had been spreading with alarming rapidity. General Beyers, who at the outbreak of the war had resigned his command of the Union Forces, had joined him, and De Wet was raising the back veldt commandoes with the declared intention of re-establishing the old Boer Republics. General Botha was taking the field in person against them, but so serious was the situation that it was felt he should not be left to his own resources. From one quarter only could assistance come. The New Zealand troops had just reached Australia under escort of the *Minotaur*, *Ibuki*, *Philomel* and *Pyramus*, and the combined convoy was in process of concentration at Albany, where the two fast light cruisers *Melbourne* and *Sydney* replaced the *Philomel* and *Pyramus*. With such a force and its powerful escort the situation in South Africa could be met, and on October 25 the British Cabinet decided that as a precautionary measure the whole combined convoy must come to Europe by way of the Cape instead of Egypt. On October 28 the New Zealand contingent joined the concentration at Albany, and the final arrangements were made for the troops to proceed to their new destination in three groups, according to the speed and coal endurance of the transports.

It meant, of course, a very serious distortion of our Imperial concentration, but until South Africa was made secure again that concentration could never be consummated. The necessity had to be faced, but not for long. On the day the decision was taken the cloud was lifted. At Commissie Drift, near Rustenberg in the Transvaal, General Botha had soundly defeated the rebels. Both Beyers and Maritz were in flight over the German border, and so far as they were concerned the rebellion was over. As soon as the news was fully known it was clear the internal situation was well in hand, and on October 30 the convoy was ordered to proceed as originally intended to Colombo, escorted by *Minotaur, Ibuki, Melbourne* and *Sydney.*

Though the reversion to the original plan left the naval defence of the Cape as unsatisfactory as ever, there was no suggestion of decreasing the Australian convoy's powerful escort. It was a suggestion that could hardly be made at the moment, for although there was nothing near the convoy track except the *Königsberg* and the *Emden*, the latter had just reappeared in a manner to shake confidence in the ability of the local forces to deal with her.[1] The shock was all the greater because since her disappearance after her raid on the Minikoi Area at the end of September the operations against her had met with considerable success. On October 9 Admiral Jerram heard that a Greek ship was lying off Pulo Tapak, an island on the west coast of Sumatra near the south end of Simalur—that is, in the waters from which he had always believed the Germans would operate. He at once warned Captain Grant, who promptly detached the *Yarmouth*, then on patrol off Acheh Head, to investigate. On the 12th she reached Pulo Tapak, and there she found the *Emden's* Greek prize *Pontoporos*, and not only her but the *Emden's* regular tender *Markomannia* taking in coal from her. The *Pontoporos* Captain von Müller had ordered to Simalur after his raid on Madras. On leaving the Minikoi area, he had taken his other prize, the Admiralty collier *Buresk*, down to Felidu Atoll in the Maldives, and having coaled from the *Markomannia*, which he had also kept with him, he sent her off to Simalur to refill with coal, while he himself continued down the Maldives to the Chagos Archipelago, taking the *Buresk* with him. Both the vessels at Simalur were now captured, the *Markomannia* with 1300 tons of coal and the *Pontoporos* with 5000. The latter ship the *Yarmouth* took away to

[1] See Map 13 in case.

Penang, the other she sank, and thus the *Emden's* fuel was reduced to the coal in her bunkers and what was left in the *Buresk*.

Meanwhile Captain Grant, having searched the Laccadives and Maldives as far south as Male, was patrolling south of Ceylon with the *Hampshire* and *Empress of Asia*. No tidings of the *Emden* were to be had beyond the fact that from September 28 to October 1 she had been coaling off Felidu Atoll. After hearing of the capture of her colliers at Simalur, Captain Grant was convinced she must still be somewhere to the southward, and decided to make for Diego Garcia in the south of the Chagos Islands. As this place had till recently been a coaling station of the Orient Liners engaged in the Australian frozen meat trade, it was a likely point for her to make, and at daylight on October 13 he started in search of her, taking his merchant cruiser with him in accordance with the recent standing orders. The scent was now hot. After coaling off Felidu Atoll from the *Markomannia*, Captain von Müller had actually gone on to Diego Garcia. He had in his possession an old chart which showed the abandoned trade route as still existing, and for the best part of a week he cruised south and west of the islands expecting a rich harvest. But not a ship was seen, and on October 9 he went into Diego Garcia to coal from the *Buresk*. The reception was all he could desire. In that remote and now lonely British colony the inhabitants were still unaware that a war existed, and instead of his visit being opposed or even resented, a cordial interchange of courtesies took place, and Captain von Müller was given every facility for heeling his ship to clean her bottom and for coaling at his leisure. The work was completed by the morning of the 10th, and he sailed again northward in search of fresh adventures, apparently straight into the arms of the two British cruisers. Unfortunately, however, while the *Emden* made her way northward through the Maldives, Captain Grant, in his eagerness to reach Diego Garcia, was steaming down well to the eastward on the direct route from Colombo to the Chagos Islands, and he passed the *Emden* at a distance of about 300 miles. On the 15th at Diego Garcia he learnt the truth—that the *Emden* had gone north five days before—and he immediately started back for Colombo.

Scarcely had he coaled there and resumed his patrol south of Ceylon when, on October 20, the *St. Egbert* put into Cochin on the Malabar coast with the crews of six more British ships which the *Emden* had captured between Minikoi and Ceylon. With considerable daring Captain von Müller had returned to the scene of his last exploits, and from the 16th to the 19th, during Captain Grant's sweep to the southward, there was no British cruiser on the spot. True, an attempt had been made to recall the *Askold*, which in company with the *Dupleix* was escorting a Franco-British convoy to Suez, but the message reached her so late that she was obliged to go on to Aden to coal.[1]

The miscarriage was the more regrettable, for amongst the new batch of captures was the *Exford*, an Admiralty collier with 6000 tons of Welsh coal for Hongkong, and thus at the moment when the *Emden's* career was practically at an end through the capture of her supply ships, she received a new lease of life. All the other prizes, except one, which was a dredger, were large, and the number included the *Troilus* of the Blue Funnel Line, a vessel of 7500 tons, homeward bound from Yokohama, and only twenty-five hours out from Colombo, with a cargo insured for £130,000.[2] The first two ships of the new haul were captured close to Minikoi, and the third in the Nine Degree Channel. The *Emden* then steamed eastward and captured the rest off the coast of Travancore, between the direct tracks from Aden and Bombay to Colombo. All were sunk except two, the *St. Egbert*, to which, on account of her neutral cargo, the prisoners were transferred, and the Admiralty collier *Exford*, which was kept as a tender. Most of the ships captured were duly following the routes given to them officially. But, as we have seen, effective deviation at this nodal point was practically impossible. Still, as evidence of how well-advised were the Admiralty instructions, it is to be noted that during the four days the area was left unguarded while the *Emden* was at work in it nineteen steamers passed unmolested.[3]

Not only did the Admiralty instructions keep most of

---

[1] The convoy was *Arcadia*, *Nile* and *Carnarvonshire* with British troops from Tientsin, Hongkong and Singapore, *El Kantara* with French troops, and *Cordillère* with munitions from Japan.

[2] The captures were:—

Clan Grant	(3,948 tons), Clan Line, outward bound to Calcutta, War Risks £30,600.
Benmohr	(4,806 tons), Ben Line, Leith to Yokohama, valued at £50,000.
Chilkana	(5,146 tons), British India, Middlesbrough to Calcutta, War Risks £77,000.
Exford	(4,542 tons), Tatem S.N. Co., Cardiff to Hongkong with Admiralty coal, War Risks £32,500.
Ponrabbel	(473 tons), dredger for Tasmania from Port Glasgow.
Troilus	(7,562 tons), Blue Funnel Line, War Risks £129,115.
St. Egbert	(5,596 tons), Yokohama to New York, War Risks £54,500, neutral cargo.

[3] See note at end of chapter, p. 340.

the trade out of Captain von Müller's way, but the cruiser dispositions that were immediately made came within an ace of punishing his bold return with disaster. The moment Captain Grant heard the news he went off again with both his ships to Felidu Atoll to search the Maldives. This he could now safely do, for the *Yarmouth*, having taken over from the *Zhemchug* off Penang a convoy of four French transports with troops and stores, had brought it on to Colombo, leaving the Russian cruiser to search the Nicobars and Andamans for any German colliers that might be there, and the *Yarmouth* was now ordered to the Minikoi area. The result of Captain Grant's movement was that the *Emden* had another miraculous escape. Still, her luck stood by her. After sinking his last prize and dismissing the *St. Egbert* with his prisoners, Captain von Müller stood to the southward, with the *Buresk* and *Exford* in company, till about noon on the 20th, when he was in the latitude of Colombo. He then turned to the south-eastward to give Dondra Head in Ceylon a wide berth. As he came on, the *Hampshire* and *Empress of Asia* began their sweep west-south-west towards Felidu Atoll, so that they must cross the *Emden's* track. By midnight it looked as if nothing but a miracle could save her. At ordinary speed they would have clashed just after sunrise. But, eager as Captain von Müller was to make off as fast as possible, he could not get more than nine and a half knots out of his prizes. From his log it is clear the trouble caused him considerable anxiety, but, in fact, it was the stroke of luck that saved him. Had he done a knot or so more, or even had he kept away another point or two to the southward, he must have run right into Captain Grant. As it was, about 7.30 the two British cruisers passed across his course from ten to twenty miles ahead of him. The morning was dark, with heavy clouds and passing showers. A spell of rain must have come on in the nick of time, for neither captain saw the other, and once more the *Emden* escaped the *Hampshire*, this time by minutes.

Yet she was only out of the frying-pan into the fire. Captain von Müller had decided the time had come to shift his ground altogether to the eastern part of the Indian Ocean, and in the afternoon of the 21st he detached the *Exford* to a rendezvous north of the Cocos, which had also apparently been given to his colliers at Simalur. He was still quite unaware of what had happened to them. Indeed, his intelligence all through was very meagre. His success was won by very simple means. The stories that prevailed at the time of ingenious wireless calls and the like had little or no foundation : he had not even a direction meter to locate the calls he heard.   His method had simply been to take up a position in a fertile area and hunt smoke, which from a crow's nest on his foremast he could see at a distance of thirty-five miles. But now whenever smoke was seen he turned his stern to it and hurried on.   It was not till he had made a point 200 miles south of Dondra Head that he held up for the Nicobar Islands, where he intended to coal before commencing operations in the new field.   Here, as we have seen, the Russian light cruiser *Zhemchug*, of almost equal force, was carrying on a search for the *Emden's* colliers.[1]   The Japanese light cruiser *Chikuma* was also in the vicinity working the Acheh Head Patrol.   At Singapore the light cruiser *Yahagi*, of the 2nd Japanese Squadron, had just arrived with the French transports from Saigon, but she was under orders to join the Australian Convoy at the Cocos Islands in place of the *Nisshin*, which had run on an uncharted rock outside Sandakan and had to go into dock at Singapore.   In Penang, the base of the Malacca Strait Patrol, was the *D'Iberville* with three destroyers, *Fronde, Pistolet* and *Mousquet*.   Here, on October 26, they were joined by the *Zhemchug*, who, after completing her search of the Nicobar and Andaman Islands, had come down the coast of Burmah through the Mergui Archipelago, and received permission for a week's overhaul of her main engines.   On the previous evening Captain von Müller anchored with the *Buresk* at Nankowry Harbour in the Nicobars.

What was in his mind was a raid on Penang, where he expected to find the *Dupleix*, though she was actually at Aden, and after coaling he dismissed the *Buresk* to a sea rendezvous and started on his daring enterprise.   Though the port contained three French destroyers, it had no fixed defences, and for this reason our cruisers when visiting the place, having in mind the fate of the *Pegasus* at Zanzibar, were in the habit of laying out anchors so that the ship could quickly bring her broadside to bear on the entrance.   The Harbour Master, Commander McIntyre, R.N.R., and Lieutenant Maund, R.N., who was serving in the *Zhemchug*, urged this and other precautions on the Russian captain, and Lieutenant Maund each night took charge of the signal station at the military headquarters.   Little else, however, seems to have been done, except that one French destroyer went out to patrol at night and a picket boat was on guard. The other two destroyers were alongside the quay, and the *D'Iberville* was overhauling her engines.

		Tons.	Knots.	Guns.
[1]	*Zhemchug*	1904	3,130	23	8 4·7″
	Emden	1909	3,544	25	10 4·1″

This was the position when, shortly after 5.0 a.m. on October 28, a cruiser with four funnels (for Captain von Müller had just rigged a dummy one) appeared entering the harbour. She was painted dark grey like our own ships, and was flying a flag that was taken for the white ensign. The picket boat let her pass without challenge or giving the preconcerted warning, and the *Zhemchug* did not shift her position. When within three-quarters of a mile of her the supposed British cruiser hoisted German colours, and directly afterwards fired a torpedo. It took the *Zhemchug* aft and flooded the engine room, and then, as the *Emden* ran past her, Captain von Müller opened fire at 300 yards. The surprise was complete and resistance hopeless. Scarcely any of the Russian guns were even cleared away, nothing but a perfunctory harbour watch was being kept on board, and the *Emden* ran on untouched past the French destroyers, who were equally unready. On coming abreast of the *D'Iberville*, which was the innermost ship, she turned and, without firing on the French gunboat and destroyers, ran out again to pass the *Zhemchug*, which was now burning fiercely. At point blank range the *Emden* fired into her again and gave her another torpedo. There was a huge column of flames and debris, and in a minute the *Zhemchug* went down, only a quarter of an hour after the first shot was fired. Such was her inglorious end, as though the curse of the ill-fated Baltic Fleet, in which during the Russo-Japanese War she had seen her first service, still clung to her.[1]

As for the *Emden*, content with her bold and brilliantly executed exploit, she ran on out till, at the northern entrance, she came upon the Glen Liner *Glenturret*, which was just stopping for a pilot. This ship was bound for Yokohama with Government ammunition for Singapore and Hongkong, and was flying the Explosive flag. Regardless of the two destroyers in the harbour, the *Emden*, with fine effrontery, stopped to take possession of her, and had already lowered her boats when what appeared in the still dim light to be a cruiser was seen coming in. The boats were recalled, and the *Emden* stood on to face the expected action. But it proved to be only the French destroyer *Mousquet* returning from patrol. She made a gallant fight of it with guns and torpedoes, but all in vain, and in seven minutes she went down. So the affair ended. There was no time to go back to the *Glenturret*, for the other French ships were getting under way. Still, the *Emden* stopped long enough to pick up the survivors

[1] Out of a complement of 340 she lost 1 officer and 90 men killed, and 2 officers and 106 men wounded.

of the *Mousquet*, from whom she heard the *Pontoporos* had
been captured, and then she made off to the northward and
disappeared.

Such was the tale that reached the Australian Government as the great convoy was finally assembling for its
departure. It was tempered, indeed, by the news that on
the day after the Penang raid General Botha's victory at
Commissie Drift had been completed by the dispersal of the
Eastern Transvaal rebels at Treurfontein; and furthermore, by
the time it was settled that the convoy was to proceed after
all to Aden, all danger from the *Königsberg* was over. Ever
since, on September 20, she had destroyed the *Pegasus* at
Zanzibar she had been lost, and had consequently remained
a standing menace to the convoy route, and absorbed an
annoying amount of our cruiser force. From the last day
of September onwards an extremely active search had been
kept up by a division of three light cruisers, *Chatham, Dartmouth* and *Weymouth,* under the direction of Captain Drury-
Lowe of the *Chatham,* and there was also at Mombasa the *Fox,*
waiting for the expedition from India to German East Africa,
which had been long delayed owing to the need of getting the
main force to Egypt as soon as possible. She, of course,
could not move far, but the other three ships hunted out every
conceivable hiding place on the German coast and in the adjacent islands again and again. There was little result, except
that the *Königsberg* seemed paralysed by their activity. No
capture had been reported since she took the *City of Winchester,* nor had our cruisers much luck in finding her tenders.
On October 9, however, the *Dartmouth,* which was looking
round Casuarina Island in the Mozambique Channel, captured a German tug from Beira, which was supposed to be
serving the missing enemy. Ten days later Captain Drury-
Lowe anchored in the Lindi River to search it for the fourth
time, and sending his cutter up the river, found the German
East African Liner *Präsident,* a ship of 3,385 tons. She, too,
was believed to be communicating with the *Königsberg.*
She was flying the Red Cross flag, but not being painted white
or on the list, she was captured and disabled. From her papers
it was found that on September 15 coal had been sent to the
Königsberg in lighters from Lindi to Sarari, six miles up the
Rufiji, and German charts seized on board showed the river
was navigable by a ship of the *Königsberg's* class. Accordingly, after being called elsewhere by a false report, Captain
Drury-Lowe arrived at the Rufiji Delta on the 30th, and
there he found her lying up at Sarari with her collier and
three small steamboats. It was impossible for the *Chatham*

to reach her, and as natives reported that the creek up which
she lay was mined and defended by guns and entrenched
troops, Captain Drury-Lowe sat down to blockade her till he
could make arrangements for a flotilla attack.

It was on the last day of October that he was able to
report he had run the *Königsberg* to earth, but to the Australian
Convoy, which was to sail next day, it could make no difference. Pressing as the need was for reinforcing the Cape
station, the wide extent of sea which so large a convoy
must cover rendered it dangerous to reduce the number of
ships allotted for its escort. As it was, the *Yahagi*, which
should have joined the convoy at the Cocos Islands, was no
longer available, for Admiral Jerram had found it necessary,
so soon as he heard of the *Emden's* exploit at Penang, to
divert her to join the *Chikuma* in hunting down the irrepressible raider. The arrangements therefore stood, and on
November 1, before the news of the *Königsberg* reached
Australia, the great convoy sailed for Colombo under escort
of the *Minotaur, Ibuki, Melbourne* and *Sydney*. Nor was
any call made upon Admiral Patey. With the *Australia,*
Montcalm and *Encounter* he was still at Suva maintaining the
covering position which he had been ordered to take up, and
hourly expecting instructions to proceed to South America
in chase of Admiral von Spee. He had urged to be allowed
to do this in the middle of the month, but no fresh orders
came, and he had to continue cruising in the Fiji–Samoa area.

The Japanese were still occupied with the main part of
their fleet in the siege of Tsingtau, and so was the *Triumph*.
Their two South Sea Squadrons, as arranged, were operating
in concert with Admiral Patey on either side of longitude 140°,
which is roughly the dividing line between Polynesia and the
Malay Archipelago, and there they were keeping an eye on
the as yet unoccupied German islands to the eastward and
the numerous German ships in neutral ports to the westward,
as well as Honolulu, where the long-lost *Geier* had appeared.[1]

[1] The fate of most of the small German raiders was by this time known.

The *Planet* had been found at Yap by the Japanese Second South Sea
Squadron, when on October 7 they went there to take possession of the island,
and she sank herself as they approached.

The *Komet* early in October was found to be hiding on the North coast
of New Britain, and using her wireless for intelligence purposes. An expedition against her was organised at Rabaul consisting of the captured Government Yacht *Nusa* under Lieut.-Commander J. M. Jackson, R.N., and some
Australian infantry under Lieut.-Colonel J. Paton. Between them they
managed a very clever surprise, and on the 11th the *Komet* was seized undamaged with her wireless gear intact. She was added to the Australian
Fleet as the gunboat *Una*.

The *Eber* put into Bahia on September 4, and was in due course interned
there with her officers and crew by the Brazilian Government.

In that port she had been making good her defects, and so lax were the American rules about internment that the Japanese thought it necessary to watch her, not only with the armoured cruiser *Asama* but also to detain there the small battleship *Hizen*, which had been under orders for Esquimalt to reinforce the Anglo-Japanese Squadron on that coast. They had also agreed to take over the eastern part of the Indian Ocean—that is, from 90° east longitude, which took in the Andamans and Nicobar Islands, to the Sunda Strait, and for this purpose were detaching Vice-Admiral Tochinai with two armoured cruisers, *Tokiwa* and *Yakumo*, to form a third squadron with the *Nisshin*, *Chikuma* and *Yahagi*.

Nothing, therefore, was available for the Cape except the *Goliath*, which, on the day the *Königsberg* was run to earth, had arrived at Mombasa with the main force of the German East African Expedition; but she had developed serious defects which needed attention, and before she could move a disaster had occurred which rendered much more drastic measures in the highest degree urgent.

NOTE.—According to the German Official History the total known losses up to October 24 amounted to 39 vessels. Of these, 17 were captured by the *Emden*, 13 by the *Karlsruhe*, 2 each by the *Leipzig*, *Dresden* and *Kaiser Wilhelm der Grosse*, and one each by the *Königsberg*, *Kronprinz Wilhelm*, and *U 17*. British Admiralty returns to the same date show total losses by surface craft in all waters as 43, including one vessel sunk by a torpedo boat, 2 by the *Kronprinz Wilhelm*, 14 by the *Karlsruhe*, and a Russian vessel sunk in the Black Sea by the *Hamidieh*. Both lists include vessels captured but not sunk.

CHAPTER XXV

THE BATTLE OF CORONEL, NOVEMBER 1[1]

WE have seen how on October 22 Admiral Cradock left Port Stanley in the Falklands to make a sweep round the Horn, leaving the *Canopus* to meet him at the other side of the Straits. We have also seen how the Admiralty instructions seem to have left him no doubt that he was to operate with his squadron on the west side, while Admiral Stoddart guarded the east, and how he considered himself still bound by the order of October 5 (received by him on the 7th) to search for the enemy. That this was so is made quite clear by a further message which he sent home late on October 26. He had just joined Captain Luce's detachment at the secret base, and was now more deeply impressed than ever with the impossibility of doing what he understood was expected of him. With the force at his disposal he could see no way of bringing to action a squadron so fast, efficient and homogeneous as that of Admiral von Spee. Referring to the order of October 5 and the importance of an early success, he submitted that with the *Canopus* in company it was impracticable, owing to her slow speed, to seek out and destroy the enemy's squadron. The *Canopus* was only fit for escorting and guarding his colliers. He intended, therefore, to employ her on that duty and had ordered Admiral Stoddart to send him the *Defence*. In doing so he cited his own failure to bring the *Karlsruhe* to action on August 6, and suggested that her depredations should be ignored till a ship of superior speed could be sent to deal with her.[2]

---

[1] See Maps 14 and 15 in case and Appendix D II.

[2] The telegram as received was as follows, but there is reason to believe its text was mutilated in transmission:—

"With reference to orders contained in Admiralty telegram received October 7 to search for enemy, and our great desire for early success, consider it impracticable, on account of *Canopus's* slow speed, to find and destroy enemy's squadron. Consequently have ordered *Defence* to join me after calling at Montevideo for orders. *Canopus* will be employed on necessary convoying of colliers. From experience of August 6, most respectfully submit not to oppose depredation of *Karlsruhe*. May it continue until she meets vessel of superior speed."

The mean trial speed of the *Karlsruhe* was 27·6 knots—that of the *Defence* 23·3. From Admiral Cradock's first orders (see *ante*, p. 309 *note*) it would appear that the *Defence* was to be given him not to deal with the *Karlsruhe*, but to make his squadron strong enough to meet Admiral von Spee.

When the message came to hand next day (the 27th) it was found, owing to mutilation in transmission, difficult to see precisely what Admiral Cradock wanted, and after due consideration a plan was adopted, which differed radically from that which it is now evident the Admiral had in mind. It was decided definitely to keep the force available in the South American area divided into two squadrons of about equal strength. The immediate reason seems to have been fresh news of the *Karlsruhe*. The *Defence* had reached Pernambuco on October 25, and next evening there arrived a Norwegian ship which had been stopped by the *Karlsruhe* three days before. She reported that as late as October 23 the German cruiser was still on the trade route, and with this information the *Defence* had at once put to sea, but not to hunt the *Karlsruhe*. Her immediate orders were to relieve the *Cornwall* as base guardship at Abrolhos Rocks and send her to join the *Bristol*, *Macedonia* and *Edinburgh Castle*, who were engaged in a thorough search of the Fernando Noronha area and the north coast of Brazil. Directly the Admiralty knew of Admiral Cradock's call for her they countermanded it.[1] Quite apart from the heavy demand which the hunt for the *Karlsruhe* made upon Admiral Stoddart's squadron, they did not consider that Admiral Cradock required any addition to his force. Their plan was to move the North Pacific Squadron—that is, the *Idzumo*, *Hizen* and *Newcastle*—southward to the Galapagos Islands, and by this means they calculated that if Admiral von Spee had gone north he would meet a superior squadron and be forced down to the *Glasgow* and *Monmouth*, and that these ships would be able to draw him on to the *Good Hope* and *Canopus*.[2]

The telegram to Admiral Cradock, which was sent off in the evening of October 28, perhaps never reached him— in any case it was too late to affect his movements.[3] On the 27th, still hoping, it would seem, to receive a modification of the instructions which, as he conceived them, appeared impracticable, he detached the *Glasgow* northward again to

[1] The telegram ran : " *Defence* is to remain on East Coast under orders of Stoddart. This will leave sufficient force on each side in case the hostile cruisers appear there on the trade routes. There is no ship available for the Cape Horn vicinity. Japanese battleship *Hizen* shortly expected on North American coast. She will join with Japanese *Idzumo* and *Newcastle*, and move south towards Galapagos."

[2] The *Monmouth's* speed was inferior to that of all the German ships except the *Leipzig*. (See *post*, p. 350.)

[3] It was received by the *Glasgow*; and Captain Luce is of opinion it probably did reach the Admiral.

Coronel, where he could expect to hear from the Admiralty by way of Montevideo. Captain Luce's further instructions were to send telegrams, to obtain intelligence and to intercept a German sailing ship which was said to be making for Santa Maria Island off Coronel. Next day he called up the *Canopus* and her colliers from the Straits, his intention being, as soon as he heard Captain Luce's intelligence, to proceed northward with the squadron and coal at Juan Fernandez, where there were friendly French interests; and while awaiting the *Glasgow's* report, he detached the *Otranto* to look into Puerto Montt, the southern terminus of the Chilian west coast railway.

The *Glasgow*, in her search for the German sailing ship, arrived off Santa Maria on the evening of the 29th, but with the Admiral's approval waited till next morning before going into Coronel. During the afternoon she took in many wireless messages in cipher, apparently German. This she reported to the Admiral, who at once decided to sail at 6 a.m. on the 30th with the *Good Hope* and *Monmouth* and stand to the northward. The *Canopus* was also close at hand. Indeed, just as he was coming out he met her with the two colliers she was escorting. Unfortunately, however, he found she required a twenty-four hours' repair on her high-pressure piston gland, and he had to order her into the anchorage to carry out the work. At the same time he informed Captain Luce, in view of the indications he had taken in, that the visit to Coronel was a consideration secondary to the search for the enemy, and accordingly, as the wireless signals continued strong during the night, the *Glasgow* cruised to the westward and north-westward of Santa Maria Island during the 30th and the night of the 30th–31st. Next morning the *Otranto* rejoined the flag. She had reached Puerto Montt in the afternoon of the 30th, and finding the place entirely pro-German, had left again at 6 a.m. on the 31st, without having obtained any information. The *Glasgow* was more fortunate. At 1 a.m. on the 31st, being then off Coronel, she had heard the *Leipzig's* call sign, apparently addressing a merchant ship very close, but saw nothing then or at daybreak. Upon this or other indications Admiral Cradock seems now to have formed the opinion that Admiral von Spee was making for the Northern objective area— that is, the Galapagos Islands and the approaches to the Panama Canal. So far as is known he was not yet aware of the Anglo-Japanese Squadron that had been told off to that area, and he may well have believed, on the information he had, that the duty of protecting it rested on his shoulders. Whatever his motive, what he now did was to call up the

Canopus to proceed with her two colliers to St. Felix (Lat. 26° 18′ S., Long. 80° 11′ W.), a lonely island over 500 miles to the northward of Juan Fernandez, the place where previously he had intended to coal.

His immediate anxiety was for intelligence, and his next step was to order the *Glasgow* definitely to go into Coronel, to dispatch and collect telegrams, with instructions to sail on November 1 as convenient. On reaching the port at 6.20 p.m. on the 31st, she sent off the telegrams which the Admiral had drafted at the base, in one of which he explained his dispositions and his intention of moving northward, coaling at St. Juan Fernandez, but without again mentioning that the *Canopus* had been devoted to the escort of his colliers. By the time it reached the Admiralty the new Board was installed, with Lord Fisher as First Sea Lord, and one of their first acts was an effort to improve the precarious position in which Admiral Cradock found himself. The *Defence* was immediately ordered to join him, and in informing him of this they made it clear he was not expected to act without the *Canopus*. He was to keep his squadron concentrated on her, detaching the *Glasgow* to get touch with the enemy, and to make every effort to form a junction with the *Defence* at the earliest possible moment. He was also told that the Germans believed him to be in Corcovado Bay—an impression which must have been due to the *Otranto's* visit to Puerto Montt.

Prompt as was the action taken it was too late—the telegram never reached him. Before it could arrive he had given the *Glasgow* an order to meet the squadron at noon next day (November 1) at a rendezvous fifty miles west of Coronel. , By the time she arrived both she and the squadron were taking in strong German signals. They still seemed to indicate that the *Leipzig* was somewhere to the northward, calling up merchant vessels, and the Admiral formed a line of search. On the orders he had he could hardly do less. Doubtless if he had received the last explicit telegram from the Admiralty defining exactly what was expected of him, he would have left the *Glasgow* to investigate and prepared to fall back on the *Canopus*. But he had been previously told to "be prepared to have to meet" the enemy and to "search"—expressions, which, taken together, a British officer in his position could only interpret as an order to "seek out the enemy and destroy him." As this could not be done if he had to drag the old battleship along with him, he appears to have felt that by the unwritten law of the Service an order to seek out must override all others. It may be, of course, that as a fortnight had gone by from the date at which the *Scharnhorst* and *Gneisenau* had been expected to appear in Chilean waters, he was confirmed in the belief that they must have gone north to the Panama area. The probability of being ordered to co-operate with our North Pacific squadron may therefore have influenced his decision to take the risk he did. Otherwise it is scarcely credible that with a squadron relatively so weak and with his two best units, *Good Hope* and *Monmouth*, newly commissioned and still quite raw at their gunnery, he would have gone to meet two of the smartest and most seasoned cruisers in the German Navy, each of them of equal force with his flagship.

If this was indeed his belief, he was soon to be undeceived. On October 12 Admiral von Spee had arrived at Easter Island with the *Nürnberg* in company, and there he found the *Dresden*. This ship, after her failure to capture the *Ortega*, had cruised up the trade route nearly as high as Coronel. As she found nothing, she turned back, keeping further from the coast, till September 29, when she went off to Mas-a-Fuera. There she coaled from the *Baden*, which had been acting as her tender ever since she left West Indian waters, and which now proceeded to tow her to Easter Island. She reached it two days before Admiral von Spee, and on October 14 the *Leipzig* turned up and completed the concentration. For a week the squadron lay there resting, revictualling and making its preparations without hindrance, for in that lonely Chilean possession, which was nothing but a cattle ranch, the semblance of authority that existed was quite unable to assert neutrality. Thence he was therefore able to obtain all he required, and on October 18, while Admiral Cradock was still waiting for the *Canopus* at the Falklands, he sailed, fully replenished, for Mas-a-fuera. There, on October 27, he was joined by the *Prinz Eitel Friedrich*, driven from her proper cruising area in New Guinea waters by the Australian Squadron. By this time he must have heard that British cruisers had been at Valparaiso; for the same day (the 27th) that Admiral Cradock reached his secret base, he sailed again, and at noon on the 30th he was fifty miles west of Valparaiso. In that vicinity he cruised out of sight and sent in the *Prinz Eitel Friedrich*, who chased a British ship, the *Colusa*, so close into the port that a Chilean gunboat had to intervene. Next day, having certain news that the *Glasgow* was at Coronel, Admiral von Spee at once decided to move in to cut her off, but, as we have seen, she left just in time to escape him and just too soon to be able to inform the flagship of his presence. Thus about the time Admiral Cradock

23

began his sweep northward, believing he had nothing but the *Leipzig* before him, the whole German Squadron was about sixty miles north of Arauco Bay. They too believed they had a single enemy cruiser (the *Glasgow*) in their clutches, and the intention was, as they neared Coronel, for the *Nürnberg* to steam past to see if she was still there, while the rest formed on an arc twenty miles distant from the harbour.

Such was the strange position at 2.30 p.m. on November 1, by which time the *Glasgow* had rejoined. Neither admiral knew that the other was present, and each believed he had nothing more serious in hand than cutting off an isolated cruiser. While the British flagship proceeded N.W. by N. (mag.) at ten knots, the squadron was ordered to take up stations on a line N.E. by E. (mag.) from the flag in the order *Good Hope, Monmouth, Otranto, Glasgow*, at fifteen miles apart. For some time past it had been blowing strong from the south-east, and it was in a fairly heavy sea that the squadron proceeded to take up the prescribed formation. Two hours later, at 4.20 p.m., the line of search was still incomplete when the *Glasgow* sighted smoke on the starboard bow, and a few minutes later altered course to S. 84° E. towards it. Five minutes later the *Otranto*, which was then about two miles W. N. W. of the *Glasgow*, signalled to her that she also had seen the smoke. In another quarter of an hour the *Glasgow* knew the long-expected crisis had come. She had made certain what ships were causing the smoke, and at 4.40 reported them as the *Scharnhorst, Gneisenau* and a German light cruiser. In another five minutes she was able definitely to determine their course. They had turned towards her, and signalling to the flagship, "Enemy's protected cruisers in sight steering between S.E. and S.," she turned away at full speed to S. 65° W. in order to close the *Good Hope*, which had promptly turned towards the enemy. The *Monmouth* and *Otranto* followed her lead. The *Canopus*, which had left Vallenar Roads at 9.0 the previous morning, was still nearly 300 miles away to the southward, toiling slowly with her colliers through the heavy weather on her long voyage to St. Felix, and quite unable to give any support.

It is not without emotion that one contemplates the feelings of so fine an officer when suddenly he found himself face to face with the hopeless situation into which, against all his protests and better judgment, he clearly believed himself to have been forced. A cloud that can never be lifted has fallen on one of the most tragic moments in our Naval history. All we can ever know is the silver lining.

For whatever he thought and felt, Admiral Cradock did not flinch.

When about 4.30 the *Glasgow* located the enemy, they were still coming down the coast in order to take up their encircling position off Coronel. The flagship *Scharnhorst* was outermost and the *Nürnberg* innermost, but, having chased a small steamer, she was out of sight to the northward, and as the *Dresden* had been told to keep touch, she, too, was twelve miles astern. Admiral von Spee's squadron was thus a good deal dispersed, and he only had steam for fourteen knots, but as soon as he sighted two of the British squadron to the S.W. he ordered all boilers to be lighted, recalled the two light cruisers, and, without waiting for them, began to chase with his other three ships in line ahead, working rapidly up to twenty knots. He was careful, however, to keep his enemy four points on his starboard bow. "The wind was south," he says, "force 6, with a correspondingly high sea, so that I had to be careful not to be manœuvred into a lee position. Moreover, the course chosen helped to cut off the enemy from the neutral coast." [1]

In anticipating such a manœuvre by his enemy he was not far wrong. Widely as Admiral Cradock had allowed himself to be separated from the ship which the Admiralty relied on to give him strength for the encounter, there is no sign of his having attempted to avoid action. It is probable that having regard to the relative speeds and positions of the two squadrons he judged it impossible to fall back on the *Canopus* without first being brought to action, and thought his best chance, as the sun was setting behind him, lay in forcing an engagement while he had the advantage of the light.

As we have seen, as soon as the *Glasgow* had made out what the enemy were and that they were steering for her, she turned back, and with the *Monmouth* and *Otranto* steamed at full speed towards the flagship. This was at 4.47, and about 5.0 Admiral von Spee saw them running off to the westward, the *Glasgow's* course being actually S. 65° W. As well as she could for the enemy's continual jamming, she was reporting the character and movements of the Germans. She had sight of the *Good Hope* at 5.0, and ten minutes later Admiral Cradock signalled for all ships to raise steam for full speed and to concentrate on the *Glasgow*— that is, on the ship which was nearest the enemy. The course

---

[1] Admiral von Spee's Official Report. This report, with that of the *Glasgow*, is the main authority. The two are in substantial agreement as to ranges, movements and the general course of the action.

of the three cruisers in closing the flagship was about W. by S.,
and to this Admiral von Spee conformed about 5.10, altering
again to the S.W. ten minutes later, but it was not till nearly
6.0 that he sighted the *Good Hope*. By this time Admiral
Cradock had his squadron in line ahead in the order *Good
Hope, Monmouth, Glasgow, Otranto*. The signal had been
made at 5.47 and he was leading about S.E. to cross in front
of the enemy, who was then distant about twelve miles.
As, however, the *Otranto* could do no more than 15 knots, he
seems quickly to have found that on the course he was steering
he could not effect his purpose, for at 5.55 he inclined away
to starboard (S. 20° E.).[1] Even this would not do, and
judging apparently that nothing was left to him but to force
an action on parallel courses he signalled to alter to south
(mag.). There can be little doubt what his intention was,
for no sooner was the squadron steady on the new course than
he made an obvious effort to close the enemy. At 6.04,
according to the report of the *Glasgow's* navigator, the " British
Squadron turned four points together to port towards the
enemy, with a view to closing them and forcing them to action
before sunset, which, if successful, would have put them at
a great disadvantage, owing to the British Squadron being
between the enemy and the sun." The enemy, however,
refused by immediately turning away in succession to port,
and so kept the range at about 18,000 yards.

So at least it appeared to our squadron. According to
the published German track chart, Admiral von Spee certainly
did turn away about three points at this time, but it is
not certain that he saw the British movement clearly, or
that he realised an attempt was being made to force an
action. His own account was that, having frustrated what
he took to be an attempt to get inshore of him and to
windward, and having in the effort drawn well ahead of
his squadron, he was content to wait for the rest to come
up. " The enemy," he says, " was amiable enough not to
disturb us in this." [2] This, however, is tantamount to
saying he did avoid action at this time, and Admiral Cradock,
finding he could not close in the direct manner he had attempted, turned back in about five minutes into line ahead
to a course that was south (mag.). But he had not given
up the idea of forcing an action, or, at least, he must have
realised that an action was now inevitable practically on

---

[1] Captain Luce in his report says the enemy had turned S. when the signal
was made, but the published German chart shows them still keeping S.W.

[2] This is from his private letter. The British turns are not shown on the
German track chart.

the enemy's terms, and that the little chance he had was to bring it on while he still had the advantage of the light.

The two squadrons were now steaming to the southward on slightly converging courses, and at 6.18 Admiral Cradock ordered speed to be increased to seventeen knots, and then, after making the general signal for close attention to the flagship's movements, altered one point towards the enemy, signalling to the *Otranto* to proceed at her utmost speed. He next called up the *Canopus* and informed her he was going to attack the enemy there and then, giving his position as Lat. 37° 30′ S., Long. 74° 0′ W.[1]   This signal the *Canopus*, who was steering to the northward at 10 knots, took in, and replied at once : " My position 41.10 S., 76.20 W., Course N. 10 W.,"—that is, she was over 250 miles away.

By this time the *Dresden* had come up into the line, and Admiral von Spee, who when Admiral Cradock last altered towards him had answered by a corresponding turn away, now (6.47) altered back again one point towards the British, and as Admiral Cradock saw that both the German light cruisers were in station, he reduced speed to sixteen knots, possibly to cover the *Otranto*.   He still kept pressing her to use her utmost speed, but she could only reply that against the head seas she could do no more; but she was coming up on the *Glasgow,* and when the Admiral slowed down she hauled out to starboard, and, seeing an action was imminent, asked if she was to keep out of range. No clear reply could be had, and, having no battle value, she kept away on the *Glasgow's* starboard quarter.

The sun was now setting in a stormy sky.   The Germans tell of heavy clouds with driving showers that obscured the failing light, but the western horizon was all aglow.[2]   So long as the sun was still visible the light was all in Admiral Cradock's favour, but in these circumstances the Germans refused to fight.   As soon, however, as it had gone down the advantage was turned against him, for while the Germans were almost lost in the obscurity of the eastern horizon, he was clearly silhouetted against the afterglow. For this Admiral von Spee had been working.   " I had manœuvred," he says, " so that the sun in the west could not disturb me.   The moon in the east was not yet full, but promised good light during the night, and there were rain squalls in various directions."   Under such conditions of light, with heavy seas breaking over their engaged bows,

---

[1] This position was actually fifty miles south of where he was.

[2] British officers state that they saw nothing of the clouds and rain on which the German authorities insist.

what chance had our comparatively old ships, which had had no opportunity of doing their gunnery since they were commissioned for the war, against the smartest shooting squadron in the German service, and that squadron superior in numbers, design, speed and gun power ? [1]

It was a minute or two after 7.0, when the sun had just set, that Admiral von Spee opened fire at a range of about 11,400 yards. Even then his line was not properly formed. While the British ships were accurately placed at two cables apart, in the German line there were five cables between the *Gneisenau* and *Leipzig* and seven between the *Leipzig* and *Dresden.* Notwithstanding that all ships were rolling heavily in the ugly seas, the shooting of the two big German cruisers was excellent from the outset. The *Scharnhorst's* first shots were a salvo of three guns, which burst on the water beautifully together and 500 yards short of the *Good Hope.* Her third salvo apparently hit the *Good Hope's* forward 9·2″ gun,

[1]

BRITISH					
Ship.	Classification.	Completed.	Tons.	Trial Speed.	Armament.
Good Hope (Flag) . (Capt. P. Francklin)	C.	1902	14,100	23·0	2 9·2″; 16 6″
Monmouth . . . (Capt. F. Brandt)	C.	1903	9,800	22·4	14 6″
Glasgow . . . (Capt. J. Luce)	L. C.	1910	4,800	25·3	2 6″; 10 4″
Otranto . . . (Capt. H. M. Edwards)	A. M. C.	—	—	—	4 4·7″

GERMAN					
Scharnhorst . . .	C.	1907	11,420	23·2	8 8·2″; 6 5·9″; 18 22 pdr.
Gneisenau . . .	C.	1908	11,420	23·5	8 8·2″; 6 5·9″; 18 22 pdr.
Leipzig . . .	L. C.	1906	3,200	22·4	10 4·1″
Dresden . . .	L. C.	1908	3,592	24·0†	10 4·1″
Nürnberg . . .	L. C.	1908	3,400	23·5†	10 4·1″

Total in action ⎰ British = 28,700 tons.   2 9·2″; 32 6″; 10 4″ guns.
           ⎱ German = 29,632 tons.   16 8·2″; 12 5·9″; 20 4·1″; 36 22 pdr. (3·4″) guns.

The *Scharnhorst* and *Gneisenau* had both a great reputation for good shooting; the latter had won the Kaiser Prize for the Cruiser (China) Squadron the previous year.

       * Not in action.   † Designed speed.

for the *Otranto* observed a sheet of flame near the forward
six-inch casemate, and the big gun was not fired throughout
the battle.   The *Gneisenau* fired salvoes at the *Monmouth*,
whose forecastle also was on fire in three minutes, although
she is known to have been stripped of paint and woodwork.
The *Leipzig* fired on the *Glasgow*, but failed to hit her, as
the range was too great for her smaller guns.   By this time
our ships had also opened fire, each on her opposite number
in the enemy's line, except the *Otranto*, who, owing to the
range at which the action was fought, was unable to take
any effective part in it.   Her captain was quick to realise
that, owing to the great size of his ship and the relatively short
range of her guns, she could serve no purpose, except as a
mark for the enemy to range on.   For a time, therefore, he
tried to confuse their aim by zigzagging and altering speed,
but finally, after the *Gneisenau* had put two shells over his
fore bridge, one salvo fifty yards on his starboard bow and
another 150 yards astern, he drew right out of the line to the
westward and stood by, watching the action.

It quickly became general.   By 7.10 the *Leipzig* was
straddling the *Glasgow*, and the *Dresden* was also firing at
the *Glasgow* and possibly at the *Otranto*, while the two big
cruisers dealt with the *Good Hope* and *Monmouth*.   And
every minute the tactical disadvantages under which our
ships entered the fight increased.   The heavy seas were
sending up bursts of spray in the faces of our gunners, their
telescopes were obscured, and in the growing darkness our
spotters in the tops could not mark the fall of our shot.   The
smoke of the leading German ships driven down their line
by the strong south-east wind, frequently veiled the *Leipzig*
from view of the *Glasgow*, the only British ship of whose
firing we have any detailed account, but the rest can have
fared no better.   She had opened fire at 7.5, when the range
was estimated at 10,000 yards.   From the first the impossibility of observing the fall of the shot and the indistinctness
of the target reduced her chance of hitting to a minimum,
and her firing was consequently very slow.   At 7.14, finding
she was getting astern of station, she increased speed, but
reduced again at 7.19, about which time a 4·1″ shell from
the *Leipzig* broke up, without bursting, against the conning-
tower support in the Captain's fore cabin.   All this time the
Glasgow could see the two leading British ships were being
heavily punished without being able, in the adverse conditions,
to make any effective reply.   The *Monmouth* had yawed
out of the line to starboard, and she never quite got back
into station.   Another fire broke out in her after part, and

she began to lose distance. The *Glasgow*, in order not to mask her fire and to avoid the projectiles intended for her, had to conform by keeping on her port quarter, but later on she moved back and steamed on a line midway between the courses of the *Monmouth* and *Good Hope*.

The Germans were now almost invisible. There was nothing to lay on except the flashes of their guns, while they continued to hit their well-defined targets with salvoes fired at the rate of about three a minute. The result could be seen upon the *Monmouth*. She had managed to subdue her fire aft, but at 7.25 her forecastle burst into flames again and burned for five minutes. At 7.30 the *Leipzig* ceased fire, and was thought to have changed places with the *Dresden*. In any case both of them soon started firing on the *Glasgow*, and she could see neither. All she could dimly make out were the two large cruisers, and with her forward 6″ gun she was firing on the *Scharnhorst*, and claims several hits and a conflagration in the fore part of the enemy. Her after 6″ gun was trained on the *Gneisenau*, and is credited with a hit under the enemy's after turret with a lyddite shell.

As for the *Good Hope*, who had received salvo after salvo as the two lines kept converging, she was by this time in a forlorn condition. Almost constantly since the commencement of the battle she had been on fire, and at 7.35, when, although Admiral von Spee for the past quarter of an hour had been edging away, the range was down to 5500 yards, she was seen to be altering course to port towards the enemy, as though in a last desperate effort to sell her life dearly. But five minutes later another large conflagration started in her, perhaps a recrudescence of the original fire near the forward 9·2″ gun. The *Monmouth* was in little better condition, but the *Glasgow* was still practically untouched and able to hit back. The moon was rising, and right under it she kept catching sight of a light cruiser, upon which she fired. In return she got her first bad hit—a 4·1″ high explosive shell, which burst fair on her water line below the seamen's mess deck over the port outer screw; it stove in the ship's side and made an irregular hole about six feet square, in appearance almost as if the ship had been rammed, but it did nothing to stop her fighting on.

But by this time it was evident the flagship was nearing her end, though she was still firing. She could be clearly seen very close to the enemy, with her funnels lit up by flames around her bridge. At 7.45 she began to lose way, and dropped from about eight cables on the *Glasgow's* port bow till, five minutes later, she was midway between the *Glasgow* and the enemy. It was now quite dark; the moon was obscured by clouds and occasional rain squalls, when suddenly the gloom was rent with an immense explosion where the *Good Hope* was dimly burning. It took her amidships; her fore part gave out a huge sheet of flame rising 200 feet high; her firing ceased; but what looked like her after part could be faintly seen in the glow of flames which occasionally rose out of it. For a moment so near was the *Good Hope* to the enemy that some of the *Glasgow's* gunners thought it was the German flagship that had gone and not our own, but they were soon undeceived.

By 7.52 the converging courses had brought the range down to 4,600 yards and Admiral von Spee had drawn slightly ahead and was edging inwards. The *Good Hope* was silent, and he was now concentrating on the *Monmouth*, but whenever the *Glasgow's* guns flashed she received the attention of the whole German line. Shortly after 8.0, therefore, she ceased fire. It was now just an hour since the first shot had been fired, and the action was clearly decided. The *Good Hope* was nowhere to be seen, and the *Monmouth*, having turned away to the westward and succeeded in extinguishing her fires, had also disappeared from the Germans' view. The *Glasgow* followed her round, and by 8.15 found her turning to the northward. She had continued her turn nearly sixteen points in order to get her stern to the heavy seas, as she was down by the head and making water badly forward. But by this time the moon had risen above the driving clouds, and under it the *Glasgow* could make out the enemy coming up from E.S.E., as it seemed, in line abreast. Admiral von Spee had, in fact, ordered his light cruisers to make a torpedo attack as soon as the British ships ceased fire, but hitherto they had not been able to find anything. Now it was clear that in a few minutes they must sight the three British ships unless they got away at once. The *Glasgow* therefore warned the *Monmouth* to keep as much as possible to the northwestward. She was unable to do anything to help her— her own escape had, indeed, been almost miraculous. Throughout the action, unarmoured as she was, she had been fighting in the line, and she calculated that some 600 shells had been fired at her; of these five had hit on the water line, but not fatally, as the coal had saved her, and though the Captain's cabin had been wrecked, she had not been on fire. Now that the flagship was gone, escape was the only possibility, and she made off at full speed to the westward, followed by the *Otranto*. So for the time the three ships escaped; for Admiral von Spee was endeavouring to make a circuit round his enemy's line to get them against the moon, but, owing to the course the British ships had taken, they foiled the manœuvre, and he found nothing. About 9.0, however—at which time he was going north-west—he heard firing some ten miles off to the northward, and carried on for the sound of it.

It was the *Nürnberg* engaging the ill-fated *Monmouth*. Having been thrown out of the chase in the early part of the day, the German cruiser had been making desperate efforts to get up with her squadron, and since dark had been steering for the flashes of the guns. When they ceased there was nothing to guide her, and by ill luck, as she was groping her way through the dim moonlight, she came near enough to the *Monmouth* to make her out. By this time the damaged ship had a list of ten degrees to port, and steam was escaping dangerously amidships. As the *Nürnberg* approached her the list increased so much that she could not use her port guns, and the Germans could open fire on her with impunity at close range. " To me," wrote Admiral von Spee's son, who was a sub-lieutenant on board, " it was dreadful to have to fire on the poor devil no longer able to defend herself; but her flag was still flying." The *Nürnberg*, in fact, ceased firing for several minutes to let her surrender, but in the *Monmouth* there was no such thought. From the earliest Tudor days British ships had established a reputation that they would always sink rather than surrender. In later times the tradition had not always been maintained, but in the present war there was in this respect, as in so many others, a reversion to the old indomitable spirit—not only, it must be said, in our own Service, but in that of the enemy as well. Had the *Monmouth* chosen to surrender she could easily have done so. As it was, there was no choice for the *Nürnberg* but to give her the only end she would accept. It came quickly. The *Nürnberg* had to make but one more run, pouring in a lacerating fire at point-blank range, and then the defiant British cruiser capsized. To the last her flags were flying and still flew as she went down. Every soul on board was lost, for the sea was too high to permit of the *Nürnberg* lowering her boats. Smoke, too, was seen to the south-east, and the German had to be careful. It proved, of course, to come from the rest of her squadron, and so the action ended with a combined search for the lost *Good Hope*, while the *Glasgow* and *Otranto* gradually swept round to the southward, and made off independently to join the *Canopus*.

Whether it was by interpreting the *Glasgow's* signals to her or by direct intelligence from Valparaiso, Admiral von Spee had reason to suspect there was a British battleship in the vicinity. He believed her to be a "Formidable" ("Queen" class, as he calls her), and appears to have been uneasy about his position. "Against this ship," he wrote the day after the action, "we can hardly do anything. If they had kept their forces together we should most likely have come off second best." [1] From this remark it is possible to infer that he considered the Admiralty plan might well have involved him in an action against superior force, but whether he meant that he would have avoided action if the battleship had been present is not clear. His subsequent conduct seems to imply that he was not inclined to take the risk. His squadron was practically untouched. He had suffered no hits of any importance, and, it is said, had only three men wounded. Yet the day after the action he proceeded with his two large cruisers and the *Nürnberg* northward to Valparaiso, leaving the other two light cruisers at sea to look out for some colliers which he was evidently expecting, and incidentally perhaps to search for the *Glasgow* and *Otranto*. After staying there the permitted twenty-four hours he went back to Mas-a-Fuera, while the three British ships were making their way with all speed to the Falklands; and at Mas-a-Fuera, for some unknown reason, he remained inactive, making no use of his victory, while the British Admiralty was stung into an activity which, for reach and completeness, had never been equalled in our annals.

On whom the responsibility for the disaster lay must always be a difficult question to decide, since we can never tell what was in the Admiral's mind. It can be urged on the part of the Admiralty that even if their instructions lacked something in precision and completeness, they had a right to expect he would never suffer himself to be separated from the ship they had given him specially to ensure his safety; but "safety" was a word he hardly knew. Whether under the conditions of the meeting it was possible for him to have declined action till he had fallen back on the *Canopus* is doubtful. If it was, then his conduct may be regarded as Quixotic; but even so we can do no less than remember him as we remember Sir Richard Grenville of the *Revenge*. Possibly no better judgment will ever be passed than that which was pronounced by Mr. Balfour, when as First Lord of the Admiralty he unveiled the Admiral's memorial in York

---

[1] *Kieler Neueste Nachrichten,* April 20, 1915. It is said he had heard from Chile that *Canopus* had passed through the Straits.

Minster. It was a year and a half after the event, when opinion had had time to mature, and this is how he concluded his eulogy:—" What, then, was his design in attacking a force obviously greatly superior to his own; a force which, except by some extraordinary accident, some stroke of unexpected fortune, he could not expect successfully to cope with? Was it that he refused to count the risks? Such deeds of uncalculating daring make our blood tingle within us. Yet there is, after all, a higher wisdom than such calculation, and a higher courage than such daring, and that higher courage I believe Admiral Cradock to have possessed. Why, then, you will ask me, did he attack—deliberately, designedly, intentionally—a force which he could not have reasonably hoped either to destroy or put to flight? I think a satisfactory explanation can be given. Remember what the circumstances of the German squadron were. The German Admiral in the Pacific was far from any port where he could have refitted. No friendly bases were open to him. If, therefore, he suffered damage, even though in suffering damage he apparently inflicted greater damage than he received, yet his power, great for evil while he remained untouched, might suddenly, as by a stroke of the enchanter's wand, be utterly destroyed. . . . Admiral Cradock could only judge by the circumstances that were before him, and if he judged that his squadron, that he himself and those under him, were well sacrificed if they destroyed the power of this hostile fleet, then I say that there is no man, be he sailor or be he civilian, but would say that such a judgment showed not only the highest courage, but the greatest courage of unselfishness; and that Admiral Cradock, by absolute neglect of personal interests and personal ambitions, had shown a wise judgment in the interests of his country. . . . If I am right—it must be to a certain extent a matter of conjecture—, but if I am right in the account which I have given of the motives which animated him, there never was a nobler act, unsuccessful though it was, than that which he performed off the coast of South America. We do not know, we never shall know, what were the thoughts of Admiral Cradock when it became evident that, out-gunned and outranged, success was an impossibility. We shall never know what he felt when the setting sun on that evening threw his own ships up clearly against the bright western sky, a mark for his enemies, and at the same time rendered his own fire difficult and ineffective by placing them in the shade. He must have realised then that his hopes were dashed for ever to the ground, that his plan had failed. . . . His body is separated from us by half the world, and he and his gallant comrades lie far from the pleasant homes of England. Yet they have their reward, and we, looking at what they attempted, and judging what they did in the light of what they attempted, are surely right in saying that theirs is an immortal place in the great roll of naval heroes."

CHAPTER XXVI

CRUISER REDISTRIBUTION AFTER CORONEL—THE TURKISH
INTERVENTION—FATE OF THE *KÖNIGSBERG*, *EMDEN* AND
KARLSRUHE—FALL OF TSINGTAU.

REALISING all that the Coronel disaster meant, the new
Board as it entered office had to face an ugly situation.
For reasons, which now seem insufficient, the available force
in the decisive area had been divided into two inadequate
squadrons and the normal result had followed. Coming, as
the disaster did, on the top of the still unpunished exploits
of the *Karlsruhe* and *Emden*, it had inflicted a serious blow
to our naval prestige, at a moment when, as it happened,
prestige was peculiarly important, and in addition to the
moral effect it had exposed our command of the Atlantic to
real menace.

Had the trouble stood alone it would have been grave
enough, but it was far from standing alone. There were
several complications which gravely deepened the sinister
impression and increased the difficulty of removing it. As
we have seen, the activity of the German submarines had
recently made the Grand Fleet's bases for the moment
untenable, with the accidental consequence that we had lost
one of our finest battleships. But as a new battle cruiser,
the *Tiger*, and three more powerful battleships, *Benbow*,
Emperor of India and *Queen Elizabeth*, were just completing
for sea, and as the preliminary anti-submarine defences for
Scapa were well forward, this difficulty was not very serious.
The gravest complication was that affairs at Constantinople
had just reached the final crisis.

Early in October it had become clear that the Germans,
in collusion with Enver Pasha, the Minister of War, were doing
their best to force the Porte into joining the Central Powers
openly. The special ambition of Enver and his party was
the re-conquest of Egypt. It fell in precisely with the
German plan of dealing a mortal blow to the British Empire
by wresting from us the Suez Canal. This adventurous
policy the Turkish Neutrality Party, headed by the Grand

Vizier, were resisting with all the obstinacy they could muster. Unfortunately, as was known only too well to the Entente Embassies, there was no personality amongst them fit to cope with Enver and Talaat, and by the middle of the month it was admitted to our Ambassador that they had not been able to stop preparations for an Egyptian expedition. Bedouins were being employed to dig wells on the frontier, and there were strong indications of a scheme for mining the Canal and Gulf of Suez in order to catch our transports that were passing to and from India. The second large convoy from Bombay was entering the Red Sea, and the Wessex Territorial Division was due, outward bound. The latter had even to be held up at Port Said till adequate patrols could be established against the threatened danger, not only on the line of passage, but also in the Gulf of Akaba, at the head of which the Turks were concentrating troops, and apparently intended to establish a flotilla base. So inflammable was the situation that the War Office ordered our outposts at El Arish and Nekhl to be withdrawn, but on October 27 the Wessex Division was allowed to sail under escort of the *Dupleix*. Next day 2000 Bedouins were reported to be advancing on the Canal from Nekhl, and it was quickly recognised that the crisis was at hand.

The truth was that the Germans had come to realise that the hour had arrived when the hand of the reluctant ministers must be forced. Owing to the judicious way the almost hopeless situation had been handled at Constantinople, the Entente Powers were still holding their own. The Grand Vizier and the Heir Apparent were as stubbornly opposed to the Germans as ever, and so was the truculent Jemal Pasha, Minister of Marine, out of his professed sympathy with France and his personal antipathy to Enver Pasha. The majority of the Ministers, indeed, were inclined the same way, and so sullen and widespread was the anti-German feeling which our Ambassador and his colleagues were fostering that the Germans saw it could not be overcome by fair means. Accordingly, they and their apt pupil, Enver Pasha, fell back on the notorious Prussian device. Sir Louis Mallet some weeks earlier had warned our Foreign Office that he might be beaten by the Ministers being unable to prevent the *Goeben* committing an act of provocation in the Black Sea, and his apprehension was well founded. In the last days of the month Admiral Souchon, without saying a word to Jemal and without the knowledge of the opposing Ministers, suddenly took the combined German-Turkish Fleet into the Black Sea. On October 29 the

Ministers received a wireless message from the German Admiral to say that his flotilla had been treacherously attacked by the Russian Fleet, and that in retaliation he had bombarded some of the Russian coast towns. The message was false—no such attack had taken place—, it was all an unscrupulous device to force the hand of the Turkish Government.

So glaring, indeed, was the pretence, that the Germans themselves did not adhere to it. Another justification was afterwards put forward, entirely different and equally false. The *Breslau* and the Turkish cruiser *Hamidieh* had gone to sea first with a division of destroyers, and the *Goeben* followed with two minelayers. The new story was designed to give the impression that in the morning of October 28 they encountered the Russian minelayer *Prut*, with a couple of destroyers, about to lay a minefield in territorial waters off the entrance of the Bosporus so as to prevent the two sections of the Turkish Fleet uniting. As this was an act of war, the *Goeben*, it was asserted, sank her by gun-fire on the spot and took her crew prisoners, to the number of three officers and seventy-two men, and proceeded at once to attack the Russian coast.[1]

What really happened was that after steaming eastward about 100 miles, presumably to join the *Breslau* and *Hamidieh*, Admiral Souchon headed himself for Sevastopol with a mine-layer, while the rest of his ships made for other objectives. The Russian Fleet, as he knew, had just returned there to coal after a cruise, and during the night of the 29th he proceeded to mine them in. Then with two destroyers sweeping in front of him, he began to draw in in order to bombard the port. But before he was in really effective range he was fired on, and after a fifteen minutes' bombardment at long range he was hit three times and made off. The Russian Fleet was in no position to pursue, but three destroyers gave chase, and before they were shaken off had killed fourteen men on board the *Goeben* by gun-fire.[2] Admiral Souchon, according to the plan he had conceived, was now making for the Strait of Kertch, where another minefield was to be laid, and on the way he fell in with a large ship of 5,500 tons. This was the *Prut*, which, according to the Russian Staff Report, was at this time a transport and unarmed.[3] She tried to run herself ashore, but her commander, Lieutenant Roguzski,

---

[1] Ludwig: *Die Fahrten der Goeben und der Breslau,* pp. 87, *et seq.*; Otto von Gottberg, *Kreuzerfahrten und U-Boots Taten,* p. 73.

[2] Ludwig, p. 98.

[3] *Morskoi Sbornik,* December 1914.

finding it impossible to escape, opened his Kingstons, blew a hole in the bottom of his ship and perished with her. The prisoners that were taken were the survivors rescued from the water by the Turkish destroyers.[1]

The *Prut* story, therefore, affords no better justification of the cynical attack than the other. She was not a mine-layer, she was not caught off the Bosporus, nor was she encountered till after the treacherous bombardment had taken place not only at Sevastopol but elsewhere. For the *Goeben's* crime was intensified by what the other ships were doing. While the Admiral was before Sevastopol, some of the destroyers were raiding the harbour of Odessa, where they surprised and torpedoed a gunboat and damaged the electric works before they were driven off. The *Breslau* and *Hamidieh* went north-east, and after bombarding the open town of Theodosia in the Crimea, they proceeded to Novorossisk, an oil port on the Circassian coast. There a gunboat had preceded them with a summons to surrender, and on the demand being refused they together bombarded the place for two hours, and practically destroyed it, with its oil tanks and all the shipping in the port. Having thus ruthlessly involved the Turks in unpardonable outrage, the ships returned severally to Constantinople.

The news of what had happened, as it was falsely telegraphed by the German Admiral, threw the Ministers into a state of great agitation. The Allied Ambassadors had just demanded an explanation of the Bedouin raid across the Egyptian frontier. The Ministers could give none, for they denied all knowledge of it; but as to the naval incident, since they had not yet fathomed the shamelessness of their protector, they could not doubt the Admiral's word, and ended in endorsing his action. Still the Allied Ambassadors, suspecting a trick, counselled patience, and it was in this highly critical situation that the British Cabinet consented to keep the loss of *Audacious* secret for a time. In the evening of the 30th, however, Sir Louis Mallet was instructed to present an ultimatum. It was to the effect that unless the Turkish Government dissociated themselves from the unprovoked acts of hostility on Russia by carrying out their repeated promises to remove the crews of the *Goeben* and *Breslau*, and undertook to do this within twelve hours, he was to ask for his passports. Before the time expired the fleet had returned, and the German trick was laid bare. It was quickly found that Admiral Souchon's story would not bear

[1] The German Official History states that the *Prut* was sunk by gunfire and that her commanding officer was included among the 75 survivors.

24

a moment's examination. A stormy meeting of the Ministers followed, at which the Grand Vizier and his friends struggled passionately to retrace the fatal step. In the end a resolution in favour of neutrality was carried, but one for dismissing the German officers was lost. There was still some hope that the sullen weight of opinion behind the Grand Vizier and the Minister of Marine might yet save the situation, but it was quickly shattered by the action of the Russian Imperial Government. Not for the first time, they took a grave step regardless of their Allies. On September 18 they had concluded an agreement with Rumania which had never been communicated to London nor, so far as is known, to Paris. Now they went still further, and without a word to anybody they declared war on Turkey. This independent *démarche* was, in the circumstances, not unexpected, and it had been so far anticipated that both the French and British Ambassadors had received instructions to follow the lead of their Russian colleague. Accordingly, on November 1 they left Constantinople, and in pursuance of the terms of the joint ultimatum delivered the previous evening, Admiral Carden was given orders to commence hostilities.

So Sir Louis Mallet's prolonged struggle ended in defeat, but much had been gained. With the scales weighted against him by the requisition of the two Dreadnoughts and the failure to stop the *Goeben*, and with his eyes open to the insidious character of the opposition that surrounded him, he had by skill and patience postponed the evil day till Egypt was safe and the Navy had secured the Eastern highway. As the two highest authorities in the British Government and those most nearly concerned declared, when all the facts were before them, he had fought a splendid rear-guard action, and its value to the Empire was as great as the struggle had been desperate.

Since September 20, when Admiral Carden had been appointed to the Mediterranean command, he had been watching the Dardanelles. The *Indomitable* had rejoined the *Indefatigable*, and he had also the French battleships *Vérité* and *Suffren*, and the light cruisers *Dublin* and *Gloucester*, with three submarines, twelve destroyers, and their parent ship *Blenheim*. The *Defence*, as we have seen, had been sent to Admiral Stoddart. Of the three remaining ships of the 1st Cruiser Squadron, the *Black Prince* and *Duke of Edinburgh* were on escort duty in the Red Sea, and the *Warrior* on guard at Alexandria as senior officer's ship in Egyptian waters, and to these minor services these three fine ships had been tied, notwithstanding the critical situation in South

American waters.[1] With the Home Authorities there was still a forlorn hope that a prompt demonstration by the Dardanelles squadron might yet cause a reaction against German influence and save the situation. Accordingly, late on November 1, while the battle of Coronel was being fought, Admiral Carden was instructed, on the earliest suitable day, to bombard the outer Dardanelles forts with his armoured ships at a range which would render the Turkish guns innocuous.

Already on the previous day, in anticipation of hostilities, he had received authority to cut out a minelayer which was reported to be in the Gulf of Smyrna, and two destroyers, *Wolverine* and *Scorpion*, were detached for the purpose on November 1. On entering the Gulf they found a large armed yacht lying at Vourlah Jetty. On her being summoned to come out she was set on fire by her own people, and burned so rapidly that there was nothing to do but sink her by gunfire. Half a dozen heavy explosions which occurred before she went down proclaimed her to be a minelayer, and a smaller vessel alongside, which seemed to be carrying mines, was destroyed by similar explosions. The destroyers rejoined the flag on November 2.[2]

At dawn next day, November 3, Admiral Carden approached the Dardanelles to carry out the bombardment. He himself, with the two battle cruisers, took the batteries at Sedd-el-Bahr and Cape Helles on the European side of the entrance, while the French battleships dealt with those on the opposite side at Kum Kale and Orkanieh. Each group of ships made one run at long range, lasting about ten minutes, during which time the British fired forty-six rounds of 12″ and the French thirty rounds. The practice was very good; salvo after salvo fell into the forts, while, though the Turkish fire came near, no ship was hit. Towards the end of the run a violent explosion was seen on the European side, and Admiral Carden withdrew.

The actual results were, of course, difficult to ascertain, but Mr. Palmer, our Vice-Consul at Chanak, was able to give some idea of it. The magazine at Sedd-el-Bahr certainly blew up, and an American ship, which came out shortly afterwards, reported the fort in ruins. At Kum Kale, though

---

[1] On November 1, the day Coronel was fought, an Admiralty memorandum pointed out that the best value was not being obtained from these ships, and directed that as soon as possible they should be relieved by older light cruisers from the Irish Station and reconstituted as a squadron for Home Waters.

[2] The German account states that a Turkish gunboat and two transports were destroyed on this occasion.

the material damage was less, the casualties were severe. The highest estimate was 600, the lowest 150, including 40 Germans. Turkish officers reported the men to have been demoralised by the accuracy of the fire, but the moral effect was purely local. At Constantinople it was put about that the ships had been driven off, and as the attack was not renewed it is to be feared that the impression made was rather the reverse of what had been intended.

Simultaneously steps of less doubtful import were being taken for the security of Egypt. At Port Said was the *Black Prince*, who, since she had brought up her convoy from India, had been engaged with the *Warrior* in taking possession of the enemy ships which had sought refuge in the Canal at the outbreak of war to the number of twelve large German steamers, including the Norddeutscher Lloyd *Derfflinger* of 9000 tons, and one smaller one, as well as two large and one small Austrian. She was now ordered to relieve the *Warrior* at Alexandria, and Captain Borrett, in the *Warrior*, was instructed to proceed off El Arish, stop any troops advancing on the coast road, and generally to act in place of the withdrawn outpost. The *Minerva*, which with the *Northbrook* had arrived on October 30 with a convoy containing the Ist Indian Cavalry Division, was ordered to Akaba on similar service. Two destroyers were sent to Port Sudan as a patrol against minelayers, and the Malta torpedo boats were ordered to the Canal to relieve the patrol destroyers for more active duty.

These arrangements sufficiently secured the situation for the time, but no one could foretell how much heavier the intervention of Turkey would make our naval responsibilities in the Eastern Mediterranean. The new war, which was actually declared on November 5, meant an immeasurable complication of the duties of the fleet, and it asserted itself as a culmination of all the rest at the moment when the new Board learned that the whole existing scheme of distribution had been thrown out of gear by Admiral Cradock's defeat. Apart from fresh anxieties in Home Waters and the Mediterranean, every vulnerable point all over the world lay exposed to a telling blow from Admiral von Spee. It was widely felt that, whatever the cause, the whole problem created by the existence of his squadron had not been successfully managed, and nothing but the widest grasp, a bold realisation and acceptance of risks and the utmost promptitude of action could avail to restore our command.

But the Admiralty were equal to the occasion. At all costs the exposed positions must be protected; and not only this— at all costs the danger must be ended once for all. It must be seen to, that whatever might be Admiral von Spee's objective, in whatever quarter he might choose to appear he should find himself confronted with a squadron not merely superior, but so superior as to leave no possible doubt as to the result. All chance of failure must be eliminated and a blow given so prompt and decisive as to bury the memory of all past miscarriages. The material, if rightly used, was sufficient. Already on the day the new Board had taken over their duties they had done their best to mend the faulty disposition they had found by immediately ordering the *Defence* to obey Admiral Cradock's orders to join him. It was, of course, too late. Not till November 3 did she arrive at Montevideo, and next day the news of the disaster reached the Admiralty. Their first step was to order Admiral Stoddart to concentrate his armoured ships, *Carnarvon* and *Cornwall*, on the *Defence* at Montevideo, and at the same time the *Canopus*, *Glasgow* and *Otranto*, whose fate was not yet known, were told to go there too, without making the Falklands, if they possibly could. The *Kent* from the Canary–Cape Verde Station was also directed to join as had been originally intended. In company with the *Highflyer* she had been hunting for the *Karlsruhe*, on persistent reports that that ship had been seen on the Moorish coast. She had just come to Sierra Leone to coal, and was able to start next day. So much was done for the immediate safety of the ships which had survived the action and to protect the trade which was most directly exposed. For the moment the Falklands were abandoned in order to secure the essential concentration at the immediately critical point, but it was only for the moment.

On the same afternoon drastic steps were taken to deliver the retaliatory blow. In the utmost secrecy Admiral Jellicoe was called on to send two of his battle cruisers, *Invincible* and *Inflexible*, to Berehaven for urgent foreign service. The Admiral commanding the 2nd Battle Cruiser Squadron to which they belonged was to shift his flag to the *New Zealand*, for the *Invincible* was now to carry that of Admiral Sturdee. He was now handing over the duties of Chief of the Staff which he had carried out since the beginning of the war. For he it was who had been selected to command this splendid force and restore the situation. To further his mission he was given the fullest powers. His command indeed was unprecedented, embracing as it did a wider extent of sea than had ever yet been committed to a single admiral. He went out as Commander-in-Chief in the South Atlantic and Pacific. In the Atlantic his northern limit was 5° north latitude—that is, the line from the north of Brazil to Liberia; but if the movements of the enemy should cause him to come north of that line the Admiral of any station he entered would come under his orders. The idea was that he should proceed with the utmost dispatch to South America, take Admiral Stoddart under his command, and carry on with the concentrated force to the key position at the Falklands to seek out and destroy the enemy. With such a squadron he could count on being able to deal decisively with Admiral von Spee if he came south to break into the Atlantic. If, however, he should go north, either to pass through the Panama Canal or attack Canadian territory or Japanese trade, it was intended he should encounter a no less formidable opposition. The *Newcastle* and *Idzumo* were already there, the *Asama* and *Hizen* were at Honolulu watching the *Geier*, and Admiral Patey, in the *Australia*, was at Suva with a fast collier which he was keeping intact in anticipation of the orders he now received. The Admiralty plan was for the *Idzumo* and *Newcastle* to come south as far as San Clemente Island, off the south end of California. There, unless later information of the German movements permitted a more southerly concentration, the *Hizen* would meet them and also the *Australia*. Admiral Patey on arrival would take command of the new squadron, which would then move south to find the enemy. To this project the Japanese agreed, and not only this, but they also expressed their readiness to send their First South Sea Squadron to replace Admiral Patey between Fiji and the Marquesas in case the Germans should break back. They even went beyond their word; for on November 8, when the American authorities at Honolulu finally interned the *Geier* and her tender, the Japanese ordered both the *Hizen* and *Asama* to proceed to San Clemente. They also reinforced their First South Sea Squadron with another armoured cruiser, so that it now comprised *Kurama*, *Tsukuba* and *Iwate*, and was superior to that of the Germans.

The Pacific, as well as our South American trade, was thus well provided for, but in South-West Africa lay another possible objective at which Admiral von Spee might strike. It offered a promising field, and was now quite inadequately guarded. De Wet and other Boer leaders were still keeping alive the embers of the rebellion which General Botha's victory had damped down, and the appearance of the German Squadron on the coast in superior force would certainly fan the flames and as certainly upset all the Union plans for the conquest of German South-West Africa. There was no time to spare, and the day the news of Coronel arrived the *Goliath* and *Dartmouth*, which were on the East African Station looking after the *Königsberg*, were ordered to join the *Albion* at the Cape.   But as two days later it was found that the battleship could not start at once, other arrangements were made. The only ship of force which could arrive as soon as Admiral von Spee was the *Minotaur* (Captain Kiddle).   She had left St. George's Sound on November 1 in charge of the Australian Convoy, with the two light cruisers *Melbourne* and *Sydney* and the Japanese battle cruiser *Ibuki*.   Now that the German squadron had been located so far away it was impossible for any one to contend that so powerful an escort was necessary, and on November 6 Captain Kiddle was ordered to leave the convoy in charge of Captain Silver of the *Melbourne*, and take his ship by way of Mauritius to reinforce the Cape Squadron.

Had this arrangement stood alone it would have left the South-West African coast with a squadron whose constitution was as defective as that of Admiral Cradock.   It was good enough to defend the exposed bases of the Union Expedition, but if concentrated it would not have speed enough to force an action on Admiral von Spee.   But, in fact, it was only part of the disposition that was actually made, for it was combined with certain steps which had to be taken to guard the waters to the northward.   Besides our West Coast Colonies there was the Cameroons Expedition, which was still in progress and might possibly furnish an objective for Admiral von Spee.[1]   During the past month substantial progress had been made.   In the extreme north our Maidugari column had succeeded in joining hands with the French, and reinforced by them with about 500 Europeans and natives and a couple of guns, had, by a concerted operation, driven the enemy out of the whole of the Lake Chad region down to the 11th degree of latitude.   Here, however, the Germans held a strongly entrenched position at Mora, and the French commandant sat down before it to await reinforcements.   It was clear, therefore, that the complete reduction of the colony must be a prolonged affair, since in the south the enemy clung to their baffling policy of retiring into the Hinterland as the pressure on the coast increased.   On October 12 another mixed column had started up the river from Duala for a second attempt on Ybassi.   It was about the same strength as the first, but this time a clever surprise was effected by landing the troops on both banks, with the main force on the opposite bank to that which had been tried before.   The result was

[1] See Map 16 in case.

that on the 14th the place was occupied with very little loss and left in charge of a garrison, while the flotilla returned to Duala. Meanwhile, the *Bruix* and *Surprise* were down the coast bombarding the ports Kampo and Kribi, but without landing. They then proceeded northward to the Nyong River, where they found the *Ivy* had already effected a landing and destroyed the telephone. She was, in fact, engaged with the flotilla in making a thorough survey of that and the Sanaga River in preparation for the next important operation. Its objective was Edea, and the plan was of some elaboration in order to obtain a concentric movement. While a French column with a British naval 12-pounder was to advance along the railway, two flotilla columns with allied troops would converge on the place from the south-west and south. The first, with which went the *Mole*, the 6″ gun lighter, the armed tugs *Remus*, *Sir Frederick* and *Porpoise* and the dispatch vessel *Vigilant*, was to move up the Sanaga River, the larger vessels from the sea and the lighters, one with 150 British troops, direct from the Duala Estuary by the Kwakwa Creek, which joins the Sanaga River at a mission station called Lobetal. Here the two sections would combine. The main body of the troops, to the number of about 1000 French infantry and as many carriers under Colonel Mayer, was to go by the Nyong River in six transports, escorted by the *Cumberland*, *Dwarf* and *Surprise*, and to proceed by river as high as Dehane, some twenty miles south of Edea.

One great advantage of the scheme was that the Germans believed that Edea could not be approached from this side by any serious force. It was only the admirable and patient survey work that made it possible, and even so the navigational difficulties were so great that progress was slow. It was on October 20, after the Northern Railway had been cut six miles up by a small British force sent to occupy Maka, that a start was made. The Kwakwa column left early, and the rest at sundown, and next day the main or Nyong column succeeded in crossing the bar, but not without loss. A German prize tug that was towing the 6″ gun lighter took the ground and had to be abandoned, and to prevent further delay the lighter was sent back to Duala with the *Dwarf*. But this was not all. A whaler, in which was Captain Fuller with some of the chief staff officers, capsized in crossing the bar, and the Director of the Nigerian Marine and two other very valuable lives were lost.[1] Still, it was a fine piece of

[1] Lieutenant H. A. Child, R.N. (Retd.), Director of the Nigerian Marine; Commander S. B. Gray, R.N.R. (Retd.), Chief Transport Officer; Captain A. A. Franqueville of the French Military Staff.

work, considering that ships of the size of the transports had never been known to enter the river before.   So rapidly was the feat performed that the advanced guard of the French was able to start up the river the same evening towards Dehane.   The success was only emphasised by what happened to the Sanaga column.   It, too, arrived off the river to time, but in the bad weather that prevailed was unable to attempt crossing the bar till next day.   As for the Kwakwa column, it met with such sharp opposition from entrenchments short of Lobetal that it decided to retire for the night.

This, however, was the last check.   On the 22nd the Nyong column, in spite of every kind of navigational difficulty, was able to occupy Dehane, and next morning began to advance on Edea, leaving a small British garrison behind it. The same day (the 23rd) the Kwakwa column, having evacuated its wounded at Duala, tried again, and this time reached Lobetal unopposed and occupied it.   Simultaneously the Yapoma column began to advance along the railway.   The following morning the Sanaga column, after bombarding suspicious points at the entrance of the Kwakwa creeks without drawing any reply, joined hands with the Kwakwa column at Lobetal, and next day began its advance towards Edea on both banks of the river.   Twice, so thick was the bush, the troops had to be re-embarked.   About midday on the 26th, as they were seeking a final landing-place amidst loud demonstrations of friendliness from the natives, they heard that the Nyong column had occupied Edea a few hours earlier. It afterwards transpired that the sound of the 6″ gun at Lobetal, combined with the surprising news that a large force had reached Dehane by river, was too much for the fortitude of the garrison, and that they had retired hastily by rail and road eastward towards Yaunde, which lies up the Nyong river about 100 miles above Edea.   It was not till next day that the Yapoma column, which had been delayed by breaches in the railway, arrived to join hands with the other two.

So at small cost, thanks to the well-combined plan which the surveying officers had made possible, the surprise had been effected.   The operation was a complete and almost bloodless success, and no sooner was it ended than preparations were begun for treating Buea and the Northern Railway in a similar manner.   In the meantime, however, it was necessary to do something for the Ybassi garrison.   The Germans had been showing increased activity, and on November 1 a small column was sent to relieve it.   This was successfully done on the 3rd, but as the river was rapidly falling and water

transport would soon be impossible, it was decided to withdraw
the garrison temporarily. The evacuation was carried out
on the 9th, and nothing left but a minor post at the junction
of the Dibamba River with the Wuri, twelve miles below
Ybassi. While this was going on the *Ivy* and *Vigilant*
looked into the various small ports lower down from Kribi
to Kampo and, sending parties ashore, destroyed or removed
all the telephones with little or no opposition.

From the impunity with which these operations were
carried on it was clear the Germans had practically abandoned
the coast, but the power of reaction they had been displaying
emphasised the need of keeping up the pressure. The new
combined operations against Buea were to begin on November 10, and the latest experience had shown how much
depended on naval co-operation. But since the fall of Edea
the Admiralty had been pressing more strongly than ever
for the release of the *Cumberland* in order to complete their
distribution to meet Admiral von Spee. To this General
Dobell urgently demurred. The *Pothuau* was coming to
relieve the *Bruix*, and as her captain was senior to the captain
of the *Challenger* it would mean change in the naval command.
Seeing in what cordial harmony he was acting with Captain
Fuller, the General regarded such a change as highly undesirable—a view in which the captain of the *Bruix* concurred.
Not only were the *Cumberland's* 6″ guns essential to success,
but as the main part of the combined work fell to the Nigerian
Marine it was highly inconvenient not to have a British
officer in command. Eventually, on General Dobell's repeated entreaties, representations in this sense were made to
the French Government, who readily agreed that the *Pothuau*
should pay no more than a flying visit for the present. Till the
end of November the existing arrangement was to stand.
Not till then was it possible for Admiral von Spee to appear,
but by that date the *Cumberland* was to have all her main
armament on board again ready to join the new West Coast
Squadron which it had been decided to form.

This was the furthest to which the Admiralty could go.
It was necessary to provide ere long for the area, and ships
were very hard to find. The Cape Verde Squadron, deprived
as it was of the *Kent*, could lend but little assistance. Indeed,
it was in obvious danger itself. The only possibility was to
draw upon the Mediterranean, and there at the moment ships
could ill be spared. It had already been decided in principle
that, to make up for Admiral Jellicoe's loss of the two battle
cruisers, the whole of the 1st Cruiser Squadron was to join
him. In any case, two such fine ships as the *Black Prince*

and *Warrior* were wasted as guardships for Egypt, and on November 6 they were ordered to proceed to Gibraltar, the French consenting to supply their place till other British ships arrived.   Two of their older units, the battleship *Bouvet* and the cruiser *Amiral Charner*, were told off for the service, and to relieve them the *Vengeance* had been called down from the Channel, the *Doris* from the Irish Station and the *Proserpine* from the Gibraltar Patrol.

Urgent as was the call of the Grand Fleet for the 1st Cruiser Squadron, the *Warrior* and *Black Prince* were not to join it at once.   The plan was that they should first form, with three French ships of similar type, a new squadron for the Southern Atlantic.   It was to be under a French Admiral, and was to sweep down the African coast so as to protect the weak Cape Verde Squadron, the French and British West Coast Colonies and the Cameroons, and if Admiral von Spee tried to strike north of the German South-West African Colony to drive him on to Admiral King-Hall's squadron.   On the proposal being laid before the French Government, they referred it to Admiral de Lapeyrère, their Commander-in-Chief in the Mediterranean, but he was only able to express his great regret that he could not spare the ships, and we had to rest on our own resources.   Admiral de Robeck was therefore directed to shift his flag to the *Warrior*, and, taking the *Black Prince*, *Donegal* and *Highflyer* under his orders, to proceed to Sierra Leone and await orders.   Here he would be able to call on the *Cumberland* if necessary, and so a fifth squadron was provided superior to that of the Germans.

This arrangement was not completed till November 12, and on that day the last link in the vast chain was forged. The only area that had remained unprovided for was the North American and West Indies Station, which Admiral von Spee might possibly strike through the Panama Canal. By the rules which governed its international status it was permitted for three warships of any one nation to pass through at one time, while three others, even of the same nation, could wait at either end.[1]   It was therefore possible for Admiral von Spee to take his squadron through without seriously breaking his concentration.   As it was also known that he

[1] The 10th Rule, established by President Wilson's proclamation of November 13, provided that " there shall not be, except by special arrangement, at any one time a greater number of vessels of war of any one nation including those of the allies of a belligerent nation, than three in either terminal port and its adjacent terminal waters, or than three in transit through the Canal; nor shall the total number of such vessels, at any one time, exceed six in all the territorial waters of the Canal Zone under the jurisdiction of the United States."

had put into Valparaiso with the *Scharnhorst, Gneisenau* and *Nürnberg* after the action, and had left again the following day (November 4), it was possible he could reach Panama before Admiral Patey, with the new North Pacific Squadron, could get into position to stop him.

In such an event the West Indian Division, as well as allied ports in the islands, would be in danger. Besides his own ship, the *Berwick*, Captain Clinton-Baker, who was still in command of the division, had only the *Essex, Condé* and *Descartes*. In the New York area Admiral Hornby had his flag in the *Glory*, which had just rejoined from escort duty with the Canadian convoy, and besides he had the *Lancaster, Suffolk, Caronia* and the Canadian cruiser *Niobe*. The two divisions, if concentrated, might together be able to give a good account of the German squadron; single-handed, neither could face it, nor could either area be left unwatched. In this difficulty Admiral Hornby's orders were to watch the Canal from November 12 onwards with two of his fastest cruisers, which were to keep touch with the enemy should he appear, but were not to get engaged with superior force.

These orders were issued on November 8, at which time Captain Clinton-Baker was about to search certain points in the Caribbean Sea where the *Karlsruhe* was reported to have a base. The probability of her appearing in those waters was increased by the fact that on November 2 the captain of the *Vandyck*, a new 10,000 ton ship of the Lamport and Holt Line, reached Para and reported that he had been captured by her on October 26 between Ceara and Maranham.[1] We now know that Captain Köhler was actually on his way to raid Barbados and Fort de France in Martinique. At the British island he would have found no ship to meet him, but Fortune was weary of her favourite, and after bestowing the finest windfall that had yet fallen to his lot, deserted him.

On October 26, the day after he left his old ground and was approaching the track from Trinidad to Brazil, he was surprised to sight the high white superstructures of a large passenger ship, and by noon she was captured. This was the *Vandyck*, then bound from Buenos Aires to New York, and, besides over 200 passengers, mostly American, she was carrying mails, treasure and a rich general cargo, including 1000 tons of frozen meat. It was an extraordinary stroke of fortune. Having been warned by the *Bristol* after passing Rio, she was keeping away from the route, and using no light or wireless. It was a pure chance that the *Karlsruhe* fell in with her in changing

[1] See Map 12 in case.

stations, and the worst of it was that she was by far the finest prize the lucky raider had yet encountered. The ship was retained till she could be gutted, but next day (October 27) the passengers, together with the crews of the last two prizes taken on the old ground, *Glanton* and *Hurstdale*, were crowded into the *Asuncion*, which was sent away to Para with orders not to make the port till November 1. During the night, as the *Karlsruhe* was taking in provisions from the *Vandyck*, another ship came quietly up to them and was taken. She was the *Royal Sceptre* of London, with a cargo of coffee valued at a quarter of a million; but it was neutral, and as the ship was old and worn out they had to let her go. At daylight the *Vandyck* was sunk.

Captain Köhler then proceeded on his way. His intention was, besides making surprise attacks on British and French possessions, to disturb the trade routes to Trinidad and Barbados. It was at the latter place he meant to make his first attempt. He knew there were several large passenger steamers lying there, and was calculating on a resounding blow to our prestige like those which the *Emden* had dealt in the East Indies. On November 1 he coaled from the *Farn*, and, leaving her behind, carried on for his objective with the *Rio Negro* and *Indrani*. By sunset on November 4 they were only 300 miles short of Barbados, and in high expectation of what lay before them. Captain Köhler was on the fore-bridge, and the greater part of the crew were assembled forward to listen to the band, when suddenly a terrible explosion shattered the ship. There were cries of " Torpedoed," but as the flame and smoke cleared it was seen that the whole fore part had been blown off, and with it had gone the captain, one lieutenant and 259 petty officers and men. For twenty minutes more the after-part floated— just long enough for the tenders to take off all the survivors, to the number of 17 officers and 129 petty officers and men— and then all was over.[1] The cause of the tragedy is a mystery that cannot be solved, nor was it till a month later, when the *Rio Negro* with the survivors succeeded in evading our blockade and reaching home, that it was known even in Germany that the *Karlsruhe* was no longer a danger to our trade. Even then her fate was kept secret, and for long after she had ceased to exist she continued to occupy our cruisers and hamper our dispositions. The measure of success she had achieved was too great for her possibilities of further damage to be ignored. In the three months of her career as a commerce raider she had taken or sunk sixteen British

[1] The cause of the explosion has never been ascertained.

vessels, and one Dutch on British charter. Their gross burden totalled over 76,000 tons. The value of ships and cargo was over a million and a half, and with our West Indian cruisers preoccupied with watching the Canal, she might well have added considerably to the total. As it was, by the time the great combination for dealing with Admiral von Spee was well on foot, one source of complication was removed, and within a few days at the other end of the world another clearance had been made.

Since the daring raid on Penang on October 28 the *Emden* had not been heard of, but on the same principles of co-ordinating all the available material in a comprehensive scheme for her destruction, a disposition had been worked out for the Indian Ocean from which she had even less chance of escape than had Admiral von Spee. It was not done without difficulty, for in the same theatre of operations there were two other preoccupations which could not be neglected, and in a measure tended to cramp the combination against the *Emden*. The first was the failure of the expedition against Tanga in German East Africa.[1] On October 31 the *Goliath* and *Hardinge* had arrived at Mombasa from India with the Bangalore and Imperial Service Brigades, and here, unfortunately, the *Goliath* broke down, so that when on November 2 the expedition reached its objective it had nothing but the *Fox* to support it, for the *Chatham, Dartmouth* and *Weymouth* were absorbed in the first efforts to get at the *Königsberg* in the Rufiji River. Still, the landing at Tanga was successfully effected. On the 4th it was completed, and an advance on the town began. During the attack, however, owing partly perhaps to insufficient artillery support from the sea, the raw troops were not able to face the fire they met, and so complete was the rout that there was nothing to do but bring them away. This was very cleverly managed without the enemy's knowledge, and by the 6th the troops were all in their transports again.

It was at best a most regrettable affair. The work of rendering the *Königsberg* impotent, which the Admiralty had directed was to take precedence of all military considerations, however urgent, had better success. The first object of the operations, which were under Captain Drury-Lowe of the *Chatham*, was to block her in, and this he proposed to do by sinking the collier *Newbridge* in the mouth of the branch up which she lay. On November 6 the *Kinfauns Castle* arrived with a seaplane, with which the enemy's position could be determined. At daylight on November 10 the collier was

[1] See Map 7 in case.

taken in by Commander Fitzmaurice of the *Chatham,* escorted by the armed steamer *Duplex,* and the steamboats of the three cruisers armed and protected. On entering the river they came under a hot fire of Q.F. and machine-guns which the guns of the ships could not subdue, but in spite of it they carried on, and succeeded in sinking the blockship fairly across the channel and getting off the men with very few casualties. Having by this skilful operation imprisoned the *Königsberg,* at least for the time, the next step was to endeavour to destroy her. But this was no easy matter. She lay so high up amongst the tall jungle that fringed the river that the cruisers' guns could not reach her and gunboats could not see her. She could only be got at with the aid of troops or by bombing. But no troops were available, and the seaplane that had been sent was unequal to bombing attack. Till better machines could be procured or troops became available, nothing further could be done. But the cruisers had still to remain to blockade the river, not only to prevent supplies reaching the *Königsberg* but to see she did not clear the obstruction and break out.

On this side of the Indian Ocean, therefore, the situation was far from satisfactory, and no end could be seen to the preoccupation it was causing. On the Asiatic side, where lay the other preoccupation, there was quite another story to tell. For there had been carried out one of the best-managed combined operations of the war.

Since the end of September it had become clear that in view of the increasing hostility of Turkey something definite must be done to uphold our interests in the Persian Gulf, and particularly to protect the refinery and pipe line of the Anglo-Persian Oil Company, in which the Government had recently acquired a large interest. The terminal and refinery had been established at Abadan, an island which lies in the Shatt-al-Arab—that is, in the channel by which the Tigris and Euphrates reach the sea after their junction at Kurnah. So great were the interests at stake that no sooner was the danger realised than it was decided to send up a military force to the Gulf by way of a demonstration to check German propaganda amongst the Arabs. But it was obvious that it must be done in such a way as not to alienate the Sheikhs or prejudice the delicate situation at Constantinople by committing a provocative act against Turkish territory. At the same time it was necessary that the force should be of considerable strength, and that it should be on the spot ready to act before anything was known of its movements. It was decided, therefore, to detail the whole of the VIth Indian

Division, and to send off one of its brigades under Brigadier-
General W. S. Delamain, with the next Indian Convoy
as though it was required for Egypt.[1] When well to sea it
would break off and proceed straight to the *place d'armes*
that had been selected. This was the island of Bahrein, which
lies in a bight on the south side of the Gulf, midway between
the entrance and the Shatt-al-Arab.[2] It had been claimed at
various times by Turkey, Persia, and ourselves, but now,
although not actually a British Protectorate, we had a Political
Agent established there, and the Sheikh had practically
entrusted his foreign relations to the Indian Government.
Only 250 miles from the Shatt-al-Arab, it was well-situated
as a *place d'armes*, but so long as the *Königsberg* or the
Emden was at large it would require naval cover.

The key of the situation in the Gulf area was the ancient
and still famous port of Basra in the Shatt-al-Arab, a little
above Abadan, and it was likely enough that one or both of
these cruisers might seek to repeat there the part which the
Goeben had been playing so successfully at Constantinople
ever since she had found it impossible to keep the sea. What
gave colour to this possibility was that the Turks were protesting with all the effrontery of their German masters against
the ships of our Gulf Division remaining in what they called
Turkish waters. The division now consisted of three ships,
which had been ordered to patrol the Shatt-al-Arab. In the
middle of October, when after the Allies' failure to save
Antwerp, things looked specially critical in the Bosporus,
the sloop *Espiègle* (Commander Nunn), which had been taken
away from the Colombo area just before the *Emden* appeared,
was in the Karun River off the friendly Persian town of
Muhammera, below Basra [3]; the Indian Marine ship *Dalhousie*, which had been guarding the oil works at Abadan, had
come out of the river to establish a watch at the entrance
of the Gulf, while the sloop *Odin* (Commander Wason) was
outside the outer bar of the Shatt-al-Arab; but as all of
them were too inferior to the *Emden* to afford the cover the
expedition required, it was arranged to give it the support
of a battleship. In this case, of course, where, as at Luderitz
Bay, it was a question of covering a combined expedition, the
device was unexceptionable. The ship selected was the *Ocean*,

---

[1] 16th Brigade: 2nd Bn. Dorset Regt., 104th (Wellesley's) Rifles,
20th Infantry, 117th Mahrattas, and H.Q. and two batteries of the 1st.
Brigade, Indian Mountain Artillery.

[2] See Map p. 394.

[3] Though nominally a Persian subject the Sheikh of Muhammera was
at least semi-independent, and in 1910 we had given him a special assurance
against infraction of his autonomy by Persia or any other Power.

which had just reached Aden from Gibraltar, and Captain Hayes-Sadler, who commanded her, was to be in charge of the naval operations.

On October 16 the Gulf transports sailed in company with the main convoy for France and the Mombasa Expeditionary Force. The first or Bombay section of the great combined convoy was escorted by the *Swiftsure, Goliath* and *Dufferin,* and the second or Karachi section by the *Duke of Edinburgh* and *Hardinge.* On the third day out, at the rendezvous where the two sections came together, the *Ocean* met them, and she with the *Dufferin* and the Gulf contingent parted company, while the *Goliath* and *Hardinge* went off with the East African Force. Reaching Bahrein on October 23, the Gulf Expedition waited there till on the 30th news came of the German attack in the Black Sea. General Delamain was immediately ordered on to the Shatt-al-Arab, and the India Office directed that a second brigade was to be got ready to follow him. Next day, the 31st, the Admiralty sent authority to commence hostilities against Turkey, together with special operation orders for the disposition of the ships. The *Espiègle* was to come down to protect the oil works, the *Odin* to remain off the bar, and the *Dalhousie* to be at Bushire as a wireless link with the Indian cable. By the evening of November 3, the day the Dardanelles forts were bombarded, the convoy was off the outer bar, which the *Ocean* could not cross, and Captain Hayes-Sadler devoted the following day to arming the tugs and launches, fitting the minesweepers, and to general preparations for forcing a passage past the guns which guarded the entrance of the river near the old Turkish fort at Fao. On the 5th, the day war was declared, the outer bar was crossed. Next morning Captain Hayes-Sadler in the *Odin,* with an armed tug manned from the *Ocean,* silenced the guns outside Fort Fao—the fort itself being in ruins—and then landed some 600 troops, with a party of the *Ocean's* Marines and a section of Mountain Artillery, under Colonel Rosher. There was no opposition. Reinforcements followed quickly, and during the night the fort was occupied and the guns thrown into the river.

In the meantime the *Espiègle* had dispersed a Turkish force that had established itself higher up opposite the ruined village of Abadan, and on the 7th, while the landing force at Fao, having completed its work, was being withdrawn, General Delamain with the rest of the brigade moved up the river till he was in sight of the oil refinery works at the north end of Abadan Island. Next day he went on board the *Odin,* and with Captain Hayes-Sadler searched for a suitable landing place.   A firm high bank with deep water was found two or three miles further up on the west or Turkish side, at the point where the river begins to bend round Muhalla Island.   Here lies a village called Saniyeh, and at this spot the whole brigade, with the exception of a small garrison left at Fort Fao, was encamped by the evening of the 10th.   The brigadier had been instructed not to advance further till the arrival of Lieutenant-General Sir A. A. Barrett, who was in command of the force, and had already left Bombay with the 18th Infantry Brigade, the 10th Brigade R.F.A., and the bulk of the divisional troops.   General Delamain, therefore, decided to entrench himself where he was and cover the oil works till his chief appeared.   The position that had been secured was all that was required for the moment.   It had been attained easily enough, thanks to a very smart piece of work, creditable alike to the foresight of those who prepared it and to the readiness and resource of the naval and military officers who carried it out.

Simultaneously an equally rapid and unexpected blow was delivered in the mouth of the Red Sea.   At Sheikh Syed, opposite Perim, and just outside the northern limit of the Aden Protectorate, a mixed force of Turks and Arabs was reported to be assembling.   Here a strong work known as Fort Turba was in a position, if adequately armed, to command the passage between Perim and the mainland.   The force which the enemy had assembled was also strong enough to threaten Perim itself, and Aden and the Indian Government thought it advisable to deal with it at once.   The means were at hand. Another large convoy with five infantry brigades and the Imperial Service Cavalry Brigade had left India for France and Egypt on November 2, under escort of the *Duke of Edinburgh, Swiftsure* and *Northbrook*, the *Duke of Edinburgh* being under orders for home to join the Grand Fleet.   The troops were urgently required in France, but the assent of the Home Authorities was obtained for a detachment of them to undertake the operation on their way, provided it would not delay the convoy more than twenty-four hours.   Accordingly, on November 8, as the convoy approached Aden, Captain Henry Blackett in the *Duke of Edinburgh*, with the *City of Manchester* and two other transports, containing three battalions of Indian Infantry under Brigadier-General Cox, was sent ahead at full speed.   At daybreak on the 9th he closed the fort, and after laying it in ruins without drawing a reply, he led the three transports to a point within the Strait near Sheikh Syed.   Here a landing was at once effected in the face of considerable opposition and a galling fire, and the *Duke of Edinburgh* was able to keep it under sufficiently for a covering position to be seized without much loss. The disembarkation could then proceed, and early in the afternoon, when half the troops were ashore, an advance was made, still in the face of opposition, to clear the enemy away from the vicinity of Fort Turba. The enemy, however, eventually made off before it, and by night all the surrounding heights were occupied. Then, the following morning, without any interference, Captain Blackett was able to land a demolition party at the fort. It was found to contain only five light guns. These were destroyed, the work itself was completely dismantled, and by 6 p.m. all the troops were on board again, and the transports hurrying on to rejoin the convoy after a very clean and rapid piece of work.

It was subject to these preoccupations arising out of the new Turkish war that the plan for ending the *Emden's* career had to be elaborated. As soon as Admiral Jerram heard of the Penang raid he sent the *Yahagi*, which had been intended to meet the Australian convoy, to join the *Chikuma* and maintain with her a patrol from Rangoon to Acheh Head. He also sent on the *Empress of Russia*, which had just reached Singapore, to Colombo, so that for the Colombo–Minikoi area and the Colombo–Calcutta trade route Captain Grant soon had the *Hampshire, Yarmouth, Askold, Empress of Russia* and *Empress of Asia*, while the Admiralty ordered down the *Gloucester* from the Mediterranean to increase the force of fast light cruisers. Now that the *Königsberg* was blockaded, they intended also to use the *Weymouth* and *Dartmouth* who had been hunting her with the *Chatham*, but as soon as the news of Admiral Cradock's defeat arrived they ordered the *Dartmouth* to the Cape. The *Weymouth*, on her way to join Captain Grant, was to proceed by Providence Island, Diego Garcia, the Maldives and Minikoi. To complete the scheme they requested that all the Japanese squadrons not engaged in the von Spee combination should draw to the westward into the vicinity of Sumatra and the Dutch Indies, so as to deny to the *Emden* every loophole and every place of shelter as far westward as the 90° meridian, which runs through the middle of the Bay of Bengal. This the Japanese Government readily undertook to do, and the whole scheme was to be complete by the middle of November.

Meanwhile, over the only area of the Indian Ocean which was as yet unguarded, the Australian convoy would be passing with its powerful escort. The focal point of this area was the cable centre at the Cocos Islands, where the Eastern Telegraph

Company's cables to Mauritius, Batavia, and Perth in West Australia diverged, and where there was also a wireless station. Admiral Jerram had for some time regarded it as a likely place to attract the *Emden's* attention, and being unable to place a cruiser there he had instructed the station staff how to give immediate warning of a surprise attack, and had furnished the officials in charge with the call signs of all the ships in the surrounding waters. The convoy was steering off the usual track on a course that would take it past the east side of the islands, and at dawn on November 8— being then a week out—it was about 230 miles south-east of them. Here the *Minotaur* received the order which, as we have seen, had been sent out on the 6th, that she was to proceed to the Cape in place of the *Goliath*. Captain Kiddle at once handed over his charge to Captain Silver of the *Melbourne*, and parted company, while the convoy held on with the *Melbourne*, *Sydney* and *Ibuki*; and not without anxiety, for they had lost the *Minotaur* just as they were approaching what was regarded as the most dangerous point, where, for all they knew, the *Königsberg* as well as the *Emden* might be on the look-out for them.

In fact, at that very hour the *Emden*, with the *Buresk* in company, was rejoining her other collier, the *Exford*, at the rendezvous Captain von Müller had given her forty miles north of the Cocos. The *Exford* had been waiting there since October 30, expecting other ships, probably the *Pontoporos* and *Markomannia*. That the former had been captured Captain von Müller learned from the survivors of the French destroyer *Mousquet*, and after dismissing them in a prize called the *Newburn*, which he had taken after leaving Penang, he went away to meet the *Buresk* at Simalur, his original coaling-rendezvous, on the coast of Sumatra. Having picked her up there he carried on as far as the Strait of Sunda hoping to find ships in the East Asiatic trade using that route. In this he was disappointed ; he cruised in the area from the morning of the 4th to the evening of the 5th when he turned to the southward and made for the *Exford's* rendezvous with the intention, as Admiral Jerram expected, of raiding the Cocos cable station, but in entire ignorance of the Australian convoy. During the morning of the 8th he passed across their course about 250 miles ahead of them. They had been keeping rigid wireless silence, but Captain von Müller must have heard the *Minotaur* acknowledging her orders for the Cape, for in dismissing the *Exford* preparatory to his attack he warned her to steam north-north-west, as there was British wireless in the opposite direction.

For himself, however—over-confident, perhaps, in the luck that had clung to him—he took no precautions. In the harbour there was nothing but the proprietor's schooner *Ayesha*, and seeing all clear, he went close in at daybreak on November 9, with his dummy funnel again set up, and a landing-party of forty-seven, with maxim guns, in boats under his quarter. But the dummy funnel was so badly rigged that the telegraph officials immediately realised the situation, and with admirable promptness sent out the S.O.S., and calling up the *Minotaur*, told her *en clair* that a strange ship was entering the harbour. Then they were jammed, but they got a message through on the cable to Admiral Jerram as the German boats made for the shore. He at once ordered the *Hampshire* and the two " Empress " liners, which were in the Colombo area, to steam at full speed to meet the convoy, and directed the *Yakumo* and three destroyers to the Sunda Strait to meet the *Philomel* and *Pyramus*, who were approaching it on their way from Fremantle to Singapore.

During the night the convoy had passed forty miles east of the Cocos, and was about fifty-five miles north of them when, shortly before 7.0 a.m., the *Melbourne* got the warning. The problem which Captain Silver then had to decide immediately was not without difficulty. Though he had been told by Captain Kiddle that the *Emden* was expected at the Cocos, he did not know the *Königsberg* was located and held. For all he could tell the two cruisers might be in company. Should he, therefore, carry on or should he attempt to destroy the cruiser known to be in reach? There was little doubt he should follow the old rule of attacking " the enemy in sight." But what should he detach for the purpose? By an equally venerable rule he must not leave his convoy himself. If two enemy cruisers were present it would be best to detach the *Ibuki*, as the most powerful ship, but, on the other hand, the two might attack the convoy, and for that reason the *Ibuki* should remain. Accordingly, with no little self-control, which the Admiralty fully approved afterwards, he detached Captain Glossop in the *Sydney*. By 7.0. she was away, but to the urgent entreaties of the Japanese captain he had reluctantly to turn a deaf ear, and the two remaining cruisers took station to the southward to cover the convoy.

Meanwhile, the German landing-party had seized the station and smashed the instruments, but not before the Superintendent had got off a message to London and the three stations with which he was in cable communication. The Germans then blew up the wireless mast and demolished the whole installation. Thorough as was the work of destruction, it was done with all possible consideration, and little that was not connected with communications was touched. With the cables they were not so successful. They had no proper tools for cutting and were confused by spare lengths laid out to sea to save burying ashore. They had, in fact, only succeeded in cutting that to Perth when smoke was seen on the horizon and the *Emden* sounded the recall.[1] This was shortly after nine o'clock in the morning. A quarter of an hour later the two ships could see each other, and so rapidly was the *Sydney* coming down from the north-east that Captain von Müller found it necessary to abandon the shore party and put to sea without delay in order to get room for manœuvre. For his intention was to fight, and believing he had only one of the comparatively weak light cruisers of the East Indies Squadron to deal with, he steamed out to the northward to meet her.[2]

As the *Emden* crossed the *Sydney's* bows at less than 10,000 yards Captain Glossop turned to the northward on a parallel course, and so at 9.40 the unequal action began by the *Emden* opening fire at 9,500 yards.[3] It was a calm, clear morning, and her shooting was brilliant from the first. She straddled the *Sydney* at once, while the *Sydney*, having over-estimated the range by 1000 yards, began by sending everything far over. It was not till the twelfth round, so the Germans say, that she secured a hit; but, on the other hand, though the enemy's shell showered all round her, the danger-space of the *Emden's* 4″ guns at that extreme range was very small, and, hot as the action was, the *Sydney*, beyond having one control station disabled, suffered very little. Moreover, though nominally the *Sydney* had little more than a knot the advantage in speed, she had at least four knots actual superiority, and Captain Glossop was able to keep the range open as he liked. Maintaining his speed, he rapidly drew ahead, until about ten minutes after the action had begun the *Emden* circled 8 points to starboard and stood to the eastward as though to cross him astern. By this time she had been repeatedly hit. As her range-finder had been shot away her firing was less accurate and her troubles rapidly increased. Very soon after her turn, her steering gear seems to have been disabled, and her first funnel and foremast were shot away. She could only steer with her engines, and fire slackened.

---

[1] See *The Zodiac* (Eastern Telegraph Co.'s Journal), Vol. VIII, p. 125, February–March 1915.

[2] *Emden*, 3592 tons, 1908–9, 24·12 knots (T.S.), 10 4·1″ guns, 2 torpedo tubes. *Sydney*, 5400 tons, 1912–13, 25·7 knots (T.S.), 8 6″ guns, 2 torpedo tubes.

[3] See Plan p. 384.

For so terrible was the effect of the British lyddite that whole gun crews were swept away together, and, seeing how many men she had had to leave behind at the Cocos, she had no reserves. Still, in spite of losses and constant fires, she continued the hopeless action gamely.

To counter her last movement the *Sydney* made a corresponding turn to port and slowed down, and so for a short time they were fighting on opposite courses. But soon the *Emden* doubled back north-west. She was burning fiercely aft and was clearly in great distress. Her fire, which at first had been at the rate of ten shots a minute per gun, was slackening more and more and growing wilder. Her object seemed to be to close, and Captain Glossop did not seek to thwart her. Keeping his course and low speed he let the range fall to 5,500 yards, and then, having fired a torpedo which missed, turned away 12 points to starboard and, increasing to full speed, opened out the range again. The *Emden*, who could not reply, since both her torpedo tubes had been put out of action, conformed with a similar turn, and the two ships were once more fighting at long range on parallel courses, with the British cruiser somewhat ahead.

The action had now lasted about forty minutes, and both the *Emden's* fire control positions and her two remaining funnels were gone. She was holed all over and was burning fiercely fore and aft. Indeed, so smothered was she in smoke that at one time it was believed she had gone down. But she was soon seen again making to the eastward, and the *Sydney*, who had drawn well ahead of her, held on the same course, till about 10.30 the *Emden* suddenly turned away and doubled back 16 points to starboard. Captain Glossop promptly conformed with a similar turn and continued to engage her with his port battery at about 7000 yards. The *Emden*, though she still kept firing with the few guns she had left, was now at his mercy. Both ships were heading about north-west as though to pass on either side of North Keeling Island, but in another half hour (11.20 a.m.) it was clear the German was sinking and was endeavouring to beach herself on the island. Captain Glossop then put on full speed to cut her off, but it was too late, and with her flag still flying she ran hard on the reef on the south shore.

For an hour and forty minutes she had made a gallant fight against superior force, but it was clear she was helpless. Captain Glossop therefore left her and gave chase to the *Buresk*, which could be seen making off to the northward. She was quickly overhauled and forced to strike her flag, but when a prize crew was sent on board it was found the

Germans had opened her inlet valves and so damaged them that she could not be saved. Having taken off her crew and the British prisoners he found on board, Captain Glossop left her, and at 4.0 p.m. returned to the *Emden*. Her flag was still flying, and as no answer was made to his repeated summonses to surrender, he had to open fire again. The result was a useless massacre, and it was not till after the second salvo had torn the helpless ship that she showed white flags and sent a man aloft to haul down her colours. Why this was not done before was never explained.

Pitiable as was her condition, Captain Glossop had now to leave her for the night in order to get back to the Cocos to deal with the landing party before dark. On the way, however, he felt compelled to stop to pick up men who had been blown out of the *Emden* during the action and were still keeping themselves afloat. Owing to this delay it was nightfall before he reached the island, and he then found that the landing-party, when they saw how the action was going, had seized the proprietor's schooner and had escaped with her in the dusk.

The structural damage which the *Sydney* had suffered was very slight. Of her crew she had lost only four killed and twelve wounded, and she returned at once to the North Keeling to rescue the survivors of the *Emden*. The wreck was found to be in a pitiable condition. Her decks were a shambles, and the work of rescue was extremely difficult, for she had beached herself on the weather side of the island, and the send of the sea was very heavy. As the prisoners were numerous their parole had first to be taken, that " while in the *Sydney* they would cause no interference with the ship or fittings and would be amenable to the ship's discipline." The work then commenced and lasted till 5.0 p.m. As soon as it was done the *Sydney* went round to the lee side to pick up some twenty men who had managed to get ashore. But it was not till next morning (November 11) that all were on board and she could follow the convoy to Colombo. Captain von Müller himself was saved, and it is stated that the dead numbered 8 officers and 126 men. The prisoners on board were 11 officers, 9 warrant officers, and 191 men, of whom 3 officers and 53 men were wounded. In the crowded decks little could be done for them. Four died of their wounds, and it was no small relief when at midnight on the 12th, thanks to Admiral Jerram's prompt orders, the *Empress of Russia* met them, and it was possible to transfer to her all the prisoners except the few most serious cases which it was dangerous to move.

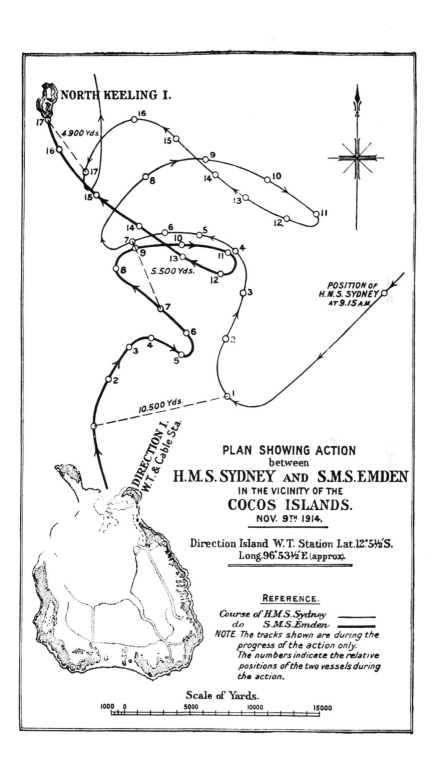

NORTH KEELING I.

4.900 Yds.

5.500 Yds.

POSITION OF
H.M.S. SYDNEY
AT 9.15 A.M.

10.500 Yds.

DIRECTION I.
W.T. & Cable Sta.

PLAN SHOWING ACTION
between
H.M.S. SYDNEY AND S.M.S. EMDEN
IN THE VICINITY OF THE
COCOS ISLANDS.
NOV. 9TH 1914.

Direction Island W.T. Station Lat.12°5½'S.
Long.96°53½'E (approx).

REFERENCE.

Course of H.M.S. Sydney   ————
  do   S.M.S. Emden   ━━━━
NOTE. The tracks shown are during the
progress of the action only.
The numbers indicate the relative
positions of the two vessels during
the action.

Scale of Yards.
1000 0   5000   10000   15000

So ended the episode of the *Emden*, which recalls the most famous exploits of the old French raiders. Not only had Captain von Müller obtained a high measure of success both in the actual damage he had done and the strategical and economic disturbance he had caused, but he had won the admiration of his enemy for the skill, resource and boldness with which he had maintained his position so long, and for the chivalry and humanity with which his duty had been discharged.

So striking, indeed, was the career of the *Emden* that her end almost overshadowed a much greater success. The news of her destruction followed within two days that of the fall of Tsingtau. The combined operations against the German Pacific base had occupied little more than two months, compared with the eight which it took the Japanese to capture Port Arthur from the Russians. The first landing began on September 2 in the Gulf of Pe-chi-li, eighty miles north of Tsingtau. Moving southward across the Shantung Peninsula, the cavalry seized the railway at Kiao-chau, and then, on the 18th, the rest of the troops were landed in Lo-shan Bay, about fifteen miles north-east of the German defences, and the fortress was isolated. On the 22nd the British troops arrived from Taku and Wei-hai-wei under escort of the *Triumph*, and on the 27th the attack on the advanced German positions began.

Most important of them was a hill on the German right, known as Prinz Heinrich Berg, which overlooked the whole place. The experiences of Port Arthur and 203 Metre Hill had taught that in combined operations of this kind the vital necessity was a good observing position. Without such a position the guns both afloat and ashore could do little more than give a covering fire for the infantry. Upon the fixed defences they could make no decisive impression. Accordingly Prinz Heinrich Berg appears to have been the primary objective of the Japanese, and on October 17 it was captured in a night attack. Siege guns were then called up from the Japanese base, while an observing station was rapidly organised on the hill. By the 31st all was ready for the grand attack and, although for three days the weather was too bad for the ships to take part in the bombardment, the place surrendered in a week (November 7).

Thus three months after the war began, Far Eastern Waters were permanently barred to the enemy, and the Japanese were free to take their place in the world-wide combination that had been designed in Whitehall.

CHAPTER XXVII

SECURING THE COMMAND IN EGYPT AND THE EAST—THE
PERSIAN GULF OPERATIONS AND PROGRESS OF THE
CAMEROONS EXPEDITION

THE embarrassing effects that can be produced by a single
well-handled raider have seldom been better exemplified
than in the career of the *Emden*, and in her case the extent
of the disturbance may be measured by the relief which her
destruction afforded in almost every area of our naval operations. It happened at a most opportune moment, when the
demand for cruisers and torpedo craft had become specially
insistent. The number of ships of these classes whose attention she had been occupying, directly or indirectly, on the
convoy and trade routes was very considerable. The greater
part of them were now released at a stroke, and they were
streaming towards and up the Red Sea for the stations where
they were required.

The principal calls were in Home Waters and the Mediterranean. At home the increasing activity of the German
submarines and the exigencies of a closer blockade demanded
every light cruiser and destroyer that could be spared, while
the detaching of the two battle cruisers—and it soon became
clear that a third would have to be taken—in order to deal
with Admiral von Spee raised in the Grand Fleet a specially
insistent demand for the powerful ships of the 1st Cruiser
Squadron which hitherto had been allotted to the defence of
Egypt and the Red Sea. The need for removing these ships
made the call of Egypt particularly urgent. It was just a week
after the opening of hostilities with Turkey that the *Emden*
had been destroyed, and during that time the menace of an
immediate invasion from Syria had been growing stronger
every day. Long before the war it had been settled in view of
such an invasion that the proper line for the defence of Egypt
was not the desert frontier but the Canal, and the merits of
that line depended materially on the fact that it lent itself
to naval co-operation with the land forces. Since the main
new fact in military tactics which the experience of the

war had brought out was the increasing importance of heavy artillery, such co-operation was more than ever essential, and owing to the removal of the *Emden* from the board, ships were now available.

Chief amongst them was the *Swiftsure*.   As we have seen, she, together with the *Duke of Edinburgh*, was at the moment escorting a large convoy of Indian reinforcements—the same convoy which dealt with Sheikh Syed.   As usual, her limit was Aden; but, as her services would now no longer be required for escort in the Indian Ocean, she was immediately ordered to carry on with the convoy to Suez.   In the meanwhile the Home Counties Territorial Division, which reached Port Said for India on November 11, was ordered to stand fast in Egypt.   Further security would be provided by the cruisers proceeding homewards, for the *Gloucester*, *Melbourne*, *Sydney*, *Hampshire* and *Yarmouth* were all ordered to the Mediterranean for further instructions, while the *Dartmouth* and *Weymouth* carried on for the Cape.

This left in the Indian Ocean nothing of importance except two groups, both of which were engaged in coastal work: one, under Captain Drury-Lowe (*Goliath*, *Chatham*, *Fox* and *Kinfauns Castle*), was operating against the *Königsberg* in the Rufiji River and in support of our troops in East Africa; the other, consisting of the battleship *Ocean*, the sloops *Espiègle*, *Odin*, and attached armed vessels, was attending the Persian Gulf Expedition.   As both were independent combined operations there was little to require the presence of Admiral Peirse on the station.   The Egyptian zone was far more important, and as it was obviously impossible to conduct the defence of the Canal and the Red Sea from India, it was decided to form a new station in the threatened area, and recall the Admiral to command it with his flag in the *Swiftsure*.   The only doubt was the Persian Gulf, but on being consulted he agreed that the conduct of those operations could well be left to Captain Hayes-Sadler of the *Ocean*, and accordingly he proceeded to Suez with all speed to take personal charge of the new extension of his command.

The Gulf operations had, in fact, been going as well as could be desired, thanks to the foresight and secrecy with which they were instituted.   We have seen how, by the evening of November 10, General Delamain and Captain Hayes-Sadler had their whole force ashore at Saniyeh above the oil works on Abadan Island, about ten miles below the junction of the Karun River at Muhammera.   There they had entrenched to await the arrival of General Barrett and the reinforcements he was bringing.[1] He reached the camp early on the 14th, and hearing that a Turkish force was concentrating at Saihan, four miles up the river, he at once ordered General Delamain to push out a reconnaissance in force. The enemy were found entrenched at the edge of the palm groves that fringed the river, but, with the help of the *Odin*, they were quickly turned out, and, as soon as they were seen to be in full retreat, the force returned to camp.

The way was now clear for an advance. It was essential to continue the initial success as speedily as possible, for under German influence a Jehad had been proclaimed, and to prevent the movement taking hold of the Arabs, General Barrett had been authorised to push on to Basra as soon as he was in a position to do so. This port—the " Bussorah " of the old East Indian trade—had been from time immemorial the great emporium of Mesopotamian trade.[2] Lying seventy miles from the mouth of the Shatt-al-Arab, it was the highest point that sea-going vessels could reach, and it was here the wondering Eastern poet came in touch with the men " that go down to the sea in ships." The place it had always held in Arab imagination was enshrined in some of the best-known tales of the Arabian Nights, and it still held good. Its occupation, therefore, quite apart from its strategical value, could not fail to make a deep and lasting moral impression. Accordingly, although owing to the difficulties of the landing place General Barrett had not been able to get all his artillery ashore, he decided to move on November 17. Prompt action was everything, and the difficulty of the guns could, in a measure, be compensated by the sloops and gunboats in the river. Captain Hayes-Sadler arranged that he should move with the troops with the *Odin*, *Espiègle* and two armed launches. The only trouble was that owing to the screen of palms, ship fire could not be relied on to any great extent— indeed, it could only be controlled by megaphone from the masthead—but it was General Barrett's design to get on the right flank of the Turks and drive them on to the ships.

[1] The Persian Gulf Expeditionary Force (" Force D," as it was called) consisted mainly of the VIth (Poona) Division. It comprised the 16th Brigade under Brigadier-General Delamain (2nd Dorsets, 104th (Wellesley's) Rifles, 20th Infantry, 117th Mahrattas); the 18th Brigade which came with General Barrett under Major-General C. I. Fry (2nd Norfolks, 120th Rajputana Infantry, 7th Rajputs, 110th Mahratta L.I.); and the 17th Brigade under Brigadier-General W. H. Dobbie, which left India about November 20 (1st Oxford and Bucks. L.I., 119th Infantry, 22nd Punjabis, 103rd Mahratta L.I.). The Divisional Troops were the 33rd Cavalry; 10th Brigade R.F.A., two batteries Indian Mountain Artillery, 48th Pioneers. The transport included the 52nd Camel Corps and the Jaipur and Bharatpur transport.

[2] See Map, p. 394.

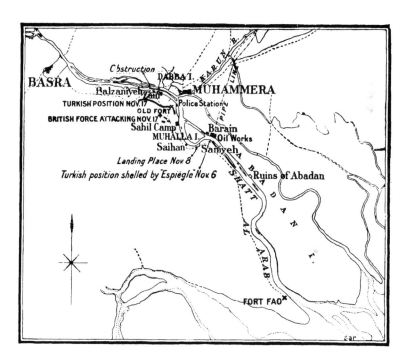

Scale of Miles

5   0   5   10   15

OPERATIONS NEAR BASRA

At dawn the troops were moving, and by 9.0 the enemy was located, to the number of 4,000 Turks and 1,500 Arabs with twelve guns, some six miles up the river. They were entrenched at an old fort a little above Sahil, but their right extended so far to the westward and into such difficult ground that it' was impossible to turn it, and the plan of attack had to be changed. Rain had made the open ground in front of the position very heavy, but, nevertheless, General Barrett determined to attack their centre and left on either side of the old fort, which seemed to be the key of the position. He was met with a damaging fire from well-served field guns and machine-guns, which, beyond dropping a few shells into the old fort, the ships could do little to counter. Still, by 1.15 p.m., in spite of every difficulty and some considerable loss, he had put the enemy to flight. The ground was too heavy, and the artillery fire which covered the rout too formidable, for immediate pursuit. The ships, however, were able to shell and set fire to the enemy's camp which lay inland from the Police Station in rear of the position, and General Barrett decided to form an entrenched camp on the river bank at Sahil in order to clear his wounded and get up stores preparatory to striking at Basra.

It was soon found that the enemy had fallen back to another position at Balzaniyeh, just beyond the long island of Dabba, whose lower end is opposite Muhammera and the mouth of the Karun river. It was from our loyal adherent, the Sheikh of Muhammera, that all the information was coming, and he had to tell also that an obstruction had been formed in the main or north channel of the river at the head of Dabba Island. Here a Hamburg-Amerika liner, which had been engaged in the Gulf trade till the war forced her to take refuge in the Shatt-al-Arab, had been sunk in the fairway with smaller vessels on each side of her. As General Barrett had to rely entirely on river transport, this was a very serious obstacle. Still, in order to protect the Sheikh from an Arab attack with which he was threatened, General Barrett resolved to push on as soon as he could move, and meanwhile, on the 19th, Captain Hayes-Sadler went up in the *Espiègle* to see what could be made of the obstacle.

As he approached it he was fired on by a 500-ton gunboat, the *Marmariss*, by an armed launch, and by a battery of four 15-pdr. Krupp guns which had been established on the left of the Turkish position at Balzaniyeh and commanded the obstruction. The fire was returned with such effect that the armed launch was quickly sunk, the *Marmariss* put to flight up the river, and the battery silenced without the

Espiègle having received a single hit. The obstruction was then examined in peace, and it was found that the channel was not completely blocked, a possible passage having been left between the sunken liner and the island. On his return to the General, therefore, it was arranged that an advance on Balzaniyeh should be made at daylight on the 21st. The armed launches would support the right of the force by proceeding up the boat channel, which ran south of Dabba Island, while the *Espiègle, Odin,* and the Indian Marine ship *Lawrence,* which had just arrived, engaged the fort and endeavoured to force the obstruction.[1] Till the evening of the 20th, however, it was very doubtful whether the advance could be made as arranged, since it had still been found impossible to land all the guns. The question was in debate when a boat came down from Muhammera with the surprising intelligence that the Balzaniyeh position had been evacuated. Whether or not as a result of the *Espiègle's* action of the previous day, the Arabs had begun to desert, and a retreat up the river had been decided upon. Nor was this all. The gunboat *Marmariss,* which after her short action with the *Espiègle* had retired to Basra, had gone on up the river. With her had fled the Valis of Basra and Baghdad, and the whole garrison of Basra had embarked in dhows and river steamers and was in full retreat on Amara, a hundred miles up the Tigris. To ascertain the truth, Captain Hayes-Sadler went up again to the obstruction next morning. Finding the position deserted, he proceeded to clear the passage of the wire hawsers that barred it, and scarcely was the work done when a launch appeared with a deputation from Basra confirming the news that the place had been evacuated and begging for the British to come up and save it from looting Arabs.

Captain Hayes-Sadler at once returned to the camp and suggested embarking two battalions in river steamers. The General agreed, and the ships *Espiègle, Odin* and *Lawrence* immediately started for Basra. By 3.0 p.m., in spite of great difficulties from the tide rushing past the obstruction, all three of them had passed up. Stopping only to dismantle the guns which they found abandoned in the fort, they pressed on, and by 5.0 p.m. were anchored off the Custom House of Basra. It was on fire and beset by looting Arabs. One blank round sufficed to disperse them, and a party was landed to take possession of the quays and extinguish the fires. Next morning (November 22) further large parties went ashore and

---

[1] The *Lawrence* was the last of the six Indian Marine ships to join. She was transferred to the Navy on the outbreak of war with Turkey.

set to work systematically to clear the town and to hoist British flags on all the public buildings, including the German Consulate, whose staff were made prisoners. A few hours later the two advanced battalions arrived under General Fry to relieve them, and thus order was completely restored before any serious harm was done. In the course of the afternoon the main force appeared, and on the 23rd General Barrett made his formal entry into the town. Under the British flag, surrounded by the paraded troops and bluejackets, Sir Percy Cox, the British Resident and Chief Political Officer, to whose knowledge and skill much of the success was due, read a proclamation. It announced that the British had now replaced the Turkish flag and administration, and at the same time the neighbouring friendly sheikhs were assured by letter that Basra would never again be allowed to pass under Turkish authority. To complete the consolidation of our position, steps were next taken to secure Kuweit, which lies at the head of the Gulf on the Arabian side. The Sheikh, an old friend, to whom we had just sent an increased garrison for his protection, was now informed that his territory would be recognised as an independent principality under British protection, and this was done by treaty shortly afterwards.[1]

Thus, to the high credit of all concerned, in less than three weeks after the declaration of war with Turkey we had a firm hold on the water gate of Mesopotamia.[2] The effect could only be to enhance our local prestige so materially that we could regard the allegiance of the friendly Arabs as confirmed, while at the same time we had secured a *place d'armes* from which we could deal with any attempt of the Turks to seize the oil fields at Ahwaz through Persian Arabistan. So far-reaching, indeed, was the moral effect likely to be that Sir Percy Cox urged that the flowing tide should be used to its utmost, and an immediate advance made on Baghdad. In some quarters the idea received considerable support; but both the India Office and the Government of India, though fully alive to the political importance of ultimately occupying the old Arab capital, regarded the project as premature. They therefore suggested the less ambitious scheme of further securing the defensive position already attained by occupy-

[1] Kuweit, or Koweit, was claimed by the Turks as part of the Ottoman Empire. In 1899, however, the Sheikh placed himself by treaty within the British sphere, and later on, by a further treaty, we secured all the points within his country to which the terminal of the Baghdad railway might be brought.

[2] For a full account of these operations see *Official History of the Great War, The Campaign in Mesopotamia*, Vol. I.

ing Kurnah, a place some forty-five miles above Basra, where the Euphrates and Tigris flowed together into the Shatt-al-Arab. It was naturally a point of high strategical importance, which from its situation was not only easily defensible but also covered the whole of the fertile tracts along the Shatt-al-Arab. On November 27 this plan was sanctioned, and General Barrett was authorised to undertake the operation with one brigade, or so much of his force as he deemed necessary. Accordingly, the General decided to commence the new movement on December 3, by which time his 17th Brigade and the remainder of his divisional troops would arrive at Basra to complete his force.

The difficulties of the operation were mainly navigational. For above Basra sea-going ships did not proceed, and the river was uncharted. There was nothing to go by but military maps without soundings, and it was the season of lowest water. Captain Hayes-Sadler had, however, already made a reconnaissance in anticipation of the advance to ascertain whether Kurnah was occupied. On the 25th he groped his way up in the *Espiègle*, with the *Odin* and the armed launches *Miner* and *Mashona* in company, till six miles below Kurnah he sighted the *Marmariss* retiring up the Tigris. Pursuit was impossible, for three miles further on they were brought up by shoal water and an obstruction against which the *Odin* disabled her rudder. Here they came under shell fire from Kurnah and rifle fire from the banks. It was soon silenced, and they were able to locate a lighter sunk in the fairway. At dusk they returned, without any casualties, to report that they had selected a good defensible landing place at Um Rash, a friendly village on the left bank about two and a half miles below the junction of the rivers and out of sight of Kurnah. Accordingly, in the afternoon of December 3, as the remainder of the division was reaching Basra, the Kurnah detachment started up the river under Colonel Frazer in four steamers, escorted by the two sloops, the *Lawrence* and three armed launches, *Miner*, *Lewis Pelly* and *Shaitan*, two of the transports being also armed, each with two 18-pdr. R.F.A. field guns.[1]

Anchoring for the night ten miles below Kurnah, they proceeded again at daylight next morning (December 4), and as they approached the landing place were fired on by two guns at the village of Muzereh, which lies back on the left bank some two miles or more from the selected landing place.

[1] The column consisted of one company Norfolks, half company Sappers and Miners, 104th Rifles, and 110th Mahratta L.I., with the gun teams of the R.F.A.

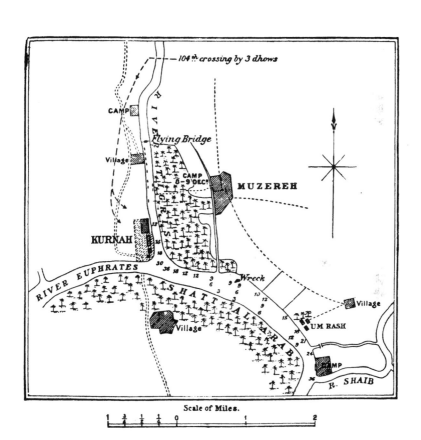

Scale of Miles.

OPERATIONS NEAR KURNAH

As Kurnah itself stands in the fork of the two rivers, it could not be reached without crossing one of them. From the left bank of the Shatt-al-Arab, on which the troops had landed, it was the Tigris that barred the way, and at Muzereh the Turks had entrenched a position to prevent access to its bank. Under cover of the ship fire, however, the troops were all safely landed by 9.0 a.m., and an immediate advance began against the Muzereh position. While the *Odin*—which in spite of her disabled rudder had accompanied the force—guarded the camp, the *Espiègle* and *Lawrence* with the two armed transports supported the attack. It had to be made over a perfectly flat plain without cover of any kind, but the ships managed to draw most of the artillery fire till it was silenced, and about 11.0 the position was carried. The troops then began to push on, and the launches were ordered to advance with them. But so hot was the fire as soon as the bend of the river brought them in sight of Kurnah, that the *Miner* was soon holed and had to return and beach herself. But by this time the troops were also withdrawing. It had been ascertained that the Turks had escaped across the Tigris into Kurnah, and it was, moreover, clear that, whether or not the bulk of the Turkish forces were retiring as high as Amara, they had left an unexpectedly strong rear guard at the junction of the rivers. It was now, indeed, Colonel Frazer's opinion that Kurnah could not be taken except by crossing the Tigris and attacking it from the north. This he could not do with his existing force. He therefore decided to return to the Um Rash camp and ask for reinforcements.

The river steamers, with the wounded and prisoners, were sent down to fetch them, and at dawn on the 6th General Fry arrived with the rest of the Norfolks, two more Indian battalions and another battery R.F.A., which brought the whole force up to 2,300 men with sixteen guns, and made it slightly superior to the estimated strength of the enemy.[1] As the General intended to establish himself at Muzereh before trying to cross the Tigris, he had to wait for a mule transport train to work between the village and the Um Rash camp. No movement was therefore made that day, and in the interval the Turks reoccupied the Muzereh position. In the afternoon they even attempted to attack the camp, but the effort was promptly crushed by the ships and the artillery. Early next morning (December 7) the mules arrived, as well as a mountain battery for which the General had also asked, and at 9.0 the advance began. As the troops moved out of camp the ships and launches weighed and anchored again further up, where

[1] Actually the enemy had a total of about three thousand.

26

they had a clear view of the town. They were met with a heavy fire both from Kurnah and Muzereh, which they returned, while under cover of the ships' guns the attack developed, supported by a wide turning movement on the enemy's eastern or left flank. Still, so severe was the rifle fire from Muzereh that Captain Hayes-Sadler scraped his way over the soft mud still further up to assist the field artillery in subduing it. In this they were successful, and about 1.0, as the turning movement on the east developed, the village was stormed by the Norfolks. Pursuit through the palm groves towards the Tigris followed without pause, and to support it Captain Hayes-Sadler sent the launches ahead and determined to move on till the mud and the obstruction stopped him. This he did, but by 3.30 he had to recall the launches, for the *Shaitan* had been disabled and her commander killed by the heavy fire that had been encountered. Still, by this time the action was practically over, for it was found the Turks had made off up the Tigris, and the General decided to bivouac at Muzereh for the night, where were collected 130 prisoners and three guns.

The work of the following day (December 8) was to get the troops across the Tigris, and at 8.30 a.m. Captain Hayes-Sadler sent the launch *Lewis Pelly* up to reconnoitre. In spite of the enemy's fire she got within a quarter of a mile of the junction, but was then forced to withdraw, and as he could not get at the obnoxious guns where he was, Captain Hayes-Sadler decided to try to pass the obstruction. This, by careful sounding, he accomplished soon after 11.0, and, with the two armed transports on his port beam, began firing on Kurnah with lyddite. The result was all that could be desired. At an early hour half a company of Sappers, covered by the 104th Rifles, had been dispatched to the northern edge of the palm groves to arrange a means of crossing the river, and the Norfolks and 110th Light Infantry were moved up in readiness. By the time the flotilla opened fire the Sappers, by swimming the Tigris, had run a wire hawser across to the opposite bank, and having got hold of a dhow from a friendly Arab, were establishing a ferry or flying bridge a mile and a half above the town. By this slender means the 110th Light Infantry began to cross, while about a mile higher up the 104th Rifles, which was the wing battalion, found three more dhows and received permission from the General to go across also. Thanks, as it would seem, to the Turks' preoccupation with the *Espiègle's* lyddite and the field guns in the transports, as well as an infantry diversion in the palm groves opposite the town, neither movement was observed

LOWER MESOPOTAMIA
TO THE HEAD OF THE
PERSIAN GULF.

P E R S I A

MESOPOTAMIA

A R A B I A

PERSIAN GULF

BUSHIRE

CABLE TO. BUSHIRE & INDIA

Bushire

Bebahán

Rámúz

Hindiyan R.

Bamní I.

Ras Baháragan

Ahwáz

Wais

Kerkha R.

PERSIAN CREEK PIPE

Bachín Division

Amára

Ali the Sea

Kut

Old Rash

Nasiriya

EUPHRATES

Qurna

Hammar

Shadadan

Salih

Dabbal

Balzaniyeh

Samiyeh

Zobeir

Muhailah

Shahudei

BASRA

Fadia I.

KARÚN

Fort Fào

KUWEIT KADAMEH

Kuwait Kadameh

SHATT-EL-ARAB

EL BATIN

Prepared in the Historical Section, Committee of Imperial Defence

Ordnance Survey, 1919.

1540/38.

by the enemy, except for some snipers in dhows moored under the bank lower down. As soon as the passage was complete both battalions and a mountain-gun section advanced under Colonel Frazer on Kurnah, the 104th making a wide sweep to take it in rear. They actually captured three towers which formed part of the defences, but so slow had been the crossing with the means at hand that the General thought it too late to press the attack and engage in street fighting that day, and at 3.30 he ordered Colonel Frazer to break off and bivouac at the flying bridge.

The ships continued to fire till sunset, and then held their ground in readiness to support the attack next day. But, in fact, Kurnah had had enough. Early in the middle watch a small steamer was seen coming down the river with all lights burning and blowing her siren. She carried a flag of truce with three Turkish officers wishing to discuss terms of capitulation. As Captain Hayes-Sadler could not communicate with the General, he insisted on surrender at discretion. To this the officers agreed, and promised to return and meet the General in the morning. They kept their word, and during the afternoon of December 9 the British flag was hoisted over Kurnah. With the surrender of the place the number of prisoners was brought up to forty-five officers and nearly 1000 men, including the Vali of Basra and the Turkish Commandant. The British casualties ashore in the three days' fighting were twenty-seven killed and 292 wounded. Afloat they were very slight, amounting to no more than two killed and ten wounded, but amongst the killed was Lieut.-Commander Elkes, R.N.R., who had so gallantly commanded the *Shaitan*.

From a defensive point of view the operations had given at small cost all that was required. Anything further would be in the nature of offence, and for that it was necessary to wait till the situation in France and Egypt and the maturing of the New Army permitted a sufficient force to be allotted to this subsidiary theatre. With Kurnah firmly in our possession we had definitely secured at the head of the Persian Gulf a sound strategical position which, besides all its other material and moral advantages, finally clenched our command of Eastern waters.

In the Cameroons a similar situation had been reached, which, though less satisfactory from a military point of view, served to deprive the colony of any naval value to the enemy. As we have seen, it was on November 10, the same day that General Delamain disembarked his force in the Shatt-al-Arab, that the carefully elaborated plan against

Buea was set in motion.[1] As in that which had been so successful against Edea, it was based on three columns, but in this case the troops were almost entirely British. While the French held Yapoma and Edea, the main column, of over a 1000 men, under Colonel Gorges, was to go by water to Tiko, the nearest point of the Duala creek system to Buea, and thence it would advance by land a distance of about twelve miles.[2] The second column, about 600 strong, under Lieutenant-Colonel R. A. de B. Rose, would move from Susa westward to the Mungo River, where a flotilla would meet it.   A combined advance would then be made to Mpundu, where they would be within six or seven miles of Colonel Gorges's line of advance, and would come under his command.[3] The third column, under Lieutenant-Colonel A. H. W. Haywood, also starting from Susa, was to push up the Northern Railway to Mujuka, a military post west of Ybassi and some thirty miles inland from Buea on the German line of retreat.[4] Besides the flotilla work on the Mungo River and for the capture of Tiko, the Navy had special functions of its own.   Its main business was to seize the port of Victoria and the shore end of the Buea light railway, and it was also to make a demonstration further north off the port of Bibundi " to cause the enemy to withdraw towards the Northern Railway."

It was with this demonstration that the operations were begun on November 10 by the *Dwarf*. The next two days she spent in visiting two small ports that lay beyond Victoria, and in the night of the 12th she anchored in company with a transport off Bibundi. On the same day the main column started for Tiko with the flotilla in which were the *Cumberland's* two 6″ guns, under Captain Beaty-Pownall of the *Challenger*. The two other columns also left Susa, and during the afternoon Colonel Rose's column met the Mungo Flotilla, headed by the captured German gunboat *Sokoto*, at Mbongo. In company with it they continued to advance the same day on both banks of the river, and halted for the night at Diongo. Simultaneously the *Ivy*, with the *Porpoise*, *Vigilant*, and a

[1] See Map, *ante* p. 276.

[2] *Main Column :* Colonel Gorges.   Two naval 12-pdr. guns; 1st Battery Nigerian Regiment; 1st Battalion Nigerian Regiment; one Pioneer Company Gold Coast Regiment; one company Senegalese; Signal Detachment West India Regiment.   Total, 70 Europeans, 1077 natives, and six guns.

[3] *Second Column :* Colonel Rose.   One section artillery, Gold Coast Regiment; Composite battalion; two sections Pioneer Company Gold Coast Regiment; Signal Detachment.   Total, 590 rifles, six guns.

[4] *Third Column :* Colonel Haywood.   Two Mountain Guns ; 2nd Battalion Nigerian Regiment ; Signal Detachment.

transport conveying the *Cumberland* and *Challenger's* Marines, with the *Bruix* as supporting ship, left the Suellaba base for Victoria.

On the following day (November 13) the *Dwarf* with her own boats and those of the transport made an elaborate pretence of landing, and after waiting till dark for the alarm to spread, sent a party ashore to cut the telephone wires. The demonstration seems to have had the desired effect, for it was learnt later that news did spread in the interior that a landing in force had taken place. In any case there was nothing left to give trouble at Victoria. At daylight the *Ivy* and her squadron appeared and sent in a summons to surrender in an hour on pain of bombardment. It was refused, and at 9.0 a.m. all the ships, including the *Bruix*, opened on Victoria and the adjacent port of Bota. Under cover of the fire the latter place was occupied by the Marines without opposition, and by 10.30 they were advancing on Victoria. The elaborate entrenchments which defended it were found unoccupied, and within the next hour the place was in their possession. The railway was undamaged, a quantity of rolling stock was captured intact, and next day was devoted to clearing the beach of land mines and restoring the leading marks of the port.

Everywhere else the combination was also going like a clock. Even before the landing at Bota had been effected, the main flotilla had driven the enemy from their trenches at Tiko, and that point, too, was occupied without opposition. On the Mungo River there was the same story to tell. At Mpundu the Germans would not face the flotilla, and by the time the troops arrived the *Sokoto* and her mosquito consorts had cleared it, so that the same afternoon the column could begin its march to join hands with the main column, which started at daylight the next morning (the 14th) from Tiko. While the Marines were making themselves at home in Victoria the two columns met. Very little opposition was encountered. The enemy seemed demoralised by the bewildering complexity of the operation and the speed with which it was carried out. The result was that by the afternoon of the 15th not only was Buea occupied, but the railway column was in possession of Mujuka, and the Force could be warmly congratulated on an exceedingly well-planned piece of combined work, skilfully and boldly executed.

On the British side, then, all was clear for a further advance into the interior, but on the French side the situation was not so satisfactory. Reconnaissances from Edea, in which Colonel Mayer had been engaged, proved that the country between Edea and the sea, including Dehane and a place called Ebea, near the mouth of the Lokundje River, had been reoccupied by the enemy, and it was necessary to clear the district before the Allied right could move in harmony with the left.   To this end General Dobell concerted a plan similar to those which had already succeeded so well.   A French force was to advance from Edea on Dehane, where an armed vessel proceeding up the Nyong River was to meet it. Another French column was to land at Longji and march on Ebea, while a flotilla with the British Marines made for the same objective up the Lokundje.   When these operations were complete the French coast column would march to the port of Kribi, the headquarters of the district, and occupy it with the support of the *Dwarf* and *Ivy*.   A reconnaissance conducted by the *Ivy* on November 19 and 20 as high as Dehane confirmed the report that the enemy were in force both there and at Ebea, but she could also give the satisfactory intelligence that the larger vessels of the flotilla could still reach Dehane in spite of the falling waters.

On November 26 the movement began from both directions.   Next morning the Lokundje Flotilla entered the river, and during the day the French coast column was successfully landed at Longji.   But here progress was checked by news that the Ebea column had been repulsed above Dehane.   The coast column, therefore, hesitated to advance on Ebea till the Longji district had been thoroughly reconnoitred.   This was not our way of conducting coastal operations ; our best masters of the art had always set surprise higher than reconnaissance.   The French Service, however, did not distinguish so clearly between coastal and regular land operations, so our Nyong Flotilla had to be withdrawn and the lighter part of it sent up the Lokundje to expedite matters.   There it found no trouble in dealing with the outposts it came across.   They were all dislodged and one of the posts occupied.   But by the 30th the French commander was convinced he could not carry on without reinforcements, and the flotilla returned down the river to await their arrival.   Next day, however, word came that none were available.   General Dobell, in fact, was about to launch a column he had been organising at Mujuka to follow up his success at Buea.   Its object was, by clearing the rest of the Northern Railway, to strike a blow at the Germans who had retreated that way and at the same time to relieve the persistent pressure which the enemy was maintaining on the central sections of the Nigerian frontier, and thereby preventing the Nigerian Column from co-operating with him. He had, therefore, no troops to spare.   Consequently, to the great regret of the British Staff, the attempt on Dehane and Ebea had to be abandoned, and the French contented themselves with occupying Kribi while the operations on the left wing proceeded.

It was on December 3, the day the port was occupied, that the Mujuka Column started under Colonel Gorges. Some little opposition was encountered, but by the 10th the railhead at Nkongsamba was in his hands, with a quantity of rolling stock and two aeroplanes.[1]

With this success, what may be regarded as the first stage of the operations was brought to a conclusion. Its general effect was that, although in the occupation of the interior less progress had been made than was hoped, the whole of the coast that had any importance, with all the ports, was denied to the enemy, and the Cameroons had ceased to be a naval factor before the time expired when the *Cumberland* was due to leave. But Captain Fuller did not go with her. The *Pothuau* had arrived, and the conference with the British officers had convinced Captain Chéron, who had come out in command of her, that a change of naval command was highly undesirable. He suggested, therefore, that while he remained as Senior Naval Officer, Captain Fuller should exchange ships with Captain Beaty-Pownall and continue to issue naval orders as Senior Naval Officer on General Dobell's Staff. In this arrangement, which the Governor of Nigeria and General Dobell warmly supported, the Admiralty and the Ministry of Marine concurred; and not only this, but it was agreed that the *Cumberland* should leave behind her the guns she had lent, as well as all officers, steamboats and gear which were essential to the working of the flotilla, and that Captain Beaty-Pownall should take her straight home to have them replaced. Accordingly, on December 4, the *Cumberland* sailed and the *Pothuau* took her place. But scarcely had she arrived when it was known that the main danger to the success of the further operations was past. On the other side of the Atlantic the blow had been struck which finally made all serious interference from the sea impossible.

[1] With Nkongsamba was surrendered the country up to and including Bare, at which place the two aeroplanes—the first to reach West Africa—were captured.

CHAPTER XXVIII

OPERATIONS LEADING UP TO THE BATTLE OF THE FALKLANDS [1]

WHILE Captain Hayes-Sadler and General Delamain had been making their final preparations for forcing an entrance into the Shatt-al-Arab, and Captain Fuller and General Dobell were making theirs for the capture of Buea, the great combination for redressing the consequences of the Battle of Coronel was starting into action. At midnight on November 5 the *Invincible* and *Inflexible* had left Cromarty. Their original orders were to go to Berehaven to fill up with coal, but as the *Invincible*, which was to carry Admiral Sturdee's flag, required docking and repairs, and as it was necessary to take out all possible stores for Admiral Stoddart, both ships were directed to go to Devonport. Proceeding round the west of Ireland, they arrived on the 8th. Here, when the dockyard officials had examined the *Invincible*, they reported that the work which was required upon her could not be completed till the 13th. For the Admiralty a week's delay was inadmissible, and an order was immediately telegraphed that she must sail at latest on the 11th, and that if her defects had not been made good by that time the necessary dockyard hands must go with her and be sent back as opportunity offered. So fine was the response that the two ships put to sea at 4.45 p.m. on the 11th.

Two days earlier—just as the *Sydney* was finishing off the *Emden*—Admiral Sturdee received his sailing orders. They directed him to proceed to St. Vincent, Cape Verde, but, as it was just possible Admiral von Spee might move north to the Panama Canal, he was warned that he might be diverted on passage to the West Indies. On existing indications, however, the German squadron was expected on the southeast coast of America, and in default of further orders Admiral Sturdee was to proceed to the Abrolhos Rocks rendezvous, where he would find Admiral Stoddart's squadron concentrated, and on his way down he was to call to his flag the *Bristol* and *Macedonia*, which were then searching in the

[1] See Maps 2 and 14 in case.

Rocas area for the *Karlsruhe* and her colliers. For the sake of perfecting the concentration against the main body of the enemy and providing Admiral Sturdee with light cruisers, that ship was to be left to do her worst. But only for a time. The morning after Admiral Sturdee's orders were signed news came in of the *Emden's* destruction, and within a few hours it was decided to bring the *Sydney* and *Melbourne* into the Atlantic. Seeing that the *Australia* had already been ordered to the Californian coast, it was a serious draft on the Commonwealth Navy. There were still German auxiliary cruisers at large, and further contingents of troops for Europe would soon require escort. The Australian Government were naturally anxious, and asked to have the whole situation explained. In reply the Admiralty informed them of the measures which had been taken, by means of the two Japanese South Sea Squadrons, to secure the safety of Australian waters and to meet the eventuality of Admiral von Spee breaking back, and explained that the two Australian light cruisers were far too valuable to be used for anything but the most active work that had to be done. The Commonwealth Government at once agreed. So, leaving the Australasian convoy to the *Ibuki* and *Hampshire*, the two light cruisers hurried on to Malta.

There still remained one further step to take to complete the world-wide combination, and before Admiral Sturdee sailed arrangements had been made which would render his diversion to the West Indies unnecessary in any case. The fact was that the old apprehension for the North Atlantic trade routes had been re-awakened. Since the first week in the war they had been undisturbed, but now there were rumours that the Germans intended to send out battle cruisers to raid them. It was reported, indeed, that the *Von der Tann* had actually broken out. The reports came from sources that could not be ignored, especially as a bold stroke against the slender British force which was watching the large German liners at New York might well let them loose to prey on our trade. It was difficult to believe that Admiral von Spee's movement across the Pacific was not part of some larger plan, and quite possibly the idea was to combine an attack on our Plate and Brazil trade with one on the northern routes. The stopping of both these arteries of commerce at the same time—even for a few weeks—would place us in a very difficult position, and it was certainly the most effective plan for influencing the war that appeared to be within the resources of the German Navy. In any case the menace was too probable to be neglected, and even at the cost of still further weakening the Grand Fleet it was decided to draw upon it for another battle cruiser. Accordingly, on November 10, Admiral Jellicoe had orders to detach the *Princess Royal* to reinforce our New York division, but so secret was the matter kept that even Admiral Hornby was not informed she had been ordered to join him.

Coming, as it did, so closely after the loss of the *Audacious* and the Gorleston Raid, the demand was a very serious one to make upon the Commander-in-Chief. True, the splendid new battle cruiser *Tiger* had just joined him, but it would be some time before so raw a ship could be regarded as an efficient battle unit, and as for the promised 1st Cruiser Squadron, there seemed little prospect of its being able to join him till Admiral von Spee had been dealt with. All that could be done was to lay the whole situation before him and show how the possibility of Admiral von Spee coming through the Panama Canal, defeating the West Indies Squadron and releasing the armed liners in New York, rendered the detaching of the *Princess Royal* imperative. The risk, such as it was, had to be run. It was entirely in accordance with the old principle that the Grand Fleet was not only our main concentration, but the reservoir on which we had to draw to meet all such eventualities, and on November 12—the day on which it was calculated the Germans might be off Panama—the *Princess Royal* secretly left Cromarty for Halifax.

By this time all anxiety as to the surviving ships of Admiral Cradock's squadron was at an end. On November 8 the *Canopus* and *Glasgow* had reached the Falklands, and on orders already issued they carried on to join Admiral Stoddart, who was concentrating at the River Plate. The third ship, *Otranto*, having sufficient coal, was proceeding there direct from the Strait. The first appreciation had naturally been that Admiral von Spee would follow up his victory by delivering a blow at the east coast trade routes. This was now doubtful. He had not been heard of since November 4, and the only new information was an intercepted message which seemed to indicate that his rendezvous was Mas-a-fuera. It was possible, therefore, that he would have to be sought out on the west coast, and if this was so the Falkland Islands became essential as a coaling base and must be protected. In these circumstances the previous orders of the *Canopus* were cancelled, and on November 9 Captain Heathcoat Grant was directed to remain at Port Stanley, moor his ship so as to command the entrance, and co-operate with the Governor for the defence of the place. On receiving these orders from Admiral Stoddart he turned back and reached Port Stanley on the 12th to find the Germans had not yet appeared.

Meanwhile Admiral Stoddart, with his flag in the *Defence*, was off the Plate with the *Carnarvon, Cornwall*, and *Orama*. The *Otranto*, which had come direct without going to the Falklands, had also joined him. On the 9th—the day the *Canopus* was turned back—he received orders to remain where he was long enough for the *Glasgow* to join, and, as it was still possible the Germans would appear on his station, to fall back northward to the Abrolhos coaling station and protect the colliers. If Admiral von Spee should appear there and attempt to destroy them, he was authorised to engage him. On the 11th the *Glasgow* arrived, and Admiral Stoddart sailed next day for Abrolhos Rocks, sending the *Orama* to search Trinidada Island on the way. It was a happy inspiration, for almost immediately she sighted a ship which ran from her south-eastwards. The chase was soon overhauled, and the crew, after setting her on fire, took to their boats. She proved to be the *Navarra* of the Hamburg-Amerika Line, which had left Pernambuco on September 24 with munitions and supplies for the German cruisers, and seems to have been wandering in search of them ever since. On October 9 she had been seen entering the Strait of Magellan, and next day was at Punta Arenas. She seems to have left immediately, probably to meet the *Kronprinz Wilhelm*, who detached a tender to look for her about this time. The *Navarra* was steering towards Trinidada, and the *Kronprinz Wilhelm* appears to have been moving down to meet her, for on October 7 she had captured the British steamship *La Correntina* 270 miles east of the Plate.[1] This vessel was one of our defensively armed merchantmen, with two 4·7″ guns, but, having left home before the outbreak of war, she had no ammunition on board. Her fate, however, was not known till more than a month later, when a German steamship brought her crew into Montevideo, together with those of two French sailing ships, the *Union* and the *Anne de Bretagne*, which had also been captured. After seeing the *Navarra* sink and rescuing the crew, the *Orama* carried on for Abrolhos. In reporting the fortunate occurrence Admiral Stoddart begged that it should be kept secret.

Up till this time he had not heard that Admiral Sturdee was coming out, but on November 11, the day the battle cruisers sailed, he was informed. On November 17 Admiral

[1] *La Correntina* was sunk on October 14.

Sturdee put into St. Vincent, Cape Verde, to coal, and on the same day Admiral Stoddart reached Abrolhos Rocks. He found there the *Edinburgh Castle*, which had been left on guard, and the *Kent*, so that besides the *Defence* he had three armoured ships with which to meet Admiral von Spee should he appear. But he had no light cruisers. The *Bristol* and *Macedonia* were still searching for the *Karlsruhe*, and the *Glasgow* had to go into Rio to dock and repair the damage she had received in the Coronel action. So exasperated were the Brazilian authorities by this time, as were also those of Chile, by the insolent disregard of their neutrality which the Germans had been displaying, that for the *Glasgow* they extended " benevolence " to its utmost limits. She received the most cordial welcome, was allowed to remain six days till she was in a better condition than when she began the war, and when she left she was not permitted to pay the dock charges. Considering how strong was German influence in Brazil, and that the cruiser was part of a defeated force, it was high testimony in a neutral of a desire to be just, and the exhibition of good-will was one which our Navy should be slow to forget.

While Admiral Stoddart was thus getting into position and the *Canopus* was completing arrangements for the defence of the southern base, Admiral Hornby to the northward was disposing his squadron to meet the eventuality of Admiral von Spee coming through the Panama Canal. His intention was to concentrate the *Glory, Essex, Lancaster, Berwick*, and *Condé* as a fighting squadron in the West Indies, leaving the *Suffolk* and *Caronia* to watch New York. But, on informing the Admiralty of his plan, he was told the *Princess Royal* was coming, and that he was to shift his flag from the *Glory* to the *Suffolk*, and send the *Glory* down to join the *Lancaster* and *Berwick*. He at once suggested keeping the *Glory* for New York and sending the battle cruiser to the West Indies. But he was told that the *Princess Royal* must remain north to meet the contingency of a heavy cruiser breaking out of the North Sea, though, as the *Suffolk* required dockyard repair, the *Glory* was ordered not to move south for the present. Whatever grounds there were to anticipate that the enemy's plan was to send out battle cruisers, it seems certainly to have been expected by the Germans in South America. Some weeks later the Plate wireless station was intercepting daily calls to the *Seydlitz, Moltke* and *Von der Tann*, although we knew that all these ships were then in the North Sea. An additional reason for not being in a hurry to send the *Princess Royal* to the West Indies was that such indications as we had pointed to Admiral von Spee not having moved to the northward.   On November 13 the *Leipzig* and *Dresden* appeared at Valparaiso.   They left again next day, but the whole German squadron was reported to be off the port, and a suspicious collier was known to be at Punta Arenas, apparently waiting for the German squadron to come south.

But, in fact, the report of Admiral von Spee being off Valparaiso was false.   On leaving that port, as we now know, on November 4 he had gone back to Mas-a-fuera, which he had appointed as a rendezvous for his two detached light cruisers.   There he arrived on November 6, to find that on the previous day the *Leipzig* had arrived in company with two of his own colliers, *Amasis* and *Santa Isabel*, and also with a prize, the *Valentine*, a French four-masted barque of 3000 tons.   The following day the *Baden* joined, with another, the Norwegian ship *Helicon*, of 1,600 tons.   Both prizes were full of Welsh coal, which Admiral von Spee proceeded to transfer to his cruisers and regular colliers. The work was still in progress when, early on the 8th, the *Prinz Eitel Friedrich* joined, followed later by the *Dresden* with the *Sacramento*, carrying 7,000 tons of coal and 1,000 tons of stores ; her meeting with the light cruiser appears to have been definitely prearranged.   Her, too, it was decided to clear in spite of the delay it would involve and the continued violation of Chilean territory.   Why Admiral von Spee waited so long before following up his success is not apparent.[1] It can hardly be that the captured coal was essential for further operations, for he had several colliers awaiting orders in Chilean ports.   Possibly he, too, may have received the rumours that German battle cruisers were breaking out of the North Sea to join hands with him.   There was certainly an expectation to this effect prevalent in the squadron, for under date November 23 an officer of the *Gneisenau* entered in his diary that he had been told that the *Seydlitz* and *Moltke*, loaded with ammunition, were making their way into the Atlantic, and about three weeks later, as we have seen, the Montevideo wireless station was making daily calls to these two ships, as well as to the *Von der Tann*.   Admiral

[1] On November 4 the German Naval Staff telegraphed to Admiral von Spee : " You are advised to try to break through with all your ships and return home."   That this message reached its destination is certain, though on what date is unknown, for on the 16th he answered a further message asking " What are your plans ? " by telegraphing " The Cruiser Squadron intends to break through for home."   This intention was the foundation of his subsequent movements, modified only by his desire that the squadron should take every opportunity of fighting in order to bear an honourable share in the activities of the German Navy.

von Spee may, therefore, have been simply standing by to give them time to appear, so that nothing was lost in transferring the captured coal. By the 15th—that is, after over a week's stay—the work was complete, and he sailed for St. Quentin Bay in the Gulf of Peñas, about 300 miles north of the Magellan Strait, where his other colliers were to meet him. Two days later—the 17th—he met the *Dresden* and *Leipzig* at a sea rendezvous about 400 miles south of Mas-a-fuera. Their news was that on the way from Valparaiso they had captured the *North Wales*, the collier which Admiral Cradock had ordered on to Juan Fernandez from his secret coaling base near the Straits and which they caught making her way back to the Falklands with 700 tons of coal on board. She, too, was sunk, but her consort, the storeship *Crown of Galicia*, which was three days ahead, got through without being sighted.

On November 21 the squadron reached St. Quentin Bay, and there they found two large colliers awaiting them. One was the Norddeutscher Lloyd S.S. *Seydlitz*, which had stolen out of Valparaiso without a clearance shortly before the battle of Coronel. The other was the Kosmos liner *Memphis*, which had come from Punta Arenas, also without clearance. Two days later a third ship joined them. This was another Kosmos liner, the *Luxor*, which had been lying in Coronel since September 6. On that day she began taking in 10,000 tons of coal, and she had succeeded in getting 3000 tons on board before the Chilean authorities put a stop to it. Still, in defiance of them, she managed to slip out during the night of November 18 with a large supply of provisions besides the fuel. Her departure from Coronel was at once reported to the Admiralty, and they thus became aware that Admiral von Spee was still trying to take in coal somewhere on the west coast, but nothing further was yet known of his movements. It was enough, however, to assure them that Admiral Sturdee would be in time to deal with the German squadron if it attempted to attack the Plate routes, since by the time Admiral von Spee reached St. Quentin Bay, Admiral Sturdee had left St. Vincent and was well on his way to Rocas Reef, which he intended to search as he passed down.

The situation was thus so well in hand that a modification of the combination was possible. It was specially important to find something to take the place of the battle cruisers in the Grand Fleet as soon as possible, and it was now felt that the *Warrior* and *Black Prince* could be spared. The formation of a new African squadron under Admiral de Robeck was no longer necessary. It was therefore cancelled. On November 19 he was ordered to return to the *Amphitrite* and resume the command of the 9th Cruiser Squadron, while the *Black Prince*, *Warrior*, and *Donegal* were ordered to join Admiral Jellicoe. In their place the *Defence* was to reinforce the Cape Station. With the *Defence*, *Minotaur*, and *Albion*, as well as the light cruisers *Weymouth* and *Dartmouth* from the East Indies and the *Hyacinth* and *Astræa* of the original squadron, it was strong enough. Orders went out accordingly on November 22, Admiral Stoddart being instructed that as soon as Admiral Sturdee arrived he was to remove his flag from the *Defence* and send her away to St. Helena at fifteen knots to join the Cape Squadron.

Her presence at the Cape was urgently required, for until she arrived it was impossible to resume the plan of operations against German South-West Africa. Ever since the rebellion had broken out these operations had been suspended, but it was now mastered. The successes of the Union forces had continued without interruption. On November 13 the back of the movement had been broken, when General Botha, assisted by Colonels Brand and Brits, had defeated De Wet at Bantry, Mushroom Valley and Honderkop, and on that day, with a view of freeing the Union forces for opening the campaign against the Germans, a notification had been issued offering an amnesty to all rebels who surrendered by November 21. By that time De Wet had suffered two more reverses, and the rebels were coming in in such large numbers that the Government decided they need no longer delay operations. On November 23, therefore, they informed Admiral King-Hall that they proposed to send an expedition to Walfisch Bay about December 12, a date which was next day advanced to the 2nd. But they had calculated without the far-reaching effects of the German Pacific Squadron. Admiral King-Hall at once saw the dangers that beset the project so long as Admiral von Spee was unlocated, and telegraphed home for instructions. The difficulty was that, owing to the mystery which surrounded the movements of the German Admiral after the Battle of Coronel and the unhappy experience of the battle itself, the Admiralty had felt compelled to send him a strict order to keep his squadron concentrated. In the middle of the month, therefore, he had recalled the *Albion*, which had been stationed as guardship at Walfisch Bay, and had gathered all his ships at Simonstown and Table Bay. As the two East Indies light cruisers *Dartmouth* and *Weymouth* had arrived and the *Minotaur* was close at hand, it would, of course, be possible for him to escort the expedition to Walfisch Bay; but as the place had still no adequate coast defence, he would have to protect it, and in view of his orders to remain concentrated, the only way to do it was to keep the whole squadron there. This would leave the southern base at Luderitz Bay exposed to attack, as well as the whole line of supply from the Cape, 750 miles long. The crucial trouble was the difficulty raised by endeavouring to act from two bases 250 miles apart, and the nearest 500 miles from the main source of supply. The risk, however, would be greatly reduced by using the nearer base alone, and he was ready, if the Union Government chose to take the lesser risk, to convey an expedition to Luderitz Bay, but he could not take it to Walfisch Bay till the *Defence* joined, which meant he could not sail till December 14. So entirely, however, did General Botha's plan of campaign depend on acting from both bases simultaneously that the Union Government decided to postpone the expedition for a fortnight.

Thus was the old law exemplified, and a conspicuous modern instance afforded of how a belligerent by keeping a force concentrated at sea may hamper military operations even in a quite distant theatre by forcing a corresponding concentration on his enemy. In this case the reaction of our enemy's concentration was strengthened by the mystery which continued to shroud his movements. At the Cape vague rumours led to a belief that Admiral von Spee was then actually crossing the Atlantic. But this the Admiralty soon ascertained to be untrue. On the same day that the Union Government decided to re-open operations, our Consul-General at Valparaiso was able to report that he had information direct from Mas-a-fuera with the names of all the ships present on November 15. He also stated that it was believed they had been depositing a store of coal on the island, and that the Chilean Government, to assert its neutrality, was going to send ships to destroy it. The information was amplified next day (the 23rd) from an intercepted German message, which left little doubt that Admiral von Spee was at St. Quentin Bay.

The news had a marked effect on Admiral Sturdee's instructions. It seemed to indicate that if he was to bring the German squadron to action he would have to seek it on the west coast. On November 24, therefore, orders were sent out that after joining up with Admiral Stoddart he was to move south to the Falklands, which he was to use as his base, and then move to the Chilean coast, searching the channels and inlets of Tierra del Fuego and keeping his big

ships from being seen in the Straits. He was further informed
that the *Australia* and Admiral Patey's Anglo-Japanese
Squadron would be at the Galapagos Islands on December 2,
ready to move south, and that the Japanese First South
Sea Squadron would probably be moving eastwards from
Fiji to the Marquesas Islands.[1]

These orders Admiral Sturdee received at the Abrolhos
Rocks rendezvous when he reached it on November 26. He
found there the *Carnarvon*, to which Admiral Stoddart had
just shifted his flag, *Cornwall*, *Kent*, *Glasgow* (now thoroughly
repaired), *Bristol*, and *Orama*. The *Defence* was also waiting
there in order to transfer to the *Invincible* the Poulsen
wireless gear with which she had been fitted. As a link the
afterwards famous *Vindictive*, similarly fitted, was on her
way to Ascension, and by this means it was hoped to get
over the difficulty of communicating, which had been found
so troublesome in Admiral Cradock's case. Admiral Sturdee's
first care was to select his three fastest colliers and dispatch
them in advance on separate courses to the Falklands. Then
having rigged the Poulsen gear and coaled, he arranged for
the *Orama* to escort the rest of them—five in number—to
his new base, while he took the united squadron down inshore
of them.

To any one who at this moment could have surveyed the
vast theatre of operations it would have seemed that, in

[1] This squadron was being reinforced by the light cruisers *Chikuma* and
Yahagi from the Indian Ocean after the destruction of the *Emden*. The
Ikoma was also to join. The *Iwate* was being transferred from the 1st to
the 2nd Squadron, which was concentrating at Truk Island in the Eastern
Carolines. The *Ibuki* and the *Nisshin* were also to join it there, while the
other two cruisers which had been under Admiral Jerram—*Tokiwa* and
Yakumo—were recalled to Japan to join the First South Sea Squadron.
The two squadrons were, therefore, now constituted as follows :—

FIRST SQUADRON

Vice-Admiral Yamaya (*Base*, Suva, Fiji)

Kurama ⎫	
Tsukuba ⎬	battle cruisers
Ikoma ⎭	
Iwate	armoured cruiser
Chikuma ⎫ . . .	light cruisers
Yahagi ⎭	

SECOND SQUADRON

Rear-Admiral Matsumura (*Base*, Truk, Carolines)

Satsuma	battleship
Ibuki	battle cruiser
Nisshin	armoured cruiser
Hirado	light cruiser
Umikaze ⎫ . . .	destroyers
Yamakaze ⎭	

spite of the rapidity with which the British combination had been organised, it was too late. For on the day Admiral Sturdee reached Abrolhos Rocks, Admiral von Spee left St. Quentin Bay for the Falklands. Besides the two large cruisers he took with him the *Dresden, Leipzig,* and *Nürnberg*. The *Prinz Eitel Friedrich* was detached, as the *Emden* had been, to act independently as a commerce raider on the west coast. The three colliers *Seydlitz, Baden,* and *Santa Isabel,* and possibly another, remained with the squadron. The *Memphis* and *Luxor,* after having been swept, were dismissed, and both on their arrival in port were interned, the *Memphis* at Coronel by the Chileans and the *Luxor* at Callao by the Peruvians. So, as Admiral Sturdee came southwards, the German squadron was steaming towards the Horn, but in weather so tempestuous that they could sometimes make no more than five knots; the colliers were unable to keep touch, and so no formation could be preserved.

It was on November 28, two days after the Germans started for the Falklands, that Admiral Sturdee left the Abrolhos rendezvous. By that time the crews of *La Correntina* and of one of the French sailing vessels which the *Kronprinz Wilhelm* had captured had been brought into Montevideo by her tender, the *Sierra Cordoba,* and it was thus known that a fortnight earlier she had been working some 300 to 400 miles off Santos. Admiral Sturdee, therefore, decided to make a sweep for her, and went down the route with his squadron in extended order, covering a front of fifty miles. But, in fact, she was no longer there, for after her second French capture, the barque *Anne de Bretagne,* she had gone to the northward to take up the *Karlsruhe's* old cruising ground, from which the *Bristol* and *Macedonia* had just been withdrawn.[1] Had he held on, therefore, he would have found nothing, but, as it was, a report from Rio the same evening that the Von Spee squadron was 400 miles from Montevideo drew him off in that direction. It was not till December 1 that he knew the report was false, and he then set his course for the Falklands.

But, meanwhile, another report of the whereabouts of the German squadron had come to hand. It had been received on November 29 from Iquique in the extreme north of Chile, and it stated that at least three cruisers had been off that port the previous day. This looked so much like a move for the Panama Canal that Admiral Hornby was

---

[1] Here the *Kronprinz Wilhelm* made two captures on December 4 : the British collier *Bellevue* (sunk on the 20th) and the French steamship *Mont Agel,* immediately sunk by ramming. On the 28th she captured the British steamship *Hemisphere* (sunk 7 January, 1915).

ordered to send the *Princess Royal* to Jamaica at once.
Captain Osmond Brock, who commanded her, was to become
Senior Naval Officer for the West Indies, and his orders were
to keep up communication with Admiral Patey, with whom
wireless contact had just been established by the *Berwick*.

The news, which was false, made no difference to Admiral
Sturdee. He continued his way down, and on December 3
his squadron was completed by the junction of the *Macedonia*,
which had been away at Sierra Leone to coal and make good
defects. On November 25 the *Canopus* at Port Stanley had
taken in a signal that Admiral von Spee had actually rounded
the Horn, but this was unknown to Admiral Sturdee, and on
December 4 he got a message which left him in no doubt he
could safely carry on as he was. It came from our Consul-
General at Valparaiso, and stated that the *Prinz Eitel Friedrich* had been sighted off the port early that morning.[1] From
this fact the Admiral concluded that the whole German
squadron was probably there.

His deduction was erroneous. Admiral von Spee had
actually rounded the Horn at midnight on December 1–2,
but, instead of going on, had called another halt. In the
morning his light cruisers sighted and captured the British
four-masted barque *Drummuir* about thirty miles from Staten
Island, and, as she had on board 2,800 tons of anthracite,
which she was taking to San Francisco, she was towed into
the mouth of the Beagle Channel, and there, under Picton
Island, the squadron anchored to discharge her cargo into
the cruisers and colliers. The work took three days, and it
was not till noon on December 6 that they put to sea again.
The *Drummuir* was towed out and sunk, and then the course
was finally set for the Falklands.

It is evident, therefore, that but for his delay in clearing
his last capture Admiral von Spee would have reached Port
Stanley at least two days before Admiral Sturdee. What
he expected to find there was a British squadron coaling. It
was believed to consist of the *Canopus*, *Carnarvon*, and possibly the *Defence*, *Cornwall* and *Glasgow*. According to
two of the survivors of the *Gneisenau* he obtained this information from a Dutch ship the day after leaving Picton Island.
On the strength of it, so the two men asserted, his intention
was to draw the British to sea and destroy them. He could
then occupy the Islands and demolish the wireless installation, and for this operation landing-parties were told off.

---

[1] The *Prinz Eitel Friedrich* sank the British steamship *Charcas* on December
5 : on the 11th she captured the French barque *Jean* (sunk on the 31st), and
on the 12th she sank the British barque *Kildalton*.

Assuming the prisoners' statement to be correct, it may
be taken as certain that, as the *Canopus* was there alone, he
would have attempted to destroy her.   Whatever success he
might have met with, his power of fighting Admiral Sturdee
must have been seriously crippled; for Captain Grant had
had full time to complete his preparations for defence.

Having returned to the Falklands on November 12, he
attempted to place the ship in position in Port William, the
outer harbour, but, finding the weather rendered this impracticable, he moved into Port Stanley, the inner harbour,
which is practically a lagoon accessible from the outer harbour by a very narrow entrance.[1]   At one end lies the little
settlement, at the other he moored his ship, and eventually,
finding it impossible to keep her steady, berthed her on the
mud, as he was specially authorised to do by his instructions.
The outer entrance was closed with a row of electric mines
constructed out of old oil drums, and a picket boat with
dropping gear patrolled outside.   Three batteries were also
established and armed with 12-pdrs., and an observation
station set up ashore as a fire-control position for covering
all points from which an attack could be made on the wireless
installation.[2]   The work was exceptionally laborious, and it
had to be done in a continuous succession of hurricanes of
snow and hail.   In the midst of the work the storeship,
Crown of Galicia, came in after her escape from the German
squadron, and her stores were cleared and stowed in the
Admiralty sheds which had been built some years before
but never yet used.   The new King Edward Memorial
hospital was also equipped by the medical staff of the ship,
and all through the weather never ceased to justify its evil
reputation.   It was not till December 4 that all was done
and the *Canopus* was snug in her mud berth at the eastern
end of the harbour.

Thus sturdily prepared, the deserted little colony was
waiting for the blow to fall.   Ever since November 25, when
the message came that Admiral von Spee had doubled the
Horn, they had been expecting attack.   Day by day the
anxiety grew, but not till the forenoon of Monday, December 7,
did the signal station report a single sail.   Then without
warning Admiral Sturdee's whole squadron appeared, to
the great relief of all concerned.   His intention, as signalled
to the squadron the previous day, was to commence coaling at once and leave again on Tuesday the 8th, in the

---

[1] See Map 17 in case.

[2] The wireless station was at the eastern end of the Murray Heights,
about three-quarters of a mile W.S.W. from Hooker Point.

evening, in order to get round the Horn before the enemy
came east. As his own colliers had not arrived and there
were only three in the harbour, the whole squadron could
not coal simultaneously, and, moreover, the *Bristol* required
engine repairs. The arrangements, therefore, were that the
Carnarvon, *Bristol*, and *Glasgow* should coal first, and the
two battle cruisers next. These five ships could then sail,
if desirable, on Tuesday, leaving the *Kent* and *Cornwall* to
follow. The orders for the squadron, except the *Bristol*,
were to keep steam for twelve knots at two hours' notice,
and for the guardships, to be ready for fourteen knots at
half an hour. Till Tuesday morning the *Inflexible* was to be
guardship and afterwards the *Kent*. On arrival all the ships
anchored in Port William within the minefield, except the
Bristol and *Glasgow*, which went into Port Stanley, and the
Macedonia, which was told off to patrol during the night ten
miles from the entrance.

After anchoring, the Admiral signalled for all captains,
and a conference was held. Of news, beyond persistent
rumours from Brazil, probably spread by Germans, that
Admiral von Spee intended to make for South Africa, there
was very little. Since, however, the German squadron had
not appeared, it seemed obvious the report of their having
passed the Horn must have been false. The last indication
the Admiral had to go upon was the appearance of the *Prinz
Eitel Friedrich* off Valparaiso, and there seemed little doubt
that the squadron should get to the west coast as soon as
possible. The arrangements, therefore, stood as settled the
previous day.

By 6 a.m. the *Carnarvon* and *Glasgow* had finished coaling,
but a hitch had occurred with the *Bristol*, for the coal in her
collier was found to have deteriorated so badly that it could
not be used, and she had to wait for the *Glasgow's*. There
was thus only one left for the battle cruisers, but, fortunately,
one of the squadron colliers now appeared, and she was
ordered at once to the *Inflexible*, who was able to begin
coaling at 7.20. The *Bristol* still had her fires drawn, the
Cornwall had an engine opened up at six hours' notice, and
neither she nor the *Kent* nor *Macedonia* had begun to coal.
Thus the squadron was in no condition for action, when,
half an hour later (7.50), the signal station which the *Canopus*
had established on Sapper Hill above the town reported the
startling news that two strange ships of war were approaching
from the southward.

CHAPTER XXIX

WHEN Admiral von Spee was at Valparaiso after the action off Coronel, it is said he refused to sanction any celebration of his victory by the German colony. Even at the club he declined to drink to the confusion of the British Navy, and in conversation seemed to be impressed with a foreboding that his career would soon be brought to an end. From the first his movements showed that he was under no delusions as to the crushing superiority of the Allies on the high seas, and now he could scarcely doubt that swift retribution must follow the blow he had been fortunate enough to deliver to British prestige. It was a blow certain to let loose all the latent energy and resource of the oldest and most powerful of the navies. On December 6 he told his captains that he might attack the Falkland Islands, destroy the wireless station and arsenal, and also take the Governor prisoner as a reprisal for the capture of the Governor of Samoa. His officers were not unanimously in favour of the project; his Chief-of-Staff and the captain of the *Nürnberg* agreed with it, but the captains of the *Gneisenau*, *Dresden* and *Leipzig* considered it strategically correct to avoid the islands.

In all the circumstances he naturally approached the islands with caution. The captain of the *Gneisenau*, with his own ship and the *Nürnberg*, was sent ahead to reconnoitre, and as a first step to destroy the wireless station by gun fire. It was this detachment which at 7.50 on December 8 was sighted from the signal station. The surprise was complete. Admiral Sturdee was not intending to sail till the evening, and there had been so many false alarms of late that little notice was taken at the moment. Indeed, so busy was the flagship coaling that the *Glasgow* in the inner harbour, who took in the signal, fired a gun to ensure immediate attention.[2] That

---

[1] See Maps 17 and 18 in case.
[2] *Canopus* passed the alarm at 7.50. *Invincible's* signal log records the *Canopus* signal at 8.0. It also notes that *Glasgow* fired a gun at 7.56. *Kent* was ordered by signal to weigh at 8.10, and the general signal "to prepare to weigh" was made at 8.14.

Admiral Sturdee had reached the Falklands just in time was a stroke of luck which the judgment and energy of the Admiralty fully deserved, but he had been caught at a disadvantage, and the prospects, should the Germans press home an attack without delay, were far from pleasant. Still, but for the Admiral's foresight it might have been worse. After a long run down from Brazil the engineer officers would naturally expect the ships to be put at long notice to give them a fair chance of overhauling. But in view of the uncertainty of the situation Admiral Sturdee had felt obliged to put them at two hours, and but for this precaution the end might have been very different. The *Glasgow* and *Bristol* were at once ordered to raise steam for full speed, but as the *Glasgow* was also repairing machinery she could not be ready for two hours, while the *Bristol*, who had both engines opened up, reported she would be unable to move till 11.0. The battle cruisers had not completed coaling, but the general signal to prepare to weigh was made, and at half-past eight " Action " was sounded off and coaling ceased.

By this time the signal station reported more smoke away to the south-westward, and a quarter of an hour later the *Kent*, who had just taken over guard duty, passed down the harbour. Her orders were to join the *Macedonia*, which was now anchored at the entrance, and observe the enemy. At the same time the *Canopus* reported the *Gneisenau* and *Nürnberg* were eight miles away and the main body of the enemy twenty miles. As the leading ships continued to come on, the *Macedonia* at 9.15 was recalled inside the harbour, and the colliers were cast off so as to leave all ships free to fire. While this was going on a third patch of smoke was reported by the signal station. It must have come from Admiral von Spee's three colliers, which apparently had orders to make for Pleasant Road, about twenty miles south-west of Port Stanley.

Meanwhile the two advanced ships were coming rapidly on, steering, as it seemed, for the wireless station near Hooker Point, and the *Canopus* could hope that the precautions she had taken might avail to avert the surprise taking effect. Having previously made all preparations for indirect laying from his fixed platform, Captain Heathcoat Grant at 9.0 asked leave to fire. A quarter of an hour later the two advanced ships could be seen to turn to the north-east, and off the Wolf Rocks, some six miles short of Cape Pembroke, they eased down with their guns trained on the wireless station. By this time Admiral Stoddart had the *Carnarvon* ready, and was ordered to clear for action and engage the enemy as they

rounded Cape Pembroke. But the *Canopus* had first to say
her word. Her gunnery officer was established ashore in an
extemporised observation hut, and as soon as he judged the
range to be down to 11,000 he gave the signal. She fired with
both guns of the fore turret. The shots fell a long way short,
but the Germans hoisted their colours, and putting their
helms hard aport, made away to the south-east. As they
did so she tried again, this time with a salvo at extreme
elevation. Again the shots were short, but only by a hundred
yards or so, and to many observers it seemed that some frag-
ments of shell or a ricochet hit the *Gneisenau* at the base of
the after funnel. It was useless to fire again, and in a few
minutes (9.31) the enemy altered back 8 points and slowed
down as though intending to engage the *Kent*, which was now
well outside the entrance of Port William. So menacing was
the movement that the Admiral signalled the exposed cruiser
to close the flag. But before she could act on the order the
danger was past; for five minutes later (9.40), as the *Gneisenau*
opened the harbour, the dense columns of smoke that hung
over it from the British ships firing up showed there must be
something more than had been expected inside—and, worse
still, there could be made out what looked like tripod masts.

Seldom, perhaps, did naval commanders receive a severer
shock. Though reports of the *Invincible* having come out
had appeared in American papers, no word of what was in
store for him had reached Admiral von Spee. She had last
been heard of in the Mediterranean, and nothing was further
from the thought of the captain of the *Nürnberg* when he
advised an attempt on the Falklands than her sudden appearance at the islands. Fully understanding what he had helped
to bring upon the squadron, he turned with the *Gneisenau*
directly away from the port and made off at high speed in
response to a signal from the Admiral to rejoin the flagship.

It was now a quarter to ten, nearly two hours since the
enemy's smoke had first been sighted, and all ships, except
the *Bristol*, had steam up. The *Glasgow*, which had already
weighed, was ordered to join the *Kent*, and Admiral Stoddart
was directed to go out and take charge of the look-out ships.
At 10.0 the rest of the squadron weighed and proceeded
through the minefield in the order *Inflexible*, *Invincible*,
Cornwall. As they came down the harbour the *Glasgow*
reported the enemy going off to the south-eastward as hard
as they could, and she and the *Kent* put on full steam to keep
touch.

The foul weather that had been so persistent had now
passed away. The sea was calm, with a clear blue sky and

a light cold breeze from the north-west.   Visibility was at its maximum, and as the squadron cleared Cape Pembroke Light the enemy's five ships could be clearly seen on the south-east horizon hull down.   The *Glasgow*, which had passed the *Kent*, was well ahead signalling their movements.   As Admiral von Spee saw the British ships and could clearly make out the tripod masts of the battle cruisers, he had increased speed to join his advanced division, and the nearest ship was judged to be over fifteen miles from the harbour mouth.   This must have been an over-estimate, but in any case the enemy had secured a long start, and in those latitudes no one could count on the favourable weather lasting.   So without more ado Admiral Sturdee at 10.20 made the signal for " general chase." The moment recalls many others of famous memory when the same exhilarating signal was made; it had been the prelude of some of the most decisive successes in our records, but conditions had changed, and it was soon found that it could not be strictly followed.   In the effort the battle cruisers had made to work rapidly up to full speed, they were belching forth such volumes of dense smoke that in half an hour the Admiral found it necessary to do something to reduce the trouble.   The enemy could not be seen, but at 10.48 the *Glasgow* reported them twelve miles distant.   It was clear our ships were gaining, and the Admiral thereupon (10.50) signalled to the *Inflexible* that he was easing speed to 24 knots to lessen the smoke, and to the *Glasgow* to keep three miles ahead.[1]   He then took the further step of ordering the *Inflexible* to get gradually on his starboard quarter and keep clear of the smoke.

The freedom of " general chase " was thus already broken into, but more was soon to come.   The *Carnarvon* and *Cornwall*, in spite of the reduction of speed, were lagging far behind, and to an inquiry from the Admiral (11.7) as to how fast they could go the *Carnarvon* replied 20 knots and the *Cornwall* 22. He had just ordered the *Cornwall* to take station on the *Carnarvon's* starboard quarter, and informed the *Inflexible* he had reduced to 19 knots.   His idea was to avoid getting his squadron scattered too widely, and there seemed no reason for excessive hurry.   The enemy were now well in sight from the flagship, their funnels and bridges showing above the horizon, and the *Glasgow* reported them doing no more than 15 knots.   It was clear he had the speed of them and could follow their motions.   Accordingly, as it was very desirable that the *Carnarvon* and *Cornwall*, which were now some five

---

[1] There is a clerical error here in the official despatch.   It gives two miles, but the logs of both *Invincible* and *Glasgow* record the signal as three miles.

miles astern, should be given a chance of getting up, he decided not to press the action at once. With this object, at 11.26 the signal was made to proceed at 20 knots. The effect of it, combined with the previous signals which had given the squadron a tactical formation for the approach, was finally to annul " general chase."

At the same time his attention was called in another direction. The *Bristol*, who by the extraordinary exertions of her engine-room staff had managed to get out, signalled that three strange ships were off Port Pleasant. The information had come from two ladies at Port Darwin who had been watching the proceedings, and had seen Admiral von Spee's colliers arrive.[1] While one remained on the look-out the other went to the telephone and warned the Governor. The message, which reached the *Canopus* at 10.50 just as the *Bristol* was coming out, was passed on to her. Owing to the German jamming of our wireless much time had been lost, and prompt action was needed. There had been numerous reports of German reservists gathering at South American ports, and though the strange ships might be colliers, it was quite possible they were transports carrying a landing force to seize the islands. Captain Fanshawe of the *Bristol* was therefore ordered to take under his command the *Macedonia*, which was not intended to follow the squadron, and with her to seek out and " destroy the transports."

Having made up his mind not to press the action at once, Admiral Sturdee, at half-past eleven signalled that there was time to take the next meal. Ships' companies had thus an opportunity of cleaning up, for in some of the ships every one was still black with coal-dust and in coaling rig, a very undesirable condition for going into action. At the same time he altered course to close the enemy, and the affair settled down to a plain stern chase. At first the movements of the enemy had been difficult to make out. Up till 11.15 Admiral Sturdee had been steaming parallel to them, approximately eastward. Then the *Glasgow* was able to report that they were altering to starboard, and at 11.25 he conformed by an order to turn together to east by south (mag.). This brought him again on a course parallel to the enemy, but as soon as he had given the signal for a meal he inclined 2 more points together to starboard, which brought him to south-east by east on a converging course. It could be seen that the enemy was well concentrated, with the *Gneisenau* division leading, but Admiral Sturdee's efforts to close up his own squadron proved

1 Port Darwin is in Choiseul Sound, south-west of Port Pleasant.

12.51 P.M.
"OPEN FIRE"

Scale of Yards.

1000   0   1000 2000 3000 4000 5000 6000 7000 8000 9000 10000 11000

Carnarvon

Cornwall

Kent

Inflexible ⚹ Invincible   Glasgow

Leipzig

Nürnberg   Scharnhorst
                Gneisenau
                Dresden

unavailing. In spite of the reduction of speed Admiral Stoddart was unable to get up. He could force no more than 18 knots out of the *Carnarvon*, and as the *Cornwall* had 4 knots in reserve she was ordered to go ahead (12.5). Still, Admiral Sturdee kept his speed down to 20 knots, but at 12.20 the enemy could be seen altering to starboard, and their formation to be breaking up as though they were reforming. Admiral Sturdee decided to seize the moment to press the chase. It was impossible to wait longer for his unfortunate colleague—he was now about 6 miles astern—and speed was increased to 22 knots.

The enemy was now going south-eastward, direct before the wind and shrouded in their own smoke.[1] Admiral Sturdee could only hold on as he was, but at the same time he ordered the *Inflexible* to open to 5 cables. Speed was being quickly worked up, till by 12.50 it was 25 knots, and as they were fast overhauling the enemy the Admiral made the general signal to engage. The *Leipzig*, being the rearmost and slowest ship, could not stand the increasing speed and was falling astern, and shortly before one o'clock, when the *Inflexible* had her at 16,000 yards, Captain Phillimore opened fire. The flagship joined in a minute or two later, and at the same time course was altered 2 more points together to starboard in order to close, and speed increased to the utmost possible. No hits were obtained, but as the range diminished shots fell so close that at times the *Leipzig* was lost to view in the splashes.

It was clear things could not last as they were : something had to be done to save the lagging German cruiser, and Admiral von Spee took a decision which did him and his Service the highest honour. Determined to sacrifice himself and his two heavy cruisers to save the rest, which after all could do the greatest service to his country in harrying our trade, he resolved for the honour of the flag and to facilitate their escape to accept action. About 1.20, therefore, he signalled to his light cruisers to scatter and make for the South American coast, while he with the armoured ships fought it out to the end. With that the three light cruisers broke off to the southward, and the Admiral turned his two ships about

---

[1] In order to prevent his ships hindering each other and to increase their speed as much as possible, the German Admiral signalled that they need not remain in line ahead. The *Nürnberg* kept up well with the *Gneisenau* ; the *Dresden*, at her own request, was allowed to steam at her utmost speed and soon came up with them. The *Leipzig*, the oldest of the ships, dropped a little astern.

6 points into line ahead, and headed away at his utmost speed to the north-eastward out into the ocean.

It was a fine manœuvre, but Admiral Sturdee had provided for it in his battle instructions, and without any signal being made his light cruisers broke away in chase of those of the enemy, while the two battle cruisers turned together through 7 points, and were thus brought into line ahead abeam of the enemy before he could complete his turn.

So about 1.20 the main action began with the *Invincible* ranging on the *Gneisenau* and the *Inflexible* on the *Scharnhorst*, and Admiral Stoddart now ten miles astern trying vainly to get up with them by cutting the corner. During the turn the *Gneisenau* had slowed down to let the flagship pass ahead and as soon as the Admiral had taken the lead he began to return the British fire. The range, however, which was still about 14,000 yards, was too great, and the enemy's shots fell about 1000 yards short. But it quickly diminished, for Admiral von Spee promptly led four more points inwards, and as soon as it was down to about 13,000 yards, he altered outward again to a course parallel to the British, and just as our two battle cruisers had exchanged targets with the change in the German line the *Invincible* was hit. The hit appeared to be due not to straddling but to the flagship having come within the extreme range of the German guns. Admiral Sturdee therefore at once (1.44) turned away 2 more points together to port, and the range rapidly opened out again as the action continued. The enemy were firing deliberately to husband their ammunition, which had not been replenished since Coronel, but the range was now too great for the fire to be effective. The British did little if any better, the fire of the *Inflexible* being specially loose since, stationed as she was, she was so smothered with the flagship's smoke that spotting was impossible. The after guns of the *Invincible* were almost as badly blinded, and very few hits had been scored when, by two o'clock, the range had opened out to over 16,000 yards and both sides ceased fire. In order to renew the action Admiral Sturdee led round 4 points to starboard, and then signalled for 4 points more together (2.5). While the evolution was proceeding the enemy was blotted out in the smoke, and when he was in view again he was seen to have altered some 10 points to starboard and to be making off to the southward 17,000 yards away in the direction in which his light cruisers had disappeared. Admiral Sturdee at once increased speed again, and another stern chase began. As it proceeded at the utmost speed he kept altering a point or

Carnarvon

1.30 P.M.

Scale of Yards.

1000   0   1000 2000 3000 4000 5000 6000 7000 8000 9000 10000 11000

Cornwall

Kent

Inflexible
Glasgow
Invincible

Leipzig   Nürnberg

Gneisenau
Scharnhorst

Dresden

two together to starboard—that is, towards the flying enemy's course. This was done, we are told, partly to clear his own smoke, which was as dense as ever, but the effect was that by 2.45 the range was down again to 15,000 yards, and turning a couple of points to port, so as to bring all his broadside to bear, he re-opened fire.

For five minutes Admiral von Spee held on as he was and made no reply, but then he began to turn to port through about 9 points, and coming thus into line ahead again made as though to cross the British course. Admiral Sturdee promptly responded with a parrying turn through 6 points to port, and as the two forces came once more broadside to broadside the enemy re-opened fire. They were now abaft the beam on a converging course, and the range was rapidly falling. Still Admiral von Spee held on. His object evidently was to close to his own distance in order to bring his secondary armament into play. It was here lay his only possible advantage over his enemy, and by many it was regarded as a real advantage. The omission of secondary armament from the early Dreadnought ships was the point on which critics had most severely condemned the type. One of the sharpest recent controversies had divided specialists on the question, and it must have been perfectly familiar to Admiral von Spee. Now for the first time an opportunity had arisen of subjecting the difference of opinion to the actual test of battle. From this test Admiral Sturdee did not flinch. Keeping on as he was he allowed the range to fall, and when it was down to about 12,500 yards (2.59) the Germans began to fire with their 5·9″ guns. All Admiral Sturdee did was to signal for 2 more points together to port to keep the range as it was, and presently (3.10) as the range continued to fall he edged away another couple of points and brought it back to about 12,500.[1] During this period the action was at its hottest. Both sides were securing hits, but the British ships appear to have suffered little. With his superior speed Admiral Sturdee was easily able to keep his distance, and the enemy's 5·9″ guns at their extreme range did little to affect his fire. Though some immaterial damage was done to superstructures, no casualties occurred. The gunnery conditions, however, were very bad. The smother of funnel smoke from the battle cruisers made accurate spotting or laying impossible for either side. Still, the British 12″ so far asserted their mastery that by 3.10 the *Gneisenau* had taken a list, and in another five minutes the *Scharnhorst*, which was burning in places

---

[1] Admiral Sturdee in his despatch says it fell by 3.15 to 10,000 yards, but this is not in accordance with German observations.

and whose fire was slackening, had her third funnel shot away.

By this time (3.15) the smoke interference had become so intolerable that Admiral Sturdee turned together sharply through 16 points outwards and to windward to clear it. He thus came on the opposite course with the *Inflexible* leading. For the first time she had a clear view of her target and was able to make more satisfactory practice. But in five minutes, as they drew abreast of the enemy, Admiral Sturdee turned 4 points together to port to head across their wake, and this brought the *Inflexible* abaft the flagship's beam, and smoke interference was almost as bad as ever. Still, hitting continued, and the *Gneisenau's* list had increased so much that her secondary armament would no longer reach, and it ceased fire. As for the *Scharnhorst*, she was even in a worse condition, as could now be plainly seen.

At 3.27, by which time the battle cruisers were well on his port quarter, Admiral von Spee turned suddenly 16 points to port in succession and stood to the north-westward, as though to parry the British manœuvre by crossing Admiral Sturdee's bows. If so it was a desperate expedient, for as the Germans went about the flagship was almost hidden by the smoke from bursting shell and internal fires. " Her upper works," writes an eye-witness, " seemed to be but a shambles of torn and twisted steel and iron, and through the holes in her side, even at the great distance we were from her, could be seen dull red glows as the flames gradually gained the mastery between decks." [1] She seemed to many to be entirely beaten, but as soon as the turn had brought the guns on her starboard side to bear, she renewed her fire almost as briskly as ever in spite of the condition she was in. The range even permitted her to bring her secondary armament into play again. For when the Germans made their sudden manœuvre Admiral Sturdee had countered with a 4-point turn inwards and held that course, so that the two antagonists closed on courses that converged almost at right-angles. The range was then down to 12,000 yards or less, and Admiral Sturdee turned outwards again and increased the range to 15,000 yards to open out beyond the reach of the enemy's 5·9″ guns.

The crisis of the action was now at hand, but the precise movements till it culminated cannot be determined with any certainty. According to the Admiral's despatch the *Inflexible* during the last turn had edged into the flagship's wake. On the other hand, the *Inflexible's* officers say she

[1] *A Naval Digression*, by G. F., p. 196.

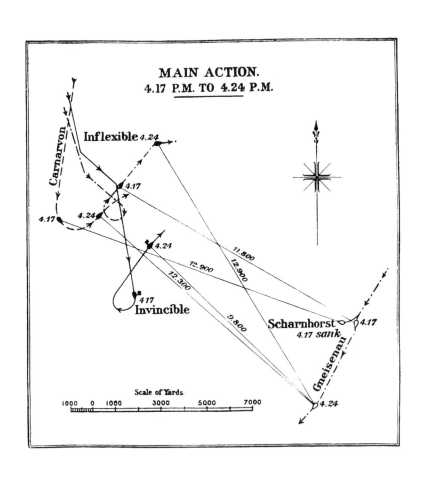

MAIN ACTION.
4.17 P.M. TO 4.24 P.M.

gained the lead by the 3.15 turn together and maintained it. "Then," says her gunnery officer, "for the first time I experienced the luxury of complete immunity from every form of interference," and that from the time Admiral von Spee made his sixteen-point turn he fired on the *Scharnhorst*, which had become his opposite in the line. "I was now," he wrote, "in a position to enjoy the control officer's paradise : a good target, no alteration of course and no next aheads or own smoke to worry me."

Owing to this and similar conflicts of memory all that can be said with any confidence is that after Admiral Sturdee had opened out the range he began to incline inwards to maintain his selected distance from the enemy. During this period both British ships, whatever may have been their relative positions, record firing on the *Scharnhorst*. She was suffering more terribly than ever, and losing speed so rapidly that by 4.0 our ships had fairly overhauled her and had begun to turn more sharply inwards.[1] She was still firing gamely with her remaining guns when, in the words of the gunnery officer of the *Inflexible*, "she suddenly shut up as when a light is blown out." At the same time she lurched away to starboard, heading for our ships, and it could be seen she had a heavy list and was in her last throes.[2]

The *Inflexible*, which at this time it is agreed was leading, at once turned back to starboard to get at her old adversary, the *Gneisenau*, on the opposite course and then to cross her wake and engage her from leeward. Captain Phillimore thought the Admiral would do the same, but he had just turned towards the *Scharnhorst*, and was holding on for the beaten ship. By this time, with her flag still flying, she had turned over on her beam ends, and it looked as if the *Gneisenau* were going to stand by her. But Admiral von Spee's last signal to her was to save herself, and she was seen to be carrying on.

Admiral Sturdee had promptly inclined to starboard to deal with the *Gneisenau* at closer range, and this course he kept till at 4.17 the *Scharnhorst* disappeared. Not a soul of her crew was saved : there could be no thought of rescue, for the *Gneisenau* demanded all his attention. The smoke was now drifting straight down the range between the *Invincible* and the enemy, and Admiral Sturdee, being scarcely able to see his target, turned back to starboard to get out of the smother. Then as soon as he was clear he began to

---

[1] Between 3.25 and 3.57—the decisive half-hour—*Invincible* logs 6 signals to alter course, but it cannot be determined whether they were seen or obeyed by *Inflexible*, for none of them appears in her signal log.

[2] At 4.15 the *Carnarvon* came within range and opened fire.

engage the *Gneisenau* on the opposite course at ranges of
from 10,000 to 12,000 yards. At this time she suffered
severely from both battle cruisers. Shell after shell got
home; her No. 1 turret was knocked out and one stokehold was full of water. When the *Invincible* had run on
thus for about ten minutes and the range opened out as she
passed the enemy, Admiral Sturdee began to circle right
round again, as though to get on a parallel course. But
owing apparently to the difficulty of seeing exactly what
the *Gneisenau* was doing, he continued the manœuvre till
he was heading nearly westward and on a course which
diverged from that of the enemy.

His movement, however, enabled the *Carnarvon* to get
well up. The *Inflexible* had also rejoined, for when the
flagship had run back to her she conformed to the Admiral's
last turn and so came up on the flagship's starboard beam.
Thus all three ships were together again, and the Admiral
signalled to form line ahead. But so badly was the smoke
drifting down the range that in this formation neither the
Inflexible nor the *Carnarvon* could get any clear view of the
target. At last, so completely was the *Inflexible* blinded by
the smother, that after trying to pass the flagship to windward, she broke back in desperation right out of the line
14 points to port and held away to get clear. She had no
order to do so, but Admiral Sturdee afterwards expressed
approval of her independent action. He himself held on,
inclining to port sufficiently to bring his course parallel to
that of the *Gneisenau*. Then by putting on full speed and
making further small turns inwards he began to get into a
position well on her bow. The *Carnarvon*, being unable to
keep up with the flagship, dropped astern. The *Inflexible*,
having run through the smoke, found herself, at 4.50, heading
to cross astern of the *Gneisenau*. As she was seen to be still
firing vigorously on the *Invincible*, the *Inflexible* kept her
course and re-opened fire with her starboard guns. During
the next few minutes many hits were marked, but the
Gneisenau still held on, and at 4.58 the *Inflexible* checked
fire and turning 12 points to starboard towards the Admiral
brought her port battery to bear at about 12,000 yards with
a clear target (5.01). As the enemy's speed dropped the
Carnarvon was soon able to join in, and in this way the ill-
fated *Gneisenau* was receiving a concentrated fire from three
separate bearings.

It was high time to make an end. Over four hours had
passed since the first shot was fired, and a drizzling rain had
come on in which the target was growing fainter every minute.

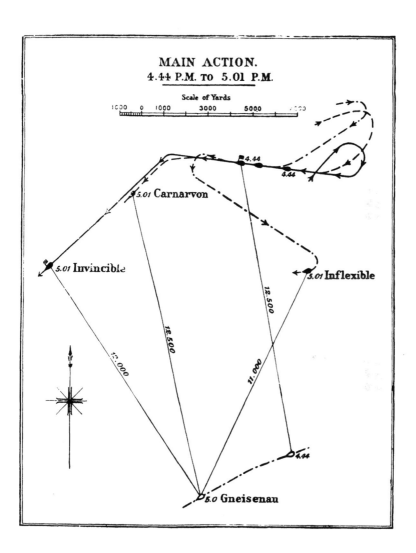

MAIN ACTION.
4.44 P.M. TO 5.01 P.M.

Scale of Yards

But the end was very near. In the first ten minutes of the new phase the *Gneisenau* had lost a funnel; she was evidently suffering severely; her speed had dropped to 8 knots; fore and aft she was burning, and her shots came slower and slower. Still, for half an hour she endured the concentrated fire, replying with well-timed but badly spotted salvoes, till all her 8″ ammunition was spent.   Then at 5.30 she was seen to turn towards the *Invincible*, which had reached almost ahead of her, and to stop with a heavy list to starboard.   Admiral Sturdee at once swept round to close.   At the same moment the *Inflexible* was making a similar movement.   After his independent turn Captain Phillimore had run on for about ten minutes, taking full advantage of the clear target.   He had then turned back 12 points to starboard, bringing his other broadside to bear, and presently began, like the Commander-in-Chief, to make small successive alterations to port to keep on a course parallel to the *Gneisenau*.   At 5.30, seeing the distress she was in, he, too, turned towards her.   She was listing more and more and burning furiously, but, still undefeated, she from time to time fired a gun, and her fire had to be returned.   After a few rounds, however, she was again silent.   She was thought to have struck, and " Cease fire " was signalled.   But in another minute she began again, and the signal had to be annulled.   The *Inflexible* then continued her turn through 16 points to run past her with her starboard broadside bearing.   The Admiral at the same time was coming up on the enemy's starboard quarter.   But, in fact, there was no more to be done.   The *Gneisenau's* gallant struggle was over at last.   In about a quarter of an hour she was again silent and was seen to be going.   All the British ships at once turned in to close at 20 knots; but they were still 3000 or 4000 yards away, when very suddenly she heeled over on her beam ends.   For a minute or so the remnants of her crew could be seen walking on her side, and then she plunged down to join her sister.

It was a splendid fight she had made against hopeless odds, and the British ships pressed on eagerly to the work of rescue.   Some 600 of her men had been killed or wounded, she could no longer fire a gun, but even so there had been no thought of surrender.   When there was no longer any hope of escape, her sea-cocks, it seems, had been opened and all hands ordered on deck.   So they made sure she should sink fast enough to avoid falling into British hands; otherwise, perhaps, many lives might have been spared.   As it was, by lowering all boats that would float and throwing out ropes and life-belts the moment the spot was reached, some 200 of her complement of 850 were picked up, but of these many failed to survive the shock of the icy cold water, and all these were buried next day with full military honours.

How unequal had been the contest is shown by the little the British squadron had suffered. In spite of the enemy's excellent gunnery, the only casualties were one man killed and three wounded in the *Inflexible*. The *Invincible*, who received most of the enemy's fire, was hit about a score of times, and though much knocked about above the armour belt, had suffered no material injury worse than having a strut of her foremast carried away. The *Inflexible* had only a few scratches, and the *Carnarvon* was not touched.

By 7.30 the work of rescue was completed. It so happened that the scene of the last act had already witnessed part of the general action, for some three hours before the last shot was fired the chase of the enemy's light cruisers had passed close to the spot. Since they broke away nothing had been heard of them. Anxious to pursue his success, Admiral Sturdee had called up his three cruisers as soon as the *Gneisenau* went down. From the *Kent* and *Cornwall* there was no reply, and it was not till the boats had returned to the ships that he received a message from the *Glasgow* to say how her chase had sped.

When about 1.25 the German light cruisers broke away they headed at first to the southward, and when the chase began they were ten or twelve miles ahead of their pursuers. As the British ships had nominally no superiority of speed over the enemy, the result could only be doubtful. Of the German ships the *Dresden* was the fastest, for, although her designed speed was given out to be 24 knots, she seems to have been capable of a sea speed of 27. Next to her came our own light cruiser the *Glasgow*, good for over 25 knots, but our two armoured cruisers, *Cornwall* and *Kent*, were 23-knot ships, and even so the *Kent* had the reputation of being the lame duck of her class, and had seldom attained her designed speed. Of the other two German cruisers, the *Nürnberg* was a 23.5 knot ship, and the *Leipzig* by design had 22 knots, but she was a bad steamer, and really slower by a knot or so. Fortunately, none of the German ships was in a good condition when the war broke out, and after four months' continual cruising their boilers were not calculated to stand severe pressure. This was unknown to us at the time, but the outcome could not be doubtful if we could only get to grips. For the German light cruisers had nothing heavier than 4.1″ guns, and excellent as these guns were, not only as compared with our own inferior 4″, with which

the *Glasgow* was mainly armed, but even outranging our older
pattern of 6″, they were no match for the weight of metal of
the fourteen 6″ which the two armoured cruisers carried.

At first the enemy kept together, and when about 1.30
the chase had fairly begun the *Nürnberg* was the centre
ship, with the *Leipzig* about a mile away on her starboard
beam, and the *Dresden* perhaps 4 miles ahead on her port
bow. The *Glasgow*, doing under her 25 knots, rapidly overhauled and passed our two armoured cruisers, which were
going neck and neck, and crossed ahead of them after the
Dresden. But this idea Captain Luce, who was senior officer,
soon had to abandon. It was quickly evident that our
armoured cruisers, if they were gaining at all, were gaining
so slowly that the only chance of bringing the enemy to
action before it was too late seemed to be to attack the rearmost ship. At 2.15, therefore, he slowed down sufficiently
to allow his two consorts to close without ceasing himself to
gain on the *Leipzig*.

By 2.45, as the enemy had been continually edging to
port, the direction of the chase was about south-by-east,
and so it was they all passed close to the spot where the
Gneisenau afterwards sank. Captain Luce, who was still
nearly 4 miles ahead of our armoured cruisers, was, in fact,
actually in these waters when, at 2.53, finding himself within
12,000 yards of the *Leipzig*, he opened fire on her with his
forward 6″ gun. She accepted the challenge with spirit, and,
turning to starboard to bring her broadside to bear, replied.
It was evident at once that her 4·1″ guns were equal to the
range, while the *Glasgow's* 4″ were not. As soon, therefore,
as the enemy began to straddle him, Captain Luce also turned
to starboard to open out the range, and carried on thus till
the *Leipzig* ceased fire and turned back again to follow her
consorts. Once again the manœuvre was successfully performed, and though the enemy's fire was very accurate as
long as she could keep the range down, the *Glasgow* was only
hit twice, and her casualties were very light. Thus at small
cost Captain Luce's object was attained, for each time the
Leipzig turned and tried to close she lost more ground, so
that our armoured cruisers gradually crept up. They were
still neck and neck, the *Kent* doing wonders at 24 knots, and
after 3.30, in reply to a query from the *Glasgow*, they could
signal they were gaining.

This must have been obvious to the enemy, for soon after
they began to scatter, the *Nürnberg* inclining away to port
while the *Dresden*, who had maintained her lead, went to
starboard and soon disappeared in the south-west. Already

(3.36) Captain Ellerton had settled with Captain Allen of the *Kent* that he would take the *Leipzig* with the *Cornwall*, while the *Kent* took the *Nürnberg*. As for the *Dresden*, it was clear that her speed left nothing to be done with her.

By 4.0 the two armoured cruisers were nearly within range. Captain Luce was now holding on after the *Leipzig* on her starboard quarter, and seeing his supports coming up he kept his speed till the range fell to 9000 yards and his 4″ guns would tell. The two armoured cruisers were coming up slightly on the enemy's port quarter and had them almost in range. About 4.15 both of them opened fire, but their shots fell short. The *Nürnberg* was making away to the eastward with the *Kent* after her. The *Leipzig* had inclined to port till she was heading about south-south-east, and the *Cornwall* followed, continuing to fire on her, but receiving no reply, as the enemy was still fully occupied with the *Glasgow*. In another ten minutes the *Cornwall* began to straddle her fairly, and seeing the chase thus well in Captain Ellerton's grip, Captain Luce circled round to starboard to join him, his idea being to produce the maximum effect of fire by both ships engaging her on the same side. As he passed athwart the *Leipzig's* wake he smothered her with his other broadside, and ceasing fire as he neared the *Cornwall*, passed under her stern, and came into action again when he was clear.

The *Leipzig* was already heavily engaged with the *Cornwall* and was clearly doomed. She was being hit time after time. In less than a quarter of an hour her fore-topmast was shot away, and the same shot killed her gunnery lieutenant. At this time Captain Ellerton was steering a slightly diverging course from the chase so as to keep his starboard guns bearing, but just before 5.0, as the range was opening out unnecessarily, he turned sharply to starboard and brought his other broadside into play. Already the *Leipzig* was suffering severely under the cross fire of the two British ships, for, owing to the tactics adopted, there was no mutual interference. Her speed, too, was falling so fast under her punishment that they were able to turn as they liked and to keep the range anywhere between 10,000 and 7000 yards. For nearly an hour these tactics were continued, the *Cornwall* from time to time closing in and firing her foremost group of guns, and then, as soon as the *Leipzig* began to hit, altering outwards again and giving full broadsides till the range became too great. This went on till 6.0, when the drizzling rain came on and began to obscure the target, and as the chase was still fighting gamely Captain Luce signalled to close. The range was soon reduced to 8000 yards, and then the *Cornwall* began to fire lyddite. The effect was immediate. A surviving German officer described it as terrific, and the loss of life fearful. She was in an inferno of dark smoke and flashes from the bursting shells, every salvo hit, and in a few minutes she was burning. Still she continued to fire, and still her pursuers closed. By 6.35 the range was down to 7125 yards, and the *Cornwall*, being now again in position to bring her whole port broadside to bear, was doing worse damage still and starting fresh fires, till the *Leipzig* was ablaze fore and aft. Her fire now came only in gasps, but still she fought on, and continued to hit as her assailants drew closer and closer. Nor was it till past 7.0, four hours after the *Glasgow* had first opened fire, that her last gun was silent. She then fired three torpedoes from her starboard tube, but all missed.

No ship could have done better against such odds. As the two British cruisers drew in to ascertain if she had struck, she was seen to be a wreck. Her mainmast was gone as well as two funnels; she was all ablaze, from where her mainmast had stood to her stern, as well as right forward, but her ensign was still flying defiantly on what was left of her foremast. It was difficult to know what to do. She seemed still to be moving through the water, and might yet be able to fire a torpedo. Captain Luce, therefore, after waiting for half an hour, decided he must finish her at close range. At 7.50 both ships re-opened fire. There was no response. It was known afterwards that, having fired her last remaining round, the beaten ship had opened her sea-cocks and about 150 men had collected amidships between the two burning ends hoping to be saved. The slaughter in consequence was terrible, but soon they succeeded in burning two green lights; then the British ships ceased fire and stopped, believing it was a signal of surrender. Presently, as nothing further happened, they crept on again, coming up directly under her stern out of torpedo danger. At a quarter to 9.0 boats were ordered out, and Captain Luce signalled to her he was sending to save life. Still there was no reply, but by this time she was heeling over heavily to port, a mass of flames and smoke, and, when the boats were already picking up the survivors who had taken to the water, she turned on her beam ends and quietly disappeared (9.23).

Prompt as was the work of rescue, and though many men had been seen to leap into the sea, only four officers and fourteen men were saved alive. The intense cold and choppy sea that was getting up had done for the rest. Amongst those lost was her gallant captain, who although he was one of the few unwounded and had been cheering on his men till the last, could not be found, to the great regret of all who had seen his unflinching fight. As for the British cruisers, in spite of his prolonged resistance, they had suffered very little. The ships themselves were not materially damaged. Though the *Cornwall* had been hit eighteen times and had a list to port, she had not a single man hurt, while the *Glasgow* had not been hit more than twice, and her casualties were one man killed and four wounded.

The last scene had been enacted between 70 and 80 miles to the southward of where the *Gneisenau* had gone down. As soon as the Commander-in-Chief heard of it, being anxious to pursue the chase of the *Dresden* and *Nürnberg*, he asked for the position, but after so many turns our cruisers could give nothing definite. Both of them, moreover, had been holed, and as both ammunition and coal were very low, they were in no condition for a further chase, even if they knew in what direction to go. But of the *Kent* and *Nürnberg* they could give no news at all, having completely lost them since the *Kent* parted company, nor could they get any answer to their calls.

But, in fact, there was no cause for anxiety, though when the chase began there seemed little prospect of success. A notoriously bad steamer, the *Kent* was nearly seven miles astern and her engine-room staff were already strained with eight hours' full speed. But when once she had settled down they performed miracles and made her surpass herself. By forcing fires with all her woodwork they soon had her steaming as she had never steamed before, doing, they said, up to 25 knots. For nearly an hour she thus flogged along, till by 5.0, when the sky became overcast and the wet mist was beginning to obscure the horizon, the range was down below 12,000 yards, and the *Nürnberg* opened fire with her stern guns. The shells went right over, while the *Kent's* 6″ would not yet reach. Even ten minutes later, when the *Kent* opened fire, the shells seemed still to fall short, but as the mist and rain thickened spotting became very difficult, and owing to the tremendous vibration set up by the hard-pressed engines, range-finders were of little use.

The shooting of the *Nürnberg* was excellent, but although during this part of the chase her shells fell thick round the *Kent*, only one got home. In spite of the difficulty of spotting, the *Kent*, as was afterwards known, scored two hits, one in the after steering flat below the waterline, which killed all the men in it except one. But in less than half an hour things began to improve very fast. For some reason she found herself rapidly overhauling the chase. The fact was that the *Nürnberg's* boilers were in such bad condition that in her

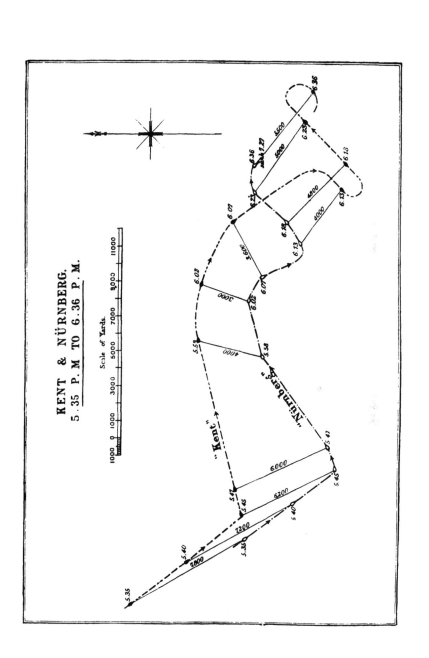

KENT & NÜRNBERG.
5.35 P.M TO 6.36 P.M.

effort to escape she had burst two of them, and her speed
had dropped to 18 knots.   So rapidly then did the *Kent* gain,
that in a quarter of an hour it was obvious an action could
not be avoided, and at 5.45 the *Nürnberg* turned boldly
8 points to port and brought her broadside to bear.   As the
light was fast failing in the drizzle, Captain Allen was only
too glad to accept the invitation.   He had no thought of a
long-range action at that hour—it was a case of quick work
or failure—and, responding with a turn of only 6 points, he
settled down on a converging course.   By the time the two
turns were complete the ships were abreast at only 6000
yards.   The action was now very hot, and as the range fell
the *Kent's* shooting could be seen to be all that was desired.
Being able to keep before the enemy's. beam, Captain Allen
had no fear of torpedo, and continued to close the range till,
at 6.0, it was down to 3000 yards; then, unable to endure the
punishment, the *Nürnberg* turned sharply away to starboard.
Captain Allen responded, but in order to keep his guns bearing
he turned rather less and the range opened again.   Still he
continued to hit, and in ten minutes the enemy was on fire,
with her fore-topmast gone and only two guns alive.   Moreover, she had been losing speed so fast that the *Kent* had been
able to run right past her, and begin to circle 8 points to starboard to cross her bows.   Unable to parry the movement, the
Nürnberg responded with a similar turn to port, as though to
ram, as some thought, but possibly also because it was necessary to bring her other broadside into action.   It was a fatal
movement, for as she came bows on Captain Allen was able
to rake her with all his starboard guns at 3500 yards.   The
effect was decisive.   Amongst other hits, two 6″ shells burst
together on her forecastle and destroyed all her forward guns.
Still she completed her turn, and for a minute or two the
action was on opposite courses; but before he was quite abeam
Captain Allen swung round outwards to keep out of torpedo
danger, and having in this way gained a position on her starboard bow, he gave his fresh gun crews on the port side their
turn.

The end now could not be far off.   By 6.25 the *Nürnberg*
had lost nearly all her way, and the *Kent* had to come round
16 points so as not to draw away from her.   Before the turn
was complete she was seen to be quite silent, and Captain
Allen ceased fire.   The shattered enemy was lying stopped
and a wreck 5,500 yards away.   She had a heavy list, was
down by the stern and burning fiercely under the bridge and
forecastle, without any sign of life.   But apparently she was
not sinking, nor in the bad light could it be seen whether she

had struck. Captain Allen, therefore, steamed towards her, and not till he had closed to 3,300 yards could he see that her flag was still flying. There was nothing to do but open fire again, but it was only for five minutes, for just before 7.0 she hauled down her colours.[1] It was no shame to her after fighting so gallantly for an hour and a half against so superior an adversary. Only two of the *Kent's* boats could possibly float, and they had been hastily patched up and were already gone to the rescue when, just before 7.30, she turned over to starboard and sank quite quietly. Search for survivors was kept up till 9.0, when it was quite dark. A few men were found floating lashed to hammocks, but many of these were dead from the cold, and only seven men were saved alive. The *Kent*, on her part, suffered very little. She had been hit nearly forty times, but beyond having her wireless room wrecked so that she could not communicate, there was little structural damage done. So well, indeed, had her armour and casemates served her, that in spite of the excellence of the enemy's gunnery she had lost only four men killed and twelve wounded, and of these casualties ten occurred in a casemate through a lucky shell igniting some cartridges.

Though the *Nürnberg* was the last ship of the German squadron to be brought to action, she was not the last to go. Some forty miles to the south-westward the *Leipzig*, though she had ceased fire, was still afloat when her sister went down.

The colliers had already been captured some hours earlier. When at 11.45 Captain Fanshawe of the *Bristol* received Admiral Sturdee's order to chase them with the *Macedonia*, he had run some fifteen miles to the eastward after the squadron. Turning at once to the west-south-west, he met the *Macedonia* at 12.30, and the two ships ran on in company to the southward past Port Pleasant.[2] Though they passed it at a distance of only a dozen miles to the southward they could see no sign of the colliers. For another hour Captain Fanshawe kept on as he was, but still sighting nothing, at 2.0 he turned south-east—that is, the direction in which he had seen the German squadron disappear. Then almost directly he received a signal to say that the ships he was seeking had been seen from Fitzroy, the settlement near Port Pleasant, retreating at full speed. A minute or two later he could make out the smoke of two steamers on his port bow, and made away east by south in chase.

There were, in fact, only two of them, the *Baden* and

---

[1] This is denied by the Germans. See *Der Krieg zur See : Kreuzerkrieg*, Vol. I, pp. 312–13.

[2] See Inset to Map 17 in case.

Santa Isabel. When they saw the squadron being chased they had remained at anchor awaiting orders. The third ship, the *Seydlitz*, had been ordered to keep in sight of the squadron as hospital ship, but finding the British cruisers were nearer than her own, she had made off to the east-south-east to avoid them.[1] By 3.0 Captain Fanshawe had the other two in sight, and after chasing for half an hour more fired a couple of guns and ordered them to stop. They were then taken possession of, but owing to the wording of Admiral Sturdee's order some doubt arose as to what to do with them. The signal had said " Sink the transports," but they proved not to be transports; on the contrary, they were full of coal and a rich cargo of stores, which would be of great value to the fleet. Captain Fanshawe, however, considered himself bound by the letter of the signal, and without waiting to report the nature of his captures, he removed the crews to the *Macedonia* and ordered her to sink the *Baden* by gun fire, while he dealt with the *Santa Isabel.* At 7.0, after both of them had been riddled on the waterline and were seen to be settling, he hurried off eastward to try to rejoin the Admiral, leaving the *Macedonia* to stand by till the prizes sank and then to take the prisoners to Port Stanley. It was not till half an hour later that he knew the result of the action, and that the sacrifice of so much valuable material had been quite unnecessary.

The news of the victory had been sent to the *Bristol en clair*, and the *Seydlitz* took in the signal. She had just heard from the *Baden* that her two consorts had been captured, and was hurrying off at her utmost speed on a southerly course. The result was she had a very narrow escape, for some time after 8.0, through the thickening squalls of rain, she was aware of a man-of-war firing slowly some four miles away on her beam. It must have been the *Cornwall* or the *Glasgow* firing the last shots into the *Leipzig*. But in the gathering darkness they could not see her, and she finally hurried off to the southward. She was subsequently (January 1915) interned at Puerto Militar by the Argentine Government.

Of the *Dresden* no trace could be found. So soon as the *Gneisenau* had sunk, Admiral Sturdee had endeavoured to find out from his cruisers in what direction she had gone, and in the meanwhile, to ensure the safety of the *Orama* and the eight colliers she was bringing down, at 8.30 he ordered the *Carnarvon* away to the northward to meet them and escort them to Port Stanley. He himself, with the two battle

[1] *Blumenthaler Zeitung,* June 6, 1915, and *Kieler Neueste Nachrichten,* August 3, 1915.

cruisers and the *Bristol*, was sweeping in a south-westerly direction at 18 knots for Staten Island to cut off the *Dresden* if she tried to round the Horn, and he had ordered the *Bristol* to follow him.   Of the *Kent* and *Nürnberg* he could get no news, but when he knew that the *Glasgow* and *Cornwall* had settled the *Leipzig* he signalled to them (11.25 p.m.) to proceed to the Magellan Straits.   The *Glasgow* replied that both ships had fired away nearly all their ammunition and that the *Cornwall* had only 250 tons of coal.   Admiral Sturdee therefore directed them to return to Port Stanley and coal, and he himself held on as he was, keeping the *Inflexible* with him. Nor was any fresh order at this time given to the *Bristol*, so that the Straits were left without any British ship to watch them.   As he afterwards explained, his appreciation of the situation was that, so far as he then knew, two of the enemy's light cruisers had got away, for as yet he had had no news of the *Kent* and *Nürnberg*.   With only three ships available, he considered he could only search a limited area, and as he knew that the German squadron had coaled in the south of Tierra del Fuego before the battle, he judged that was the most likely area in which to find the missing ships.   For these reasons he continued on as he was, keeping all three ships with him, and by 10.30 a.m. on the 9th was within fifty miles of Staten Island.   Here the weather turned so hopelessly thick that further search seemed useless, and as by this time he had also heard that prisoners from the *Leipzig* had said the light cruisers' orders were to make for the south-east coast of America, he turned and made a wide sweep to the north-north-west, signalling to the *Bristol*, who had not yet been sighted, to steer north and search the western group of the Falklands.   For twenty-four hours the sweep continued, but with no result, and about 10 a.m. on the 10th he gave up the search and made for Port Stanley north-about.   Here the *Kent* came in soon after to report how she had sunk the *Nürnberg*, but it was not till the second day after his arrival that he had any news of the lost *Dresden*.

His intention was, after coaling and repairing damages, to divide his squadron into three divisions to search for her— one for Tierra del Fuego, one for the east coast as high as Montevideo, and the third for the coast of Brazil.   On the 11th, however, he received other instructions from the Admiralty, where the escape of the *Dresden* was not yet fully realised.   These instructions laid down a scheme of operations against the three cruisers not forming part of Admiral von Spee's squadron, which were still believed to be working in South American waters, namely, the *Prinz Eitel Friedrich*, now known to be near Valparaiso, the *Karlsruhe*, whose end was still unknown, and the *Kronprinz Wilhelm*, which had not been heard of since she sank the *Correntina* off Montevideo. The *Prinz Eitel Friedrich* was to be dealt with by the Allied North Pacific Squadron—that is, less the *Australia*, which was to pass into the Atlantic by the Panama Canal. The rest, *Newcastle*, *Idzumo* and *Asama*, were to sweep south from the Galapagos Islands, but Admiral Sturdee was also to send the *Kent* and a merchant cruiser to work up the Chilean coast to meet them. The Admiral himself was to deal with the other two raiders, and for this purpose was to divide the squadron into two parts. For the south-east coast area the *Carnarvon*, *Glasgow* and two merchant cruisers would remain where they were under Admiral Stoddart. All the rest were to move north, the *Canopus* returning to her duty as guard-ship at Abrolhos Rocks, and there also the *Dartmouth* would shortly arrive from the Cape.

The following day, however (December 12), these orders were modified on news of the failure to find the *Dresden* and a growing anxiety for the situation in Home Waters. The two battle cruisers, he was informed, were wanted for the Grand Fleet as soon as possible. He was therefore to leave Admiral Stoddart in command of all the other ships to search for the *Dresden*, and as soon as she was dealt with they were to move north to look for the other two. He was further told that the *Australia* being too big to go through the Canal was coming home by way of the Falklands. At the same time the *Melbourne*, which after reaching Gibraltar had been ordered to the Azores, was directed to hasten to Bermuda for instructions, as the *Karlsruhe* was reported to have been seen at the Bahamas.

An hour or so after these orders were sent off an urgent message reached Whitehall from our Consul at Punta Arenas to say that the *Dresden* was there in the Magellan Strait. Admiral Sturdee's orders were immediately modified so far that he was authorised to use his discretion for taking action against her in spite of the need of getting his battle cruisers home as soon as possible (December 13, 4.45 p.m.). Four hours later, when it was known that the Chilean Authorities meant to allow the *Dresden* to coal, he was definitely ordered to press the chase so that she might be destroyed and not interned.

These instructions Admiral Sturdee had anticipated. The news that the *Dresden* was at Punta Arenas reached him at 3 a.m. on December 13. It was thirty-six hours old, and so busy was he coaling and repairing the damages suffered in the action that the *Bristol* was the only ship ready for sea.

In less than two hours she was away, and at 8.30 the *Inflexible* and *Glasgow* followed, the division being under the orders of Captain Phillimore of the *Inflexible*. Later on Admiral Stoddart, with the *Carnarvon* and *Cornwall* was sent to search the Patagonian coast, and next morning, according to Admiralty instructions, the *Kent* and *Orama* left for the west coast in search of the *Prinz Eitel Friedrich*. He himself decided that he could best meet the general requirements by proceeding home at once, leaving the *Inflexible* to follow not later than December 29. Accordingly he started home on the 16th, but next day the Admiralty sent a final order that both the battle cruisers were to come home at once, filling up with ammunition at St. Vincent, Cape Verde, on their way, and that the search for the *Dresden* was to be left to Admiral Stoddart. In the meantime it had been found at Punta Arenas that the bird had flown, and on the 19th the *Inflexible*, which had passed out into the Pacific, turned back for home, leaving Admiral Stoddart to direct the unending search for the *Dresden*.

So ended the series of chases and actions known as the Battle of the Falklands. Of the five cruisers and three tenders which composed Admiral von Spee's squadron one cruiser and a tender had escaped, and by British tradition the victory could not be regarded as quite complete. Since one of them was a light cruiser, it had not rendered those waters free, but it had removed the squadron which had so long and so seriously disturbed our strategy. It was, in fact, as the Germans admitted, a fine strategical victory. Tactically it had less claim to distinction owing to the marked superiority of the British squadron, but Admiral Sturdee could claim that by his method of conducting the action he had destroyed a powerful enemy squadron without material injury to two capital ships which it was essential to return to the Grand Fleet with their fighting power intact. The risk of detaching them had been considerable, but the Admiralty by sure judgment accepted it and so had succeeded in bringing to bear at the right time and place an overwhelming superiority of force. It may be said that the fortunate meeting at the Falklands was mainly a point of luck, but it was luck fairly won on Nelson's golden rule of never losing a wind, and in any case those who designed the operation fully deserved all the credit due to plans which obtained so large a measure of success without any diminution of naval strength. What the action meant to the course of the war was that in little more than four months the command of the outer seas had been won, and we were free to throw practically the whole weight of the Navy into the main theatre.

APPENDIX A

The actual constitution of the High Seas Fleet on the eve of war was as follows, but it is doubtful whether the whole of it was ready for sea. It is believed that four of the twenty-three battleships and the *Derfflinger* did not join till some months later.

GERMAN HIGH SEAS FLEET

Commander-in-Chief, Admiral von Ingenohl.

FLEET FLAGSHIP
Battleship, *Friedrich der Grosse* (10 12″)

FIRST BATTLE SQUADRON
In command, Vice-Admiral von Lans.
Second in command, Rear-Admiral Gädeke.

1st Division.	Guns.	2nd Division.	Guns.
Ostfriesland (flag) .	12 12″	*Posen* (2nd flag). .	12 11″
Thüringen . .	12 12″	*Rheinland* . .	12 11″
Helgoland . .	12 12″	*Nassau* . .	12 11″
Oldenburg . .	12 12″	*Westfalen* . .	12 11″

SECOND BATTLE SQUADRON
In command, Vice-Admiral Scheer.
Second in command, Rear-Admiral Mauve.

3rd Division.	Guns.	4th Division.	Guns.
Preussen (flag) .	4 11″	*Hannover* (2nd flag) .	4 11″
Schlesien . .	4 11″	*Schleswig-Holstein* .	4 11″
Hessen . .	4 11″	*Pommern* . .	4 11″
Lothringen . .	4 11″	*Deutschland* . .	4 11″
Reserve ships . .		{ *Elsass* 4 11″	
		{ *Braunschweig* 4 11″	

THIRD BATTLE SQUADRON
In command, Rear-Admiral Funke.
Second in command, Rear-Admiral Hebbinghaus.

5th Division.	Guns.
Kaiser	10 12″
Kaiserin	10 12″
König Albert	10 12″
Prinzregent Luitpold (flag) . .	10 12″

CRUISER SQUADRON

In command, Rear-Admiral Hipper.
Second in command, Rear-Admiral Maass.
Third in command, Rear-Admiral Tapken.

BATTLE CRUISERS

	Guns.
Seydlitz (flag)	10 11″
Moltke	10 11″
Blücher	10 11″
Von der Tann (3rd flag) . . .	8 11″
Derfflinger	8 12″

LIGHT CRUISERS

Roon .	. 4 8·2″	*Mainz* .	. 12 4·1″	*München*	. 10 4·1″
Hansa .	. 2 8″	*Stralsund*	. 12 4·1″	*Danzig* .	. . 10 4·1″
Vineta .	. 2 8″	*Kolberg*	. 12 4·1″	*Stuttgart*	. 10 4·1″
Köln .	. 12 4·1″	*Rostock*	. 12 4·1″	*Frauenlob*	. 10 4·1″
Strassburg	. 12 4·1″	*Hamburg*	. 10 4·1″	*Stettin* .	. 10 4·1″

APPENDIX B

GRAND FLEET

Commander-in-Chief : Admiral SIR JOHN R. JELLICOE, K.C.B., K.C.V.O.
Chief of Staff : Rear-Admiral C. E. MADDEN, C.V.O.
Fleet Flagship : *Iron Duke* (ten 13.5″; twelve 6″), Captain R. N. Lawson.
Attached ships { Light Cruiser : *Sappho*, Commander G. V. C. Knox.
{ Destroyer : *Oak*, Lieutenant-Commander D. Faviell.

FIRST BATTLE SQUADRON

Vice-Admiral SIR LEWIS BAYLY, K.C.B., C.V.O.
Rear-Admiral H. EVAN-THOMAS, M.V.O.

Marlborough	(10 13·5″)	flag of V.A.	Captain E. P. F. G. Grant.
St. Vincent	(10 12″)	flag of R.A.	Captain W. W. Fisher, M.V.O.
Collingwood	(10 12″)	. .	Captain J. C. Ley.
Colossus	(10 12″)	. .	Captain The Hon. E. S. Fitzherbert.
Hercules	(10 12″)	. .	Captain H. H. Bruce, M.V.O.
Neptune	(10 12″)	. .	Captain A. T. Hunt, C.S.I.
Superb	(10 12″)	. .	Captain P. Vaughan Lewes, C.B.,D.S.O.
Vanguard	(10 12″)	. .	Captain C. S. Hickley, M.V.O.

Light Cruiser : *Bellona*, Captain Percy M. R. Royds.

SECOND BATTLE SQUADRON

Vice-Admiral SIR GEORGE J. S. WARRENDER, BART., K.C.B., K.C.V.O.
Rear-Admiral SIR ROBERT K. ARBUTHNOT, BART., M.V.O.

King George V	(10 13·5″)	flag of V.A.	Captain G. H. Baird.
Orion	(10 13·5″)	flag of R.A.	Captain F. C. Dreyer, C.B.
Ajax	(10 13·5″)	. .	Captain Sir A. J. Henniker-Hughan, Bt.
Audacious	(10 13·5″)	. .	Captain Cecil F. Dampier, A.D.C.
Centurion	(10 13·5″)	. .	Captain M. Culme-Seymour, M.V.O.
Conqueror	(10 13·5″)	. .	Captain N. C. Palmer, C.V.O., A.D.C.
Monarch	(10 13·5″)	. .	Captain E. H. Smith.
Thunderer	(10 13·5″)	. .	Captain T. Jackson, C.B., M.V.O.

Light Cruiser : *Boadicea*, Captain L. C. S. Woollcombe, M.V.O.

Third Battle Squadron

Vice-Admiral E. E. BRADFORD, C.V.O.
Rear-Admiral MONTAGUE E. BROWNING, M.V.O.

Eight battleships of " King Edward VII " class : 4 12″ ;   4 9·2″

King Edward VII	flag of V.A.	. Captain Crawford Maclachlan.
Hibernia	flag of R.A.	. Captain A. Lowndes.
Africa		. Captain H. J. O. Millar.
Britannia . . .		. Captain H. G. G. Sandeman.
Commonwealth . . .		. Captain Maurice Woollcombe.
Dominion		. Captain H. L. Mawbey.
Hindustan . . : .		. Captain J. Nicholas.
Zealandia		. Captain W. H. Cowan, M.V.O., D.S.O.

Light Cruiser : *Blanche*, Captain R. Hyde, M.V.O.

Fourth Battle Squadron

Vice-Admiral SIR DOUGLAS A. GAMBLE, K.C.V.O.

Dreadnought	(10 12″) flag of V.A.	Captain W. J. S. Alderson.
Bellerophon	(10 12″) . .	Captain E. F. Bruen.
Temeraire	(10 12″) . .	Captain E. S. Alexander-Sinclair, M.V.O.
Agincourt	(14 12″) . .	Captain D. R. L. Nicholson, A.D.C.

Light Cruiser : *Blonde*, Captain A. C. Scott.

First Battle Cruiser Squadron [1]

Vice-Admiral SIR DAVID BEATTY, K.C.B., M.V.O. D.S.O.

Lion	(8 13·5″) flag of V.A.	Captain A. E. M. Chatfield, C.V.O.
Princess Royal	(8 13·5″) . .	Captain O. de B. Brock, A.D.C.
Queen Mary	(8 13·5″) . .	Captain W. R. Hall.
New Zealand	(8 12″) . .	Captain Lionel Halsey, C.M.G.

Second Cruiser Squadron

Rear-Admiral The Hon. S. A. GOUGH-CALTHORPE, C.V.O., C.B.

Shannon	(4 9·2″ ; 10 7·5″) flag of R.A.	Captain J. S. Dumaresq, M.V.O.
Achilles	(6 9·2″ ; 4 7·5″) . .	Captain A. L. Cay.
Cochrane	(6 9·2″ ; 4 7·5″) . .	Captain W. G. E. Ruck-Keene, M.V.O.
Natal	(6 9·2″ ; 4 7·5″) . .	Captain J. F. E. Green.

Third Cruiser Squadron

Rear-Admiral W. C. PAKENHAM, C.B., M.V.O.

Antrim	(4 7·5″ ; 6 6″) flag of R.A.	Captain V. B. Molteno.
Argyll	(4 7·5″ ; 6 6″) . .	Captain J. C. Tancred.
Devonshire	(4 7·5″ ; 6 6″) . .	Captain E. V. Underhill.
Roxburgh	(4 7·5″ ; 6 6″) . .	Captain S. S. Hall, C.B.

---

[1] The Grand Fleet cruisers were officially designated " Cruiser Force A," and of this force Sir David Beatty was " Vice-Admiral Commanding."

FIRST LIGHT CRUISER SQUADRON

Commodore W. E. GOODENOUGH, M.V.O.

Southampton	(8 6″)	pendant of	Commodore Goodenough.
Birmingham	(9 6″)	. .	Captain A. A. M. Duff.
Nottingham	(9 6″)	. .	Captain C. B. Miller.
Liverpool	(2 6″; 10 4″) .	.	Captain E. Reeves.
Falmouth	(8 6″)	. .	Captain J. D. Edwards.
Lowestoft	(9 6″)	. .	Captain T. W. B. Kennedy.

APPENDIX C

MEDITERRANEAN FLEET

Commander-in-Chief: Admiral SIR A. BERKELEY MILNE, Bt., G.C.V.O. K.C.B.

Chief of Staff: Commodore RICHARD F. PHILLIMORE, C.B., M.V.O.

SECOND BATTLE CRUISER SQUADRON

Inflexible	(8 12″)	flag of C.-in-C.	Captain Arthur N. Loxley.
Indefatigable	(8 12″)	.	Captain Charles F. Sowerby.
Indomitable	(8 12″)	.	Captain Francis W. Kennedy.

FIRST CRUISER SQUADRON

Rear-Admiral ERNEST C. T. TROUBRIDGE, C.B., C.M.G., M.V.O.

Defence	(4 9·2″; 10 7·5″)	flag of R.A.	Captain Fawcet Wray.
Black Prince	(6 9·2″; 10 6″)	. .	Captain Frederick D. Gilpin-Brown.
Duke of Edinburgh	(6 9·2″; 10 6″)	. .	Captain Henry Blackett.
Warrior	(6 9·2″; 4 7·5″)	. .	Captain George H. Borrett.

LIGHT CRUISERS

Chatham	(8 6″)	.	Captain Sidney R. Drury-Lowe.
Dublin	(8 6″) . . .	.	Captain John D. Kelly.
Gloucester	(2 6″; 10 4″) . .	.	Captain W. A. Howard Kelly, M.V.O.
Weymouth	(8 6″)	.	Captain William D. Church.

APPENDIX D

In view of the criticism passed upon the then First Lord of the Admiralty (Mr. Churchill) in connection with the loss of the three "Cressy" or "Bacchante" cruisers (September 22, 1914) and with the action off Coronel (November 1, 1914), it has been thought desirable to reproduce the two following minutes written by Mr. Churchill shortly before the events—

I

"The force available for operations in the narrow seas should be capable of minor action without the need of bringing down the Grand Fleet. To this end it should have effective support either by two or three battle cruisers or battleships of the Second Fleet working from Sheerness. This is the most efficiently air and destroyer patrolled anchorage we possess. They can lie behind the boom, and can always be at sea when we intend a raid. Battle cruisers are much to be preferred.

"The 'Bacchantes' ought not to continue on this beat. The risk to such ships is not justified by any services they can render. The narrow seas, being the nearest point to the enemy, should be kept by a small number of good modern ships.

"The 'Bacchantes' should go to the western entrance of the Channel and set Bethell's battleships—and later Wemyss' cruisers—free for convoy and other duties.

"The first four 'Arethusas' should join the flotillas of the narrow seas.[1]

"I see no sufficient reason to exchange these flotillas now that they know their work with the northern ones.

"As the 'M' boats are delivered they should be formed into a separate half-flotilla and go north to work with the Grand Fleet.

"The *King Alfred* should pay off and be thoroughly repaired.

September 18, 1914.

(*Initialled*) "W. S. C."

II

Extract of Telegram from Rear-Admiral Cradock, *via* Montevideo, to Admiralty. (Received October 12, 1914, 6.15 p.m.)

"Intelligence received re *Gneisenau* and *Scharnhorst*. *Good Hope* revisited Orange Bay October 7, found evidence of presence of *Dresden* there September 11. Indications show possibility of *Dresden, Leipzig, Nürnberg* joining *Gneisenau* and *Scharnhorst*. Have ordered *Canopus* to Falkland Islands, where I intend to concentrate and avoid division of forces. Have ordered *Glasgow, Monmouth* and *Otranto* not to go north of Valparaiso until German cruisers are again located. *Karlsruhe* apparently operating in

---

[1] These four light cruisers were not immediately available. One had been delivered, but was then under repair; the construction of the others was being accelerated and they were due for completion shortly.

South American waters; suggest therefore *Essex* be now detached and relieved by *Cornwall* and remain as S.N.O., *Cornwall* then proceeding south. With reference to Admiralty telegram No. 74 does *Defence* join my command ?

"Do regulations of Panama Canal permit passage of belligerent ships at present time ? "

October 8.

Mr. Churchill (First Lord of the Admiralty) minuted the above telegram as follows—

" In these circumstances it would be best for the British ships to keep within supporting distance of one another, whether in the Straits or near the Falklands, and to postpone the cruise along the West Coast until the present uncertainty about *Scharnhorst* and *Gneisenau* is cleared up.

" They, and not the trade, are our quarry for the moment. Above all, we must not miss them."

October 12, 1914.

(Initialled) W. S. C.

INDEX